Death
Daring
and
Disaster

Death Daring and Disaster

Search and Rescue in the National Parks

REVISED EDITION

Charles R. "Butch" Farabee, Jr.

TAYLOR TRADE PUBLISHING

Lanham • New York • Dallas • Boulder • Toronto • Oxford

Published by Taylor Trade Publishing
An imprint of The Rowman & Littlefield Publishing Group, Inc.
4501 Forbes Boulevard, Suite 200, Lanham, Maryland 20706

Distributed by NATIONAL BOOK NETWORK

Library of Congress Cataloging-in-Publication Data

Farabee, Charles R.
  Death, daring, and disaster : search and rescue in the national parks /
Charles R. Farabee, Jr.— Rev. ed.
     p. cm.
  Includes bibliographical references and index.
  ISBN 1-58979-182-7 (pbk. : alk. paper)
  1. National parks and reserves—Search and rescue operations—United States—
History. 2. United States. National Park Service—History. I. Title.
  SB486.S53F37 2005
  363.34'81'0973—dc22
                                                                    2005002019

♾ ™ The paper used in this publication meets the minimum requirements of American National Standard for Information Sciences—Permanence of Paper for Printed Library Materials, ANSI/NISO Z39.48-1992.

Manufactured in the United States of America.

Cover photograph: July 17, 1980. After lowering a crewman down to assist a man trapped on a rock in the middle of roaring cascades, a Lemoore Naval Air Station "Angel" lifts the hypothermic victim from between Upper and Lower Yosemite Falls. Moments after this photo was taken, the helicopter lost power and the pilot was barely able to fly free of the mist-shrouded area. Kennan Ward Photo

DEDICATED TO

all those who save life or limb;

Bill Butler, John Dill, Ernie Field,
and Doug McLaren;

the "Yosemite Mafia;"

AND

Adam and Lincoln

CONTENTS

CHAPTER THREE   55
1920–1929

CHAPTER ELEVEN
2000–

FOREWORD

As Secretary of the Interior for most of the 1960s, I had an opportunity to help orchestrate the beginning of the environmental movement. And I also played a role as nearly 50 areas were added to our National Park System.

Perhaps second only to liberty, our national parks, which are set aside "in such manner and by such means as will leave them unimpaired for the enjoyment of future generations," may very well be one of our nation's finest legacies to future generations. These areas herald the delicate strands of nature and history that bind us together as a land. The story of our national parks, embodying the finest in our natural and historical resources, has been inspiring in ways many times. In *Death, Daring, and Disaster,* however, veteran ranger Butch Farabee uniquely chronicles the one unsung chapter in the unfolding story about our park lands: search and rescue.

By 1961, when I became a member of President John F. Kennedy's cabinet, 80 million people enjoyed these majestic benchmarks of our heritage; eight years and two terms as the Secretary of the Interior later, this number had nearly doubled. By the end of the millennium, this figure will again have more than doubled, with some 350 million people visiting our National Park System. Tragically, there is mishap: In 1997 alone, 4,500 of these visitors needed to be rescued, 14,000 required emergency medical aid, and 300 died.

These statistics are not surprising when you consider that the collective size of our National Park System—84 million acres—is greater in scope than every state in the Union except four and is infinitely more complicated and diverse than all of them. And each year, several million people tempt fate and risk misfortune in dozens of ways in such wondrous but potentially deadly places as the Grand Canyon, Denali, Yosemite, Shenandoah, Gateway, Glacier, and Lake Mead. These visitors boat, drive, climb, hike, camp, dive, ski, swim, hang-glide, and even illegally parachute.

Search and rescue and emergency medical assistance on our public lands are performed by an elite, small cadre of civil servants and dedicated volunteers. It wasn't always so. Beginning in 1870 when a blind man was lost and bewildered for thirty-seven days in what became the world's first national park, *Death, Daring, and Disaster* chronicles over 400 sagas highlighting more than 125 years of drama and heroic sacrifice. Additionally, Butch Farabee traces the evolution and use of such milestones as helicopters, emergency medicine, rescue techniques, volunteer SAR groups, valorous awards, and scuba in our parks—and provides a record of engaging landmarks of technology and events for historic search and rescue missions.

I remember many of the tragedies and events Butch recounts: the midair collision over the Grand Canyon that killed 128 people in 1956; the massive rescue requiring fifty world-class mountaineers to fly to Alaska in 1960; the two scuba divers who disappeared in Death Valley in 1965; the forty-two hikers trapped by floodwaters in Zion that same year; and the 1967 three-day rescue of two climbers trapped on the north face of the Grand Teton. Vice President Hubert Humphrey wrote in a personal letter to the rescuers about this last mission, saying, "I still don't see how you did it, but I am told that Mr. Campbell will live, so I guess you did!" A highlight in my career as the Secretary of the Interior was to honor with Valor Awards many of the men and women who participated in these perilous rescues. These and many other well-deserved recognitions, hard earned over the years, are cataloged in *Death, Daring, and Disaster*.

Butch looked for his first lost person in 1958 as an Explorer Scout at the age of 16. He went on to become a national park ranger. During his more than thirty-year national park career, he has participated in nearly 1,000 search, rescue, and emergency missions while stationed at Glen Canyon, Lake Mead, Death Valley, Yosemite, and Grand Canyon. He served as the first Washington-based emergency services coordinator for four years. As such, he worked with dozens of local, state, and national medical and rescue response groups, as well as representing the Secretary of the Interior on the government's Interagency Committee on Search and Rescue. With a career spanning many dramatic life-and-death operations over four decades, Butch Farabee has an insight into search and rescue that is matched by few people today. In my view, he is the perfect person to write this book.

Stewart L. Udall

For many decades the National Park Service has been a leader in search and rescue (SAR). This is the manual for the country's first SAR school. DOUG MCLAREN COLLECTION

INTRODUCTION

In my days as Chief Ranger at Grand
Canyon, we had a lady undertaker in
Williams. She used to complain. "Those
park rangers! They bring those bodies
out draped over a mule; they don't seem
to realize how hard it is for us to
straighten them out."

—Retired Grand Canyon
Superintendent Howard Stricklin

Death, Daring, and Disaster is about search and rescue, heroes, and an
untold chapter in the history of our nation's parks.

When Yellowstone was guaranteed to the world in 1872, just 300
adventurers came to revel in the first national park. In 2004, the eve of the
136th anniversary of the "Mother Park," more than 266 million people
enjoyed the 388 areas now within our country's playgrounds. But some of
those visitors didn't live to tell about it.

Among the very finest in the world, the National Park Service (NPS) has
always been a leader in search and rescue (SAR). Decades before the public's zest for the great outdoors exploded in the 1970s, and local and state
governments were forced into rural rescue, the favorite places for most
campers, boaters, and hikers were our parks and monuments. Rangers of
the National Park Service had to be the best.

*Beverly Johnson leaping onto Yosemite's El Capitan at the start of a Big Wall rescue,
circa 1973.* NPS PHOTO/AUTHOR'S COLLECTION

Search and rescue in isolated areas—compared to urban SAR—is generally more complex and often made much more dangerous by rugged terrain, adverse weather, nonexistent communications, lack of nearby sophisticated medical aid, extremes in elevation and environment, and a scarcity of readily available resources.

With early records sketchy or even absent and pioneering tourists largely self-reliant and not apt to report any misadventure short of death, SAR details and related numbers for national parks over time are merely guesstimates. Since its beginnings in Yellowstone, however, there is a rough figure of 130,000 mishaps. In 2003 alone, there were 3,108 SAR missions: lost children, fallen climbers, downed aircraft, drowning bathers, frozen skiers, trapped cavers, overdue boaters, injured hikers, and exhausted mountaineers stranded on hundreds of distant rugged peaks.

National Park Service rescuers in 2003—the last year for which there are accurate accounts—saw 124 deaths but also 427 saves: lives spared by a timely, expert SAR team. Routinely risking life and limb, these brave men and women walked, ran, climbed, flew, or swam to 3,251 people in need of help that year. They also answered 13,693 calls for emergency medical assistance while administering advanced lifesaving skills to 1,590 people, as well as progressive cardiac care to 319. These dedicated teams—spending nearly $3.5 million—labored 82,683 long hours saving lives.

Here are some examples of the immense workload in our national parks. In 1996: The Grand Canyon had 482 SARs, involving 377 injured or ill people and 18 deaths. These accidents alone cost taxpayers $555,000. The place is busy; the record for dispatching an SAR helicopter into the mile-deep world wonder is reputed to be 12 times in one day. Lake Mead National Recreation Area, nearly 1.5 million acres straddling Nevada and Arizona, saw 332 SARs and 36 deaths. In their spare time, the rangers there also made 516 criminal arrests. The professionals on Grand Teton's highly decorated SAR team responded to 148 missions; sadly for them, they had to deal with 13 traumatic deaths as well. Alaska's Mt. McKinley, at 20,320 feet high, with winds greater than 200 mph and temperatures routinely several dozen degrees below zero, is among the world's most uncompromising rescue challenges. With more than 1,000 mountaineers now eagerly seeking the high point of North America each year, the park weathered 16 SARs and 6 extremely difficult body recoveries in 1996. The internationally recognized climbing staff of the Denali National Park SAR team deserved every federal penny they were paid.

Beginning with a blind man, lost and bewildered for 37 days in what would soon become Yellowstone National Park in 1870, *Death, Daring, and Disaster* highlights over 400 life-and-death sagas. It also documents the arrival of formalized rural SAR in this country: helicopters, volunteer rescue teams, the Mountain Troops of World War II, valor awards, Big Wall rescues, SCUBA, medicine, and technology.

Most of these SARs are long forgotten, but all were dramatic and demanded sacrifice; many were, as you can well guess, heroic. Some received wartime-sized headlines: a Japanese national hero, still missing on Mt. McKinley; the publicity-seeking adventurer who parachuted onto Devils Tower in 1940 with no planned way off; and the worst accident of its time, the midair plane collision over the Grand Canyon that killed 128 people in 1956, to name but three.

There are hundreds of other epics: an injured climber lowered 2,000 feet off an overhanging Yosemite wall; a last-second save of a little boy trapped beside his dead parents in a plane being buried by a raging Sierra blizzard; 50 men aboard a Russian freighter being shredded to pieces on the rocks of the Olympic Coast during World War II; the recovery of an unrequited love affair from the heart of an active Hawaiian volcano; a jet pilot who bailed out over Kings Canyon in 1956 and crawled out, six weeks later; 26 illegal aliens left to die in the 130-degree July heat of southern Arizona; 1,400 people desperately looking for a seven-year-old boy lost forever in the wilds of the Smoky Mountains; and the river runner in 1950 who fell into a Grand Canyon rapids (later christened "Necktie Willie" in his honor) and was "hanged" not once, but twice, by his trailing boat rope. He somehow survived!

There are tens of thousands of stories left to be told.

In September 1884, the first two people died on Longs Peak. In the 1990s, rangers respond to more than 14,000 medical emergencies; all require a team effort. (Left to right) author, Rick Smith, Walt Dabney, George Durkee, and Mark Forbes on a Yosemite trail, circa 1972.

CHAPTER 1

Before 1900

Or like the ghost of that lost dusky maiden,
Whose hapless feet too near its' torrent stray'd;
Across the precipice her form was swept . . .

—<u>Mariposa Gazette</u>, September 30, 1865

EXPLORATION of a new world is granted to only a few. In the nineteenth century it awaited those caught up in the excitement of western expansion. An eclectic body of settlers, scientists, and soldiers, their motives ranged from excitement to exploit. Much of what they saw was deemed worthless. For the curious and challenged, however, adventure drew them to the summits.

In October 1519, Spanish explorer Hernando Cortes ordered Diego de Ordaz up Mexico's erupting 17,887-foot Popocatepetl, the continent's fifth highest peak. Regardless of whether Ordaz really reached the snow-covered summit (debated even today), climbing had arrived. Then in 1642, a man named Darby Field scaled New Hampshire's weather-dominated Mt. Washington, becoming what is generally credited as this country's first documented mountain climb.

There were few accidents because of the pioneering, self-reliant nature of those brave few visiting the seven national parks of the nineteenth century (Mackinack Island was soon ceded back to the State of Michigan), coupled with the relatively infrequent visitation to these isolated areas (including 1899, Yellowstone had registered only 113,876 guests in its then 28-year existence). They took care of themselves quickly, efficiently, and with little fanfare. With poor or almost nonexistent communications, little notice was given the few authorities stationed in these solitary and isolated places. There was virtually no paperwork.

By 1900 most of the more obvious points in the Lower 48 had been explored; early daredevils, requiring fitness and tenacity, were satisfied to travel the simplest, safest routes.

PRE-1900 MILESTONES

August 1540	Directed there by Hopis, 13 Spanish explorers of Coronado's expedition view what is now known as the Grand Canyon.
August 27, 1650	Expedition of Englishmen begins exploring westward across the Allegheny Mountains.
March 19, 1669	German explorer John Lederer reaches the crest of the Blue Ridge near what is now Virginia's Shenandoah National Park.
1694	First recorded volcanic eruption in the U.S.: California's Lassen Volcano.
April 3, 1776	Pedro Font, a Franciscan missionary, looks eastward some 30 leagues and sees the snowcapped great western divide of the Sierra Nevada in what is now Sequoia National Park.
1786	Country's first rope is commercially manufactured by machine.
August 4, 1790	Revenue Cutter Service (Coast Guard) is organized.
February 23, 1791	"Life Saving Station for Distress Between Mariners" is incorporated by the Humane Society of the Commonwealth of Massachusetts; huts are erected on Nantucket.
January 23, 1793	Although actually established in 1780, the Humane Society of Philadelphia, the country's earliest first aid emergency organization, is incorporated. Its objective is the "recovery of drowned persons and those whose airstream may be suspended from other causes, as breathing air contaminated by burning charcoal, hanging, exposure to the choke-damp of wells, drinking cold water while warm in summer, strokes of the sun, lightning . . ."
May 14, 1804	Lewis and Clark start westward across the country.
June 14, 1834	Underwater diving suit ("water dress") is patented.
1839	Five unidentified fur trappers are killed probably by Indians near what is now Yellowstone National Park's Indian Pond.
1841	First record of skis being used in the U.S.

PRE-1900 MILESTONES

November 13, 1843	Washington's Mt. Rainier erupts.
August 14, 1848	Federal lifesaving service effectively begins when Congress appropriates $10,000 to "provide surf boats, rockets, carronades, and other necessary apparatus for the preservation of life and property from shipwreck on the coast of New Jersey, between Sandy Hook and Little Egg Harbor."
Winter 1849	En route to goldfields, a forty-niner dies crossing what in a decade will be labeled "Death Valley."
July 2, 1850	Self-contained breathing apparatus mask is patented.
March 21, 1851	Mariposa Battalion "discovers" Yosemite Valley, although Walker party reached the valley rim in 1833.
June 12, 1853	Crater Lake is "discovered."
June 1855	Mt. Rainier is possibly climbed by two unknown men.
1857	One of the earliest U.S. mountaineering deaths is 60-year-old University of North Carolina professor Elisha Mitchell. He perishes while exploring in North Carolina; Mt. Mitchell, the highest point east of the Mississippi River, is named for him.
1862	Austrian Alpine Association is founded.
August 2, 1862	Army Ambulance Corps is established.
1863	Virginia Alpine Club is formed; it is never heard from again.
June 30, 1864	President Lincoln grants Yosemite Valley and the nearby Mariposa Big Tree Grove to the State of California to be "held for public use, resort, and recreation . . . for all time."
October 1864	Clarence King made the first serious reconnaissance of Yosemite Valley and climbs easier summits along its rim.
Before 1865	Hospital ambulance service is introduced to the U.S. by Commercial Hospital (General Hospital) in Cincinnati.
May 21, 1866	At the age of 52 and for 22 subsequent years, Galen Clark is named "Guardian of Yosemite," the first person formally appointed and paid to protect a great natural park.

PRE-1900 MILESTONES

Galen Clark, on patrol near Nevada Falls. Clark was the first guardian of Yosemite National Park and this country's first park ranger, serving from 1866 to 1880 and from 1889 to 1897.

YOSEMITE NATIONAL PARK
RESEARCH LIBRARY

August 23, 1868	Civil War veteran Major John Wesley Powell, along with six others, first to climb Longs Peak, the highest point in what is now Rocky Mountain National Park.
1869	John Muir, 31, climbs Yosemite's Cathedral Peak.
May 24, 1869	In three boats and with nine men, Major Powell begins floating down the Green River and, ultimately, the 278 miles of the Grand Canyon's Colorado River. On August 29, three of his crewmen leave the expedition and hike out; they are never seen alive again; their departure point will eventually be called Separation Canyon. The next day, Powell and his party drift onto what in 70 years will become Lake Mead.
1870	During the Franco-Prussian War, French balloonists rescue 160 wounded soldiers from Paris; these may be the first air medevacs.
August 17, 1870	First recorded climb of Mt. Rainier; only 30-some parties will reach the top by the turn of the century.
August 29, 1871	First climb of Mt. Lyell, high point of Yosemite.
1872	Inconclusive proof suggests the first climb of Grand Teton.
March 1, 1872	President Grant establishes world's first national park, Yellowstone; 300 visitors are recorded that year.

PRE-1900 MILESTONES

August 18, 1873	First record of Mt. Whitney being climbed—highest point in Lower 48, now in Sequoia National Park.
1874	Carlyle Lamb becomes first guide on Rocky Mountain's Longs Peak; he eventually charges $1 per person for trip up and back.
October 12, 1875	Scottish carpenter and trail builder George C. Anderson engineers his way to top of Yosemite's Half Dome; 10 years before, it was written that this peak was "perfectly inaccessible . . . and never will be trodden by human foot."
1876	Country's first topographic map is made: the Grand Canyon.
January 1876	Appalachian Mountain Club is founded; it "will carry on a systematic exploration of the mountains of New England."
June 19, 1876	L. M. Clemmons receives first Life Saving Medal.
July 10, 1877	Cork life preservers are awarded Patent #192,832.
1877	Yellowstone submits its first report to the Secretary of the Interior; the park is allotted $10,000 for its operations in 1879.
August 26, 1877	Yellowstone tourist Charles Kenck, shot by fleeing Nez Percé Indians, is the first documented death in a national park.
June 18, 1878	President Hayes signs the United States Life Saving Service into law; between 1871 and 1915, when it rejoins the Revenue-Cutter Service to form the Coast Guard, the USLSS will have aided in 28,121 disasters and shipwrecks and preserved the lives of 174,682 persons and $288,871,237 worth of vessels and cargo.
1880	Yellowstone's Harry Yount is appointed gamekeeper and becomes first NPS protector; his $1,000 annual salary is a major slice of the $15,000 appropriated to the park by Congress for 1881.
January 20, 1880	James Mooney is killed in a fall over a cliff near the falls now named for him in what will become Grand Canyon National Park.

PRE-1900 MILESTONES

May 21, 1881	American Red Cross is organized in Washington, D.C.
December 1, 1881	Yellowstone superintendent proposes to use guides who need "only the expense of badges, license, and record."
August 1882	Walter Watson, surviving a fall into a Yellowstone hot pool, becomes first SAR-related victim in a park.
1883	Adventure climbing, with the ascent of Flattop Mountain, begins in what soon becomes Glacier National Park.
September 23, 1884	Carrie Welton becomes first person to die on Rocky Mountain National Park's Longs Peak.
1885	Associate Society of the Red Cross of Philadelphia, a unit of the national Red Cross, institutes training on "bandaging."
	First First Aid course is taught at the annual encampment of the New York State militia. Idea proposed by George R. Fowler.
September 5, 1885	Forty-six-year-old M. D. Scott, a U.S. Geological Survey (USGS) employee, is struck in the head by lightning and dies on Yellowstone Lake.
August 17, 1886	Company M, First United States Cavalry, arrives at Mammoth Hot Springs to begin protecting Yellowstone.
February 21, 1888	Frank Hess, killed by a Yellowstone avalanche, is first documented SAR-related death in a national park.
August 9, 1888	John Coyle, a Yellowstone Army private, earns first SAR-related award for valor in a national park.
May 31, 1889	Pennyslvania's Johnstown flood kills 2,209 people; American Red Cross's first disaster relief effort.
August 10, 1890	Len Longmire begins 20 years of professional guiding on Mt. Rainier; he ultimately charges $1 per person.
September 25, 1890	Sequoia becomes second national park; Yosemite and General Grant become third and fourth on October 1.
1891	Telephones are installed in Yosemite Valley. By 1911 10 ranger station outlets are linked to superintendent's office.

PRE-1900 MILESTONES

April 6, 1891	Troops I and K of the 4th Cavalry are selected for "fighting fires, backcountry patrol, mapping, constructing trails, fish planting, and maintaining order" in the three recently established national parks in California.
June 4, 1892	Sierra Club is founded; John Muir is first president.
July 4, 1893	Local rancher Will Rogers, using precut wooden pegs and playing to an audience of 1,000 picnickers, makes the first ascent of Wyoming's Devils Tower, the first monument in the NPS.
1894	Summit registers are placed on peaks of the Sierra.
July 19, 1894	Oregon's Mazamas Mountaineering Club is founded; meeting on top of Mt. Hood—193 men and women make the summit.
	Serving as a guide on the mountain since 1891, Harold Langille leads group up the 11,245-foot-high peak.
July 24, 1895	Eighteen-year-old Blachley H. Porter is struck by lightning and dies on the edge of the Grand Canyon, a park first.
1896	Denver-based Rocky Mountain Climbing Club is founded.
	Rudiments of organized mountain rescue in the Eastern Alps first appear in Vienna, followed in 1898 at Innsbruck, Austria.
July 27, 1897	Professor Edgar McClure, descending after making weather experiments, becomes first death on Mt. Rainier.
September 23, 1898	Yosemite's Archie Leonard and Charles Leidg are appointed "forest rangers," the first to hold the "ranger" title in a national park. National park "forest" rangers will not become designated "park" rangers until 1905.
1899	Systematic instruction in civilian first aid begins in Jermyn, Pennsylvania, when a small group of miners forms a club to "take up the study and practice of first aid."

```
               September 9, 1870
        (pre) Yellowstone National Park
      --------------------------------------
```

RESCUED . . . AFTER 37 DAYS

VESTED with considerable wilderness seasoning, Truman Everts wasn't overly concerned the first night he was separated from his party. Moving out early the next morning, he soon "dismounted to examine his surroundings when his horse took fright and bolted with his gun, blankets, matches—everything except the clothing he wore, a small knife, and an opera glass." Everts passed that second night sheltered sleeplessly in a wooded thicket; nearsighted and seriously handicapped without his missing glasses, he literally stumbled onto the shore of Heart Lake that afternoon. The steaming geyser basin there became Everts's home for some days to come.

Almost three weeks before, the Washburn-Langford-Doane Expedition— honored later by historians of the National Park Service for its philosophical foresight—had departed Fort Ellis on August 22 with provisions for 30 days "to make the first official exploration of the Yellowstone country." Included in this 19-person band were six soldiers, two animal packers, two cooks, and nine of the area's more "influential gentlemen," including one Truman C. Everts.

President Lincoln had appointed Everts as Assessor of Internal Revenue for the Montana Territory in 1864; when President Grant came into office, Everts lost the post. Now in between pursuits, he was on vacation. Annoyed by poor eyesight, Everts was still robust and at 56, a dozen years senior to the next oldest man.

The explorers entered what is now the park near Mammoth Hot Springs and then followed the Yellowstone River south to Yellowstone Lake, where they then traveled around its eastern edge. For the 19 days before Everts became lost, their route was fraught with impenetrable lodgepole thickets, tangles of fallen timber, and later, swampy marshes near the lake. On the afternoon of September 9, after straggling far behind—somewhat his habit—Truman Everts became separated from his comrades.

Everts's only mildly concerned companions—trusting in his outdoor experience—believed he had most likely ridden on to a previously discussed rendezvous deeper into Yellowstone. Having set a beacon fire on the ridge top and discharging guns after dark, they pushed on. Not finding any sign of their friend on the south shore of Yellowstone Lake that third night, the now-worried party agreed to lay over and look for him. It snowed that night and any hint of the hapless man's trail disappeared.

On the 12th, three days after the deposed assessor was last seen, 15 members of the party went searching; traveling in pairs, they systematically probed probable routes. Henry D. Washburn, a major general in the recent Civil War as well as a distinguished congressman, and Nathaniel P. Langford, who had nearly become governor of the Montana Territory the year before, slowly worked their way toward the southwest.

. . . a half mile of the shore of Heart Lake when Langford's horse broke through a thin turf into the underlying hot mud. The animal's legs were so badly scalded they had to turn

back when actually within sight of the geyser basin where
Everts was lying in his wet clothing.

Until he was found five weeks later, this was the closest anyone would get
to the hapless Everts. Huddled among wet, slippery rocks in a crude refuge of
branches and reduced to eating thistle roots, he called the vapor-filled area
home for the first seven days. "At first this was barely preferable to the storm,
but I soon became accustomed to it, and before I left, though thoroughly par-
boiled, actually enjoyed it." Two feet of snow fell on him.

On September 16, "after seven days [of] unavailing search," the expedition
moved on to present-day West Thumb Junction. They "concluded that Mr. Everts
had been shot from his horse by some straggling Indians" or, with a little luck,
had followed a tributary of the Snake River and had reached some settlement.
Three men remained "to still prosecute the search": pioneer merchant and probably the best outdoorsman
among the expeditioners,
Warren C. Gillette, and two
troopers, Privates Charles
Moore and John Williamson.
After considerable effort and,
although coming nearly as
close to the almost-blind man
as had Washburn and Langford,
the three failed to find the missing Everts.

In the October 6 *Helena
Daily Herald*, a law partner of
one of the expeditioners offered
$600 to anyone who could find
what remained of poor Everts.
Taking Judge Lawrence up on
this lucrative reward, George
Pritchett and John "Yellowstone Jack" Baronett proposed
to look "until the deep snows of
winter drove them back." On
October 16, Baronett stumbled
across Everts.

The Rescue, reproduced from Thirty-Seven Days
of Peril *by Truman C. Everts, published in*
Scribner's Monthly, *November 1871.*

There was icy sleet falling . . . but I noticed that my dog had
found some kind of a trail. . . . I saw that something had
dragged itself. . . . I decided that some hunter had wounded
a bear . . . trailed . . . for a mile or more, my dog began to
growl, and looking across a small canon. . . . I saw a black
object upon the ground. . . . My first impulse was to shoot
him. . . . I saw I should have no difficulty in overtaking him. . . .
When I got near it, I found it was not a bear, and for my life
could not tell what it was. It did not look like an animal
that I had seen, and it was certainly not a human being . . .

it was making a low groaning noise, crawling along upon its knees and elbows, and trying to drag itself up the mountain.

Lost for 37 days, Everts weighed "no more than fifty pounds" and truly owed his life to many days of tender nursing by a very caring Yellowstone Jack. Judge Lawrence, however, now refused to pay the reward, claiming the live and grateful man should do so. Everts, declaring he would have extricated himself eventually, declined to pay as well. Before dying in Maryland in 1901 at 85, Truman C. Everts married a second time at 65 and sired a son at 75.

```
August–September 1882
Yellowstone National Park
```

FIRST SAR WITHIN A NATIONAL PARK

TRAVELING amidst the wonders of wild Yellowstone, Walter Watson and his three friends were examining "a geyser about two and a half miles from the Firehole River" when the curious vandal "volunteered to attempt a descent and secure a piece of the beautiful colored work on the interior for each member of the party."

When the knob with his weight gave way, the hapless Watson became the first documented subject of an SAR within a national park, as his chilling, albeit slightly implausible account in Bozeman, Montana's September 7, 1882, *Avant Courier* documents.

A TOURIST FALLS INTO THE CRATER
OF A GEYSER—TRUTH STRANGER THAN FICTION

. . . When I struck the water, feet first, I experienced a feeling of relief. I seemed to sink thousands of feet, but of course sank but a short distance. I grasped around wildly, but nothing but the water could be felt. I was rising to the surface and knew it, and a feeling came over me that I was saved. How, I knew not, but still I was certain that I was not to be left in the crater. On coming to the surface I reached out and a friendly rock gave me support. I heard the shouts of my friends, but could see nothing and was unable to call out in reply. After what seemed to be ages . . . I realized that my friends had given me up for lost.

It was just after noon when we reached the crater; I suppose it was nearly five o'clock when I heard what sounded like distant thunder. The noise grew more and more distinct, and the water surrounding me began to be troubled. I then realized that I was in the crater of an active geyser, and that in a short time the entire space would be filled with water.

Suddenly I discovered that the water was rising. This gave me the hope that I might be able to keep afloat until the surface was reached. The water continued to rise more rapidly, and I at last found myself at the point from which I had fallen. Although well nigh exhausted, I exerted my remaining strength in climbing to the surface. This reached, I managed to crawl some distance away from the mouth of the crater when I lost consciousness. When I recovered I was being cared for by the strangers, the men who conducted me to my comrades.

In 2003, 121 years after Walter Watson became the first, there were over 3,100 SAR missions within the National Park System.

February 21, 1884
Yellowstone National Park

FIRST SAR DEATH

BY this point in the new park's short history, at least seven people had already met untimely ends. In 1877 two tourists were slain by the retreating Nez Percé Indians under Chief Joseph. In 1883 two men drowned while swimming their horses across the Yellowstone River; once they disappeared, the duo was hardly looked for (more people die in Yellowstone from drowning than from anything else other than vehicular accidents and illness). Five days later, John Zutavern was shot in nearby Gardiner in a petty quarrel over a razor and some blankets. While working on the National Hotel in Mammoth Hot Springs, an unidentified construction worker fell from a scaffold and died on July 7, 1883. Finally, on January 27, 1884, 27-year-old Emily Moore took too much morphine and thus became the park's first suicide.

Jacob Hess, number eight, was truly Yellowstone's first SAR-related death; a "Finlander," he would suffocate in an avalanche.

UP-RIVER MISHAPS

A FATAL SNOW-SLIDE

GARDINER, Mont., February 22—Last evening a snow slide occurred at a point half way between this point and Mammoth Hot Springs, as a sled and seven men were passing. The slide carried the team and men down the mountain side a distance of one hundred yards, burying them all underneath the snow. The occurrence was witnessed by Jas. Wrist, who went promptly to the assistance of the unfortunate men and succeeded in getting four of the men out, and came on here for assistance. As soon as the alarm was given, nearly all of the able men of the town turned out, and succeeded in finding the remaining three men. One was dead, and the other two will recover. They were Swedes, in the employ of Oscar Swanson.

—*Livingston (Montana) Enterprise*, 2-23-1884

A short follow-up in the next week's paper said Hess and his party "had been drinking heavily at Gardiner and were not in condition to manage the team." Another account goes on:

> When in drink he was quarrelsome and dangerous. It is said he had killed one of his companions while under the influence of drink and had served a term of years imprisonment for that offense. When sober he was a good workman and was well liked by his comrades.

Jacob Hess was the first SAR-related death within a national park and, arguably, also has the ignominy of being its first drunk-driving death as well.

In 1996 the National Park Service recorded its single worst year for SAR-related deaths: 297.

Summer 1884
Yellowstone National Park

"WILL KILL EVERY BLOOD-SUCKING BIRD OR BEAST OF PREY"

THE wife of Prof. Wm. Allen, of Madison, Wisc., while at the Grand Canyon (of the Yellowstone), was attacked and fearfully bitten by wild beasts. Her two sons came to her assistance, and with much difficulty succeeded in rescuing her. They had no arms with them, having been informed at the Mammoth Hot Springs Post Office that hunting in the Park was strictly prohibited. She was terribly bitten on her hands and face before the insatiable blood-suckers could be choked or smoked off. Mrs. Allen is highly indignant at the secretary's order prohibiting the killing of animals in the National Park. She declares they ought to be shot, no matter how enchanting their song may be. These were the only wild beasts she encountered during her tour in the Park. When she comes again she gives fair notice that she will come armed to the teeth, and will kill every blood-sucking bird or beast of prey, unless the assistants are on hand to furnish them with food sufficient to amuse them while she is tending to her own business.

—*Livingston (Montana) Enterprise,* "Park Notes," 8-4-1884

September 23, 1884
(pre) Rocky Mountain National Park

FIRST TWO PEOPLE
TO DIE ON LONGS PEAK

AT 14,256 feet, Longs Peak is the 15th highest of Colorado's 53 fourteeners. Immense and imposing, it is also challenging and rugged: a spectacular mountain with many moods. Named for Major Stephen H. Long, the frontiersman who saw it from the rolling eastern plains in 1820, it has a commanding view: Kansas and Nebraska to the east, Wyoming to the north. First climbed on August 23, 1864, by one-armed Civil War veteran Major John Wesley Powell and six of his expedition, it proves to have several relatively easy routes to the top. Anyone in reasonably good physical condition and some determination, can climb it.

Carrie Welton, a wealthy and cultured woman from Connecticut, hired the area's first climbing guide to get her to the top. Over the past 10 years, Carlye Lamb, charging $1 for each person assisted, had made more than 55 safe and successful ascents. He had never lost a person.

The adventuresome young woman reached the summit, although not without some coaxing on Lamb's part. On the way down she collapsed at the Keyhole. Unable to go on, she insisted her guide go for aid. Returning with assistance some hours later, he found she had perished from exhaustion and exposure. Carrie Welton became the first person to die on Longs Peak. The next to perish on the park's highest peak was an ignominious death as the August 31, 1889, *Rocky Mountain News* reports.

> An unfortunate accident occurred on Wednesday [August 28] by which Frank Stryker, a young man 28 years of age, lost his life in a most unusual manner. . . . Last Tuesday they started . . . to ascend Long's peak . . . and were amusing themselves joking and laughing.
>
> Frank Stryker . . . had enjoyed starting big boulders down the precipitous mountain side and watching them bound out of sight. When within 400 feet of the summit he announced his intentions of sending off a particularly huge stone. While . . . doing this his revolver fell out of his pocket and struck violently against a stone. One of the shells exploded and the ball struck him on the neck, passing almost completely through it.
>
> His friends . . . formed a rude litter of poles . . . messenger . . . dispatched . . . to procure medical assistance. This was at noon. Progress was . . . slow . . . wounded man was in great pain and every movement caused him intense agony. For ten long hours the mournful party labored over rocks before death came to relieve the moaning sufferer.

On August 25, 1995, after falling 400 feet, Jun Kamiura became the 48th person to die on Longs Peak; he will not be the last.

```
        August 9, 1888
    Yellowstone National Park
```

FIRST VALOR AWARD

PRIVATE John Coyle of the 22nd United States Infantry was on routine foot patrol at Castle Geyser, within sight of Old Faithful; only 19 days before, he and his colleagues—called the "Immortal 15"—had arrived from Montana Territory's Ft. Keogh. To the soldiers, still unsure of what was expected of them, the 6,000 Yellowstone visitors that year were proving an engaging challenge.

Contrary to park rules—and common sense—an adventuresome young woman had climbed the geyser cone to look inside. A wind shift suddenly enveloped her in a cloud of steam, confusing and terrifying her. Unable to safely descend and fearful of falling into the yawning hot vent, she screamed out for help.

Dreading the worst, the soldier clawed his way up the steep wall of the wet, slippery cone. Wrapping his blue coat around the frightened woman, Private Coyle brought her safely down. In so doing he suffered a serious scalding of his face.

On August 25, Orders No. 52 were issued by Army headquarters at Ft. Keogh. They read in part: "The colonel commanding is pleased to announce to the regiment an act of heroism and gallantry displayed by Private John Coyle, Company B, 22nd Infantry, while on duty in camp at the Old Faithful Geyser, Yellowstone Park." Citing details for the commendation, the colonel concluded by saying, "[S]uch commendable and exemplary conduct entitles Private Coyle to great praise and the thanks of the regimental commander are hereby extended to him."

As a result of this act of heroism—risking serious injury and even death—he was granted the **U.S. Lifesaving Service Silver Medal.** Private John Coyle thus became the first person to be formally recognized for a rescue within a national park area.

A federal lifesaving service effectively began on August 14, 1848. On that day Congress identified $10,000 for "surf boats, rockets, carronades, and other necessary apparatus for the better preservation of life and property from shipwreck on the coast of New Jersey, between Sandy Hook and Little Egg Harbor." Over the next several decades there were numerous laws and appropriations but not until the Life-Saving Stations Act was enacted on June 20, 1874, did the system get full recognition.

> Between 1871 and 1915, when the Life-Saving Service rejoined the Revenue-Cutter Service to form the U.S. Coast Guard, the service assisted 28,121 disasters and shipwrecks and preserved the lives of 174,682 persons and $288,871,237 worth of vessels and cargos.

In 1913 there were at least 285 lifesaving stations on the waters surrounding the United States as well as the Great Lakes.

According to Lee Whittlesey in *Death in Yellowstone,* at least 19 people have died in the park's 10,000 hot springs.

July 10, 1889
(pre) Grand Canyon National Park

WORKING ON THE RAILROAD—THREE DROWN

SUFFERING inexperience, hunger, suffocating heat, poor equipment, and, most important, the unknown, the eight men pushed steadily into the heart of the Grand Canyon. Frank Brown, expedition leader and the president of the Denver, Colorado Cañon and Pacific Railroad Company, believed it might just be possible to run tracks along the Colorado River all the way to California. This, the third expedition to enter Marble Canyon, was studying the feasibility of building a line the length of the deep gorge.

Brown launched his small boat first that morning. Neglecting to bring life preservers along, he admitted trusting to a higher power—despite the "earthly" pleas of his nonswimming engineer, Robert Stanton. Soon Stanton, nearing what is now River Mile 12 shortly after pushing into the current himself, "noticed a crewman running up the shore and waving both arms. The frantic man shouted, 'Mr. Brown is in there!'" Drowned.

Crewman Peter Hansbrough carved an epitaph to Frank Brown near that fatal point, five days before he himself would die. On July 15, having just lowered their small craft through what later would be called 25-Mile Rapid, Hansbrough and fellow boatman Henry Richards capsized against the rocks of the north wall and vanished. Demoralized and unable to continue, the remaining five men of the ill-fated campaign halted and prepared to leave.

About to start up South Canyon, Stanton "gazed up the main stream. At that moment the muddy, rain-swollen river bid his crew one last, ghastly farewell: beyond their reach, the body of Frank Mason Brown swiftly passed downstream."

Six months later, Stanton's second expedition discovered the skeleton of Peter Hansbrough 18 miles farther downriver. On January 17, 1890, they laid the unfortunate boatman to rest.

Robert Stanton eventually surveyed the river all the way to the Gulf of California. Fortunately, a railroad was never built down through what is now Grand Canyon National Park.

The Kolb brothers, Emory C. and Ellsworth L., shown here on their 1,400-mile-long trip down the Colorado River in 1911, were much luckier than the ill-fated 1889 Brown-Stanton expedition.

GRAND CANYON NATIONAL PARK RESEARCH LIBRARY

<pre>
                    January 1, 1890
          (pre) Grand Canyon National Park

</pre>

STILL WORKING ON THE RAILROAD

ROBERT Stanton, on his second expedition into the Grand Canyon (the fourth ever to enter the deep gorge by river), was again charting a possible route for a railroad. He, along with his not-quite-veteran 11-man crew, had just spent New Year's Eve above what is now River Mile 14. Near this spot, on Stanton's ill-fated earlier trip, two of his men as well as Frank Brown, the group's coleader, had disappeared in the Colorado's muddy waters.

On that first day of the new year, the expedition's photographer, Franklin A. Nims, was busy documenting the explorers running Sheer Wall Rapid. Along with a fellow crewman, Nims had worked his way up on the cliffs above the river when "he fell 22 feet . . . struck his foot on the shelf below where he was and turned back and fell on his back and head." Although unconscious much of that first day, Nims's only real injury would soon prove to be a broken leg.

> Two men sat up with him all night. This morning his color is good. The bleeding at ear and nose has stopped. His pulse seems good. His hands feel natural, and he has no fever. About noon he asked for a drink of water. . . . We put his leg in a box made by Mac, and bandaged it in the best way we can. We have made a stretcher of two oars and canvas bed cover.

Stanton, watching as Nims was strapped onto a boat and thus unable to fend for himself if they should capsize in the frigid water, must surely have shuddered while recalling the deaths he witnessed on his first trip. The expedition's leader now faced a difficult—not to mention terribly labor-intensive—decision.

Not blessed with helicopters, mountaineering equipment, or even a solid litter, Stanton chose to drag—sometimes literally—the injured Nims up Rider Canyon to the rim, a distance of 4 miles and 1,500 vertical feet. He then had to go 35 miles upstream to Lee's Ferry and enlist the aid of the kindly Johnsons living there.

Stanton took two days to work his way out, but for the rest, getting Nims up the cliffs and to the top—lashed to two willow poles—must have been a serious trial of the most unwieldy sort.

> . . . the little bench . . . was so sloping that a man could not stand on it alone . . . they carried him by men going up, lying down on the slope catching on with toes and fingers and holding on to ropes . . . while the rest held to the stretcher and shoved him along . . . the climb of about 900 feet on the slope of loose rocks . . . at about 45 degrees. At top of this for about 100 feet the way out was through a huge crack in the cliff, filled with immense sharp boulders.

July 27, 1891
Yellowstone National Park

LOVELORN, THE WILDERNESS SCOUT
COMMITTED SUICIDE

IF Yellowstone's Harry Yount is to be credited as the first park ranger (a title actually not used until about 1905), then Ed M. Wilson probably should be remembered as the first consummate protector of its unique, world-famous natural resources. Hired likely in 1885 as a "mountaineer assistant," the noted Army scout brought much-needed, hard-earned talent to the wild new park.

That same year, seizing two poachers in August and then five more in November, he made Yellowstone's (and thus the National Park System's) first arrests. In January 1887, Wilson joined the first winter trip through the park and in February 1888 instituted a winter backcountry law enforcement patrol, proving it viable for many generations of park rangers to follow.

Park Superintendent George Anderson would write: "[Wilson] preferred to operate alone by night and in storms; he knew every foot of the Park, and knew it better than any other man has yet known it; he knew its enemies and the practical direction of their enmity." Once, departing after dark and battling what Anderson would claim was "as bad a storm as I ever saw," the lone scout made a 40-mile trip into the rugged Yellowstone wilderness to apprehend a trapper harvesting beaver, which was illegal in the newly protected area. "Wilson came upon him while sleeping, photographed him with his own kodak, and then awakened him and brought him to the post."

Within a year of arriving in Yellowstone, bachelor Wilson fell under the charms of Mary R. Henderson, a 16-year-old beauty and the youngest daughter of a local hotel keeper. In 1891—she now 20 and he nearly 40—Wilson, so agonized from what quickly had become an unrequited love, walked up a hill and faded into the woods above Mammoth Hot Springs on the evening of July 27. Locals searched, reward posters went up, and the press wrote of the heralded scout's sudden, mysterious disappearance. Discovered the next June, his fully clothed skeleton lay next to an empty bottle of morphine.

At least the third to perish by his own hand in Yellowstone National Park, Mountaineer Assistant Ed M. Wilson was the first to create such an enigma as to generate an actual search.

The two ignominies of being the park's first suicide as well as death by drug overdose (morphine was easily obtainable in those days) belong to 27-year-old Emily Moore, who killed herself in 1884.

March 14, 1894
Yellowstone National Park

"BECAME CRAZED AND PERISHED FROM COLD"

PRIVATE David Mathews, first thought to be the victim of a poacher, disappeared on a routine mail run. It was later believed, although never conclusively proven, that his untimely mishap was due to the severe elements. He was the second of at least seven of Yellowstone's early soldiers to die of freezing or avalanches.

Captain George Anderson, Yellowstone's fourth superintendent and its first West Point graduate, wrote in his *Annual Report to the Secretary of the Interior:*

> In my last report, I noted the death of Private Mathews, of Troop B, Sixth Cav. while on detached service from the Riverside station to the Lower Basin for the mail. A most thorough search for his remains was continued for almost six months after his disappearance. His body was found early in June of this year on the south side of the Gibbon River about three miles from its junction with the Firehole. It was evident that he became lost, and while in that condition became crazed and perished from cold.

A handwritten note on the inside cover of the park's cemetery registry, the *Yellowstone Book of Interments,* states:

> This man was last seen alive March 14, 1894 when he left one of the patrol stations . . . enroute for another. His remains (identified by his clothing, watch, etc.) were found June 9, '95. He undoubtedly lost his way and perished from exhaustion and exposure.
>
> DAVID L. MATHEWS, Grave #9, Private

Captain George S. Anderson, shown here in this mid-1890s photo with one of his many trained bears, was acting superintendent of Yellowstone National Park from 1891 to 1897.

YELLOWSTONE NATIONAL
PARK PHOTO

Captain Anderson, caring and actively interested in the welfare of his men, was a vigorous and aggressive administrator of the park's law. Because of Mathews's death, the Army's mail carriers were required to travel in pairs in the future. This necessary dictum by Anderson was either disobeyed or soon forgotten, however, as evidenced by the death of Private John W. H. Davis late in 1897.

July 25, 1895
(pre) Grand Canyon National Park

"LAST PIECE OF NATURE'S HANDIWORK HE SHOULD EVER BEHOLD"

THE earliest recorded death by lightning at the Grand Canyon was that of 18-year-old Blachley H. Porter, a visitor from Connecticut. On a cloudless, unusually bright Thursday morning, Porter, his brother Louis, and their friend Arthur Renton left the south rim's Tolfree Camp and hiked to Bissell Point, some 4 miles away through thick underbrush and over a dim, rough trail.

Arriving at their destination just before noon, a sudden rainstorm set in, and the young men sought shelter under a projecting rock some distance into the canyon. Jagged and intimidating, lightning flashed all about them . . .

> They had only been under the rock a few minutes when there came a blinding flash, and Lewis [sic] [and] Arthur . . . were hurled down the incline unconscious. Renton first recovered consciousness—in about half an hour, he thinks—and dragged Lewis [sic] Porter behind a log, to prevent him falling over the precipice. When the two men recovered consciousness they were still so dazed they could not realize where they were, and started . . . their way from the canyon, thinking it was a scorching fire.
>
> Crawling and creeping as best they could, they made their way back to the rock. They were horror-stricken to find Blachley Porter dead. He lay with face turned towards the canyon, which he so shortly had admired and which was fated to be the last piece of nature's handiwork he should ever behold.

```
             July 27, 1897
      (pre) Mt. Rainier National Park
  ----------------------------------------
```

HEADLINES FROM THE JULY 30, 1897,
SEATTLE POST-INTELLIGENCER ANNOUNCE
THE MOUNTAIN'S FIRST CLIMBING VICTIM:

HIS LAST ASCENT

Edgar McClure Perishes on Mt. Rainier

Falls over a Precipice
His Bruised and Mangled Body Found Among the Rocks

AN experienced mountaineer and a professor of chemistry at the University of Oregon, Dr. Edgar McClure was among the 57 people who summitted the 14,410-foot peak that day, the greatest number to reach the top in one day to date. Electing to descend after dark, McClure

> stumbled and fell and went rolling and tumbling down the snow fields on the rocks below. His momentum was so great that his body went pitching on over the rocky slope forty-yards distant, striking stones, bruising and mangling him. Death must have been almost instantaneous.

Searching all night, Dr. Cornell, McClure's traveling companion,

> could plainly see the lanterns of the rescuing party. Just at daylight, I saw them from where I stood. They stooped down among a pile of rock and picked up the body of their professor. I hurried down, and upon reaching the spot found that he had fallen down the icy cliff fully 300 feet.

Cornell would continue, "[McClure was] held in high esteem as a profound thinker and a noble exponent of his favorite science"—he had taken thermometers and wind gauges to the summit.

> The experiments were satisfactory . . . the professor remarking . . . that every thermometer . . . taken up the mountain had been broken . . . and he would take good care that his glass should not meet with a similar fate. Poor fellow! He little thought that not only his glass would be broken, but every bone in his body as well.

While the large party was descending the next day, Mt. Rainier almost claimed more club members when two slid into a crevasse 200 feet above where McClure met his end. Badly cut, W. C. Ansley managed to struggle from the frozen crack and report the accident. The second man, Walter Rogers, although "thoroughly chilled," was narrowly saved by a rescue team after midnight.

Fay Fuller, the first woman to scale Mt. Rainier and a true trailblazer in the male-dominated sport of "peak bagging," remained on top through the night, "as sensational a piece of mountain work as ever done by a woman in this or any other country."

Almost 80 years after Professor McClure was the first to die on the slopes of Mt. Rainier, climbing guide Marty Hoey digs two other victims from the ice and snow. She would later die while climbing Mt. Everest. WALT DABNEY PHOTO

December 14, 1897
Yellowstone National Park

SKIED 132 MILES IN EIGHT DAYS

FOR sanity from isolation and boredom, the soldiers guarding Yellowstone depended on the undependable: flimsy telephone wires and the twice-monthly mail drops. The Army garrisons at Mud Geyser and Snake River had agreed to meet on the 15th and 30th of each month to exchange reports, gossip, and mail.

Lulled by a mild December and thus lightly clad, Private John W. Davis and a companion left on the 13th; relying on skiing for warmth, they reached the Lake Hotel that first night. It dropped to below zero; with a dawn departure, the 19 miles yet to be covered now seemed much farther. Exertion and frigid temperatures took their toll. Halfway, one man turned and hastily retreated; he finally made it back the next day—suffering nearly frozen fingers, ears, and toes. Now, violating Captain Anderson's ban of not traveling alone, Davis continued on . . . a fatal mistake.

The commander of Fort Yellowstone was not unduly concerned at first, "undoubtedly sharing the opinion that there was plenty of dry wood along the route and the man would surely have matches." On the 16th, the thermometer registered -35 degrees at Norris; now, most certainly overdue, a search was begun for Davis.

An hour after midnight, Sergeant Max R. Welch, the officer in charge at Norris, started toward the Canyon Hotel; 29 miles and 16 hours later, he stopped at the Lake Hotel. Over these next eight days he would ski 132 miles, most of it in subzero cold. By dawn he was en route to West Thumb.

With an increase in winter sports, hundreds of SARs take place each year that require ice and snow skills. Rocky Mountain National Park rangers Bob Haines (left) and Jim Randall skiing into an accident site in 1969.

ROCKY MOUNTAIN NATIONAL PARK RESEARCH LIBRARY

Ten miles out, near a small bridge, they found the body of Davis where he had frozen to death in the road. The corpse could not be moved, so they returned to Lake Hotel. . . . The sergeant then began construction of a sledge, using a pair of skis for runners while the soldier went back to the Mud Geyser station for assistance. . . . Sergeant Simmons . . . brought the animals . . . and he, with Welch and Akers, went out . . . to recover the body. . . . At the same time, scouts Whittaker and . . . Morrisson left Fort Yellowstone in a sleigh . . . and four-mule team to bring in the body. It took eight men and another four-mule team to get them through Snow Pass . . . and found the canvas wrapped body there.

Fighting bitter cold and drained by the 4 feet of fresh snow, the six-man rescue team delivered the frozen mail carrier to Ft. Yellowstone on the 23rd. Fearing a thaw, they buried him in Grave Number 12 in the post cemetery that very afternoon.

There is no indication that Sergeant Welch, Private Akers, or any of the other men ever received even the simplest of recognitions for their distinguished and arduous efforts.

July 1, 1899
Yosemite National Park

LADIES SHOWED NO FEAR
**Intended to Remain All Night on
Columbia Rock, in the Yosemite**

YOSEMITE, July 2—There was for a time last night at the Curry camp some anxiety for the safety of Miss Helen M. Brown of Utica, N.Y.; Mrs. Mary A. Knapp of Boston and twelve-year-old Hazel Knox of Merced. The ladies had reached Columbia rick [sic] on the trail to Eagle Peak at nightfall. The rock is on the edge of a precipice and an iron railing has been put there to give nervous people a sense of security while viewing the valley beneath. The ladies concluded to remain on the rock for the night instead of taking chances of a misstep on the mile or more zigzag path along the edge of a precipice by returning to their camp.

Worried over their absence a searching party with lanterns set out to look for the ladies. At 12:30 the searchers by firing pistol shots announced to the watchers at the camp that the women were safe.

—*The Examiner (San Francisco)*, 7-3-1899
(reprinted by permission)

Hoping to generate interest in Yosemite National Park, 36-year-old Oliver Lippincott and his Locomobile entered the park on June 23, 1900. Actually driven by Edward Russell, this is probably the first automobile to enter the national parks. HANK JOHNSTON COLLECTION

CHAPTER 2

1900–1919

There are some as is doomed to die, and
some that are not. Some as are, die;
such are as not, we save. It's the
day's work...and the men
does their best.

—Anonymous veteran of the
United States Life Saving Service, 1878

FOR the first 50 years of recreational travel in the "Wild West," national parks catered largely to the "first-class" trade and became, by default, the semi-exclusive resort for the wealthy. Despite the affluence—but not long removed from their life of frontier survival—most visitors to these rugged, isolated areas knew that to endure they must rely on skill and good judgment.

This was an era in which, when someone dared scale Yosemite's Half Dome, it made the front page of local newspapers. In 1916, the year the National Park Service was created, 356,000 tourists journeyed, often at great expense and hardship, to the 14 parks and 21 monuments then in existence. There were rangers and/or custodians in just 11 of these areas to care for the mushrooming numbers of travelers: Search and rescue and related protection were minimal at best. Fortunately for all concerned, these early voyagers were both self-contained and self-sufficient. There were no well-equipped rescue teams, government agencies watching, satellite-based radios for help, or helicopters for quick evacuation.

MILESTONES OF THE EARLY 1900s

1900

Yellowstone is visited by 8,928 tourists: 2 casualties, 1 from scalding and the disappearance (to this day) of L. R. Piper.

To protect Sequoia, 61 enlisted Army soldiers summer there.

June 23, 1900

First automobile, a 1900 Locomobile owned by Oliver M. Lippincott, enters Yosemite Valley: an NPS first. On January 6, 1902, he also chauffeured the first auto, a Stanley Steamer, to the South Rim of the Grand Canyon: also a first.

1901

Now world-famous, New Mexico's Carlsbad Caverns are "discovered." It will be made a national monument on October 25, 1923.

March 15, 1902

American Alpine Club is founded with 45 members.

May 22, 1902

Crater Lake becomes a national park; Superintendent W. R. Arant is the only search and rescue force for four years.

September 15, 1902

Prior to this date all rangers in parks are Forest Rangers until a memorandum in Sequoia referenced "Park Rangers." Later, in a June 3, 1904, letter to the Secretary of the Interior, acting superintendent of Sequoia National Park requests an individual be appointed as a "Deputy Park Ranger."

1903

Mountaineering guide concession opens at Mt. Rainier. Eight people try—but fail—to climb Mt. McKinley.

Tourists climbing out of the Grand Canyon of the Yellowstone in 1903.

YELLOWSTONE NATIONAL PARK
RESEARCH LIBRARY

MILESTONES OF THE EARLY 1900s

January 7, 1904	Radio distress signal CQD ("Stop sending and listen") is formally instituted by Marconi Company.
April 15, 1904	Carnegie Hero Awards are established. From 1904 to 1920, three people earn this prestigious prize for rescues within a national park: two in Yosemite and one in Glacier.
May 24, 1904	Driving a Stanley Steamer, Mr. and Mrs. Luper from Vallejo, California, are the first to drive into Sequoia.
1905	California enacts a law on birth and death certificates; recordkeeping until this time has been haphazard and anecdotal.
	"Observing visitors continually risking the dangerous climb to the top of Moro Rock, Captain O'Shea [Sequoia superintendent] recommended that crude steps be cut to the top for their safety."
June 5, 1905	While scaling western edge of El Capitan, 50-year-old Charles Bailey becomes Yosemite's first climbing fatality.
July 24, 1905	One-hundred-twelve climbers from the Sierra Club, Mazamas, American Alpine Club, and Appalachian Mountain Club, reach the summit of Mt. Rainier; included is Stephen T. Mather who, in a decade, will become the NPS's first director.
December 7, 1905	In a letter to the Secretary of the Interior, Sequoia's Walter Fry writes: "If you have any badges that indicate our official title, would be pleased to have them. The badges now worn, designate us as Forest Reserve Rangers."
1906	Three rangers guard Sequoia and General Grant National Parks.
May 8, 1906	"Stokes" splint-stretcher is issued Patent #820,026.
June 11, 1906	Yosemite Valley annexed into Yosemite National Park.
August 25, 1906	John W. Rhodes is first recorded death in Sequoia.
June 15, 1907	Sequoia Post Office is officially designated "Ranger."
August 12, 1907	First Carnegie Hero Award to be earned in a park—Yosemite.

MILESTONES OF THE EARLY 1900s

November 13, 1907	Twenty-four-hp helicopter is first flown in France.
1908	Lectures by Major Charles Lynch of the Army's Surgeon General's staff are issued: the first Red Cross First Aid Manual.
July 24, 1908	First automobile permit, a $5 annual fee sold at Mt. Rainier, to be issued in a national park; motorized vehicles usher in the era of emergency and rescue work.
September 17, 1908	Lt. Thomas E. Selfridge of Army Signal Corps at Ft. Meyer, Virginia, becomes world's first person to die in a plane crash.
November 22, 1908	SOS distress signal is adopted by seafarers.
1909	Civil Aid Services Mountain Rescue Unit is founded in Hong Kong.
1910	First aid as a national program is launched by Red Cross.
	Yellowstone has 19,575 visitors; Yosemite, 13,619; Crater Lake, about 5,000; and General Grant, 3,585.
	To guard Sequoia, the Army uses 3 officers and 50 men.
April 10, 1910	Two men from the Sourdough Expedition plant a spruce-tree flagpole on lower of two summits of Mt. McKinley.
1911	After two men disappear in a storm in August 1909, Mt. Rainier Superintendent Edward Hall introduces "Official Guide System" for climbing the peak. "Those . . . are mountaineers of known ability, and no accidents of a serious nature have occurred where parties have been accompanied by these official guides." In 1914 three of the four guides will be paid $25 per summit trip.
	First Boy Scouts of America Honor Medal for Lifesaving is presented to Charles Scruggs of Cuero, Texas.
	Deployed from 15 stations, 350 soldiers protect Yellowstone.
June 1911	Two are killed in four-horse stagecoach wreck in Yosemite.
September 11, 1911	First Conference of National Parks is held in Yellowstone; one topic on agenda is need for visitor safety.

MILESTONES OF THE EARLY 1900s

1912	Statue of Liberty, although not yet part of National Park System, is "violated" when a man parachutes from the top: the first of many such headaches for the NPS.
March 1, 1912	World's first parachute jump from an airplane.
April 1912	Colorado Mountain Club is founded with 25 members.
June 7, 1912	Top of 20,320-foot-high Mt. McKinley, highest point in North America, is finally reached.
1913	Water-oriented lifesaving program is initiated by Red Cross.
	There are at least 285 lifesaving stations along sands and shoals of outer United States as well as Great Lakes.
	Rangers cannot transfer from park to park; they must resign from one area before moving to another.
February 22, 1913	California's *Mariposa Gazette:* "Considering the number of visitors and the ruggedness of the country it is gratifying . . . that accidents [in Yosemite] . . . are very rare. Unceasing vigilance . . . is exercised by the park authorities and those engaged in serving the tourists who enter the wonderland."
August 13, 1913	Dr. Fletcher, killed while climbing on Blackfoot Glacier, is first death documented in Glacier National Park.
1914	Mountaineering concept of "belaying" is introduced to United States.
	Just nine NPS areas have park rangers.
June 14, 1914	Lassen Volcano erupts; one person is believed killed.
June 25, 1914	Straining to reach 15,700 feet, Silas Christofferson is pilot of first plane to fly over Sequoia's 14,495-foot Mt. Whitney.
1915	Visitation to Yosemite is 31,548; Mt. Rainier, 30,000.
July 26, 1915	With an annual salary of $900, 22-year-old Richard "Dixie" MacCracken begins as Rocky Mountain National Park's first ranger.
August 1915	The American First Aid Conference is formed.

MILESTONES OF THE EARLY 1900s

August 1, 1915

Automobiles are finally allowed into Yellowstone; before the close of the season, 985 cars will make the circuit of the park's roads; this is the end of the horse-drawn stage era.

September 3, 1915

First motor vehicle death in Yellowstone, very probably a first within the NPS.

1916

Yosemite has 1 chief ranger, 1 assistant, 1 special ranger for maintenance, 1 for timber cutting, 3 regular rangers, and 19 temporary rangers. Rocky Mountain National Park has 1 chief ranger and 4 other rangers.

Stigler Stretcher, developed by Vienna's Dr. Robert Stigler, is first used by Austro-Hungarian troops. It will eventually be used by rangers in the mountainous West for litter evacuations.

Largely because of the sinking of the *Titanic* in 1912, life belts with lights attached for visibility at night are invented.

July 15, 1916

Official census of campers in Yosemite Valley counts 1,115 people on this day; most are tenting out of autos.

August 1, 1916

Hawaii National Park is established, but there will be no rangers until 1922. Eight days later, Lassen Volcanic National Park is established; there will be no money to administer it for four more years.

August 25, 1916

National Park Service is established by President Woodrow Wilson. Law provides for a director at $4,500 annually, an assistant director at $2,500, a chief clerk at $2,000, a draftsman at $1,800, a messenger at $600, and as many employees as needed—so long as total cost for new agency does not exceed $19,500. Congress allows the existing 35 parks and monuments $500,000.

October 16, 1916

"By mutual agreement of the heads of the departments, troops were withdrawn from the park [Yellowstone], and a civilian supervisor, with a corps of 25 rangers for patrol and protection work, and a few civilian employees necessary for other duties, appointed by the Secretary of Interior replace them."

1917

Red Cross Safety First program is adopted in national forests. Through correspondence courses, concerned foresters begin first-aid instruction. There are 100 questions in 10 papers; by 1922, 100 rangers will be enrolled in 32 isolated stations in California and 2 in Nevada.

MILESTONES OF THE EARLY 1900s

April 1917

As reported in the *Philadelphia Press,* fog bells are devised for placement along Rocky Mountain trails from a quarter to a half mile on top of Flattop, Longs Peak, Hallet's Glacier, and Hallet's Peak. The bells will be of a deep tone; suspended over them will be a small, lightweight paddle; the slightest breeze will tilt the paddle and ring the bell. These bells are a response to the 1915 disappearance of President Wilson's friend, Dr. Sampson.

May 16, 1917

Steven T. Mather is appointed first director of NPS; only 99 people staff all the NPS field areas. Superintendents are only responsible to NPS director.

August 14, 1917

Dorothy Haskell is killed in a fall into a crevasse. To date, 14 people have died in Mt. Rainier National Park: nine climbing, three avalanche, one gunshot, and one motor vehicle.

August 18, 1917

First two-way air-to-ground radio message.

October 1917

First plane to land in an NPS area—Yellowstone. A plane is known to have landed in East Glacier in 1913, within just feet of the park. The evidence that it actually landed inside of Glacier National Park is inconclusive, however.

Fall 1917

Organized winter sports begin in Yosemite, Rocky Mountain, and Mt. Rainier National Parks. Rangers handle traffic control, accidents, and searches for lost skiers.

1918

Prior to becoming superintendent in 1921, Roger Toll publishes *Mountaineering in Rocky Mountain National Park,* a manual on recreational climbing for the general public.

U.S. Army Air Service modifies several combat planes into "flying ambulances" for medical evacuations during World War I.

Summer 1918

Five women are hired as seasonal "Rangerettes": Yosemite, Mt. Rainier, Glacier, Sequoia, and Yellowstone National Parks.

1919

Glacier National Park is visited by 22,449. Up to this date, six people have died in the park.

February 26, 1919

Grand Canyon National Park is established; 37,745 visitors are recorded that year. First death from a vehicle accident on October 4.

```
July 30, 1900
Yellowstone National Park
```

THE DANDY DISAPPEARS . . . FOREVER

IN 1900, 8,928 visitors were recorded in the park. Among them was 36-year-old LeRoy R. Piper.

A bank cashier from Ohio, Piper was en route to California to settle an uncle's estate. Fashionably dressed in a blue suit, monogrammed white shirt, patent leather shoes, and derby hat, the sartorial dandy was sporting two diamond rings, a Knight Templar emblem, and a Shriner's button when last seen stepping onto the porch of the Fountain Hotel at Lower Geyser Basin. He vanished.

L. R. Piper walked away from Yellowstone's Fountain Hotel and was never seen again.

YELLOWSTONE NATIONAL PARK
RESEARCH LIBRARY

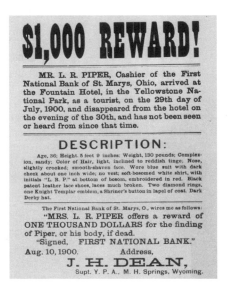

$1,000 REWARD!

MR. L. R. PIPER, Cashier of the **First National Bank of St. Marys, Ohio,** arrived at the Fountain Hotel, in the Yellowstone National Park, as a tourist, on the **29th** day of July, 1900, and disappeared from the hotel on the evening of the **30th,** and has not been seen or heard from since that time.

DESCRIPTION:

Age, 36; Height, 5 feet 9 inches; Weight, 130 pounds; Complexion, sandy; Color of Hair, light, inclined to reddish tinge. Nose, slightly crooked; smooth-shaven face. Wore blue suit with dark check about one inch wide; no vest; soft-bosomed white shirt, with initials "L. R. P." at bottom of bosom, embroidered in red. Black patent leather lace shoes, laces much broken. Two diamond rings, one Knight Templar emblem, a Shriner's button in lapel of coat. Dark Derby hat.

The First National Bank of St. Marys, O., wires me as follows:

"MRS. L. R. PIPER offers a reward of ONE THOUSAND DOLLARS for the finding of Piper, or his body, if dead.

"Signed, FIRST NATIONAL BANK."

Aug. 10, 1900.   Address,

J. H. DEAN,

Supt. Y. P. A., M. H. Springs, Wyoming.

In his *Annual Report to the Secretary of the Interior* for 1900, the superintendent of Yellowstone wrote:

> [Piper was] reported . . . some twenty-four hours after he was first missed. My men were . . . fighting fire at . . . Shoshone Lake, and I could render little or no help. My patrols were instructed to do what was possible, and some days later a searching party was organized by friends of the lost man. Nothing being accomplished, however, the day following the return of my men from the scene of the fire I sent out a detachment, and some days later a second detachment, but with no better result.
>
> . . . my belief that Mr. Piper, when he arrived at the Fountain Hotel, was in a partially demented and irresponsible condition and that he wandered away from the hotel, fell in with some camping outfit, and got out of the park.

Despite the offer of a $1,000 reward and a one month search by the Army, no clue to Piper's fate was ever found. Lee Whittlesey, in his book *Death in Yellowstone*, theorizes that the man "walked out into the night and inadvertently stumbled into one of the many hot springs . . . located nearby."

```
July 6, 1901
Yellowstone National Park
```

FELL WAIST DEEP INTO HOT MUD

**A Shocking Accident Befalls Two Women Travelers
in the Yellowstone**

WERE VIEWING THE "PAINT POTS" AT THE THUMB

When Pulled from the Boiling Spring They Were Terribly Burned

**They Were Completing a Tour of the World and Visiting the Park
on Their Way from This City**

Special Dispatched to the "Chronicle."

HELENA (Mont.) July 9—A report was received to-day from Mammoth Hot Springs in the Yellowstone National Park, of an unusual accident which occurred there Saturday afternoon. Two women, Mrs. Zabriski [sic: LaBriskie] and daughter of Brooklyn, N.Y., fell into one of the boiling "paint pots" at the Thumb on the lake, and before they could be rescued sustained injuries from which they may not recover.

The paint pots at the Thumb are huge natural caldrons of clay, each one colored mud. Similar phenomena are found in various places in the park, [these] giant paint pots being near the fountain geyser. The women, who were touring the park by way of the Modia route, were inspecting the boiling mud springs Saturday afternoon. They were unaccompanied, and all the details of the accident may never be known. One of the women fell into the boiling mud caldron, and it is presumed that the other also fell in while trying to rescue her companion.

Both women were submerged in the boiling mud almost to their waists, and neither was able to extricate herself. Friends who were some distance away heard the unfortunate women cry for help and rushed to their assistance. They were pulled out of the boiling spring in an almost unconscious condition.

There is no telephone or telegraph line to the Thumb, but as a steamboat happened to be there at the time of the accident, the women were put on board and conveyed to the Lake Hotel. Medical assistance was summoned from Mammoth Hot Spring. Both women were frightfully burned and it is reported that their injuries will probably prove fatal.

—*San Francisco Chronicle,* 7-10-01

(reprinted by permission)

```
July 7, 1901
Yosemite National Park
```

DROWNED IN THE RAPIDS

DARING YOUNG LADY LOSES HER LIFE

A Canvas Craft Upset Among the Rocks of the Merced

Companion Endeavors to Save Her, but She Slips from His Grasp and Her Body Disappears

SPECIAL DISPATCH TO THE "CHRONICLE."

YOSEMITE. July 7—The body of Miss Sadie Schaffer, one of the waitresses of the Sentinel Hotel, lies in the rapids of the Merced this evening near El Capitan bridge. At about 2:30 o'clock this afternoon a party of three—Miss Schaffer, Miss Sadie Young and Johnny Van Campen—left the Sentinel Hotel in the latter's boat. This is a frail, canvas-covered craft. When starting out into the stream they were warned of the treacherous waters of the Merced. They jokingly bid their friends good-by.

At about 4 P. M. they reached the beginning of the rapids above El Capitan bridge. There they landed, Miss Young going ashore. Miss Schaffer and Van Campen, however, concluded to continue through the rapids. A short distance below that point Van Campen saw that they could not do this with safety, so pulled toward the shore, catching hold of a root.

At this moment Miss Schaffer, in a spirit of daring took one of the oars and shoved the boat again into the stream, saying that they would shoot the rapids anyway, at the same time dropping the oar into the water. In a moment the boat became unmanageable and upset, throwing the young lady out on one side and Van Campen on the other. For a moment both held to the upturned boat. Then he caught her hand and floated down with the current 100 feet or more. Unfortunately they struck a large bowlder [sic] and thus became separated, both going under. When he came to the surface he could not find any trace of her.

Two men were on the riverside a short distance below but they did not see her body float by. Her hat was found about half a mile below the scene of the accident. A large force of men examined the river but at dark they abandoned the search. It will be resumed again in the morning by Guardian Stevens and a force of men.

The young lady was an expert swimmer. Her parents are dead but she has a sister living in Oklahoma Territory. She was a general favorite with the tourists.

—*San Francisco Chronicle,* 7-8-01
(reprinted by permission)

February 17, 1904
Yellowstone National Park

CHRIST MARTIN AND CHARLES NELSON, CORPORALS

CHRIST Martin and Charles Nelson, Corporals of Troop C, 3rd Cavalry, intended to ski southward to the Riverside Station (the first name for West Yellowstone). Lou Bart, an old prospector from the nearby Apex Mine, had always warned the local soldiers to give wide berth to the base of a nearby mountain during the winter because of avalanche danger. Within a half mile, their route from the Specimen Creek Gallatin Soldier Station would take them by a steep slope near the river.

> Heedless of Bart's warning, they veered over to the west side of the valley and were caught by a thunderous avalanche. Corporal Nelson, who was some distance behind Martin, was not entirely engulfed and managed to free himself and go to Jim Trail's cabin for help. Jim and Ed Moorman, who was [sic] staying with him that winter, immediately went to the slide area and searched for Martin, but with no success.

After two months of significant effort by several search teams, including a detail of U.S. Cavalry, 38-year-old Christ A. Martin, a career soldier of more than 20 years, was found on April 16. He was subsequently interred in the Mammoth Army Cemetery in Grave 21.

July 26, 1904
Sequoia National Park

"STRUCK BY A THUNDER BOLT AND INSTANTLY KILLED"

MT. WHITNEY, the highest point in the contiguous United States, was originally named Fisherman's Peak by the first Europeans to reach its summit; Messrs. Johnson, Begole, and Lucas stood on the 14,495-foot granite crest on August 18, 1873. Within another month five other intrepid adventurers had worked their way up, including the most celebrated mountaineer of that era, John Muir.

> This peak, Mt. Whitney, was this day [September 19, 1873] climbed by Clarence King, U.S. Geologist, and Frank F. Norris of Tule River. On Sept. 1st in N.Y., I first learned that the high peak south of here, which I climbed in 1871, was not Mt. Whitney and I immediately came here. Clouds and storms prevented me from recognizing this in 1871, or I should have come here then. (C. King)

On July 18, 1904, a trail to the top of Mt. Whitney was finally completed; it cost a total of $275.55, including wages of $199.00. G. F. Marsh blasted a rough route up the eastern face of the peak. He reported, "I can not find words to thank the gallant little band that stayed with me through frozen snow banks and the bitter north wind and worked so hard and cheerfully amid the treacherous rocks."

Killed by Lightning

(July 29, 1904, *Inyo Independent*) A terrible fatality occurred on the summit of Mt. Whitney last Tuesday. A party of eight people, being the U.S. Fish Commission and attendants, made the ascent of Whitney from the west slope. While on the summit a thunder shower broke over the mountain, and the party sought shelter under a shelving rock. . . . [T]he packer for the party, a young man named Byrd Surby, remained standing on a high rock and was struck by a thunder bolt and instantly killed. Two others were rendered unconscious from the shock. Two of the party went to Lone Pine for assistance and the remains were taken to that place the next day. Dr. Woodin went to Lone Pine yesterday to prepare the body for shipment to the young man's home at Three Rivers.

This is the first recorded traumatic death in what is now either Sequoia or Kings Canyon National Park. The remote Kern River Canyon and the 14,000-foot Sierra Nevada crest were part of the Roosevelt-Sequoia National Park Bill before the 69th Congress. The name Roosevelt, in memory of the recently departed Teddy, was ultimately dropped in a Senate amendment adopted only the day before. Thus finally, on July 3, 1926, Mt. Whitney became a part of Sequoia rather than Roosevelt-Sequoia National Park.

```
                    June 5, 1905
              Yosemite National Park
    ---------------------------------------
```

PARK'S FIRST CLIMBING DEATH

WHEN Charles A. Bailey "was dashed to death" trying to make a "record climb up a cliff west of El Capitan," the 50-year-old real estate dealer from Oakland became the first in a long list to die challenging the vertical world of Yosemite granite.

No stranger to the park's perils, the adventurer had spent 16 summers hiking the area during which he "discovered" Sierra Point. Bailey, a prominent member of the newly formed Sierra Club who was particularly enamored with Yosemite Valley, had authored several articles heralding its charm and beauty. He had just returned from a 14-month trip around the world on which he had conquered several notable mountains, the Matterhorn among them.

Along with J. C. Staats, his 22-year-old partner from Ohio, he started early on the "almost perpendicular face of the cliff where there is no trail and where man has never placed foot before."

Midafternoon the two novice climbers halted for a breath after scaling nearly half of the stately cliff's 3,000 feet. "Bailey was sitting on a narrow shelf and Staats was clinging to the face of the rock below. Suddenly Bailey began to slide. He shot downward a few feet to Staats' left and fell headlong out of sight, striking his head several times before he disappeared."

"Horror-stricken" but mustering his courage, Staats cautiously worked his way down to where he found a hat and blood-spattered rock. Unable to go farther and with "almost superhuman efforts," he managed to reach the top and then proceeded back to the village. "Staats was almost prostrated by the physical and mental strain."

> The party searching for the body of Baily [sic] located it at 11 o'clock to-day [June 6]. J. A. Snell of Calistoga and H. Spaulding and F. Curry of Palo Alto were lowered by rope 600 feet and by 1 o'clock had brought the corpse to a point where it could be taken by others. The body was badly mangled and most of the bones were broken.

Charles A. Bailey was the first climber to fall to his death in Yosemite. According to historian/author Hank Johnston in *The Yosemite Grants, 1854–1906: A Pictorial History,* Giacomo Campi, an Italian restaurateur from San Francisco, fell to his death in June 1871, the only known fatality resulting from climbing the rickety old ladders up the cliff beside Vernal Fall. The two ladders were replaced that summer by a more sturdy wooden stairway.

On June 14, 1897, according to the *Sierra Club Bulletin* for that year, Charles Bailey and two other men located a spot on the western flank of Grizzly Peak just above Yosemite Valley where five of the park's major waterfalls could be seen at once: Vernal, Nevada, Lower Yosemite, Upper Yosemite, and Ililouette.

1905 or 1906
(pre) Glacier National Park

EARLY REMEMBRANCES OF A FOREST RANGER

IN the Forest Reserve Act of 1891, Congress authorized U.S. presidents to set aside large tracts of areas of the public domain. Prior to its establishment in 1910, what is now Glacier National Park was such a forest reserve, or national forest, as they were retitled in 1907. Ranger Frank F. Liebig worked for the Forest Service from 1902 until he retired in 1935. The following is from a letter he wrote in 1944 to a Forest Service historian about a rescue mission he was on in the soon-to-be-established Glacier National Park.

> On one of these trips coming in across Gunsight Pass, I came in late one evening into Sperry Glacier basin with my horses, ready to set up my tent for the night. I saw a crowd of people a little ways off and heard someone saying,

"There is the ranger now." And soon some people came running over and said a woman had fallen into a crevasse in Sperry Glacier and they didn't know how to get her out. In the meanwhile they had sent a man down to the hotel ten miles away to get some ropes.

When the people told me about the woman falling into the crevasse, I turned the horses loose in a hurry, and grabbed two lash ropes and the ax, and told the men to come on. The place was a quarter of a mile to the edge of the glacier, and about 250 yards across the ice to the crevasse. I cut a stunted green fir tree four or five inches and five feet long, and had the men pack it along. When we got to the place three or four men stood at the place where the woman slid in. Two women and three more men came along, with them a minister of the gospel by the name of Falls—a real mountaineer. . . . I selected a place on the lower side of the crevasse, and set the green post into the hole and packed ice all around to make it fairly solid. Then tied the two lash ropes together and tied a number of knots into the rope for a good hand hold. Then tied the rope to the post sticking above the ice and told a couple of men to hang onto the post so it couldn't slip out and threw the rope into the crevasse.

I could see the woman lying almost horizontal in the ice. The crevasse was about four or five feet wide on the top, and came together to a knife edge on the bottom, about 35 feet down. She was wedged in at about 30 feet, and dead as a door nail. (So we thought.)

I slid down the rope, and had some sweat worked up, and when I got down (Was it cold!) I tried to hang onto the rope and pull the woman loose, but couldn't budge her. The walls of ice were smooth as glass and I could not get a foothold. We thought she was dead anyhow, so I stepped on her body to rest my feet, and told the men to haul up the rope and send the ax down, which they did. Then I chopped a hole on each side of the ice big enough to put my feet in for a hold, then sent the ax again to the top. When the rope came down again I started to pull the woman loose and nearly pulled her arm out, she was wedged in so tight. But I finally got her loose, having a foothold chopped in the ice, then managed to get the rope around her waist and the men pulled her up to the surface and then let the rope down again.

I was so frozen by this time I was in doubt that I could climb the rope, so I put it under my arms and was hauled out by the men too. When I got out I could hardly stand up I was so cold, and had to stamp around a bit to get my blood in circulation again.

We had plenty of help by this time. Someone brought a lantern and candles from camp, and it was getting dark. There was no stretcher, so four men got hold of the woman, one on each leg and one on each arm, one ahead with the lantern. When we got to the edge of the ice there was a narrow trail leading down through the rocks and around some cliffs, one over 20 feet high. We thought it would be safer for all of us to let the body down on our rope over the cliff. Someone went ahead to receive the body below. When the body was half-way down, the woman began to spin around and hit her head on the rocks, cutting quite a gash in her head, which must have brought her to. Because she let out an awful yell, which scared us half to death, as we had all thought she was a goner for sure. Then she fainted again.

We got her to the camp finally, where they had a big fire going and lots of hot coffee and lots more of hot drinks, and we all had our share of the hot brandy. Even the minister of the gospel and yours truly, even if I was on the water wagon. I had my share and don't know today how I got into my sleeping bag only half undressed. I think someone else must have helped me.

A doctor came up towards morning and pronounced the woman o.k. Some men and women filling her up all night with hot brandy, until she was gloriously drunk. We sure had a late breakfast next day. All thought I had done a wonderful job. But I pulled out ahead of the crowd in order not to attract so much attention. I didn't even stop at the hotel and went direct to the ranger station. The woman never even said thank you for getting her out of the glacier. She surely would have been dead if she had stayed in the ice all night. But such is the world.

```
                August 12, 1907
             Yosemite National Park
-------------------------------------------
```

THE FIRST CARNEGIE HERO AWARDS

ON March 12, 1904, philanthropist and steel tycoon Andrew Carnegie, in signing a Deed of Trust to establish the Carnegie Hero Fund Commission, said:

> We live in an heroic age. Not seldom are we thrilled by deeds of heroism where men or women are injured or lose their lives in attempting to preserve or refuse their fellows; such the heroes of civilization. The heroes of barbarism maimed or killed theirs.
>
> I have long felt that the heroes and those dependent upon them should be freed from pecuniary cares resulting from their heroism, and, as a fund for this purpose, I have transferred to the Commission five million dollars of First Collateral Five Per Cent. Bonds of the United States Steel Corporation, the proceeds to be used . . .

On August 12, 1907, the first **Carnegie Awards** granted in a national park area were:

> #429—**Harry L. Masser**, aged seventeen, student, helped to save Bertha L. Pillsbury, aged seventeen from drowning. . . . Masser swam fifty feet to Miss Pillsbury, who had become frightened when carried beyond her depth in the Merced River. She grasped him, and they struggled together until another man arrived and relieved Masser, who then swam to shallow water, almost exhausted.

> #430—**J. Parks Jones**, aged seventeen, student. . . . Jones, who shortly before had sprained his neck, witnessed the struggle between Miss Pillsbury and Masser, and swam seventy-five feet to them. He grabbed Miss Pillsbury, and swam forty feet with her, being dazed and weak when he got to the bank.
> —*Carnegie Hero Fund Commission 1907 Annual Report*

The first award (#1) bestowed by the Pittsburgh-based Carnegie Hero Fund Commission was for a July 17, 1904, save of a drowning person in Pennsylvania. Beginning with Messrs. Masser and Jones, 48 **Carnegie Awards** have been bestowed for various acts of valor in our national park areas.

```
                  August 3, 1908
        (pre) Grand Canyon National Park
------------------------------------------------------------------
```

BRUSH SAVES HIS LIFE

Survives Greatest Dive Ever Made into the Great Gorge—Lands on Thick Brush on Narrow Ledge

THE escape of D. Johnson last week [August 3] from certain death, when precipitated over the rim of the Grand Canyon by the roots of a falling tree at Grandview was certainly miraculous.

Johnson was thrown in the air ten feet or more and out into the canyon head foremost, passing through two narrow projecting ledges of jagged rock, landing on a three-foot ledge a hundred feet below. Tons of rock came tumbling down following the fall of the tree, but still conscious he had presence of mind enough to crawl underneath a projecting ledge of rock and escape it. Had he struck the projecting ledges of rock death would have been certain; the heavy growth of brush on the narrow ledge was placed exactly right to break his fall and prevent his rolling off the ledge.

Had he fallen from this ledge his fall would have been a thousand feet or more sheer to the rocks below. Johnson, with two others were working on a tree about eight inches in diameter standing on the edge of the rim. It gave way suddenly when he was standing directly behind it. A heavy root broke and caught him in the bark as the tree fell, throwing him upward and out into the canyon.

He was brought up by a round about trail to the rim. A physician happened to be stopping at the hotel and an examination was hurriedly made. It was found that no bones had been broken and aside from minor bruises and shock of the fall he was perfectly sound. He was brought to Flagstaff the day following his fall.

—*The Coconino Sun*, 8-14-08 (reprinted by permission)

June 17, 1909
Yosemite National Park

"A PREY TO BIRDS AND WILD BEASTS"

LEAVING the comfort of the Glacier Point Hotel, 37-year-old F. P. Shepherd headed for nearby Sentinel Dome. When a thick, water-filled fog rolled in, the jeweler's two women companions quickly abandoned the adventure; the recent immigrant from England went on.

For days, these soldiers in Yosemite National Park "scaled the faces of dizzy precipices" searching for F. P. Shepherd. The 37-year-old jeweler was never found.
YOSEMITE NATIONAL PARK RESEARCH LIBRARY

For almost a week, readers of the *San Francisco Chronicle* keenly traced the efforts of the Army's Yosemite Cavalry detachment.

> Nothing seemed to daunt these brave soldiers. They scaled the faces of dizzy precipices, they were lowered with windlasses over the rocky walls where not even a goat could get a foothold, and dangled between earth and heaven without fear or complaint. They shrank from no risk, no matter how perilous, for their hearts seemed to be in the search.

Led by Lieutenant Lynch, a detail of U.S. Cavalry spent the next four days "with ropes and grappling irons . . . descending the sheer cliffs which look down on the Illilouette falls and the rapids in the upper Merced canyon." The danger of what they were doing was not lost on the soldiers—or the newspaper.

> It is a task attended with the utmost danger, as one slip on the part of the soldiers would send them to a terrible death thousands of feet to the rocks below. It is feared now that he may have been attacked by wild beasts or that in trying to find his way in the thick fog at night he may have fallen over some cliff and been dashed to death. If he is still alive he will be in a deplorable condition, as he is without food and blankets . . . the chilling rain which has fallen in and around the valley will leave him in a badly weakened physical state.

Using field glasses, one well-intentioned but ill-informed Army officer steadfastly watched a flock of large black birds for hours, thinking they might be carrion-seeking vultures; they weren't.

> There was always the faint hope that should Shepherd be found, life might not be extinct, and it was this hope that spurred on the brave cavalrymen. . . . Every nook and cranny, every clump of brush, not only on the face of the cliffs, but on the upper levels was diligently searched for traces of the unfortunate man.

On June 21, the search for the ill-fated hiker was terminated.

> Shepherd is now considered to be beyond human aid, and the only object in continuing the hunt would be to save the unfortunate man's body from being left in the wilderness, a prey to birds and wild beasts.

August 14, 1909
Mt. Rainier National Park

ALL THAT WAS EVER FOUND OF THE TWO CLIMBERS

ALL that was ever found of the two climbers were their alpenstocks perched at the lip of the 14,410-foot summit's steaming crater. Disappearing in deteriorating weather, J.W.Stevens, 30, and T.V. Callaghan, 50, became the second and third to die while trying to reach the mountain's crest. A third member of the party, L. M. Sterling, turned around at the 13,000-foot level. A less experienced climber than his associates, Sterling descended to Paradise, where he waited. They never showed up and are still on the mountain.

In 1909, there were only four men on the ranger force to handle the 3,782 people who registered in the park that year. Two years later, in a belated reaction to these two deaths, park boss Edwin S. Hall instituted an "Official Guide System" for those visitors wishing to climb on the mountain; that first year there were four authorized guides.

On August 12, 1912, Charlot Hunt became the fifth to perish while attempting to reach the top of Mt. Rainier and the 10th fatality recorded in the park. The following day's story, courtesy of the *Seattle Post-Intelligencer*, describes her demise.

Stevens and Callaghan were the second and third victims to die climbing Mt. Rainier. After sliding 1,000 feet in 1977, this 47-year-old victim was the 23rd. The pilot of the Chinook helicopter did an amazing job holding the rear of the ship in place for 20 minutes.

JOHN CONOBOY PHOTO

SEATTLE GIRL FALLS TO DEATH ON MT. RAINIER
**Body with Every Bone Broken, Found in Valley and
Placed on Litter of Alpenstocks and Sweaters—Party of 15 from Tacoma
Y.M.C.A. Made Ascent in Safety**

About 10:45, not long after the start downward, Miss Hunt reeled and plunged forward, falling about fifteen feet. Clinging on the side of the mountain a moment, she seemed to break her fall, and her startled companions had half formed thoughts that a tragedy had been averted when she lunged forward a second time and in the sight of her horrified fellow-climbers, tumbled and rolled down the mountain over, and among the rocks, until with a crash her battered body came to a stop at the bottom of the incline.

Unnerved by the scene of horror they had witnessed, the other young women in the party of sixteen . . . were unable to continue the ascent . . . and the other young men . . . let the shuddering girls down with ropes and the remainder of the party reached the valley shaken but unhurt.

Professor Edgar McClure was killed in 1897 while climbing Mt. Rainier; in the 100 years since then, 66 others have joined him.

```
                    1909 or 1910
              Sequoia National Park
    ----------------------------------------
```

THE LEGEND OF LOST SOLDIER CAVE

CLEAR and cold, the South Fork of the Kaweah River raced toward the San Joaquin; fleecy clouds drifted silently overhead and summer breezes rippled the hillsides lush with wildflowers. The legend of Lost Soldier Cave was born on one of these lazy Sierra days.

For the few soldiers garrisoned along the South Fork at the tiny camp at Clough Cave—with little to occupy their time but checking an occasional fisherman or keeping stray sheep from trespassing into the park—it was easy, if not somewhat isolated, duty.

When the young warrior returned from his explorations upstream, the others in camp didn't share his excitement at finding a new cavern. They were living across the stream from one cave, and with several other small ones nearby, this discovery was no great surprise. Saying the waist-high opening was in a small side canyon a mile away, he described what he knew: With the entrance tunnel slanting steeply downward, a rolled rock seemed to bounce a long time before its rattling sound faded away to nothing.

Having generated little or no interest in his adventure, the soldier set out alone the next available free day. Along with ropes, candles, and a lantern, he was armed with a gun for "hibernating bears or demons of the underground." Tying his rope to a sturdy nearby tree, he entered the dark hole.

After sliding 20 feet down a precipitous, sewer-sized, and mud-slicked chute, he lowered himself over an abrupt overhang to the rocks 30 feet below. Then, working his way cautiously along the uneven and jagged ledges, he came to an even lower passage. On his hands and knees, the intrepid explorer left his lantern perched at the top. Not noticing that the tunnel curved a little, the soldier went onward; casting shadows, his candle flickered.

Stopped by a yawning "bottomless" pit, he dropped a rock; the noise echoed back up. Excited and with the wax quickly melting down, he started the short distance back toward the light. With cool sweat misting from his brow, he looked forward to the summer freshness outside. But he couldn't find the kerosene lamp.

By evening his friends became worried; firing their rifles throughout the night, they got no answer. After enlisting nearby campers who surprisingly took charge, the group was soon following tracks up the ravine. They almost stumbled over the outstretched rope.

Over time, the mystery of the lost soldier and his cavern grew more quixotic. At park headquarters there was no record of the cave or the incident; local lore shed little light. Finally, after nearly 40 years, the cave was rediscovered: Byron Allen of nearby Visalia slid down the mud-caked rope to find the "Lost Soldier."

PHOTOGRAPHER NEVER FOUND

B. B. BAKOWSKI specialized in photos for scenic postcards. Intent on capturing the frozen fairyland of Crater Lake deep in an Oregon winter, he loaded his sled with cameras and other supplies and struck out for the park's white wilderness.

The first notice of the misadventure appeared in the February 22 *Medford Mail Tribune:* "PHOTOGRAPHER LOST IN SNOWS OF CRATER LAKE."

Failing to make a prearranged meeting date, several search teams looked for Bakowski over the next month. They found a canvas tarp sagging across the opening of a 10-foot-long snow tunnel, inside of which were shoes, underwear, and extra clothing. They found papers, letters, and 60 rolls of unexposed film. They found a pencil stuck in the snow. But they found no B. B. Bakowski.

The headlines of March 3 read:

GALE RAGING CRATER LAKE
Blizzard Has Prevailed for Three Weeks
Little Doubt That Photographer Perished

Whether he plunged to his death over the snowy precipices of Crater Lake or was frozen to death in the blizzard which held the lake in its embrace for three weeks will not be known until the summer sun has melted away the huge drifts of snow.

The searching parties have been greatly hampered by the severe blizzard which is raging at the lake. It is impossible to see over 200 yards ahead and snow is drifted many feet deep. A high gale prevails.

Conditions at the lake are such that if Bakowski remained in the neighborhood it is impossible for him to be alive.

By March 9 all search parties had given up; "the melting snows of summer would have to succeed where they had failed." Snows have melted for years, but the fate of B. B. Bakowski, the young photographer from Bend, Oregon, remains a mystery.

After all the publicity and effort this strange disappearance received, Park Superintendent Arant wanted to bar all visitor access during the winter. He failed.

WITH ROPES AND GRAPPLING HOOKS

SWELLED with the water from the melting snow fields, the canyon was so clouded with spray that it was impossible save for a water weasel [sic: ouzel]. Lured on by the rare beauty of the wild, white water, confident of their own skill and judgement, [sic] they had gained the brink of a dizzy ledge when suddenly young Pohli missed his footing. In an instant the mad torrent seized him and hurled him into the choas [sic] of the cascades and bowlders [sic].

Austin Ramon Pohli, a popular senior at the University of California, "slipped on a spray-drenched boulder and fell over 100-foot Snow Creek falls." His three school friends made a valiant effort to find him without any success.

Learning of the disaster, the park superintendent, Army Major W. T. Littlebrandt, quickly "dispatched fifteen of his troopers, who toiled in the midst of the torrents at great personal hazard. Indian guides were sent . . . with ropes and grappling hooks to endeavor to recover the body."

His body was recovered the second day "thereafter by First Sergt. Louis Dorn, Troop A, First Cavalry, who had himself lowered by rope to the pool of water beneath the fall. He secured the body by diving for it."

The February 22, 1913, *Mariposa Gazette* read in part: "Considering the number of visitors and the ruggedness of the country it is gratifying . . . that accidents in Yosemite are very rare. Unceasing vigilance for their prevention is exercised by the park authorities and those . . . serving the tourists who enter the wonderland."

Despite space age technology, mules and cacolets (litter on pack frame) are still used today on SARs. The victim on this mule was recovered from Yosemite National Park's Snow Creek Falls 72 years after Austin Pohli died there.

HUGH DOUGHER
COLLECTION

August 19, 1913
Glacier National Park
- -

DR. FLETCHER IS INSTANTLY KILLED

While Exploring in Glacier Park He Makes Misstep and Falls

GLACIER Park, Mont., Aug. 20—While exploring one of the deepest crevasses in the glacier body, Dr. Clavis [sic] I.

Fletcher, of Indianapolis, a well known explorer, whose research in glacier formation had been extended, fell 600 feet, and was instantly killed. When the fatal accident occurred the doctor was exploring the Blackfoot glacier.

Since earliest boyhood he had traveled constantly and had visited every country in the world, becoming an accomplished artist under foreign masters in his youth.

All of his travels partook of adventure for him and a collection of photographs from all parts of the world that he made is a long story of daring and constructive study of country and people wherever he went.

—*Helena Daily Independent*, 8-21-13

Beginning with the death of Dr. Fletcher and up through and including four deaths in 1997, 208 people have died in Glacier National Park since it was created in 1910.

```
              June 14, 1914
        Lassen Peak National Monument
    --------------------------------------
```

LASSEN'S VOLCANO TAKES HUMAN LIFE

Shower of Rock and Ashes Rain upon Party Investigating Mouth of Crater

RED Bluii—Lassen peak drew human blood for the first time since the old volcano burst into its present eruption.

[Lance] Graham of Viola was killed Sunday by a shower of huge rocks from the crater, and buried in a rain of cinders and ash.

Lloyd Stipple of Manton was caught in the same downpour of bowlders [sic] and was terribly hurt. His skull was fractured, his chest crushed and his arm broken by the fearful pelting of rocks. His companions . . . found him a raving maniac.

. . . Two new craters opened, one on the north and one on the west side of the peak, each more than a mile from the original vent. Fire, smoke, steam, volcanic ash, rocks and heavy gases belched forth from all three of the craters.

[They] went up Saturday afternoon from Viola to Manzanita lake, four miles from the northwest side of Lassen, intending to climb the crater peak as a Sunday excursion. Long before daylight the party of eight left the lake and, following the old Supan trail, climbed on to the west shoulder of the mountain.

They reached the crater in safety, looked down upon it and, noting the heavy outpouring of steam and smoke that boiled up between the three peaks that mark the ruined walls of the ancient crater, decided to get away as quickly as possible.

They were too late. Hardly had they gone a quarter of a mile from the crater when the black mass of rock and ash rushed up from the crater with a mighty roar and stood high above them.

They ran in terror before the awful threat, but there was no refuge. With a crash the hail of rock fell upon them. At the same moment the storm of ash came down with the midnight blackness.

As the men ran down the slope they lost each other in the darkness. When the survivors came out of the storm and met below the line of rock and ash four men were missing. They could not go back then to search for their comrades.

—*Mariposa Gazette,* 6-20-14 (reprinted by permission)

Lance Graham did not die, as was related in the above news account. "They started to carry my supposed dead body down the mountain. . . . At this time I was fully aware of what they were doing and of the fact that they thought me dead . . . it seemed to me that I was for the time being a disembodied spirit."

August 5, 1915
Yosemite National Park

DAMSELS IN DISTRESS

A PARTY of three eastern girls were overtaken by darkness Thursday, while returning from Cloud's Rest. A man companion brought word of their plight to park headquarters with the further information that one young lady was too fatigued to walk further. Mr. Gaylor, with a horse for the tired woman, was detailed to the relief of the party. Finding a second member of the party exhausted only one course was open to the perplexed "policeman"—to surrender his own mount.

But there was this obstacle—the lady knew not how to ride and the horse had never borne a burden fair. The hour was nearly midnight and darkness solved the keener perplexity—a dearth of riding skirt. Casting truth aside, to allay the lady's fear, boldly the ranger declared that the steed's maneuvers were the regulation acts of every horse at starting and without this snow white lie to spur her courage, who can speak the result? Not until 3 o'clock in the morning were the tourists landed at their destination, Camp Curry.

—*Mariposa Gazette,* 8-7-15 (reprinted by permission)

The *Annual Report to the Secretary of the Interior: 1915* stated of the SAR events in Yosemite for that year:

A few accidents occurred, but none were serious. These were caused by tourists leaving trails in trying to make short cuts or in climbing about the face of cliffs. In these cases they were rescued by the use of a rescue harness built by Park Superintendent George V. Bell.

One individual, as noted in that year's June 12 issue of the weekly *Mariposa Gazette,* was very lucky.

Ranger F.S. Townsley last Wednesday had the happy experience of rescuing a man lost in the snow of the mountains. Mr. Townsley discovered the man, by name Miller, in a dazed condition. He was coming from Mono Lake and lost the road in the deep snow at Soda Springs. There he wrote on a box a farewell message and set out for a last attempt to locate the road. He owes his life to the timely appearance of the ranger.

Forest S. Townsley, shown in this 1934 photo using a new, 30-pound "portable" two-way radio, was chief ranger in Yosemite National Park for 27 years.

YOSEMITE NATIONAL PARK RESEARCH LIBRARY

Forest S. Townsley was born in Greeley Center, Nebraska, on August 24, 1882. Starting his career at Platt National Park (Chickasaw National Recreation Area in Oklahoma) in June 1904, he was transferred to Yosemite in 1913; he became the park's chief ranger in May 1916. Handpicked by Director Stephen T. Mather, he was temporarily assigned to the recently authorized Grand Canyon National Park to help organize its new ranger force. Townsley, chief ranger of Yosemite for 27 years, died of a heart attack on August 11, 1943, while on a fishing trip in the Tuolumne Meadows area at what is now known officially as Townsley Lake.

September 3, 1915
Rocky Mountain National Park
- -

PASTOR'S FATE CALLED DIVINE

U.S. MAY AID SEARCH FOR MISSING PASTOR

Attorney General Gregory Wires Regrets and Offers Government Help in Quest

ROCKY Mountain National Park was signed into law by President Woodrow Wilson on January 26, 1915. On the very day of its formal dedication,

September 4, the disappearance of one Thornton R. Sampson soon plunged the park into a mystery unsolved for years. It was one of the most political as well as extensive search efforts in National Park Service history.

An avid fisherman, Dr. Sampson was on vacation near Grand Lake with the intention of attending the formalities in Estes Park the next day. Sampson was a professor of church history as well as the first president of the Texas Presbyterian Theological Seminary in Austin. The 63-year-old minister, an accomplished outdoorsman, was also a very good friend of President Wilson's.

Clifford Higby, the colorful owner of a local hotel and the last man known to see Sampson alive, declared: "[I]n the storm that broke . . . it would have been impossible for even an experienced mountaineer to find his way. I doubt very much if his body will be located until the snow melts in the spring."

The search turned into a national effort. "When President Wilson learned of Dr. Sampson's disappearance he ordered every available park official in this section to help in the search. Day after day guides, mountaineers, rangers and citizens tramped the hills hunting for the missing educator." But winter's fury eventually arrived and the ardent labors were abandoned.

Reconciled to her husband's probable fate, a pious Mrs. Sampson declared that "if God willed it was his time to go there could have been no more fitting setting." Seventeen years passed . . .

On the evening of July 8, 1932, an engineer working on a Fern Lake-to-Bear Lake Trail, found a knapsack, a watch, and portions of a human skeleton. Only the skull, scattered in a slope of loose rock in Odessa Gorge, was on the surface. Sampson's son would soon claim the remains and then surmise about his father:

> I am positive he built a fire, became warm and fell asleep—
> from which . . . his Maker never aroused him. I am convinced
> that had he been [only] injured prior to his death, with suf-
> ficient strength left . . . he would have used up all of his
> tobacco. In all my experience with injured or hungry men I
> have never known one that didn't invariably call for tobacco
> even to the last.

```
              September 8, 1915
           Grand Canyon National Park
    ----------------------------------------
```

CRAZED IN GRAND CANYON

New Hampshire Tourist Wanders Without Food or Drink

GRAND CANYON, Ariz., Sept. 12—After wandering for three days in the depths of the Grand Canyon without food or water, W.H. Harvey, a retired merchant of Manchester, N.H., was rescued yesterday in Hell's Half Acre, one of the most perilous parts of the canyon. Mr. Harvey was crazed from thirst and hunger.

Mr. Harvey and James H. Hyde of New York started down Hermit Trail, eight miles west of Grand Canyon Hotel, several days ago. They took neither food, water, nor guide, intending to follow the river along the bottom of the canyon back to the foot of Bright Angel Trail, which leads to the canyon bottom from here.

Soon after leaving the foot of Hermit Trail they became lost in the waste of rock formations. The alkali water which they were forced to drink caused both men to lose their minds temporarily. Mr. Hyde became separated from Mr. Harvey and found his way out of the canyon, but was unable to direct searchers to the spot where he had left his companion.

Parties searched the canyon for two days and found no trace of Mr. Harvey. Yesterday he was discovered in a delirious condition, his outer clothing gone. He was brought out of the canyon on a pack burro. He is recovering from his hardships.

—*New York Times,* 9-13-15,
The New York Times Company (reprinted by permission)

May 26, 1916
Yosemite National Park

LOST FOR TWO WEEKS

LYING on a cot at the government hospital, Wm. Burke, the Sonora man who was lost in the mountains and without food or warmth for twelve days, has a harrowing tale to relate. Sixteen days before his rescue by park rangers last Sunday [June 11], Mr. Burke set out to cross the mountains in search of employment. He lost his way, fell through the ice into a stream thereby ruining his matches, likewise most of his provisions, became blinded by snow, encountered rats and hungry bears at night and scaled heights where one misstep meant death, all this and more he survived. Two Berkeley students crossing the mountains brought word of his plight to government headquarters. Mr. Burke is loud in praise of the treatment accorded by park authorities and by government hospital staff.

—*Mariposa Gazette,* 6-17-16 (reprinted by permission)

In 1916, Yosemite had one chief ranger, one assistant, one special park ranger in charge of maintenance, one park ranger in charge of timber-cutting, three regular park rangers, and 19 temporary park rangers.

August 12, 1917
Mt. Rainier National Park

"GIRL LOST IN CREVASSE"

THIS 3-inch-high front-page headline in the *Seattle Post-Intelligencer* summed it up. C. H. Haskell brought his family for a Sunday outing in the snow. Unroped, as was customary in that day, the family of five and their friend, M. Horace Palmer, climbed to the 7,000-foot mark on the Nisqually Glacier. Intending to traverse the steep, icy slope to its lower end, the party slid along marveling at the view and breathing in the sparkling air. It was 11 A.M.

By August, summer heat generally has unveiled most of the mountain's countless deep crevasses. Most . . .

> Miss Haskell and Palmer were walking together and she was holding his hand when a snow bridge broke under her. She went down and dragged Palmer with her. He stuck in the ice and snow a few feet down and she lost her hold and disappeared.
>
> Word reached the ranger station at 3 P.M. and rangers with equipment "hurried" to the scene. The newspaper reported, "A guide was lowered by rope 300 feet, but was unable to see her. It is estimated the crevasse is at least 600 feet deep."

The 1919 *Annual Report to the Secretary of the Interior* differed a little from the newspaper on the details: "The park ranger was lowered into the crevasse to a depth of more than 100 feet and finally recovered the body on a ledge about 35 feet below the surface, under several feet of snow."

Regardless of who actually found the 15-year-old and exactly how deep they had to go, these early rescuers displayed a great deal of courage and deserve a great deal of credit.

On September 15, 1916, J. A. Fritsch, described by a news article of the event as a "Salt Lake City Capitalist," fell 50 feet into a hidden crevasse. Rescued, he was brought out only "dazed." Guide Jules Stampfler remained with him through the night. Eventually carried down the mountain by guides and rangers, Fritsch was examined by three doctors, who declared he was not seriously injured, although still somewhat "dazed." He died two days later. This rescue cost $297.31, including $150.00 for the services of the park's contract doctor, $131.45 for the mountaineering guide's costs, and 86 cents for a telegram notifying the director of the National Park Service of the fatal incident.

August 2, 1918
Rocky Mountain National Park

MISS F. E. FROST

. . . **AGED** 19, of Sterling, Colo., in company with Mr. Homer Thomson, attempted to cross a snow bank above the Fall River Road. Miss Frost lost her footing and in falling pulled Mr. Thomson off his feet. Before they could recover, they were sliding head foremost down the bank. Approximately 500 feet from the start of the slide a large rock protruded above the snow.

Miss Frost struck this rock and . . . roll[ed] for a distance of approximately 100 feet finally falling over a ledge and lodging in a snow bank at the base. In some manner, a rock weighing in the neighborhood of 400 pounds, fell . . . killing her instantly. She also received a death-dealing wound on the head. Mr. Thomson continued to slide approximately 500 feet, lodging in the trees at the base of the snow bank and receiving 50 slight wounds.

—*Annual Report to the Secretary of the Interior*—1918

August 6, 1919
Glacier National Park

SILVER CARNEGIE HERO MEDAL

HERBERT Aaron Friedlich, aged twenty-six, lawyer, saved Raymond Kraft, aged twenty-one, clerk, from an impending fatal fall, Glacier Park, Mont., August 6, 1919. Kraft alone ascended a mountain known as Pinnacle Wall for three hundred and fifty feet; and in attempting to cross a glacier thirty feet wide, he lost his footing and slid about seventy-five feet, injuring his ankle. He then attempted to descend the mountain on narrow ledges and finally reached a short ledge two feet wide. Kraft could go no farther and was greatly frightened. The face of the mountain below Kraft sloped down for one hundred and fifty feet at an angle of about twenty degrees from a perpendicular and was bare of vegetation. Friedlich with extreme caution and difficulty climbed toward Kraft from the base of the mountain. At two points in the ascent, where there were projections to surmount, he was forced to lean back for handholds, swing out with his feet unsupported, and pull himself up. He reached Kraft after climbing two hundred and fifty feet and with great difficulty helped him to descend. Two and a half hours were required to reach Kraft and descend with him.

—*Carnegie Hero Fund Commission 1923 Annual Report*

Mary Buck Farrow sits in the plane with her now unknown pilot standing by. Taken in East Glacier in 1913, this may be the first plane to both fly over a national park as well as possibly land in one. GLACIER NATIONAL PARK RESEARCH LIBRARY

CHAPTER 3

> They [rangers] are a fine, earnest,
> intelligent, and public-spirited body of
> men, those rangers. Though small in
> number, their influence is large. Many
> and long are the duties heaped upon
> their shoulders. If a trail is to be
> blazed, it is "send a ranger." If an
> animal is floundering in the snow, a
> ranger is sent to pull him out; if a
> bear is in the hotel, if a fire
> threatens a forest, if someone is to be
> saved, it is "send a ranger."
>
> —Horace M. Albright, <u>Oh, Ranger!</u>

THE 1920s began with the chopping of blocks of ice from Yosemite's frozen Merced River, to be stored in sawdust for refrigeration in the heat of summer. Mules still pulled plows to clear dirt streets of snow. This decade also saw a young National Park Service and the 20th century come together.

Despite the absence of staff to care for 11 of the country's 25 national monuments, visitation in 1920 to the 43 existing units of the National Park System reached 1,058,455, the first time it had exceeded one million. In just five years this figure doubled, reaching 2,108,089 in 1925. Thanks to the convenient and relatively affordable family car, as well as passionate advertising by the automobile, railroad, and tourist industries, parks were in. So was the airplane.

AVIATION

Aircraft, still novel and of undetermined value for resource and visitor protection, arrived. Although planes had flown over and around national parks since at least 1913 (such as in Glacier), the first to intentionally land in a park did so in Yellowstone in 1917. Documented elsewhere, this event went unreported in the park's *Superintendent's Annual Report to the Secretary of the Interior—1917.* Yosemite, however, made no such mistake and chronicled its first experience with the unique machines in the park's 1919 report.

> After much discussion . . . the commanding officer of the [Mather] field finally consented to permit . . . an Army plane to negotiate . . . landing . . . Yosemite Valley. . . . [O]n the morning of May 27, [1919] Lieutenant J. S. Krull, flight commander at Mather Field, in a Curtiss biplane . . . dropped down into the valley from the direction of Half Dome and made a perfect landing on . . . field . . . prepared for the purpose. . . .

> [F]ollowing morning . . . Krull effected an equally successful take-
> off, and although a forced landing due to gasoline trouble, was
> necessary . . . he arrived safely at Merced after having made the
> round trip of about 150 miles in less than two hours. . . . . [T]he
> hazards . . . lurking along the rim . . . in the way of dangerous air
> currents do not exist . . . a flight into the valley is little . . . more
> dangerous than elsewhere.

A superintendent of vision, Yosemite's W. B. Lewis concluded in his *Report to the Director,* "I believe also that feasibility of the use of the aeroplane for fire patrol from the valley is one that should be immediately considered." Lewis knew that two years before Lieutenant Krull made Yosemite National Park history, the Forest Service, in cooperation with the U.S. Army, had begun experimenting with aerial fire patrols over mountainous California. "Hap" Arnold, legendary leader of the Army Air Forces during World War II, figured very prominently in these early trials.

According to the 1920 annual *Sierra Club Bulletin,* "26 planes, 29 officers, 15 cadets, and an average of 92 enlisted men" and "31 national forest officers" were dedicated to aerial fire patrol that summer. A total of 659 fires were first detected in this way. On June 20 that year, and applying only to Yosemite, the director released the first NPS regulations about aircraft landing and commercialization in parks. The next year, a three-passenger biplane landed in Yellowstone between the Lake Ranger Station and Yellowstone Lake. After breaking a propeller on August 7 and being down for two weeks, the owner asked the park permission to charge $25 per passenger for a 15-minute flight over Yellowstone. It was denied.

By sheer good luck, the first real aircraft accident in a national park was narrowly averted on July 21, 1921. When his engine suddenly stopped at 15,000 feet, Raymond G. Fisher, a Forest Service pilot on fire patrol, force-landed on rugged Wizard Island, a rocky dot in the middle of remote Crater Lake. The resourceful, skilled aviator somehow safely "dead-sticked" his way onto the jagged shores. Fisher discovered that all four spark plugs of his craft's motor were broken. Using the plane's recently installed wireless set, he contacted a fellow pilot. Rescuers, not foolish enough to try to land themselves, soon parachuted in the needed parts. The next day, Fisher managed to wing his way up and out of the extinct volcano.

One day later, Yosemite experienced its first plane wreck; no one was hurt when a flight from San Francisco crashed on takeoff in Leidig Meadow on July 23. Five years later, however, on July 24, 1926, someone died in a plane wreck in a national park. LeRoy Jeffers became the NPS's first fatality when a biplane piloted by Dr. Bunnell crashed in the Yosemite resort of Wawona.

Not counting the aid provided to Crater Lake's lucky aeronaut and thus not considered a rescue, probably the first documented use of an airplane for SAR was over the Grand Canyon in the fall of 1923. Expeditions down the Colorado River were rare and the world feared for their safety. When Colonel Birdseye's U.S. Geological Survey trip became unaccounted for, the governor of Arizona asked the Army to look for them. Eventually turning up safe, the river party was never seen from the air, although Grand Canyon explorer and photographer Emory Kolb had spotted the Army plane above them.

OTHER AVIATION MILESTONES

February 24, 1919	Army Lieutenants E. D. Jones and R. O. Searle are the first to dare to fly over the mile-deep Grand Canyon.
1920	Portable radio is packed in by horse to the 12,000-acre Mill Creek Fire in California's Lassen National Forest. Firefighting operations are then directed by wireless from above. Concerned about ongoing boundary clashes with Mexico, the Army flies patrols out of Glenn Springs, in what is now Texas's Big Bend National Park.
August 13, 1921	Carrier pigeon flies from Yellowstone to New York City—2,000 miles—with a note saying a naturalist needs rescuing.
August 8, 1922	R. V. Thomas, with Ellsworth Kolb serving as cameraman, finally lands inside Grand Canyon near Indian Gardens. Ten days later they duplicate the feat with a movie company shooting aerial footage.
August 1923	World War I "Jenny" crashes into a boulder in Great Smoky Mountains: park's first plane wreck.
June 17, 1924	Ben Eielson, hired by gold prospector Jack Tobin, is first to pilot a plane into Mt. McKinley National Park; the World War I "Jenny" lands on a gravel bar just below Muldrow Glacier.
August 1925	First plane to fly over Mt. Rainier.
December 28, 1928	Several planes land inside Hawaii Volcano National Park's still-active Kilauea Crater.
October 21, 1929	First civilian ambulance air service to transport sick people is organized in New York.
August 13, 1930	First flight over summit of North America's highest point, 20,320-foot Mt. McKinley.
August 26, 1930	Goodyear Blimp is considered for body removal from Sequoia backcountry; it is never used. This SAR also spawns park's first plane wreck; no one is injured.
February 1, 1932	Sequoia National Park is site of largest air search in NPS history; 10 percent (50) of entire Army Air Corps looks for hapless pilot of downed military plane.
April 25, 1932	First plane to land on a Mt. McKinley glacier.

Ranger Dan Kirschner and wildfire specialist Doug Ottosen during short-haul rescue training below the Grand Canyon's south rim in October 1992.

KEN PHILLIPS PHOTO

OTHER AVIATION MILESTONES

May 22, 1932	First autogiro to land in a park—Yosemite.
July 1932	First plane to land in Rocky Mountain National Park. Officials are stymied by how to classify such adventuresome visitors; finally listed under "miscellaneous" arrivals, not having come on foot, horse, motorcycle, or automobile.
June 18, 1937	First seaplane to land on Lake Mead.

MILESTONES OF THE 1920s

1920	There are 1,058,455 visitors to the 43 units in the NPS.
	With a high of some 1,000 people per day on the valley floor, visitation to Yosemite is 60,906; of 192 reported accidents, only two are serious: a broken arm and a broken leg. Autos profoundly increase the workload of park staff.
May 1920	Essential to SAR in years to come, a mechanical snowplow is invented in Yellowstone, a conversion from 75 hp Caterpillar.
1921	Yellowstone has 1 chief ranger, 3 assistant chiefs, 24 rangers, 42 temporaries, 12 ranger stations in winter, and 17 in summer. Sequoia has 1 chief, 1 assistant, and 1 ranger. Glacier has 1 chief, a "first assistant chief, 2 assistant chiefs, and 12 to 15 park rangers."

MILESTONES OF THE 1920s

March 1921	Department of the Interior's Bureau of Mines begins organizing thousands of first-aid- and rescue-trained miners into local teams for formalized mine rescue efforts.
Summer 1921	Professional hiking guides still work in Yosemite. They apparently do not stop Secretary of the Interior Fall, along with NPS Director Mather, from shooting a rattlesnake and taking the forbidden rattles back to President Harding.
1922	Rope is fixed up Yosemite's Half Dome to make it easy for tourists.
October 1922	First National Lifesaving Conference, Washington, D.C.
July 4, 1924	Tasker L. Oddie officially becomes a Yellowstone ranger to "recuperate" from his other job as Nevada's junior U.S. senator. Along with the other seasonals, he reports to the chief ranger each morning for his assignment.
August 22, 1924	First life to be claimed by Yosemite's Vernal Falls.
1925	Visitation to Yosemite exceeds 200,000 for first time. "The park is operating with a smaller ranger force than in 1916, with the travel more than six times as large."
January 12, 1925	In trying to save Agnes Vaille—first woman to scale Rocky Mountain National Park's Longs Peak in the winter—Herb Sortland becomes first formal rescuer killed in a national park area.

Woman climbing cables on Longs Peak in Rocky Mountain National Park, circa 1927.

ROCKY MOUNTAIN NATIONAL PARK
RESEARCH LIBRARY

MILESTONES OF THE 1920s

January 30, 1925	Trapped in a coffin-sized tunnel, Floyd Collins ultimately dies in Sand Cave. This drama, in what will soon become Mammoth Cave National Park, is voted by national media as the third most notable news event between the two world wars.
January 18, 1926	First NPS Chief Ranger's Conference is held in Sequoia; safety, SAR, and visitor service are big topics.
November 22, 1927	Snowmobile is awarded Patent #1,650,334.
1928	Rangers begin snow surveys in California national parks to assist State Water Resources Division. Winter SAR skills advance.
1929	Glacier has only one serious accident (a man thrown from a horse) among its 70,742 visitors that year.
February 20, 1929	Two rangers die in Grand Canyon; one not found.
February 26, 1929	Grand Teton National Park is established. Five are on staff to attend to 51,000 people: one superintendent, one permanent ranger, two temporary rangers, and one temporary clerk.
March 1929	Grand Canyon superintendent first proposes permits and bonding for Colorado River rafters after disappearance of Hydes.
July 1, 1929	First permanent ranger is appointed to Lassen Volcanic; only two temporary rangers in Bryce Canyon that summer.
September 27, 1929	Through heroism during the "Greathouse Rescue," temporary ranger Charlie Browne becomes first of two to ever receive a presidential appointment as a permanent park ranger.

January 1920
Yellowstone National Park

"THE BURIAL SERVICE BEING READ BY RANGER WINN"

ON April 21 Forest Ranger F. R. Johns and another Forest Ranger who with Johns . . . had occasion to return from one of their patrols, through the park, and about 1½ miles inside of the park, on Hellroaring Creek, they found the body of a man, the snow . . . having melted so that a little of his clothing showed.

Park Rangers George Winn, of the Soda Butte Station, and Ralph Harr, of Tower Falls Station, were directed to go to the point, make full investigation and report, and bury the body near the point where it was found, as it was impracticable to move it under present winter conditions. This they did on April 24, the Burial Service being read by Ranger Winn from the Episcopal Prayer Book.

Due to snow conditions and lack of pack animals, it was found to be impracticable to convey lumber to the place for making a box, but the body was carefully wrapped in a strong canvas before burial, and this will last for several years in case of identification through any means.

The body was buried four feet deep, as a large rock was encountered at this depth, which prevented going deeper. The grave is located 1½ miles inside of the park from the north boundary, on the right bank of Hellroaring Creek. It is marked with stakes at the head and foot, and the tree near by is blazed. . . .

This incident explains the report made by Mr. C. O. Davis, of Gardiner, Montana, made to our rangers on January 31, to the effect that while he was trapping not far outside of the park line on Hellroaring Creek, he had found tracks of a man outside of the park and leading into the park on Hellroaring; that he found indications that this man had lived at the Forest Ranger's cabin on Hellroaring Creek for about a month, as he had consumed all the rations that had been placed in the cabin by the rangers for winter use. Also that the tracks and signs indicated that he was crippled, probably from frozen feet. He took the pains to follow the peculiar trail until he reached the park line, but Divis [sic] having firearms did not want to go into the park as he had no authority to carry arms unsealed in the park. He said he believed a dead man would be found in the park when the snow melted.

Ranger Harr, stationed at Tower Falls, was sent to this vicinity four times afterwards to investigate the report, but the deep snows had covered up all traces, and he found nothing to report. . . .

The man was apparently a foreigner. There were no signs of violence, and it was apparent that he had perished from exposure and cold.

—*Chief Ranger's Monthly Report*—April 1920

```
July 7, 1920
Yosemite National Park
```

PROMINENT ELK FAILS TO SAVE RIVER VICTIM

Los Angeles Man Slips on Rock, Fractures Skull, Killed Instantly
CAMP CURRY TRAGEDY
Attempt to Drag Stream in Search of Body of 12-Year Old Girl

CAMP CURRY, Yosemite (Cal), July 7—Gertrude Kistler, twelve-year-old daughter of Sedgwick Kistler of Lock Haven, Penn., a delegate to the Democratic National Convention, was drowned in the Merced river here today and H.J. Pink of Los Angeles, who went to her rescue, slipped on a rock as he entered the stream and fractured his skull, death resulting instantly. The accident occurred above Happy Isles.

The girl's body had not been found this afternoon, and an attempt to drag the stream was started.

Witnesses of the double accident worked over Pink's body in the hope that he could be resuscitated, but Dr. F. L. Stein, on examination, reported that he had not been drowned but was killed by the fall. Pink was well known in the Yosemite. This was his fourth trip into the valley this year.

—*San Francisco Chronicle,* 7-8-20
(reprinted by permission)

The tally for 1920 (ending June 30, seven days before these deaths) was 60,906 registered visitors; there were "192 accidents with only two being serious—a broken arm and a broken leg."

```
August 28, 1920
Sequoia National Park
```

FAT MEN BARRED FROM CRYSTAL CAVES; MUST REDUCE

IF you measure more than 32 and a quarter inches around the waist, keep away from Sequoia National Park—that is, if you want to visit its famous Crystal Cave.

Superintendent John White today notified the Auto Club's touring bureau to warn all fat tourists that they must reduce their waist measure or keep out of mysterious Crystal Cave.

Fat motorists have as much chance of getting into the crystal grotto, world famous since it imprisoned Thaddeus Brown of Lemoore for three days, beginning August 28, as a camel has of getting through the eye of a needle.

Mr. Brown, it will be remembered, is the stout gentleman who stuck for three days in Hell's Crack, about half a mile from the Crystal Cave entrance, deep in the bowels of the earth near the motor road through the national park.

All attempts on the part of the park rangers to drag him out of the hole with ropes were unavailing.

Starving was resorted to. In three days Mr. Brown's waist measurement was reduced 14 [sic] inches and he slipped through the crack.

All prospective visitors to the cave will henceforth be measured at the administrative building at Giant Forest and those whose waist measurements are over 34¼ inches will be debarred from entering what is said to be America's most beautiful cavern.

Methods used to reduce the waist line 14 [sic] inches in 3 days, adopted by Uncle Sam's forest rangers, are to be investigated by many motion picture stars.

—Unnamed newspaper, 9-13-20

With the transportation swell generated by the combustion engine just starting to be felt, the western parks near centers of population were being barraged by tourists and automobile associations. If staffed at all, most areas of the young National Park System were not ready for the influx of people. At this time, Sequoia National Park had one chief ranger, one assistant chief ranger, and one park ranger to handle this incident.

```
July 21, 1921
Crater Lake National Park
----------------------------------------
```

HOW SCIENCE OUTWITTED DEATH IN WILD

PARACHUTES SAVE FLYER MAROONED ON CRATER LAKE
Forests Aviator Forced to Land in Deep Crater

SAN FRANCISCO, July 23—When the engine suddenly stopped 15,000 feet in the air above remote Crater Lake, Ore., Thursday, Raymond G. Fisher, forest service pilot, was forced to land on a tiny island in the lake, which is in the pit of an extinct volcanoe [sic] with walls 1,000 feet high surrounding it. . . . The plane was not damaged in the descent and Fisher, upon examination, found four of the spark plugs of the engine broken.

Using the wireless set which the machine was equipped, he succeeded in getting in touch with another forest service plane on duty in the vicinity.

This second flyer hastened to Medford, Ore., with news of Fisher's landing on the island and obtained new spark plugs for Fisher's machine . . . the rescue pilot found it impossible for another plane to land on the island. . . . Other forest service planes came up and sets of spark plugs were sent to earth by means of parachutes. Hunting with a torch Thursday night Fisher found one of the parachutes and yesterday morning repaired his machine.

Working carefully and swiftly Fisher started his giant machine alone. Then the big plane bumped over the rocky island, left the ground and shot out over the lake. Before he would be free he had to climb 2,000 feet in that constricted space. He circled, gathered speed, fought the twisting air currents, circled again and again and at last shot over the rim of the crater and headed for the west.

—*San Francisco Examiner*, 7-24-21
(reprinted by permission)

Aviation and aircraft came to the forefront and to the attention of the Forest Service in World War I: Why not use them for patrolling the rugged, wooded areas of the country? In August 1915, research was begun in Wisconsin. Jack Vilas and E. M. Weaver flew experiments in a Curtis flying boat to demonstrate the feasibility of finding fires from the air; poor weather and communications forced the abandonment of the project. In 1917, Henry Graves, chief forester, consulted with the Army Air Corps, suggesting that the Army begin fire patrols over western forests. The first successful flight was over California that same year. Missions were extended to cover Montana, Idaho, Oregon, and Washington.

July 25, 1921
Yosemite National Park

S. F. CLUBMAN PLUNGES OFF YOSEMITE PEAK

2 Companions Risk Lives to Save F.H. Morley, Held Suspended by Boulder over Deep Gorge

Merry Sierra Club Hikers Party Ends in Disaster; Victim Lies Near Death at Club's Lodge

FRED H. Morley, wealthy retired engineer and clubman of the city, lies at the point of death in the Sierra Club Lodge at Lake Tenaya in the remote section of the Yosemite National Park, following a fall from the precipitous summit of Cathedral Peak.

The accident took place on Saturday when Morley, with 2 companions, left the main body of the Sierra Club—now on their annual outing—and ventured among the towering peaks to the east of the Meadows.

Rounding a dizzy curve on the mountain top at over 10,000 feet elevation, Morley lost his footing and plunged outward into space. His fall was broken by projecting boulders 75 feet below, where he lay unconscious.

At the time of the disaster Morley was accompanied by Al Orcutt G. Haskell, Christian Science Practitioner, . . . and Professor F.E. Crofts, principal of a Berkeley grammar school.

RESCUERS RISK LIVES

The two men, equipped with the regular mountain climbing outfit of the Sierra Club made their way along ropes down the cliffs to where Morley's senseless body lay.

At the risk of their lives they constructed a rude sling of rope and lowered the injured man 500 feet down a sheer precipice to safety. Regaining the summit with difficulty they circled the base of the rock, finding Morley breathing, but unconscious.

Haskell left for the Sierra Club lodge 12 miles away over rough country, to summon help, while Crofts stayed with the victim. . . .

Several hours later Haskell returned with a pack train of mules and a litter. Medical care was administered. Morley, still unconscious, was placed in the litter and carried by slow stages across the rugged, "duck" [rock cairns] trails to the Meadows. The journey ended late at night.

—San Francisco Examiner, 7-27-21
(reprinted by permission)

Yosemite rangers are training in this 1923 mock cliff rescue. Left to right: Forest Townsley, Henry Skeleton, Charlie Adair, John Wegner, and John Bingaman. The "victim" is unknown. Note the size of rope.

MRS. JOHN BINGAMAN COLLECTION

Morley died of a basilar skull fracture the next day.

August 11, 1921
Yellowstone National Park

TWO ESCAPE WHEN PLANE PLUNGES INTO YELLOWSTONE LAKE

ORA E. Phillips and W.C. Brooks of Hemingford, Neb. escaped uninjured when their airplane plunged into Yellowstone Lake in Yellowstone National Park. . . . They landed in the shallow water and were able to reach shore without difficulty.

This was the first plane to land within the park boundary. Congress has not made any regulations relevant to the entrance of the flying craft and park officials are at a loss as to how to collect entrance fees for it.

—*Denver Post*, 8-12-21 (reprinted by permission)

Despite the newspaper's claim, according to Aubrey L. Haines in *The Yellowstone Story: A History of Our First National Park*, a Captain Smith and a Lieutenant Blanton landed a stick and string "Jenny" on the flat northwest of the old Fountain Hotel in October 1917. They had almost rolled to a stop when a wheel hit a soft place and the craft nosed over. No harm was done, and with some help to get the nose up, the plane was made operational and flown out of the park. This was the first plane ever recorded as landing in a national park, although at least one small aircraft landed in East Glacier (within feet of Glacier National Park) in 1913.

The first NPS policy governing aircraft was for Yosemite; issued on June 19, 1920, it regulated the landing, takeoff, and commercial aspects of flying into that area. This guidance was the direct result of Army Lieutenant J. S. Krull's landing in Yosemite Valley on May 27, 1919, followed less than a month later by that of Lieutenant Bud Coffee.

```
            August 13, 1921
        Yellowstone National Park
-------------------------------------------------------------
```

MAN LOST IN YELLOWSTONE SENDS N Y CRY

NEW YORK, Aug. 17—(By Universal Services)
A cry for help from a man lost and starving in the wilds of Yellowstone Park over 2000 miles away was brought to Broadway tonight by a carrier pigeon.

The pigeon, bound for the Hotel Belleclaire, dropped to the wet pavement of Columbia Circle shortly after 10 P.M., exhausted when its long journey was almost completed. Picked up by a policeman, the following message was found under the bird's wing.

> Notify Ben Singer, Belleclaire Hotel, New York; am lost on Hoodoo mountain, Yellowstone. Send help, provisions and pack horse. Heller.

Singer, when the message was given to him, sent the following message to Ned Frost, a noted guide at the Wapegi ranch, Cody, Wyo. "Edmund Heller lost southeast of Yellowstone Park in Big Hoodoo Mountain. Start at once. Spare no expense. Take food and provisions and find Heller."

Singer explained to the police that Heller, a noted naturalist, author and friend of Colonel Roosevelt, left the Belleclaire Hotel ten days ago to photograph wildgame in Yellowstone. Singer said Heller took a number of carrier pigeons, which he had trained on the roof of the Belleclaire, with him.

According to Singer, Heller was well equipped with provisions, pack horse, and everything necessary for the trip. He feared a fall into a canyon. Pigeon fanciers . . . declared that this was an extraordinary feat for a bird to perform.
—*New York Times,* 8-17-21, The New York Times Company
(reprinted by permission)

The note was dated August 13; thus the bird flew more than 2,000 miles in four days. On August 20, 1921, Yellowstone Superintendent Horace M. Albright stated that Heller was no longer lost since he had recently been seen talking to employees for several days.

According to the June 13, 1924, Colton, Washington, *News Leader:*

An interesting application of carrier pigeons . . . is soon to be tried . . . in the opening up of the large region east of the Grand Canyon . . . uninhabited except for wandering bands of Navajo Indians. Touring cars will take passengers. . . . To guard against delays from breakdowns and to keep park headquarters informed of them, carrier pigeons will be carried in these cars and released in case of difficulty. This service may be increased to include private messages from passengers.

```
          September 16, 1921
      Rocky Mountain National Park
    ----------------------------------
```

ELEMENTS DISINTER UNKNOWN'S BODY
ON FLAT TOP MOUNTAIN

(Special to *The News*)
GRAND LAKE, Colo., Sept. 18—Disinterred three times in the past four years from its shallow grave on top of Flattop Mountain near here, the body of an unidentified man was again brought to light this week, it was learned here yesterday. An attempt to bring the body down from its lofty grave for a fitting burial probably will be made, according to Forest service officials.

Two Eastern physicians came upon the body, which now consists of little more than a bleached skeleton. At first it was reported that the remains were those of the Rev. P. E.

Samson [sic], Austin, Texas minister, who was lost near the scene ten years ago, but a later investigation proved this report erroneous, according to Fred McClaren, forest ranger [Park Ranger] of this district.

Four years ago, according to Ranger McClaren, a man believed to be the one whose skeleton was again found this week was lost near Randall glacier. His dog was later found wandering near and subsequently led to the discovery of his master's body. The discovery was made by Forest Ranger Giles, who, because it was winter when the body was found, was forced to bury it where it lay.

The man was later partially identified as a prospector of this section of the country and who had worked the few weeks preceding his death as a ditch digger. The theory advanced at that time was that he had worked until he received enough money for a grubstake and then set forth, only to fall victim of the trail.

Three times since the elements have uncovered his body and each time forest rangers [Park Rangers] returned to the scene to bury it again. A boulder, upon which is carved a crude cross, sets at the head of the grave.

—*Rocky Mountain News,* 9-19-21
(reprinted by permission)

Ten days later, on September 26, 55-year-old H. F. Taggett told Longs Peak Inn Manager Emerson Lynn that he was going to hike up to Chasm Lake; that was the last time the man from Los Angeles was heard from. His disappearance remained a mystery—that is, until 1940 when a skull was discovered at nearby Peacock Pool. Nineteen years after Taggett's disappearance, park rangers believed these to be the last remains of the fourth recorded death on Longs Peak.

```
           July 21, 1922
        Yosemite National Park
------------------------------------
```

YOUNG LADY INJURED ON GLACIER POINT TRAIL

MISS Frances Killam of Palo Alto . . . was seriously injured and ten others slightly injured, by a slide which swept down on the upper end of the ledge trail to Glacier Point Friday morning. . . .

Miss Killam's injuries consisted of a compound fracture of the left leg and numerous cuts and bruises.

There were 60 hikers on the trail at the time of the slide and there was great excitement in the Valley for a time when it was believed, by the people below, that all had been buried under the slide or carried to death over the cliff.

The entire ranger force was rushed to the scene and the injured and excited were properly cared for.

The slide was caused by the heavy rains of the previous two days. The ledge trail is now closed.
—*Mariposa Gazette*, 7-29-22 (reprinted by permission)

The Ledge Trail was permanently closed in 1960.

Hikers traveling up the Ledge Trail to Glacier Point in Yosemite National Park, circa 1924, were met by this warning: "It is 3,000 feet to the bottom and no undertaker to meet you. Take no chances. There is a difference between bravery and just plain ordinary foolishness." YOSEMITE NATIONAL PARK RESEARCH LIBRARY

August 1, 1922
Rocky Mountain National Park

A.E. KITTS, BANKER OF GREELEY, INSTANTLY KILLED BY LIGHTNING ON CRESTS OF LONGS PEAK TUESDAY AFTERNOON

A.E. KITTS . . . instantly killed by lightning on top of Longs Peak Tuesday afternoon. Joe Bullas, of Topeka, Kansas, was knocked unconscious and severely burned at the same time.

Mr. Kitts, along with Rev. Dando . . . son . . . Joe Bullas . . . at the cabin at Timberline . . . arriv[ed] at the Summit at 12:30.

They were standing within a few feet of the cairn when a thunderstorm came up. The first stroke of lightning struck Kitts, killing him instantly, burning off half his clothes. Bullas' head was badly seared and his shoes were burned off his feet. Dr. Dando and his son tried to revive Bullas but failed, so went down to Longs Peak Inn for help where they notified the Chief Ranger Allen. . . . Allen rushed to the Peak, accompanied by Dr. Wiest who dressed the wounds of Bullas, who, in the meantime had regained consciousness and started down the mountain.

Superintendent Toll formed a party and started at once to bring down Kitts' body. They did not return until four o'clock on Thursday morning.
—*Estes Park Trail-Gazette*, 8-4-22
(reprinted by permission of the Estes Park Trail)

A year later, lightning stuck again. On September 4, Ethel Ridenour and Miss Edwards, a doctor friend from New York City, were hiking among the rocks at the base of Longs Peak when a severe electrical storm came on swiftly. Ridenour remarked to Dr. Edwards that it would be well for them to separate in the event one of them should be struck by lightning the other could render assistance. The doctor did not give much thought to the suggestion, but Ridenour insisted. They had only proceeded a few steps when the crash came and both were knocked unconscious.

The bolt from the heavens struck Ridenour on the left side of her head and then went down her spine; the flame's path marked the hiker's body by broad burned streaks. All breathing and heart action had ceased when Dr. Edwards—all of her clothing shredded by the electrical blast—regained consciousness. Still dazed, she at once started artificial respiration and then screamed for help.

In the rare atmosphere of that elevation, sounds carry great distances, and the keeper of the Timberline Cabin heard the cries. By miracle and probably the proximity of Dr. Edwards, the lucky young woman from Kansas City survived the lightning strike.

September 1923
Grand Canyon National Park

SEARCH FOR
EARLY COLORADO RIVER EXPLORERS

THE twenties saw visionary land reclamation, including the irrigation of the waterless Southwest through the taming of the Colorado River. The mighty river, overflowing its banks in the disastrous winter flood of 1905, had formed Southern California's Salton Sea. Now, with the government considering several huge dams in the West, a nine-member team from the U.S. Geological Survey led by Colonel C. H. Birdseye, was tasked to study the river's largely uncharted waters for harnessing.

Within 48 hours of their launch on August 1, the Colorado's fury broke upon the team in Badger Creek Rapids; a hole was smashed through the first boat to dare the plunge. It was the maiden adventure among the many perils awaiting them on their nearly 300-mile route. In camp that night—over the first radio on the river—they learned of President Harding's death only 45 minutes after it occurred.

Danger soon became a part of their daily life. "We put on life jackets made of cork and lay face down on the planking, clinging hard to the life-lines that were stretched across the deck. The waves seemed mountainous." Waves 20 feet high broke overhead as the tiny boats shot among the rocks and whirlpools. Treacherous eddies clutched at them; water "boils" welled up suddenly from beneath. There were risks of every variety, including a cloudburst. In one 24-hour period, the raucous river rose 21 feet; every minute was a battle against disaster.

Huge logs borne on the roaring waters threatened the fragile little boats—and the men in them. Below Kanab Creek the photographer's boat was drawn into a hole and turned over, imprisoning him beneath it. He somehow escaped unhurt.

Colorado River exploration, rare up to this time, was an event of national importance and chronicled accordingly. So, when the nine men were not heard from for weeks, Acting Arizona Governor McGillian asked the Army to fly the canyon to search for them.

Nonplussed, the director of the Geological Survey said, "I see no reason to be stampeded from a strong belief that all is well with the party. Disaster . . . is inconceivable." On September 24, a follow-up article in the *New York Times* added to the drama.

> Two Deputy Sheriffs of Mohave County, veteran cow men, left this morning with several Indians to search the country north of Peach Springs. . . . [S]couts asserted the river still was on a rampage, shooting water fifty feet into the air. . . . The scouts cut short their search on word from . . . the USGS, instructing them not to venture too far into the canyon . . . no trace of the surveyors.

Birdseye and his band of eight, enduring harrowing conditions, ably survived the trip.

July 13, 1924
Yellowstone National Park

CAR PLUNGES 800 FEET

AUTOMOBILES began entering parks when Oliver Lippincott and his Locomobile arrived in Yosemite on June 23, 1900. It wasn't until July 24, 1908, however, that the first horseless carriage was officially permitted into a national park, Mt. Rainier. Seven years later, cars were allowed into Yellowstone. That same year, 1915, also saw its first motor vehicle fatality—and probably the

Automobile accidents, like this one in Yosemite National Park's Merced River in 1926, will always keep rescuers busy.

YOSEMITE NATIONAL PARK RESEARCH LIBRARY

earliest one in the National Park Service. On September 3, Sarah Edith Higgins, a 49-year-old woman from Helena, Montana, fractured her skull when the large

Maxwell in which she was riding rolled over onto her after it went off a slick road and crashed down a steep, 60-foot embankment between Tower Junction and Mammoth.

The following newspaper account records another bizarre accident demanding an intense, dangerous rescue effort by both rangers and employees of the Yellowstone Park Transportation Company.

BACK OVER BRINK OF GRAND CANYON

Minneapolis Couple in Yellowstone Park Drop 800 Feet

LIVINGSTON, July 14—Mr. and Mrs. Earl J. Dunn of Minneapolis, traveling in a light enclosed car, were almost instantly killed Sunday afternoon when the car in which they were touring got out of control of the driver and backed over the brink of the Grand Canyon of the Yellowstone river in Yellowstone park. The car and occupants took a drop of 800 feet sheer before landing on the sandstone base of the canyon and rolled fully 200 feet, coming to rest at the river's edge.

Hudson was the first to reach the wrecked car, which lay, a twisted mass of steel, at the base of the canyon and he and McLean dragged the mutilated forms of the occupants from under the wreckage with the aid of ropes from above, and finally succeeded in getting the bodies to the top of the precipice.

According to eye-witnesses, the Dunn party were evidently attempting to turn around and it is thought that the driver gave the car more momentum than necessary and in some manner that baffles observers, managed to slip between the trees at the brink of the canyon and made the plunge to death.

—*Butte Montana Miner,* 7-15-24

July 25, 1924
Mt. Rainier National Park

HONEYMOONING NEW WIFE OF MAN WITH SIX OTHER WIVES FALLS OVER CLIFF

THE following is from a letter by Park Superintendent Tomlinson to F. B. Kutz of the Long Beach Police Department's Bureau of Records. The Hills, two park visitors, were

on their way out of the park from Paradise Valley [when] they stopped at Christine Falls and while there met Mr. Jordan. They talked with him casually at first but on learning that he was from Long Beach, California, became more interested in him. They discussed for some time matters of interest to both with reference to California and their trips.

After some time Mrs. Hill asked Mr. Jordan what he was doing there. He replied that he was "watching the river" as he had lost his wife and he had expected to see her come floating down the river. This struck Mr. and Mrs. Hill as a very strange attitude to say the least and on further questioning Jordan he told them that the Rangers were up the trail somewhere looking for Mrs. Jordan, who had been lost for several hours and that the rangers had told him to remain there. Mr. and Mrs. Hill waited around there for some time and talked further with Jordan who kept watching the river but who appeared to be extremely calm under the circumstances.

After being lowered by rope down a steep cliff, Ranger Edward Anderson recovered a dead Sadie Jordan from the creek below. Apparently, the 48-year-old Mr. Jordan was still married to:

Bess ("whom he deserted");

Minnie ("complained against him and he served one year in federal prison at Leavenworth, Kan. for this bigamy");

an "unnamed laundry worker, a widow";

Cora ("woke up one morning after having been drinking and found I was the husband of a girl . . .");

Grace ("I corresponded with several hundred women through a national matrimonial agency" while serving six months in jail for "living with a woman to whom he was not married");

Edith ("another 'jail letter' sweetheart"); and

Sadie (whom he met at a dance).

Jordan was eventually convicted of bigamy for the second time by a California court.


```
           August 22, 1924
       Yosemite National Park
----------------------------------------
```

"GIRL GOES OVER FALLS TO DEATH"

CAUGHT in a swift undercurrent when she lost her footing while wading in the Merced River, 16-year-old Lucille Dullig of Hollywood, was today swept over the crest of Vernal Falls and plunged 325 feet to death in the swirling water below.

The girl's death plunge was witnessed by her father and a girl friend . . . they arrived in the locality just before noon and waded across the crest of the falls to take photographs.

In returning, Dullig and his daughter walked a few feet apart. The girl stumbled and was engulfed in the swift current. She rose to the surface, screaming, just as the avalanche of water carried her over the crest of the falls.

Horror stricken, Dullig and Miss Straub climbed down to the base of the falls. Dullig braved the strong current to rescue his daughter's body. She was dead when taken from the water. Dullig carried the body 2½ miles to Camp Curry.
—*Stockton Record,* 8-22-24 (reprinted by permission)

This is the first recorded death from plunging over Vernal Falls. From 1924 through 2003, at least 11 other people died in this way (in 1929, 1946, 1947, 1968, 1970, two in 1971, 1973, and 1977). In two of these cases, (1946 and 1970), a second person died trying to help the first.

Protective railings for the safety of tourists at Vernal and Nevada Falls were erected in 1892 by Galen Clark.

Yosemite chief ranger Forest Townsley (left) with two unidentified men (one wearing a badge) poses with bloodhounds in this 1924 photo.

August 24, 1924
Glacier National Park

EVEN J. EDGAR HOOVER COULDN'T FIND THEM

THOUGH seven years apart, the two Whiteheads looked like the brothers they were—the same height, facial features, and dark brown hair; both wore glasses. Joe, 29, was an engineer for the Universal Battery Company in Chicago, and William, 22, attended MIT in Boston.

On Sunday morning, dressed for cool, moist weather and intending to fish along the way, the pair left Many Glacier and began hiking toward the Lewis Hotel. They never registered that night.

Chief Ranger Brooks and Superintendent Kraebel, notified of the men's disappearance after a week had passed, quickly launched a massive effort. "Thirteen rangers, two famous Indian guides, and seven mountaineers tried for more than two weeks, and this has been supplemented by all the visitors in the Park." The U.S. Biological Survey detailed a famed lion hunter with his dog to help find them. The lakes and streams along the way were thoroughly searched; all the trails in the rugged park were walked.

The Secretary of the Interior tried to assure a distraught mother: "There never has been a search in the National Parks conducted with more vigor and effort than this one, and nothing has been left undone that could be humanly anticipated."

$1,700.00 REWARD
For
JOSEPH and WILLIAM WHITEHEAD

Brothers disappeared Sunday, August 24, on the trail between Granite Park Chalets and the Lewis Hotel in Glacier National Park, Montana.

Despite an intensive two-year search involving J. Edgar Hoover, not one clue was ever found of the whereabouts of the Whitehead brothers.

GLACIER NATIONAL PARK RESEARCH LIBRARY

With the coming snows, the search shifted to include a few criminal possibilities. For more than two years, the new chief of the young Bureau of Investigation personally oversaw the efforts of his "G-Men." Almost every month, J. Edgar Hoover filed a detailed progress report with the director of the National Park Service or the Secretary of the Interior. Clues for the investigators quickly ran out, as did the patience of Dora B. Whitehead, the missing men's mother.

> I want my two sons, dead or alive. Surely I am not asking too much. They belong to me—I have a right to have them. My two sons were murdered or kidnapped in a National Park, and I am pleading with the Government of the United States to find them.

The government of the United States never did find them.

Although the probe for the two Whitehead brothers was massive and intense for its day, numerically the largest ground search ever to take place in the United States. was probably the search for one or more of the 14 African-American children who were murdered in Atlanta over a 15-month period in 1979 and 1980. On October 25, 1980, an estimated 3,000 searchers in 30 teams scoured vacant lots and other deserted parts of the city for several of the homicide victims.

January 12, 1925
Rocky Mountain National Park

AGNES W. VAILLE

AGNES W. Vaille wanted to be the first person (actually the second) to scale the 1,600-foot-high East Face of Longs Peak in the winter, a climb accomplished only a few times even in the summer. After three failures, the 35-year-old joined veteran Swiss alpine guide Walter Kiener on a fourth attempt.

A graduate of Smith College and secretary of the Denver Chamber of Commerce, Vaille was a stalwart in the Colorado Mountain Club: a "true lover of Colorado, a devotee of its wild and inaccessible places, a votary of canon and chasm, of peak and precipice, with the courage and strength of a man and the soul of a naturalist."

Leaving Denver late at night, she and Kiener reached the Timberline Inn at 3 A.M. After only "a scant amount of rest," they started for the top; the climb was a slow and difficult one. At 4 P.M., as darkness approached, they were so far along "it was just as easy to complete the trip as it was to return." Weather had been favorable, but as the day wore on, a strong wind began to blow and the cold grew more intense; their thermometer that Sunday night registered 14 degrees below zero.

Reaching the top of Longs Peak at 4 A.M., the windchill neared 40 below. Not daring to stop, they chose to descend the peak's shorter, though more difficult, north side. Progress was excruciatingly slow—their continued exertion for 24 hours "with but little rest the night before" was exacting its toll.

Five hours after leaving the summit, the two came to the most perilous part of the descent. A misstep sent Vaille tumbling 150 feet down a steep face of rock and snow. She repeatedly assured Kiener that she was okay, but she was clearly exhausted and nearly stretched to her limit.

Quietly, Vaille confessed to Kiener that her hands and feet had been frozen most of the night. "She mentioned this only because of her inability to loosen a strap, and apologized for asking for help. Her courage and pluck never failed her from the first moment of the trip to the last." Staggering along once again, she finally collapsed after only 50 yards.

After hearing her say she could "proceed after half an hour's sleep," Kiener knew he had no choice. Reaching the inn just after noon, he found several men willing and waiting; assembled quickly from nearby, they were ill-dressed and without snowshoes.

Kiener, Hugh Brown, Jacob Christen, and Herb Sortland quickly started out. Within a half mile, Brown admitted defeat and returned. Minutes later Sortland "found that he could not make the trip at the rate of progress that was necessary" and he too turned back. A caretaker from the Longs Peak Inn, Sortland was freezing his face. "All of them, of course, were running a very great risk on account of the severe wind and bitter temperature." Christen and Kiener watched him walk away and saw that he was making good progress—they believed he was in no more danger than they were. But Sortland never made it back.

> Kiener and Christian [spelling differs] had an exceedingly difficult and dangerous trip. Occasionally they had to clear the sleet from each other's faces before they could proceed further. For a time Kiener was partially snow-blind, due to wind and sleet, so that Christian had to lead him. Christian told me [Superintendent Roger W. Toll] that at times he had but little hope of returning alive.

Now waging their own battle of survival, the two men reached Vaille shortly before dark. When Kiener had left her, she had been on her back using her knapsack as a pillow. Now they found her face down on a sloping rock, her pack on her back and an ice axe hooked to her wrist. It's doubtful she lived another hour. Reluctantly leaving the lifeless woman, the two men battled their way down to the inn.

Two hours before midnight, Assistant Superintendent Tom Allen and Rangers Jack Moomaw and Walter Finn arrived at the tiny inn. Word had also been sent to Roger Toll, Vaille's cousin, as well as the park's superintendent. "I was able to get only five miles from Estes Park. After getting stuck in the snow two or three times, we finally abandoned the car and proceeded on foot the four remaining miles to Longs Peak Inn." He and coworker Edmund Rogers reached the inn just minutes after word of Vaille's death.

> . . . we started for Timberline Cabin, which we reached at 4:30 A.M. I found the trip a hard one . . . when we got into the open, about 1,000 feet down the hill from Timberline Cabin, we received the full force of the wind. The wind-blown snow stung like sand and it was almost impossible to see anything ahead during the heavy gusts. . . . Every step up the hill was a struggle against the wind. The last thousand feet, we could not use either snowshoes or skis, but went first over wind-blown rocks and then wallowed, often on hands and knees, through deep snow drifts. So far as I am concerned, I could not have gone any further that night.

Timberline Cabin is paltry protection at any time, but it is almost useless during a blizzard. The men had a fire, not in the stove but on top of it, in order to get all the possible heat from the fuel. Most of the building's thin, insulating chinking was gone and the floor was covered with snow that had blown through the cracks. The gale howled all night—the rescuers feared that the south wall, "loose and rattling," would blow off.

Walt Kiener suffered from very badly frozen feet and hands—they were swollen and blistered "in a most pitiful manner." (Toll, in an article to the hiking club's magazine, *Trail and Timberline,* later stressed that they were "FROZEN—not frost-bitten.") Although nearly exhausted, Kiener was ready to return for his friend if the wind should die down. His "endurance and determination could not have been greater."

> One could not have lain down on the floor or tried to sleep without being frozen, so we huddled around the fire for the remainder of the night. The head and back of each person was covered with snow that blew into the cabin and which remained unmelted if more than two feet from the fire. We hoped that the wind would die down at sunrise, but as it did not slacken in the least we decided to wait until 9 o'clock and then return to Longs Peak Inn if it was impossible to ascend higher. At 9:50 the wind still being at its height, we started down.

Since Vaille was dead, the search for Herb Sortland began. For the next two days, 13 experienced winter mountaineers looked for the 23-year-old. They scoured the peak's lower slopes and visited all the possible shelters, including several deserted mining cabins. No trace was found until February 25, when a caretaker at Longs Peak Inn, the person who sounded the original call for additional help, discovered Sortland's body only 300 yards from the inn. Having broken a hip, the would-be rescuer had frozen to death where he had fallen.

On Thursday morning the men rose at 3:15. Seeing clouds shrouding Longs Peak, they could only guess at how the day would unfold. For the first hour, the moon helped them greatly, and even above timberline, they encountered little wind. A gentle snow settled on them most of the day. The worst was over.

> . . . at 12 o'clock we reached Agnes's body. Two skis were laid end to end. A third ski put across the joint and lashed together. The body was then strapped to these skis and carried with the aid of ski poles. The body was at an elevation of about 13,300 feet. This is about 900 feet in elevation below the summit of Longs Peak and rather less than half a mile distant. . . . At least eight men were required to carry the body across the Boulder Field.

After four months in the hospital, the lionhearted and severely frostbitten Kiener lost all his toes and fingers.

> Kiener's work was almost superhuman. No man could have done more. Not one in ten thousand. . . . He ploughed through drifts, ascended steep ice slopes, climbed up and down slick and frozen cliffs, in an arctic temperature and part of the time in a howling blizzard . . . forty-seven and a half hours of grilling struggle.

To help Kiener with his medical expenses, Park Superintendent Toll hired him as a ranger for five summers while he was earning a doctorate in botany from the University of Nebraska. Kiener died in 1959.

January 30, 1925
(pre) Mammoth Cave National Park

GREATEST CAVE RESCUE EVER

TRAPPED in a coffin-sized tunnel deep within a cave for 17 days, Floyd Collins soon became a household word. The spirited fight for his release—ranked only behind the first trans-Atlantic flight and the Lindbergh baby kidnapping—was judged by national journalists to be the third biggest news story between the two world wars.

> At the narrowest part of the fissure he again moved his lantern . . . it toppled over and went out. Floyd had been plunged into darkness many times before and it did not bother him. . . . He tucked his arms along his sides, compressed himself as flat as possible, and again began to combine shoulder and hip motions to wiggle through. Bringing his feet into play, he dug them hard into the sides and floor of the crack for better leverage. . . . Inadvertently, he struck the hanging rock that he had so carefully avoided on the way in. It broke loose.

By noon, two hours after squirming into dank Sand Cave, the 32-year-old was stuck, his left foot locked fast by a 26-pound rock. Over the next two weeks, while the media painstakingly described every nuance of Collins's torturous misadventure, the country grew obsessed with the tragedy unfolding 54 feet beneath central Kentucky.

At first, friends tried to dig the hapless man free while preserving his body heat and energy levels; they believed sinking a shaft from the surface would take too long and that pulling him out by rope would be inhumane. All too soon they discovered that, if they slid into the chute head first, they had to work upside down and on their back; if they climbed in feet first, they couldn't bend to his level without twisting into a superhuman position.

Conditions were ripe for Collins to become national news—an epic of "man against nature." To a public locked in winter and with time to focus on headlines and the radio, this drama proved irresistible—a lone victim suffering from who knew what kind of indescribable torment. Before it was over, newsmen from almost every state and even a few foreign countries were on-site.

William B. "Skeets" Miller was a 21-year-old, untested reporter for Kentucky's largest newspaper, the Louisville *Courier-Journal.* Weighing just 117 pounds and only 5-foot-5, Miller soon became the trapped man's voice to the world; it was an experience Skeets would never forget. Although terrified at being in the tiny hole, Miller's first 75 minutes of talking to a not-quite-panicked Collins altered his life forever. He knew that Collins might die before being freed, and this evolving sense of utter helplessness struck a nerve deep in the young journalist. Skeets's genuinely touching insight into the despair that lay belowground would earn him a Pulitzer Prize for the best reporting of that year.

By February 3, the Sand Cave sideshow was in full swing. At least 16 big-city papers and six film studios were there. For the next two weeks, the *Washington Post* gave Collins full front-page treatment, and the *Chicago Tribune*'s lead story soon became coverage enlarging to wartime-like head-lines—eight columns long and 2 inches high. The Associated Press claimed that Skeets's touching articles were being used by more than 1,200 other newspa-pers; one New York paper said it hawked in excess of 60,000 extra copies each day from February 7 on.

One wealthy reader, learning that amputation of Collins's leg was being considered, sent her own doctor. A fellow physician from the same Chicago hospital said, "The operation would be unprecedented if successful." He cau-tiously went on to say that "it would have to be performed under a local anes-thetic and, because of the impossibility of obtaining freedom in which to work, it would be extremely difficult." Because the dismemberment would involve cut-ting the femur off at nearly waist high, the doctor was bringing the most advanced surgical tools to stem the outpouring of blood he expected in the poor light. By the seventh, 17 volunteer doctors were either at the cave or on call. They didn't amputate.

On February 5, the state interceded and the Kentucky National Guard took over; by evening a steady stream of gear was moving in. The rail line serving the area added extra cars to its trains and expedited the arrival of all sorts of materials. More than 200 companies volunteered various forms of specialized equipment. When the shaft from the surface finally began, Collins had been stuck for 144 hours and hadn't eaten or drunk for a day and a half.

Eventually, a crew of 75 men was in place—engineers, miners, drillers, surveyors, day laborers, college students, even hobos joined the dig. A team of football players from Western Kentucky Normal arrived, "excused from classes until the race against death at Sand Cave was finished." Drilling in ankle-deep mud, only two men could work in the pit at a time; the walls kept falling in. Initially the good weather was welcome, but it soon unlocked the water frozen in the ground and digging became even more difficult.

Nationwide, churches held all-night prayer vigils and Collins's salvation was the topic of numerous Sunday services. A San Francisco radio station began its broadcast day by asking its audience to pray for the trapped caver. Three attention-seeking women claimed that the bachelor intended to marry them; several marriage offers came in while one woman even offered to inch down the nearly impossible passageway to be wedded on the spot.

Halfway through the ordeal, the national office of the American Red Cross began paying all routine expenses at Sand Cave after the local chapter quickly went broke feeding 200 people each meal. From Kentucky and Tennessee, 59 National Guardsmen were on post to ensure order among the 500 people visiting the area every day. Five-strand barbed-wire fencing was erected around the shaft and the Guardsmen nervously stockpiled extra ammunition nearby.

Daily film clips of the rescue were shown at movie houses all across the country. Louisville's WHAS aired eight radio updates a day and other stations soon followed suit. If announcers were late with news releases, they were flooded by angry callers, and managers interrupted scheduled programming for bulletins. To augment the telegraph line to nearby Cave City, a 500-watt radio base was created with a call sign of 9-BRK. Western Union eventually set up an office at the cave and brought in at least a dozen operators.

Near the end, the *Chicago Tribune* estimated that it had answered 4,000 telephone calls about Collins per day. President Calvin Coolidge followed the story while members of Congress left debates on the House and Senate floors for updates. Hotels, public assemblies, eateries, and theaters posted "Collins' Reports." People continued to believe that American brilliance for organization and engineering could easily save a man trapped belowground.

On February 8, the Sunday before the shaft was finished, Collins's plight escalated from sideshow to full carnival. With less than a 90-mile drive from Louisville, an estimated 4,500 autos from at least 20 states as well as hundreds of horse-drawn buggies clogged the narrow, clay-covered lane to Sand Cave. After adding four extra coaches from Louisville to Cave City, the local railroad sold 2,500 additional tickets to weekend revelers.

Having traveled from near and far, 10,000 to 50,000 gawkers milled in the fields near the tragedy; guards and barbed wire kept them away from the slowly deepening rescue shaft. Skillful entrepreneurs hawked to a willing swarm, offering food, drinks, chairs, games, medicinal elixirs, and balloons saying "SAND CAVE."

When the shaft neared completion, 20 telegraph circuits stood by to handle the news. All the major newspapers planned special editions; journalists believed that when Collins was finally reached, all records for newsprint devoted to one story would be surpassed. Only a few miles away, in a pasture dubbed "Collins Field," seven airplanes stood by to carry rescue and cadaver photos to leading eastern cities such as Chicago, Cincinnati, and Atlanta. A young Charles Lindbergh was one of the pilots.

At 1:30 P.M. on February 16, at the bottom of a 54-foot shaft, diggers broke into the passage—still 6 feet above the recently departed. Disheartened and without momentum, they filled the hole in. In a day when hamburgers were 5 cents, the whole rescue cost an estimated $200,000. In April the shaft was redug and on the 17th, Collins's body was finally freed. Buried already for three months, he was finally put to rest in nearby Crystal Cave, a cave he had discovered.

The tragedy aroused considerable interest in the area, and on May 25, 1926, President Coolidge authorized the creation of Mammoth Cave National Park. On September 9, 1972, spelunkers joined Crystal and Mammoth Caves; at nearly 350 miles in length, this is the longest cavern system in the world.

```
                    June 7, 1925
              Yosemite National Park
      ----------------------------------------
```

WEIRD SUICIDE UNEARTHED BY PARK RANGERS

Member of Europe's Nobility Plunges 2600 Feet to Instant Death

(Special Dispatch to The Chronicle)
YOSEMITE, Aug 18—Evidence of a weird suicide by a 2600-foot plunge over Yosemite falls in the Yosemite National Park led to the disclosure today of the death of

Count Theordore James Jackowski, a Polish nobleman and former resident of San Francisco. Discovery of the nobleman's tragic leap was made by forest [park] rangers, who found fragments of bone at the base of the giant waterfall.

Search for the body was started last week when two hikers . . . found a coat at the top of the fall in which was a will, scribbled in pencil on notebook paper and signed by Theordore Jackowski.

"Last night saw wonderful firefall," the will read. "Now see me fall. Don't get shocked. I am at end of trail. Please plant some redwood on me."

Two rangers prepare for a trip into the Yosemite backcountry, circa 1925. Notice the pistol on the hip of Forest Townsley.

YOSEMITE NATIONAL PARK
RESEARCH LIBRARY

A $20 travelers' check was found in the coat, made out to Sheriff Finn of San Francisco. In the will were instructions to Finn to pay $5 each to two policemen who arrested Jackowski, recently, and $10 to a jail trusty who was good to him while in jail.

Sheriff Left $5 to Plant Redwood

Five dollars Jackowski left to the "Sheriff of Yosemite to pay for planting redwood trees over my grave."

Jackowski, it was learned today . . . was a Polish count who, after a tour of this country, returned to Poland upon inheriting a huge fortune, estimated at a quarter of a million dollars.

Returned to U.S., Living Luxuriously

He then came back to the United States. In his travels . . . Jackowski lived luxuriously and his inheritance rapidly dwindled. He had just spent his last cent . . . and in a fit of depression leaped to his death over the high waterfall.

The suicide will was dated June 7. After the finding of the coat, rangers searched about the foot of Yosemite falls and found fragments of bones which Dr. C.H. Church, resident physician, declared to be those of a human.

—*San Francisco Chronicle*, 8-19-25
(reprinted by permission)

```
August 14, 1925
Glacier National Park
```

SEARCHING GLACIER FOR MISSING PAIR; GONE SINCE AUGUST 12

BELTON, Aug. 25—National [park] service rangers in the vicinity of Sperry chalets are engaged in a search into the remote recesses of the mountains . . . [for pair] who disappeared in that section of the park. . . .

They left the camp August 10, leaving word they were going to Lake Ellen Wilson. . . . They did not return to the campgrounds, where they had left their outfit, and it was not until August 19 that the camp cook notified the park officials of their disappearance.

A search was at once instituted and it was ascertained they had not returned to Whitefish and their camp remained untouched. Two parties headed by park rangers and one trail crew were sent out to search for them, but up to Monday night no trace of the missing couple had been discovered.

—*Helena Daily Independent*, 8-26-25
(reprinted by permission)

Perishing during the severe early-season snowstorm of August 14, the two were later found near remote Lincoln Pass by rangers.

Glacier National Park had been given the stigma of being a rich man's pleasuring ground catering to the elite. One article of the day, largely prompted by the much-heralded and never-solved mystery of the Whitehead brothers (August 24, 1924), suggested that all hikers register as they moved along from camp to camp.

```
June 27, 1927
Zion National Park
```

THEIR FIRST BIG RESCUE

THEIR first big rescue ended happily, but Park Superintendent Ev Scoyen was sorry

to state that there remains no doubt but that he [Evans] succeeded in reaching the summit of our greatest mountain. I had hoped that no one would ever succeed in this climb, but nothing seems impossible anymore, and if he had failed, it would only be a question of time until some one did succeed.

Driving a big Chrysler with California plates 1-270-476, the two young men spent their first week sightseeing among the amazing red and gray cliffs. Douglas Graham wasn't very husky, being "crippled by sickness"; W. H. W. Evans "was distinctly of the daredevil type, and a seasoned mountaineer." He was a constant worry to his friend Graham, wanting to scale anything and everything that looked difficult and dangerous.

Like a colossal sandstone tombstone, the Great White Throne towers above Zion Canyon. Told it was impossible to climb, Evans took the challenge and succeeded. However, when the young adventurer was not heard from for more than 24 hours, rangers started tracking him. As they searched, they kept a watch on the autocamp far below for the prearranged bonfire, a signal to them should anything develop.

After considerable effort in the June heat, the rescue team "noticed a notebook at the foot of the cliff, and at practically the same moment saw Evans stretched out in some brush and sand a few feet away. . . . Gifford appeared on the cliff about 2,000 feet up and shouted down that the man had been found." Broken, bruised, and barely alive, the young climber had had nothing to drink for more than 38 hours. "His canteen was half full but was so badly smashed that it was necessary to cut the top off before he could be given a drink."

Within 35 minutes, two doctors, six horses, and four extra men were on their way up; a crude stretcher was made from poles, shoestrings, and Chief Ranger Reusch's donated overalls. Although eventually successful, Evans's rescue proved extremely difficult and Superintendent Scoyen glowingly wrote of his men:

> The daring and nerve of Evans in this climb is matched by that of the rescuers. Dangerous chances were taken by these men, especially those who followed his trail up over the cliffs. There was no glory in this work, only another days work, distinguished by the fact it was harder than usual. The men . . . deserving commendation are Reusch, Woodbury, Schiefer, Russell and Gifford.

June 29, 1927
Yellowstone National Park

HISTORICAL ENTRY IN
CANYON RANGER STATION LOGBOOK

. . . **TWO** boys . . . employed by the Hotel company as dishtable men . . . went down into the Canyon just below Red Rock. The boys traveled up the Canyon in an attempt to reach the base of the Lower Falls. The canyon is deep at this point and the north side is practically impossible to scale due to high cliffs. The boys were unable to retrace their steps and were stranded.

One lad was able to climb to a point where a rope could be gotten to him and he was taken out in that manner. The other boy in his attempt to scale the canyon fell about thirty feet. In his fall he cut a deep gash in his right hip and many abrasions on the body. Because of his injuries and the heavy, cold mist from the falls he soon became half frozen and exhausted. Attempts were made to reach the lad from the North rim . . . but lack of rope prevented a successful attempt. . . . Every possible means was tried but all attempts proved futile.

Word had been sent to Lake for rope and it reach[ed] a point above the lad at about 5:45 P. M. Ranger Kell was the only ranger on that side and he was let down over the cliff into the canyon. Remus Allen, an employee of the Transportation Company, followed Kell. The rope which they went down on was too short and the two rescuers found it necessary to strike a trail to the stranded lad.

In one place it necessitated their wading into the river to get around a small bluff . . . it was necessary to take the lad to a position where another rope could be let down. This was a very perilous undertaking as it was necessary to cross several patches of open rock and much loose shale. The canyon is very steep all along this part and a slip would have meant a fall into the river.

Kell and Allen finally got the boy to the right of Red Rock and to within 150 feet of the top where they reached a rope. . . . The three were pulled out from this point. . . . Allen, due to the severe strain, coughed up some blood from his lungs and worked loose a silver plate which he carries in his shoulder.

Too much credit cannot be given Kell and Allen for their very manful attitude. They truly risked their lives in their attempt to save a fellow man.

The rangers at Canyon feel that some means of rescue should be furnished them for future use. We have had similar experiences to this in the past and have always been handicapped by the lack of rope. At least 1000 feet of rope on a rope cart and two body harnesses are needed. This lad could have been rescued at least three hours sooner and with much less work if the necessary equipment had been at hand.

—*Canyon Ranger Station Logbook,*
entry by Ranger Karl J. Hardy

```
              April 7, 1928
          Yosemite National Park
-------------------------------------------
```

MUFFLED, THE WORDS SOUNDED
FAINTLY LIKE "HELP"

SPRING winds carried the cries of fright down the dark, deep cliffs. Campers, hotel guests, and local residents heard them; John Bingaman, a Yosemite ranger for many years, heard them.

Edna Wilbur, the bold daughter of the Secretary of the Navy, and her friend Ona Ring had become trapped. "After crossing the water course they lost the trail and got down far on the cliff to a sheer drop-off of 200 feet. . . . They were in a place covered with snow and mud, wet and very uncomfortable."

It took Bingaman and Ranger Reymann two hours to reach the two young women on the Ledge Trail. Now a treacherous, boulder-choked gully, in years gone by it had masqueraded as a real pathway. Before the trail slid into disrepair, hardy souls made quick work of the 3,000 feet between the valley floor and Glacier Point.

Tying two ropes together, Ranger Reymann was lowered 75 feet to the ledge. "They certainly appreciated our coming after them."

Mr. Stephen T. Mather   Yosemite, Calif.
Washington, D.C.   April 30, 1928

Dear Mr. Mather:

I read your telegram to Mr. Leavitt in regards to Miss Wilbur's rescue. It is good to receive praise from our superior officers. It makes us feel that our efforts are worth while.

I have always tried to give my best to the Service. And certainly will continue to do so.

Since Mr. Albright's return he has told me about the excitement the rescue created back in Washington. I received a very nice letter from Secretary Wilbur in his own hand writing, which I prize very much. And was most pleasant to receive.

Thanking you,
Yours very truly

John W. Bingaman

Director Mather and Superintendent Leavitt, trying to convince the Civil Service Commission of the need for "having our patrolling rangers retired at 62 years of age," cited this rescue as an example. "Only men of youth, experience, and ability are qualified to participate in such strenuous and dangerous work as this is."

Climbing onto treacherous cliffs at night, rangers Bingaman and Reymann went to the aid of two young women stranded on a ledge high above Yosemite Valley.

YOSEMITE NATIONAL PARK
RESEARCH LIBRARY

December 1, 1928
Grand Canyon National Park

THE MYSTERY OF BESSIE AND GLEN HYDE— 70 YEARS LATER

BESSIE'S husband of six months called it a belated honeymoon; others heralded her as the first woman to brave the Colorado River. Focused on "fame and fortune," Glen persuaded his 23-year-old bride to write a book while they toured the country thrilling audiences. Bessie was a poet and artist, and the adventure before her held great promise. She was eager to test herself, and she soon would do so.

October 20 saw the novice boatman and woman shove off from Green River, Utah, in a homemade, flat-bottomed scow; at 20 feet long, 5 feet wide, and a scant 3 feet deep, it was prophetically labeled a "floating coffin" by local skeptics. Among their stores were bedding, a mattress, and a sand-filled box for a kerosene stove, but no life preservers.

They did surprisingly well, despite cold weather, a maze of rapids, and Glen's catapult overboard when his oar caught a hidden rock. Bessie became the first woman to run both Cataract and Marble Canyons. After 26 days they put in at the foot of the Bright Angel Trail and hiked to Grand Canyon Village for supplies and a taste of comfort. Again, Glen was beseeched to stop—or at least to take some life preservers. Setting out two days later, he had done neither.

Ten days after they failed to meet Glen's father in Needles, the Hydes' empty scow was easily spotted by two Army search planes 3 miles above Separation Canyon. Floating quietly in an eddy, it was held fast by a towrope snagged in the riverbed. Their last "calendar" date, notches carved daily into the boat's sideboard (a hatchmark for each day and a cross for each seventh day), was cut November 30. Everything inside the undamaged boat seemed in order—yet there was no sign of life anywhere.

A three-person search party, using the only other vessel afloat in the entire Grand Canyon, launched from Phantom Ranch. This boat, abandoned the year before by the Pathe-Bray Expedition, a floating publicity stunt with a live bear aboard, was really just a derelict used to pull driftwood in for the ranch fires. These three, facing dangerous rapids, soon became the subject of a second search. Eventually a large Ford Tri-Motor airplane, gingerly steering between the mile-high cliffs, found the trio safe 69 miles downstream.

A second, separate, search effort for the missing honeymooners was mounted far downriver at Glen's father's insistence. Ellsworth and Emory Kolb, veteran canyoneers and early-river runners, along with Chief Ranger Jim Brooks, volunteered. Diamond Creek, one of the few side canyons by which the river can easily be reached, was only 11 miles upriver from where the Hydes' boat lay deserted. The three men borrowed a wagon and saddle horses from the local Hualapai Indians and on December 21 rode the 22 miles in. Here they found a small abandoned craft from the James Girand Dam Site Survey Party of years before.

Making this craft "seaworthy" took clever improvising, but in two days they were able to push off, floating 9 miles that Christmas Eve. As they moved along, they landed at likely beaches but could find no tracks or other human traces.

Glen and Bessie Hyde's boat did not appear to have drifted very far, certainly not through much rough water; the sweep oars were bobbing alongside the craft. Personal effects were found lying on a seat or stowed neatly away—including Bessie's diary. It gave full daily accounts through November 30 and described all the points of interest. It also indicated that they had successfully run all the rapids and that none of them had to be lowered through by means of ropes from the shore. The three investigators felt sure that the deserted vessel could not have traveled more than a mile or two before it became caught in the rocks.

Cutting the boat free, the search team followed; while running Separation Rapids, however, their own dinghy swamped and all three were thrown into the frigid river. They clung to the overturned craft as it sailed down the remaining 400 yards of whitewater. The weather was freezing; the rocks were glazed with ice.

> They had managed to retain the oars so that when the boat reached still water . . . they clambered to the top of the flat-bottomed boat, sculled it to shore, got it turned right-side up, bailed it out and continued 6 miles further to Spencer Canyon without being able to dry out their clothes or provisions.

Despite continued searching by both fathers, the Hydes seem to have vanished.

Forty-three years later, on a beach not far from Diamond Creek, an engaging tale began to tantalizingly unfold around the campfire. A local boat guide regaled tourists with river days gone by. Among the party sat a diminutive woman in her sixties, named Liz, who took particular interest when the Hydes were mentioned. Partway through the guide's story, Liz began adding completely unknown and unverifiable details. To the mounting curiosity of her fellow passengers she was soon telling a stirring new version of what happened.

Then she claimed to be Bessie Hyde. She said that the 1928 trip had been hard on her. Once on the river, Glen was no longer the man she had married. She wanted to leave when they reached Phantom Ranch. "He was a son-of-a-bitch who beat me all the time." She told the captivated audience that when she and Glen later beached near Diamond Creek, she wanted off. He refused.

At least one boatman listening to her yarn that warm fall evening thought she was joking. O. C. Dale didn't believe her, although she did seem to know more about the river than a first-time passenger should. Another guide, George Billingsley, was convinced that Liz was actually Bessie, however. He heard her declare that she had stabbed Glen with a kitchen knife, dragged him into the river, and set the boat adrift. She then hiked out the easy 22-mile Diamond Creek and caught an eastbound bus.

Intrigued several years later by Billingsley's tale, Scott Thybony, investigative writer and noted Arizona historian, located and phoned "Liz." She repeated details from that evening campfire her river guides had forgotten. "When I asked about the Hydes' disappearance she denied having told the story. She hesitated a moment and then said matter-of-factly, 'I don't remember that at all. I'm not Bessie. I don't even know the name, Hyde.'"

Thybony states in his story "The River Mystery" that the "circumstantial evidence is intriguing. Liz is Bessie's age and height; she lives near Bessie's hometown. And on her first Colorado River trip she was able to relate a convincing story about Bessie Hyde on the spur of the moment."

Without life preservers, both the Hydes were simultaneously dragged to a watery grave in their heavy winter clothing? Did one go to the rescue of the other? Why were there no tracks or telltale signs upstream? How did Liz know so much about the river and early river lore? Why did she later deny having heard of the Hydes? Was Liz Bessie?

Superintendent Tillotson, because of the hardship placed on the park by publicity and thrill-seeking boaters of that era, proposed the following text for a Special River Running Permit.

BOAT TRIPS DOWN COLORADO RIVER

The rapids of the Colorado River can at no time be traversed by boat in safety. Many lives have been lost in attempting such a trip and for this reason trips of this nature . . . may be undertaken only by those holding a special permit from the Director . . . for this purpose. Such a permit may be issued . . . to those who can make a satisfactory showing as to their previous experience as boatmen in a rapid water and whose boat and other equipment is deemed satisfactory and safe. Applications . . . shall be accompanied by a good and sufficient bond of not less than $2,500.00 which shall be available to cover expenses up to that amount in case it should be necessary to send out rescue parties.

Director Albright forwarded it to the Assistant Secretary of the Interior. On March 30, 1929, Solicitor Edwards rejected it, saying, "It would be impracticable to enforce such a regulation."

February 20, 1929
Grand Canyon National Park

TWO RANGERS DROWN

CASUAL readers could easily have overlooked the following short news story on the back pages of the *Phoenix Republic.*

> The swirling waters of the muddy Colorado River are believed to have claimed two more lives when the boat of Fred Johnson, 30, U.S. Forest [sic] Ranger, and Glen Sturdevant, 31, park naturalist, was caught in the rapids of Horn Creek yesterday morning. James P. Brooks, chief ranger of Grand Canyon Park, the third occupant of the boat, was carried many yards down stream, but was able to reach the shore.

Hiking down the steep, rocky Bright Angel Trail, the three rangers headed toward Phantom Ranch, 4,000 feet below. Even with their heavy wool clothing, they must have shivered as they passed through early-morning shadows cast by the canyon walls from oceans dead eons ago. Their canvas packs, cumbersome and heavy, were full of scientific recording equipment.

For nine days they collected fossils, inspected Indian ruins, surveyed wildlife, and logged animal conditions; there was much to learn about this new park. On the 20th they broke camp at 9 A.M.

The trio easily rowed the mile upstream; their collapsible, 13-foot boat was built for quiet water, not for the rapids for which the Colorado River of the Grand Canyon is famous. After they portaged to the top of Horn Creek Rapids, the narrowing walls, 500 feet high at this point, forced them back into the water sooner than they really wanted. Only 75 yards of swiftly moving current now separated them from the first huge wave of the rapids downstream.

Days later, the six jurors at the coroner's inquest listened closely as Chief Ranger Brooks testified.

> Mr. Sturdevant was rowing, Fred in the bow and I was in the stern. The boat swung around and I told Glen to pull and I would try to turn it. We began to lose distance. The shore current swung the boat around . . . and drifted us towards the rapids, and we could see then it was impossible to do any more rowing. I believe I said that we were going to go over, seems as if I said that, and then Glen lost one of the oars. We went over the side and we did not have a chance and it could

not have been a very short distance, probably about the second cascade which threw all of us in.

Brooks had been able to grab a kapok life roll just as he was thrown out. Sturdevant had a life belt already on. "I thought if I could reach him I could crowd him to the shore. That was the last I saw of Fred or either one of the boys. I believe I did come up once or twice because I did get a breath of air and I came up below the foot of the rapids."

Frantically, Brooks scoured beach and boulder alike for the other two. He climbed onto the cliffs to gain a vantage point; his shouts were answered only with echoes. He took his clothes off, thinking that the shining sun would help dry them out, but it was too cold so he put his damp heavy wools back on. Late in the afternoon, after looking for seemingly endless hours, he worked his way up through the broken layers of ancient rock and stumbled into Phantom Ranch long after dark.

Mike Harrison volunteered to search the river for his friends. That first day, his party of four found Sturdevant's body floating in a dark eddy surrounded by the ill-fated group's provisions. Bobbing nearby was Brooks's water-soaked, leather, mackinaw-lined jacket; it now weighed 75 pounds. Harrison remembers putting "Glen's body on the stern of the boat, lying athwart the stern, and I sat there with my hands on the rope and my two feet over Glen's chest, and that is the way we went through Monument Creek Rapid, back to Hermit, and he was taken out on that tram."

The next four days were spent searching; the 800-pound boat had to be taken out at the foot of every rapid. ". . . hitching the block and tackle onto a big rope, and pushing, we skidded that boat around every one of those rapids over the rocks from baseball size to as big as a desk, and then put it in at the head of the rapid." Originally, this craft had been cut in two and then abandoned by a Hollywood movie company using it to film *Bride of the Colorado,* which was never released.

Ranger Bert Luzon rode deep into the canyon with instructions from Superintendent Tillotson. "Look, Bert, we've had one hell of a time coming up here. Two men have already been lost. We're in a boat that was spliced together with a piece of copper." Efforts continued and Mike Harrison recalled:

> . . . never found Fred's body, although we dynamited the head and foot of Horn Creek Rapid. Never brought up a body . . . we thought it might be lodged in the rock in that rapid, but it wasn't. Brought up some dead fish, but that is all. Shot up a geyser of water in the air . . . we threw in a . . . full case of dynamite . . . and all we brought up was water and a few dead fish.

On February 26, the 10th anniversary of the creation of Grand Canyon National Park, a double military memorial was held in the village. Volleys were fired over Sturdevant's grave and a bugle sounded "Taps." The rifle escort then proceeded to the canyon rim at Powell Memorial Point, "where another round of rifle shots was fired over the Grand Canyon, Fred's grave, and where again the notes of 'taps' echoed and re-echoed from the Canyon walls."

```
                    March 6, 1929
            Carlsbad Caverns National Park
        --------------------------------------
```

RESCUED FROM 800 FEET BELOW SURFACE

UNTIL Emily Mobley was hauled from nearby Lechuguilla Cave in 1991 with a similarly broken leg, the 4-mile carry of Park Engineer Tom Vint from the 800-foot level of Carlsbad Caverns was the deepest rescue ever performed in the National Park System.

Vint, on an inspection tour of two recently discovered rooms in the Left Hand Tunnel area with Superintendent Tom Boles and Chief Ranger White, fell when his feet slipped out from under him. Boles, in his *Monthly Report* for March, described the event.

> The breaking bone was distinctly heard . . . each of us thought it was the crunching of a formation. Mr. Vint however asked us to wait a minute while he examined his leg; we soon ascertained that one if not both bones were broken just above the ankle. Chief Ranger White was sent to the Lunch Room for the cot-stretcher, and returned in one hour, with the cot and the trail crew, and Mr. Vint was laced on it and carried to the surface, a distance of nearly four miles. First aid had been given by an improvised splint made from a leather puttee, which was so effective that he suffered comparatively little from the rubbing of the broken ends.

```
                    July 2, 1929
              Mt. Rainier National Park
        --------------------------------------
```

DEPARTMENT OF THE INTERIOR'S FIRST VALOR AWARD

LEON H. Brigham, the park's chief alpine guide and a veteran of 45 Mt. Rainier ascents, described the blizzard that engulfed his six-person climbing party that day as "the worst that I have ever experienced . . . particles of ice swept into our faces and eyes. It was necessary to chop steps all the way up."

For almost seven hours, Brigham, apprentice guides Ray Strobel and Forrest Greathouse, and their three clients forced their way from Camp Muir up the 14,410-foot peak. Although the day had dawned pleasantly, clouds soon capped the summit; fierce winds blew so hard that for the last 100 yards "they all had to crouch low and crawl the remaining distance." After only 10 minutes inside the summit crater, they grew numb and quickly started down.

Edwin Wetzel proved a laborious client from the start. Being from Milwaukee and not used to the thin air, he had to be supported between Brigham and Strobel on the way up; on the way down he grew even worse.

Powerless to stand, he continually sat down, wanting to slide. Wetzel complained that he was too cold to hold onto lifelines; his sharp, pointed axe didn't help much and he was unable to place his feet into the steps that Brigham had chopped. Then, without warning, Strobel started to slide.

> I am unable to say what caused me to lose my footing. I may have been blown over, jerked off my feet, or missed a step. . . . As we went down the steep snow and ice I screamed. Greathouse tried to dig his axe in but in vain. In an instant we were all being swept down at a great speed. I got but one glimpse of the side of the crevasse as we went over and in. I welcomed the darkness and the shelter of unconsciousness. When I awakened my first thought was to get from under the individuals piled on top of me.
>
> We were all in a terrible daze and had to move very slowly. We realized there was extreme danger of the great blocks of snow and ice coming in from overhead or the false floor that we were resting on caving through. All about was porous and rotten snow and ice. Some seventy-five feet above . . . I could see light.

Strobel, miraculously suffering only bruises and cuts, somehow climbed from his near-tomb and went for help. When Brigham regained consciousness, he found Greathouse lying on his side, his labored breathing the only sign of life. Clients Bradshaw and Weatherly were barely conscious and Strobel was gone.

With years of experience and a strong instinct to survive, Brigham faced the ordeal ahead.

> It is impossible to judge the exact time that we were in the crevasse. It was at least two hours. Nine hours were required to make the trip from the crevasse to Muir, and in crawling most of the way, Bradshaw and I were unconscious a good part of the time.

Charlie Browne loved the mountain and loved to climb. At 33, the 5-foot-8 temporary ranger was tough and wiry after seven years at sea. When he saw the dazed man stagger into the shelter of Camp Muir, he quickly reacted. Gathering what he could, the new ranger pushed his way out into the blinding storm.

The news of the disaster was quickly carried down to the Paradise Ranger Station, and within an hour a rescue party was moving up. District Ranger John Davis, three alpine guides, and four others packed stretchers, ropes, and first-aid gear. Passing Camp Muir, the rescuers soon found the two injured men; both had already been examined by Ranger Browne. Urged by Brigham to nurse those still above, Davis climbed onward into the gale.

Alone on his mission of mercy, Ranger Browne found a shocky Weatherly; he helped him down the steep, icy chutes below Camp Comfort. Then, believing Weatherly to be sufficiently safe to leave, Browne went back for Greathouse and Wetzel.

Faced with an unrelenting blizzard, Browne was lucky to find the correct crevasse. Unable to enter, he soon discovered drag marks leading away from the hole.

> Following these a half mile down the Ingraham, he found Wetzel unconscious, his clothing nearly torn from his body, and apparently breathing his last. Browne could not move Wetzel so he dug a trench in the snow and rolled him into the hole to keep him from falling farther down the steep glacier.

Frustrated by the darkness, the main rescue team continued upward into the storm. Not knowing which crevasse was correct, they warily looked at each as they crossed. After three hours of finding nothing, they returned to Camp Muir; two weary hours of step-cutting later, Ranger Charlie Browne joined them.

On the next day a party led by mountain guide Johnny Day located the dead Wetzel. When the body was retrieved and then lowered, it slipped from their grasp and fell into another crevasse. Recovered with great difficulty, Wetzel finally arrived at Paradise late that night.

After several fruitless days of trying to find Greathouse and to prevent more loss of life, the guides asked that no further attempts be made. Four days after the tragedy, however, Park Superintendent Tomlinson dispatched a team of 12 experienced mountaineers—their leader was Temporary Ranger Charlie Browne.

> Even after we arrived we felt the situation was almost hope-less. Many tons of ice had fallen into the crevasse. We finally decided that there was only one thing to do if the body was to be recovered—to crawl through the hole in the snow and be lowered into the pit. We had a conference then. We all agreed it was a foolhardy thing to do—but all of the fellows volunteered to go down.
>
> As I was in charge I thought I should go if anybody did . . . so they let me down. They used a ninety-foot rope, and I guess I went down all but twenty feet of it. . . . Then I found the body, buried in the ice and snow. I could only see his shoulders, the back of his head and the upper part of his left arm. . . .
>
> Where he was lying there was a sort of false bottom and I decided it was likely to fall farther into the crevasse, so I put a rope around the body.

Apprentice guide Forrest G. Greathouse, a Seattle high school football coach on his very first climb on Mt. Rainier, was finally brought back to Seattle.

On July 22, 1929, Temporary Charlie Browne received a promotion and pay increase from $1,740 to $1,800 per annum.

On July 24, 1929, Washington's official press release read: "The first citation for heroism ever issued by the Department of Interior was made to-day by Secretary Wilbur in the case of Park Ranger Charles E. Browne." On August 1, 1929, he received the award "in the presence of the Park Headquarters Staff and the Park Rangers on duty on the South Side of the Park." In a follow-up letter to the director, Superintendent Tomlinson wrote that "only members of the Nat. Park Service were present because Ranger Browne and I felt that enough publicity had been given the matter."

Charlie Browne also received The Mountaineers' prestigious **Acheson Cup,** "to be awarded each year to the Washington member accomplishing the most notable achievement in mountaineering for that year."

On September 27, 1929, President Herbert Hoover appointed Charles E. Browne as a national park ranger—the first of only two to ever achieve this distinction.

On May 10, 1930, Mt. Rainier climbing guide Ray Strobel received the **DeMolay Medal** from Tacoma's Fredric W. Keaton Chapter of the Order of the DeMolay for his heroic efforts on the rescue. It was only the 12th time this award had been bestowed and the first time it was ever received by someone living.

This 31-year-old California man was lost in Yosemite National Park in 1966 but not found until 1971. His remains were buried in place, per the request of his widow. PHOTO BY AUTHOR

CHAPTER 4

1930–1939

...as I was looking at him there was a
flash of some dark object in the air
above him, and most of his head just
disappeared. Instantly he was on the
ground, having been struck by a rock
the size of a football.

—former Longs Peak guide, Hull Cook

EARLY VOLUNTEER MOUNTAIN RESCUE GROUPS

Rescue groups have well served this country since at least 1780, when the Humane Society of Philadelphia was established. Their objective was, among other things, the "recovery of drowned persons." Ten years later, on August 4, 1790, the marvel of the U.S. Coast Guard, the Revenue Cutter Service, was founded and a sterling tradition of ocean rescue began. The following year, the Life Saving Station for Distress Between Mariners, was founded on the shores of the East Coast and shelters dedicated to saving souls from the seas were erected on Nantucket. In 1848, to further safeguard sailors from the angry shoals off New Jersey, a federal lifesaving service began when Congress appropriated $10,000 to provide "surf boats . . . and other necessary apparatus for the preservation of life and property from shipwreck."

The history of our country's westward expansion is full of mishaps and perilous journeys. At least 20,000 emigrants, about 1 of every 17 who started, were buried beside the Oregon Trail. And few of us haven't heard of the luckless Donner Party; trapped by snow in the Sierra Nevada, nearly half of its 87 members died by starvation before being rescued in 1846. When Yellowstone was set aside in 1872, however, touring recreationists in the wilds began facing trouble, particularly eastern "dudes" arriving by train in 1883. For 60 more years, soldiers, climbing guides, and rangers saved the stranded and found the lost, at least in the rugged national parks being created in the West.

Avocational climbing organizations started to emerge, beginning with the Virginia Alpine Club in 1863. Because the latter was never heard from again, the Appalachian Mountain Club, founded in 1876, is considered the oldest extant major group dedicated to playing in this country's alpine areas. Eventually to follow was the Sierra Club in 1892, then the Oregon-based Mazamas in 1894, the Rocky Mountain Climbing Club in 1896, the American Alpine Club in 1902, and The Mountaineers (based in Seattle) in 1906. Blessed with machines and weekends of leisure, these societies assailed the national parks in earnest.

Although a few mountain rescue teams were alive and well elsewhere in the world—the eastern Alps in 1896 and Hong Kong in 1909—it wasn't until

Portland's E. C. Loveland was rescued on the Sunshine Trail on Oregon's Mt. Hood in 1926 that organized mountain rescue began in this country. Three Hood River Guides, a promotional group of the Hood River Chamber of Commerce, took part in this labor. One of these men, Andy Anderson, a local lumberman and outdoor enthusiast, recognized the necessity to more formally deal with the occasional lost child or injured hunter. On July 31, 1926, he sent postcards to fellow scramblers requesting that they meet on August 3. The "Crag Rats," a name jokingly suggested by Anderson's wife, inferring "they were just a bunch of rats climbing around on the crags on weekends, instead of staying home with their families," was established with 24 men on August 30, 1926. Initially made up of lumbermen, ranchers, and local businessmen, they remain today the oldest active mountain rescue team in the United States.

The San Diego Mountain Rescue Team, shown resting on September 6, 1974, after a successful four-day search for a 17-year-old girl lost in Yosemite.

AUTHOR'S PHOTO

Over the next several years they sporadically went on calls for aid but not until a message arrived from national park superintendent A. O. Tomlinson that their expertise was needed on the glacier-covered slopes of Mt. Rainier did their name spread far and wide. They played a prominent role in one of the most famous life-and-death dramas this country had seen: the Greathouse-Wetzel rescue on the Fourth of July weekend of 1929. This was also the mission that prompted the Department of the Interior's first Valor Award, issued to Park Ranger Charlie Browne.

On the night of January 13, 1936, 23-year-old Delmar Fadden surreptitiously skied around Mt. Rainier's White River Entrance Station. For two long weeks, 15 rangers and assorted local alpineers endured brutal conditions looking for the young man who wanted to be the first to conquer the 14,410-foot peak in the winter. Climber Ome Daiber, now acknowledged as the "Father of American Mountain Rescue," spotted the dead man from the air and then, along with several park rangers, scaled the windswept slopes to claim the frozen body of the former Eagle Scout.

Over the next decade Daiber, appreciating the need for rescue expertise in his beloved Cascade Mountains, put together a quasiformal list of fellow outdoorsmen to aid on climbing misadventures. On March 9, 1944, the superintendent of Mt. Rainier met with The Mountaineers and reviewed the challenges presented by lack of manpower due to the war; the climbing club readily agreed to assist.

Fifteen days later, Daiber's inventory was presented to the strapped park to assist with its increased rescue pressures.

On December 1, 1947, three Colorado University Hiking Club members went winter climbing on Navajo Peak west of Denver. Two didn't make it, despite massive but uncoordinated heroic measures by the military as well as many well-intentioned locals. Still reeling from this disaster, neighbors soon agonized over a fruitless search for three-year-old Alice, who died less than 150 yards from her father's cabin on nearby Sugarloaf Mountain on January 26, 1948. From these two catastrophes sprang Boulder County Rescue on March 5, 1948. The name was soon changed to Rocky Mountain Rescue Group (RMRG) and was officially organized that fall. The mentor and chief instructor for this young group was veteran SAR ranger Ernest Field of nearby Rocky Mountain National Park.

In the spring of 1948, Wolf Bauer, along with Ome Daiber, called Daiber's group together to screen *Bergwacht,* a short foreign film on technical rescue. Produced by the famed Austrian SAR team of the same name, the movie was created by Dr. Rometsch of the Bavarian Bergwacht and Wastl Mariner of the Austrian Alpenverein. Mariner is now acknowledged to be the "Father of Mountain Rescue." With Daiber's inventory serving as the nucleus, and called by the Mountaineering Development Committee of the Seattle Mountaineers with support from the Washington Alpine Club and National Ski Patrol, the Pacific Northwest's Mountain Rescue and Safety Council officially came into being on June 26, 1948. In attendance were rangers from both Mt. Rainier and Olympic.

OTHER CLIMBING AND RESCUE TEAM MILESTONES

1906	Canadian Alpine Club and what evolved into the British Columbia Mountaineering Club are founded.
December 19, 1906	The Mountaineers, originally called "The Seattle Mountaineers Club, Auxiliary to the Mazamas," is established.
March 26, 1922	Club de Exploraciones de Mexico is founded—a climbing first for Central America.
1931	Argentina's El Club Andino Bariloche is established—a climbing first for South America.
1933	Britain's mountain rescue organization begins as the Joint Stretcher Committee by Rucksack and Fell and Rock Climbing Clubs.
November 28, 1934	Britain's Central Rescue Organization is formed.
1935	Mazamas begin teaching climbing, as do The Mountaineers.
1939	Colorado Mountain Club hosts its first climbing school.
May 1939	Speleological Society of the District of Columbia is organized; it eventually becomes the National Speleological Society (NSS).

OTHER CLIMBING AND RESCUE TEAM MILESTONES

1945	Created to look for downed pilots in the nearby mountains, an SAR team is formed by the Navy on Puget Sound's Whidbey Island.
1947	Colorado Mountain Club begins a technical climbing school and soon teaches mountaineering first aid and self-rescue.
1948	Sierra Club, Potomac Appalachian Trail Club, Chicago Mountaineering Club, Harvard Mountaineering Club, and Phoenix, Arizona–based Kachinas begin formally stressing rescue skills.

Mazamas organize a mountain rescue group.

International Commission for Alpine Rescue (IKAR—Internationale Kommisia für Alpines Rettingwesen) is founded by group of doctors and alpine specialists from five countries: Austria, France, Germany, Italy, and Switzerland.

Dartmouth Mountaineering Club, mentored by faculty advisor and former Grand Teton Ranger John Montaigne, initiates safety program on alpine safety and rescue. |
September 13–17, 1948	Mt. Rainier hosts NPS's first technical Mountain Climbing and Rescue Training School. Thirty-eight rangers representing 12 areas participate, along with 11 from the National Ski Patrol, Coast Guard, Army, Air Force, Navy, Forest Service, and The Mountaineers.
1949	Sierra Club institutes its own callout list for climbing accidents, similar to that of The Mountaineers.
June 4–5, 1949	Second Northwest Mountaineering Conference takes place at Snoqualmie Pass in Washington, dedicated to safety and SAR. Sponsored by Mountain Rescue Council and hosted by Washington Alpine Club and The Mountaineers, 32 groups with more than 120 delegates attend. Coast Guard gives the first formal helicopter demonstration for mountain rescue.
1951	Oregon's Inter-Mountain Rescue Council is formed: ten agencies belong, including Mazamas, Crag Rats, and Cascade Ski Club.
September 1, 1951	Sierra Madre Search and Rescue Patrol is organized for mountaineering accidents in Southern California.

OTHER CLIMBING AND RESCUE TEAM MILESTONES

December 1951	Southern California's second mountain SAR unit is formed: Altadena Mountaineers.
Fall 1955	Group of local Seattle rescuers meet; integration of Explorer Scouts into the Mountain Rescue Council begins. Older Boy Scouts will perform such duties as base camp operations and eventually "move up" to litter handling. Explorer Scouts were used for SAR as early as 1948 (Phoenix) and had even been considered for a formal SAR group (Sierra Madre) in 1951.
November 10, 1955	Oregon's Mountain Rescue and Safety Council (MORESCO) is established in Portland.
February 18, 1956	Overflow crowd of 500 Seattle-area Scouts enthusiastically voice interest in SAR. This gathering, the initial one for the now nationwide Explorer Search and Rescue (ESAR) program, makes its field debut by looking for a fellow scout lost on August 19, 1956, in Mt. Rainier National Park.
October 1956	Mountain Rescue Council and park rangers from Mt. Rainier meet to discuss SAR; the idea for some form of national mountain rescue organization is discussed.
June 6–7, 1959	More than 400 people attend training at Timberline Lodge on Oregon's Mt. Hood, and Mountain Rescue Association (MRA) is formed. Eleven Oregon and Washington SAR teams initially sign MRA's bylaws. Dick Pooley of Oregon's Mountain Rescue and Safety Council is group's first president.
	In addition to these formally organized teams of the 1950s, there were semiofficial sheriff's posses, ham radio groups, church cliques, and others doing search and rescue in addition to their regular activities. Lack of policy, structure, and coordination often resulted in gross confusion and competition in the field.
1960	Tucson-based Southern Arizona Rescue Association is created.
Spring 1961	Colorado Rescue Association is established.
February 2, 1966	Colorado Search and Rescue Board is formed.
December 3, 1973	Himalayan Rescue Association is founded.

MILESTONES OF THE 1930s

1930	NPS's 55 units are visited by 3,246,656.
April 11, 1930	Alvin Brooksly becomes first fatality in Zion.
November 17, 1930	Crater Lake chief ranger is killed in blizzard.
1931	Visitation to Yosemite is 461,855.
Summer 1931	NPS begins use of two-way radios at Mt. Rainier; a portable weighs 15 pounds and transmits 10–20 miles.
July 2, 1931	First roped climb in Sierra (Yosemite's Unicorn Peak), followed by ascent of difficult east face of Mt. Whitney.
July 12, 1931	Woman dies after her leg is struck by a rattlesnake in Yosemite. For a short time, superintendent considers introducing wild hogs into the park to eliminate this "menace."
1932	"Four people [are] arrested by Park Ranger Oscar Sedegren for climbing [Mt. Rainier] without first registering and having their equipment inspected.... [F]ined $2.50 each after pleading guilty . . . first case of the sort ever brought to the Commissioner . . . believed the act will have a salutary effect on other climbers who seek to evade . . . climbing regulations."
May 9, 1932	First death on Mt. McKinley.
May 12, 1932	Charles Lindbergh's baby is found after 72-day search; this is possibly the largest such effort in U.S. history.
1933	First "Walkie-Talkie" is built.
November 5, 1933	First "artificial aid climb" in Yosemite.
1933–1942	Civlian Conservation Corps enters the parks.
May 1934	"Modern" climbing era begins: Bestor Robinson, Jules Eichorn, and Dick Leonard climb Yosemite's Higher Cathedral Spire.
Fall 1934	First use of artificial air for diving in NPS. First underwater archeology work to be undertaken in North America is in Colonial National Historical Park; artifacts are recovered by a hard-hat diver from numerous British warships of Cornwallis's fleet, sunk in the York River in 1781.

MILESTONES OF THE 1930s

November 1934	Already enigmatic and paradoxical at 20 years old, Everett Ruess vanishes in what is now southern Utah's Escalante-Grand Staircase National Monument; his disappearance is still one of the National Park Service's most baffling mysteries.
1935	Sequoia's protection staff consists of 1 chief ranger, 1 assistant, 7 permanents, and 13 temporaries.
1936	Rocky Mountain's Chief Ranger John McLaughlin serves as model for Dorr Yeager's NPS book series, *Bob Flame: Ranger.*
January 20, 1936	For his impressive efforts on perilous Delmar Fadden search, Mt. Rainier's Bill Butler is appointed permanent national park ranger by President Roosevelt.
April 3, 1936	Executive Order grants permission to "employees of the National Park Service . . . to serve as deputy sheriffs."
July 13, 1936	Fred J. Overly is appointed first ranger at Olympic.
July 18, 1936	Second person to be killed by lightning in Yosemite.
1937	No accidents occur on Mt. Rainier and no one is lost; 238 attempt summit, 153 are successful.
February 8, 1937	Oren P. Senter, formerly of the Bureau of Reclamation, becomes the first park ranger at Boulder Dam Recreation Area (Lake Mead). Park also receives its first patrol boat from U.S. Coast Guard; a 45-footer, it is christened the *NPS-1.*
February 16, 1937	Nylon (Fiber 66) is awarded Patent #2,071,250.
April 21, 1937	First drowning (three boaters) in Lake Mead.
July 2, 1937	Amelia Earhart, 39, disappears after taking off from New Guinea for Howland Island. Pressed into the probe, 4,000 men, 10 ships, and 65 planes scour 250,000 square miles for 16 days in what is probably the largest such effort on record.
March 1, 1938	TWA airliner with nine people aboard disappears in a snowstorm over California's Sierra Nevada. Massive search effort ensues; it is found in Yosemite three months later.
June 30, 1938	Resolution HR-8143 is passed by Congress. Bill appropriates funds for developing the autogiro. Original $2 million is for research on rotary-wing and other aircraft. U.S. Forest and Park Services are involved.

MILESTONES OF THE 1930s

July 3, 1938	Four-year-old boy vanishes in Rocky Mountain, prompting perhaps the park's most intensive and enigmatic search.
Summer 1938	NPS, as recommended by the American Alpine Club in 1937, adopts three loud sounds as the Universal Distress Signal.
November 13, 1938	Death Valley National Monument deploys a plane on loan from Sequoia on a search for the first time.
January 28, 1939	First snowplane is shown to rangers at Yellowstone; it has a 65-hp, airplane-type motor and operates on three 7½-foot skis.
March 6, 1939	One-dollar climbing fee is instituted during Mt. Rainier's three-month climbing season; $214 is collected. Toll will be eliminated on November 13, 1939, by NPS director.
April 9, 1939	First recorded use of artificial air for NPS SAR diving for a drowning at Lake Mead—a hard-hat diver searches for a 19-year-old boy 1 mile above Hoover Dam.
May 31, 1939	Conference with chief of Air Corps is attended by various agencies, including U.S. Forest Service, Biological Survey, and NPS. "These men laid the foundations for a new-type experimental rotary-wing aircraft [helicopter]."
September 3, 1939	Difficult east face of Sequoia's Moro Rock is climbed by Howard Kaster, Art Johnson, and Dr. Carl Jensen.
September 1939	Marion Steffens, 33, disappears and becomes Olympic National Park's first recorded death.
October 5– November 15, 1939	U.S. Forest Service evaluates parachuting of men onto forest fires; seven experienced jumpers, using a five-place, high-wing aircraft, are used. This paves the way for future use of Pararescue.

Found on June 12, 1935, Carl Meyer died of starvation during winter at a Yosemite Creek cabin.

YOSEMITE NATIONAL PARK
RESEARCH LIBRARY

July 8, 1930
Zion National Park

PARK'S FIRST
SAR FATALITY

VACATIONING from St. Louis, Mrs. Faust, son John, and school chum Eugene were on a popular guided saddle trip to the park's West Rim. Awed by the spectacular vertical beauty they were riding through, a fascinated Eugene grilled the wrangler about other exciting trips among the red sandstone cliffs.

With plenty of summer light left for more adventure, the energetic 19-year-old explorer announced he was off to see Emerald Pool, a gentle, two-mile hike.

An anxious Mrs. Faust notified Chief Ranger Jolley when the youth failed to show that evening that "he was not one to miss his supper." Armed with lanterns, Rangers Russell, Thornton, and Woodbury easily followed the boy's tracks around the pool and back to near the lodge. Stymied, they waited till dawn.

Checking all the likely trails in the warm, early-morning sun, the boy's whereabouts were still a mystery. Jolley went into nearby Springdale and hired 15 men, and a "detailed search of the canyon floor, the slopes below the ledges, and the river was carried out and was completed late in the afternoon." Thinking the boy may have entered "some temporary mental derangement," officials sent wires to Las Vegas and all of southern Utah.

A large reward, $100, was posted; 40 more men soon volunteered. During the night, searchers were stationed to listen for cries of help.

As a last "forlorn hope," a small party rechecked Lady Mountain Trail. Overlooked the first time up, Eugene's name and address were found in the trail register on top. Descending, the party found where he had left the trail. With this news relayed to the rescuers below, 14 men started up with a stretcher and first-aid gear. "At a point about 500 feet below where the trail starts down, Ranger Russell noticed the boy's knees sticking up above some brush, and in a few minutes the party reached him and found him dead."

Superintendent Ev Scoyen, in his official report to NPS Director Steven Mather, wrote: "As far as I am concerned, when such cases occur in the future, it seems that it would be well to gather all available evidence as to where it is thought that the person had gone, and then hunt *every place else* except there [emphasis added]."

This was Zion's first fatality involving some form of search and rescue effort. The park's only other death had occurred three months before. On April 11, Albine Brooksly of nearby Orderville, Utah, was killed when a large lumber anchor slid down the "old Mormon cable" and struck him on the head.

August 4, 1930
Sequoia National Park

HERO DARES EXPLOSION

Rushes into Blast to Save Friend
PARALYZED MAN IS RESCUED

THREE RIVERS (Tulare Co.), Aug. 7—Stricken with paralysis after lighting the fuse on the last of twelve powder blasts and lying helpless before the horrified gaze of his fellow workmen, Fred West, powder man for the Buck Canyon High Sierra Trail crew, waited with resignation for the series of terrific detonations which would blow him to eternity.

From behind the safety of trees and rocks his companions watched the sputtering fuses, breathless and appalled with the impending tragedy which was unfolding before their horrified eyes.

Suddenly one of those things happened which renews one's faith in human nature—one of those things which ages ago evoked the beautiful phrase, "Greater love than this hath no man."

A man stepped out from behind the protection of the rocks and tree, rushed to the side of [the] stricken man as the fuses sputtered almost at the hip of the power, and dragged him behind the protection of a nearby abutment just as the earth rocked with twelve ear-splitting detonations in rapid succession.

Huge rocks and trees hurtled in all directions, spelling death and destruction to everything in their path, but the man who risked his life and the man for whom he chose the risk lay safely behind the protecting bank.

The man who risked his life was Marvin Murphy. Today he refused to boast or to pose as a hero. He merely said, "I just couldn't let Fred West die like a rat in a trap."

West was struck on the hip by a stone a few days previously. It is thought that the sudden attack of paralysis was caused by the injury, of which West had made light.

The injured man was rushed over the mountains to the Giant Forest hospital by stretcher, his companions shouldering the stretcher in panting relays over steep hills and down precipitous canyons. Today it was reported at the hospital that he is expected to recover.

—*The Fresno Bee*, 8-7-30 (reprinted by permission)

Assistant Secretary of the Interior John H. Edwards applied to the Carnegie Hero Fund Commission for recognition of Marvin Murphy's heroism. On November 19, they denied the consideration because "there were no eyewitnesses to Mr. Murphy's act."

August 26, 1930
Sequoia National Park

SEEKS BLIMP TO BRING BODY OUT

DONALD DOWNS, SIERRA SLIDE VICTIM, DIES

FIGHT AGAINST INFECTION LOST MONDAY NIGHT

Runner Covers 28 Miles in Twelve Hours to Bring out News

Fighting far into the night to save the lives of two boys injured in a landslide in the wildest of the Sierra, the doctor and two nurses and the anxious mother had to admit defeat when death stepped in . . . and took the life of Donald Downs.

—*Fresno Republican,* 9-3-30

AT 13,180 feet, the trail over Forester Pass was surely a challenge to build. With but a few winter-free months each year, the construction crews made each day count; that Tuesday was no different. The young men, most from the nearby San Joaquin Valley, quickly grew expert in the skills necessary for the back-breaking work; explosives were just one of them.

Safely tucked away under a rocky ledge, 23-year-old powderman George Carey waited for the peak-rattling blast. Others, now grown almost casual toward the dangerous dynamite, hid under nearby granite shelves. A large boulder, dislodged from somewhere above, bounced down the mountainside; ricocheting one last time, it landed under the overhang shared by four youthful workers.

"It pinned Downs' arm under it. His life was despaired of, but another boy gave the boulder a blow with a pick and dislodged it enough for Downs to get his arm out. It was found to be crushed and his collarbone broken." Three others also suffered serious injury, and the 12-day nightmare began.

George Carey, hardened from the summer's heavy labor and acclimated to the mountain's thin air, ran 28 (other local newspapers said he ran 22) miles for help. Park Ranger Sam Clark, receiving the report at Whitney Creek, immediately rode to the Forest Service station at Tunnel Meadow. Just past midnight, 13 hours after the accident, the unfolding drama in the backcountry was phoned to Chief Ranger Lawrence Cook at headquarters: ". . . send Doctor, men and equipment to pack out the four injured men."

After a seemingly short night, Clark remounted for a five-hour ride back to the waiting Carey. "We made the trip from Whitney Creek to Tyndall Creek with only one horse, taking turns at riding, arriving . . . after dark . . . unable to locate the trail camp."

By light they found the camp handling the emergency as best it could. Then, retracing most of his route, Clark intercepted the approaching Dr. Fraser. After giving directions, he rode many more miles to get help from the distant Mt. Whitney trail crew.

At sunset he sent word to Lone Pine, 15 miles away. "Locate U.S. Forest Service Ranger Shellenbarger, and secure men to assist in packing out the injured men." Leading 12 other men, Clark saw Friday dawn over the 14,000-foot peaks of the Sierra.

The next nine days must have blurred for Ranger Sam Clark. His report to Sequoia Chief Ranger Cook read, in part:

> We started for . . . camp, arriving . . . 6:10 A.M. We constructed three stretchers, using . . . iron cots and tent poles. . . . The Griffin boy . . . able to ride . . . put him on my horse . . . to Independence, . . . I started Robert Rankin on a stretcher, with six men to carry him. . . .
>
> I also started Edward Jordan on a stretcher with four men to carry him. . . . Taking three men and myself, we carried Donald Downs . . . arriving . . . 7 P.M. Dr. Fraser amputated the left arm of . . . Downs . . . four inches from the shoulder, last night after gangrene . . . set in. Mrs. Lawson . . . nurse, stayed with Donald . . . entire trip.

Saturday, August 30, 1930

> I went to Independence with . . . Shellenbarger. . . . Dr. Fraser said we would be unable to move either Jordan or Downs for seven or ten days.
>
> I met Mrs. Downs and Miss Moore, nurse . . . at foot of trail . . . they were enroute to Baxter Cabin with a guide.
>
> I purchased supplies and medicine . . . and reported to Chief Ranger Cook.

Sunday, August 31, 1930

> I started with pack mule and medicine at 7 A.M., packer with supplies following me. Met Government packer Jones 9 miles from here with order for medicine . . . said Downs was very low, and another operation was necessary, so I took the order for medicine. . . .
>
> I took a car at the foot of the trail . . . to Independence, instructed . . . put in relay of horses while I went . . . for medicine. Instructed . . . Shellenbarger . . . to phone Colonel John R. White [Superintendent] for permission to obtain plane and rush duplicate order of medicine to Baxter Cabin. 12:30 P.M. . . . started with relay of three horses . . . arrived at 4:15 P.M. . . . Plane with Shellenbarger arrived 4:30 and dropped medicine o.k. Downs better, operation unnecessary.

Monday, September 1, 1930

> I returned to Independence and phoned message from Dr. Fraser to Col. White . . . obtain Goodyear volunteer Blimp. . . . orders . . . White . . . take plane . . . to Los Angeles.
>
> . . . Shellenbarger and Jack Snicer [sic] left here in airplane No. NC705V to drop medicine . . . The plane crashed at 5:30 P.M. after dropping medicine. . . . not injured . . . plane . . . did not return at 7:10 P.M., I reported . . . received orders . . . secure aid from Army at March Field . . . I communicated with Lt. Sharon . . . dispatch a ship . . . following morning . . . at my disposal.

Tuesday, September 2, 1930

. . . Shellenbarger arrived here 1 A.M. . . . reported to Chief Ranger . . . cancel ship . . . Government packer Jones arrived here with telegram as follows, to-wit, "To Dr. William D. Adams, Fresno. Come by plane to Independence bring instruments and sterrile [sic] dressings stop shoulder ressection [sic] stop Morton W. Fraser."

. . . Carey left cabin 3 A.M. on foot . . . word . . . death of Donald Downs at 2:04 A.M. . . . I sent Albright Undertaking Parlor . . . with packer and instructions . . . bring . . . body . . . out and Mrs. Downs to precede the body.

Wednesday, September 3, 1930

Mrs. Downs arrived 1:15 P.M. . . . the body arrived here 8 P.M. Received waive of inquest . . . from Deputy Coroner.

Thursday, September 4, 1930

Made arrangements to bring out Edward Jordan. Fifteen men from the Department of Water & Power . . . 6 men from . . . and 21 boys from Bishop High School.

Friday, September 5, 1930

I took twenty of these men to Baxter cabin and twenty-one near Shepherd pass to . . . assist us the following day.

Saturday, September 6, 1930

7:10 A.M. we started . . . Jordan on a stretcher . . . arriving 6:20 P.M. . . . put . . . Jordan . . . Doctor . . . party in the Winnedumah Hotel for the night . . . Jordan talked to his mother.

The September 1 crash of NC705V in Tyndall Creek was the first of many in Sequoia and Kings Canyon National Parks.

```
                November 17, 1930
            Crater Lake National Park
        ----------------------------------------
```

DEATH OF A CHIEF RANGER

FROM Canada to Mexico, the massive winter storm tightly locked the land in its grip. After five days, 44 inches of snow had accumulated at the park's summer headquarters. Old-timers had never seen such an early, heavy blow.

Accompanied by his wife, Bill Godfrey had transferred to Crater Lake in May as the chief ranger. Fresh from 19 months in Yosemite, he was a "man of fine character, well read, high-minded and determined." When he started something, he was very persistent.

Godfrey, 41, absent when the blizzard first hit but feeling compelled to retrieve some files at work, entered the park's west entrance. Walking through 18 inches of new snow for 3 miles, he grew weary and was barely able to return to his car.

Superintendent E. C. Solinsky, talking with his chief by phone the next day, was informed that the tenacious Godfrey "had learned just how far he was able to walk in the snow and survive, that his trip the previous day was a severe one and he was just able to get back to his car." Godfrey tried again, despite being chastised by his worried supervisor for not waiting for better weather.

Passing through the south entrance, he went only a mile before his progress stalled once again. Hindered but not stuck, he chose to spend the night in his small coupe rather than the comforts of town. Godfrey started anew at 6:30 the next morning, having passed the freezing night without food or even a blanket.

Now extremely concerned, Superintendent Solinsky wanted the park's brand-new rotary snowplow to start for the south entrance; the machine had no radio and was already headed in the other direction. He asked a local garage owner "to take the necessary help and . . . follow Godfrey until they found him." Owing to several false and fatal assumptions, this never happened; Godfrey kept on walking.

At 7 that night, Rudy F. Lueck was assisting with plowing the heavy snow when he learned that his good friend Godfrey was defiantly trying to hike into headquarters. Even 60 years later, longtime retired Ranger Lueck could still feel the sorrow from that night.

> I found a pair of skiis . . . started out to find Godfrey . . . I was alone. I found Godfrey at about 10:30 P.M. He was about two miles from Anna Springs, had been down in the snow for hours but was still alive. I tried my best to revive him by rubbing circulation back into his arms and legs. He knew I had found him but the exertion and his effort was too much. He died in my arms. He called my name just before he died.

```
              June 28, 1931
        Mesa Verde National Park
-----------------------------------------
```

SECRETARY OF THE INTERIOR
BECOMES EMERGENCY SURGEON

MESA Verde National Park, Colo., June 29—Donning the white robe and mask of the skillful surgeon, Dr. Ray Lyman Wilbur, secretary of the interior, stepped into the emergency hospital operating room of Spruce Tree camp here Sunday and saved the life of V.M. De Merschman of Grand Junction, Colo.

... Secretary Wilbur and his party in Spruce Tree house, watched Navajo Indians enact an ancient tribal ceremony.

Secretary Wilbur saw De Merschman put his hand to his side and collapse in sudden agony. The stricken man's face had a ghost pallor in the grotesque flicker of the Indian torch light.

Immediate Operation Ordered by Wilbur

Immediately the distinguished member of President Hoover's cabinet stepped back into the familiar role as physician and surgeon, in which he won national distinction before an appointment to high office in Washington.

—Unnamed newspaper, 6-30-31

Prior to becoming Secretary of the Interior, Ray Lyman Wilbur had been both president of Stanford University and president of the American Medical Association.

```
                 July 5, 1931
          Mt. Rainier National Park
```

"HE SLID OVER A MILE, DROPPING AT LEAST 2000 FEET"

USING a ¾-inch cotton rope, guide Clem Blakney still did not have enough to tie all 11 of his party in. Although five were unroped and not everyone had crampons or ice axes, however, the climbers reached a point 800 feet from the summit. They took a rest.

Almost before anyone noticed, Robert Zinn started sliding down the steep, crusted snow; disregarding his own safety, his brother charged after him. Quickly losing balance, brother tumbled after brother. The screams of "dig in" went unheard. Three hundred feet later, Kenneth hit a snow hummock and stopped.

Superintendent Tomlinson, in his official report to the National Park Service director, said, "It has been estimated by the rescue party which found Robert's body among the crevasses above the Nisqually ice wall, that he slid over a mile, dropping at least 2000 feet in that distance."

Blakney and two other Mt. Rainier National Park guides spent several hours searching crevasses along Zinn's fateful path. Blakney was lowered into one: nothing. Finding only part of an alpenstock and a pair of scissors from Zinn's first-aid kit, the trio of climbers "decided he [Robert Zinn] had 'jumped' the crevasses and fallen onto the top of the East Nisqually Glacier, 1500 feet below."

At 4:30 P.M., searchers departed Paradise under the leadership of District Ranger Charlie Browne. Two years before—almost to the day— Browne had proven to be one of the heroes of the Greathouse tragedy. The rescue team also included Chief Ranger John Davis, senior guide "Swede"

Willard, two horse wranglers, and second-year mountain guide William J. "Bill" Butler. This marked the beginning of Butler's 30 years of rescue heroics on Mt. Rainier.

At 1:00 A.M. the men left Camp Muir, making a sweep of the broad area below the East Nisqually ice wall. ". . . the party was split and only part were permitted to approach the ice wall in order that those remaining could give them aid in case of a mishap." Avalanches forced them to retreat to Camp Muir at daybreak.

On July 7 the search resumed. Starting where Zinn began his death slide, Butler was lowered into each crevasse they came to. He found equipment—but no Zinn. Finally, at midmorning and only 25 yards from the edge of the huge ice cliff, a hand was visible in a crevasse. News was flashed by mirror to Paradise below.

"Swede" Willard and Bill Butler received letters of praise from Secretary of the Interior Ray Lyman Wilbur. Butler's reply symbolizes his long career: "Those of us who were engaged in the rescue did nothing more than any other group of mountaineers would have done under similar circumstances."

```
July 25, 1931
Zion National Park
```

THE BODY WAS PACKED
IN 100 POUNDS OF ICE

THE body was packed in 100 pounds of ice and arrived at park headquarters "in very good condition."

Despite the desert's intense, almost suffocating heat, Ronald C. Orcutt wanted to climb Cathedral Mountain. Having already scaled the nearby and more difficult Great White Throne, this should have been easy. Leaving at 10 A.M., Orcutt told a neighboring trail construction crew he would soon be back. When he had not returned by dinner, four of the trail crew went in search of the young man from Los Angeles.

> We found the body at 12:00 midnight and after spending about thirty minutes getting the body prepared to carry out, started down the canyon. . . . The way was very rough and we had to let the body down two places by ropes. One drop was sixty feet and another was twenty-five feet. We were two hours and forty minutes getting to the trail camp and all were nearly exhausted. Some other men joined us here to help down the trail and as soon as construction of an improvised stretcher was under way . . .

February 1, 1932
Sequoia National Park

"DEATH WAS CAUSED BY MAKING AN EMERGENCY PARACHUTE JUMP"

"I CLIMBED upon the cowling and told Hoffman I was going over. He shook his head, showed me a map, and said 'bad country.' I felt I would rather hit bad country in a chute than in a plane—so I told him to throttle down. Then I jumped." That morning, when Army Lieutenant William A. Cocke stepped into the swirling whiteness engulfing him and Hoffman, a two-month-long search began.

Lieutenant Edward D. Hoffman was lost somewhere in the harsh, winter-locked Sierra Nevada. Ten percent of the Army's Air Corps would look for the experienced bomber pilot. The hunt would pit hermitlike mountain men, throwbacks to Carson or Fremont, against the present. Fueled by good intentions, eager locals and tested rangers spent weeks battling blinding snowstorms, 15-foot drifts, and incredibly brutal terrain chasing half-hopes and false leads.

San Francisco's Crissey Army Air Field, Hoffman's destination that Monday morning, had forecast clear skies the length of California's Central Valley. Shortly after lifting off from Los Angeles, however, clear became cloud. Observer-passenger Cocke, a world record–holding endurance glider pilot, would later recall:

> About one hour out we were at 18,000 feet when our plane would not climb. Then Hoffman turned around—but the clouds had closed up behind us. I watched the instruments and saw he was using all the power we had as he circled around, flying blind, looking for some opening in the clouds. We lost 2,000 feet and I decided to bail out—to go over the side in my chute.
>
> I had no sensation of falling although I did seem to be spinning about. When the chute opened it seemed to be below me so I must have been upside down. I don't know how long it took me to get down.
>
> At first I was surrounded by the mist of clouds and then by snow falling so thick that the ground was not visible at 200 feet. When I landed, a high wind caught the chute and dragged me several feet through brush. I took off the harness, tied the chute to a tree and started out.

Fifty paces, gasp—rest—pray; fifty paces. . . . Knee-deep snow, steep mountainsides, thin air, and clothes-ripping underbrush taxed Cocke to his limit. Miraculously, within hours the exhausted parachutist stumbled onto some telegraph wires leading to a deserted but partially stocked ranger cabin.

Cocke, after using the only match he could find, spent the night warm and safe, praying that Hoffman had experienced a miracle too. The next morning, after "slogging" only a few miles, Cocke and Chief Ranger Lawrence Cook crossed paths. The search for Lieutenant Hoffman would now begin.

The February 4 headlines of the *Fresno Morning Republican* would claim, **"150 Planes to Join Search for Lost Fliers."** Searchers were now looking for two aircraft downed in the storm. An airliner with eight on board burned on impact would be gruesomely revealed elsewhere within a few days. The fortune of the 24-year-old Hoffman, however, father of a four-month-old baby, would not unravel for another two months.

The search continued . . .

A report that a signal fire was sighted late one afternoon near Panther Peak was investigated by World War I combat aces Captain Hunter and Lieutenant Dawson. The promising signal fire turned into mist. A group of five woodcutters camped near Dunlap reported hearing an airplane about 1:45 P.M., the day Hoffman disappeared. Army aircraft and light bombers launched, but again nothing was found.

Forest rangers, game wardens, and local cowboys joined in the spirit to save a soul: "Every step meant a plunge downward in soft snow to the waist. It became the plan to progress by stages of 200 feet, each one taking his turn helping to break the best trail possible." From many vantage points, field glasses were turned hopefully upon rugged mountainsides, but everywhere the snowy covering returned the same monotonous glare.

Since the park service experienced its first fatal plane wreck in 1926, hundreds of planes have crashed in the remote areas of our national parks. This wreck, investigated by Yosemite rangers in February 1975, involved two deaths. NPS PHOTO/AUTHOR'S COLLECTION

Chief Ranger L.F. Cook and Ranger Tom Williams returned last night from a two-day search up the south fork of the Kaweah . . . twelve feet of snow on the level at the Garfield cabin, at . . . 8,200 feet. The cabin, they said, was completely covered with snow and they were obliged to dig their way into it for a night's shelter.

Hundreds of the curious milled around the airport while special police guarded the transient fleet of search planes and the impromptu overnight Army post. Wild rumors spread around the flying field that the two pilots were carrying a woman passenger. Officials considered using sled runners on a few of the planes, but this was deemed "inadvisable since the scattered meadows in the park are covered with from ten to thirteen feet of snow."

On February 21, Hoffman's father, a Tacoma mineralogist, drove for 25 agonizing hours to reach the Fresno search base. He was vexed with the government's efforts, despite the 53 aircraft flown by the Army's best, the use of aerial photorecon, and the efforts of professional outdoorsmen. He "just knew" his resourceful son, locked somewhere in the frozen wilderness, was alive; the right "key" would bring him home.

Walter "Shorty" Lovelace, 44, knew the mountains better than the beaver he trapped. Traveling by mule in summer and ski in winter, he was rock-solid like the gray Sierra granite around him. Needing doors only 4 feet high, he had built a string of 15 log cabins along the sparkling streams and flowering alpine meadows he so dearly loved. Shorty had become a living legend, relic mountain man, and hermit; he was also the last thin hope a father had of finding his son alive.

> Jeff Davis, an army flier, was planning to fly over the Sugar Loaf district to-day to drop off three copies of a message addressed to Walter (Shorty) Lovelace. . . . The messages which will be dropped will ask Lovelace to build a fire signal in the event he has news of the plane, and a party will mush in. He is promised a reward. He is to build three fires. If he has no information, he is to walk in an easterly direction, holding both arms above his head. This will show he has found one of the notes.

Shorty Lovelace never struck a match; no fires were necessary. The silent, desperate prayers of a tortured parent—afraid of forever losing a child—went unanswered.

On April 2, the United Press headlines read, **"Wrecked Plane of Army Flier Found in Hills—Evidence Found That Lieutenant Hoffman May Be Alive."** The unburnt wreckage was found a half-mile from a cabin—there were no signs of Hoffman, alive or dead. The search was renewed; hope, and maybe even Hoffman, were alive.

A fragment of a parachute was found in the top of an 80-foot pine tree more than 3 miles from the downed plane. Trappers tracked not for lion, but for man. Bits of charred paper and the remains of an almost-fire were found farther along, abandoned before it could provide any lifesaving heat. The long, cold trail finally led to a pair of abandoned flying boots.

The promise of life was short-lived; hope—and Hoffman—were dead. Wet, freezing, and worn out by his struggle against a raging snowstorm, the lieutenant had laid down beneath a clump of bushes and quietly slept his life away.

> The body was found a few feet from a winding trail that led around an irrigation canal to habitation. Only three-quarters of a mile down the trail from the spot the body was found is the Lake Canyon Lodge on the Mineral King Highway, where lives Lowell Van Allen.

The coroner's inquest for Army Lieutenant Edward D. Hoffman lowered the final curtain on one of the longest, most intensive air and ground searches ever conducted. " . . . death was caused by making an emergency parachute jump from an airplane while in a snowstorm . . . the flier died from exposure to the elements."

```
              May 10, 1932
        Mt. McKinley National Park
----------------------------------------
```

FIRST TWO TO DIE ON MT. MCKINLEY

ON MAY 7, 1932, the Liek-Lindley Expedition became only the second party to ever reach the top of North America: 20,320-foot Mt. McKinley. Harry Liek was the superintendent of the park and Alfred Lindley was a Minneapolis attorney who had crewed for Yale in the 1924 Paris Olympics. Joined by Park Ranger Grant Pearson and Norwegian skier Erling Strom, this party climbed not only the highest point, but the separate 300-foot lower North Peak as well.

Also on the mountain at that time was the Carpe-Koven Cosmic Ray Expedition. Allen Carpe, at the behest of both the University of Chicago and the Carnegie Foundation, was gathering data on the nature of cosmic rays. He was joined by Theodore Koven, Edward Beckwith, Nicholas Spadavecchia, and Percy Olton.

Unlike the Liek-Lindley Expedition, which had freighted all of its supplies over 105 miles by two dogsleds, Carpe had most of his supplies airlifted onto the glacier by airplane. Joe Crosson, flying a Fairchild 71 monoplane, thus became the first person to land on Mt. McKinley and probably the first to supply a mountaineering expedition anywhere by air.

After descending all night from their successful summit bid, Liek and company had strong misgivings as they entered Carpe's seemingly deserted camp. The fresh snow all around it had not been disturbed in several days: "It looked queer. . . . We all had a feeling that something was wrong." They knew that on this mountain nobody goes far from the warmth of sleeping bags or the protection of tents. Anxious to move on, they hurriedly ate their first meal in 24 hours, put on their skis, and started down the icy slope.

> First, we saw wandering footprints in the snow and then Mr. Koven's body, lying face down. He had been severely injured before he died of exposure and we wondered whether the cause had been an avalanche or a fall into a crevasse. Following his tracks a short distance we found the answer. A big crevasse with crampons and an ice axe at one end and many tracks around it, both of skis and feet, told the story.

In the May 18, 1932, *New York Times* front-page article—"**CARPE, KOVEN DIED IN A FEAT OF DARING**"—Lindley surmised that the two men, concerned for their overdue teammates farther down the glacier, started after them unroped. A heavy snowfall had obliterated the previously safe trail and now concealed the ice field's hidden crevasses. One of the two dropped into an unseen pit and the other, going to his aid, also fell in. Koven, mortally injured, managed to climb out, only to soon perish. Carpe was never found.

With Koven's body firmly strapped to a sled, the Liek-Lindley Expedition continued on down the glacier toward the survivors of the ill-fated party. Strom pulled the sled and Lindley walked behind to act as a brake and rudder. With all of their rope being used to haul the dead man, Liek and Pearson followed—unroped.

They had only gone 100 yards when Pearson disappeared into a crevasse. "I had time to let out a feeble shout. Then, for a couple of long, long seconds, I plummeted downward." With his huge pack scraping against the ice, he came to a sudden stop 40 feet down. With Pearson safe and realizing the dangers of continuing with their frozen cargo, they left Koven wrapped in a tent and marked the spot with the 8-foot sled tipped on end. In August, Pearson would return; only inches of sled were still visible.

After 40 hours without sleep, Superintendent Liek and his now-weary party climbed off the Muldrow Glacier and into the rocks of McGonagall Pass, where they found Olton and Beckwith. Spadaveccia had left, coincidentally on the day of the deaths, to get help for Beckwith, who was very sick from food poisoning. Realizing there was little they could do to help Beckwith, the skiers continued out to Cache Creek and then on to headquarters. As soon as they could, they radioed an emergency message to Fairbanks asking for an airplane for the sick man. Pearson would later recall in his autobiography, **My Life of High Adventure**:

> . . . the snow had melted off the field in Fairbanks. A consultation was held immediately between the Fairbanks Fire Department and the only pilot available at the moment, Jerry Jones . . . the fire department came clanging out to the landing field with hoses, pump and water wagon, and sprayed that field until it was all mud. Jerry then whooshed the ski plane through the slop until it was airborne, flew to Mt. McKinley and picked up the sick man waiting in a tent on the glacier. His splash return landing is probably the only one on record ever accomplished in a man-made mud pie.

When Beckwith became ill, his teammate, Spadaveccia, started for the nearest phone some 45 miles away at Mt. Eileson (Copper Mountain). With Beckwith safe in Fairbanks courtesy of the "mud pie" flying skills of Jerry Jones, the search for Spadaveccia, now missing for over a week, began. Alaskan Airways pilot S. E. Robbins flew in to retrieve Olton. He would also look for the now missing 35-year-old engineer; Robbins didn't come back either.

After a second day of bad weather, Jones anxiously returned to look for Robbins and Spadaveccia. When the bush pilot flew over the camp, he saw 3-foot letters crudely stamped into the snow and highlighted in lampblack, saying that all was well. Robbins had broken an axle while trying to take off with Olton. Spadaveccia had retraced his footsteps to the camp, after being lost for 10 days in search for a telephone. In tracking Spadaveccia during his 10-day odyssey, Rangers John Rumohr and Lee Swisher had made a 180-mile hike on snowshoes before "finding" him at the camp.

June 2, 1932
Hawaii National Park

HAWAIIAN LOWERED 900 FEET INTO ACTIVE VOLCANO

THE locals considered the recent tidal waves and ongoing earth tremors bad omens from Madame Pele, the Hawaiian Goddess of Fire. They hailed the slight man standing in the wooden cage before them as a hero. A native of Japan,

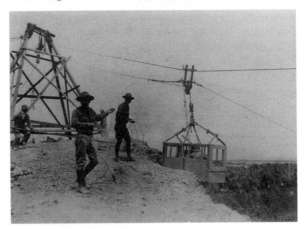

Readying himself inside the wooden gondola, 43-year-old Rikan Konishi is about to be lowered into the crater for the adventure of a lifetime.

NATIONAL ARCHIVES

Rikan Konishi, now dangling high over a molten lake that bubbled and smoked, was only moments away from the most unusual adventure of his life.

Silent in death, almost 1,000 feet below and at the edge of the fiery fluid lay 17-year-old Margaret Enos and the jealous young man who had shot her. Sylvester Nunes, terminating an unrequited affair of the heart, had hurled himself into Halemaumau Pit with his dead, never-to-be girlfriend locked in his arms.

Islanders were stunned by the crime's passion, friends grief-stricken. The coroner's inquest—one of the strangest ever convened—was sworn in on the crater's edge where the six jurors viewed the bodies through a telescope. Officials proposed that funeral services be held on the rim and that the youths be buried by exploding dynamite near them; the families weren't satisfied.

Understandably distraught, the girl's father asked to be lowered into the crater, but he was refused. Volunteering to go over, "rangers brought paraphernalia to the rim . . . to devise a means of descent." Building a trail to the bottom was soon ruled out for fear that loose rock would cost the life of a worker. "Police were forced to guard the rim to prevent curious onlookers from approaching too near to the edge, where the danger of collapse is constant."

National Park Service Director Horace Albright, remembering the 16-day circuslike recovery of cave explorer Floyd Collins (see story of January 30, 1925, in Chapter 3), issued a nationwide call "for men to descend into the crater." Offers poured in.

A Florida man proposed to do the job for $1,000, two round-trip tickets, and all other expenses. One day later he cabled, "If it is alright with you I would like to change the bid to 'Five Hundred Dollars for said job.'" Two from Louisiana said, "We are both ex-marines, both are able-bodied men, ready to start at once. $400/body delivered to the rim of Volcanoe." Weldon Ubery wrote, "I am only 16 but feel capable of the hazardous job." A man from Quebec merely wanted expenses for the bizarre odyssey.

Behind large-rimmed glasses, Rikan Konishi was an unassuming and modest 43-year-old contractor from Hilo. As the successful bidder, the 5-foot, 100-pound man undertook the perilous task out of a gracious sense of gratitude for a past kindness shown him by a relative of one of the victims. He wanted only $1,000 and some local lending of cable, rope, tractors, hoists, and other heavy equipment needed to descend into the unexplored crater.

Aided by dozens of helpers and using spotlights donated by the Army's nearby Camp Kilauea, Konishi worked night and day building platforms and stringing cable. Initially estimating he could remove the bodies in just two days, his efforts dragged on for more than a week. Using three tractors and two caterpillars and with a mile of cable loaned him by the Oloa Sugar Plantation, he somehow stretched the unwieldy, ¾-inch metal line . . . 3,500 feet.

After several false starts, including a particularly harrowing incident in which the tractors failed to pull the steel cable sufficiently taut, the cautious Konishi was ready. The open wooden cage in which the tiny man now stood was only 30 inches wide, 6 feet long, and just over 3 feet high with doors at either end. Dressed in a bulky gray sweater, khaki trousers, old yellow shoes, and a dirty straw hat tied under his chin, he addressed the gathered crowd in Japanese. Grateful for their cooperation and support, he told his neighbors they could now further assist him "by keeping back."

Crouched on a short stool, the diminutive Konishi was further dwarfed by the volcano that surrounded him. Packed about him were two bags of earth, hooks, a rake, lunch, binoculars, a movie camera for the unvisited bottom, red and white signal flags, two canvas slings, a coil of heavy rope, and a phone connected by cable to his brother-in-law. He wore no gas mask for the "dangerous fumes."

Lighting a cigarette at 10 A.M., he signaled for the winches to start. Somewhat loosely attached to the cage with a cotton rope held by a slip-knot, Konishi was pulled out over the abyss.

Sluggishly the cable paid out, and after 20 minutes he slowly began the vertical descent. The rope fouled 75 feet down. Gingerly climbing free of safety he freed the guideline; "spectators were breathless." At one point he asked to stop and take motion pictures of the crater. He removed his hat and wiped his brow. Two hours later he landed on the black slope, 35 feet from the girl. "Mr. Konishi got out, calmly surveying the situation."

After wrapping the 11-day-old corpses in canvas and hooking them below the wooden crate by a long line, he sat down and ate his lunch, "a guest of Madame Pele in her awesome home." At 2:15 P.M. he placed the white flag in the prearranged signal for success. Because of the victims' weight and Konishi's small frame, the cage was raised just enough to have the two bodies dragged directly underneath. Lowered back down, Konishi then carefully tied the bodies alongside the frame. At 4, he signaled to ascend. An hour later, after climbing onto the top of the coffin-sized swing twice to make some minor adjustments, he reached the top. The Hilo Iron Works sounded its work siren, loudly hailing Konishi's success.

Benefit and fund-raising events over the next two weeks added $1,114 to the $1,000 guaranteed by the National Park Service so that Rikan Konishi could meet his expenses.

```
            July 18, 1932
    Rocky Mountain National Park
```

PUT HEADLESS MAN OVER SHOULDER
AND CARRIED HIM DOWN

HULL Cook, today a noted surgeon in Nebraska, spent some brief summers of his youth as a climbing guide on Longs Peak. Along with others, he led his clients from the Boulderfield Cabin, a mountain-style rock hut located in the shadow of the peak's north face.

According to Cook, he had occasionally been involved in a rescue that was straightforward and without much risk. And, as he would later write, carrying someone out who actually had minor injuries or was just exhausted was simple.

> Put the victim on my shoulders, say "Hang on around my fore-head, but keep your hands out of my eyes" and start walking. This was so much easier than having two or more persons struggling, some up, some down over the jumble of rough rocks that had to be traversed. Having the injured one sitting on your shoulders freed your chest for deep breathing. The passenger from his high perch would often be terrified, since we would be walking upright where he felt cautious creeping was necessary; but our heavy Swiss edging nails helped give sure footing.

One event—involving a man named Robert Smith from Indiana—that Cook vividly recalls even 63 years later was not so lighthearted.

> As we progressed across the Boulderfield . . . we were passed by two vigorous teenagers who were three or four hundred feet above us by the time we reached Chasm View, where everyone stops to enjoy the spectacular view across the east face. Mr. Smith was standing next to me asking questions about the hazards that he felt were inherent in rescue work, and although I explained that most rescues were not dangerous, he modestly expressed a lack of interest in such activities. In fact his very last words were "I'd rather be a live coward than a dead hero."
>
> Seconds later, as I was looking at him there was a flash of some dark object in the air above him, and most of his head just disappeared. Instantly he was on the ground, having been struck by a rock the size of a football. I jerked off my pack and laid it over his gruesome injury before Mrs. Smith could witness a macabre sight that would have tormented memory for the rest of her life.
>
> She at once asked about a doctor, and I had to explain that her husband was absolutely, beyond all possible hope. This was to her a shockingly unfathomable fact. Seconds before he had been standing there in the prime of his life. I waited until I saw them depart . . . before shouldering the body and carrying it down.

```
July 19, 1932
Sequoia National Park
```

"LIKE A CHAPTER OUT OF A BRET HARTE TALE"

. . . on a mountain-climbing trip with the Sierra Club. . . .
They started out with the club party, but a few days later,
about July 19, Miss Spalding suffered an acute heart attack
and was left at Ralph Merritt's camp on Roaring River. . . .
The progress of her illness was reported to her family in letters received from John R. White, superintendent of Sequoia
National Park, and Dr. Fraser, who made his first trip into
the mountains to treat her July 21.

—*Los Angeles Times,* 8-5-32 (reprinted by permission)

LITTER CREW LOSES GRIM PARK DASH

Woman Hiker Expires as Stretcher Bearers Battle Way Back to Civilization

VISALIA, Aug. 4—A tense drama of life and death played
against the rugged background of Sequoia National Park
ended tragically today when Miss Jane Spaulding [sic] of Los
Angeles died while being brought out of the wilderness by
stretcher bearers.

Like a chapter out of a Bret Harte tale, the grim race
with death was run by four latter-day "frontiersmen," walking in twenty-minute relays. It began early yesterday at an
elevation of 7000 feet, where the woman had lain upon a
rude hospital bed for several days with a few friends and one
or two mountain women in attendance night and day.

Stricken at Camp

A mountain man, reared in a rugged atmosphere that draws
men and women together in adversity, raced through the wilds
to carry the message to Dr. Morton W. Fraser, park physician.

Dr. Fraser trekked to her side with a train of pack
mules, but found her sinking fast and in dire need of hospital care. He returned to his starting point and arranged for
the stretcher bearers.

Overtaken by Death

With them he plunged back into the mountain fastness, the
woman was placed on a portable canvas cot, and the strange
caravan began to fight its way back to civilization.

But only a few miles from Scaffold Meadow death over-
took the party. The stretcher bearers turned around to carry
a dead woman back to camp.

—*San Francisco Chronicle,* 8-5-32
(reprinted by permission)

April 19, 1934
Grand Canyon National Park

TWO PARTIES FIGHT TO SAVE LIFE OF INJURED MAN IN GRAND CANYON

**Adventurer Hurt When Rope Slips and He Falls 80
Feet Down Walls to Tiny Ledge; Nearest Habitation Is Fifty Miles Away**

GRAND CANYON, Ariz., April 21—(I.N.S.)—Over the sacred trails of the Hopi Indians, never before trod by white men, two rescue expeditions toiled ceaselessly Saturday in the 1,500-foot gorge of the Colorado River canon in an effort to save the life of an injured adventurer, H.S. Moulton, 40, of Flagstaff, Ariz.

Fifty miles from any habitation, Moulton, accompanied by three friends had attempted to trace the "sacred salt" trail of the Hopis, when, lowering himself down the precipitate canon walls, his rope slipped, and he was hurled eighty feet to a tiny ledge. His right leg was broken and he was badly hurt.

One of Moulton's companions scrambled seventeen miles over rocks and desert to a telephone to contact Chief Ranger James P. Brooks of the Grand Canon [sic] National Park. Brooks organized a rescue party of five rangers and fifteen CCC [Civilian Conservation Corps] boys from a company on the southern rim of the national park.

Saturday morning a second relief expedition of National Park Service employees and another group of fifteen CCC youths left here as sunrise burst over the painted desert. For twelve hours Moulton's companions, one of whom is James Gregg, deputy sheriff of Coconino County, attempted to make their way up the precipitous canon while awaiting the arrival of the first rescue party.

Finally the first relief expedition arrived at the scene of Moulton's accident, and, risking their lives, took him from the tiny ledge on which he had fallen and placed him on a stretcher. That was Friday. . . . For the remainder of the day and most of the night, the rescue party slowly worked their way up the deep canon.

Their objective is a point twelve miles distant from where Moulton fell, and where the steep canon walls are only 300 feet high. From there he can be taken with comparative speed to the Grand Canon National Park hospital fifty miles away.

Down the canon is toiling the second relief party, seeking to contact the first one. Moulton has been working in the Grand Canon since Dec. 1 as foreman of the park CWA [Conservation Work Administration] work, as have his three companions. Their work finished Thursday evening, the group, with provisions for ten days left for the venturesome exploration of the Little Colorado River gorge.

—*The Denver Post*, 4-21-34 (reprinted by permission)

June 22, 1934
Yosemite National Park

TENDERFOOT RANGERS

INCREASES in the ranger force in the national parks this year are bringing into the service a lot of young Democrats who may be deserving but who are totally inexperienced in the ways of the woods, instead of the forest-wise men who have heretofore been appointed to such posts.

One of these tenderfoot rangers got lost in Yosemite a few days ago and it required a two-day search by the whole park force to find him. The regular ranger force in Yosemite is six; thirty-seven temporary rangers have been added, drawn largely from eastern cities. These green hands will not only be useless until they learn—which cannot be done in a hurry—but they will be a burden to the regular force, which will have to look after them as well as the public. By the time they are beginning to learn their work the season will be over.

The object of having a ranger force is to protect the parks and the visitors to the parks, not to provide summer-vacation jobs at $100 a month to young politicians.

—Unnamed newapaper, 6-34

William L. Carless, Jr., a temporary ranger from Kansas City, was lost for two days in Yosemite's treacherous Tenaya Canyon and was the embarrassed subject of a 40-person search party.

July 6, 1934
Grand Teton National Park

WITHOUT A SHRED OF EXPERIENCE—
OR COMMON SENSE

The two men left friends and set out to do the 13,770-foot Grand Teton in one day, an adventure for which seasoned mountaineers allow the better part of two. They knew nothing of the route, took neither rope nor ice axe, wore leather-soled shoes, and did not register. Not surprisingly, they didn't come back . . .

Ranger Fritiof Fryxell spent that first evening fruitlessly scanning for signal fires from the overdue men. At first light, he, fellow rangers Hanks and Hayden, and local mountaineer Whipple Andrews started up. Ascending Glacier Gulch, they fired shots, shouted, and with field glasses surveyed the east ridge of the Grand. Well up on the north slope of Teepe's Snowfield and dwarfed by the distance, they spotted a sprawled figure.

The body "was lying face up and head downslope, and was greatly mutilated," having fallen at least 1,000 feet. A recent German emigrant, the 20-year-old was minus a shoe. Rocks on the snow suggested an avalanche as the cause. While Hanks and Hayden "sewed the body into canvas," the other two climbed the steep snowfield following the obvious slide marks. The missing shoe was found—the fall had violently snapped the laces.

After skirting ice-covered rocks and scrambling up dangerous, boulder-filled gullies, the team returned to help scoot the body down to a waiting support crew. The following day, the search resumed without success. Fighting biting wind and numbing cold all the way, they reached the top of the Grand on the ninth. The register there proved that Ohlendorf and Leese were not among the 25 to summit that summer. Fryxell and Hanks then descended to the edge of the snowfield and inspected extensive areas on the south face. Only rock and snow.

> We rejoined the rest on top. The eastern extremity of the summit offered a perfect view of the upper part of the east ridge, yet here too, we could find only rock and snow. But finally on Teton Glacier 3500 ft. beneath us, at the base of the north precipices of the gendarmes, through the glasses I noted an object that looked like a prone figure or a broken tree trunk. So distant it could not certainly be identified, but clearly it was not a rock and the chances were against a broken tree lodging here. That Ohlendorf might be found on the opposite side of the peak from Leese had not been anticipated.

After seven days of backbreaking searching and dangerous climbing, the team brought the dead 20-year-old off the mountain and took him directly to the Jackson Cemetery. With Ranger Fryxell escorting "while the sunset colors were still bright behind the Tetons, we laid Ohlendorf to rest beside Leese."

```
                   August 2, 1934
                 Acadia National Park
------------------------------------------------------------------------
```

CARNEGIE HEROS
#-2882 AND #-2883

CHRISTINE STEWART, aged thirty-five, house-maid, attempted to save Emily McDougall, aged thirty-one, from drowning, Bar Harbor, Me., August 2, 1934. Miss McDougall, Miss Stewart, and Miss Ellen Geaney in bare feet stood on a flat rock at the shore of the Atlantic Ocean near Thunder Hole, on which surf and spray were thrown by

incoming waves that dashed over lower rocks for thirty feet from the shore. There was a strong undertow. The water was very cold. Miss McDougall, who was on a slightly lower part of the rock than the others, suddenly was washed off by receding water from an unusually high wave and was carried back and forth in the turbulent water. Miss Stewart, without removing any of her clothing, plunged from the rock, swam a short distance toward Miss McDougall, and then was carried back toward the rock. Miss Geaney also plunged from the rock and swam toward Miss McDougall. Miss Stewart reached Miss McDougall, who threshed frantically, thirty feet from the rock in water thirty feet deep and took hold of her; and Miss Geaney soon reached the two and took over the support of Miss McDougall, Miss Stewart remaining and swimming near by. Miss Geaney was unable to swim closer to the shore, and after several minutes Miss Stewart at Miss Geaney's request again took hold of Miss McDougall. The three then were forty feet from the shore. Miss Geaney was suffering from severe nausea and swam or drifted toward the shore and got hold of a rock twenty feet from the point she entered the water. Later she was pulled out of the water. After Miss Stewart again took hold of Miss McDougall, Miss McDougall threw her arms around her neck, but Miss Stewart pulled them loose. Both were washed back and forth. A man, who was a strong swimmer, was attracted and swam to Miss Stewart and Miss McDougall, who then were fifty feet from the shore, tried briefly to render aid, was affected by the cold water, released his hold, and turned on his back to float. He was rescued later. Miss Stewart, supporting Miss McDougall across her body, drifted farther out until a policeman with a rope tied around him swam to them, reaching them eighty-five feet from the shore. The three were drawn to the shore by men who held the rope. Miss McDougall was dead. Miss Stewart had been in the water forty minutes and was exhausted. She suffered from inflammation of the lungs and was disabled two months.
   —*Carnegie Hero Fund Commission 1934 Annual Report*

Christine Stewart received the **Carnegie Hero Award** (#-2882) Silver Medal and "$500 for a worthy purpose as needed." Ellen Geaney received the **Carnegie Hero Award** (#-2883) Bronze Medal and "$500 for a worthy purpose as needed."

July 25, 1935
Yosemite National Park

SEWED UP HEAD WITH NEEDLE AND THREAD
FROM ANIMAL STUFFING KIT

CARL Sharsmith, both a professor of botany at Berkeley and a seasonal park naturalist, had warned of the hike's dangers at the previous evening's campfire. Now, on the Yosemite Field School day trip, he slowly led the way up Mt. Lyell; at 13,114 feet it is Yosemite's highest point.

Victorious in their ascent, Sharsmith soon asked if there was any interest in climbing nearby Mt. McClure; a few of the more hardy students took him up on his challenge.

Once again successful and now resting near McClure's knife-edge top, Sharsmith talked about the hazards of rolling rocks.

"I looked around to see Carl falling back with arms outspread, trying to get hold of something . . . a hundred feet down . . . Carl disappeared from view."

Bud Ashcraft and "Tex" Bryant found the semiconscious ranger sitting on a ledge, blood streaming down his face and his feet dangling over a 1,500-foot sheer drop. He wanted the rock that was painfully poking him removed, but the "rock" was a broken hip.

"I wanted to tape the gash on Carl's forehead, but Bud said that it wouldn't hold on the return trip and thought it best to sew it up. He had his animal stuffing kit with him. Bud sewed it up with a needle and thread." Dr. "Tex" Bryant remembered:

> We decided that the best way to get Carl back to the top of the mountain and down to the Lyell Glacier was to prepare a rope swing. A rope went under his thighs and another around his back. Four long ropes led up from this. By putting a man on the end of each rope and one holding Carl, we got him down to the Lyell Glacier just at dark.
>
> Lucas was back with a stretcher improvised from an army blanket and two poles. We started back to camp four miles away over the Lyell Glacier in the dark. The going was tough and we had to change carriers often. We decided on a route back to camp, but Carl kept insisting that we were not going the best way. Since he was raving quite a bit, we thought he was wrong about this, too, but he wasn't.

On August 25, 1991, the 75th anniversary of the National Park Service, a spry Carl Sharsmith, standing proud and in full uniform, was honored by Director James M. Ridenour as the longest continually working employee in the Park Service. At the age of 91, after 63 years of duty, this country's oldest national park ranger died in San Jose, California, on October 14, 1994.

January 19, 1936
Mt. Rainier National Park

"I AND THE CADAVER WENT FREE-WHEELING DOWN THE MOUNTAINSIDE"

DELMAR Fadden, an accomplished outdoorsman from Seattle, wanted to be the firstever to climb Mt. Rainier in January. Loaded down with food and equipment to survive the harsh cold and wind, the 23-year-old former Eagle Scout cautiously skied around the White River Entrance Station on the night of January 13 to avoid being turned back. When Fadden's twin brother eventually reported him overdue on this, his third such winter summit attempt, one of the most publicized mountain searches in history was set in motion.

For two long weeks, 15 rangers and assorted volunteers endured awesome hardships on the frozen 14,410-foot peak.

Three of five rescuers at the 10,500-foot level on January 31, 1936. Left to right: Ome Daiber, Seattle mountaineer; John Davis, chief ranger; Paul Gilbreath, Seattle mountaineer. Out of sight are Bill Butler and Bob Buschmann. JACK DAVIS COLLECTION

> A bitter cold wind full of snow was blowing . . . exposure along the wind swept ridge started hands and feet freezing and was very discouraging . . . progress was slow searching our way over the heavily crevassed and broken surface of the glacier . . . were caught by dark and fog on . . . the glacier. Headlights were useless and we cautiously found our way.

Fadden had confided to a friend "that he was going to make every effort to throw rangers off his trail and that if he was taken Rangers would have to shoot it out with him." Although the threats were soon discounted as idle boasting, nervous rangers still anxiously checked nearby patrol and shelter cabins. For improved communications, broken summer telephone lines were fixed and large, 40-pound "portable radios" were dragged into place. Rescuers forced their way through miles of chest-deep snows just to reach the 11,000-foot level.

On the third day, Chief Ranger John Davis knew his small team of rangers needed help; Ome Daiber arrived the next day. Daiber was a mountain "hard man"—a talented and untiring climber capable of intense efforts. Eulogized upon his death in 1989 as the "Father of Mountain Rescue," Daiber became the driving force behind volunteer rescue in the Pacific Northwest. Over the next two decades—before structured and formal search and rescue teams—officials often called on Daiber and his looseknit cadre of volunteers for assistance. They eventually became the nationwide Mountain Rescue Association.

On day nine, Daiber spotted Fadden's body from the air, sprawled on the snow about 1,000 feet below the summit. Two climbing parties were formed the next day: Daiber, Chief Ranger John Davis, and Paul Gilbraith in one team, and Ranger Bill Butler and Bob Buschmann, a former climbing partner of the dead man, in the other.

Their trip was "just a hard steady grind up the Glacier." Clouds had completely covered the country beneath them and higher clouds between 10,000 and 11,500 feet were quickly closing in as well. "These were a real threat and kept continually worrying us. At about 1:30 P.M. we passed into the shadow of the mountain and from then on low temperatures estimated from thirty to forty below zero were our concern." In fewer than 10 hours they climbed 8,000 feet in elevation.

> At the 12,500 foot elevation the pace began to get too stiff for me [John Davis]. My legs just wouldn't move any faster and time was beginning to be a serious consideration with our goal almost in sight. We re-roped with Daiber, Gilbraith and Buschmann forming one party and Butler and I the other. The first party went ahead slowly and reached the body at 3:10 P.M. and Butler and I only ten minutes behind . . . Butler could easily have kept up with the rest of them and he was behind only because of me.

The 23-year-old Fadden was found face down, head downhill, "and of course solidly frozen." His left foot was minus a crampon, the right sleeve of his parka was torn in a number of places, and snow had forced its way into his mouth and nose. His pack was up over his head, his hands were bare, and his ice axe was missing. "It was evident that he had lost his footing and slid down the mountain, knocking himself unconscious and freezing to death before he could regain his senses."

After lashing the body in a canvas tarp, the men started slowly down. Chief Ranger Davis recalled their descent.

> . . . we had to traverse a slick ice, glare ice, very steep slope, quite a long one. Our ropes were not long enough to reach to the bottom of the slope. . . . I had to anchor and let Bill and [the] body down. My legs did not have any strength left in them and my knees started to bend. We were standing on a terrifically steep slope . . .
>
> . . . my feet went out from under me and I started down the mountainside at [missing] miles an hour. I got to the end of the rope that Bill was tied to and of course yanked Bill off his feet, and Bill and I and the cadaver went free-wheeling down the mountainside with very little chance to stop. . . . But apparently through the grace of God—and I can't think of any other reason—the three of us did stop in a patch of corn snow.

In one final but illustrative indication of the strength of character of that rescue team, 15 of the men served as pallbearers, carrying "his body to its last resting place."

Temporary Park Ranger William Butler received an appointment as a permanent park ranger by Franklin Roosevelt for his efforts on this rescue. This was the second and last time a ranger was granted such a prestigious recognition by the president.

August 19, 1936
Grand Canyon National Park

"AS THE GREATEST HONOR"

WE owe the Civilian Conservation Corps an unpayable debt of gratitude, and so do the six people they helped rescue one night . . .

"The call for volunteers came at 5:45 P.M., Ranger [Perry] Brown selected the party; the packs were ready, and we were on our way at 6:30 P.M." A young Louis Purvis, stationed at the CCC camp at Phantom Ranch in the canyon's bottom, remembers that he was scared.

> With the canyon narrowing to 25 feet and the water cresting to 22 feet, few people on the rim, and none of us in the rescue party, believed that we would find them alive. The darkness soon fell on the trail, due to increased cloudiness that threatened to continue the down pour. In the extreme darkness, the occasional landslide, along with the uncertain footing, our progress was very hazardous. We were unaware of the great dangers that lurked all about us.
>
> The trail was obliterated. In several places the rock wall that supported the trail gave away and fell into the canyon, a thousand feet below. We were all very grateful when we reached Roaring Springs. The shoulder straps on our packs were cutting into us badly, our knees were very painful and weak from checking the weight of the packs as we descended the canyon wall. We rested for a very short time, realizing the urgency of our mission.
>
> We were approaching the "Narrows," and needless to say, the trail was entirely gone. We went to the creek bed for better footing. Time-after-time we crossed Bright Angel Creek, somewhat abated, it was still on a rampage.
>
> We reached the party about one in the morning, eleven miles from the North Rim and about mid-way through the "Narrows." The people were on a ledge that gave them some shelter and enabled them to survive the raging torrents that threatened to sweep them off the ledge to their death. After ministering to them, we helped them to reach Phantom Ranch safely.

The letter that Purvis and his three CCC co-rescuers received from the CCC Director Robert Fechner prophesied, "As the years pass, you can look back with commendable pride upon the fact that you maintained the fine spirit of the Civilian Conservation Corps by your unselfish service and courage." On the 50th anniversary of the CCC, while revisiting the Grand Canyon, Louis Purvis recalled that rescue "as the greatest honor, and the most satisfying experience that ever happened to me."

April 21, 1937
Boulder Dam National Recreation Area

PARK'S FIRST DEATHS

THE trio of inexperienced sailors set out at night, broke a rudder, and then, tragically, swamped in rough water.

In what is now known as Lake Mead National Recreation Area, the search for the park's first fatalities fell to its first ranger. On duty since only February 8, Oren P. Senter led the hunt for Charles R. Lillibridge, Herbert Bowen, and Milo A. Slawson. The missing men, employed locally by the Bureau of Reclamation, were, ironically, former coworkers of Ranger Senter's.

For the next week, as many as 75 men from Boulder City CCC Company 573 were stationed at lakeshore vantage points to look for the bodies. The 45-foot NPS-1, the recreation area's first and only patrol boat, was a recent acquisition from the Coast Guard. Arriving the same day Senter did, it was quickly pressed into service without any success. The three men were never found.

Almost two years later, probably the first attempt at recovering a drowning victim in the National Park System by using an artificial air source took place at Lake Mead on April 9, 1939.

> Tom Haake, 19-year-old Las Vegas youth, fell from the stern of his father's speedboat about one mile toward the Dam from the Hemenway Wash Boat Landing. Unable to swim, the young man drowned before it was possible to get aid to him. . . . Intensive searching, dragging the lake, a search by a deep sea diver hired by the father of the youth, and other efforts . . . proved of no avail.
>
> —*Monthly Report*, 4-39

On May 5, Haake was found floating on the surface.

The first recorded use of surface-supplied diving in the National Park Service, as well as the first documented underwater archeological work in North America, was undertaken at Virginia's Colonial National Historical Park in 1934. Under the joint sponsorship of Newport News' (VA) Mariners' Museum and the NPS, artifacts were recovered from two British revolutionary warships of Cornwallis's Fleet sunk in the York River. Navy hard-hat divers were used there during 1934 and 1935.

March 1, 1938
Yosemite National Park

"ICE IS FORMING ON THE WINGS
AND I AM TURNING BACK"

IT was the most devastating storm to hit Southern California in 64 years. The cloudburst-driven floods brought ruin to more than 100 communities in five counties. Highways, utilities, and train tracks were destroyed—$79 million worth. Among the 208 known dead or missing were nine in a small TWA airliner.

Popular around the Stanford campus, the two young people were en route to Ohio to see their critically ill father. Tracy Dirlam, president of Phi Gamma Delta, had to cancel a lecture on "Hell Week" that night. Mary Lou, an ardent student and Tracy's sister, was an outstanding athlete who excelled in golf and horseback riding. M. H. Salisbury, off from his duties as a TWA pilot, was returning from a visit to his mother in Walnut Creek. Also Chicago-bound, Mr. and Mrs. Walts had just kissed six-year-old Lucius goodbye; they would never again kiss their only child hello . . .

Two hours into the flight, pilot John Graves radioed his company about the rapidly deteriorating conditions; an hour later he was ordered to land wherever he could. The headlines in the *San Francisco Chronicle* the next day said the rest.

S.F. TRANSPORT PLANE, WITH NINE ABOARD,
UNREPORTED ON LOS ANGELES FLIGHT

Big TWA Ship Last Heard from Flying Near Bakersfield

Carrying six passengers and a crew of three, a transport plane of Transcontinental and Western Airlines was believed to have crashed. . . . The plane, northbound from San Francisco airport, was unreported for more than five hours on a scheduled flight to Winslow, Ariz. It left here at 6:30 P.M., but because of storm conditions . . .

The first of many clues gave promise. "Mystery lights and a white object were reported sighted at nightfall near a mountainside scar in the area where the plane was last seen." It is thought that aerial flares were seen, that shots were heard.

The effort then focused on the foothills east of Fresno. With snow down to 2,000 feet, cloud ceilings only 500 feet higher, and more than 2 inches of rain locally, the rescuers were seriously hampered. "Unable to penetrate beyond the Sierra foothills, a half dozen planes . . . were forced to abandon the search an hour later."

By the third day, more than 50 planes were committed to the mission. United Airlines sent large ones, Los Angeles County small ones. Army bombers and Navy fighters flew. "The searching planes were to cover an 88-square mile area . . . 60 to 80 miles east of Fresno." Outlined by the earlier sketchy reports, the probe was divided into 22 sectors. Each pilot and attending observer was assigned one very rugged four-square-mile section.

More than 400 searchers combed the foothills, "including 300 CCC enrollees, with several hundred additional CCC camp youths waiting." Conditions were miserable: wet, windy, and cold.

False reports abounded: "We were at Bass Lake Tuesday night and heard a crashing sound like a plane might make hitting a mountain." Half-hopes persisted: "The plane's lights blinked off and a white flare dropped from it and fell out of view behind the ridge." Over three months passed and the $1,000 reward went unclaimed. Until . . .

WRECK LIES ON YOSEMITE PEAK

Long Lost Plane Found—Nine Dead

Park Hiker Locates Shattered Air Liner, Missing Since March 1, in Melting Snow; Searchers Leave Today to Get Bodies

Yosemite, June 12, (U.P.)—A youth who followed a "hunch" today found the wreckage of a missing Transcontinental and Western Airways plane lost since March 1. . . . The discovery was made by 24-year-old . . . of Fresno . . . [who] had decided it would be found somewhere in the vicinity of Buena Vista peak, twelve miles northeast of Wawona in Yosemite Park. . . . This morning he found bits of wreckage. Tracing them he came to the wrecked plane and inside he counted the bodies of eight of its nine victims. The plane lay partially buried in the snow on the southern side of the 9,000-foot peak. It was about 200 feet from the tip of the peak.

—*Los Angeles Times*, 6-13-38 (reprinted by permission)

The "finder" was a CCC employee who worked in Yosemite when the plane disappeared and, as such, was ineligible to claim a reward. Even 45 years later, retired ranger Tom Tucker vividly recalled rumors that the plane had been found much earlier, but the youth did not announce it until later in order to fraudulently collect the bonus.

A plaque dedicated to the dead passengers was placed on Buena Vista Peak by the mother of the two Stanford students.

The first fatal plane wreck in Yosemite, and possibly the NPS, occurred on July 24, 1926. Le Roy Jeffers was killed outright when a small craft piloted by Dr. Sterling Bunnell crashed trying to land in Wawona; Bunnell later died from his injuries as well.

With nine people on board, this TWA plane crashed on a remote peak in the Yosemite backcountry. Lost on March 1, 1938, it was not found until June 12.

YOSEMITE NATIONAL PARK
RESEARCH LIBRARY

July 3, 1938
Rocky Mountain National Park

"I'M COMING, MAMA"—BUT HE NEVER DID

ROARING River, born of countless snows from high in the nearby Mummy Mountains, deserves its name; after plunging 3,000 feet in 7 short miles, the foaming waters that summer morning tumbled past aging pine, bugling elk, and a happy little boy.

Camped in Horseshoe Park, William Beilhartz, his wife, 10 children, assorted in-laws, and friends enjoyed the July Fourth weekend. After Sunday breakfast, the Denver nurseryman walked 50 yards to the crystal cold river to wash up. His four-year-old tagged along; others did the same, and again the child followed. When his mother finally summoned him, by the last words she heard from her curly-headed son were "I'm coming, mama." Alfred Beilhartz, the subject of the park's largest search, was never seen again.

The search for Alfred Beilhartz is among Rocky Mountain National Park's most enigmatic. The four-year-old was never seen again. ROCKY MOUNTAIN NEWS

Within 45 minutes of the alarm, 110 CCC enrollees led by District Ranger Jack Moomaw were combing the area for the boy. They dragged the river at several places, but the swift water made these operations almost impossible. "One CCC youth, wading in the roaring stream, was swept from his feet and nearly drowned." By dark, more than 150 people were looking for little Alfred.

Governor Ammons volunteered the Colorado National Guard; airmen and airplanes assisted. State prison bloodhounds arrived. Officials instructed new workers to look for "blue denim overalls, a brown sweater, brown tennis shoes, or anything else that may seem to have a bearing on the case." Searchers checked all vacant cabins in the area. They stretched huge "fishnets" across both the Fall and Roaring Rivers, 5 miles below the campsite. A large bonfire was lit in hopes the boy would see it in the dark.

Tuesday's *Rocky Mountain News* read: **"Rangers to Divert River in Hunt for Lost Denver Child."**

D.H. Canfield, superintendent of Rocky Mountain National Park, said the attempt to divert the river, now running at flood stage, would be made tomorrow. . . . George Fry, assistant chief ranger and an engineer, estimated the diversion could be accomplished in six hours with the crew of 110 CCC enrollees engaged in the search.

"We'll need between 200 and 400 sandbags for the job,"
he said. "By felling some big spruce trees and using the bags,
we can divert the river in the narrow neck of the cañon a mile
above the camp. We'll simply run the water down the other
side of the valley."

They deflected the river; considerably emptier, the 35-foot-wide boulder and
log-choked riverbed were crawled through for miles, not once but six times. Mud-
filled rocky crevices 15 to 20 feet deep were probed. Six beaver dams were dyna-
mited in order to look inside; swimmers dove under overhangs and into narrow,
dark beaver tunnels. "Two tourists told Park Service rangers they thought they
heard a child crying near the Fall River bridge a week after the search began."

Two hundred fresh CCC men were brought in from Grand Lake to assist the
men from Camp One. The operation was directed through a system of shortwave
radio sets. A recent innovation in communications, the "portables" were so
large they had to be carried on the searchers' shoulders.

The search took a new, but logical, twist: kidnapping. "The best place to
begin is with an investigation of all persons who were in this region last
Sunday." Superintendent Canfield ordered the screening of all cars entering and
exiting the park. Several persons were under "surveillance."

Mediums and mystics as far away as Iowa were sent photos. Rangers drove
to Denver to follow up on leads. A gauze bandage, thought to be from a cut on
Alfred's heel, was found a mile away and was quickly sent to the FBI.

In final desperation, Cascade Lake, a power company dam on the Fall
River, was drained. Using grappling hooks, the 5 feet of water in the lower end
was repeatedly dragged.

Finally, after 11 days of intense and heroic efforts, the search was suspended. Every weekend for months afterwards, the boy's parents would return
and call out Alfred's name. Nothing . . .

"I'm coming, mama."

On July 16, 1938, Superintendent Canfield was named to the *Denver Post's*
Gallery of Fame for directing this massive effort. Born in 1904, and following a
32-year career, David Canfield died in 1977. At the time of the search he was
the National Park Service's youngest superintendent, so posted in 1935.

Even more than 50 years later, retired ranger George Fry, a key player in
this massive, heartbreaking search, would still recall the little four-year-old . . .
and wonder.


```
                    January 25, 1939
              Carlsbad Caverns National Park
        -----------------------------------------
```

SURVIVAL SENT TO RIPLEY'S "BELIEVE IT OR NOT"

SUPERINTENDENT Thomas Boles titled the following "Believe It or Not" when
he recorded it on page 13 of his January 1939 *Monthly Report* to the director
of the National Park Service:

. . . Ranger Leslie Thompson, assigned to elevator duty, brought the elevator to the surface about 12:30 to bring down the tourists who were in the lobby of the elevator tower at that time. Thompson closed the elevator door and stepped to the next room and during his absence Electrician Carpenter took the elevator on a special trip in[to] the Cavern in order that Auditor Marlow Glenn and Chief Clerk VanKirk might get into the Cavern before the tourist party.

Thompson returned to the elevator door and although the indicator showed that the elevator was at the bottom . . . he automatically reached for his key and unlocked the door and opened it a couple of inches. He . . . hung up the key . . . and requested the tourists have their elevator tickets ready . . . he reached behind him and opened the door and stepped back into the shaftway which is 754 feet deep.

For nearly 100 feet he fell head first but had presence of mind to clasp his arms around the five elevator cables which caused his body to reverse itself so that he clasped his legs as well as his arms around the cables, which had been recently tarred over with rust preventive and were quite sticky. After sliding 25 or 30 feet he brought himself to a full stop 125 feet below the surface and called to the people at the top that he was all right and to come down in the other elevator and get him.

After blocking the elevator door open so that the Pacific elevator could not be moved until the rescue had been effected, Handyman Bob Miller and Ranger Hieb took the other car and pulled Thompson into the other elevator and brought him to the surface none the worse for wear except slightly skinned fingers and a thoroughly greased uniform.

While the tourists waiting to go down on the elevator were shocked to see Thompson fall backwards in the shaft, they were even more astonished when he appeared in the doorway of the other elevator just a few minutes later none the worse for wear and probably the coolest one of the outfit.

I attribute this miraculous escape to Thompson's cat-like activity and his cool head under all circumstances. He had worked for many months in this elevator shaft and though falling head down he knew just which way to reach . . . and realized at once that it was the cables—and not the beams— which must be grasped.

```
              August 7, 1939
        Rocky Mountain National Park
-------------------------------------------
```

LOWERING THE DYING MAN FROM LEDGE TO LEDGE

GERALD Clark had already climbed Longs Peak seven times. Despite his mother's deep concerns, the 39-year-old photographer went again anyway; he had been up every route except one.

Cascading water and spray-covered rocks made this steep section of the Second Chimney extremely severe. Needing just a little slack in the rope to inch up the next few feet, Clark untied from his two companions. Although successful with this difficult move, he found himself trapped—he could go neither up nor down.

Dressed in a light flannel shirt and denim trousers, the veteran climber was not prepared for the water tumbling down the steep gully, nor for the unexpected summer snowstorm. "The east face, which has claimed several victims in a score of years was in league with a driving snowstorm to balk rescuers. Mr. Clark was marooned for 20 hours in a water-drenched trough high on the side of the peak."

Ranger Ernie Field, one of the most seasoned mountain rescue men in the country, was on a Colorado Mountain Club day trip nearby. Leading four other experienced CMC climbers, he quickly responded to the faint cries for help.

"The elements seemed to be against all of us that night, however, and our climbing was retarded by darkness, rain, and fog." Cold and wet, the rescuers spent a long night. As soon as they could get the cramps and chills worked from their own muscles, three men went over the edge of the sheer cliff. "Mr. Clark was so hidden by the storm and trough that the rescuers could not find him when they started down at dawn."

Conscious when reached, "he passed out the first time we lowered him out on a rope." Snow and sleet swirled all about. For five hours, Ranger Field and two expert Denver climbers "worked down the cliff, lowering the dying man from ledge to ledge on the rope. The descent by each rope maneuver averaged only about 40 feet." Lower, tie, descend, lower, tie . . . 1,500 feet.

Despite the heroic labors of the rescue team, risking death themselves from sheer cliffs, falling rocks, and freezing snows, Clark died just after reaching the bottom.

Ranger Ernest Field and Colorado Mountain Club members Robert Boyd and Robert C. Lewis Jr. were named to the *Denver Post* **Gallery of Fame** on August 12, 1939, for their efforts.

August 28, 1939
Olympic National Park

WOMAN LOST ON PENINSULA

Rangers Seek Missing Woman
Mass Search Opens for Trace of Botanist on Mt. Olympus;
Actions Mystify Officials

FOURTEEN rangers and fire guides [guards], working from a base camp at Glacier Meadows, were searching the west side of Mount Olympus yesterday for some clue to the strange disappearance of thirty-three-year-old Marion Frances Steffens, Chicago botanist.

Twelve days ago rangers found, in a neat bundle near the end of the Hoh River trail on the west side of the mountain, some of the woman hiker's camping equipment and food with this note: "In emergency the following were offered and belong to these persons. Please see they are returned to the proper owners . . . sleeping bag, . . . logger's boots, . . . packboard . . ."

. . . was given a lift up the Hoh River road . . . to within a few rods of the ranger station. She got out of his car at that point, . . . explaining that she wanted to avoid the rangers.

Rangers reported via short-wave radio from the scene of the search the ice about Blue Glacier field has broken up, and there are many large crevasses, some as deep as 200 feet, the bottom of which cannot be seen from above.

Unnamed and undated newspaper

The Vassar graduate was never found, despite a concerted effort by a great many people, including several overflights by the U.S. Coast Guard. In response to a September 23 letter from Park Superintendent Preston P. Macy to the victim's father, Robert Steffens, brother of the victim, said:

I was astonished . . . you had sent my father a statement of $151.65 as the full amount of the bill for groceries. . . . When you first mentioned . . . this bill . . . the total amount was $125, and you inquired whether I thought my father would be willing to pay the $25 in excess of the $100 you were permitted to purchase without competitive bidding. This, you stated, was to relieve your office from a somewhat embarrassing situation created by the emergency. . . . I seriously doubt if he will do so. . . . As for . . . the total amount, there are federal appropriations . . . and it seems to me these expenses . . . covered, even though they be of an emergency nature.

There were two other major searches—using overflights and bloodhounds—that year. On February 19, a 20-year-old CCC enrollee fell to his death climbing a glacier. Then, on February 27, a 23-year-old student died after sliding down a snowfield.

Precursor to the U.S. Army's famed Tenth Mountain Division, members of the 15th Infantry Ski Patrol pull a pico rescue sled while training at Mt. Rainier National Park in November 1941.

CHAPTER 5

Back in those days, by taking the bull
by the horns we could and did make a
workable and responsive rescue
organization. We had practically no
equipment except some Army surplus
(which we thought was great!), no good
radio communications, damn little money,
not too much support from the higher
ups; we did volunteer a lot of overtime
and . . . we made it work.

—retired Sequoia Ranger Dick Boyer

THE best thing ever to happen to search and rescue was World War II. The events—and many of the men and women—are now history, but the shadows of this legacy are apparent every time a lost child is found or an injured mountaineer is lowered from a cliff.

MOUNTAIN TROOPS

On January 6, 1940, the War Department asked Army Chief of Staff General George C. Marshall about equipment, food, transportation, special clothing, and other essentials for an effective winter mountain field force. Simultaneously, "Minnie" Dole, the leader of the newly formed National Ski Patrol, and Roger Langley of the National Ski Association wrote the Secretary of War: "If foreign troops should attack our northeast coast in winter . . ." Not many believed the United States would, or even could, be invaded. "Thank you," said the Army. "We'll take your offer under consideration."

After a year, Dole finally heard from Secretary of War Stimson; on November 15, 1941, the 1st Battalion, 87th Infantry Mountain Regiment, was activated. America now had its Mountain Troops. The day after the attack on Pearl Harbor, the first inductee, a young ski racer from Dartmouth, reported. Dole's ski patrol became a nationwide recruiter, the only civilian group thus designated.

"Wanted by the Army": men able to pass a night in the winter woods without dying of exposure or fright—outdoorsmen, cowboys, and lumbermen. The Park Service contributed dozens. Rangers such as Dick and Doug McLaren, Ernie Field, Bob Frauson, Bob Weldon, Laury Brown, and Bob Bendt had to answer a questionnaire as well as submit three reference letters testifying to their abilities. For the next three years they skied and climbed on Mt. Rainier and at Wisconsin's Camp McCoy. Ranger "Pat" Patterson became the director of the 87th Mountaineering School at 9,000-foot-high Camp Hale in Colorado.

Sam Clark, an old-time Yosemite ranger who mustered out as a lieutenant in the engineers after the war, was reputed to be the one to lock the gate when they finally closed down Camp Hale.

An elite detachment went to West Virginia's Seneca Rocks in the spring of 1943 to train in mountainous terrain. Regimental combat teams of 3,000 to 4,000 men eventually passed through there each month. Determined crews worked with pack animals; engineers improvised river crossings; and budding medics specialized in mountain medicine, first aid, and tricky evacuations from cliffs. And, of course, there was rock climbing.

Every month for a year, 150 greenhorns scrambled over Seneca Rocks during an intensive two weeks of training. Within days, these men were climbing, rappelling, and practicing the skills required to save each other. More than 75,000 metal pitons were driven into those craggy cliffs. Classified by the Army when first written, the *Manual of American Mountaineering*, by Ken Henderson of the American Alpine Club, became a climbers' bible for decades to come.

Outdoor gear that defined the standard for the next 50 years was developed and streamlined. Late in 1941, the War Department marshalled some of this country's foremost mountaineers to design and refine this equipment, men like Brad Washburn, Bill House, Bob Bates, Terris Moore, Dick Leonard, and James Ford.

Laminated skis replaced the long, old-style, wooden "planks," and quick-release bindings were perfected. Feltlike mukluks—"Bunny Boots" to be used for high-altitude combat—were still worn on Mt. McKinley well into the 1980s. New rucksacks and tents evolved—prototypes for today's lightweight models. Miniature stoves, cook kits, and dehydrated foods arrived for the troops.

A new rubber sole with cleats led to a bulky but versatile mountain boot that could be used for both skiing and rock climbing. Better crampons, ice axes, pitons, and carabineers surfaced. Pile-lined parkas and light, eider-down sleeping bags, with heavy zippers guaranteed to open in a hurry, were invented. The "weasel," the first successful, large, over-the-snow vehicle, was built especially for troop and supply transport. Studebaker's Eliason Motor Toboggan was America's first real snowmobile.

By far the greatest single contribution to mountain rescue was the nylon rope; the halt in Philippine hemp manufacture dictated an emergency substitute for the manila line. Plymouth Cordage Company tested the new synthetic; it stretched 39 percent before breaking: $\frac{7}{16}$-inch-diameter, 120-foot lengths were adopted—a standard today.

Just before shipping overseas, the full 10th Mountain Division was finally created and became fully operational. In February 1945, the battles of Riva Ridge and Mt. Belvedere would make the division legendary. Hundreds scaled 1,500-foot Riva Ridge under cover of darkness to catch the Germans by surprise. They cracked the "Gothic Line" stretching across northern Italy and opened up the Po River Valley to the Allied forces. This remarkable effort soon led to the capture of 20,000 enemy soldiers.

Today, the 10th Mountain Division members are heroes. Paying the supreme sacrifice, 990 of them never made it home; the legacy they leave, however, endures. Every time a lost child is reunited with a terrified mother or a careless climber is given a second chance, the specter of the legendary Mountain Troops is there.

HELICOPTERS

With the possible exceptions of the two-way radio and the continuing refinement of emergency medicine, there is no milestone in the evolution of search and rescue more significant than the arrival of the helicopter. Thousands are alive today because pilots and crews have performed with dedication and daring.

The German Focke-Wulf (FW-61) first flew on June 26, 1936, but it wasn't until Igor Sikorsky designed the VS-300 that the truly modern helicopter finally got off the ground. Even while this novel gadget was being tested, its use on a bizarre rescue in a remote NPS area was suggested. On October 1, 1941, daredevil Charles Hopkins parachuted onto the top of 865-foot Devils Tower; he had no way off. He was eventually saved by man, not machine.

The XR-4, the military's version of the VS-300, made its maiden flight on January 13, 1942; with a 36-foot blade diameter and a 165-mph motor, it had a range of 130 miles. On April 20, with his chief pilot at the controls of a hovering craft, Sikorsky lowered himself to the ground on a thick rope and another man soon climbed back up using a 25-foot rope ladder.

In December 1943, Ladd Field in Fairbanks received the "Arctic Jitterbug," one of only 131 R-4s built during World War II. The first helicopter in the frozen north, this YR-4B was tested as an air ambulance; flying into small, snow-covered landing areas, it took out "patients" in practice missions. The Jitterbug was once considered for the rescue of a civilian who had crashed in an isolated spot. Fixed-wing reconnaissance, however, soon determined the pilot was dead and officials chose not to risk using this new tool.

Finally, on January 3, 1944, the Coast Guard's first helicopter pilot, Commander Frank Erickson, performed the world's first helicopter mercy mission.

> A United States destroyer blew apart near the entrance of New York Bay today with an explosion so terrific it hurled men and guns into the sea. The blazing ship sank in 40 minutes, as Coast Guard craft edged to her side to rescue 163 men, including 108 injured.

Lifting off from nearby Floyd Bennett Field, Erickson battled weather and winds. Using a rescue hoist he had developed, he delivered a cargo of much-needed plasma to the 100 badly burned men of the USS *Turner.* Helicopter rescue legends began.

On April 23–24, 1944, Lieutenant Carter Harmon of the Army Air Corps flew a YR-4B from India into Burma to save three British soldiers trapped behind enemy lines after their Stinson had crashed. The pilot of the downed aircraft, Sergeant E. M. Hladkovkak, welcomed the newfangled apparatus with "You look like an angel." The usefulness of this new tool was not lost on the NPS. In a May 1946 report about the NPS and World War II, Director Newton B. Drury described the machine's unique virtues and potential contributions and forecast its use in rescue.

The Forest Service first used helicopters on a nonmilitary rescue. On August 5, 1946, a Bell 47-B removed an injured radio operator trapped on a mountain in the path of the Bryant Fire in California's Angeles National Forest.

The first chopper involved in an NPS SAR was not the rescuer, but the rescuee. On October 5, 1948, while "rubbernecking" on a body recovery on

Olympic's rugged west side, an SAR helicopter based at McChord Field suffered engine failure and crash-landed in Upper Lena Lake. Uninjured, the crew of three was guided out of the area the following day by District Ranger Dewey Webster.

The first helicopter actually deployed on an NPS mission had to fly into an active volcano. On April 27, 1949, a soldier on temporary duty near Hawaii National Park walked away from his car after becoming stranded in the dark, only 100 yards from the edge of 500-foot-deep Kilauea Crater. The next day, the

On August 5, 1946, this Bell 47 pulled an injured radio operator from the path of the Bryant Fire in Angeles National Forest. This was the world's first civilian medevac. SMITHSONIAN INSTITUTION

body of Lieutenant Stephens was discovered while a small military helicopter scanned the rugged walls from inside the crater.

Four days later, a Lieutenant Frost set down at Boulder Beach to demonstrate the machine at a Nevada Boy Scout Camporee; named the "Rescue," it was the first helicopter ever to land at Lake Mead. One hopes the Army officer was a better pilot than navigator, for the scouts were camped in Las Vegas—30 miles away.

One of the last significant NPS helicopter events during the 1940s occurred on August 2, 1949, when a stripped-down craft made an unsuccessful rescue attempt at Yosemite's Benson Lake for an injured 12-year-old boy. The next day, a disassembled second ship was trucked into the park, reassembled, and was flying 4,000 feet above its rated altitude; it made the first-ever NPS medevac.

In the 1940s, thousands of military planes crashed and hundreds died; many of these tragedies occurred in units of the National Park System. During World War II, four wrecks killing 22 aviators occurred in Arizona's Saguaro National Monument alone.

One notable accident resulted in the most heralded recognition of the decade. It involved a persistent Bill Butler, Mt. Rainier's assistant chief ranger. On December 10, 1946, a Marine Corps plane with 32 on board vanished between California and Washington. After six months, Butler located the craft in a glacier. He was subsequently granted a **Department of the Interior Distinguished Service Award**; a **Navy Public Service Certificate**, its highest civilian award; an **NPS Superior Accomplishment Pay Increase**; and a check for $5,000 (twice his annual salary) from appreciative relatives of the missing aviators. The latter was returned uncashed.

Allowed under the provisions of Section 14 of 1946 Public Law 600, "Honor Awards," the Department of the Interior presented the first **Distinguished Service Award** (DSA) at its First Honors Convocation on April 28, 1948. Assistant Chief Ranger Bill Butler's gold-embossed **DSA** and accompanying gold medal were presented personally by Secretary of the Interior Krug on October 24, 1948, at a superintendent's conference at the Grand Canyon.

MILESTONES OF THE 1940s

1940	Visitors to 161 units in the NPS total 16,755,251.
July 15, 1940	Chet Derry makes world's first rescue parachute jump: a downed plane in Montana's Bitterroot National Forest.
November 16, 1940	The first time an NPS SAR training is suggested, Sequoia Ranger H. B. Blanks develops an agenda. World War II prevented the training from taking place.
Fall 1940	Mountain rescue caches are established at Rocky Mountain by Ernest Field: two 120-foot ropes, 20 assorted pitons, two piton hammers, four carabineers, two pairs of crampons, one ice axe, one rappelling hook, four headlamps, and four flares.

One of two climbing rescue caches located in Rocky Mountain National Park in 1940.
ROCKY MOUNTAIN NATIONAL PARK RESEARCH LIBRARY

MILESTONES OF THE 1940s

April 8-13, 1941	Seasonal ranger and avid mountaineer Jules Eichorn teaches rock climbing to 14 other Yosemite rangers.
December 1, 1941	Civil Air Patrol (CAP) is founded as an auxiliary of the Air Force. By 1944 it will be the world's largest nonmilitary aircraft fleet, with 520 planes, 22 gliders, and two hot-air balloons.
November 1943	Federal government creates Suggestions System and among other things, the **Award of Outstanding Achievement.** The honor is accompanied by a $25 war bond contributed by three federal employee unions.
November 19, 1943	First "routine" honors of any kind bestowed by the Department of the Interior are presented in simultaneous ceremonies: Washington, D.C.; Denver, Colorado; and Portland, Oregon.
1944	Dogs are "parachuted" to downed Army aviators in Alaskan outback.
March 9, 1944	The Mountaineers Climbing Committee pledges to help the NPS with rescues on Mt. Rainier. A list of the Seattle area's best climbers who are not at war is furnished to the park.
May 1944	Military's Air Sea Rescue detachment is formed.
May 22, 1944	Olympic National Park Ranger Dewey Webster is presented an **Award of Outstanding Achievement,** a $25 war bond, and a personal letter of appreciation from Secretary of the Interior Ickes for locating a Navy plane that disappeared in April 1943. Webster is one of just three Department of the Interior employees and the first from the NPS to receive this new award.
July 1944	Oren P. Senter assumed duties as Big Bend National Park's first ranger.
December 1944	*Field Manual 70-10: Mountain Operations,* a primer for SAR and climbing, is published by the War Department.
1946	Federal Tort Claims Act (28 U.S.C., sec. 2671 *et seq*) is enacted.
March 13, 1946	Headquarters Air Rescue Service is established; it will eventually evolve into the Air Force Rescue Coordination Center.

MILESTONES OF THE 1940s

December 23, 1946	NPS's first Annual Mountain Climbing Report is submitted by Mt. McKinley National Park.
March 5, 1947	Boulder (Colorado) County Rescue, one of the first volunteer mountain rescue teams in the country, is formed. This is the nucleus for today's Rocky Mountain Rescue Group.
June 21, 1947	Three rescuers from Yellowstone die trying to aid 70 people trapped in an unseasonable blizzard near the park.
October 4, 1947	Safety Committee of the American Alpine Club is established, which plays a major role in rescue education. Fifteen climbing accidents and 11 deaths are reported that year.
October 24, 1947	Fifty-two are killed in an airliner crash in Bryce Canyon, the world's seventh greatest air disaster to date.
1948	U.S. Border Patrol initiates the "Man Tracking" program.
	Code of Federal Regulations (2.14)(d) states that no one "will be permitted to start alone for the summit of Mount McKinley, Mount Rainier, Grand Teton, South Teton, or Devils Tower."
April 12, 1948	Transporting a hut into remote Supai Village, a helicopter lands for the first time in the Grand Canyon.
June 26, 1948	Seattle Mountaineers call a meeting of Pacific Northwest climbers—the Mountain Rescue Council is born.
July 1948	A request is made to initiate helicopter sightseeing flights over the Grand Canyon; it is rejected by the director.
September 13-17, 1948	Mt. Rainier hosts the National Park Service's first mountain rescue training.
December 1948	Management's first formal guidelines for climbing Mt. McKinley are drawn up and sent to various mountaineering groups.
January 1949	Yellowstone sees the recreational use of snowplanes begin; this will eventually lead to a proliferation of snowmobiles.
April 1949	A Sikorsky helicopter lands on Mt. McKinley to assist in survey conducted by scientist Brad Washburn—a first.
May 9, 1949	NPS Director Drury recommends that "pitons, which have been used in connection with rock climbing, be removed."

"A THOUSAND FEET OF ⅜ INCH MANILA ROPE, A REGULAR DOUBLE-BITTED AXE, NERVE, CARE, AND CAUTION"

WHEN the two boys didn't return for supper, neighboring campers reported them overdue. And at midnight, after finding footprints leading into the hard, snow-packed crater, rangers knew they had to climb down the wall of the treacherous, dormant volcano.

> A descent . . . was . . . begun. This was accomplished by means of a thousand feet of ⅜-inch manila rope, a regular double-bitted axe, nerve, care, and caution. The descent of the slide was not possible on the side from which the approach had been made; consequently, it was necessary to cross it.
>
> Park Naturalist Doerr proceeded down the slide. . . . Ranger Foiles crossed over onto the opposite side, and it was he who discovered . . . young men . . . it was obvious they were not in good physical condition.

David, 20, and Kenneth, 17, had somehow negotiated the nearly vertical cinder slope to the lakeshore and then, incredibly, managed to climb halfway back up before being overtaken by dark. Awake all night, the boys tried to keep "cool, calm, and collected." At first light they discovered they could go no higher and were climbing back down to water when they were found by the rangers.

> Ranger Foiles, under the most difficult and definitely dangerous conditions, assisted them in their arduous climb back to where the rescue rope could be used. In one particular instance, young Campbell was on his all-fours trying to make progress ahead, but . . . was slowly slipping back over the cliff, when Ranger Foiles hurried to his aid by stretching out his leg for Campbell to hold on to and pull himself back.

In order to search along the water's edge, park crews would have ordinarily needed to laboriously lower a boat down to the lake by means of hoists and cables—over 1,300 feet.

July 20, 1940
Mt. Rainier National Park

THE PERILS OF BERNADETTE

THE other 17 were already an hour ahead of Bernadette Wright and her companion. Along with others in The Mountaineers' party, she was intent on reaching the 14,410-foot summit. At the mountain's 9,500-foot level, she

> was leading at the time she slipped from a narrow snow
> ledge of cornice wall which was hung next to the wall of pro-
> truding rock . . . [her] pack caught on the rocks in such a
> manner that she lost her balance and toppled over. Her
> slide was approximately 65 ft. in total length. The slide car-
> ried her through a narrow cleft in some rocks and thence
> down the steep snow slope of the crevasse.

Only badly bruised, she was stranded between the icy walls.

Leaving the Paradise Ranger Station just past midnight, Temporary Ranger Patterson led a crew of five others on the tedious, five-hour, uphill slog. Wright was quickly extracted from her trap. With a thin tarp as a lining for the "cadavar [sic] basket" and sleeping bags on top and bottom, "triangular bandages were used to firmly hold her in position . . . [with] ties around the groin and up at an angle to the sides of the basket to hold her steady."

The rescue team elected to carry her straight down the steep snowfields rather than attempt a dangerous side traverse. "At all times the head was kept up-hill, and at all times . . . a climbing rope, with competent men to anchor and snub the basket, was kept made-fast to the head of the basket."

Almost three years later, Ranger Gordon "Pat" Patterson became the Director of the Army's 87th Mountain Infantry Mountaineering School at Camp Hale, Colorado. He later became one of the key instructors of the Special Mountain Warfare Detachment, which trained British troops in Italy in World War II.

August 11, 1940
Boulder Dam National Recreation Area

AVIATOR KILLED IN LAKE MEAD

LAS VEGAS, Nev., Aug. 11—(AP)
In a newly delivered army airplane, Lt. Laurence E. Wernberg of New York City plunged to his death today in Lake Mead behind Boulder Dam near here.

The B-T13 ship was one of five which Wernberg and fellow officers picked up at the Vulter Aircraft Factory near Los Angeles to fly to Kelly Field, Tex.

Shortly after take-off today for Winslow, Ariz., Wernberg's plane dived into 500 feet of water, a quarter of a mile of the dam.

. . . apparently was having motor trouble and was gliding toward the lake when the plane hit a cable stretching across the canyon about 40 feet above the water and plummeted into the lake. He apparently failed to see [a] large sign on the cable.

Dragging of the lake for the plane and . . . body was started.

—*Arizona Republic,* 8-12-40
(reprinted by permission of Associated Press)

OTHER MILITARY PLANE WRECKS DURING THE 1940s:

On September 9, 1941, a twin-engine B-18A hit the 6,000-foot level of Olympic's Mt. Constance; all six crewmen were killed.

On July 30, 1943, a B-24 slammed into Saguaro's Tanque Verde Ridge, killing all nine aboard; a 510-acre fire was started.

On October 17, 1943, a P-47 "Thunderbolt" fighter fell from 32,000 feet into Shenandoah; its sole occupant was killed.

On April 13, 1944, an Army plane with two onboard crashed into the Given's Creek area of Yosemite; both died.

On February 2, 1945, a twin-engine Navy C-46 crashed into Sequoia; five months later, eight bodies were brought out.

On March 29, 1945, an AT-11 pilot barely survived when he crash-landed onto Death Valley's "Devils' Golf Course."

On June 12, 1946, a four-engine B-29 "Superfortress" hit the Great Smoky Mountains' Clingman's Dome; all 12 died instantly.

August 15, 1940
Crater Lake National Park

RESCUERS USE 3,000 FEET OF ROPE

TWO young men, David and Kenneth, had been pulled off the same cliffs exactly two months before. In a sense it was the park's warmup for what Chief Ranger J. Carlisle Crouch would label as a "most difficult, hazardous and concededly thrilling rescue."

Three 17-year-old boys, tired of taking photos from the top of Garfield Peak, decided to make their way down the 1,700-foot slope to the lake. Shortly after reaching the water, however, their luck ran out. Scrambling along the shore, they were halted by cliffs rising hundreds of feet above the lake. The youths start-ed up one of the most difficult and dangerous ridges on the crater's wall. Devoid of vegetation, it is composed of unstable volcanic ash, small loose rocks, and hardpan clays.

In spite of these obvious hazards, they persisted, doing much of their climbing on all-fours. By nightfall, two had reached a point only halfway up; unable to move, they cried out to anyone above. More agile—or maybe just more nervy—the third boy reached a small sloping ledge 400 feet higher. Trapped now as well, he joined in the chorus. "Help!"

The rescue team, convinced they needed to climb up from the lake, hiked down to the boat landing and the two waiting dinghies with outboard motors. The seven rangers started across the lake, only to encounter perilous, 6-foot, white-capping waves.

After searching at length for a reasonably safe route up, a rockslide some distance away was climbed as far as possible. Then, using a rope, Ranger Foiles was able to reach the same level as the two youths. Having just clawed his way up cliffs composed of treacherously loose rock and now facing hardpan and a deep ravine, he spent what little remained of the night on a narrow over-hang. Daylight . . . rope . . . two down, one to go.

George was up so high—1,000 feet above the water, but still 700 feet from the top—that communications were impossible. From their vantage point on the lake, the rescuers believed it would be easier to lower the boy from the top. Back up the trail . . .

> Looking over the crater wall, down the precipitous and unstable cliffs to this lonely and helpless human form was, to say the least, quite terrifying and discouraging. An effort was made to weigh all of the . . . difficulties and hazards which might be encountered, as well as the fatigued and weary condition of the young man.

Back down the trail . . .

> Ranger Mann elected to act as the lead man with the rope. He was equipped with an ice axe and was able to negotiate the first part of the steep climb in comparative ease. He was followed by Ranger(s) Huestis . . . Miller . . . Hay . . . Douglas . . . Kartchner . . . and Armentrout.
>
> The total rope used in making the climb was 3,000 feet, made up of ½" and ¾" strands. . . . Perfect cooperation of and coordination between the various men . . . along the rope line, coupled with efficient paying out and splicing by Ranger Finch, together with natural mountain-climbing ability, caution, and judgment on the part of Ranger Mann, resulted in reaching Buser exactly at 4:00. . . .
>
> The rescue was effected without any serious injury. . . . Ranger Ordwein received a blow on the head from a small falling rock, while Ranger Branaman's head broke the fall of another rock . . . the first night. Falling rocks, precarious

hand and foot holds, together with inadequate lights make
. . . the Crater at night extremely dangerous; such work in
the day time is sufficiently dangerous.

Superintendent Leavitt stated in his *Monthly Report,* "For sheer thrill, this
was probably the most dangerous rescue we performed on the crater walls."
The location of the boys and the route taken by the rescue party were plainly
visible from several spots east of the lodge. These vantage points resulted in a
banner crowd in attendance throughout the day, cheering the rescue party on
and shouting words of encouragement to the boys.

```
                    May 19, 1941
              Grand Teton National Park
        ----------------------------------------
```

SUPERINTENDENT'S LETTER TO THE CCC

Lieutenant H. C. Leach,
Company Commander,   May 22, 1941
Company No. 5498,
Jenny Lake, Wyoming.

Dear Lieutenant Leach:

I have just read with much interest the account of two
enrollees in your Company who saved the life of a drowning
man on Jenny Lake Monday afternoon, May 19.

These two enrollees, Ashford H. Simmons and V. A.
Cooper, were out on Jenny Lake some three-fourths of a mile
with a rowboat when they noticed a canoe overturn about a
half mile from them. They saw a man struggling in the icy
cold waters of the lake and Cooper, having the oars in his
possession at the time, began rowing as fast as possible in
that direction.

Mr. Simmons states that when they were within about
one hundred yards, the man disappeared under the water
and that when within about fifty feet of the swimmer he
went down for the second time and stayed under water, as
it seemed, at least forty-five seconds. Just as they neared
him, he went under for the third time but Mr. Simmons,
who was in the bow, reached far under the water and luckily caught the drowning man by the hair. The boys had a
hard time getting him into the boat as he was totally limp
by this time, but when they reached the boat landing he
had revived enough so that he could stand. They gave him
hot coffee and wrapped him in blankets and he apparently
suffered no ill effects.

This man was Jim Stevenson, an employee of Boat Operator Reimers, who was trying out a canoe, and the boys undoubtedly saved his life for he would have soon perished in the ice-cold water of the lake.

These boys should be commended highly for their resourcefulness and quick action in this situation, which enabled them to save a human life.

I shall bring this matter to the attention of the Director of the National Park Service at Washington immediately.

Sincerely yours,

Chas. J. Smith,
Superintendent.
cc: The Director
Region Two

August 10, 1941
Mt. Rainier National Park
_-_---

A MOTHER'S LONELY VIGIL

PASSIONATELY praying while dreading the worst, Juney's mother sat impatiently by the telephone. She clearly recalled the nightmare only 12 years before when her husband—and Juney's father—had barely survived a similar fall on the same mountain. (See story of July 2, 1929.) Now she anxiously awaited word of her 21-year-old son.

Leon Brigham Jr., or "Juney" as his friends called him, led the unroped group; all buddies from high school, the five young men were on an overnight climbing trip. Having just finished lunch and on their way down, they came to a narrow snow bridge. "Juney went out to test it with his pole. I held on to his ice ax. Then the snow bridge broke and the ice ax shot through my fingers like a gun." Plunging 90 feet straight down, the boy probably died instantly in the narrow, frozen crevice.

Ascending by moonlight, the team of rangers and mountain guides—Juney's father among them—cautiously scrambled over the rock and ice by headlamp. Without benefit of a trail, their steep route was hazardous and always difficult. They hefted a stretcher, a rope, and survival gear for the unpredictable weather and a 50-pound, "portable" two-way radio.

With one of Juney's shaken friends leading the way, the rescue party easily found the telltale hole in the snow. Rangers Bill Butler and Gordon Patterson were soon lowered down. "[T]he body was frozen by the intense cold at the bottom of the crevasse, and was covered to a depth of eight feet with snow that had been dislodged in the fall. Young Brigham had discarded his shirt and was bare from the waist up." After chopping the boy free of his icy tomb, the task of raising the two rescuers began.

Two ropes were lowered to each man. These the rangers strung through rope belts about their waists and fastened to their feet with loops. The man being brought up would rest his weight first on one foot, then the other. While one rope bore the weight, the party above would pull in the other rope a short distance, then the ranger would switch his weight to the second rope. The procedure, repeated, allowed the men to "walk" out of the crevasse.

With his ashes spread two weeks later on the mountain's summit, Juney, a student at the nearby University of Washington, was the 13th person to die on Mt. Rainier. Professor McClure was the first, when he fell in 1897.

Victims like Juney often partially disrobe—despite their very cold surroundings—as they unconsciously sink into advanced stages of hypothermia and freezing.

```
          October 1, 1941
   Devils Tower National Monument
-----------------------------------------
```

PARACHUTED ONTO DEVILS TOWER

WITH its tiny fuselage glinting in the Indian summer dawn, the Aeronca banked steeply to the north; the silence, with the plane's 65-hp motor momentarily throttled back, was short-lived. Grinning and waving from his perch below the wing, a slightly built Hollywood stuntman nonchalantly stepped backward into 2,000 feet of cool morning air. It was 8:11 A.M.

"Imagine my surprise . . . when Mechanic Heppler came to headquarters with a statement that a man had just parachuted to the top of the Devils Tower." Newell Joyner, custodian of the country's first national monument, had only the day before been discussing just such a publicity stunt. "We decided that it was probably just another rumor; surely there was nobody foolish enough to contemplate such action, 'because how could they get down?'"

To jump out of a perfectly good airplane, let alone aim for a tiny, boulder-studded acre on top of an 865-foot rock pedestal, might seem foolish to most. To the 30-year-old Royal Air Force transport pilot making his 2,348th leap, this was merely business. Not only did Charles George Hopkins hold the world record for the total number of jumps, he also held world records for the longest freefall (20,800 feet), jumps in one day (25), as well as the U.S. record for the fall from the greatest height (26,400 feet). To him a "buck was a buck," whether he was stunting for movies like *Hell Divers and Here Comes the Navy* or teaching combat jumpers for Nationalist China's Chiang Kai-shek. This U.S. veteran of the Battle of Dunkirk was anything but a fool.

Pulling his rip cord a scant 200 feet above and away from the tower's edge, the barnstormer hung in the webbed harness for only 15 seconds. To keep from overshooting the tiny target, he partially collapsed his 24-foot chute early, dropping onto the rocky top. The grimy nylon shroud lines fell twisted to one side of a bush; the patched white canopy settled over another one nearby. Hopkins, massaging a black-and-blue, slightly swollen ankle, waited for pilot Joe Quinn to drop the 1,000-foot rope, sledge, pulley, and iron spike on the plane's next flyby.

Yelling up from the parking lot, Ranger Joyner asked the obvious: "How will you get down?" Years of daredevil cockiness were reflected in Hopkins's reply: "Why worry about getting off? It's no problem, is it?" That was not long before the bulky coil of half-inch manila rope, arching from Quinn's blunder and the plane's momentum, skipped and bounced over the cliff's southeast edge. It stopped on a narrow ledge just out of reach of the luckless parachutist.

Earl Brockelsby was a reptile-farm owner and the promoter of this Rapid City Chamber of Commerce stunt. He released the prepared publicity statement to more than 400 radio stations before learning that Hopkins's descent rope had missed its mark. With something more than a glitch in his plan, he raced to the airport, intent on dropping another line. He found the plane, sans pilot. Not until 4 P.M. was Clyde Ice of nearby Spearfish hired as a replacement. Actually, Ice had been approached several days earlier for the flying job; but he had refused because he felt that the winds were too tricky and the feat was surely destined for failure.

The pilot's opinion proved to be prophetic; strong gusty winds and moisture-laden clouds settled in at 6 P.M. Despite the turbulent air and dangerous downdrafts, however, Ice was able to make several drops; a 2,400-foot line with a grappling hook landed near George. With this aid he was able to retrieve the first 1,000-foot rope; both lines were now terribly tangled. Hopkins, bundled in thin blankets and silhouetted against a beautiful sunset ablaze with reds and oranges, settled in atop the rock pedestal and sorted out the ropes.

Joyner awoke to a dreary morning. Even at 5:30 A.M., he knew fog was rolling across the top of the tower. An early skiff of snow mantled the area. Years later Clyde Ice said, "I kept Hopkins alive on the Tower the days he was stranded there . . . he wouldn't have lived through the first night without the blankets I dropped to him." Hopkins claimed later that the blankets did little good because they quickly became wet from rain and snow.

Headlines called his perch "an Island in the Sky" and solutions to his problem came rolling in. One telegram read: "Drop Hopkins four quarts of whiskey; get him drunk. Then he'll fall off the ledge. The Lord takes care of drunks." As the story spread, some letters contained more serious suggestions and diagrams. In Akron, Ohio, the Goodyear Tire and Rubber Company began preparing its famous blimp for the rescue. Company officials believed that it could hover over the top of the tower and drop Hopkins a ladder from the gondola. A violent storm halted them in Indianapolis. Elsewhere, a newfangled machine being tested by the Navy and called a helicopter was seriously considered but eventually rejected.

Aerial photos and diary notes from the tower's few previous climbers were air-dropped. A third 1,000-foot rope was sent; it missed. Understandably dubious, Hopkins tried to climb down at several likely points but quickly gave up. Finally grasping his plight, he asked for a portable radio, a crossword puzzle, a tarp, more blankets, and a blond. Over the next few days, a tent, fur-lined flying suit, boots, helmet, hot water bottles, portable stove, wood, axe, flashlight, and enough food "to outfit a country store" were dropped to Hopkins. A Wyoming coal company seeking free publicity donated several bags of fuel.

Somehow a fifth of whiskey miraculously survived a drop, but "Devils Tower George" was a teetotaler. No blond ever arrived.

When the stunt's organizers gave up on reaching Hopkins, mountain climbers were suggested. Hopkins was advised to cease any further descent attempts; no dummy, he happily agreed. The rescue now fell to Joyner—a first for both the tower and the ranger.

Unlike Devils Tower, Rocky Mountain National Park near Denver has a long history of complicated, dangerous rescues. Ernie Field, an expert climber who was known as a "ranger's ranger," led many of these missions. In 1940, the year before George Hopkins decided to tempt fate, Field had serendipitously spent three weeks helping Custodian Joyner plan for eventual rescues. Over the years, Field was a cornerstone, a "godfather," to the nation's budding mountain rescue community. He coauthored one of the country's first rescue manuals, taught climbing to the Army's elite 10th Mountain Division, and midwifed the birth of the Rocky Mountain Rescue Group. In 1954 the Army asked him to lead a team for a planeload of flyers enmeshed on a jungle wall inside a South Pacific volcano.

After battling a blizzard all night, Ernie Field and his friend Warren Gorrell, a seasoned mountaineer and licensed Longs Peak mountain climbing guide, arrived at 10:15 A.M. on October 3.

As Field and Gorrell were leaving Denver, Ranger Joyner received a telegram saying, "Unique first descent, need any help completing it? Regards." The signer of the message was a young Dartmouth medical student, Jack Durrance. In 1940, three years after the tower's first technical ascent, Durrance had pioneered what would become the most popular route. Over the next several decades, he would go on to climb many of the world's major mountains.

Field and Gorrell started up for Hopkins 45 minutes after arriving. Climbing cautiously, they were laden with an assortment of gear. Ranger Field remembered, "The first two hundred feet presented no difficulty, but before long we found ourselves gazing up, straight up, some six hundred feet to the nonchalant Hopkins perched on the rim of the Tower's top." Field slipped but slid his way up while Gorrell held the safety rope from below. Ranger Field fell 15 feet, nearly breaking his ribs.

The crux of the "Durrance Route" is a 60-foot vertical stretch about halfway up the tower. It involves two thin, parallel cracks 3 feet apart. Field later recalled:

> We looked at it, and then at each other, and then back up the pitch again. It was difficult, more difficult than either of us had expected. Both of the vertical cracks were too small for any wedging, and there were no horizontal cracks or other handholds in evidence. We both tried to ascend this pitch, frontwards, backwards, sideways, and endways—with no luck. The climb involved friction holding and wedging for a long unsecured vertical distance with no intermediate resting points . . . made mental notes to learn more about friction climbing, established a fixed rope . . . and descended.

Stymied, Field encouraged Joyner to accept Durrance's offer. The next two days, cloudy and wet, saw the climbers preparing spikes and wedges and placing more ropes on the previously climbed section. They watched as State

Patrolman Hendrickson, aided by 20 Boy Scouts, herded the 3,500 curiosity-seekers around each day. The national press, no longer treating this as simply a local publicity stunt, quizzed the rescuers about techniques and equipment.

Hopkins refused an offer by Joyner to have traps dropped to him to catch mice for a scientific field study. The critters were now his constant dinner guests. Hopkins kept "airmailing" notes, informing the mud-bound group far below of his status. "How is everybody down there?—Just eating breakfast, pulse and temperature normal, disposition has been better. Need a good bath and shave. Write me at the same address you know." In another he wrote, "Dear Folksd: [sic] Pardon my fancy stationery, but they are just out of it up here. . . . Boy, it got so cold up here last night and so dern dreary with all that fog I would have gladly settled for a brunette or even a red head."

On Sunday morning, Paul Petzoldt, a veteran Grand Teton climber, arrived. At age 16, he'd made the fifth ascent of the Grand Teton. Later he founded the National Outdoor Leadership School and went on to teach climbing for the next 30 years. Petzoldt was accompanied by Harold Rapp, a 6-foot-10 seasonal ranger nicknamed "Altitude." Both had been lured to the challenge by the 3-inch headlines in the Wyoming newspapers. Escorted from Denver by the Highway Patrol were Merrill McLane, Chappell Cranmer, and Henry Coulter, Durrance's brother-in-law. Delayed a day by weather, Jack Durrance finally joined the circus.

Durrance led the climb most of the way. At 3:15 Monday afternoon, he and Petzoldt shook hands with Hopkins; an hour later the top of Devils Tower seemed crowded with nine people. At 4:35 P.M., after throwing most of the donated stores over the edge and hiding the rest under boulders, they started down. With darkness now upon them, a sound equipment truck from Denver radio station KLZ turned on its large floodlamps; spotlights from two police cruisers were used, as were headlights from several tourists' cars.

Four hours after they began, one nonplussed daredevil, "baby-sat" by eight rescuers, slid from the gloom into the glare. On the edge of the limelight were some of the world's best. Petzoldt had reached 26,000 feet on the First American K2 Expedition; Cranmer and Durrance had just returned from the Second Expedition to the same unconquered peak. Field, Rapp, and Gorrell were veterans of some of the toughest and most demanding rescues in the Rockies. Coulter and McLane had previously pioneered difficult routes on the tower.

Relieved, relaxed, and ever the showman, world parachute record-holder Charles George Hopkins spoke into the waiting microphones.

In 1986 the American Alpine Club honored Dr. John R. Durrance with the prestigious **David A. Sowles Memorial Award** for his major role in the rescue.

```
           October 24, 1941
       Kings Canyon National Park
----------------------------------------
```

FIGHTERS "RAINED" FROM THE SKY

THE squadron of P-40 "Warhawks," tasked with testing the nation's defense system only 44 days before the bombing of Pearl Harbor, was nearly finished with its routine, five-day, cross-country journey. Lifting off from Riverside, the 19 young pilots confidently pointed their sleek, single-engine fighters toward Seattle.

Within two tragically short hours, 4 of them would die in crashes, 4 would bail out over the rugged High Sierra, and 11 would make forced landings. In addition, two bombers soon crashed while searching for the downed fighters. Between October 24 and November 2, the U.S. Army Air Corps suffered 13 plane wrecks in California—with 13 dead and 3 missing.

Weather reports that ill-fated Friday indicated that most of the California skies were solid with heavy fog and clouds. With few electronic aids available, navigation was by direct ground reference using marginal aerial maps. Playing "follow-the-leader," the last man, Lieutenant John Pease, trusted his more experienced commander, Major C. E. Hughes. Climbing to 15,000 feet to avoid the overcast, ground references soon disappeared below the cloud cover. Still dressed in lightweight summer gear, cockpits grew colder; the fliers had neither survival training nor equipment.

After being airborne for less than an hour, the confused crew grew disoriented and the planes separated. Without the telltale earthly landmarks below, their short-range radio communications became useless. Enveloping clouds added to the rapidly growing chaos, and it now became an "every man for himself" race against death.

Without warning, Pease's powerful Allison engine quit. After a restart, it failed again. Pease was the first of four to safely jump. Lieutenants Jack West and Leonard Lydon, forced to leave planes that were quickly losing altitude, bailed out in a blinding snowstorm. Incredibly, the two pilots from Iowa stumbled into each other in Sugar Loaf Meadow the next day. They spent seven more harrowing nights trapped amidst the remote and towering peaks of the Sierra. Along with Pease, they were finally spotted by one of the 22 searching Army aircraft. Lydon's P-40 was never found.

One Warhawk crashed south of Yosemite near Bass Lake. It was so badly mangled that the G.I. dogtags were the only clue to the pilot's identity. Another doomed aircraft was flown by Second Lieutenant Richard N. Long; before his flight orders were changed, this was to have been his wedding day.

In 1959, near Kings Canyon's South Guard Lake at 11,000 feet —18 years after the plane had disappeared—two hikers stumbled across burned wreckage, human bones, and a gold second lieutenant's bar.

June 1, 1942
(pre) Lake Clark National Park

RESCUE TOOK 25 DAYS

ALMOST within sight of Anchorage when last heard from, the B-18 and its four-man crew were over an area marked "unsurveyed" on the maps. The search for the small bomber proved fruitless.

Seventeen painful and labored days later, Sergeants Don Harris and Charles Michaelis struggled into Anchorage. They had crashed into Mt. Redoubt, an 11,000-foot dormant volcano; left behind were their pilot, Lieutenant Ed Clark, and his copilot, Lieutenant Joe Donaldson. Clark had grossly sprained or broken an ankle and Donaldson had a very serious compound fracture of the lower leg.

From the air early that morning, searchers soon spotted the wreckage at the 7,500-foot level. Major Milo Fritz, ordered to lead the difficult rescue attempt, saw no signs of life. But, by two that afternoon, Dr. Fritz, along with a local hunting guide and seven other soldiers, was under way. They bore plasma, glucose, 12 rolls of plaster splints, dressings, painkillers, and two extremely awkward 25-pound Stokes litters. Each man carried 60 pounds and took turns helping with the cumbersome wire-mesh stretchers.

Over the next seven days, the rescue team of nine would endure awesome hardships. Almost immediately after leaving their 30-foot boat, they had to start chopping their way through dense stands of wrist-thick spruce and horizontally growing alders. Then, after leaving the almost impenetrable thickets, they came to meadows of stubby grass growing through 3 inches of water. Dark clouds of mosquitoes and little black no-see-ums covered the tired and frustrated men. After 12 hours of very difficult bush-whacking, they stopped to rest.

In the "Land of the Midnight Sun," rest was both fitful and all too short. One man awoke with his eyes swollen shut by insect bites. They abandoned sleeping bags and precious food. A second man turned back, his kidneys punished by an ill-fitting pack. Determined, the team crisscrossed the freezing Redoubt River several times. Forgotten in haste, extra footwear and vital sunglasses soon exacted a grave toll from the rescuers.

Meadows and rivers gave way to small glaciers. What appeared from the air to be relatively easy walking was actually dangerously steep snowbanks and tortuous crevasses. In the increasingly thinning air, the exhausted men would take five steps and then rest. Winds gusted and clouds swirled around them. Major Fritz pushed ahead, carrying only the urgently needed lifesaving medicine.

On the third day, they reached a pathetic, gangrenous Donaldson; Clark had limped off for help just five days before. Incredibly, 25 days after crashing on a remote, unsurveyed Alaskan mountain, Clark would reach Anchorage—just one day after the rescuers and his much improved copilot.

```
                    June 19, 1942
              Grand Teton National Park
     -------------------------------------
```

ON THE GO FOR 24 HOURS

A PARTY of four, all experienced mountaineers and belonging to the Sierra Club, attempted Grand Teton. As daylight disappeared, Mr. and Mrs. Everett turned around 500 feet below the 13,770-foot summit. Dr. Clyde Nelson and William Rice—one wearing hobnailed boots and the other wearing rubber-soled Keds—continued struggling toward their goal; they soon became the park's first climbing fatalities in eight years.

The Everetts, after spending a bitterly cold night high on the mountain waiting for their companions to come down, reported the two overdue.

With a rescue team, Chief Ranger Allyn Hanks started up to investigate the report. Going as far as they could by horse, the three men then continued up the mountain in the dark.

After considerable searching the next morning, the rangers could "see in the snow field on the southwest side of the mountain evidence that objects of some sort had slid down the snow field." It didn't take long to reach Nelson and Rice.

"The bodies were wrapped in canvas and Chief Ranger Hanks and his men worked all that day under terrible difficulties getting the bodies down over vast snow fields." They had been "on the go continuously for twenty-four hours."

On July 2, 1942, NPS Acting Director Demaray sent letters of commendation to Chief Ranger Hanks "and the men who assisted him."

On July 5, 1943, the clerk of Local Board #-248 of the Selective Service System for Los Angeles County wrote the superintendent to ascertain that William B. Rice, Order No. 2675, had in fact been killed and was "not failing to report for military service for other reasons."

Grand Teton ranger Paul Kenworthy said, "Bill was just too long for the amount of canvas we had with us. We had to leave his feet out." This 20-year-old man was killed on Mt. Owen in 1947.

NPS PHOTO/GRAND TETON NATIONAL PARK

April 1, 1943
Olympic National Park

RESCUERS QUICKLY REMOVED
THEIR BOOTLACES

BUILT in Ohio, the homely, 252-foot, gray freighter now flew the flag of the USSR. Originally christened the *Lake Elpueblo* in 1919, the *Lamut* was bound for Vladivostok out of Washington's Puget Sound. Its Russian captain, mistakenly thinking he was 16 miles farther south on the rugged Olympic coast than he really was, would soon hear the vessel's death knell.

Gripped by mountainous seas and a snarling gale, the 2,700-ton ship and its helpless crew of 54 were driven toward the towering Quillayute Needles, a rocky trap of jagged ocean cliffs. When the "jaws" closed, monstrous breakers quickly turned the transport onto its port beam; the squealing of the shearing hull pierced the howling wind and crashing waves.

Almost freakishly, the *Lamut* was wedged between a 270-foot-high mainland cliff and a long, narrow rocky island. Had it been just a few hundred yards either way, the ship would have been driven safely onto a broad sandy beach.

Frantically the crew tried to launch a lifeboat, but a cable snapped and the bow of the small craft dropped into the raging surf; foaming surge quickly swallowed the one young woman who fell overboard. Frightened, they waved flashlights and fired rifles trying to attract attention in the rain-shrouded darkness.

Although they made a valiant effort, rescue craft were useless on the open sea—they could get nowhere close to the rocks of the "boiling maelstrom." The captain knew they could not get off without help; he also knew they could break up before it came.

Coast Guard Chief Specialist William Nyquist led his 12-man Beach Patrol through the swampy, almost impenetrable forest. High above the roiling waters, they cautiously scrambled across the tricky ground of the wet cliffs.

At dawn, rescuers looked 200 feet straight down onto the dead *Lamut*. Untamed seas smashed at it while the crew huddled on the steep-pitched deck. On one side of a deckhouse, large orange letters painted an ominous message: "1 WUMAN ILL."

Rescuers threw a rope down the cliff; it was short by only a few feet. Forced to improvise, they quickly removed their bootlaces, adding precious inches to the lifeline. Climbing hand over hand across the now anchored route—dangling far above a watery grave—46 men and 7 women escaped death.

Nyquist and fellow-rescuer Frank Kowski eventually returned to their prewar careers as Yellowstone National Park rangers.

May 15, 1943
Shenandoah National Park

"THE BALLAD OF DORIS DEAN"

"**THE** Ballad of Doris Dean" had at least 40 verses; to the tune of "The Death of Floyd Collins," a Harrisonburg hillbilly radio station played them all that summer. The four-year-old had been found . . . alive!

Doris tagged along with her two older brothers when they went for the milk cows at 5 on Monday evening; the boys chased her back toward the house. After putting the animals in the barn, they found she had not made it home. Retracing their steps with their frightened mother, the family frantically looked for the little girl until dark.

Rangers from nearby Shenandoah were called the next morning, and soon the police, neighbors, Forest Service, Boy Scouts, Virginia Protective Force, Soil Conservation Corps, and a host of others began combing the wooded hills and grass-covered glens. Three inches of rain, locally heavy thundershowers, cold nights, and gusty winds reduced the girl's odds over the next several days. Searchers killed 21 deadly rattlesnakes and copperheads; Doris would eventually tell one of the rangers that she had "seen three snakes but had kept out of their way."

An astonishing number of volunteers assisted in the search—1,200—but by the fourth discouraging day, most of them were returning home. Briars and underbrush were so dense that many feared the child would lie hidden in a thicket forever.

Disheartened, the chief ranger went to Superintendent Dixon Freeland and recommended pulling out. Freeland disagreed and told the remaining searchers to go to the top of the highest point and work downward. The chief ranger argued against this tactic, but fortunately for the little girl, he lost.

Doris was found Saturday afternoon; suffering from bruises, scratches, and dehydration, she had walked more than 6 miles from her home in those five fear-filled days. She said that she had "drinked the water from the leaves." Searchers had been very close on several occasions, but the little girl could not call loudly enough to attract their attention. And thus, A. B. Cline's "Ballad of Doris Dean" was born.

> But Doris still is living she is happy now again
> The God who watched above her, took away her pain
> And we will all remember as the future years go by
> That it was only by the will of God, that Doris did not die.
> No man will ever follow the trail this baby made.
> Only the God in Heaven saw where Doris laid
> Her life will have some pleasure, a part of it will be sad
> But little Doris will always need, the faith her mother had.

```
                        May 23, 1943
                  Yellowstone National Park
        ----------------------------------------
```

A FORGOTTEN GIANT . . .
UNTIL YELLOWSTONE BURNED

"**THIS** IS IT! GET OUT!" Half asleep when he heard the alarm, the B-17's 24-year-old bombardier instinctively rolled out of the hatch and, as he fell into space, frantically grabbed for his rip cord.

The Yellowstone fires of 1988 seemed unstoppable when seen on the 6:00 news. For months the nation watched transfixed as thousands of yellow-shirted firefighters and scores of aircraft futilely battled the towering walls of flame. When finished, Mother Nature had "massaged" 794,000 acres. One of her gentler "caresses" uncovered the skeleton of an almost forgotten metal giant, swallowed by brush, erased by time.

Second Lieutenant Roy E. Thompson had received his pilot's wings only the previous November; he and the crew of #42-30260, five lieutenants and five sergeants, along with a passenger, had been en route from California to their home base in Lewistown, Montana. The War Department's official accident investigation reported:

In the vicinity of Reno, Nevada, the pilot climbed to an altitude of 15,000 feet. Shortly after reaching this altitude, rough air was encountered and soon thereafter icing conditions. Somewhere over Yellowstone Park, the pilot ordered the crew to prepare to bail out.... The plane was on fire while in the air. The Bombardier, the only survivor, did not see a sign of the airplane after he bailed out other than two fires on the ground below.

Ranger Tom Ela and his wife, Betty, had just returned from a birthday party when they heard the plane go over. "I went to the window because I knew it wasn't sounding right. We could hear it go into a scream as it went down." Burning fuel lit up the sky.

The B-17, a potent weapon against the war machine of the Third Reich, exploded on impact; it dug a crater 20 feet deep. The wreckage scattered everywhere. A search for survivors, because of confusion over the actual number onboard the craft due to the last-minute passenger, hurriedly began.

Ela remembered, "On the third day, when I climbed a tree and hollered 'Halloooo' for the hundredth time, an answering call came back. He said his name was McDonald, he was very, very cold, and he asked, "Where am I?'"

After wandering through the dense lodgepole forest for two days, Second Lieutenant William F. McDonald began wondering "if he had [had] a nightmare and bailed out by mistake."

For 45 years this B-17—attached to the 2nd Bomber Command, 2nd Air Force, 385th Bomb Group, 548th Bomb Squadron—lay buried and overlooked . . . until the Yellowstone fires of 1988.

December 5, 1943
Kings Canyon National Park

BOMBER LOST IN MOUNTAIN LAKE FOR 17 YEARS

NEVER hinting at any onboard trouble, the young radioman routinely reported in as the B-24's weary six-man crew approached the 14,000-foot Sierra Crest. Minutes later, after a multihour, laborious round-trip training mission to Tucson, the four-engine "Liberator" neared Fresno's Hammer Field.

When it was learned that 22-year-old Second Lieutenant Charles Turvey hadn't landed as scheduled, Captain William Darden, in a second B-24, launched early the next morning to look for Turvey and the first huge plane. This seven-man crew, despite the thick winter storm clouds and the snow showers that swirled around the ridges and peaks of the rugged Sierra, was eager to find its missing sister ship.

Moments after liftoff, as the turbulence abruptly quickened, the search craft's hydraulic pressure failed. Forced to set down promptly on a seemingly snow-covered clearing, Darden ordered his men to make a fast choice: bail out now or crash-land with him in the narrow, meadowlike opening directly ahead.

The copilot and radio operator miraculously walked away from their tree landing, but the plane vanished. "Meadowlike" Huntington Lake, drained for repairs in 1955, would finally reveal the second B-24 and its remaining crew 190 feet below.

On July 27, 1960, Leroy Brock was leading a two-man Geological Survey party along an obscure ridge high above LeConte Canyon. The buck ranger hardly knew that the tiny lake, hidden between the barren granite walls at 11,264 feet, even existed when he first saw the splash of yellow from the oxygen bottles, the parachute canopy billowing underwater, the logbook with the 1943 entry, and the leather boot with the still-preserved foot inside.

The remote lake, nameless and unattractive to even the most avid fisherman, had kept its secret for 17 years. Twisted and broken metal, now hidden by the stunted alpine flowers and large gray boulders, was proof that Turvey and his ill-fated B-24 had crashed near the top of the 12,500-foot ridge and then slid into the water.

Ranger Brock, despite his dive into the submerged wreckage using snorkeling gear, was unable to probe the plane. Only after a special team of Army hard-hat divers was flown in from the Presidio was the mystery of bomber no. 41-28463 and its six crewmen solved.

The father of the 23-year-old copilot, Second Lieutenant Robert M. Hester (for whom the tiny Sierra lake is now officially named), had died the December before the plane was discovered. He had spent 10 summers scouring the jagged peaks for traces of his young soldier-son. "Mountain romance" has it that as Hester was dying he declared, "Now, I'll find out where Robert is."

June 20, 1944
Grand Canyon National Park

"GREETINGS . . . YOU ARE IN THE GRAND CANYON"

AT 20,000 feet and with engines sputtering, the bomber pilot ordered his crew to jump. The young men, shrouded immediately by the midnight darkness and dangling from parachutes they couldn't see, focused on the scattered, tiny lights twinkling afar. Then, as if a giant curtain were being lowered, the lights disappeared one by one. The three jumpers, their link with the world gone, kept dropping—their first hint that they were actually floating into a canyon.

Heralded by national headlines as the **"Greatest Rescue in History of Army Aviation,"** the 10-day epic began after the B-24's five-man crew finished a routine celestial navigation exercise and were headed back to the Tonopah (Nevada) Army Air Field.

Cruickshank was the first through the plane's large bomb bay. He never saw the others above him, nor the ground below him. Smashing into a steeply sloping cliff, he miraculously broke only his right foot. Pain and his perilous position kept the navigator from Massachusetts from stirring until daybreak.

Bombardier Goldblum, ricocheting from rock to rock, "came down within the arms of death when his chute was caught by a jagged cliff." Stopping on a tiny,

3-foot-wide shelf, the Second "Luey" was lucky to be alive. One newsman reported, "If he had unhooked his 'chute and looked around they would have picked him up about 1,200 feet below and carried him out in a shroud. As it was, he spent the night on the ledge in forced uncuriosity." By dawn's light he would climb up his fortuitously snagged parachute to safety.

Embanks wasn't even scheduled for this flight; the instructor aerial engineer took his ill student's place at the last moment. By his own estimate, he delayed pulling his rip cord "about four seconds and floated for 14 minutes" before landing unhurt. Even after the rescue, the corporal from Montana still had the rip cord.

Just as soon as the plane's engines stopped, they started. The "malfunctioning mechanism controlling the propeller's pitch" corrected itself. Nursing the craft slowly along, the pilot landed at the Kingman (Arizona) Army Air Field, 100 miles away.

At first light, Embanks saw "time frozen in rock": a canyon a mile deep and more miles wide, cast in a thousand shades of red and gray. Seeing nothing familiar, he heard himself say, "Embanks, it looks like you're in one hell of a spot." Climbing up 1,200 feet to the plateau he narrowly floated by the night before, he anchored his 24-foot, white canopy down as a signal.

Cruickshank and Goldblum were luckier. They found each other the first thing the next morning when each was heading for Tuna Creek. Using a crutch made from a small tree, the injured navigator hobbled along. When the first formation of 20 search planes flew directly overhead, "Embanks waved everything he could find and even tried to build a signal fire." Engine roar surrounded them, the deafening noise bounced from wall to wall, the planes soon faded from view. "'That,' [Embanks] said, "was probably the most disheartening sight I ever saw.'"

While Cruickshank lay aching in the shade, Goldblum was looking for an escape through the prisonlike canyon walls, but he could find no break in the seemingly endless tiers of cliffs. They spent the night in a bobcat den and used G.I. boots for dipping their first small drink. Although the South Rim, 4,000 feet above, had had a killer frost only a few nights before, the reflector oven–like heat became oppressive where they were. Water soon became critical.

On the third day, Goldblum and Cruickshank spotted Embanks's parachute and made their way toward "his" plateau. Still trapped but at least together now, they could do little but wait and hope.

The first smoke bombs dropped from high overhead told them that their desperate signals had finally been seen. On their sixth day in the gorge, they were dropped K-rations, blankets, water, a walkie-talkie, and a note: "GREETINGS . . . YOU ARE IN THE GRAND CANYON."

> Those rations . . . tasted like a 4-inch prime tenderloin steak garnished with mushrooms. They were constantly running out of water, too. Luckily, Embanks found a spring, but it was about a 4-hour climb down the side of the plateau. They'd drink the spring dry, climb back up the plateau and drink parachuted canteens dry, then go back and drink the spring dry again.

Although easily supplied, the stranded parachutists wanted out, but except for a handful of river-runners and a few rangers off at war, no white man had ever set foot on this terribly isolated section of the Colorado Plateau. Efforts escalated.

Two rescue parties from the South Rim started down. In one was Dan E. Clark, chief boatswain mate with the U.S. Coast Guard. The 19-year veteran of the seas went along to shoot a cable 300 feet across the river with a line gun. In the excitement that beset the rescue, they had forgotten that someone needed to be on the other side to grab the cord; the three trapped men couldn't climb down the cliffs to the river. The plan was abandoned.

A dismantled, hard-hulled boat was packed from the rim down a steep, twisting trail on the backs of a long string of government mules. After scouting the river a little closer, the "would-be sailors" realized that what looked like ripples from a mile above were, in fact, 10-foot waves. This idea was abandoned too.

Colonel Donald B. Phillips, commander of the nearby Kingman Army Air Field, spent two hours flying circles and taking aerial photos of the cliffs, looking for a way through. Immediately upon landing, he ordered a convoy of men and materials to the North Rim to establish a base from which a new rescue attempt would be launched. He thought he had found a "chink" in the canyon walls.

Few men knew the area like Ed Laws; the 56-year-old park ranger had spent the last 30 years working at the Grand Canyon. He was summoned from Toroweap Ranger Station, an isolated post 50 miles to the west, in the hopes that he could somehow feel a way through the thousands of feet of ragged and broken cliffs.

Dr. Alan A. MacRae was savoring his 14th consecutive summer exploring the secrets of the inner Grand Canyon. The theology teacher from Delaware spent his hard-earned vacations immersed in the grandeur and mystery of the park. Volunteering his unique expertise and claiming he could find a way to the men, he was told his help was "unnecessary." He was assured that almost as they spoke, a rescue boat was being assembled on the river bank and the three trapped men would soon be reached.

Hiking across the canyon, MacRae and his new wife neared a trailside telephone near Ribbon Falls when he was intercepted. "Where's MacRae? Put him on the phone immediately. We've got to talk to him about a rescue. The attempt from the South Rim has failed!"

Laws and MacRae worked well together. The two veteran canyoneers forged their way into the depths of the canyon. "When they went around above the talus, they found that a sheer cliff of 150 feet stopped them from using [the aerial photos] . . . but across the canyon . . . they saw some greenery and went around to see whether they could camp with water." Not only did they find water, but they also came to a thin break in the red limestone wall just below their spring. A well-defined deer trail led almost directly to the downed airmen.

The two-man rescue team spent 20 hours climbing down the 10-mile, often vertical route. Except for Cruickshank's limp, the climb back to the 9,000-foot North Rim passed without incident. John Handford, a CBS employee on active duty as an Army public affairs specialist, recorded meeting the rescuers on the North Rim.

> At 10:30 we were all standing in a clearing near the canyon's
> rim wondering if we were in the right place when we looked

down a trail and saw five men walking towards us. People just stood with their mouths open. Finally somebody said, "My God! It's them!" and the spell was broken. Everybody rushed forward and started talking at once. . . . Interviewing the men was like trying to get a coherent report from a Ladies' Aid meeting, but we got enough dope to make a story.

Ranger Ed Laws was "promoted for exceptionally meritorious service" on January 3, 1947, for his part in the mission.

The three men proposed that the place where they had been trapped be named "EMOGO Point": E (Embank), MO (Cruickshank's nickname), and GO (Goldblum).

```
                     July 4, 1944
            Joshua Tree National Monument
    ----------------------------------------
```

PILOT PUTS ON PARACHUTE *AFTER* BEING THROWN OUT OF BOMBER

ALONGSIDE two other B-24s, Second Lieutenant George B. Smallfield and his nine-man crew lifted off from March Army Air Field at 8:30 A.M. for gunnery training. Instructions to the three bombers had included practicing V-formation flying to and from the nearby range. Having finished their routine mission, the planes re-formed at 10,000 feet and started for home. Smallfield, a 22 year old from Cleveland, led; Lieutenant Gerald H. Solheid flew the formation's right wing; and another B-24 was to the left.

Solheid soon turned the stick over to his copilot, Lieutenant Edwin Darland, directing him to drop back and loosen up their formation. Considerable radio traffic between the planes ensued, including joking with the lagging bomber about being in the rear and urging them to close in. As they tightened the pattern and approached the lead craft, Darland pulled the nose up to reduce speed, accidently putting the large plane into a skid to the left. Unable to correct the error, he slid swiftly toward the 10 men in the sister ship.

Passing just above the other plane, Solheid's left wing chopped Smallfield's right vertical stabilizer off. Both bombers went out of control. After his seven crewmen safely bailed out, Solheid and his copilot recovered sufficient stability and successfully forcelanded. Ten miles east of Palm Springs, the second plane had suffered several fatal blows.

The large, four-engine bomber quickly went into a violent loop, and Second Lieutenant Smallfield was ejected through a jagged hole in the cockpit. In a freakish, million-to-one incident, the pilot frantically grabbed for a still-packed parachute tumbling through space beside him and somehow managed to attach the chute to his harness. He pulled the rip cord just before hitting the desert floor . . . safely.

Unable to exit the spiraling B-24, the other nine crew members of the ill-fated bomber never had a chance.

```
           August 1, 1944
      Death Valley National Monument
```

THE SOLE SURVIVOR

IT was 8 A.M. when the large bomb-bay door flew open and the unconscious 17-year-old gunner fell 18,000 feet. Coming to just in time, Private Newton J. Steven pulled his rip cord while parts of 17 men and two B-24s rained down around him.

Chief Park Clerk Novak and his bomber-pilot brother looked up when the first six noisy B-24 Liberators flew over; in the vast expanse of Death Valley, the almost-deafening roar of 24 powerful engines ricocheted everywhere. The men were saying good-bye; one was remaining where the heat later that month would reach 123 degrees, and one was rejoining the terrible war in the South Pacific.

The sound of the droning motors above the not-too-distant Trail Canyon soon recaptured their attention: A lone bomber tightly banked, slowly circling a column of thick, black smoke just beginning to rise above the barren desert hills.

Colliding in midair, one plane had exploded and burst into flames while the other monster war machine, now rapidly spinning, had ripped apart. A huge burning crater, 30 feet across and 12 feet deep, was created in the rocky soil by the falling debris.

The two 4th Air Force pilots involved in this tragedy, Second Lieutenants Ernest J. Chapman and Sam B. Johnson, had a total of 805 flight hours between them.

Hastily joined by the disbelieving Novaks, the lucky young parachutist searched the harsh, boulder-strewn washes of the land for other favored souls. Private Steven, #-37347983, was the sole survivor of this midair disaster.

The hottest temperature ever officially recorded in the Western Hemisphere was in Tomesha ("ground afire"), as the natives called Death Valley, on July 10, 1913. It was measured by Oscar Denton, caretaker of the Furnace Creek Ranch.

> On that day that I recorded the greatest heat ever registered—134 degrees in the shade—I thought the world was going to come to an end. Swallows in full flight fell to the ground dead, and when I went out to read the thermometer with a wet Turkish towel on my head, it was dry before I returned.

```
          September 18, 1944
       Mt. McKinley National Park
```

IT TOOK 44 MEN 43 DAYS

ONE of the most extensive—and needless—rescue efforts in the archives of the NPS was for 19 men aboard an Army C-47. Piloted by a civilian from

Northwest Airlines, the twin-engine aircraft was on a routine, two-hour flight from Anchorage to Fairbanks.

The large transport fell apart as it tumbled 1,600 feet down the steep wall—both wings were ripped off, the fuselage lay in thirds, and an engine was embedded in the blue-white ice. Ironically, only a hundred yards to the west of the 11,000-foot ridge, not a single obstacle blocked the skies to Fairbanks; 140 miles away.

Over and over again, weary aircrews skimmed the ice and snow desperately seeking just one sign of life. It took three days before a reflected glint from the wreckage was seen by the discouraged searchers; the plane lay scattered on the unmapped slopes of Mt. Deception, 16 miles east of 20,000-foot Mt. McKinley.

Lieutenant General Emmons insisted that a recovery be launched, despite the obvious lack of survivors, the logistical nightmare of moving 44 men for four weeks over two dozen miles of broken glaciers, and the menace of a rapidly approaching winter.

Brad Washburn, recognized as the world authority on Mt. McKinley and also a member of the "C-47 Crash Expedition," would say years later, "There is little doubt that a good dog team and three competent climbers sent out immediately after the accident could have discovered twice as much in ten days as this behemoth of a party was to accomplish in five weeks and at incredible expense."

Park Superintendent Grant Pearson, a successful early climber of McKinley, became technical advisor. He was told, "If you do not care to lead this detail as a civilian, we are quite prepared to see to it that you are immediately drafted into the armed forces and given the assignment as a direct order from your superiors."

The Army provided trucks full of tents, stoves, food, ropes, ice axes, and other climbing gear—some useful, some not. They had "portable" radios weighing 26 pounds, one caterpillar bulldozer, two wounded personnel carriers, and two 3,000-pound over-snow jeeps. A sister ship of the one they sought would drop supplies.

After weeks spent bridging hidden crevasse fields, climbing dangerous ice walls and avalanche-prone slopes, suffering cold short days and suppers of fried Spam, and dodging "showers of fresh fruit and gunny sacks full of rolls," the C-47 Crash Expedition found not a single body.

Grant Pearson received the **Army Medal of Freedom** in January 1947 from Major General George Craig for his leadership and untiring efforts on this expedition. He died on September 8, 1978.

There are still 19 young men entombed somewhere on the 11,000-foot-high frozen ridge of Mt. McKinley National Park's remote Mt. Deception.
BRADFORD WASHBURN/
BOSTON MUSEUM OF SCIENCE

```
January 20, 1945
Saguaro National Monument
```

AIRMEN PEAK—A MEMORIAL

MAJOR Lorin D. Geil and his crew of four were on a routine navigational training flight from Texas to Davis-Monthan Air Field in the southern Arizona desert.
Nearing the end of their three-hour flight, they started to dodge scattered, fast-
moving snow squalls. Ten minutes out, the pilot contacted Tucson for landing
instructions; his hard-earned landing skills were never used.

Some 250 feet from the top of Wrong Mountain, the B-25D North American
"Mitchell" medium-bomber slammed into the appropriately named peak; fuel
and wreckage exploded over a 4-acre area.

Totalling at least 75 dead, this was just one of the region's 28 known military plane crashes since 1941, due largely to the heavy wartime training and
the islandlike nature of the scattered high mountains around Tucson. The
Rincon Mountains, the scene of this accident, witnessed four such wrecks, with
22 dying during World War II.

In 1986, retired Air Force chaplain Lawrence Tagg wrote to the United States
Board of Geographic Names: "The airmen involved in those accidents were not
big names or heroes in any dramatic sense, but surely they were as much casualties of the hot and cold wars that this country has been in as any other persons." He proposed that Wrong Mountain be renamed "Airmen Memorial Peak."

Tagg's request was denied because the name "Wrong Mountain" had
existed since at least 1910. Through the cooperation of the Forest Service,
however, a peak in the nearby Catalina Mountains was later officially named
"Airmen Peak." The Board of Geographic Names said it was "in honor of all airmen who have died in military aircraft accidents in the greater Tucson area."

```
February 7, 1945
Big Bend National Park
```

THE PARK'S FIRST SAR . . .

THE Park's first SAR albeit minor, was for an Army training plane from nearby
Marfa Air Base. "It was out of gas and merely 'bellied down' on one of our gravel
ridges. No one was injured, only minor damage to the plane and the park lost a
dozen or so bunches of greasewood."

The park's first real SAR was for George Ball, a recently tested veteran of
the Battle of Okinawa. On July 10, 1948, the 22-year-old Cornell student, along
with his friends, Evans and Mayes, day-hiked to the fire patrol cabin at Boot
Spring. Hunting for rare insects, Ball and Evans continued on to the South Rim,
where the two amateur zoologists separated. Evans, thinking Ball would catch
up, returned to their camp in the basin.

By 2 the next afternoon, Ball had still not shown up; a report was soon given
to Chief Ranger Sholly. Within minutes, he and Fire Control Aide Robinson were

off on horseback. "Messengers were immediately sent out to all rangers in out-lying districts to report to headquarters, bringing the saddle and pack stock from their districts. Plans were made to leave early the morning of the 12th for the South Rim area."

For 24 hours, mounted rangers and local concession employees scoured Juniper and Boot Canyons for clues. Nothing . . .

Twelve miles away, the former marine walked out onto the Glenn Springs' Road near Nugent Mountain. He had "lost his landmarks."

Engaged in patrolling the occasional border skirmish with Mexico, proba-bly the first airplane to land in what is now Big Bend National Park was an Army craft at Glenn Springs in 1920.

December 3, 1945
Crater Lake National Park

"SKULL, HUMAN: 1 EA"

IN 1970, the Navy aircraft accident investigator signed the chief ranger's offi-cial government property receipt for a "SKULL, HUMAN: 1 EA." Finally, after lying forgotten in a small, wooded side canyon for 25 years, the 22-year-old pilot from New Jersey would receive the military tribute due him.

Ensign Frank R. Lupo, along with six other Air Group 5 "Hellcat" pilots, lifted off from eastern Washington's Naval Air Station Pasco at 9 A.M. and headed south to Red Bluff. With a grand total of 480 hours of flying time, only 74 of which had involved the sleek, 2,000-hp F6F, the young airman was less than three hours away from vanishing for a quarter of a century.

> At 1010 Flight Leader checked with Redmond Radio Range Station & received CFR clearance to Klamath Falls & Red Bluff. At 1035 flight encountered lowered visibility in light snow flurries & returned to Redmond. Redmond again reported Klamath Falls & Red Bluff both well above contact conditions & CFR conditions enroute. Flight departed Redmond at 1100 & ran into alternate areas of haze, light snow, fluries [sic] & clear areas. Ceiling was about 6000', 1500 to 2000' above terrain. At about 1145, flying about 500' above terrain, flight suddenly ran into fog & snow so thick that it was impossible to see ground. Pilot was last seen or heard from at this moment.
>
> —Navy Accident Report

The history of this easily accessible fighter—with its blue wing and faded white star visible through the brush and its machine gun embedded silently in the rocky cliff face above—was clouded by the passage of time. Rangers, who had long known of the wreck and had even used its pieces for park proj-ects, had assumed that the military knew about it.

In August 1970, off-duty Seasonal Ranger Dave Panebaker went on a short hike to glimpse a chunk of World War II. "I went a ways into the canyon until I came to a level area with many large mountain hemlocks. While looking for pieces of the plane I happened to look on one side of a fallen tree where I saw a skull." Panebaker soon returned with military investigators.

> We scoured the debris pile and found no identifiable serial number for the aircraft. Then we found a portion of the instrument panel with holes where the compass must have been located and found a small piece of folded paper. It contained the aircraft serial number which ultimately led to the pilot.

In September 1970, the Navy found the young ensign's still-living mother; 25 years after World War II had ended, she finally learned the fate of her missing son.

```
February 2, 1946
Yosemite National Park
```

SKIER, LOST IN SIERRAS 11 DAYS, FOUND ALIVE

Rangers train to look for lost skiers from Yosemite's Banger Pass, circa 1941.

YOSEMITE, Feb. 19—William P. Jacobs, 25-year-old college student lost in a Sierra blizzard 11 days ago, was found alive by park rangers this afternoon. Even the youth's parents had abandoned hope . . . and given up their search. They left here yesterday with plans to return in the spring and seek his body, when the deep snows melt.

A Forest Service (Park Service) emergency cache of blankets and a toboggan enabled Jacobs to construct a windbreak, without which he doubtlessly would have perished. When he disappeared on February 3 while skiing at Badger Pass, veteran trackers said no man could survive more than two nights without shelter.

Jacobs was ravenously hungry and was suffering from two frozen toes, but still had the strength to walk, according to his rescuers, District Ranger Duane Jacobs (no relation) and Assistant Chief Ranger Homer Robinson.

Jacobs . . . said he became separated from his skiing companions when he accidentally lost his glasses. He is quite near-sighted and while trying to find his way back to the Ski Lodge became engulfed in a blizzard. The storm was one of two which Jacobs endured in his eleven days on the mountain. During the 36 hours of the first storm, 32 inches of snow fell. At night the temperature dropped to 5 degrees.

Fifteen rangers searched a 12-mile area. . . .

—*San Francisco Chronicle,* 2-20-46
(reprinted by permission)

July 9, 1946
Yosemite National Park

DEATH AT YOSEMITE WATERFALL

VETERAN TRIES TO RESCUE BOY, BOTH ARE SWEPT OVER CASCADE

YOSEMITE National Park, July 9—Yosemite's beautiful Vernal Falls became an instrument of death today when a boy and a Navy veteran were swept over the brink of the spectacular 325-foot cascade.

The victims were Keen Freeman, 11, son of Dr. Walter Freeman, internationally known neurologist of Washington, D.C. and Orville Dale Loos, 21, of Dayton, Ohio.

The sailor had made a heroic but futile rescue attempt and went over the falls with the lad gripped in his arms.

Witnesses, who watched spell-bound as the tragedy unfolded, said it began when the Freeman boy dropped his canteen into the water while walking with his father along the edge of the swift stream that feeds Vernal Falls.

As he reached for the container, young Keen slipped and slid into the rapids. He was about 60 feet above the falls. The fast current began dragging him toward the brink.

Loos, recently discharged from the Navy, was walking nearby with two other sailors. All three vaulted a guard-rail and plunged after the boy.

Loos managed to reach him while he was 15 feet from the edge. The sailor grabbed the youngster, fought his way to nearby rocks and began a heart breaking struggle to drag himself and his burden to safety.

But the slippery surface affected the hold. His grip broke.

With the boy in his arms he was swept over the falls and vanished in its towering plumes of spray.

Vernal Falls plunges down a sheer perpendicular escarpment approximately as high as San Francisco's Russ Building. At its base the cataract hammers itself into a cauldron of massive boulders throwing out a spume and windlike burst before the water rushes out of the huge rocks in white rapids.

After 11-year-old Keen dropped his canteen in the pool above this 325-foot waterfall, he slipped into the torrent. He and 21-year-old Orville Loos went over. This photo was taken the same month. Notice World War II servicemen on top.
YOSEMITE NATIONAL PARK
RESEARCH LIBRARY

Hours after the tragedy occurred, neither body had been recovered. Dr. Freeman, Park Superintendent Frank Kittredge, nine rangers and a number of vacationers were making the search.

—*San Francisco Chronicle*, 7-10-46
(reprinted by permission)

Freeman was recovered on July 15, and Loos on July 20. Loos received the **Carnegie Hero Award** for trying to save the young boy.

August 13, 1946
Zion National Park

TAKING OFF HIS SHOES AND SOCKS . . .

ROGER Clubb left them alongside his canteen and lunch. The 19-year-old Zion Lodge cook, intent on reaching the top of the Great White Throne, kept scrambling, even after his two wiser friends gave up and turned around. Miscalculating the time, he was forced to spend a long, cold night on a narrow, sloping ledge; he used his belt to tie himself to a small bush.

The rescue party reached the base of the cliff below the young man at noon the next day and decided that

the only safe way to get up the slope was to work their way up by drilling holes in the sandstone about three inches deep and inserting pins therein. They continued . . . up the face of the cliff, drilling a hole above them, then placing the steel with the rope in it, pulling up, resting a foot on it, drilling another hole and so on.

The men alternated in this arduous work by going up and down the rope. At 2:00 P.M. only four holes had been drilled and it looked as if Clubb would have to spend another night on his perch . . . easier going soon allowed several jumps of from 10 to 20 feet without drilling. . . . They all finally reached a small shelf about 75 feet below. . . . Ranger Dawson threw a rock with a string attached by which means Clubb drew a heavier rope up which he attached to the bush. The boys played safe, however, and drilled additional holes right up to the ledge which all four reached about 5:30 P.M. . . . nervous but in good spirits and made the descent although very shaky, with a man in front and back.

Under "Mountain Summit Climbing" in the *Rules and Regulations of the National Park Service* in effect at the time, it states, "When the superintendent deems such action necessary he may prohibit all mountain climbing in the park or monument." Superintendent Charles J. Smith proposed the following.

> . . . all climbing of any mountain, or major feature, in Zion
> National Park, not reached by a regular established trail, is
> prohibited. Provided however; that in special cases a permit,
> in writing may be granted to qualified mountain climbers by
> the Superintendent . . . shall not grant permission, as stated
> above, until he is satisfied that all members of the party are
> properly clothed, equipped, and shod, are qualified physical-
> ly and through previous experience to make the climb.

On October 31, 1946, Acting Director Hillory Tolson rejected the proposed rule.

August 24, 1946
Sequoia National Park

AFTER SETTING A CRUDE PINE CROSS

"**AFTER** setting a crude pine cross at the head, Ranger Hester and I [Wallace] dug the grave. After a few words at graveside . . . we buried Dr. Wm. Penn Tuttle, Jr., at sunset."

Tuttle, a 27-year-old World War II veteran, was last seen at 5 P.M. on the summit of 14,086-foot Mt. Russell; the peak, among the last in the Sierra to be scaled, is lethal for the unprepared.

When Tuttle had not returned to camp near Crabtree, his younger brother and a friend spent the next day searching for him. Failing in their efforts, they finally notified Acting District Ranger Wallace. Seasonal Ranger Dick Hester, dispatched at once from the Kern Ranger Station, hiked all night and then painstakingly trailed the missing man to his signature in the register box on top of Mt. Russell.

"About ⅛ of the way down the north face (which drops from 14,000 to 13,000 feet in elevation) Tuttle's tracks disappeared, where his footing had apparently given away in the loose, shifting, decomposed granite at this point." Hester, no stranger to the subtle but fatal dangers of the peaks, "narrowly escaped Tuttle's fate" several times himself.

Using binoculars, the young ranger scanned the dusky-white cliffs. Nearly 700 feet below, he saw a darkened splash of inert color. The loose, ball bearing–like granite sands on the rock's sloping edge had not been easy on the young mountaineer.

An all-but-forgotten memory now, Dr. William Penn Tuttle Jr. rests beneath the pines near the Crabtree Ranger Station, eternally shrouded by the purple shadows of the peaks above.

December 10, 1946
Mt. Rainier National Park
----

32 MARINES VANISH

BOUND for Seattle, the six C-47s lifted out of San Diego early that day; crossing into southern Washington, the twin-engine Marine transports soon hit a storm so severe they were driven to using their instruments entirely. So solid was the front—high winds at all elevations, heavy snow and extreme icing conditions—that four of the planes were forced back to Portland; one aircraft limped into Seattle; and one, with 32 young marines aboard, vanished.

Major Robert V. Riley's last radio check indicated he was over a point 75 miles west of Mt. St. Helens. Because of a 70-mph crosswind of which he was unaware, Riley was actually nowhere near where he had reported. Search officials, in calculating air speeds, ground reports, and allowing for reasonable discrepancies in the crew's plotted course, grimly determined that the World War II veteran could easily have struck 14,410-foot Mt. Rainier without ever seeing the cloud-shrouded peak, just 50 miles south of Seattle.

For the next three days, both ground and air searches were frustrated by the storm—5 feet of snow fell at the 9,500-foot elevation, the level at which the plane was believed to have been flying. For at least a month the effort was emotional and intensive. The many reports received were investigated, but no clue was found. Numerous aerial photos of the mountain were taken and analyzed carefully, while the Navy had men and aircraft continuously assigned to the area.

By July 20, eight months after the plane had vanished, the peak's lower southwestern slopes and watersheds had been thoroughly investigated from both the air and the ground. Early on the 21st, Bill Butler drove his car to the Tahoma Creek Campground and started upward. Just as he had diligently done for months, the assistant chief ranger methodically trained his large binoculars on the glaring whiteness.

Finding nothing on Success Glacier, he crossed over and climbed to the crest of Success Cleaver, dodging deadly rocks rolling from above. Not a thing. Laboring to 9,500 feet, he once again lifted his glasses and began scanning South Tahoma Glacier. This time, however, shapes didn't fit and colors seemed out of place.

Butler, appointed a permanent ranger in 1936 by President Roosevelt for the Fadden rescue (see story of January 20, 1936), knew the mountain as few others did. By moving to another vantage point, he could make out chunks of twisted plane just beginning to show above the melting snows. After taking compass bearings and orienting himself, he began the 10-mile hike back to his car.

A ground team, still unsuccessful in pinpointing any wreckage from the air and after reviewing enlarged aerial photos of the area taken the day before, was dispatched on July 23. A radio truck and two walkie-talkies were brought in by the Navy while the park installed a similar field set. A base camp was established 4 miles from the alleged wreck site.

Early the next morning, three roped teams of rangers and guides started for the place Butler had seen. The determined searchers, with sleet and snow falling most of the day, carefully picked their way between hidden crevices and confusing ice pinnacles.

The plane was scattered over 400 yards; 5 feet of the winter's snows still covered much of it. A serviceman's health record and uniform were found; insulation and tangled lengths of wire lay about. Unrecognizable shreds of metal were discovered embedded in glare ice, some as much as 50 feet below the surface of the glacier. The plane's identity tag was removed from the tail assembly. For two days crevasses were searched, but although the efforts were exhaustive, no bodies were found.

As news of the discovery spread, parents and relatives of the dead soldiers arrived in the park. Late on the 25th, because of the extreme perils involved—including the continual bombardment of falling rock from surrounding walls—the team was pulled out. When the decision to abandon the search was announced, however, the families naturally wished to know that every effort had been made to find their loved ones. Arrangements were made for them to meet with Butler and the other team members. Satisfied, they departed, knowing that all that was possible had been done.

On August 18, the regular patrol to the crash site discovered a major section of the plane; containing 11 bodies, it was at the 10,500-foot level on the South Tahoma Glacier. The Army Mountain Troops were to determine if the dead could be safely evacuated. A continual barrage of rocks—one described as high as a room—fell from the cliffs. Seasonal Ranger "K." Molenaar recalls "snuggling into the wreckage with the bodies to avoid the almost constant rock falls."

Memorial services were held at Round Pass on August 24 and a plaque commemorating the tragedy has since been placed. The 32 young Americans, ruled too risky to remove in 1946, remain entombed in the ice to this day.

For his persistent and untiring energies on the mission, Assistant Chief Ranger Bill Butler received the Navy's highest civilian award, the **Distinguished Public Service Certificate;** the DOI's **Distinguished Service Medal;** and a pay increase of $2.41 per week. He was given $5,000 by the grateful families but returned the check unendorsed.

A personal letter from Secretary Krug read, "Your extraordinary act in rejecting a large monetary reward, actually placed in your hands, impresses me as an outstanding illustration of the high caliber of men who find their way into public service."

```
             June 20, 1947
        Yellowstone National Park
----------------------------------------
```

BURIED, THREE RESCUERS DIE TRYING TO HELP

IT was a summer evening: The sun had disappeared and headlights came on, but drivers couldn't see. The road whitened rapidly; temperatures plunged to 10 degrees, winds hit 60 mph. Drifts, running-board deep, brought vehicles to a crawl. Before most of the travelers realized it, they were trapped on 11,000-foot Beartooth Pass.

A quick-moving and deadly blizzard swallowed vehicles on the highway between Cooke City and Red Lodge. For more than 24 hours, the 15-foot drifts marooned 70 summer-clad travelers. That day, heroes were born and heroes would die.

As soon as the road crews knew of the storm's severity, the pass was closed. Two plows advancing slowly from the east broke down 5 miles short of their goal. En route from the park side, a third one, a large three-auger SnoGo, slid helplessly into a snowbank. Drivers worked frantically, but nothing moved.

As night passed, car engines starved, sputtered, and died. People huddled together for warmth; one man used a hot-water bottle and rubber tubing to siphon gas from a useless snowplow to keep his family warm. The windchill was extreme.

A doctor who was pulling a trailer made the rounds of nearby cars. He found an expectant mother and a sick baby and crammed them into his small trailer. He went out again and again, looking for others who needed help.

At dawn—the three snowplows broken down—a frantic call went out for help.

Bob Helm, a national ski patrolman and ex–Army ski trooper, jammed food, coffee, and clothing into his rucksack. Plunging into the deep snowbank at the "road closed" barrier, he and a companion began their slow march toward the stranded vacationers. The 10-degree temperature and furious winds bit and blinded the volunteers.

Hours later, fighting the storm all the way, they "reached the drift covered trailer . . . found 17 persons, nine of them children, huddled around its tiny stove." Helm returned to Red Lodge for manpower, food, and more equipment. Rounding up several toboggans and a crew of cowboys, he started back up. Travelers were pulled, coaxed, and herded through the drifts. Everyone was accounted for . . . except three.

Rescuers literally fell through a drift onto the roof of a buried pickup truck and found the three missing Yellowstone snowplow crewmen. In a futile attempt to provide help for the dozens of stranded motorists, Vernon E. Kaiser, John P. Baker, and Richard N. Huckels had suffocated to death in a sealed truck cab.

October 24, 1947
Bryce Canyon National Park

FLIGHT 608—BAGGAGE FIRE ABOARD

"WE are . . . coming to Bryce Canyon—smoke filling cabin." At 19,000 feet with 52 people in his care, the captain faced a pilot's greatest fear: fire. It was 12:21 P.M. and aviation's second-greatest disaster to date was less than seven minutes away.

A $750,000 sister ship of President Truman's "Independence," the four-engine DC-6 was serviced and readied to leave Los Angeles at 8:35 A.M. One of 46 similarly new crafts, the United airliner was routed over Las Vegas, Grand Junction, and Omaha; it was to arrive in Chicago five hours and 46 minutes after takeoff.

Five minutes after 42-year-old Captain Everett L. MacMillen's strained voice was simultaneously heard in Los Angeles, Salt Lake City, and Denver, his second message came over the airwaves: "Tail-fire is going out. We may get down and we may not." An urgent teletype message was sent to the small Bryce Canyon Airport: Prepare for an emergency landing!

"Flight 608—sending blind, approaching strip. Think we have chance now." MacMillen, a veteran of 15 years, along with 35-year-old copilot George Greisbach, nursed the burning craft over the deep sandstone canyons of southern Utah. Greisbach, an Army veteran with 5,000 flight hours and two years with United Airlines, was a last-minute replacement for the sick, regular first officer.

Agonizingly, another minute passed by. "We may make it. Think we have a chance now. Approaching the strip." Moments later, one last shout was recorded from the cockpit: "The tail is gone!" Captain MacMillen's watch stopped at impact: 12:27:30.

Airport personnel were at their homes having lunch when the message came in. Yelling to his wife to call the park for all possible help, C. B. Graham and eight airport employees, armed with all the fire extinguishers they could grab, rushed toward the field and the rising black column of smoke.

Wreckage and bodies were scattered over an area 800 feet wide and 1,500 feet long, 1 mile south of the runway. With the exception of one baby boy "later determined by the medical examiner to have been born at the time of the impact . . . born, breathed and died," the 47 passengers were beyond recognition.

Over the next few days, more than 100 officials searched the burnt wreckage and the long flight path for bodies, mail, valuables, and clues. A wooden lath snow fence was erected to keep the estimated 12,000 onlookers and souvenir-hunters out of the area.

A month later, a similar but nonfatal accident revealed that the tragic midair fire had resulted from a gas leak in the cargo hatch.

March 12, 1948
(pre) Wrangell-St. Elias National Park

"THERE IS NO POSSIBLE CHANCE FOR SURVIVORS"

THIS brief radio message sent by a weather observer in one of the world's most remote places summarized the fate of 30 people.

The three seasoned flight officers in command of the chartered Northwest Airlines DC-4 had collectively logged more than 17,500 hours. Their cargo—24 seamen of Caltex Oil—had just delivered a large tanker to China. Flight 4422 was flying from Shanghai to New York, the "great circle route," when it hit 16,208-foot Mt. Sanford.

Witnesses from as far as 40 miles away reported a "terrific explosion during the night followed by flames falling down the mountainside." One Civil Aeronautics Administration employee, stationed in isolated Gulkana as a radio weather observer, took a crude bearing on the distant red glow by measuring "the exact angle with a pencil supported against a door jamb." A fellow worker then flew his own tiny, single-engine Luscombe over the area in an unsuccessful search for the source of the loud report. Both men were later recommended for raises for their initiative.

Once the aircraft was reported missing, the 10th Rescue Squadron launched a B-17 from Elmendorf AFB and a C-47 from Ladd Field that night; eight P-51s and two more C-47s were also soon deployed. A helicopter was dispatched—if not an Alaskan first, this would be at least among the earliest such uses for helicopters. Early the next morning, the mangled wreckage was spotted; the airline logo could be seen on a small but intact piece of the tail. -

Having struck the ice-covered cliff at full throttle and exploding on impact, the blazing wreckage had slid over 2,000 feet into a small glacial cirque. Resting at the base of a three-sided, 3,000-foot avalanche slope, it was both too inaccessible and too hazardous to reach, even for ski-equipped planes or dogsleds. The brother of one victim, a 29-year-old ex-paratrooper, volunteered to jump into the crash site and "then figure a way out." He never went.

Five days later, as a Northwest airliner circled high above the isolated, 11,000-foot-high crash site, people of Protestant, Catholic, and Jewish faiths conducted final rites for the 30 souls below.

Investigators from the Civil Aeronautics Board concluded that the dreadful mishap was due to "the pilot's failure to see Mt. Sanford, which was probably obscured by clouds or the aurora borealis or both while flying a course off the airway."

Buried by decades of snow and avalanches, pieces of the large four-engine aircraft are still occasionally seen. Over the years, rumors have surfaced that gold and important World War II papers lie buried there. As recently as 1989, a Northwest Airlines 747 captain tried to reach the wreckage from on the ground. No one has . . . yet.

July 21, 1948
Lake Mead National Recreation Area

Q: HOW LONG WILL A FOUR-ENGINE, 101,000-POUND B-29 FLOAT? A: JUST LONG ENOUGH!

THROTTLING back on the huge aircraft, Captain Robert M. Madison had just completed the bomber's last low pass at 1,600 feet when the World War II veteran with more than 163 combat and 3,335 total hours looked out and saw his outboard engine on fire. At 230 mph and wedged tightly between 5,000-foot mountains, Madison had few real options; ditching in the waters below seemed like a good idea at the time.

John W. Simeroth, a Bureau of Standards employee, was almost finished with his three-hour atmospheric research mission. He and the Superfortress crew were measuring cosmic rays with highly sophisticated electronic equipment from Johns Hopkins University.

Copilot Lieutenant Paul Hesler, also a veteran with 250 combat hours and a Distinguished Flying Cross, later recalled:

> The surface of the lake was just like a piece of glass, not even a ripple. This made it difficult to judge how far above it we really were. We landed on the lake going too fast, and bounced. We went up about 200 feet and then landed on the lake. When we first hit we knocked three engines off the plane.

Counting heads according to standard abandon-ship procedure, the pilot should have found five men, not four, huddled on the wing—the radioman was missing. Knowing his plane was rapidly sinking, Captain Madison swam back into the shadowy, nearly full fuselage to find Sergeant Rico already afloat. Within moments of dragging the unconscious crewman out to the almost submerged wing, the huge, four-engine plane disappeared into Lake Mead.

A startled TWA pilot, glancing down from his airliner, instantly recognized the bright green distress marker he saw below from his own recent war days. Circling lower, he waggled his wings to Captain Madison and his fellow survivors who were frantically waving from their little life raft; they had been adrift for five hours.

After only 497 hours of use, the giant B-29 Superfortress, #45-21847, sank into 300 feet of dark blue water. The cause for the fire was never determined. Due to a drought, the plane was located on August 6, 2002, by local divers.

October 5, 1948
Olympic National Park

THE FIRST HELICOPTER INVOLVED
IN AN NPS SAR

THE first helicopter involved in an NPS SAR was not the rescuer, but the rescuee.

Newspapers reported that the Army chopper out of McChord Field was flight-testing equipment when its engine failed. The pilot tried to set the ship down in a small meadow on the edge of Upper Lena Lake, when a gust of wind blowing through the pass took the tiny machine and dumped it upside down in the water about 40 feet from shore. Totally submerged, it rested with its wheels up.

The three crewmen, a detachment of the two-year-old Air Rescue Service, had been "rubbernecking"—watching the body recovery of 17-year-old Robert Thorson. An Eagle Scout and local high school student body president, the teenager had fallen about 30 feet to his death the day before while descending in bad weather off Brothers Mountain just east and outside of the park.

The area's newly formed Mountain Rescue and Safety Council, now mobilized for its first full-scale mission, was carrying the dead Bremerton youth out when the aircraft "swooped low over" them. "The climbers said they saw the craft dip behind a near-by peak and believed at the time the vehicle had crashed."

The crew, suffering only minor injuries after flipping the helicopter upside down in Upper Lena Lake, was rescued the following day by Park Ranger William D. Webster and a contingent from the Coast Guard. Superintendent Preston Macy, in an October 25 memorandum to the regional director, wrote, "The plane is completely submerged under 6 feet of water, and from our viewpoint that is the place to leave it. It is so located that a relatively small explosive charge would move it into deeper waters, which can be done at any time if felt desirable." Even decades later, much of the helicopter could still be seen.

Olympic's first use of a helicopter for an actual SAR was on Lake Crescent on June 20, 1949.

> A coast guard helicopter and forest [park] rangers were searching Friday for two sport fishermen missing from a fishing skiff. . . . The coast guard was informed that the missing men are Les Getchell, 40, and Wilbert Girt, 31, both of Port Angeles. The skiff was discovered by two boys Wednesday, the day after the two men launched the craft on the south side of the lake. Their car and trailer were found near the same spot.

April 27, 1949
Hawaii National Park

THE FIRST HELICOPTER
ACTUALLY USED ON AN NPS SAR

THE first helicopter actually used on an NPS SAR had to fly into an active volcano.

Lieutenant Stephens and his wife turned off the paved highway near Kilauea Crater sometime after midnight. A stranger to the area and unable to find the way back, Stephens left his car to orient himself. Waiting until daylight, Mrs. Stephens walked anxiously to nearby Kilauea Military Camp to report her husband missing. Joining forces, the NPS and the Army soon started to search.

Superintendent Oberhansley and Ranger Barton hiked to the crater floor to scan the 500-foot walls with binoculars. After four hours of seeing nothing, they rejoined Chief Ranger Hjort and Colonel Boardman searching near the couple's car.

Rangers and volunteers used ropes to descend into a number of narrow and extremely rugged volcanic "cracks of unknown depths," more than 100 feet deep. Hjort lowered himself over the edge of the deep crater to search the cliffs below.

By the next morning the search had escalated to more than 50 volunteers. A small party led by Ranger Orr hiked back into the crater to scan the black cliffs again. An L-5 scout plane, prison bloodhounds, and an Army helicopter soon joined in.

At noon and because of a slight shift in the sun, one spotter located what appeared to be a body one-third of the way up the black cliff. With Ranger

Gordon Bender as an observer, the small, two-place helicopter launched, and within minutes they could see someone on the wall waving a white flag. This proved to be a volunteer who had made a very daring and extremely hazardous climb up the loose volcanic rocks to the body of Lieutenant Stephens.

Navy Rear Admiral W. G. Tomlinson would later write Chief Ranger Frank A. Hjort: "[T]he willingness of the Hawaii National Park Service to continue the search, as personified by your efforts, in the face of seemingly insurmountable difficulties, sets it apart as being unusually devoted to public service."

The world's first helicopter "mercy mission" took place on January 3, 1944. Coast Guard Commander Frank Erickson (USCG #1), at the controls of a small Sikorsky R-4 helicopter and battling severe winds and a snowstorm, flew plasma to the Navy's USS *Turner* in New York Harbor, the scene of a horrible explosion injuring more than 100 men. The disaster took place just offshore of what is now Gateway National Recreation Area.

June 28, 1949
Yosemite National Park

YOSEMITE MEN HONORED FOR DRAMATIC RESCUE

YOSEMITE National Park, Oct. 17—The presentation of citations for meritorious service and certificates of honor to

Few National Park Service rescues generate awards, although many deserve them. Here, rangers lower one of two bodies from a climbing accident on the cliffs of Yosemite National Park in 1973. AUTHOR'S PHOTO

Assistant Chief Ranger Duane D. Jacobs and District Ranger
Marshall B. Evans for their rescue of two lost girl hikers in
1949 was one of the highlights of yesterday's National Park
Service conference.

The awards were presented by Dale Doty, assistant secretary of the interior.

A statement signed by Secretary of the Interior Oscar L.
Chapman said two men "performed a most courageous deed
in maintaining a persistent search from June 28th to July 2,
1949, for two young women lost in the back country of
Yosemite National Park." The girls were Miss Patti Thompson,
22, and her sister Joan Thompson, 18, of Palo Alto, both of
whom survived the ordeal as a result of the successful search.

Jacobs and Evans were commended for their "unusually resourceful tracking, exceptional ability to traverse
almost impossible terrain, and the sustained expenditure of
extraordinary physical effort. . . ."

Patti, a San Jose State College student, was found first
in an almost impenetrable part of Tenaya Canyon, with a
broken ankle. She had spent two nights without food.

Searchers headed by Jacobs and Evans picked up the
trail of Joan, a Mills College student and followed it for three
days over 10 miles of rock, brush, forest and broken country.

Joan, however, was found accidentally by three volunteer searchers just before the party reached her. She was
stranded on a ledge above Snow Creek Falls.

The girls were employed by the park service during the
Summer.

—*San Francisco Chronicle*, 10-17-50
(reprinted by permission)

"Buck" Evans and Duane Jacobs were recognized for "a courageous deed"
and became the first NPS employees to be honored with the Department of the
Interior's second highest tribute, the **Meritorious Service Award**. In addition
to silver-embossed certificates, they received silver medals.


```
                July 8, 1949
         Grand Canyon National Park
   --------------------------------------
```

"IF I WERE TO DIE TOMORROW,
I WOULD WANT TO DIE ON THE RIVER"

THIS was 79-year-old Bert Loper's reply when his doctor advised him to stop
running rivers. The doctor soon got his wish.

Born in 1869—the year Major John Wesley Powell made the first documented trip through the Grand Canyon—Loper had rafted the Colorado River in

its entirety. After more than 7,000 miles of white-water rafting over the past fifty years, destiny gave him one last date with the mighty Colorado.

The party's inflatable raft, as well as their other two small wooden boats, were well behind Loper's *Grand Canyon* as he neared 24.5 Mile Rapid. As they entered the mounting rollers, his one passenger would later report that Loper "appeared to be frozen in position." With a long history of heart trouble, the almost-octogenarian may have already been dead when his boat smashed into the madly boiling tail-waves and flipped over. Motionless in the water, the "Grand Old Man of the Colorado" floated out of sight.

Heavy-hearted but resigned to the death, Loper's friends searched the rocks and eddies for him. Sixteen miles downriver they found the *Grand Canyon*, but not a trace of Loper. The irreparably broken vessel was dragged above high water and in a salute born of generations of explorers before them, this final link to an earlier era of river pioneers was eulogized. On the boat's bow they painted this simple epitaph:

> Bert Loper
> The Grand Old Man of the Colorado
> Born July 31, 1869   Died July 8, 1949
> Near Mile 25.

In 1975 a bleached skeleton was found at the mouth of Cardenas Canyon. The remains were identified as Bert Loper; for 26 years he had rested deep in the shadows of the canyon. Then his earthly remains were taken from along the river he so dearly loved and placed in a cemetery in Salt Lake City.

Flown by Jay Deming of Palo Alto, this chopper performed the first National Park Service medevac. This is the second recorded helicopter landing in Yosemite. The first failed in its attempt to rescue 12-year-old Terence Hallinan two days before.

YOSEMITE NATIONAL PARK RESEARCH LIBRARY

His boat, for years a poetic memorial to a man who was "one with the river," was vandalized and eventually demolished by countless rafters over the years.

July 31, 1949
Yosemite National Park

PARK SERVICE'S FIRST
HELICOPTER MEDEVAC

RESIDENTS of San Francisco awoke to these headlines:

HELICOPTER TRIES TO SAVE SF BOY HURT IN YOSEMITE
YOSEMITE NATIONAL PARK, Aug. 2—A stripped down helicopter left Fresno this morning on a rescue trip designed to take it over dangerous peaks in an effort to rescue a 12-year old boy [Terence Hallinan] who is lying badly injured at Benson Lake, 30 miles north of the floor of Yosemite Valley.

Chief Ranger Oscar A. Sedergren today expressed some doubt the helicopter, which will have to fly at an altitude of 10,000 feet to reach the lake will be able to make it.

Sedergren was right to be skeptical—it couldn't fly that high.

On his second try, Knute Flint reached Tuolumne Meadows, the largest open space in the Sierra. He had "difficulty in making a takeoff and his craft bounded back to the ground several times before he could get away." With considerably more room and better takeoff conditions at Tuolumne than at the 8,150-foot-high Benson Lake, retired Army major Flint declared that "it would be impossible for him to get into the air with the boy's added weight in his craft."

After a brief consideration of landing a seaplane near the still-unconscious lad, a second helicopter was located; disassembled, it was hauled in on a flatbed truck that night. Piloted by Jay Deming and belonging to United Helicopter of Palo Alto, the two-place Hiller 360 lifted out of White Wolf at 4:30 the next morning. To save weight it was stripped of its battery and much of its gasoline. The tiny machine was already 4,000 feet above its altitude rating.

Forty-five minutes later, with the boy propped up on pillows beside him, Deming experienced even more excitement: Forced to dump 30 gallons of gas at the lake to compensate for the 100-pound boy, he was flying almost on fumes when he became lost.

A group of about 25 persons who kept vigil in White Wolf heard the helicopter, which was not in sight, bypassing the meadow and going in the wrong direction. Hastily gasoline was poured on three piles of brush and flames were sent skyward. Deming saw the fires, circled back to the meadow and landed safely with the injured boy.

After lying unconscious on the shore of Benson Lake for most of five days and four nights, Terence finally transferred to the waiting ambulance. He is reported to have said, "My head hurts and my throat is sore. But boy! Was that helicopter nifty."

Terence survived childhood and became a lawyer in San Francisco.


```
              October 9, 1949
        Rocky Mountain National Park
    ------------------------------------
```

SEARCHERS BELIEVE TWO A & M BOYS HAVE PERISHED IN ICY MOUNTAINS

ESTES PARK, Oct. 12—The icy treachery of the mountains has claimed two more young adventurous lives.

This was the almost certain conclusion tonight as the frost-bitten, exhausted, wind-lashed party of 15 Colorado A & M students came back into this tense little town after a 12-hour search for their missing college comrades.

. . . missing since last Sunday from what was to have been an initiation hike over the Continental Divide from Grand Lake, four miles from here.

These wind-burned and snowblinded students, who had spent 21 hours in fruitless search the day before, had been joined by Park Rangers and the 14th Regimental Combat Team of Camp Carson. . . .

They searched every cabin and shelter house in the deep drifted area. They had inched their way up to the top of 12,300 foot Flattop Mountain.

They had scouted the flanks of rugged Hallett and Taylor Peaks. They had cut steps for themselves across Tyndall Glacier, while the winds almost ripped the ice axes from their hands.

They had put one foot after another, to the very top of the Continental Divide against better than 60-mile-an-hour winds.

But nowhere did they find a trace of the two youths who had gone out so hopefully last Sunday morning in an effort to qualify for the Colorado A & M Hiking Club.

ODDS SEEM HOPELESS

As they started the wind increased in intensity and before they were far along the timber trail, flakes began falling.

But they plunged ahead. They were young—and youth does not have the same fears of those who have been punished by the mountains.

The wind grew heavier. It was snapping pines, rolling boulders from the ledges. But finally they stumbled to the door of the North Inlet Ranger Station.

—*Rocky Mountain News,* 10-13-49
(reprinted by permission)

Seven days, 1,240 man-hours, and "an estimated 1,488 miles" of searching produced nothing. David Devitt and Bruce Gerling had disappeared.

Helicopter SAR has come a long way since its first use in 1949. Here a Kirtland Air Force Base pararescue man performs search duties from the rear of a "Jolly Green Giant" on a 1989 search. KEN PHILLIPS PHOTO

CHAPTER 6

1950-1959

> In the event of any persons being
> injured or lost, or in distress, Rangers
> shall do all in their power to render
> assistance, and this aid shall be cheer-
> fully and promptly rendered at any time
> of day or night, and it shall be done
> without reward with those benefitted.

—Yellowstone Park Ranger Manual, 1931

VALOR RECOGNITIONS

ALTHOUGH bravery was occasionally acclaimed prior to this time, the 1950s were the decade of the "Hero Award." In addition to the Department of the Interior's **Distinguished Service Award,** the **Unit, Meritorious Service,** and **Valor Awards** were established.

An exhaustive search in June 1949 for two missing sisters eventually earned Yosemite Rangers Marshall "Buck" Evans and Duane D. Jacobs **DOI Meritorious Service Awards** on October 16, 1950. Evans and Jacobs, recognized under the same provisions of 1946 Public Law 600 that established the **Distinguished Service Award,** were the first NPS employees honored with the DOI's second highest tribute. In addition to the silver-embossed certificates, they each received a silver medal for their "courageous deed."

During the Thanksgiving weekend blizzard of 1950, 19 missionaries in a twin-engine C-47 crashed into Grand Teton's 12,549-foot Mt. Moran. Ranger Blake Vande Water and Paul Petzoldt, a local climbing guide, braved winds and avalanche conditions and boldly attempted the first winter ascent of the treacherous peak. When they reached the blackened site, they found no survivors among the few charred pieces of wreckage. The DOI accorded the **Distinguished Service Award** to Vande Water. Petzoldt, not a federal employee, hired temporarily as a "laborer-foreman," and paid $1.50 per hour, was presented with the **Conservation Service Award,** the DOI's highest civilian acknowledgment, on May 20, 1952.

On December 8, 1953, a **DOI Unit Award** was bestowed on 12 men from Sequoia and Kings Canyon National Parks for the 1951 rescue of one fisherman and the body recovery of another. This was the first NPS Unit Award for valor—in any form. The commendation, presented to Superintendent E. T. Scoyen by Secretary of the Interior McKay, used "citation" and "award" interchangeably.

As a follow-up to this mission, but received more than four years later—May 24, 1955—Rangers Thomas Adams, Richard Black, Richard Boyer, and Sequoia National Park's contract physician, Dr. Raymond Manchester, were presented with **Unit Award Certificates** for the "extraordinary risk which you all took to reach the injured men, in complete darkness. As a result, the final hours of Mr. Crawford were eased and no doubt the life of Mr. Brazil was saved." Between the time that first Unit Award was earned in 1996, the DOI has bestowed 26 similar SAR citations in 17 parks of the NPS.

A year after Secretary McKay honored Sequoia, the DOI's second Unit Award was earned by the Grand Teton Mountain Rescue Team—the first of five it has earned to date. That nine-man team, led by now-retired ranger Doug McLaren, was cited for "courageous rescue efforts involving personal risk" for the August 16, 1952, SAR of James Ayer. Less than another year later, they won their second **Unit Award**. A 22-year-old woman fell at the 13,000-foot mark on Grand Teton and broke her back. This time the incident took 27 rescuers more than 36 hours to complete. It was also the first time that rangers had used painkilling drugs to aid the victim of an accident. Her thank-you letter to the park expresses her feelings.

> although I can quote the doctor on the good condition you kept me in, I can't quite tell you how grateful I am for both the good handling [and] your cheerful and uncomplaining attitudes. . . . How I admire the character and the individual and collective skills that made the whole rescue such a darned good job.

Finally, in 1955, the **Department of the Interior Valor Award** was created. Criteria for nomination have not changed and remain very simple: The candidate must "demonstrate unusual courage involving a high degree of personal risk in the face of danger" and "be an employee of the Department of the Interior." The **Valor Award** was bestowed on two DOI (non-NPS) employees for the first time at the 15th Honors Convocation on April 16.

On May 30, 1956, a proud and long tradition in NPS SAR was started when Rangers Frank Betts, Robert Frauson, Jerry Hammond, and Norman Nesbit became the first National Park Service employees to earn the **Department of the Interior's Valor Award.** These four men, working long after dark and along treacherous and rocky cliffs, saved the life of a 17-year-old novice climber who had fallen several hundred feet onto a 3-foot ledge on Rocky Mountain National Park's remote Hallet Peak. It wasn't until the 18th Honors Convocation of April 23, 1957, however, that the team of young rangers received their tribute. Also sharing the stage that day was Cape Hatteras National Seashore Seasonal Ranger Jack W. Cahoon, who received the **Valor Award** from Assistant Secretary of the Interior Chisolm for saving a drowning man from a turbulent surf.

Since 1956, when the first NPS employees received **Valor Awards**—a citation signed by the Secretary of the Interior and accompanied by an engraved gold medal—this prestigious appreciation has been granted fewer than 200 times within the National Park Service.

Rescuers fought nightmarish summer heat and extremely tricky turbulence and displayed precision flying skills while working the tragic midair collision above the remote eastern end of the Grand Canyon, which killed 128 people on June 30, 1956. For their efforts, more than 30 airmen from Arizona's to Huachuca and Luke Air Force Base received numerous awards: At least five received the military's famed **Distinguished Flying Cross.**

MILESTONES OF THE 1950s

1950	The 182 units in the NPS receive 33,252,589 visitors. There are 52 fatalities: aircraft (19); vehicular (14); drowning (13); falls (4); accidental shooting (1); and unknown (1).
June 30, 1951	Crashing just feet outside of Rocky Mountain National Park and after NPS search, United Flight 610 is found with all 50 passengers dead.
1952	Grand Teton has 1,186 registered climbers: 390 try for summit of Mt. Rainier, 264 make it (no accidents); 109 reach summit of Mt. Olympus; 1,625 ascend Longs Peak; 750 register for climbs in Yosemite, compared to 569 in 1951 (only one minor accident); Zion registers one climber; 19 people reach top of Devils Tower; and the first ascent of Dinosaur's Steamboat Rock. NPS's Natural History Division in Washington continues to coordinate mountain-climbing activities.
November 7, 1952	An Air Force C-119 with 19 onboard crashes on Mt. Silverthrone in Mt. McKinley National Park: all are killed.
Spring 1953	First recorded use of scuba in an NPS area: Death Valley's isolated Devils Hole.
February 15, 1954	Personally requested by the Navy, Hawaii's Chief Ranger Ernest Field travels to South Pacific for body recoveries from military plane wreck inside an extinct volcano.
1955	Fewer than 300 people have floated down Grand Canyon to date.
April 24, 1955	First NPS use of scuba for fatality: Lake Mead.
Fall 1955	Boy Scouts in Seattle begin organizing for SAR; they are nucleus for nationwide Explorer Search and Rescue (ESAR) program.
June 30, 1956	Over the Grand Canyon 128 people die in world's second worst aviation disaster after 1953 crash in Tokyo.
July 1, 1956	Federal government's National SAR Plan is implemented.
July 1957	First North American Grade VI rock climb (most difficult) is completed: Yosemite's northwest face of Half Dome.
September 23, 1957	First NPS "Ranger School" begins in Yosemite.

MILESTONES OF THE 1950s

September 30, 1957	John M. Davis is appointed NPS's first chief ranger in Washington, D.C.; he will vacate on October 31, 1959.
1958	Grand Teton rangers publish *Mountain Search and Rescue Operations*, the most definitive how-to book on SAR to date.
June 7, 1959	Mountain Rescue Association is started in Mt. Hood, Oregon. Mt. Rainier National Park is original member.

June 17, 1950
Grand Canyon National Park

RESCUE CAME. WELL, SORT OF . . .

PUSHING off from Lee's Ferry on June 12, the Hudson-Marston Colorado River Expedition was attempting to break its own 280-mile downriver-running record of five days and 10 minutes set the previous year. They were trying for a round-trip record as well. The 19-foot, 125-hp *Esmeralda II* as well as the Chris-Craft speedster, the *Hudson,* were state-of-the-art. Both boats, designed to survive the incredible bashing expected by the Colorado's huge waves and unseen boulders, would all-too-soon be tested.

Composed of veteran river-runners, including Ed Hudson, Dock Marston, Joe Desloge, and Wilson "Willie" Taylor, the small flotilla experienced relatively few problems the first three days. Nearing the 100-mile mark, however, the situation changed.

Taylor was thrown out of *Esmeralda II* into Lower Tuna Rapids; swept downstream, his neck caught in the boat's drifting towrope. Not realizing this, the second boat crew also threw out a rope. Like a diabolical cartoon, the second line also wrapped around Taylor's neck. Marston motored back upstream, unknowingly dragging the poor man along underwater.

"Guess I am the only man to be hanged twice in the Colorado river and live through it!" That Willie Taylor was not even seriously injured, let alone drowned or hanged, is a testimonial to his immense good luck. Several generations of river-runners now know this rapid as "Willie's Necktie."

The *Esmeralda II* actually suffered more than Willie, being irreparably damaged when it hit rocks in the rapids. Not wishing to risk all seven men in the 19-foot *Hudson,* the boat's namesake and his 18-year-old son got out on a beach. The *Esmeralda II,* the first powerboat to go down the river, was set loose. The Hudsons, now with sleeping bags and food, waited to be rescued.

Rescue came. Well, sort of . . .

Dock Marston's wife, Margaret, along with Mrs. Ed Hudson, had trained their binoculars on the short stretches of river visible from the South Rim. One boat disappeared behind a bluff and did not reappear as soon as they believed it should. Knowing the trip schedule, the women felt something was amiss; Mrs. Marston would later learn that her husband had only stopped to fish.

The Arizona Helicopter Service had opened its doors on the South Rim only three weeks before the record river-running attempt. Consisting of two single-passenger B-1 model choppers, the young company wanted a toehold in the aerial sightseeing business. Now, with Red Carson at the stick, Margaret Marston flew into the complex canyon to relieve her concern. After a long search among the dizzying buttes, they spotted the Hudsons and their SOS.

"Sunday afternoon we saw a helicopter coming down toward us. But it ran out of gas and set down on a ledge 1,000 feet above us. Half-an-hour later a second helicopter . . . came down to our level."

The second machine refueled the first, and then both landed near father and son. The senior Hudson would remember his flight out.

We were making a left turn and had just come up over the brow of a plateau when the motor sputtered. We reached the plateau 1,000 feet above with about 100 feet to spare. Our forward motion stopped but the rotors cushioned our drop. When we hit we bounded sideways down the hill. The tail broke and bounded upward. The rotors hit and the tail assembly was spread all over the Grand Canyon. One of the blades saved us from turning over.

The Grand Canyon's first helicopter rescue—and its first helicopter crash—proved expensive. The *Esmeralda II* cost $3,500, the aircraft rentals $700, and the insurance company paid over $9,000 to lift the wrecked chopper out of the mile-deep gorge.

"Necktie" Willie's good luck continued. Four years after nearly "hanging," he died of a heart attack deep in the canyon he dearly loved. He is buried along the Colorado River at Mile 44.5.

Other NPS Helicopter SAR Firsts

Mt. McKinley—Andy Ryan, suffering from frostbite, is picked up by a contract helicopter near McKinley River on July 13, 1953.

Kings Canyon—A man injured when a horse fell on him, is picked up in Sugar Loaf Meadow by a Coast Guard helicopter on July 3, 1954.

Rocky Mountain—The search for a climber on Mt. Craig, killed on August 15, 1954, involves use of a small private helicopter.

Mt. Rainier—During the week of August 19, 1956, the search for a lost 13-year-old boy involves a helicopter from the Coast Guard.

Yellowstone—A five-day search for two concession employees, lost on June 25, 1956, involves a helicopter from Malmstrom Air Force Base.

Grand Teton—Dr. Philip Nice is lifted from Grand Teton's "Wall Street" on June 25, 1960, by a private helicopter from Greybull, Wyoming.

Great Smoky Mountains—A search for two lost Boy Scouts on December 30, 1961, involves a helicopter, although an Air Force ship picked up the two pilots of a crashed Air National Guard jet fighter on June 21, 1958, from the ranger station at Proctor.

Glacier—Climbing alone in July of 1963, a Blister Rust employee is lost and never found. Helicopters from Malmstrom Air Force Base are used.

November 21, 1950
Grand Teton National Park

MISSIONARY PLANE WRECK—21 DIE

ALL life in the *Tribesman II*—a twin-engine C-47 that smashed into cloud-shrouded Mt. Moran at 175 mph—ceased at 4:40 P.M. After clipping its right wing on a huge boulder, the 76-foot craft ended 1,000 feet below the top of the 12,549-foot peak; on board were 21 ill-fated souls, two only six months old.

Founded in 1943, the New Tribes Mission consisted of 450 dedicated, non-sectarian Protestants whose guiding principle was "reaching new tribes until we've reached the last one." This tiny band of the faithful was en route to Montana for a Thanksgiving religious rally and then on to South America to proselytize.

In Venezuela the previous June, 15 fellow missionaries were killed, ironic-ally aboard the *Tribesman I*, the mission's first plane. Sympathetic purses soon opened and within weeks $28,000 was raised for a second ship. Cy Lowrey and Bob Cramer, recent Pacific Theater B-17 veterans, now piloted for a holier cause.

Six-month-old Mark squirmed in his mother's lap; a teacher, Donna Wetherald was Brazil-bound. Her baby never knew its father—he had been at the controls of the mission's first plane. Edna Griener, with her five children, was headed to Bolivia; her mate, too, had died in that earlier disaster so far from home.

Bright but brief, the bomblike fire roughly pinpointed the accident. And so, despite plunging temperatures, a blizzard forecast for the next day, and the fact that this rugged mountain had never been scaled in winter, Chief Park Ranger Paul Judge knew a rescue team would have to try to reach the crash site.

Plane Hits Wyoming Peak
Scant Hope Held for 21 Aboard

This is the second plane wreck within six months for the New Tribes Mission, a sect dedicated to missionary work in South America. The first accident was in Venezuela, in June 1950.
COURTESY OF THE DENVER POST AND DON STERLING

With veteran climbing ranger Blake Vande Water leading, Merle Stitt, Richard Lange, and James Huidekoper, carrying only first-aid gear and survival essentials, started up. In reserve were five Air Corps Pararescuemen ready to drop onto the frozen mountain if needed. Storm and gale-force winds beat them all back.

Paul Pétzoldt, an internationally recognized climber and co-owner of the local mountain guide service, led the second attempt at the rugged peak. Having made more than 300 ascents in the area since 1924, the 43-year-old knew this rugged realm better than anyone. He and Vande Water, with three Air Rescue Servicemen stationed midway to operate a radio-relay camp, com-menced their frigid labor.

Just before dark on the 23rd, a search plane high overhead spotted burnt, mangled metal a considerable distance from where the two seasoned climbers were headed. At 1 A.M., after the Army's two-way radio equipment failed, Rangers Ashley, Huidekoper, and Lange took off on skis to catch Petzoldt and Vande Water. After the three battled their way through waist-deep drifts all night, they passed the new details on to the advance team of rescuers. Changing course toward the now-confirmed sighting, Petzoldt and Vande Water made a difficult, risky traverse to the northeast ridge, where they set up a windswept, forced bivouac. Seasoned but stressed, the two weary climbers made it to within 300 yards of the horror. Darkness forced them back for another night.

On November 25, after hammering in metal spikes to inch up a particularly icy and treacherous set of cliffs, they reached what little remained of the large plane. As they feared, there were no survivors—they found only part of one charred body. After 90 minutes of notes, photos, and reflections, they descended.

At the park's preliminary board of inquiry the next day, Petzoldt said, "Using my experience as a mountaineer as a background, I recommend to the National Park Service that any attempt to remove material from the wreckage or even to climb again to the wreckage this winter is taking an unjustifiable risk." At the request of the Civil Aeronautics Board, "it was decided that mountain climbing on the Northeast Ridge of Mount Moran would be prohibited" until the board could make an on-site investigation. (The area actually was closed for five years.)

Ranger Vande Water and Glen Exum, Petzoldt's partner in the guide service, climbed to the site on July 13, finding 8 to 10 feet of snow still present. On August 5, after allowing for added melt, an 11-man party returned one final time.

Guides Petzoldt and Exum were in charge of the climbing; Rangers Vande Water and Dick Emerson were responsible for the personal effects and disposal of the remains; Doctors F. D. Yoder and De Witt Dominick would identify the deceased; Ralph Johnson and Carl Peterson were investigators for the State Aeronautics Commission; J. Ruskin Garber and Cliff Martz represented the New Tribes Mission; and George Atteberry was the total press pool. Without the snow and ice the effort proved easier and few difficulties were met.

Only 17 of the 21 victims were ever accounted for and the remains were laid to rest in a nearby deep crack. A quiet, simple tribute was paid by the Reverend Garber; the year before, the *Tribesman I* crash had claimed his wife. Even today, a fitting shrine—the plane's tail—rises as a memorial from the rocks; still faintly discernible is the mission's painted logo: a jungle native with drawn bow.

On December 2, 1950, Paul Judge, Paul Petzoldt, and Blake Vande Water were entered into the *Denver Post* **Gallery of Fame.**

On September 27, 1951, Ranger Vande Water was given the DOI's highest recognition, the **Distinguished Service Award.** Petzoldt, although "officially" earning $1.50 per hour as a "laborer-foreman" on the rescue, was not a park employee and was therefore granted the DOI's highest civilian recognition, the **Conservation Service Award,** on May 20, 1952.

```
              March 2, 1951
       Kings Canyon National Park
    ----------------------------------------
```

GRECIAN TRAGEDY PROVES WRONG . . . OR DID IT?

GREEK mythology confers safe passage to those who travel to either side of Scylla or Charybdis—but certain death for those seeking to pass between the fabled rocks. Former Navy pilot Ted Norbury was only seconds away from the two giants when he died. His chartered four-place Stinson, crashing near the 11,000-foot level, was less than a mile from 13,077-foot Charybdis and 12,943-foot Scylla. Norbury, en route from Fresno to Las Vegas with his fiancée of only three weeks and her friend, was probably lost in a blizzard.

Three and a half years later, two "peak-baggers" stumbled across the skeletons of the three Stanford students. So remote was the crash site that it took two days for the eight-man recovery party to ride in by horse.

Ranger Bob Smith's short report said, "We worked in pairs in gathering, inventorying, and identifying the personal effects. In similar manner the corpses were placed in separate rubberized bags and labeled. The three bodies had decomposed in place."

Kings Canyon National Park was busy in 1951; another soul vanished on June 5. The Roaring River cascades 4,000 feet in two very steep miles. Snowmelt, trapped deep between shaded Sierra walls, bubbles through the gray granite gorge. Water, crystal and cold, leaps from one deep pool to the next. Rounded boulders, polished by the eons, choke the narrow and shadowed abyss. James Sisson disappeared while crossing it.

Using recently acquired climbing skills and specialized mountaineering equipment, Rangers Bender, Black, and Boyer warily roped down treacherous spray moss–covered cliffs onto dozens of inaccessible ledges. Rangers Rafferty and Pierovich examined the endless small whirlpools while Assistant Chief Ranger Schmidt poked into the dark and echo-filled caves hidden behind crashing waterfalls. Others combed tangled logjams.

For more than three weeks, countless cracks and water-filled holes were probed. The park's regularly scheduled ranger rescue school was postponed twice, and three separate large-scale efforts were made to find the 19-year-old Army private.

No trace of James Sisson was ever found.

April 12, 1951
Mt. Rainier National Park

PLANE LANDS ON TOP OF MOUNTAIN

PARK rangers soon become numb to stupid stunts. This one, however, had even Mt. Rainier's "Mr. Rescue," Assistant Chief Ranger Bill Butler, shaking his head in disbelief.

John Hodgkin, who had once boasted that he could land his tiny Piper Cub anywhere, had a long history of foolish feats. Now, having just landed only 400 feet below Mt. Rainier's 14,410-foot, ice-covered summit, the Air Force pilot wasn't sure what to do when the plane's engine wouldn't restart. A pilot since 1926, Hodgkin somehow hadn't planned on frozen spark plugs.

With strong gusty winds and temperatures well below zero, the lieutenant faced a bitter fight. Stranded in the small saddle between Point Success and the

Columbia Crest, he spent a long night "literally flying the plane as it hovered on ropes tied to small sheets of plywood he had driven into the snow."

Butler, leading three of the park's other "A-Team" climbers—Del Armstrong, Elvin Johnson, and Dee Molennar—left for the top at 2:35 A.M. Even with ideal snow conditions and starting directly from Paradise, it took them nearly 14 long hours, only to discover that Hodgkin had glided off just 30 minutes before their arrival. Ignoring directions from the Air Force rescue planes circling closely overhead, he had broken his frozen skis free and shoved the little fabric craft into motion. Skiing off, the daring pilot had "dead-sticked" to a safe but powerless landing on ice-covered Mowich Lake 8 miles away.

Landing at 14,000 feet, Air Force pilot Hodgkin didn't plan on his Piper Cub having engine trouble and being forced to spend the night. U.S. AIR FORCE PHOTO

The would-be rescuers, along with a second support group several thousand feet below, were grateful for the equipment dropped from planes from McChord and spent the night "contemplating the stars" from their "frost-lined cocoons."

District Ranger Aubrey Haines, skiing for hours while climbing nearly 3,000 feet, intercepted the brash young daredevil. Haines would not let Hodgkin take off unless it could be done safely—he said he'd rather haul out a plane than a dead pilot.

Finally deciding what the problem was, the two men stomped a message into the snow for the rescue planes still flying cover. As requested, the cans of gasoline were parachuted onto the frozen lake. Soon the engine sputtered to life and a lucky pilot flew into the afternoon sky.

When tried by the U.S. commissioner, Hodgkin's defense was that he hadn't landed on the mountain but rather only on a surface of snow—merely a transitory part of the landscape. Not buying it, the judge fined the Air Force pilot $300 and gave him a suspended six-month sentence for landing illegally in the park.

May 20, 1951
Sequoia National Park

UNIT CITATION
FOR MERITORIOUS SERVICE
SEQUOIA AND KINGS CANYON NATIONAL PARK
RESCUE TEAM

FOR heroic rescue of two park visitors on May 20, 1951.

In response to an emergency call from a member of a fishing party who reported that his two companions, Allen Brazil and Robert Crawford, both of Visalia, California, had been swept into an inaccessible canyon below a waterfall in the Kaweah River in an attempted crossing, a rescue team of eleven Sequoia employees and a contract physician was organized. Three employees and the doctor lowered themselves by ropes down 130 feet of vertical wall and traversed an additional 80 feet upstream over the face of the vertical cliff. Slippery rocks and darkness accentuated the already dangerous journey to the sloping rock ledge just above river level near the base of the waterfall where the injured men were found. Medical aid was administered to both men but Mr. Crawford died soon after the rescue party arrived. At daybreak on May 21, Mr. Brazil and the body of Mr. Crawford were evacuated across the river by means of slings on fixed lines, and by using a fallen tree. The third member of the fishing party had returned to safety and reported the emergency. In recognition of the teamwork and courage displayed by members of the rescue party in accomplishing this difficult feat under conditions that were personally hazardous, the Department's **Unit Award for Meritorious Service** is hereby granted.

Douglas McKay
Secretary of the Interior

This was the NPS's first valor-oriented **Unit Citation for Meritorious Service.** The recipients were Jeff Adams, Jack Anderson, Bob Branges, Dick Boyer, Bruce Black, Joe Davis, "Corky" Johnson, John Rutter, Hank Schmidt, Lee Stiltz, Ted Thompson, and Charley Wallace. Two days after this rescue, Sequoia National Park held its first Mountain Rescue School.

Although it took place at night and included no technical climbing or rescue training, local physician Raymond D. Manchester did not hesitate to offer his professional assistance.

Additionally, Adams, Black, Boyer, and Manchester received special letters of commendation from Conrad L. Wirth, director of the National Park Service.

```
July 21, 1951
Yosemite National Park
```

COUPLE SURVIVES PLUNGE OVER
340-FOOT WATERFALL

MRS. Norman Yeoman, 25-year old Alameda housewife, is reported to be in satisfactory condition despite critical injuries suffered last Saturday when she and her husband were swept down a steep 340-foot series of falls in the Tuolumne river. She suffered a fractured skull, broken back, fractured pelvis and lacerations.

Mrs. Yeoman was camped with her husband near the head of Waterwheel falls in the Grand Canyon of the Tuolumne miles from the rim of Yosemite Valley. Yeoman was leaning over to drink from the river at the head of the falls when he fell in and was caught by the swift current. Mrs. Yeoman, trying to reach him, fell in after her husband.

The couple were carried down the steep slope in the river bed where the water rushes into a series of scooped-out holes and then is thrown up and back to form huge waterwheels.

Yeoman crawled unhurt from the pool at the bottom of the falls. Lloyd Seasholtz, park electrical director, and Charles Davis, a vacationing Dartmouth pre-medical student, pulled Mrs. Yeoman from the water. Davis and Seasholtz' daughter Joyce, a student nurse gave first aid while Seasholtz went for help.

A dozen men, working in shifts, carried Mrs. Yeoman in a litter eight miles up a rugged trail to the nearest road. There they were met by an ambulance and taken to Lewis Memorial hospital in Yosemite. The trip took nine hours.

—*Mariposa Gazette*, 7-26-51 (reprinted by permission)

```
July 19, 1952
Crater Lake National Park
```

GENERAL MOTORS EXECUTIVES
MYSTERIOUSLY DISAPPEAR

WITH its engine still warm and keys dangling from the ignition, the empty Pontiac's right door stood wide open. Three steps away lay 300-foot-deep Annie Creek Canyon. Rangers Hallock and Packard stood at the top of the steep, pumice-covered slope.

One possibility was that the occupants had crossed the highway and become lost in the dense brush. A more logical explanation, however, was that either Jones or Culhane had made a misstep and fallen. It didn't seem likely, though, that both men went over the same sheer cliff—unless one had tried to save the other.

With additional people, two search parties were formed: one to comb the thick forest across the road and the other to scour the slopes of the precipitous canyon. If either man had been seriously injured, the passing time grew increasingly critical.

One team, using mountaineering equipment and under the leadership of Hal Packard, cautiously worked the treacherously loose cliffs below the car. After hours of fruitless searching, the assistant chief ranger decided it was far too dangerous for them to climb back up in the dark; bedrolls and food were lowered to the men.

The next day, the search area west of the roadway grew to about a half mile in width. Crews carefully spaced for "alert detection of any possible clues" worked at right angles to the road. Their efforts continued throughout the afternoon.

> The party in the canyon, after searching to a point one-fourth of a mile North of the overlook . . . retraced their steps . . . approximately one-half mile South of the overlook. The canyon search party returned to the overlook at about 12:30 P.M. They had found nothing which would assist in determining what had happened to the missing men.

The Oregon State Police and the media were informed and the mysterious circumstances were described. FBI Special Agent Linahan arrived in the park. Identification photos were received from General Motors in San Francisco. The Klamath Air and Search Rescue Unit volunteered its assistance.

Two days after the search began, it ended. C. P. Culhane, 55, and A. M. Jones, 56, were found bound, gagged, and shot to death about a half mile from their car. The killer was never caught.

```
             August 16, 1952
        Grand Teton National Park
-----------------------------------------
```

UNIT AWARD
FOR MERITORIOUS SERVICE
GRAND TETON NATIONAL PARK
MOUNTAIN RESCUE TEAM

FOR courageous rescue efforts involving personal risk.

Responding to an emergency call to the scene of a mountain-climbing accident at dusk on August 16, 1952 the Grand Teton National Park rescue team found that James B. Ayer had fallen 250 feet to his death and that his companion, Robert Saltonstall, was stranded on a ledge 400 feet above.

Night came before Mr. Saltonstall could be lowered by a series of rope belays to a point of safety, necessitating that operations during the last 150 feet of cliff be carried out in total darkness. The members of the rescue team accomplished the difficult rescue over precipitous and rough terrain under conditions involving their personal safety. By their devotion to duty, perfect teamwork, and heroism in performing this extremely hazardous undertaking, the members of the Grand Teton National Park mountain rescue team have earned the Department's **Unit Award for Meritorious Service.**

Oscar L. Chapman
Secretary of the Interior

This was the first of many such awards for Grand Teton. Those cited for this rescue were Doug McLaren (the team's leader), Dick Emerson, Robert Perkins, Walt Sticker, Bob Theodorson, and Jim Valder.

Official guidelines for Department of the Interior awards read:

This type of honor consists of a citation, not to exceed 225 words, to be signed by the Secretary; a meritorious honor award certificate; an appropriately engraved silver medal bearing the date of the Secretary's approval of the award; and an unengraved medal so that both the obverse and reverse sides of the medal will show when framed.

August 29, 1952
Hawaii National Park

WITNESSING THE SUICIDE
FROM ONLY 100 FEET AWAY

AN astonished onlooker would recall, "We were looking at the eruption, when I was told that a man was on the outside of the fence. . . . He stopped at the edge and suddenly slipped feet first. Then we heard the rolling of rocks and he disappeared." The 64-year-old man jumped 400 feet into an active volcano.

There are few places more nightmarishly dangerous for a rescue—or recovery—than the sides of Halemaumau Crater. The 500-foot, coal-black cliff is volcanic cinder and crumbles the moment a rope or boot touches it. Chief Park Ranger Ernie Field was as good as anyone in the country at mountain rescue. He knew, however, that it would be almost suicidal to try to reach the body lying only 100 feet above the lake of surging lava.

The telegram from the park's mainland superiors read, "[I]n view of extreme danger to ranger personnel if removal of body of Japanese suicide is attempted from within crater, you are authorized to bury body by covering with soil from above and to permit family to hold service in restricted area."

Field, lying on his stomach only feet from the man's last footprint and stretching as far as he dared, could just barely look over; Dr. Mosack, from the nearby Kilauea Military Camp, recorded the observations. The Certificate of Death read:

> The undersigned hereby certifies that the object examined through binoculars upon the lava on the floor of Halemamu [sic] Crater . . . was a human body lying in the prone position. Considerable quantities of blood were present in a rapidly drying pool. The body was grossly disfigured.

Reconciled to the death and convinced of the extreme hazards to the rescuers, the family reluctantly agreed to the burial of the body where it lay. After respectfully clearing the rim of all spectators, Buddhist rites were held on the morning of the 31st.

Several truckloads of gravel were parked just out of sight of the observance. Once the family left, a curving, wooden chute was constructed so that the gravel could rain down 400 feet onto the body. But as the trucks emptied, a large crack opened behind them, threatening to drop both men and equipment into the crater.

Quickly clearing the area and shoveling the gravel over the edge by hand, the staff gingerly finished the burial.

```
                    May 25, 1953
            Kings Canyon National Park
    ----------------------------------------
```

RESCUERS GET RESCUED

WITH one of his two engines dead and unable to climb from the valley they were searching, the Army captain knew they couldn't escape from the 13,000-foot, snow-covered peaks that surrounded them. Putting his plane on automatic pilot, he ordered everyone out. It was 6 A.M., the sun was just peeking over the Sierra Crest, and in moments, the rescuers would become the rescued.

Captain Seaburg, from San Francisco's Hamilton Air Base and a member of the military's highly dedicated Air Rescue Service, had quickly swung into high gear when the overdue-plane alarm was sounded. Founded in 1946, the Air Rescue Service had just been credited with rescuing 9,898 soldiers and making 996 combat saves in the Korean War alone.

Seaburg's crew was one of many in the air looking for a Beechcraft "Bonanza" that had disappeared over the weekend. The search for the small craft's two Bay Area occupants, bound for Fresno from Bishop, focused on the nearby jagged peaks rising 8,000 feet above the airport. The rugged eastern Sierra ridges form a massive granite wall for even the most experienced pilots.

Considering that two would-be rescuers settled in pine trees and two narrowly missed a river swollen with winter snowmelt, the parachutists were very lucky—all five landed safely in Paradise Valley. When last seen, their ill-fated plane was limping east into the sunrise. Corporal Asplund, their radioman, hiked the 16 miles down the south fork of King's River into Cedar Grove. Four more-senior officers, bruised and cut, waited for the horses that Ranger Bob Smith would bring later that day.

The small Beechcraft Bonanza—the object of the original search—was spotted in a blizzard later that same morning; its two occupants had met a quick death on the slopes of Mammoth Mountain.

July 14, 1953
Grand Teton National Park

IT TOOK 27 RESCUERS

THE young couple from Massachusetts had just "bagged" the highest point in the park, 13,770-foot Grand Teton. Among the 365 people to try for its summit that year, the two climbers were descending into the Upper Saddle when a knot on a critical nylon sling untied during a rappel. Falling 35 feet and landing in a sitting position, the 22-year-old broke her back; 16 long miles later, Norma Hart's tired partner finally reached help.

Broken bones are serious anytime, but an injury to the spine at 13,000 feet on this rugged peak is a grave situation. The rescue team would face both a nightmare and one of its greatest challenges. For Ranger Doug McLaren it would be one of the most satisfying missions in his 40 years with the NPS.

The first six men, armed with morphine and penicillin—the first time drugs were to be used by rangers on a rescue in this park—and given instructions by a local doctor on handling such a serious injury, were quickly on their way.

Leaving the 6,500-foot level at 7 P.M., their light soon faded. Requiring skill and daring by day, climbs by night demand even greater expertise and near-perfect vigilance. Wearing headlamps, hefting weighty packs full of rescue gear, and carrying an awkward metal litter, the team slowly labored its way up the Grand. As a new day broke at 5 A.M., the tired men finally reached Hart.

"We loaded the girl in the Stokes litter . . . on her stomach, elevating her head, her shoulders and her feet so that she was in an arched position." For the next 20 hours, she was gently lowered from one ledge to the next. At one point, Doug McLaren single-handedly guided the stretcher down a 1,000-foot snow slope. In another very awkward area, they set up a traverse by putting a fixed rope in and then sliding the stretcher down over a 60-foot cliff.

Hart's thank-you letter to the rescue team graciously read:

> . . . although I can quote the doctor on the good condition you
> kept me in, I can't quite tell you how grateful I am for both

the good handling . . . your cheerful and uncomplaining atti-
tudes . . . how I admire the character and the individual and
collective skills that made the whole rescue operation such
a darned good job.

On May 17, 1954, Secretary of the Interior Douglas McKay signed a **Unit
Citation for Meritorious Service** for the Grand Teton National Park Mountain
Rescue Team. Named were Martin Benham, Ernest Borgman, Dick Emerson,
Bryan Harry, Doug McLaren, Bob Perkins, Hadley Roberts, Dick Shaw, and
Merle Stitt.

February 15, 1954
Agrihan Island

RESCUE—300 MILES NORTH OF GUAM

ERNIE K. Field knew climbing, rescues, and volcanos, so it is no wonder the
U.S. Navy asked the park ranger for help.

Beginning in 1935 as a seasonal ranger, the Colorado State University gymnast had climbed Rocky Mountain National Park's Longs Peak nearly 150 times;
one route bears his name today. A mountaineer with tenacious talent and
exceptional judgment, he had performed dozens of rescues over the years. He
had served with the 10th Mountain Division in Italy earning a Silver Star for
gallantry. Now, as the chief ranger of Hawaii National Park, Field's unique skills
were needed once again.

Agrihan, a tiny part of the Northern Marianas Archipelago, lies 300 miles
north of Guam. After a Navy DC-3 hit the cinder island's 3,166-foot volcano, six
men lay entombed inside.

At the request of the commander of the naval forces in the Marianas and
with the concurrence of NPS Director Drury, Chief Ranger Field left for Guam
on February 22—one day after his newborn second son, Jon, came home from
the hospital.

To assist in the mission, Field had Army climbers flown in from Japan. This
crack rescue team, transported to Agrihan aboard a Navy destroyer, landed on
the remote island by rubber raft. Twisted remains of the DC-3 lay deep in the
crater, and retrieval of the bodies would require at least two roped climbers to
go down the steep, thickly vegetated, volcanic cliffs.

After studying the extreme hazards created by hauling the bodies one by
one up the crumbly walls, the veteran rescuer advised against risking any further loss of life. Field returned to Hawaii on March 16, where the following message awaited him.

Commander, Naval Forces, Marianas, wishes to express
his appreciation to Mr. Ernest K. Field for the outstanding
manner in which he led the Agrihan recovery operation.

His devotion to duty, evaluation of the dangers involved, and excellent judgment in carrying out the mission, were of the highest order. Well done.

On June 4, 1962, at the age of 48, Ranger Ernie K. Field died of a massive heart attack while serving as the midwest regional chief of Park, Forest and Wildlife Protection. Citing, among other things, his many contributions in climbing and rescue, the DOI *posthumously* gave him its highest award—the **Distinguished Service Award**—on December 12, 1962.

```
                  May 16, 1954
          Mt. McKinley National Park
-------------------------------------------
```

RANGER DIES AFTER CLIMBING
HIGHEST POINT ON CONTINENT

ELTON Thayer spent much of 1953 planning a new route up 20,320-foot Mt. McKinley. In his fourth year as a ranger for the park, he had ready access to photos and detailed journals of the few previous expeditions on the peak. Not since 1910 had anyone even attempted this particularly difficult face of the mountain; the South Buttress had never been successfully climbed.

Ranger Elton Thayer died on May 16, 1954, after reaching the top of the highest point in North America. Left to right: George Argus, Thayer, Morton Wood, and Leslie Viereck.

DENALI NATIONAL PARK RESEARCH LIBRARY

Expecting to take at least six weeks, the climbing campaign consisted of Thayer, George Argus, Leslie Viereck, and Morton Wood. Even using air-dropped supplies, they still had over 75 pounds on their backs when they started out on April 17. Blessed with fairly good weather—but overestimating the difficulty and steepness of the frozen route—the four handily made the summit on May 15. Descending the next day to the 14,000-foot level in poor snow conditions, they continued on cautiously.

> When I saw Elton slide past, I braced myself to be able to hold the point and pay out rope gradually in case Les should be dislodged from his position. In seconds he was pulled loose and my belay was not strong enough to hold two men. This all happened in a flash. After that, I only remember tumbling end over end in the loose snow, now and then being pulled by rope and always unable, because of the heavy pack, to roll onto my stomach and dig in my axe to check the fall.

After falling nearly 1,000 feet, Argus had a broken hip; Wood and Viereck miraculously escaped serious injury. Ranger Elton Thayer, dead when he stopped, was buried where he lay. (In the mid-1970s, a nearby glacial cirque was named Thayer Basin.)

Fearing avalanches and risking extremely steep ice, the two men somehow lowered their injured friend 1,000 feet to a safer spot. "To this day I don't see how we got George over that slope safely. It is amazing what one can do if the necessity is dire enough!"

After a week of rest, Army Private George Argus was still no closer to moving than before he fell. Wood and Viereck, leaving most of their food and precious gasoline in the tent with Argus, force-marched more than 40 hours during the next 48 to get help.

Under the leadership of Mt. McKinley climber Dr. John McCall, a professor of geology at the University of Alaska, a rescue team was mobilized. McCall, winter expert Fred Milan, and five men from Alaska's Army Indoctrination Center flew by helicopter to the 6,000-foot level. Exactly one week later, the rescue team reached an anxious but jubilant Argus.

Elton Thayer was the third person to die climbing Mt. McKinley.

```
                    July 30, 1954
              Grand Canyon National Park
```

WE USED MORSE CODE—
THEY DROPPED ICE CAKES

PARK Ranger Dan Davis, who died in 1997, remembered:

> Some of the toughest search and rescue operations while I was at [the] Grand Canyon were generally small and got very

little publicity. One of the toughest was for a seasonal ranger [22-year-old Ronald T. Berg] in 1954 who fell off a cliff while hiking alone down the Tanner Trail.

Al Maxie and I made the initial search and after tracking and backtracking, found where he fell off the cliff. We then cut our way under the cliff and found the body. By then it was dark so we dry-camped there. We had no radio or communications at that time, so got the message out by morse code with a flashlight to someone at the Desert View Watch Tower.

The next day, two more rangers and a trail crewman were able to get a mule down the Tanner to where the body was. The Tanner at that time was virtually impassable for stock and they put a crew on the Trail fixing the bad spots so we could get back out with the body. This particular trip we were all out of water; Maxie and I were showing symptoms of ten-percent dehydration and were in pretty bad shape.

The Park, again by signalling, was aware of our predicament and dropped cakes of ice from a fixed-wing aircraft; no one on the staff knew how to air-drop by parachute. The ice very probably saved our lives even though one cake landed on one ranger's glasses and another crunched one of our three canteens, putting us at a disadvantage at getting out.

We did get to the River and filled our three canteens with River water; camped there a night and found some gallon cans in the old River cache just upstream from Tanner Wash. So in going out, we all carried one-gallon cans of water as well as the couple of canteens we had left.

At that time, the Park did not own one body bag. By then the body was five days old, temperatures well over 100 degrees, and all we had was a mante [canvas tarp for mule packing] to wrap it in so it was pretty bad. Again, I mention this only to give an idea as to the problems we encountered before helicopters. I might add that immediately after this, I wrote my first giveaway booklet on inner-Canyon hiking and water needs.

The Grand Canyon National Park Rescue Team received the DOI's **Unit Award for Meritorious Service.**

August 22, 1954
Rocky Mountain National Park

TOLD TO WATCH FOR CIRCLING BIRDS-OF-PREY

THE *Denver Post* followed the search for 25-year-old John Dalie very closely: "A harrowing story of six foodless days and nights of aimless wandering in the ragged Longs Peak country."

Dalie, a first-year law student at Denver University, was an avid hiker. He loved climbing and "began hiking in the hills of Ohio when he was just a small boy." On a Sunday outing with 32 others from the Colorado Mountain Club, he climbed 14,255-foot Longs Peak for the first time by the standard "cable route."

> There was a lot of hail and some snow, and I was having trouble with my eyes. When I got to the top, I looked for the rest of the gang. There was no one there. I looked around for the register to put my name on it. I couldn't find it. . . . That was about 1 P.M. It was storming, and I had my knapsack. A gust of wind got hold of it and blew it over the side of the peak.

A couple of hours later, in almost zero visibility, he tried to descend a different way. Somehow he got off the marked route; that night, far above timberline, he shivered among the rocks.

Not until 9:30 that evening did the other club members discover that the tall, lean young man with gray eyes and tousled brown hair was missing. Longs Peak Ranger Bob Frauson took the report. "District Ranger Ed Kurtz and all available Park personnel were immediately enlisted in the search, and they have been working every daylight hour since."

The park pulled out all the stops. Three SA-16 search planes from nearby Lowry Air Force Base combed the area and took aerial photos. Because the sheer 2,000-foot east face is only a stone's throw from the cable route, the peak was closed while six climbers examined the base of the cliff; they felt Dalie may have walked over the edge in a whiteout. The 12 Colorado Mountain Club members who had enlisted in the search were told to watch for the telltale circling of birds-of-prey.

Most had given up finding him alive; but after six days and a loss of 60 pounds, Dalie walked into the Meeker Park Campground and asked, "What's been going on in the world?"

"They must have flown over me a dozen times. I waved my jacket, but they never saw me. I walked in high places and in low places. Up the mountain and back down."

Dalie disappeared just one week after the park used a helicopter for the first time, and for the first time on an SAR. On August 15, George Bloom had fallen 200 feet and died while descending Mt. Craig.

April 10, 1955
Grand Canyon National Park

FEAR PAIR LOST IN COLORADO SWIM TRY

River Search Yields No Clue of Frogmen

HEADLINES like these chronicled the odyssey of Bill Beer and John Daggett. Labeled "frogmen" by Flagstaff's *Arizona Daily Sun* because of their face masks and swim fins, the two surfers from Southern California later described their

26-day swim down one of the toughest rivers in the world as "a cheap vacation that got a little out of hand."

Researching their epic journey, the pair learned that in the 86 years since Major John Wesley Powell first ran the river, only 30-odd expeditions had succeeded. Others had tried, and some never returned. This expedition, the first seeking to actually swim the length of the Grand Canyon of the Colorado—originally inspired by Daggett in an idle moment of boasting—promptly took on a life of its own.

Daggett, 27, and Beer, celebrating his 26th birthday on the river, felt the key to success was simply that "if the water flowed over and around rocks, so would something floating in it." Proven eventually correct in this basic premise, they were still painfully well tested in the 160 rapids they ultimately ran. In innocence and complete ignorance of park rules outlawing such bizarre escapades, they became the 219th and 220th persons to defeat this stretch of the Colorado—and the first to do so without boats.

On April 10, wearing only thin, $15 wet suit coats, cotton sweatshirts, and woolen longjohns, the longtime allies gingerly stepped into the 51-degree water at Lee's Ferry and began paddling for Pierce's Ferry 220 miles downstream. Tethered beside them this Easter Sunday floated four 89-cent, rubberized World War II radio bags, each holding 85 pounds of sleeping bags, cooking gear, and photo equipment. They had enough food for a month and, except for the film, their supplies had cost them less than $100 in all.

In *We Swam the Grand Canyon,* a wonderfully entertaining account of their "vacation," Bill Beer remembers:

> On first getting into the water we felt pain everywhere on the surface of our bodies from the shock of the cold water. Soon after, especially if we stopped swimming, came a tingling, the first stage of numbness, and our reaction was to fight it, to shiver, to flex our arms, legs and feet, to swim—even to shake our heads. Soon the numbness passed, replaced by a weariness that made us think we were getting used to the cold. If we could stay in the sunlight and keep our heads dry we could forget for a while the cold creeping into our muscles from our necks down. But before long we would begin to feel stiff and resisted movement of any kind. It became easier to make no effort at all. Finally it became painful to move, we hurt all over.

They needed the cold, numbing water, mostly as anesthesia for all the bumps and bruises they received while swimming and floating down this muddy cement-mixer of a river. They fought inexperience, doubt, and lots of fear. At every ripple and curve of the mile-deep gorge, they knew that if anything at all went wrong, they were on their own. On a river that carried hundreds of thousands of tons of silt each day, made little stones from big ones, and flash-flooded logs 75 feet up onto the polished marble walls, Beer and Daggett had only one choice: to go with the flow.

> The possible mishaps multiplied with each rock. These were evil-looking chunks of stone with jagged edges and sharp

points where they had been broken by the mashing and grinding that continually goes on in the bed of the Colorado. Worse yet were rocks that we could see only now and then as a surge revealed dark fangs poised a few inches below the surface.

Despite the many trials they endured—and occasionally enjoyed—the two somehow reached Phantom Ranch and the 7-mile Kaibab Trail out of the canyon. In need of film, a few supplies, and time to reflect on their trip, they hiked up to the village. The 3-inch newspaper headlines Bill Beer saw when he entered the El Tovar Hotel shocked him. They were now famous.

Before leaving home and urged on by well-meaning friends, the pair had given interviews to the *Los Angeles Times* as well as a local TV station. Once revealed to the world, their odyssey promptly generated more attention than they wanted. Already given up for dead, Beer and Daggett had just been the subjects of an extensive aerial search by both Coconino County Sheriff Cecil Richardson and Park Superintendent Preston Patraw.

Celebrities now, Beer and Daggett soon found themselves at park headquarters awkwardly trying to explain their wildly illegal "vacation" to Patraw. Before the long meeting was over, not only did they get acquitted, but they had actually blackmailed the National Park Service into allowing them to continue. Patraw knew theirs was a dangerous, harebrained trip, but he also knew Beer's logic rang true. "You gentlemen realize that after all this silly publicity and stuff, you won't have a minute's peace until someone does swim down this river."

With 192 miles still to go, they swam many of the roughest rapids the river had: Salt Creek, Granite, Hermit, Crystal, and Lava Falls. "At first sight, Lava Falls seemed to deserve its ugly reputation. On second sight, it still deserved it. We had never seen such an angry, snarling maelstrom." They lived through it.

Bill Beer and John Daggett didn't start out to be famous or to set some kind of record. Despite the mediahype, local talkshow guest appearances and an episode on a long-running TV series, this had really just been "a cheap vacation that got a little out of hand."

*Bill Beer (left)
and John Daggett
at the end of
their 26-day,
280-mile, never-
to-be-repeated
odyssey.*
BILL BEER COLLECTION

June 28, 1955
Grand Teton National Park

HIKED 20 MILES—CLIMBED 22 HOURS— COVERED 14,000 FEET

OF the 1,727 recorded ascents by 844 registered climbers that year, there were only two major accidents in the park. The one involving a 25-year-old veteran climbing guide was by far the worst.

Fred Ford was a seasoned mountaineer of excellent judgment; his two clients were well trained and strong. Having reached the 13,400-foot level, they were on the steep snow slope that marks the summit's final approach. With his ice axe firmly planted in the frozen crust, Ford was 120 feet higher than his client when a 100-pound boulder struck him from above. Knocked off his feet, he now dangled, unconscious and bleeding.

Starting up at 9:45 P.M., the rescue team, led by Doug McLaren, headed for one of the most inaccessible and dangerous points on the mountain. Ten long hours later

> a severe storm descended upon the mountain with extreme wind, snow, and freezing temperatures. The storm increased in severity throughout that day and night; climbing ropes became frozen, visibility was reduced to less than fifty feet, and it became a great effort simply to survive. . . . [T]hey encountered even more severe weather conditions with wind velocities estimated in excess of 60 miles per hour and ice forming on the cliffs and ledges of the peak.

McLaren, Don Decker, Dick Emerson, and John Fonda proceeded over extremely difficult terrain to the still-unconscious Ford. McLaren and Emerson, leaving the other two above the snow-filled couloir, climbed down to a spot directly above Ford, where Emerson rappelled down a 100-foot wall. By now, Ford's client, Robert Bartholomew, had been trapped in the frigid gully without shelter for almost 20 hours and was seriously suffering from exposure and shock. It was decided to get him to safety first, and then with more help, rescue the now semiconscious guide.

After tying a rope around Ford and securing him to a rock above, Emerson and Bartholomew climbed out. When McLaren and Emerson returned, "they looked into the couloir and observed that he [Ford] was no longer there. It became apparent, that in some manner, he had loosened himself from the rope and tragically fallen an additional 1,000 feet down the sheer south face."

All the rescuers suffered frostbitten fingers in what they claimed was "the worst storm they had ever experienced."

On January 7, 1956, a **Unit Award for Meritorious Service** was granted to the Grand Teton National Park Mountain Rescue Team. It named Rangers McLaren, Adams, Balaz, Benham, Decker, Emerson, Fonda, and Krear. Fred Ford was recovered several days later.

```
          August 19, 1955
Lake Mead National Recreation Area
```

CITATION
FOR DISTINGUISHED SERVICE
RUTH M. HEARD

FOR a heroic deed in saving two lives at personal risk beyond the call of duty.

On August 19, 1955, Mrs. Heard, a supervisory lifeguard at Lake Mead [National] Recreation Area, Nevada, helped to save two women from drowning in Lake Mead and was instrumental in rescuing two small boys. During a violent storm a small boat capsized about 500 feet offshore, throwing its five occupants into the rough water. Mrs. Heard witnessed the accident and, although off duty at that time, immediately assumed charge of rescue operations. She directed a lifeguard to take a paddleboard to the scene of the accident, swam unassisted to two boys clinging to a buoy, and calmed and reassured them. Swimming to the capsized boat, she helped the older woman onto the paddleboard, directed the younger one to cling to the paddleboard and, with the aid of the other lifeguard and a ranger who swam to assist them, succeeded in taking both women to safe ground. Mrs. Heard swam back to the capsized boat and remained with the man of the party, who was clinging to the boat, until a National Park Service patrol boat arrived and rescued the man and the two boys. In recognition of her great courage without regard for personal safety, Mrs. Heard is granted the Department's highest honor, its **Distinguished Service Award.**

Douglas McKay
Secretary of the Interior

Lifeguard Sylvia S. Reeves and Seasonal Park Ranger John R. Herse also received DOI **Distinguished Service Awards.**

```
          May 30, 1956
Rocky Mountain National Park
```

CITATION
FOR VALOR AWARD
ROBERT N. FRAUSON, FRANK J. BETTS,
JERRY W. HAMMOND, and NORMAN L. NESBIT

FOR demonstrating unusual courage involving a high degree of personal risk in the face of danger.

On May 30–31, 1956, Rangers Robert N. Frauson, Frank J. Betts, Jerry W. Hammond, and Norman L. Nesbit of a Rocky Mountain National Park rescue team participated in an unusually arduous and dangerous rescue operation. On the afternoon of May 30, Patrick Dwyer, a 17-year old park visitor, fell when his rappel rope slipped as he was descending the rugged sheer face of Hallet Peak. Young Dwyer fell free for almost 200 feet, landed on a snowfield, and slid about 200 feet farther before he hit a tree on a ledge less than 3 feet wide, preventing his falling over a precipice to certain death. Ranger Nesbit was in the vicinity with another climbing group, witnessed the accident and sent a member of his party to Bear Lake, eleven miles away, to report it. He then climbed to aid the victim and await the arrival of help. Rangers Frauson, Betts, and Hammond arrived on the scene about three hours later and rescue operations, requiring ten separate belays, continued for more than four hours in the darkness through the spring snow which made footing difficult. At one point Ranger Betts crashed through a snowbridge covering a crevasse and was saved only by a sling rope tied to the litter. It was after midnight on May 31 when the trail head was reached and the victim was taken to the hospital. As a tribute to his great courage in assisting in the rescue operation with complete disregard for his own personal safety, the Department of the Interior confers upon Ranger Betts its **Valor Award.**

Fred A. Seaton
Secretary of the Interior

All four rangers received identical citations and gold medallions. These were the first **Valor Award** recipients within the National Park Service; the very first **Valor Award** given to a Department of the Interior employee was on April 16, 1955, at the NPS's 15th Honors Convocation.

June 30, 1956
Grand Canyon National Park
----
128 DIE

Until 136 people died in a midair crash over New York City on December 16, 1960, the world's worst civilian airliner disaster (aviation's second worst after the 129 soldiers killed on June 18, 1953, in an Air Force plane in Tokyo) took place over the remote eastern end of the Grand Canyon. In a Flagstaff cemetery, a modest bronze plaque lists the victims of that terrible event.

IN MEMORY OF . . . Harry Harvey Allen, Trucine Elizabeth Armbruster, Thomas Edward Ashton, Jr. . . .

With 70 people aboard Flight 2, the Trans World Airline four-engine "Super Connie" departed Los Angeles three minutes before United's Flight 718. Several minutes late in taking off for Kansas City, 42-year-old Captain Jack Gandy was assigned to 19,000 feet. Robert Shipley, at the controls of United's faster, Chicago-bound DC-7, was told to climb to 21,000 feet.

. . . Connie June Braughton, Esther Ellen Braughton, Linda Kay Braughton . . .

Well into the Salt Lake City flight leg, the TWA pilot inquired about also moving to 21,000 feet to avoid turbulence. He was denied. There was another large aircraft already at that altitude nearby.

Captain Gandy asked for "1,000 on top"; incredibly, officials granted his request. This now put the giant TWA airliner at the same level as the United, and within minutes they both were over the Grand Canyon, a spectacular sight for which even seasoned pilots were known to modify a course. Air Traffic Control heard from both planes at 10:31 A.M. as they neared Tuba City. Sixty seconds later an anxious but unfinished "We are going . . ." came over the radio.

. . . Mildred Roscoe Crick Hatcher, William Wallace Hatcher . . .

Most of the monstrous TWA burned on the shoulder of Temple Butte; a mile away, the DC-7 with 58 passengers slammed into the sheer face of 6,400-foot Chuar Butte.

A park tourist, unfamiliar with the vast canyon area, reported the vague sighting of a column of smoke. Eight long hours passed before the grim fate of 128 people was learned. Searchers, in the air for hours, had been looking farther east.

. . . Joseph James Kite, Linda JoAnn Kite, Peachie Marie Kite, Sharon Marie Kite . . .

Initially, coordination and control were understandably labored and confused. The command center was originally set up in Winslow, 150 miles away. The Civil Aeronautics Administration, Civil Aeronautics Board, FBI, NPS, Air Force, Army Air Rescue from at least five separate bases, sheriff, county attorney, coroner, and TWA and UAL officials—not to mention hundreds of members of the press—were all there. Finally, on the afternoon of the third day, Park Superintendent McLaughlin and Chief Ranger Coffin got a top official from each agency together in one room and somehow orchestrated the chaos to calm.

TWA's Super Connie was easy to get to; the DC-7 was not.

Five men from Colorado's Rocky Mountain Rescue Group were flown to the river to scale the 800-foot, chocolate-brown walls of Chuar Butte; the wind, heat, and landing spots were terrible. After two days of very demanding climbing, as one rescuer later recalled, they "had nearly reached the crash scene by slowly driving hundreds of expansion bolts into the cliff face. . . . The rock was quite rotten . . . pretty bad. I sure hope I never see anything like that again."

. . . Claire M. Maag, Howard John Maag, John Otto Maag . . .

A crack team of eight Swiss mountain climbers was flown to the United States by Swissair. They brought with them 2,000 pounds of equipment, including 1,500 feet of steel cable for the mechanical winches and parachutes they used for rescues in their native Alps.

Army Captain Walter Spriggs made an exceptionally daring chopper landing "on a narrow ledge 30 feet above the wreckage . . . where the experts said man could not land from the air and probably could not reach from the ground." One by one, the team of international climbers was placed on the 10-foot-wide ledge high on the side of the desert peak. For three days, without shade from the 120-degree heat, they pried pieces of six-day-old corpses from narrow crevices and jagged cracks.

. . . David Karn Robinson, Geoffrey Brian Robinson, Jeanette Karn Robinson . . .

Large, twin-rotored H-21 helicopters—"flying bananas"—were the only ships able to manage the treacherous, superheated turbulence of the 4,000-foot-deep canyon. "Evacuation of bodies from both sites was considered by the

The uncertainty of where these two airplanes were or what happened to them gave birth to the standardized flight following. It was eight hours before the fate of these 128 people was known.
COURTESY OF JOEL ROCHON, TUCSON CITIZEN

Army to be one of the most hazardous operations they had ever undertaken; and as a result, practically nothing but the body remains were removed."

On July 12, nearly two weeks after the tragedy, four caskets with the remains of 29 unidentified persons from United Airlines' Flight 718 were placed in the Grand Canyon Cemetery; a rock obelisk marks their final resting place today. Three days before, with an honor guard at the manicured edge of the large grave, 67 caskets had been placed in Flagstaff's Citizen Cemetery for the TWA dead. A simple plaque still pays mute tribute . . .

> **. . . Bessie Whitman, Carolyn Ruth Wiley, Elizabeth May Young**
>
> **—June 30, 1956**

July 24, 1956
Sequoia National Park

THE CHOPPER
PULLED MAXIMUM POWER

ON an outing with Explorer Post 20, Gerry and a companion were scrambling down a loose talus slope high above isolated Hamilton Lake. In the lead and walking along a sloping ledge, the 16-year-old slipped and flew 25 feet through the air, then bounced and dropped another 20 feet. A rockslide followed him— including a 1,500-pound boulder.

When Assistant Explorer Advisor Collins reached Gerry, who was planning on joining the scout group after this trip, he was lying head down in a nest of rocks. His left leg was bent over the boulder and his right leg was under it, his foot wedged in a cleft. Ironically, the huge stone that now trapped Gerry had actually saved him from being crushed by the rain of rocks.

Collins told two boys in the group to bring up what first-aid gear was in camp and then to proceed to Bearpaw Meadows, 5 miles away, to phone for help. "Hurry, but be careful!"

The most dangerous part of the trip out for the scouts was the night crossing of Lone Pine Creek—the stream was high and fast from the recent rains. Realizing the hazard, the boys crossed separately so that if one did not make it, the other one might. Both arrived safely shortly before midnight.

As word of the accident spread, nearby campers offered help. Two college men working on a trail crew at Buck Canyon hiked the 7 miles in 75 minutes to offer assistance.

Fearful of more loose granite coming down in the dark, Collins decided not to move the injured boy. It was a long vigil.

Dr. Harold Jakes, a good friend of the park, along with rangers Hal Packard and Carl Kronberg, rode all night to get to Gerry. After administering much-needed painkillers, Dr. Jakes directed the delicate move. Members of trail and blister rust crews and others gathered around the boulder and slid it away from Gerry. Eight men then carefully carried the stretcher down the treacherous slope. Time was critical, so Dr. Jakes ordered a helicopter by radio.

Not two minutes after the rescue team reached lakeside, Pete Miller, a pilot who flew local forest fires, set his craft down on a small nearby ledge. Expertly "packaged" in the Stokes litter, the injured boy was securely lashed to the landing skid. At his service ceiling of 8,000 feet, Miller pulled maximum power, and 30 minutes later Gerry was in a waiting ambulance.

```
             August 19, 1956
        Mt. Rainier National Park
    ----------------------------------------
```

"I CRIED, RICHARD'S FATHER SAID, IT WAS THE HAPPIEST MOMENT OF MY LIFE."

HIKING back to their base camp that afternoon, Richard Mizuhata was having trouble keeping up; the 13-year-old Boy Scout fell behind by skirting many of the trail's more difficult icy patches. Scrambling down another slick slope, he once again mistook a lower path for a shortcut back to the main trail; it faded out.

Now frightened, the lad quickly ate what little food he had and then burrowed deep into his sleeping bag that first night. The next day, his backpack tumbled over a cliff. Unable to retrieve his equipment, he kept moving downhill over the next several days. In spite of the fairly mild weather, Richard shivered through the nights. On day six, it started to rain.

Assistant Chief Ranger Bill Butler, an experienced rescue leader, was fearful that Richard could not signal to searchers. He knew that if the boy lost his glasses, he would be almost blind; to compound the ranger's fears, the lost teenager had a speech difficulty.

Gil Blinn, a park laborer, remembers hiking 15 miles that first day and searching 17 hours every day for the next week. It was the first of hundreds of rescues during his 40-year Park Service career.

One of the Coast Guard choppers (the first use of helicopters for an SAR in the park) had a loudspeaker installed on it. "We can give him instructions from the air on turning towards the river, so he can follow it out."

Bloodhounds were brought in but could only find a "cold" trail. The region's Mountain Rescue Council, along with dozens of other local volunteers, provided most of the ground support while the military supplied equipment and additional manpower. Seattle's Japanese community flocked to the mountain to help one of their own. By official estimates, 308 people were involved in the hunt. This was one of the largest missions in the park's very distinguished history of search and rescue.

Richard simply sat on the bare rock—terrified, exhausted, and hypothermic. It rained on him; water running underneath him went unnoticed, for he was already soaked and near death.

Finally, Japanese volunteer Paul Uno "saw a place that looked like a likely spot. It was very steep. I just had a hunch. Richard heard me sliding down through the brush. He woke up. I heard him shout." That Sunday, after a search lasting seven very long days, Paul Uno experienced the thrill of a lifetime.

So did Richard's dad: "I cried."


```
            October 4, 1956
         Olympic National Park
-----------------------------------------
```

JET FIGHTERS COLLIDE

AT 25,000 feet, the two pilots, along with their radarmen, watched the day slowly dissolve to darkness far below. And then, the fading beauty of the sky . . . eyes adjusting to the gloom . . . or perhaps another distraction caused the jets to collide. Parachutes quietly blossomed just before both F-89H Scorpion fighters crashed south of 7,954-foot Mt. Olympus.

First Lieutenant Eugene A. Hamby, adhering to his Air Force Survival Manual, spread his chute out in a small break in the almost impenetrable forest and waited. Easily spotted the next day, the lucky pilot was swiftly plucked out by the rescue chopper.

Landing almost 2 miles from Hamby, Second Lieutenant George W. Deer left his parachute in the tree he hit. Seeking the morning sun, the pilot climbed to a nearby ridgetop by the predawn light; he too was quickly spotted and hoisted into a hovering helicopter.

Still hanging below his parachute, First Lieutenant Jim B. Paschall saw the flames when the planes impacted. Having landed safely south of Mt. Dana, the young radarman waited until daybreak and then headed north down the Elwha River Trail. After one wrong turn, two days, and 30 long miles, he limped into Brinnon.

When the missing Paschall finally phoned his base on Saturday, hope surged for First Lieutenant Robert Canup. There were still no clues to the fate of the young aviator. The others were not sure if Canup had even "punched out"; it was hoped that he was afoot and, like Paschall, taking a longer but equally sure way out.

Coast Guard and Air Force SAR activated almost at the time of the midair collision and, when Canup could still not be found, their air effort went into an even higher gear. "If anyone was alive . . . able to get to any trail or make any sign or signal, the chances are almost perfect that he would have been spotted. Searching from a helicopter . . . you just don't miss much."

Primed and ready to go, both Royal Canadian Air Force and Para Jumpers from Sacramento arrived at rescue headquarters. A Navy transport collected experienced volunteers from the region's Mountain Rescue Council. Local Explorer Scouts, making one of their earliest SAR showings, eagerly swept park trails. The fifth day dawned cloudy and wet. Low overcast made it difficult to fly to a probable crash site, a hard spot to see "just over a high ridge in the shadows." Volunteers Ome Daiber, Arnie Campbell, and other veteran searchers were dropped off 4 difficult miles away and bushwhacked their way to the badly burned wreckage.

First Lieutenant Robert L. Canup had never "punched out."

```
                          May 9, 1957
                  Kings Canyon National Park
--------------------------------------------------------------------------
```

54 DAYS AFTER
HIS JET EXPLODED 6 MILES UP

LIEUTENANT David A. Steeves startled the world by limping out of the Sierra. Long given up for dead, he told a dramatic tale of endurance and gave a testimonial to faith. For some, however, it soon grew incredible. His epic was an accident . . . or was it?

To this day, the T-33 jet trainer that Lieutenant Steeves bailed out of, has never been found. SAN FRANCISCO CHRONICLE

En route from near San Francisco, Steeves's T-33 trainer climbed effortlessly to 33,500 feet. Radioing that he was over Fresno, the 23-year-old reported being on schedule. His routine flight plan called for going south to Bakersfield, east to Riverside, and then quickly on to Phoenix. He was airborne only 37 minutes that bright May morning. The jet's small explosion rocked him.

How long Steeves remained unconscious he never knew, but what happened next was surely pure reflex. With his stricken plane falling uncontrollably and with thick, blinding smoke filling the cramped cockpit, he squeezed the ejection trigger. His plastic canopy blasted into the frigid sky—and so did he.

Bracing himself as he floated all too quickly past the snow-clad peaks, he smashed into the boulder-studded side of a steep, windswept basin; his 'chute settled on the frost-chiseled rocks above him. With two painfully twisted ankles, he knew he was lucky just to be alive. He had no idea where he was but knew help would find him quickly.

The Air Force launched a massive but fruitless search. With hours of fuel still onboard and probably impacting at nearly 400 mph, a shattered, burnt aircraft would be swallowed by the surrounding gray granite. Or it might sink into one of the countless small, remote, backcountry lakes. Or . . .

One aeronautics official believed that Steeves was not really above Fresno when he called in but was instead north, heading southeast over the Sierra. Had he intentionally abandoned his flight plan or falsified his radio call? "It was a very bad navigational error for a pilot to be off course more than 80 miles after he has flown a distance of only 115 to 125 miles."

Despite the intense throbbing in his ankles, Steeves knew he needed to get off the snowfield and start helping himself. Spying two gnarled dwarf pines leaning against rocks and drifts far below, he started inching down. Bundling up his parachute, he threw it in front of him and then sat on the harness and slid. After several frustrating hours, he reached the little makeshift shelter.

Just one week before his bailout, Steeves had fortuitously become "survival conscious." He had bought a new pair of boots, had a holster sewn into one of them to carry a small .32 caliber pistol, and had stuffed several packs of matches into the other. After a childhood spent trapping and rigging snares, the athletic 6-footer felt more than prepared.

Using flight papers that first night, Steeves built a scrawny, smoldering fire in a wet stump. Inventorying his few personal possessions, he also took stock of his life. He thought of his wife, Rita, and their 14-month-old daughter, Leisa. Faced with impending divorce because of his affair with another woman, Steeves knew "he had failed himself." It grew overcast, it grew colder.

For three days he lay shivering in his canopy watching it snow lightly. As his story in the December 24, 1957, issue of *Redbook* would relate, "There were times when he told himself he had gone mad, that he was dead and this was some form of icy hell. In waves of panic he felt he was being punished for his sins; he prayed for forgiveness, despaired, then prayed some again."

While on a rescue in the area two weeks after Steeves's ordeal *ended*, Ranger Gene Balaz found a flight helmet, parts of a parachute, and a handkerchief, all with the pilot's name stenciled on them.

These abandoned items, found by chance at 11,400 feet in remote Dusy Basin, marked the start of an odyssey of pain, hunger, confusion, and fear. Dragging along, Steeves slowly picked his way between the ponds and drifts, over rocks and through brush. He spent the next night in a snowbank, and the following ones pressed up against a cliff or huddled under a rotten log. Days were long; nights were freezing.

Two weeks after landing among the 13,000-foot Sierra peaks, he stumbled into a large clearing and found a small building used seasonally by trail crews and rangers; the sign over the door read "Simpson Meadow Ranger Station." Built just the year before, the tiny shed of rough-hewn lumber now held canvas, tools, and a dozen other minor but useful items, including food.

Steeves had eaten his last meal nearly half a month before. The cans of beans, hash, and tomatoes; two packages of gelatin; a half-filled box of sugar; a coffee can partially full of rice; soups; and other assorted small items must have looked like manna from heaven to the starving pilot. He remembered "gulping ketchup hungrily from the bottle." But he had to be careful to ration the supplies.

Safe and now relatively comfortable, Steeves pulled off his flight boots for the first time in two weeks. "The pain was instantaneous and excruciating"; the ugly discoloration of pale oranges and sickly blues extended halfway to each knee.

He watched as it snowed softly over the next few days. He ate, rested, and planned. Discovering a topographic map of the park, he soon located Simpson Meadow. He was almost in the middle of the Sierra. Surrounded by 12,000-foot peaks, some towering more than 6,000 feet above him, and having already traveled dozens of torturous miles, he had only two choices.

If he continued down the middle fork of the Kings River, he would eventually reach help at Hume Lake. The other choice, a nightmare of a climb over 10,677-foot Granite Pass, led to the Cedar Grove Ranger Station. Either way, aid was still some 20 miles away; either would be hard, either would be cruel.

Hume Lake won. Many painful hours and miles later, the trail crossed the river. He stripped off his clothes and boots and entered the snow-swollen torrent. After sweeping downstream and over a 6-foot falls, he emerged, still clutching his tattered little bundle. Finally, after losing the trail one last time and dead-ending against an impassable wall of rocky cliffs, he knew he was beaten. Hume Lake lost.

Five days after struggling back to the shelter, he started up the switchbacks toward Cedar Grove, but then missed a turn and bogged down waist-deep in a snowbank. By his count, nearly a month had passed since he was exploded into the sky. Defeated once again, he grew even more desperate.

He ate dandelions and a grass snake. Finding fishhooks, he tried his fortune; he was luckier, however, when he set a snare using his small pistol. After several fruitless nights, he heard the gun, but was unable to hobble out until daylight. Coyotes had partially eaten his deer. When the deer meat ran out, he caught a few fish.

As days ran together, depression and hunger grew. He placed written signs at both ends of the meadow hoping someone would come by. On one futile fishing trip, he collapsed—he knew the end was near. Desperately hoping to attract attention, he set four small forest fires; it took hours for the wet wood to catch fire. No one noticed.

After nearly 50 tormenting days, his healed ankles barely supported his terribly skinny legs. Sensing that most of the snow was gone up high, he forced himself to try again. Off before daylight, he made remarkable time. Nearing Granite Pass, he encountered only knee-deep drifts; he kept on. When the trail finally leveled off, he rested, knowing it would soon head down.

Suddenly he looked up to see a woman on horseback 10 feet away!

At first, Lieutenant Steeves was hailed as a hero. Detailed to a mountain-survival school to teach, he appeared on TV and signed a book deal. Along with his marriage, however, the book soon fell apart when his ghost writer found too many discrepancies in his tale. Although they never publicly doubted him, the Air Force grew marginally convinced of his motives and quietly let him resign. David A. Steeves, leaving questions still unanswered, died in a small plane wreck in 1965. In 1977 a Plexiglass canopy, No. 52-9232—his jet trainer—was discovered by scouts not far from Dusy Basin. His plane has never been found.

•)

June 25, 1957
Big Bend National Park

WILMA CHISELED HER DIARY
ON A DESERT BOULDER

"June 25—Lost—Sand Storm"
AFTER gassing up their '57 Ford stationwagon and checking the air-conditioner, the couple from Houston started their "trip around the mountains." They soon turned onto the unpaved River Road—a miserable washboard of sand-filled ruts, a road to avoid in the current 114-degree Texas heat, a road not to get stuck on . . .

After 30 minutes of cramming thorny brush and blistering rocks under the tire, they were still hopelessly mired down. Turning to her 51-year-old husband, a recent victim of stomach ulcers, Wilma said, "Honey, why don't you relax here in the car while I go for help. It's not very far. And you know I have a good sense of direction." They were 30 miles from help.

". . . climbing up a peak about 75 feet high. I climbed another peak, then another and another . . . saw something that made my heart sink. It was Santa Elena Canyon, located in exactly the opposite direction." At first light she slowly retraced her steps.

"June 26—Found water—Room"
When the lodge manager discovered that his guests had not slept in their bed, he sounded the alarm with the rangers.

Wandering for hours, Mrs. White heard a faint gurgle—a tiny spring, a life-saving trickle. Refreshed, she continued to walk; at midday she sat down and tried to reason. "The best thing for you to do Wilma, is to go back to that spring and wait because, without water, you'll die. The rangers will find you in time."

At 3:30 P.M., one of the six search planes spotted Mr. White lying in the road 10 miles from his car. The heat had killed him.

"June 28—Bathed and washed lingerie"
Incorrectly, the FBI somehow found "evidence" that Mrs. White had fallen into the Rio Grande, and so dragging of the dirty-brown river was begun. A search camp was established at a nearby ranch and Ranger Rod Broyles took charge. The ground around the couple's car had been sorely trampled, obliterating any useful tracks.

"June 29—Bathed and washed shoes and cap"
A 130-degree thermometer was set under a search truck; the mercury exploded out of the top. More than 300 people now looked for the missing woman, including Animal Quarantine, the Civil Air Patrol, two sheriff's posses, the Border Patrol, Mexican Federales, and park staff. Many seriously doubted she was still alive.

On July 1, after flying countless grid patterns and bouncing and circling in the desert's violent thermals, Civil Air Patrol pilot Herb Ogle flew a narrow, remote canyon. That he even saw Wilma, frantically waving a blouse, amazed him.

July 26, 1957
Yosemite National Park

"I SAW A BIG BLACK BEAR.
I WASN'T LOST. THE BEAR WAS!"

DRESSED only in a brief sunsuit, the four-year-old was there one moment, gone the next. Shirley Ann Miller wandered away from 7,000-foot-high Bridalveil Campground late Wednesday afternoon. Now, three mornings later and within only yards of where the tot had disappeared, more than 100 searchers anxiously listened to the day's final search instructions. Some, like veteran Park Ranger Tommy Tucker sitting high astride his horse, began to fear the worst . . .

Children wander away from campgrounds all the time. Yosemite park ranger Billy Nelson, and his horse Sheik, spent a long night in 1932 looking for this little girl.
YOSEMITE NATIONAL PARK RESEARCH LIBRARY

Dan Nelson stood on a nearby stump where all could see him, exhorting all to give it another all-out effort— and reminded us that though we should continue to call out Shirley Ann's name, in reality we should now concentrate on looking for a still object—a body, or part of a body. It was an extremely gruesome and sobering aspect—but one that all of us had been mulling over, more and more.

The area was a nightmare of downed old-growth fir, steep-banked creeks, and thick, skin-ripping brush. With the unseasonably warm nighttime temperatures, the mosquitoes were "voracious, keeping up a continuous attack on anything that moved." Black bears and mountain lions were plentiful; normally not dangerous to adults, they could pose a fatal threat to a small, injured mammal.

So we strung out our searchers, not more than 10 feet apart, with those of us on horseback riding ahead on a back and forth zig-zag search pattern. About two hours into the morning, I heard a yell behind me and off to my left. Riding towards the commotion, I found Jack Nolan, holding Shirley Ann aloft and shouting "I found her—and thank God—she seems to be okay!"

Well, I will attest that it was an exceptional moment for all of us—we were emotionally fatigued, physically worn down with little or no sleep for the past three days and nights and we felt an immense sense of emotional exhilaration at finding this little 4-year-old girl, whom many of us had felt would be listed as a tragic incident.

I tried to take her up on my horse so we could hurry back to her parents—but she'd have nothing to do with my horse, and clung to Jack like she was a part of him. You can imagine the tearful, joyous reunion that took place back at camp.

Chattering almost nonstop to the assembled and ecstatic volunteers, an excited Shirley Ann exclaimed, "I saw a big black bear. I wasn't lost. The bear was!"

The area was later officially named "Lost Bear Meadow."

March 31, 1958
Yosemite National Park

"BOY, YOU'VE GOT SOME
HIGH MOUNTAINS UP THERE"

ON March 22, six young mountaineers left June Lake on a 14-day ski trip over the 12,000-foot Sierra Crest. With a near-record snow year—twice the average—they expected a great tour, and for five days they got one. That is, until one of them fell gravely ill. Ultimately found to have an inflamed heart lining, the freshman Stanford medical student grew progressively worse over the next two days. Admitting finally that they were in trouble, two of the team's strongest skiers battled the storm, making a 28-mile forced march to Yosemite Valley.

Rangers, knowing that the fickle Sierra weather could stay bad indefinitely and that a proposed helicopter landing at that elevation would be a near-miracle, started skiing toward the trapped foursome. Faced with fearsome, avalanche-prone cliffs while climbing 7,000 feet uphill, it would take them several days at best to break 28 tortuous miles of new trail.

Pilots Bill Williams and John Cooney, Army chief warrant officers from Fort Ord, had attempted one quick assault on the peak before the blizzard beat them back. The weather was so bad the next day that they couldn't even get their chopper off the ground; it was so cold that their flight mechanics had to take oil for the twin rotors of the H-21 to a nearby garage and warm it.

Bob Symons had 18,000 hours of flight time and an artificial leg. A mountain pilot extraordinaire from nearby Bishop, he started that last rescue day by slipping his little Super Cub down between the tall pines onto the narrow road of narrow Yosemite Valley. He had already spent two days dropping supplies and messages to the youths, as well as making several nearby touch-and-go landings to test snow conditions. Passing over the stranded party that dawn, Symons knew the weather could turn deadly sour, and that there might not be much warning.

After conferring with the Army pilots, Symons took off, pointing his small plane toward Mt. Lyell and the critically sick youth. He would fly communications cover while the other two would try to land. The "flying banana" soon followed.

When the huge ship started to tip over in the snow, Williams and Cooney quickly applied power and lifted off the tiny ledge. Three times they tried, each time sinking too deep. The altimeter read 11,470 feet—a helicopter rescue record. On their fourth try, the two World War II veterans set the large helicopter down. Williams got out and spent 40 minutes helping the four mountaineers up the steep slope. From above, Symons saw the clouds close—right after the chopper lifted off.

When it was all over, Chief Warrant Officer Cooney summed it up when he said, "Boy, you've got some high mountains up there."

June 15, 1958
Carlsbad Caverns National Monument

TECHNICAL RESCUE FROM OGLE CAVE

SWEATY and fatigued from hiking, the three men peered into the dusky shadows at their feet. One of many wild caves in the park, Ogle plunged 220 feet straight down. Bart, his brother Bob, and their friend Mills were excited about "dropping" into the void.

Anticipating the difficult climb out, they pre-rigged three cable ladders, locking the ends together with carabiners; a fourth, homemade ladder—was then clipped on. Bob was the first to rappel to the halfway point, a small, sloping ledge 130 feet down; his 25-year-old brother followed. Too eager, Bart painfully burned his ungloved hands sliding down the rough rope.

Incapacitated now and unable to go farther, Bart started slowly up the long, swinging ladder; he wore no safety line. Forty feet into the ascent, the homemade metal clamps on each side of the bottom ladder gave way and broke; falling cables whooshed quickly down around him. The young caver narrowly missed the deeper shaft—and death—just inches away; dropping 35 feet, he miraculously fractured only a foot and an elbow. Mills went for help.

Led by Chief Ranger Tom Ela, "the rescue operation was executed masterfully." Arriving shortly before midnight, the 12-man team quickly saw that they needed to lift Bart up without touching the walls. They set up their hoist directly over the middle of the 40-foot-wide hole by weaving a "web" of rope over the shaft. Then, covered with blankets and very tightly tied into the litter, the injured man was raised in a standing position. With their progress marked by a small lamp hooked to the foot of the stretcher, Bob pulled a guide rope from below to keep his brother from spinning wildly.

Even years later, a retired Ranger Ela would fondly recall that when Bart was safely on top, the "fun" really began.

> What made this an interesting rescue was that it was an all night affair in very tough desert country *full* of cactus, agave, yucca and sotol as well as many numerous thorny brush types in which dwell lots of live hazards (scorpions, centipedes, rattlesnakes and other desert undesirables) that lent spice to this adventure.

Lugging a litter, the men found it was a long way to the trucks; the slope was steep. Two men stumbled ahead with gas lanterns to pick the easiest route, but there really was none. Slipping and sliding, the rescuers were repeatedly stabbed by yucca and gouged by rock. Bart's ride was terribly rough, but he knew they "wouldn't let him down." Yet they did, sort of . . .

"Once he did register a complaint," Ela recalls, "when the men laid the stretcher down for a rest and a lechugilla spike came up through the wire to stick him like a hypodermic needle."

August 19, 1958
Yosemite National Park

RANGERS HAUL BOY OFF YOSEMITE CLIFF

YOSEMITE (AP)—Rangers Wednesday pulled a teen-age boy to safety up the face of a 3,000-foot cliff where he was trapped for 18 hours on a one-foot-wide ledge—600 feet up from the valley floor.

All Tuesday night 17-year-old Bill Beeghley had been kept awake by Rangers yelling at him through loud speakers. Sleep would have meant an almost certain plunge to death from the precarious perch below famed Glacier Point.

The Long Beach youth was spotted on the granite cliff-side after he became marooned during a hike with four companions. He got there while taking what he thought was a short cut around the face of Firefall Point.

Rangers equipped with special climbing gear, 2,000-pound test nylon rope and bullhorn portable loudspeakers tried to reach the boy by climbing the rock face, but could not before dark.

Then the keep-him-awake vigil over the bullhorns began. Campers were warned to be quiet. Echoes in the valley would interrupt communications.

At daylight, hundreds of campers watched as rangers moved closer. After trying an approach from below, one party of rangers got to a ledge 250 feet above him.

They lowered a ranger to within 100 feet of the stranded hiker and he managed to get ropes around Beeghley. Then began the long pulley hoist to the point's summit, 7,000 feet above sea level.

He couldn't sit down on the narrow ledge and had to lean backward throughout his 18-hour ordeal. Nor could he stand up straight.

"If I would have moved forward I would have fallen," Beeghley said. "I almost fell asleep three or four times, but the rangers kept calling me and that kept me awake."

Throughout, Beeghley had to stand on just one foot to avoid toppling off his perch. There wasn't room enough for two.

—*San Jose Mercury*, 8-22-58
(reprinted by permission of the Associated Press)

A Department of the Interior **Unit Award for Excellence of Service** was granted by Secretary Seaton to Rangers Rick Anderson, Frank Betts, Buck Evans, Dick McLaren, John Merriam, Vern Nichols, Don Potts, Dick Stenmark, and John Townsley.

September 1, 1958
Mt. Rainier National Park

NAYDENE CHEATS DEATH—
A SECOND TIME

WHIPPED by bitter winds, Naydene's vapor-soaked clothing froze to her body. The 20-year-old and her partner, unexpectedly taking longer to reach their goal than they had expected, now huddled together in the small steam caves near the summit. Exhausted, wet, and without sleeping bags, they were enduring a seemingly endless night just below the mountain's 14,410-foot rim. For the second time in exactly one year, the Stanford student faced death on this peak, this time trapped on the crater's edge. Exactly one year ago to the day, she had watched her teammate die, buried under tons of a collapsing snowbridge.

Naydene's 40-year-old friend, more experienced and not suffering as much from the moist cold, descended the next morning and rang the alarm. Chief Ranger Al Rose, no stranger to emergencies, reacted swiftly. He dispatched two climbing teams of guides, rangers, and rescue personnel and then had the Mountain Rescue Council arrange for the Navy to air-drop vital supplies.

When Ome Daiber and Dorrell Looff arrived at the Naval Air Station—rushed there in a police cruiser by the King County Sheriff's Department—the side door had already been removed from the plane. After being loaded with a rescue sled, food, oxygen, boots, sleeping bags, and extra clothing, the twin-engine craft was soon over the peak. So critical was the need for master flying skills that two senior Navy officers were at the controls. They made five free-fall drops in eight very dangerous passes—all right on target. By 4:00 P.M. Naydene was in dry G.I. clothing.

Gil Blinn and Dick McGowan started out for the young woman at 1:30 P.M. Going light ("blitzing"), they picked up equipment and a radio along the way. The two professional summit guides were well conditioned from a summer of arduous, high-altitude mountain climbing; this was McGowan's third trip to the top in three days. One hour later, a second team followed; leading was Gary Rose, ironically Naydene's guide during the tragedy of the previous year.

In reaching Naydene, Blinn and McGowan had set a speed record climbing to the top—just over seven hours for what normally takes most of two days. Naydene declared, "The sound of their voices was the most wonderful thing I've ever heard." Her father, at the Paradise Ranger Station only a half hour before the two climbers reached his daughter, said, "That scratchy voice on the radio saying 'have found her, have found her' sounded like angel music."

After spending three nights on Mt. Rainier, two of them in a cramped steam cave above 14,000 feet, Naydene walked down unscathed—courtesy of a dedicated, finely tuned rescue "machine."

```
             June 18, 1959
         Glacier National Park
-------------------------------------------
```

CITATION
FOR VALOR AWARD
DONALD A. DAYTON

FOR courageous action involving a high degree of personal risk in the face of danger.

On June 18, 1959, Park Ranger Donald A. Dayton, of Glacier National Park received word that a grizzly bear had attacked a young man, who was a summer employee at the Glacier Park Company, and had been hiking on the slopes of Mount Altyn. Picking up his rifle, Mr. Dayton, accompanied by a seasonal park ranger, made his way as fast as possible to the scene of the attack. They found a bear, a 250-pound female, on top of her victim, mauling, biting, and chewing him. After unsuccessfully attempting to scare the bear away to a point where she could be shot without further endangering the life of the victim, Mr. Dayton decided to shoot from a location where he could use all four shells in his rifle if the bear charged. Disregarding his own safety, he flattened himself on the ground about 50-yards away and aimed with the greatest of care to avoid hitting the young man pinned beneath the bear. Grizzlies are extremely hard to kill and it was only after the third shot that the bear was disabled and rolled down the slope away from the injured man. Mr. Dayton fired his last shot into the body of the fallen animal. The face and scalp of the victim, who remained conscious throughout the attack, were badly torn and chunks of flesh were missing from both legs. Mr. Dayton improvised a stretcher and made the victim as comfortable as possible until a litter arrived. He then directed the rescue operation, and assisted in transporting the badly mangled youth to the nearest hospital, where he remained in a critical condition for several days. Because of Mr. Dayton's calm judgement and his unerring action in this truly horrifying incident, the young man is alive, and will recover from plastic surgery with a minimum of facial scars. As a fitting tribute to his courageous feat, the Department of the Interior is proud to confer upon Mr. Dayton its **Valor Award.**

Fred A. Seaton
Secretary of the Interior

Of the 208 recorded deaths in Glacier National Park recorded from 1905 to 1997, nine were due to direct encounters with grizzly bears: two in 1967, one in 1976, three in 1980, two in 1987, and one in 1992.

July 23, 1959
Grand Canyon National Park

ONE FINAL PASS DOWN THE RIVER

AFTER Father Gavigan told the two teenagers about finding an old silver mine in the Grand Canyon as a kid, Walt and John saved every errand-running penny for a year. Now, after having foolishly stored their camping equipment and vital water supply at the top of the trail, the three hikers were hopelessly stranded their very first night.

The Trappist priest ordered the boys to stay put, for he would find a way out. They soon knew he was dead when they saw him fall into the deep gorge below. After realizing that no one could hear them, they finally stopped yelling. They desperately needed water, so the two worked their way down to the Colorado River far below. Momentarily safe, they both agreed upon parting to send help for the other. Walt went upriver, John went down.

Grand Canyon's helicopter "210" performing a short-haul rescue of passengers from a commercial river trip down river from Phantom Ranch in June 1991.
KEN PHILLIPS PHOTO

On Sunday, I decided I wasn't making good enough time, so I used my belt and some tough roots and made a kind of raft out of some logs. I floated down the stream—they say about eight miles—before I got into some heavy rapids . . . raft broke up . . . fell in . . . almost drowned.

I managed to drag myself out but I realized I was on the wrong side of the river. So I went up above the rapids a little and swam across to a sandbar.

There were some mesquite bushes and cactus on shore nearby. I ate some cactus pulp and mesquite beans to stop the gnawing in my stomach. The cactus tasted terrible. I drank water right from the river. When I had been on the sandbar for about a day, I collected some stones together and spelled out a big "H"—meaning "Help" and I hoped that an airplane would spot it.

Hearing echoing cries from deep within the canyon, tourists activated the search. Ranger Dan Davis, after a week of dawn-to-dusk flying in the mile-deep gorge, feared they were really looking for a third body. Davis had already found a dead priest and 16-year-old boy, and knew that the chances of John surviving the 125-degree heat or the thousand-foot cliffs were slim. On the seventh day— the last before the Army's "flying bananas" had to return to Ft. Huachuca—they made one final pass down the river.

I was on my third day on the sandbar when I heard this heli- copter coming toward me—close and low. It came within about six feet of the bar and it was kicking up a lot of sand and dust. I was never so happy in my life. A Ranger climbed down a rope ladder while the 'copter hovered above the sandbar and asked me if I felt strong enough to climb up the ladder. I told him "sure."

```
                 September 1, 1959
          Mt. Rainier National Park
     ---------------------------------------
```

"A CLASSIC EXAMPLE OF POLITICAL INTERFERENCE COSTING 3 LIVES"

"PROJECT Crater" was an Air Force summer-long geology and high-altitude research effort on top of the 14,410-foot mountain. The park, sensing problems for some of the inexperienced investigators at this storm-prone elevation, orig- inally denied permission for the camp. As is often the case however, the deci- sion was overturned by uninformed desk-bound Washington bureaucrats 3,000 miles away.

On August 30, Dr. C. T. "Tup" Bressler, chairman of the Geology Depart- ment of Western Washington College, climbed to the camp to spend a week. Bressler, a mountaineer of considerable ability after nearly 30 years in the Cascades, was well liked by his peers.

Probably suffering from a delayed but severe high-altitude edema, Bressler was already in a coma when climbing guide Gil Blinn arrived. "His condition had begun deteriorating the day after his arrival on the summit, but [the project leader] had wanted to study [Bressler's] physiological response as a part of his research project rather than evacuate him to a lower elevation."

After winds and altitude turned an Air Force helicopter around, a frantic request for an air-drop of lifesaving oxygen was made. Harold Horn, the 41-year-old operations officer for the Washington Wing of the Civil Air Patrol as well as a longtime friend of the state's rescue community, lifted off. Forced to come back once because of mechanical problems, the experienced pilot and his 29-year-old equipment dropper, Charles Carman, launched again.

Winds at the summit neared 50 knots, the air-drop never arrived, and Dr. Bressler died at 5 the next morning. A radio contact soon confirmed that Horn and Carman had failed to return home as well.

The dead professor was wrapped in tarps and everyone in camp began sliding him down. Harsh "suncupping" in the snow made the going very slow. After descending less than 3,000 feet, a severe storm rose. Hastily marking the spot with wands, the team was forced to leave the body and continue down.

During this time, the missing plane was located from the air on a ridge at 14,000 feet. Having come to a rest upside down, it was completely buried with only one wheel sticking above the fresh snow. Dick McGowan, Lute Jerstad (the NPS trail crewman who later climbed Mt. Everest), and Gil Blinn set out in the afternoon to reach it. Heavy snow made the going slow, and a ground blizzard eventually forced them to stop near midnight at 11,500 feet and sleep in a shallow crevasse. Blinn would later recall:

> The morning of September 7 dawned clear and windy. As we prepared for the summit, a team appeared below us on their way up. Lute and Dick left for the summit while I stayed behind to begin digging Bressler's body out of the snow. The support arrived shortly, led by Jim and Lou Whittaker.
>
> Eventually, Dick and Lute came back, driven down by high winds. Jim, Lou and Dick made another attempt to reach the summit and the plane wreck while Lute and I led the support party in taking Bressler's remains to Camp Muir. As we rounded Cathedral Gap, another storm hit suddenly and violently, making it difficult to find Camp Muir.
>
> The same storm stopped the summit party at about 13,700 feet. They reported that 80-mile winds, blowing snow and a lowering cloud cap reduced visibility to less than 25 feet. They too returned to Camp Muir. Bressler's body was left at Camp Muir. It was turning into a long operation.

The next day, the weather once again cleared and a recovery party was able to retrieve Bressler's body; this still left two rescuers unaccounted for. On September 9, the plane was finally reached—both men were frozen inside. After securing permission from the families, personal effects were removed and the twisted wreckage, with Horn and Carman too solidly enmeshed inside to be extracted, was shoved into a nearby crevasse.

Ranger Bob Sellers, one of the rescuers involved, is still upset after 30 years, for he believes this was "a classic example of political interference costing 3 lives."

Underwater SAR is never routine. This young air man from a nearby Air Force base went swimming in Lake Mead and disappeared in 1969. Left to right: rangers Don Chase, Orville Rogers, and the author. LARRY CLARK PHOTO

CHAPTER 7

1960-1969

John Gaylor, the veteran [Yosemite] park
ranger, thinks forest fire fighting less
strenuous than rescuing lost maids in
the woods.

—Mariposa Gazette, August 7, 1915

THE 1960s ushered in the use of scuba as a valuable tool: for search and rescue, maintenance, and resource protection.

DIVING

In the fall of 1934, the first underwater archeological work using artificial air in North America was undertaken at Virginia's Colonial National Historical Park. Numerous artifacts were recovered from British warships of Cornwallis's Fleet, sunk in the York River in 1781. A hard-hat diver was used.

Five years later, in an unsuccessful search for a Las Vegas youth who disappeared in Lake Mead on April 9, 1939, the NPS began using artificially supplied air for SAR. While France's Emile Gagnan and Jacques-Yves Cousteau were developing the "Aqua-Lung" in the early 1940s, hard-hat divers were used sporadically in the park system. This included the retrieval of a dead boy above Yosemite's Nevada Falls in 1943, as well as the first underwater archeological explorations in Arizona's Montezumas Well in 1948.

Scuba arrived in a big way off the California coast at the nearby, abalone-rich Channel Islands National Monument when 12 dive regulators from France first appeared in Los Angeles in 1948. These innovations were soon followed by another 12 the next year, all of which were successfully adapted to fit modified aircraft oxygen cylinders, crude precursors of our modern-day scuba tanks.

In 1950, again using hard-hat diving equipment, three cavers from the Southern California Grotto of the National Speleological Society (NSS) descended to 75 feet in Death Valley's Devils Hole. Their cumbersome, umbilical cord–like air hose prevented exploration of lateral passageways; however, in the spring of 1953, scuba was used there. Diving through the boxcar-sized opening in the limestone sinkhole was an aggressive young graduate student. Jim Stewart eventually became the diving officer for the University of California and the Park Service's longtime technical diving advisor. In August of the same year, William Brown, among others of the NSS, dove to 150 feet in Devils Hole. Wearing a single scuba tank, Brown discovered the large, air-filled cavern now bearing his name. He continued to breathe through his scuba system, fearing that the atmosphere in the pitch-black room was toxic (it isn't).

An early—possibly the very first—use of scuba for a body recovery in the NPS was by a marina roustabout at Lake Mead. After searching for two days, Chuck Rowland located the body of a 19-year-old on April 27, 1955. He repeated this effort several times over the next few years. Since that time there have been hundreds of recoveries in Lake Mead using scuba. It was so novel that some areas, such as Crater Lake, even required permits to use the "exotic" equipment.

On June 29, 1958, Harry Wham, a Las Vegas lounge act as well as the owner of Whamco Divers, made the first of many body recoveries for the NPS. A former member of the Navy Underwater Demolition Team (UD-10), Wham served as an advisor to actor Lloyd Bridges and *Sea Hunt*. This half-hour television show, which ran from 1958 to 1961, was occasionally filmed at Lake Mead. Wham held NAUI (National Association of Underwater Instructors) instructor rating #237 and also was a YMCA scuba instructor. He died on February 3, 1983.

On July 27, 1960, backcountry ranger Leroy Brock, while on a hiking patrol in a very remote section of Kings Canyon, discovered a crashed B-24 that had been missing since 1943. The five crewmen were soon brought out of the 11,000-foot-high lake by hard-hat divers from the Army's Presidio of San Francisco. The tiny lake was later named Hester Lake (after the copilot), and the missing aviators were interred in Arlington Cemetery.

Following the establishment of Channel Islands as a national monument in 1938 and Virgin Island as a national park in 1956, the NPS solidified its concept of underwater visitation using snorkeling and scuba when President Kennedy named Buck Island Reef National Monument an "underwater park" in 1961.

OTHER DIVING MILESTONES

1959	Ranger Jack Morehead, recently transferred from Yosemite to Colorado National Monument, is the first NPS employee to be scuba certified at government expense.
November 23, 1962	Park Rangers Art Johnson, Jim Randall, George Schesventer, and U.S. Park Policeman Ted Chittick are graduated from the three-week-long U.S. Naval School for Deep Sea Divers in Washington, D.C. "It was late November and there was ice floating on the river. One of our compass destinations from the landing craft we were diving from was a sewer outflow pipe on the south shore and we just headed for the source of the foam."
January 1963	Jim Randall, along with Millis Patton, the NPS "forms person," designs Form 10-419—the first NPS "Diving Chart." It is based on the Navy Diving Chart used for the same purpose.
June 28, 1963	Twenty-year-old Tom Dumay of Columbia Falls, Montana, a volunteer rescuer, drowns while looking for a six-year-old boy. Certified as a "shallow water diver," Dumay had run out of air. His death is a key impetus for a scuba program for the NPS.

OTHER DIVING MILESTONES

July 17, 1963	Jack Morehead and Bob White become first of many to graduate from California's Scripps Institute of Oceanography. Its dive officer, Jim Stewart, offers free training to the NPS.
August 20, 1963	First NPS Diving Policy, "Guidelines for Use of SCUBA and Other Diving Apparatus by NPS Employees on Official Business," is issued. Other than possibly the military, this is probably the first such guideline for a federal agency.
January 9, 1964	Scuba class is started at Glen Canyon; 11 days later, Bob Scott is "authorized to serve as an instructor."
August 1964	Trained by Harry Wham, first Lake Mead Dive Team becomes operational. Each diver must buy his own wet suit, face mask, snorkel, fins, and booties; tanks and regulators are purchased by the park. Knives, depth gauges, and other equipment "were also purchased by the individuals if they were wanted but were not considered essential at that time."
July 20, 1965	Two young scuba divers disappear in Death Valley's Devils Hole. Led by Harry Wham, 44 divers dive unsucessfully for three days in the search. James Houtz descends to 315 feet in the cave, and a special dive team is brought in from Washington, D.C.
May 31, 1966	Glen Canyon ranger Bob Scott is "designated as one of several in the Southwest Region to be an Examiner of National Park Service personnel who have had training and experience in the use of Self-Contained Underwater Breathing Apparatus (SCUBA)."
June 1966	Ranger Tom Hartman recovers body in Steamboat Bay for first practical use of scuba in Yosemite. One month later the park is authorized to start a dive program.
June 6, 1966	Grand Teton Ranger Jack Morehead begins teaching scuba to Yellowstone National Park staff.
1967	Lake Mead purchases its first air compressor for scuba.
1968	Gary Davis of the NPS is assigned as an "Aquanaut" to TEKTITE I, the first U.S. civilian man-in-the-sea project, Virgin Islands National Park. TEKTITE II will conclude on November 22, 1970.

OTHER DIVING MILESTONES

September 30, 1968	"First totally National Park Service Underwater Archeology project, using NPS archeologist-divers, in an NPS area, paid for by NPS funds," enters Montezumas Well for six-day effort.
1969	Lake Mead "guesstimates" they have had 2,500 hours of underwater time to this point; only one ruptured ear drum was suffered. Four years later, on August 31, 1973, Ranger T. K. Brown will die of a heart attack while on a training dive in the park's Ringbolt Rapids.
May 1970	Everglade National Park dive team is formed.

MILESTONES OF THE 1960s

1960	The NPS's 187 units receive 80,039,100 visitors.
March 9, 1960	Grand Teton Rangers John Fonda and Gail Wilcox drown on winter patrol; **Valor** and **Carnegie Hero Awards** are earned by Ranger Stan Spurgeon and posthumously by Gail Wilcox.
May 17, 1960	Greatest rescue in North American climbing annals occurs when two separate and equally demanding efforts take place at 17,000-foot level of Mt. McKinley; 50 expert mountaineers fly in from Pacific Northwest to help effect the mission.
June 25, 1960	Grand Teton's first use of a helicopter for an SAR.
November 13, 1960	Mt. Rainier National Park's "Mr. Rescue," Assistant Chief Ranger Bill Butler, is subject of *This Is Your Life* TV show—the only NPS person to be so honored.
June 15, 1961	First helicopters to be contracted for Yosemite, Sequoia, and Kings Canyon National Parks. Used for administration, fire, and SAR, they are first stationed in Fresno. In 1964 these tiny, two-place ships will cost $149.75 per hour.
1961	Mountain Rescue Association and American Alpine Club develop written form to document U.S. SAR activity.
1962	Members of German Shepherd Dog Club of Washington State establish Search Dog Committee. After three years of intensive training, they will be made available to agencies for SAR.

MILESTONES OF THE 1960s

1963	*Ashley v. United States* (215 F. Supp. 39 [D. Neb. 1963]) establishes park visitors as "invitees," a legal concept that will have serious SAR and tort implications.
	Retired Mt. McKinley superintendent and early conqueror of the peak Grant Pearson publishes *My Life of High Adventure.*
May 3, 1963	Air Force Para Jumpers drop on a wrecked B-47 in backcountry of Yellowstone—first use of PJs for NPS.
November 30, 1963	First English-language edition of *Mountain Rescue Techniques,* by Wastl Mariner, is adopted by International Commission for Alpine Rescue as its official manual.
January 1964	Dr. Harold Jakes develops portable, floatable, telescoping, 25-pound fiberglass stretcher for Sequoia National Park. The Jakes litter will be used on SARs for many years.
June 24, 1965	Climber shatters his leg high on Yosemite's Sentinel Rock and has to be winched off. This is park's first Big Wall rescue. Four climbers are used to assist. Thereafter, climbers and rangers will begin such cooperative efforts.
1966	After Mt. Rainier National Park in 1958, Rocky Mountain becomes second NPS unit to join Mountain Rescue Association (MRA). Yosemite will be third, on November 25, 1967. In 1997, 13 NPS units will be serving as ex-officio members of MRA.
May 21, 1966	Long Island's Fire Island National Seashore employees Ashley Smith and William Shaner (first day on duty) drown trying to save a surfer, three rescuers die.
June 22, 1966	First plane to fly under 630-foot-high arch of Jefferson National Expansion Memorial in St. Louis. At least seven other planes and one helicopter will duplicate this illegal act.
July 12, 1966	Dennis Johnson, 8, walks away from Yellowstone's Canyon Village. Despite an intensive search he is never seen again, and his disappearance remains one of the park's great mysteries.
July 24, 1966	First recorded injury, subsequent rescue, and possibly even first parachute jump off a cliff in an NPS area; leaping from Yosemite's El Capitan, two 26-year-old California skydivers are hurt when they misjudge hazardous conditions.

MILESTONES OF THE 1960s

Summer 1967	Commercial rock-climbing instruction and mountain guiding is begun by the Yosemite Park and Curry Company.
July 18, 1967	Seven people in one party are killed climbing Mt. McKinley—park's single worst mountaineering accident ever.
August 21, 1967	One of the earliest and most dramatic Big Wall rescues begins on Grand Teton; six men earn **DOI Valor Awards,** and park receives a **DOI Unit Award for Excellence of Service.**
December 21, 1967	Richard Slates, an experienced Mountain Rescue Association volunteer from the China Lake Team, dies while looking for a lost hiker on Death Valley's snow-covered Telescope Peak.
January-April 1968	Rangers from Mt. Rainier National Park attend first formal advanced emergency medical training.
March 9, 1969	Buried under 5 feet of snow on Mt. Rainier, a man is soon located by Jean Syrotuck and her dog Bismark, of the German Shepherd Search Dog Committee of Washington—a first for them.
April 1969	Washington State's Search Dog Committee leaves German Shepherd Dog Club and forms two groups: Search and Rescue Dogs Association (SARDA) under Bill Syrotuck and German Shepherd Search Dogs (GSSD) under Hank Wilcox—the only two air-scenting search dog groups in the United States. SARDA will disband in 1984.
June 14, 1969	Seven-year-old boy vanishes on family outing in Great Smoky Mountains—largest search in NPS history.
August 1969	First NPS SAR Report is initiated—Form 10-199b; much-needed formal recording of statistical information begins.

March 9, 1960
Grand Teton National Park

THE DEATH OF TWO PARK RANGERS

BEFORE noon that first day, 48-year-old District Ranger Gale Wilcox and his 28-year-old assistant, John Fonda, would die in the below-zero Wyoming cold. Along with Stan Spurgeon, Fonda and Wilcox had just started the three-day backcountry ski patrol. Performed in the deep of the Wyoming winter, this was a routine 25-mile trip to measure snow depth, shovel out remote patrol cabins, and record wildlife. As experienced cross-country skiers, they knew the harsh demands before them and the stark realities of survival.

Only hours before he died in the river, John Fonda took a photo of the snowplane that delivered them to the trail that morning. Left to right: rangers Gale Wilcox, Stan Spurgeon, and Clyde Maxey. JOHN FONDA PHOTO/DOUG MCLAREN COLLECTION

Heading for the Survey Peak Cabin on the west bank of Jackson Lake, the three skied away from the highway at 10:15 A.M. Within 30 minutes they reached the Snake River, where Assistant Chief Ranger Spurgeon commented on the poor state of the channel and the open patches of water. Skiing 300 more yards, they found a spot where it seemed solidly frozen over for several hundred feet.

Spurgeon carefully slid off the 5-foot bank and would later recall in his report: "I moved out onto the ice, testing ahead of me until I was approximately mid-channel, after which I poled smoothly but rapidly across. The surface of the ice was hard and windblown and free from snow." Then Wilcox, precisely matching track for ski track, cautiously poled across. Fonda, having photographed the first two crossing, gently eased onto the ice.

A University of Montana graduate in English literature and a Korean War veteran, John Fonda had served seasonally for six years until becoming a permanent ranger two years before. He loved the mountains as few others do.

Having climbed most of the park's peaks, he had performed with distinction on Grand Teton's prestigious search and rescue team for eight years.

Spurgeon spun around; to the 48-year-old veteran Teton ranger, the slight cracking noise the ice made was unmistakable; all he could see was a head 15 feet from the far shore. Wilcox, a nonswimmer, turned and without hesitation skied back toward Fonda; Spurgeon quickly followed. Six feet from the rapidly growing, dark hole, Wilcox dropped to his stomach and extended a ski pole to his floundering friend. Spurgeon slid in behind Wilcox, firmly grabbing a ski.

> Gale and I immediately wiggled out of our packs and pushed them to one side. John was hanging on to the ski pole held by Gale and trying to crawl up the ice but the ice kept breaking down with him, and as he moved forward we kept crawling backward. . . . I removed one ski and shoved it down the ice to John—who grasped it—after which the ice on which Gale and I were laying gave way and we were submerged in the water. While in the water I removed my other ski by reaching down and tripping the throw on the binding.

Speeding toward exhaustion, Spurgeon tried to release Wilcox's heavy wooden skis, which were still fastened to his boots by safety straps; diving beneath the frigid waters, Stan felt for the bottom.

> I remember trying to give Gale some support to help him crawl up on the ice. This seemed futile so I made a desperate effort to crawl up on the ice myself. A large cake of ice, perhaps . . . five feet across, broke out with me. I was able to get by it and in another desperate effort, clawing with my elbows on the ice, I was able to crawl out. I crawled for several yards, after which I got to my feet and discovered the ski pole that was left in the snow . . . came back toward Gale.

Wilcox, a 24-year veteran ranger, precariously held onto the extended pole while Spurgeon dragged him backward. When he was partially out of the water, one long ski jammed under the ice.

> By desperate efforts on both our parts we managed to break the strap and I was able to drag Gale up to safe ice. About the time I was dragging Gale away from the open water, John's head bobbed under. I yelled at him to hang on. He came up on at least two occasions before he stayed under.

Spurgeon tried to get the 6-foot Wilcox to his feet, but he was in such a state of shock and so hypothermic that he could not talk or even support himself.

> The toughest decision that I had to make was to leave Gale and proceed toward the cabin without him. My thoughts at this time were that it was obvious that I couldn't get Gale to

the cabin in his condition and the only possibility for salvation for either of us was for me to get to the cabin as quickly as possible, hoping that I would be able to get back to Gale with a sleeping bag in time.

I don't know text. The trip to the cabin is rather hazy in my mind. I can remember when I first floundered in the deep snow and tried to crawl, which soon became obviously completely impossible. I sunk the ski pole into the snow and by leaning on it with all of the weight I could I was able to continue without sinking in more than about one foot.

Exhausted and hypothermic, Stan Spurgeon was unable to return in time. Ranger Wilcox died of exposure. Ranger Fonda drowned.

Gale H. Wilcox was posthumously granted a **Citation for Valor** by the Department of the Interior on April 19, 1961, as well as a **Bronze Medal** by the Carnegie Hero Commission. Stanley H. Spurgeon received a **Citation for Valor** by the DOI on April 19, 1961, and was awarded a **Bronze Medal** by the Carnegie Hero Commission.

March 19, 1960
Yosemite National Park

WANTED TO BE THE YOUNGEST
ON TOP OF LOST ARROW

NO one saw the young blond fall; Irving Smith had moved down and out of sight of his climbing partner. The 17-year-old was on the second of two short rappels into the narrow notch behind Lost Arrow. Although frighteningly vacuous—with 1,400 feet of nothing below, and only a dozen feet to either side—Smith's descent should have been an easy, 200-foot, controlled "slide."

A faint cry echoed from below, followed by the unmistakable sounds of a body tumbling deeper into the nearly vertical gully. Ricocheting 600 feet, the young man probably died instantly.

Using a powerful spotting scope the next day, veteran climbing ranger Wayne Merry saw the lifeless form wedged in a narrow crack in the West Arrow Chimney. Aided by expert cragsman Warren Harding, Merry believed he could safely recover the body. Superintendent John Preston, however, along with the boy's parents, felt it was too dangerous and would not authorize the attempt. Smith's body remained and the area was closed to climbing for a year.

Wanting to enter the record books as the youngest to conquer The Arrow, the high-school junior from Fresno instead became the first modern-era climber to be killed in Yosemite. Between that time and 1990, at least 55 other climbers died in the valley.

On July 13, 1947, 13 years before Smith's tragedy, 24-year-old Al Baxter was the first modern-era climber to be seriously injured in Yosemite.

MAN DANGLES 2,800 FEET ABOVE YOSEMITE VALLEY

YOSEMITE NATIONAL PARK, July 14—A San Francisco mountain climber considered himself lucky he is alive today after dangling 2,800 feet above Yosemite Valley with only a slim rope holding him to his companions.

Alfred W. Baxter, 24, is in the Lewis Memorial Hospital here thankful he only suffered two broken legs in a perilous 40-foot fall down the sheer rock side of Cathedral Spire.

Two in the party of 13 rangers who brought him to the hospital also were injured. A 500-pound boulder struck them as they carried Baxter over the talus slope at the foot of the spire.

Assistant Chief Ranger Homer Robinson, in charge of the rescuers, suffered lacerations and bruises on both legs. One foot of Ranger Byrne Packard was fractured by the boulder.

—San Francisco Chronicle, 7-14-47
(reprinted by permission)

```
            May 17, 1960
      Mt. McKinley National Park
---------------------------------------
```

"MOST MASSIVE MOUNTAINEERING RESCUE OPERATION IN U.S. HISTORY"

THIS is what *Life* magazine called it. Before it ended nine long days later, more than 65 of this country's premier mountaineers had been mobilized; at least 23 world-record aircraft landings had taken place; two men had died volunteering their help; and the rescue resources of the military in Alaska had been taxed to the limit.

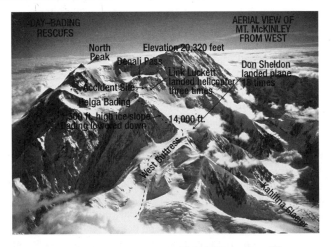

With at least three litter cases at the 12,000-foot mark on Mt. McKinley, the highest peak in North America, 50 mountaineers and two pilots assembled for these two simultaneous rescue missions.

PHOTO BY BRADFORD WASHBURN/BOSTON MUSEUM OF SCIENCE

Native Americans call it Denali; to them the massive 20,320-foot mountain is "The Great One." So it is to climbers. For the first time, two separate and successful teams—the 17th and 18th—shared the roof of North America at the same time. Four hours later and with temperatures nearing 30-degrees below zero, four men from one party lay in "a dark heap": a tangled pile at the 17,500-foot mark. One thousand feet lower, a 31-year-old woman from the other party, trying to be the second woman ever to reach the top, lay suffering in her tent from a slow, potentially fatal swelling of the brain.

A physician from Anchorage, Rod Wilson was the last in his party as they descended, and would later write:

> I kept looking back to watch the progress of the [John] Day party behind us. They were in poor shape, i.e., tired and feeling the effects of altitude from having ascended so fast. . . . I looked back one final time . . . there was a dark heap . . . perhaps 400 yards down slope.

No one is sure what happened. Jim Whittaker, who later became the first American to conquer Mt. Everest, could only recall that the ice "was like a freight train rushing by, two inches from your face." He and Lou, his twin—a senior guide and eventual co-owner of Washington's Rainier Mountaineering—escaped with only bruises and frostbite.

Pete Schoening, a veteran Himalayan climber and a recognized hero on K2 (second-highest mountain in the world at 28,250 feet) seven years before, was out of commission with a concussion and severe frostbite on one hand. The most critical of the four, however, was John Day. A 51-year-old cattleman from Portland, he snapped one ankle and ruptured the ligaments of the other; he was now at the ultimate mercy of men and mountain.

Dr. Wilson, absorbed with both his own struggle and that of his teammate, Helga Bading, would often wonder what might have happened had he not looked back one last time. Shouting back and forth, the full gravity of the situation soon registered with them all. They had devoted the last 15 hours to the highest 4,000 feet in North America and were now drained of strength; "the thought of making that return trip at that time was nearly impossible."

Team Leader Paul Crews did it anyway. Knowing how crucial their needs were, Crews gathered up a tent and forced his way back up to the injured party from Seattle. The shelter, slit open with a knife, was slipped over the injured Day, now in the group's two survival sleeping bags. The three lesser impaired men then roped up and continued down toward their camp. Schoening's concussion caused him to believe they should take another route down, so he unroped. Lou Whitaker later found his friend, gloveless and dazed, with his legs dangling over a 3,000-foot drop.

In Anchorage early the next morning, the newly formed, month-old Alaska Rescue Group received the following two-way radio message:

> EMERGENCY—All members John Day party suffered fall 11:30 PM May 17. Day injured seriously, probable broken leg. Needs air evacuation at 17,000-ft.-level top of West Buttress 200 yds from flat area. Can pack to flat area. Bring fresh

batteries for Motorola Model H 23-1 Handy Talky. Will standby your message at 8 AM and every 2 hrs. Repeat—send batteries. PAUL CREWS.

Within minutes that Wednesday morning, the callup was relayed from rescue leader John Johnston to Erik Barnes to Jon Gardey to Hans Metz, and on. The Rescue Coordination Center at Elmendorf Air Force Base reacted and a helicopter was quickly arranged for. Civil Air Patrol pilots assembled; because of rainy low ceilings, they had to follow railroad tracks. They nearly turned back.

Don Sheldon, having originally landed both parties on the mountain, immediately retook to the air. He prepared an airdrop of medical supplies and radio batteries. The Alaska bush pilot extraordinaire, at the controls of an 8898-Delta, had been in his element—and Super Cub—since early morning. But he couldn't find them.

The military Huey climbed to 17,500 feet and started to circle the peak, until smoke began seeping into the cabin. A battery had exploded, destroying part of the large helicopter's electrical system; limping back to base, it couldn't find them either.

The delirious Helga Bading was deteriorating quickly. With four, maybe even five stretcher cases at 17,000 feet on a remote peak in Alaska, the news flashed across the country.

The Northwest Mountain Rescue Council—teams from Seattle, Portland, Bremerton, Everett, Tacoma, and Vancouver—swung into high gear. Not only was it an emergency unparalleled in mountain rescue, but the injured were some of their own. Men such as Molenaar, Senner, Prater, Rose, Trott, and Wahlstrom—climbers with extensive high-altitude experience—were given only two hours to gather gear, clothing, food, and other rescue equipment.

Very early Thursday morning, the first dozen of these rescuers caught a Pacific Northern airliner for the five-hour flight to Anchorage, courtesy of John Day's son. The next loads of men and equipment went via the Air Force's free "travel service."

Dr. Wilson soon discovered just how little could be done medically and how much more important basic survival was at this time. Splinting John Day's leg and dispensing some minor narcotics, he provided little more than first aid. These were men who had endured hardship and accidents before; Wilson knew the most important thing was the will to survive. But Bading, suffering from a prolonged lack of oxygen, might die unless evacuated soon.

The one person in the world most familiar with Mt. McKinley learned about the unfolding rescue effort while at an opera in Boston. Brad Washburn had led an extensive photographic survey for the National Geographic Society in 1936. It was on this early exploration that the West Buttress Route, the one now being used by both parties, was discovered. He had been on the mountain numerous times afterward and knew it like no one else. He provided the key to the rescue to his good friend Don Sheldon.

Ski-equipped planes landed climbers on The Great One; at the mercy of 10,000 feet of elevation, they hefted heavy packs and started slowly upward. Unable to land near the victims, large, twin-bladed "flying bananas" leapfrogged the rescuers higher and higher.

On one pass, a flare was thrown out of a door to determine wind characteristics—it blew back into the helicopter. Numerous airdrops containing stoves, tents, oxygen, food, and emergency evacuation sleds were made; some even landed near their mark.

At 3 A.M. Friday, Paul Crews again started making radio calls. He was told there were now 50 men on the glaciers below and helicopters were again promised later that day. Dr. Wilson would also inform Crews "that it looked like the end of Helga" unless she was immediately taken down; roping off the nearly vertical, 1,500-foot ice wall was the only way to save her. After laboriously retrieving an emergency sled, air-dropped to a glacier far below, the ill woman was readied for the descent.

Metzger, Brauchli, and Crews, bone-weary after days of little sleep and severe strain, displayed the utmost in skilled mountaineering. They spent three long, dangerous hours lowering the dying woman down the frozen, 500-yard cliff—one short rope length at a time. Then Andy Brauchli, calling on some untapped inner strength, turned around and climbed back up.

Brad Washburn's earlier phone call from Boston kept running through Sheldon's mind as he flew upward.

> I'm certain that you can get in there with no trouble, but I can't say about coming out. Get 15,000 feet of altitude as you fly up Kahiltna Pass and fly due north . . . turn your airplane exactly 90 degrees to the right, and directly in front of you will be a large triangular pyramid of granite rock. Fly directly toward it until you are really close, drop some power, pull on your flaps, and fly around the right hand side of the pyramid. Right in front of you will be your landing spot.

That day, Don Sheldon, in bringing out Bading and then servicing the rescue effort, may have landed his plane higher than anyone had ever done; he made a total of 18 such landings in his 150-hp Super Cub. Bading, an immigrant from Germany and a founder of the Mountaineering Club of Alaska, would live to climb again.

That day, Link Luckett, starting with only 12 gallons of gasoline, landed his small Hiller helicopter three times at 17,200 feet—higher than anyone else had ever done. On his second trip, with the injured John Day aboard, he asked the 6-foot-5 Whittaker twins to lift up on the skids as he powered up on the struggling machine. Upon his command, they "threw" the ship over the edge, and the skilled 32-year-old pilot from Anchorage dove toward Peter's Glacier 7,000 feet below.

That day, an Army high-altitude specialist and veteran of previous McKinley missions, along with a private Cessna-180 pilot, crashed and burned 250 feet from the Whittakers. Although they had tried to help in their own way, Sergeant Rob Elliott and William Stevenson were not part of the formal rescue effort.

That day, with several dozen unacclimated and nearly spent rescuers strung up and down the frozen mountainside, came the frightening forecast for hurricane-force winds.

At 13,000 feet, one rescue team was pinned down by what one veteran Himalayan climber said "was the worst storm he had ever seen on a mountain."

A weatherman later determined that the winds had reached 135 mph just above the rescue camp. Tents shredded and uprooted, howling winds chiseled away 5 feet of snow, and about a dozen men eventually crammed into the one surviving five-man tent. The storm lasted 40 very long hours.

On May 26, nine days after the epic mission started, the last volunteer was lifted off the icy face of The Great One. The curtain was finally lowered on the most massive mountain rescue operation ever performed in North America.

The Alaskan press criticized the excess of manpower as a waste of time and money. But, as one rescuer responded, "The operation could have gone the other way": if the storm had hit a day earlier . . . if pilots and rescuers had not performed so bravely . . . if . . .

Link Luckett, the daring, record-setting helicopter pilot, received a **Carnegie Hero Medal** (silver), $500, and an additional "$700 to reimburse him for pecuniary loss."

```
             August 4, 1960
       Grand Teton National Park
    ---------------------------------------
```

RANGER DIES

TIM was 15 feet above and slightly to the left of his wife, Sally. Faced with an overhanging wall, he cautiously felt his way up the steep face. Having driven one piton in, he was rounding the sharp corner when his fragile friction hold failed. In just a blink of a lifetime, his fall ended below Sally.

Sapped of strength and unable to pull himself to safety, Tim cried out to his wife of less than two months for help. He was pinned tightly against the rock by his weight, and Sally desperately tried to lower him 20 feet. Thirty minutes passed before she could escape and tie her end of the rope to a boulder. Ranger Tim Bond, a seasoned climber and veteran rescuer, was probably dead before his wife started screaming for help.

Fritz Ermarth, a fire control aide climbing nearby on his day off, heard the shouts before he saw his 24-year-old friend dangling under an overhang some 25 feet below Sally. With assistance from other parties, someone was lowered to the now-still form. Using the light from a full moon, a six-man park rescue team spent all night climbing to within 300 feet of the body.

> During the night Tim's body slipped . . . 50–60 feet but was caught when the belay rope snarled at the piton anchor. The evacuation, . . . under hazardous rockfall conditions, included lowering the body nearly 500 feet down the overhanging south wall of the East Summit.

A helicopter landing at the base of the north face of Shadow Peak at the 10,200-foot level completed the evacuation. This was only the second time a helicopter had been used in a Grand Teton National Park rescue.

All the men were extremely tired. It is doubtful whether they could have completed the carry-out to the trail safely. Large boulder fields, long and strenuous traverses on steep slopes, and precipitous rotten couloirs [steep icy gullies] remained to be negotiated. The team had been without water for nearly 15 hours before a relief squad arrived.

The recovery totalled $1,561.44, with the helicopter costing the great majority of that: $1,135.42. The official report noted "that the nearest helicopter we could find for this rescue was at Idaho City, Idaho. Only 25 minutes of flying time was consumed in the actual rescue. Remaining 8 hours and 40 minutes was flying time to and from Idaho City."

November 26, 1960
Death Valley National Monument

"WAITING AND WAITING AND WAITING"

DEATH Valley's Matt Ryan, a 30-year ranger of the National Park Service, was a "living legend" among his peers; this search was, by his own account, one of his toughest assignments.

17-year-old Richard Hill was let out of his father's car on Mahogany Flat to climb Telescope Peak (11,040 foot), normally a very easy seven-mile trail that can be accomplished in four, or five, or six hours, maybe by a good strong seventeen-year old hiker. But in this case, a storm came up in mid-day, and Richard Hill did not return at the appointed time.

The storm continued until probably at higher elevations two feet of snow was dropped. Nothing could be done that night, of course, except to look for lights from distances and to check the exit roads from the Peak in case he had gotten off the trail. The search went on at a high pitch of intensity and interest for about five days. This included air search.

Air Search and Rescue sent over helicopters; we had all the help we could get our hands on . . . and of course realizing that since we found no tracks in the snow, the new snow obliterated any tracking possibilities along the trail or even off the trail, as it turned out. So we finally had to give up when a new storm hit five days later, and assume that Richard Hill had not survived, since we had no sign whatsoever that he had survived.

It was May 5 of the next year before the snow melted enough so that we could organize an all-out search for his body, and we were very fortunate to have fifty men on the mountain, including two professional mountaineering search groups; and at 4:30 of the first day his body was found only half exposed from a receding snowdrift. He was, I think you would say, perfectly preserved; he had been in deep-freeze all winter.

. . . he would have made it had he not tripped over a tree root and pitched forward down the mountain side and his head struck a cleaver-like rock that actually pierced the brain.

But from the experience standpoint, this was a heart-rending thing, with the father in the position of having released the boy and wished him well—actually walked up part of the trail with him, you know—and then waiting and waiting and waiting. . . .

Ranger Matt Ryan died on September 8, 1988, in Boulder City, Nevada.

```
                  June 18, 1961
           Mt. Rainier National Park
-----------------------------------------
```

15 MINUTES AFTER STARTING THE HIKE, HER SON WAS DEAD

"IT'S such an easy walk," Brian's mother said in the long, chilly hours before the discovery was made. "It looked so safe. It's fantastic! To think he could have gotten lost with so many people around. It was like a highway here yesterday."

A dozen searchers scoured the snowfields near Paradise for 27 hours. Stopping briefly at 4 A.M., the tired men renewed their hunt at dawn. The ordeal was made harder for some of them because of the previous sleepless night spent fighting lightning-caused forest fires. Assistant Chief Ranger Bill Butler and pilot James Beach, overhead in a light plane and dangerously close to the mountain, strained against the blinding glare of the mountainside for a glimpse of the missing teenager.

Brian's telltale, 200-foot skidmarks abruptly vanished into a fresh, jagged hole in the snow; sensing the worst as only a parent will, the boy's father remained at the top. Carefully glissading down the steep slope, Bob Sellers could see the 40-foot waterfall plunge into the mist and shadows below.

Ranger Sellers would later recall that

Jack Morehead was the smallest among us so he was unanimously elected to be belayed under the snow to the bottom of the waterfall. All of us donated our outer parkas, etc., to poor Jack and watched him disappear. He found the boy dead so tied him in and we hauled Jack up.

He [Morehead] was totally miserable and in early stages of hypothermia but in those days we didn't know what to call

his condition. We did know he needed a hot bath and a stiff
drink.

Only 15 minutes after starting what was to have been a carefree hike on
Mt. Rainier, 14-year-old Brian Cornelius died.

April 19, 1962
Yosemite National Park

THE ROPES HAD FROZEN TO THE CLIFF

IN Yosemite that year, there were 78 mountaineering SARs with 11 fatalities,
compared to four deaths the year before. The following two young climbers
should have died, but didn't.

> . . . two rock climbers—Glen Denny, age 21, and John
> Weichard, age 24—became stranded during a snowstorm in
> the notch of Lost Arrow. The party had made the accent [sic]
> of the Arrow and on the way down the storm struck. By the
> time they reached the notch on their ropes, the ropes had
> frozen to the cliff. A rescue unit was dispatched. Ranger
> Wayne Merry, with the aid of George Whitmore, a Sierra Club
> member, reached the stranded party at 1:30 A.M. The descent
> by Merry and Whitmore was made entirely in the darkness.
> Denny, Weichard and Merry were raised to safety by wench
> [sic] the following morning. The climbing party of Denny and
> Weichard knew in advance that a storm was expected.
> —*Monthly Report of the Protection Division*, April 1962

Afterward, Wayne Merry was told that they had been considered for **Valor
Awards,** "but since we were experienced and knew what we were doing, it
wasn't dangerous enough."

February 12, 1963
Everglades National Park

WITH 43 ONBOARD AND AFTER
ONLY SEVEN SHORT MINUTES IN THE AIR

NORTHWEST Orient Flight 705 disappeared. After five long hours in the air,
Coast Guard rescue helicopter 1304 found it.

Lifting off at 1:35 P.M., visibility for the state-of-the-art Boeing 720 and its
crew was swiftly reduced to only 2 miles by the fast-moving rain-squall line.

Captain Almquist, climbing through 17,000 feet, requested clearance to 25,000 feet; Chicago-bound, the jet was scheduled to be at O'Hare at 4:20 P.M.

Six fishermen floating the headwaters of Shark River looked up and were startled when they "saw a fireball in an angry thunderhead. Afterward, a streak of fire, red and smoky, emerged from the base of the cloud. After the fire fell behind trees on their horizon, the sound of a heavy explosion reached them."

Within minutes of the plane's vanishing from Miami International's radar, a huge search "machine" was in motion. Taking to the air, more than a dozen military and Civil Air Patrol pilots scoured the south and central Florida flight path of the $5 million plane. This was the first incident ever to involve the new 720-B, and only the second such incident for the Miami airport.

Like other searchers, Coast Guard Lieutenant Commander James Dillon had been ducking in and out of rainstorms and dirty low ceilings all afternoon. "It was our last pass for the night, too, because it was getting so dark we could hardly see. We knew we were somewhere south of the [Tamiami] Trail just skitting along and then Mr. Wallace saw the fires. Two of them."

Vast and flat, the 'Glades are an endless confusion of sawgrass and mangrove swamps. The radio crackled, "We've got the wreckage in sight . . . but we don't know where we are."

Hoping they were signal fires, First Officer Wallace and Crew Chief Wiechel kept them in sight while Dillon felt his way through the gloomy curtain of rain. Hope turned to wreckage.

> It was dark as hell, but we could tell it was a flat area and we could see it was above water when we got down real low. . . . We didn't see any signs of life on the outside, or any bodies either, and went ahead and made a light landing between the tail section and the main fuselage.

There were no survivors.

May 3, 1963
Yellowstone National Park

BOMBER CRASH—
FIRST USE OF RESCUE PARACHUTISTS

IT was a routine night exercise at 23,000 feet, until the large tanker's spearlike refueling boom gutted the bomber's cockpit. Three of the B-47's crew were killed outright. Captain Bruce Chapman, 33, the only one still alive in the now mortally-wounded jet, stabilized the four-engine machine and then put it on autopilot. For 60 more miles the copilot rode the swept-wing Cold War monster, until it finally ran out of fuel and went into a flat spin. Chapman "punched out" only seconds before his doomed craft "pancaked" into Yellowstone's frozen backcountry.

At 7:16 P.M., the KC-135 tanker reported a midair collision somewhere above eastern Idaho and, within 45 minutes, Yellowstone rangers had been put on standby. That night, the Air Force had three C-119s over the park, and before dawn, they were joined by four more search aircraft, including two helicopters.

Ejecting into the darkness at 10,000 feet, Chapman quickly floated into the lodgepole forest only 1,500 feet below. Having somehow escaped injury when he crashed through the trees but now faced with 8-foot-deep snow, he fashioned crude snowshoes from saplings and started to walk out. He would be found 36 hours later working his way slowly from the woods. Unknown to him, he had landed less than 400 yards from his dead comrades.

That first night, a ground party from the Targhee National Forest began laboring toward the area where the bomber was thought to be; because of deteriorating weather, they were back out by 6 the next morning. Park Rangers Gordon Boyd and Dale Nuss readied an over-snow Weasel and stood by at search headquarters. During the next day, low clouds and snow showers kept the circling search craft from spotting the wreck—but from below, they could hear Chapman's "Mayday" every hour, on the hour. On the second full day:

> 0930—"a wing tip and one man located . . . OK and will be picked up by helicopter. . . ."

> 1010—"Helicopter cannot land at crash site. They will be able to lower people by winch."

> 1405—"a 2 man para-rescue team was dropped."

The remaining three crewmen were soon recovered from the mangled giant. An Air Force captain was officially appointed Yellowstone National Park Coroner, with the explicit understanding that Supervisory Park Ranger Tom Milligan was "to serve as witness."

This may be the first record of rescuers parachuting onto an NPS SAR. Thirty years later, during the summer of 1993, the B-47, minus its classified documents and highly strategic armament, was finally removed from the Yellowstone backcountry.

June 27, 1963
Glacier National Park

"DISCONTINUE THE SEARCH FOR OUR SON, AND LOOK FOR THE DIVER"

ALTHOUGH his father had jumped into the turbulence for him, little Gregory Trenor vanished in the foam. The six-year-old had slipped on wet rocks and fallen into the swift whitewater of McDonald Creek. Along with rangers from the park, officials from the nearby Flathead Lifesaving and Rescue Association rushed to the scene.

Glacially carved Lake McDonald is over 400 feet deep, and on that first day, scuba divers, without safer, shallow waters to investigate, focused on where the creek entered the lake. Numbed by cold, searchers stopped near midnight and wearily readied for morning.

Tom Dumay, 21 and a senior at the University of Montana, was a natural for the volunteer rescue team. An athlete and leader, he had lettered in basketball, football, and track and had been the student body president of nearby Columbia Falls High School.

Dumay and fellow-diver Ron Koppang finished their first probe below. At 40 feet, the current from the inflow of McDonald Creek was certainly noticeable, but nothing to be overly alarmed about. On their second dive they were at 90 feet when Dumay's tank suddenly ran dry. After frantically signalling his partner for help, he initiated the diver's standard buddy system of sharing air. Almost as suddenly, Koppang also ran out. Fast, much too fast, he popped to the surface, but Dumay didn't .

Other divers jumped overboard and hastily tried to follow a silvery stream of scattering bubbles downward. The thin thread to life vanished. Almost before anyone realized it, Tom Dumay was gone.

Koppang was rushed to a nearby hospital. Needing specialized help unavailable locally, he was flown on to Brownlee Dam and forced to change planes twice. Using the recompression chamber of the Idaho Power Company, he was then taken down to a simulated 165 feet and slowly, safely brought back up.

Just before noon, fresh divers resumed looking—for two victims now. Gregory Trenor's distraught parents heard the tragic news and phoned the park. "Please discontinue the search for our son, and look for the diver."

On their last planned dive, and after dangerously stretching their down time that day, Jack Von Lindern and Don Elgin located friend and fellow-volunteer Tom Dumay in the blackness at 110 feet.

Young Trenor was also eventually found and laid to rest.

These deaths led the NPS to formalize a Servicewide Dive Program. In 1965, Columbia Falls High School established the **Tom Dumay Memorial Award** for athletic ability and scholarship.

September 2, 1963
Yosemite National Park

ALMOST PICTURE PERFECT,
BUT THE PATIENT DIED ANYWAY

WAYNE Merry was a member of the first climbing team to scale Yosemite's "impossible" El Capitan in 1957 and then, several years later, served there as a park ranger.

> We [Wayne Merry and John Ward] choppered on up to the shoulder of Cathedral Peak. We asked the pilot if he could put us down on the knife-edge just below the summit, a couple hundred yards from the victims. He said he would try to shuttle us up there one at a time, though it was really

stretching the altitude limits for the Hiller-12E. But he managed it—put a skid down on the edge, and one at a time we cautiously slithered out, eyeballing the drop on either side. We edged along the ridge and then climbed the face directly below the spire to where the victims were.

The leader, Earl Hsu, had taken about a ninety-footer clear past his belayer. He had fallen pretty vertically and hit a sloping ledge awfully hard. He was unconscious and obviously very critical—after a close look I figured he had multiple skull fractures and various other broken bones. He had very little chance of even making it to the hospital. Later, his belayer confirmed they were both beginners.

Carl, Earl's younger brother looked about 14 and was sitting, still belaying the motionless body. He appeared almost paralyzed by the event and obviously was without the experience even to move down to assist Earl.

We improvised a cervical collar, loaded the patient with some difficulty into a sleeping bag and the basket, and lowered him to the level of the knife-edge. Somehow or other we managed to carry him along the narrow ledge. The helicopter pilot was an absolute winner. We radioed him in and he put his skid across the crest, and somehow or other we managed to secure the basket to the skid tray without dropping it or falling off in the process. I recall leaning on the skid out over the drop with one hand while lifting the Stokes on with the other—and the skid moving slightly under my hand as we worked.

I remember glancing up at the pilot while we were doing that, and I still remember his face—pale, absolute concentration, big beads of sweat on his forehead. Between the time the accident was reported and the time that Hsu was in the hospital, less than three hours had elapsed!

After participating in hundreds of other emergencies, whether rescue, ambulance work, structural firefighting, search, or whatever, I have always thought afterward of many ways each operation could have been done better—but this one remains in my mind the only one that was almost picture-perfect. We did everything we could—but the patient still died.

```
        May 31, 1964
   Mt. Rainier National Park
------------------------------------------
```

"STEAM WAS HOT ENOUGH TO FRY A HOT DOG"

THE *Seattle Post-Intelligencer* loudly sounded the alarm with its large, front-page headlines:

12 MISSING ON RAINIER; SEARCH SET
4 Teams to Comb Peak for 3 Overdue Parties

After "hacking out shelters with their ice picks," the four men sat out the raging storm, crammed into the little holes high on the north side of the peak. Leader Paul Williams, an experienced mountain rescuer, summed up their forced bivouac: "Scared? You betcha!" But the team of strong mountaineers easily walked off when the winds lessened. The two parties on the summit's other side, however, were not so lucky.

Eight people that holiday weekend narrowly avoided freezing to death while huddling for 48 hours in Mt. Rainier's famous steam caves. These heated links to the peak's violent past are 100 feet below the top of the 14,410-foot, dormant volcano.

Karl, a 28-year-old Seattle zoologist, recalled, "We were trapped by the ice storm just about 5 minutes after we reached the summit about 12:40 Sunday afternoon. There was nothing to do except take shelter in the caves which are formed by the crater's steam jets."

Seven men and one woman "shoveled snow night and day around the clock in an exhausting battle against the elements." But it was a weird mixture of heat and cold that really sapped the climbers of their energy. Sustaining moderate burns, one adventurer later exclaimed that the "steam was hot enough to fry a hot dog."

> We were there Sunday and Monday nights. We had a tunnel, sort of an anteroom and a larger room beyond that. But we had to work continually to keep snow from burying us. If we hadn't got out yesterday morning, we never would have made it. We would have been buried and no one would have ever found the place.

A second climber, a guide with 42 successful Mt. Rainier ascents, suffered painful sulphur steam burns *and* frostbite. He explained, "It's warm and damp in the caves. . . . But you can't dry out on top of Mt. Rainier without turning into a block of ice. We knew the Mountain Rescue Council would come for us."

And come they did: 27 dedicated volunteers from Tacoma, Everett, and Seattle, joining forces with Rangers Gil Blinn and Clay Peters already on the peak. With a plane, helicopter, and recent Everest climber Dr. Tom Hornbein, they helped the eight lucky mountaineers out of their near-scorching sanctuary.

```
                    April 23, 1965
              Mt. Rainier National Park
    ----------------------------------------
```

PARA JUMPERS WERE GLAD THEY DIDN'T JUMP

THE DC-6 took off from Seattle en route to Utah's Hill Air Force Base. On a military charter with a cargo of Minuteman ICBM parts, the crew of the four-engine aircraft soon requested an Instrument Flight Plan (IFR) as they neared the cloud-covered, 14,410-foot peak. A common procedure in that area, it was treated as routine.

Captain Alvin Petry was asked for his position relative to Mt. Rainier. When no answer was received, it was assumed that the plane had flown behind the mountain where radio and radar could not pick it up. With no more radio transmissions received, it was further reasoned that the plane had found a gap in the clouds and had made it into the clear over Yakima. And, because the airplane had not actually been okayed for IFR and had not indicated any trouble, air traffic controllers assumed that it was continuing on to Utah.

When the charter failed to arrive that Friday evening, and after other alternate landing sites were checked, the Western Air Rescue Center at Hamilton Air Force Base was notified. Plotting the flight path, it was easy to see that the plane was on a crash course with Mt. Rainier. Alerted by the rescue center, the military, the Mountain Rescue Council, the sheriff, and park rescue teams swung into well-coordinated high gear.

Although the high mountain was shrouded in clouds, the Air Force put up a chopper while planes from Thun Field launched. After the weather finally cleared that afternoon, a Navy Albatross from Portland spotted the wreckage on the South Mowich Glacier.

The parachuting medics—"PJs" as they are commonly called—aboard the rescue craft wanted to jump in; "too risky" came the word from headquarters. After several loads of parachuted survival and rescue gear greatly missed their mark owing to the mountain's "squirrely" winds, the men from the 304th Reserve Pararescue Unit were thankful that their request had been denied.

A Navy Sea Sprite helicopter from nearby Whidbey Island, with George Simac and Ranger Gil Blinn onboard, tried to work in close to the crash site. This proved impossible in the thin air at 10,500 feet, and the chopper was forced to return on instruments when "they couldn't see a thing!" The next morning, two H-43 "Huskie" helicopters, better suited to the task than their larger cousins, labored up the mountain with a crack three-man climbing team aboard.

When the rescuers reached the crash site, they found the fuselage completely bare and the cockpit area gone. After considerable probing in the avalanche-prone area, they managed to find and recover all five dead crewmen.

June 20, 1965
Death Valley National Monument

WATERY
UNDERGROUND GRAVE

ONCE used as a bathtub by hard-rock miners, Devils Hole is a water-filled fissure of unknown depth. Ninety miles west of Las Vegas in an extremely isolated section of Death Valley, this limestone cavern has been only partially explored. Crystal clear, the 92-degree waters contain several hundred tiny, endangered Desert Pupfish and, sadly, two young divers.

Jack, his brother Bill, and David were skilled with scuba; 19-year-old Paul was not. Eager for the beauty and adventure that lay below, the three sank through the boxcar-sized entrance just before midnight that Sunday. Now, at 200 feet and with their air running dangerously low, they started for the small opening far overhead. Surfacing, Bill and David looked around the small pool—Paul was missing. Furiously donning fresh tanks, the two went down again to look for their unseasoned friend. Twenty minutes later, Bill broke the surface. David did not.

First to enter the waters of the unplumbed cave the next day was the Clark County Sheriff's Underwater Rescue Force—SURF—and their advisor, Harry Wham. Then the Navy came, as did volunteers from Nevada and Southern California. The Air Force flew five divers in from a trained rescue squad based in the District of Columbia.

The darkness and the energy-sapping warm water made the repeated deep diving doubly risky; the strenuous two-day effort grew complicated. Summing it up, Harry Wham said they were all devoted to the highly dangerous task "because they love to dive and freely offer to help in any emergency."

> In preparation for the night search, Navy advisors consulted diving charts to determine the maximum depth which divers could go with their limited equipment. It was estimated that a depth of 250 feet could be reached safely, but a diver could stay at that level for only five minutes.

David's mother spent her 53rd birthday watching more than 45 rescue divers look for her ill-fated son. Paul's mother said, "I'm sure he is still alive. He loved life and knew the risks and said that he would be careful." Praying their sons had miraculously managed to find one of the cave's few known air-filled rooms, the two women stood a long, silent vigil.

Divers worked around the clock, catnapping as best they could. The deepest dive, 315 feet, made by Jim Hantz of Newport Beach, failed to produce anything comforting to the survivors. No clue of the boys was ever found.

On August 15, 1991, USGS divers Alan Riggs and Paul DeLoach, along with world-record holder Sheck Exley, reached 436 feet.


```
            September 5, 1965
            Zion National Park
-----------------------------------------
```

"19 ESCAPE ZION PARK FLOOD, 26 STRANDED, HOPES HIGH"

HASTILY they lifted their terrorized sons into the branches of the small box elder. Then, clinging desperately to the tree themselves, the two fathers fought the rapidly rising floodwaters with all their strength.

The Zion Narrows, a 1,500-foot-deep scar carved in the Colorado Plateau, is world class in beauty; southern Utah's Virgin River, generally quiet and only 15 feet wide in places, has sliced its way through eons of red sandstone.

With precious little dry ground between towering walls, adventurers usually must walk in the river or swim sections of the 12-mile-long canyon. There is no alternative. There is no escape.

Otto Fife entered The Narrows for his 27th time. Leading 21 people, including sons, grandsons, friends, and several small children, the Utah sheriff knew the canyon and its moods as well as anyone. A second party from Los Angeles was spending Labor Day savoring the beauty. A Salt Lake City couple, joined by their 11- and 13-year-old daughters, was celebrating their 17th wedding anniversary. In all, 42 people were enjoying the Zion Narrows that holiday weekend.

Recalling that almost exactly four years before, five boys had drowned while taking the same trip, some of the hikers, mindful of dangerous summer flash floods, had asked the Weather Bureau about rain. None was in the forecast.

The first drops fell at 2 Sunday morning, and it poured most of the day and the next. More than just a local thunderstorm, this weather system caused the river to rise more than 18 inches. Compressed between very narrow canyon walls, this would mean depths of more than 20 feet in some places.

Two hours after awakening to the unexpected shower, the Phillips party fled to safety. Earlier warnings from skilled canyoneer Fife to "get to high ground if heavy rain occurred" probably saved their lives. At dawn, Doug Jones heard the "river crashing through the canyon below them." The Brigham Young University professor and his party were trapped for the next 30 hours.

Little Stephen was scared. "One place we had to cross deep water and daddy and the other men had to relay us boys across the river. . . . The water was over our heads and came up to daddy's chin." The nine-year-old wasn't alone in his terror.

Muted to a low rumble, the huge boulders tumbling along beneath the brown torrent were frightening to anyone close enough to hear them. Water-polished, telephone pole–sized logs, casualties of past cloudbursts, careened wildly from wall to wall.

Several people clung to cracks in the cliffs; two somehow squeezed into a hole under a waterfall. A few even climbed into frail trees rooted in the rapidly eroding, sandy banks. The river, cresting in two distinct waves several hours apart, "suckered" nervous hikers back into the swollen nightmare.

The group from Los Angeles spent a cold and fitful night. Venturing out from safety the next morning, they soon heard the unmistakable roar of another wall of water. They climbed to a high crevice, and they were trapped for another night.

Headlines from Tuesday's *Salt Lake Tribune* read, **"19 ESCAPE ZION PARK FLOOD, 26 Stranded, Hopes High."** Wading and swimming, small groups finally floated free of The Narrows; waiting friends and relatives were visibly relieved. A 16-member rescue team of rangers stood by, unable to force their way up the flooded gorge. Chief Ranger Del Armstrong, making aerial sorties, looked into the deep shadows of the threadlike canyon for signs of life.

The following day the paper heralded, **"ALL 42 HIKERS SAFE IN ZION PARK FLOODS."** Delivered from his rocky prison, one teenager said, "Boy, I'm happy to get here. What started out as a three-day pleasure hike turned into a five-day nightmare." Another said, "It was a real good place to learn about God and how to pray."

Four years before, the Zion Narrows had been terrifying too. The summer flood that hit this part of southern Utah on September 17, 1961, was the largest recorded in almost 25 years. Its crest in the park was estimated at 10 feet.

Authorities didn't know that anyone, let alone the Scotowa Expedition, a group dedicated to exploring remote tracts of the Southwest, was even in the canyon. Twenty-six people had walked into the world-class wonder, but only 21 walked out. Because of the gorge's narrowness and despite being alerted to both the storm and the hikers, rangers were helpless to even enter the flood-swollen trap.

One survivor said he "heard a sound like thunder and looked up and couldn't see any clouds. [We] turned around and a wall of driftwood, rocks and mud was bearing down on us." Another recalled, "I have been through hurricanes in Florida, but they were nothing compared to this. There were hailstones as big as half an inch, and the flood, when it came, seemed to be a great white curtain of water. The rains blotted out everything around us."

The first dead child was found three hours before any of the surviving 21 hikers swam free of the canyon. Two more were soon discovered nearby; coming to rest in Springdale, the little bodies had been dragged 10 miles by the rampaging river.

By 5 P.M., after spending up to 27 hours trapped, the last of the fortunate survivors waded out through the rushing chest-deep waters. Two teenage boys were never found.

May 21, 1966
Fire Island National Seashore

THREE DROWN IN SURF RESCUE
CITATION FOR VALOR AWARD

posthumously, for courageous action in the face of danger.

While on duty near Sailors Haven on May 21, 1966, where he was giving an interpretive talk to a group of hikers, Mr. Shaner employed as a Seasonal Ranger-Naturalist with the National Park Service, responded to a call to assist two swimmers in danger of drowning. Together with Mr. Smith, a Seasonal Maintenanceman, who had also responded to the call for assistance, they made a team effort to rescue the two swimmers drowning in the heavy surf. They initiated the rescue attempt on a fifteen foot surfboard and when it was wrested from them by heavy surf action, valiantly and heroically they continued their rescue efforts. The exertion and subsequent exhaustion proved to be more than he could physically withstand and he became a victim of drowning. For heroism and courage far beyond the call of duty in an effort to save the lives of others, resulting in the loss of his own life, Mr. Shaner is granted, posthumously, the **Valor Award of the Department of the Interior.**

Stewart Udall
Secretary of the Interior

For this rescue, on his first day of summer employment, William E. Shaner, 23, also received a **Carnegie Hero Bronze Medal Award** (posthumously).

Ashley Norman Smith, 37, park maintenance man, received a DOI **Valor Award** (posthumously) and **Carnegie Hero Bronze Medal Award** (posthumously).

James Charles Lawler, 25, a local dredge hand, received a **Carnegie Hero Bronze Medal Award** (posthumously).

James C. Del Giudice, 32, a computer engineer, received a **Carnegie Hero Bronze Medal Award.**

In an open letter to Mrs. Lawler, Judith Shaner wrote:

> The men who give their lives serving others do not always make the headlines, and unfortunately are not always remembered or even recognized by the general public.
>
> But we'll remember them always. We'll remember their courage and we'll preserve the memory of these gallant men for our own children in generations to come.

```
               July 15, 1967
        Mt. Rainier National Park
----------------------------------------
```

FAMILY OF FIVE DISAPPEARS
INTO DEEP SNOW CAVE

MELVIN, serving in Vietnam and on leave from the aircraft carrier *Ticonderoga,* was returning from the Paradise Ice Caves with his family. He and his son led. Only 500 yards from the road, they chose a shortcut down a steep snowfield. After losing control while "sliding on the seat of their pants," the two sailed swiftly off the brink of a 30-foot ledge.

Six-year-old Mark suffered a serious skull fracture; his father, also landing on the rocks at the bottom, was only dazed. After struggling up the icy slope with his injured son, Melvin couldn't see his wife or four- and five-year-old daughters anywhere.

Not knowing how far behind him the three were, Melvin did not know what to report. Rangers, who were all too familiar with the strange whims of an unpredictable mountain but who sensed the need for urgency, immediately began a search for the missing trio.

Led by Paul Haertel, 12 men looked all night for the mother and her two little girls. Using headlamps and armed with ice axes and ropes they combed the frozen slopes. After they even checked outside the park, their hopes grew dimmer. Ultimately, intensive efforts led Ranger Doug Erskine to the intimidating, shadowy hole in the snow.

The long, narrow cave had several chambers. Carved each year by melt funneling onto it, the floor was a brushy, water-covered hillside glade. Four feet high at the mouth, it tapered down to 8 inches above the water's surface, 100 feet in.

The headlines of the *Seattle Post-Intelligencer* read, **"RAINIER ICE CAVE PLUNGE KILLS TWO: Third Feared Dead."** Found the next afternoon by Erskine, the mother and her four-year-old were "in a pool of melt water under an overhang of ice and snow." Melvin, who was awaiting the outcome of his son's surgery, was not on the mountain when his wife and daughter were recovered. Still missing, five-year-old Kelly was presumed to be inside the frozen trap and was likely dead.

With tons of snow suspended above and a stream of frigid water rushing below, the cave demanded special skills and uncommon dedication. "Park rangers were prepared to dig down through the snow pack to reach Kelly's body if the other would-be rescuers were unable to reach the body by way of the tunnel."

Wanting to help one of its own, the Navy quickly volunteered. "From an icy pool less than 2-feet deep, two Navy SCUBA divers, a Marine and eight park rangers retrieved the body."

July 18, 1967
Mt. McKinley National Park

WORST DISASTER IN ALASKAN
MOUNTAINEERING HISTORY

NO one will ever know exactly how 7 of the 12-man Joseph F. Wilcox Mt. McKinley Expedition died. In *The Hall of the Mountain King,* a 1973 recounting of the tragedy as perceived by team member Howard Snyder, most of the blame is attributed to inadequate high-altitude mountaineering experience, coupled with the questionable leadership of Joe Wilcox. In *White Winds,* a 500-page 1981 rebuttal by the group's leader, Wilcox asserts that they fell victim to possibly "the most severe high altitude windstorm in the entire history of mountaineering."

Originally, the 24-year-old Snyder headed a four-man team, the Colorado Mt. McKinley Expedition, a group of friends of similar advanced experience who had trained together for this specific climb for two years. In stark contrast, Wilcox led a nine-man party, only one of whom he had ever climbed with before. It included a few who were strangers to each other as well as several who had relatively little mountaineering experience. Seven of his team would soon die together somewhere above 17,900 feet.

Only the day before Snyder was to leave for Alaska, one friend broke a hand in a car wreck and dropped out. Forced to comply with the park's regulation of no team with fewer than four people, Snyder either had to abandon the much anticipated climb or join another expedition scheduled to be on the mountain at that time. Wilcox's group was the only possibility; Snyder and his two companions reluctantly merged with them.

Details on what happened are vague because the five survivors, four of whom had successfully summited two days before, were more than 4,000 feet lower than their ill-fated mates. Just before noon on the 18th, coleader Jerry Clark radioed the rangers at Eielson Visitor Center from the summit. He said they had lost the route the night before and had been forced to bivouac. It was 6 degrees on top with a 15-mph wind. Despite whiteout conditions and with their bamboo trail markers only faintly visible, they reported no real problems.

Without question, there had been a storm of historic power. Wilcox estimated that the eight-and-a-half-day tempest had gusted to 200 mph on the peak's upper slopes. Eventually two tents were recovered: one completely shredded by the fierce winds and the other intact but partially filled with snow, a frozen figure still tragically clutching its bent center pole.

Only three of the climbers were ever seen again. To this day, all seven are still entombed high on the hardened slopes of Mt. McKinley. Regardless of what happened to the two teams, this remains the worst disaster in Alaskan mountaineering history.

```
            August 21, 1967
        Grand Teton National Park
-----------------------------------------
```

READER'S DIGEST CALLED IT
"THE IMPOSSIBLE RESCUE"

A RESCUE off the 2,700-foot, vertical north face had been nightmarishly feared for years . . . but it was inevitable. At 3 P.M., a cannonball-sized rock smashed into a 26-year-old climber and set into motion some of the most spectacular heroics ever. *Reader's Digest* would call it "The Impossible Rescue." To the crack team of rangers in Grand Teton National Park it was dangerous, difficult, and daring, but impossible? No!

Lorraine Hough watched as the careening boulder exploded like a bomb and knocked Gaylord Campbell onto a ledge 20 feet below. His leg was stained red, and the white of a bone protruded from it. Suddenly faced with a fight for their lives, they forgot that this route on the 13,770-foot Grand Teton had not been climbed many times before.

His leg grossly fractured, Campbell urgently needed medical care; nearly 72 hours would pass before he would receive it. The Grand Teton Mountain Rescue Team would mold courage, expertise, and luck in performing the longest stretcher lowering in North America. A rescue off the north face, always referred to in hushed tones, would push the art of mountain rescue to the limit.

That first night, the two doubted their screams had been heard; wind did strange things at 13,000 feet.

For the first hour of daylight, Ralph Tingey watched the tiny figures far above—one moving, one not. Even with years of experience it was still hard to steady the 60-power telescope. Yesterday he had spent an hour trying to discourage an arrogant Gaylord Campbell from attempting the 2,700-foot climb. For the next 60 hours, during the record 1,800-foot lowering of the litter, Tingey regretted having not being more persistent.

A career as an English teacher at the University of Washington had not prepared Seasonal Park Ranger Pete Sinclair for the next three days. However, 14 years of climbing, eight rescue seasons in this park, and being one of only a handful to successfully cover this route had. Now, while the helicopter pilot felt for the late summer updrafts along the impressive rock wall, Sinclair retraced the climb in his mind's eye foot by painful foot.

After a rock smashed his leg, Gaylord Campbell was lowered 1,800 feet in what Reader's Digest *would call "The Impossible Rescue."*

GRAND TETON NATIONAL PARK PHOTO

Rick Reese, veteran mountain climber and national park ranger, concentrated as he looked out through the chopper's Plexiglas. Rick was not sure how, but he knew this rescue could be—had to be—done. Vice President Hubert Humphrey would later write:

> The way you got Mr. Campbell down from the North face of that mountain after he had suffered a compound fracture of the leg is one of the most harrowing tales I have read in a long time. I still don't see how you did it, but I am told that Mr. Campbell will live, so I guess you did!

Former climbing guide Leigh Ortenburger, a mathematician by trade as well as a recognized authority on the Tetons, along with Park Ranger Bob Irvine, reached the summit at noon. With Tuesday's midday sun, this climb had been a leisurely renewal of spirit for them both. Starting down, "Okie," as his friends sometimes called Ortenburger, whispered, "Did you hear something?"

Their spines chilled; cries of help are unmistakable to those who have heard them before. Looking over the edge, they could barely make out Campbell and Hough 900 feet below.

Irvine heard the *whump-whump-whump* of the helicopter long before he saw it slowly work its way up the cliffs. They didn't know that from inside the tiny machine now fighting for altitude, Rangers Sinclair and Reese were nervously studying the unfolding drama on the table-sized ledge below. Nineteen hours had passed since the bone-crushing rock had found its mark.

Pilot and chopper, urgently commandeered from fires in nearby Shoshone National Forest, finished lifting Ranger Ted Wilson and nine others to the Lower Saddle. Wilson, future mayor of Salt Lake City, was a veteran of many Grand Teton rescues. He, Tingey, Sinclair, Reese, and Mike Ermarth would join Ortenburger and Irvine for the 1,400-foot traverse across the icy, crumbly cliffs to the scene. Four P.M. came and went.

Below, led by Doug McLaren, the support team of Dick Black, Bill McKeel, Jack Morehead, and Irv Mortenson moved into place to provide valuable aid on what one news story said was "among the most difficult technical rescues ever attempted in Grand Teton National Park and probably the entire United States."

A ragged Hough had been shouting "help" throughout the long night. As she and Campbell, now dangerously faint from pain and loss of blood, spotted the helicopter rounding the mountain, they assumed it was a routine sightseeing tour. The two battered University of Illinois students almost gave up hope.

When the noisy ship finally approached, Sinclair's voice came out garbled through the bullhorn. Help was now near. Hough wouldn't yet appreciate just how lucky they were that this particular mountain rescue team was slowly working its way toward them. Campbell would never acknowledge it, remaining aloof and condescending throughout the remainder of his ordeal.

In three hours, Reese and Sinclair had brought Hough to the Upper Saddle and the support party. And, as the gray shadows grew, Campbell's shattered leg was splinted. The team brought a litter, ropes, and two 300-foot, steel cables; they radioed for drugs. Nobody wanted to go down, but there was no choice.

District Ranger McLaren, a 15-year veteran of the Tetons, made arrangements for a more powerful chopper, morphine, and additional men and equipment. Rescuers shivered through the first of two long nights; sleeping bags and most of the food and water had been sacrificed to save on helicopter cargo. On Wednesday at 7 A.M., McLaren's aim was perfect: The morphine was pitched from the hovering ship right into Ortenburger's lap.

Who would take the wire stretcher over the edge 1,800 feet to the glacier below? Assuming his turn and knowing what to do when he stepped over, the future mayor skillfully kept the injured man from tipping over and smashing against the cliff. With the first 500 feet behind him, Campbell became disoriented and contrary, insisting that Wilson take him up. Patiently the skilled ranger ignored the added aggravation; his hands and mind were busy.

With 1,300 feet yet to go, someone dropped a rock to test the distance. It was six seconds and 600 feet to a ledge called "The Grandstand." An outcrop halfway down, even a small one, was critical for the second lowering stage, and Ortenburger volunteered to go find it. The next 30 minutes passed very slowly. The radio finally blared, "I've got one!" He quickly rappelled again, this time to ensure that the Grandstand was really only 300 feet lower. Food and water were nearly gone.

Ortenburger stood on the Grandstand; he had body-rappelled on two 150-foot ropes tied together, judging the distance to within a foot—the end of the dangling rope ended chest-high. When Reese went over this overhang, the friction from the long, single-strand body wrap left burns on his hip. Sinclair, replacing an exhausted Wilson at the end of the 300-foot cable, continued to demonstrate the great talent of this rescue team.

Campbell realized he had to spend a third, painfully long night on the north face. The rescue team was spread out over 400 vertical feet. Ortenburger and Sinclair shared a last 4-ounce can of chili. Ermarth, not so lucky, tied himself to a ledge 100 feet below the Grandstand. Falling rocks, "singing" by Reese all day, "screamed" by him all night; he still faced a dizzying 800 feet the coming day. Tired, the rescuers dug for inner strength.

By noon the men had completed two more lowerings totalling 500 feet; tasting triumph, they warmed with pride. From below, Ranger Morehead asked if the chopper could land closer to the team. Having flown similar high-altitude mercy missions before, the pilot performed superbly in the narrow, dead-end canyon.

On June 4, 1968, Secretary of the Interior Stewart Udall presented Mike Ermarth, Robert Irvine, Richard Reese, Pete Sinclair, Ralph Tingey, and Ted Wilson with **Valor Awards.** The Grand Teton National Park Support Team, with its efforts largely unheralded in the national press, received a much deserved **Unit Citation** for its role in this rescue.

Leigh Ortenburger didn't get an award because he was not a federal employee, but Vice President Humphrey sent a personal thank-you letter. Ortenburger died on October 20, 1991, in the catastrophic firestorm that raced through Oakland, California.

```
           January 27, 1968
     Rocky Mountain National Park
---------------------------------------
```

INSERTING THE FORCEPS
BENEATH THE SKULL FRAGMENT . . .

DR. Sam Luce prepared to pop the splintered bone back into place. The handful of rescuers tightly crammed into the frigid, tiny rock cabin held their collective breath. That 32-year-old Dick Kezlan was alive, even though he lay broken and unconscious on a makeshift operating table before them, amazed one and all.

Yesterday had been long, even for seasoned mountaineers. Leaving the Longs Peak Ranger Station at 3 A.M., Kezlan and his three friends had skied and hiked 8 miles, climbing through pines, across hardened tundra, and over buried boulders. Their goal was to scale the 1,800-foot east face, reach the frozen 14,256-foot summit, and make a live radio broadcast for NBC's *Monitor* in New York City. For this remote transmission they carried a pair of Park Service two-way radios for a radio-telephone relay.

Exhausted after a punishing day, the men readied for a slow retreat to the Chasm Lake Cabin; refuge for the long night before them lay a mile away. As they leaned on ice axes midway up the 800-foot Lamb's Slide, the group waited for Kezlan to inch his way back down to them. Looking off the icy, 45-degree slope, they couldn't see the ragged rocks below, but they sensed their menace.

Jim Disney, the group's leader and the most experienced of the four, heard a groan above him and "suddenly a dark form was sliding past." Instinctively, Disney screamed for his friend to dig in with his ice axe to stop the fall, but the out-of-control climber shot by.

"Then there was this indescribable crunching sound. . . . I'd never heard it before but I knew what it was." Quickly sliding down to Kezlan, Disney prayed that the results were less serious than they sounded. "I turned him over and could hardly believe what I saw. . . . It seemed like his head had been laid open. His face was a mass of blood." It was 8:30 P.M.

Seldom does such desperation get reported so rapidly. Within minutes Disney was talking to Ranger Morris Brown at park headquarters on one of the borrowed radios. Hastily the team leader described the scene and the vile conditions: temperatures near zero, 50-mph winds. Other rangers were swiftly notified of the accident, as were two nearby rescue groups and Dr. Sam Luce.

Disney did his best to make Kezlan warm. With no equipment with which to evacuate the gravely injured man, he made his way to the rock hut at Chasm Lake. Willing to settle for some blankets or even, better yet, a little first-aid gear, he miraculously found a doctor.

The pounding on the shelter's bolted door finally penetrated Dee Crouch's sound sleep. Dr. Crouch, an experienced mountaineer, was interning at Denver's Colorado General Hospital and was in the area to climb. Dressing quickly, he stepped out into the bitter cold and started up the glassy slope. He soon found "a shambles of equipment, ropes and blood"; Kezlan's forehead was crushed inward and he had lost a dangerous amount of blood. With a sense of helplessness, Dr. Crouch knew he had the training but not the tools. The man dying in front of him needed an operating room, plasma, a neurosurgeon. . . .

Sam Luce, an Estes Park physician and a good friend of the park, was a veteran of dozens of mountain rescues. Wearing headlamps and lugging 45-pound packs, he and seasoned rescue ranger Tom Griffiths battled a stinging ground blizzard. "The wind was so strong one had to lean into it in order to stand." Soaked in sweat and nearing exhaustion from the grinding uphill ski, the two faced hypothermia.

After 8 long miles and five longer hours, they reached the almost lifeless Kezlan. "The idea of treating a man who appeared half dead seemed ridiculous." Dr. Luce thought, "Kezlan's condition was such that we were no longer capable of helping this particular man." With herculean concentration, Luce found a vein for the IV, but the fluid was frozen. The windchill was 40 below zero. With the bottle now under his own parka, the doctor finally thawed the lifesaving solution and started it flowing.

An hour before dawn, more help struggled to the site. After lashing the unconscious Kezlan onto a sled, rescuers began expertly lowering him toward the cabin at Chasm Lake. Dr. Crouch, who had turned the rock shelter into a crude operating room, waited anxiously.

Ranger Griffiths, maintaining the injured man's airway, watched as the two doctors skillfully assessed the damage. Kezlan's head was a mess: a depressed fracture of the right temple, another break from right ear to right eye, and a third crack around the base of the skull. There were others . . .

Once the cup of jellylike blood was cleansed from the sunken bones, thereby relieving the pressure on his bruised brain, Kezlan's chances for life dramatically improved.

The skills of the physician gave way to those of the rescuer. By long ropes and from one ice-axe anchor to the next, the litter was lowered down steep, icy slopes toward the trailhead miles away. Tired and nearly paralyzed from the cold, the rescue machine "purred." For eight hours, more than 30 people pulled a man back to life.

May 23, 1968
Lake Mead National Recreation Area

CITATION FOR VALOR
JOE J. CAYOU

FOR the heroic rescue of Mr. Roy A. Pitchford from drowning in the Boulder Basin of Lake Mead National Recreation Area.

On May 23, 1968, when a severe, unexpected wind storm struck the Boulder Basin of Lake Mead, creating extremely heavy waves and endangering many of the small boats on the water, Supervisory Park Ranger Joe J. Cayou responded to an emergency call for help. Proceeding to the vicinity of Boulder Islands where several boats were reported to be overturned and swamped, Mr. Cayou came upon a swamped sailboat and as he proceeded to take it under tow, he heard someone yell that a man was in the water. He then heard the man cry for help and saw him disappear below the dark surface of the lake. He threw a life ring but it fell far short of the struggling man. Realizing the fruitlessness of this endeavor, he quickly maneuvered the National Park Service cruiser, *Major Powell,* to the rear of the sailboat until stopped by the sailboat lines which had become entangled in the cruiser propellers. Attempts to reach the drowning man with a rope and boat hook failed. Seeing the victim go under the storm tossed lake surface, and realizing that immediate action was needed, Mr. Cayou dove into the treacherous waters, locating the drowning man, and brought him to safety. For this heroic, lifesaving act performed at great risk to his own life, the Department of the Interior confers upon Mr. Cayou its **Valor Award.**

Stewart Udall
Secretary of the Interior

In 1996, the busy staff of Lake Mead National Recreation Area responded to 332 SARs, 176 of which were boating mishaps; responded to 442 emergency medical cases requiring skills beyond basic life support; investigated 36 deaths; and made 516 arrests.

June 1, 1968
Mt. Rainier National Park

"SHARON, I THINK DAD'S DEAD."

DAVID leaned over and shook his dad harder, again and again. The 11-year-old heard only his own heartbeats and the muffled wind outside their coffin-sized, frozen shelter. A father—loving and good—had sacrificed himself trying to save his two children.

Park rangers fear Memorial Day weekends; long and hectic, they are sometimes tragic. On this holiday, the highest mountain in Washington was particularly attractive. Storms on the 14,410-foot Mt. Rainier are legendary; the world's record for annual snowfall—1,224 inches—once fell on its impressive slopes.

James Reddick, a hardworking, 51-year-old Seattle dentist, was eager to spend time with his family. Often "camping out" on the lawn with his kids, he now wanted to take the middle two children on their first real hike. David needed a 5-miler for Boy Scouts and 12-year-old Sharon went for the sheer adventure.

Leaving the Paradise Ranger Station at 8 made them the first on the trail that Friday morning. Registered for an overnight stay at Camp Muir, 4,500 feet higher, the three settled into a start-stop-rest routine. The excited kids took their coats off and tied them around their waists. They munched candy as they climbed. This was fun.

A harbinger of storms, the wind-driven, lens-shaped clouds trying to cap the summit were soon noted at Paradise. Cautious rangers began preparing for another blow, and soon climbers were being advised to delay their trips.

At noon a party of five passed the Reddicks on the Muir Snowfield and relayed the storm warning issued below. The trail steepened, the wind quickened, the sun disappeared. Soon David spotted a cloud covering neighboring Mt. Adams; swirling snow obscured their own summit from view. Dr. Reddick continued upward, for Camp Muir was now closer than Paradise. The kids sensed their father's growing concern. Steps became less carefree, stops became less frequent. Others on the mountain who had left after the Reddicks had already turned back.

Seasoned climbing ranger John Dalle-Molle was on patrol at Camp Muir. One of the best, he knew that anyone caught up there unprepared this afternoon was in serious trouble. Sixty-mph gusts threatened to lift him off his feet as he forced his way from one small building to the other. It was 22 degrees; the windchill factor, a more accurate indicator of the danger to anyone outside, was -30 degrees. Camp Muir was enveloped in a whiteout, with fog and snow so dense that all frame of reference was lost.

Reddick knew they were in trouble—the paralyzing swiftness of the storm was swallowing them. Gale winds and swirling snows beat at them mercilessly. Eyes blinded shut, fingers numb, they piled on everything they had. A desperate father yelled to a frightened son to get out the mess kit and dig. Father and daughter scraped and kicked snow aside; almost as much blew into the trench they dug as was thrown out.

Slowly, a shallow furrow formed; in this war this was their foxhole. Reddick tried to spread their emergency tarp as a roof; crackling and snapping at each try, the flimsy little tarp was whipped loose from one hand and then almost from the other. Finally, with three packs anchoring it, the stopgap roof stayed.

Sitting on a foam pad, Reddick helped Sharon and David struggle into one sleeping bag, wet clothes and all. Having a broken zipper on his own bag, he wrapped it around himself as best he could. Then he wedged himself into the entrance with his back exposed to the raging storm, becoming a human door.

They sang, they shivered. They prayed, they dozed. Sharon noticed that, as time went on, her father talked less often and made less sense. Although she did not understand it, her father had hypothermia—he was losing heat and energy much faster than he could produce it.

The hours ran together, and the fury of the storm rose. Melting from the heat of their shivering bodies, the snow cave dripped; wet became wetter. Wind snuck in at every hole. At one point, Reddick said, "I don't think that I can make it down the mountain." The kids tried to leave; wind and blinding snow forced them back inside their tiny haven.

At noon the following day, Margaret Erskine was working at the Paradise Visitor Center. She couldn't help but notice the woman sitting across from her anxiously staring at the cloud-covered mountain. Able to "read" people, Margaret knew controlled fear when she saw it. Calling her ranger-husband Doug, she passed on what little information she could get from Mrs. Reddick. Yes, her husband and two kids were supposed to be at Camp Muir and, yes, could they please radio Camp Muir to confirm that?

Rangers Haertel and Dalle-Molle, after talking to Paradise almost 1 vertical mile below, knew their work was cut out for them. Somewhere out in this white hurricane were at least three people in desperate trouble. Even though the park rangers were willing to start, they had everywhere—and nowhere—to look. They were forced to wait the storm out. More than four inches of rain fell in Paradise that night.

Lou Whittaker, longtime senior Rainier climbing guide, earnestly readied his equipment. Nearby mountain rescue teams responded within an hour of the park's urgent request for help. Seldom did these groups fail to get called out on a major weekend. Those now rapidly assembling—rangers, guides, and mountain rescuers—were as good as they get. Among them they had hundreds of years of survival and rescue experience. Their hallmark was professionalism—they were the "A Team."

Late Saturday night, the rescuers talked strategy and studied maps. They phoned the weather bureau and alerted the nearby military base for possible helicopter support; the chances for helicopter use were slim, but they needed the machines on standby just in case. Some of the team primed gear, others snatched at sleep. If only the weather would let up.

By 5:30 Sunday morning, the weather did let up—a little. Despite lingering whiteouts, one team, led by Whittaker, started up. The storm still raged around Camp Muir, and it was 10 before Rangers Jim Valder, John Dalle-Molle, Paul Haertel, Pete Hart, and others could leave their shelter at the 10,000-foot level.

Searchers made educated guesses as to the Reddicks location. Alive or dead, they were surely covered by white; unfortunately up there, no better camouflage existed. The men strained toward the right places to look. They all hefted 45-pound packs full of personal survival equipment as well as vital lifesaving gear. Even in 30-mph winds and subfreezing temperatures, sweat dripped down their bodies. Time grew critical.

At 1:45 P.M., 500 feet below the peak's prominent Anvil Rock, District Ranger Valder saw black rocks where there should be no black rocks. A dark corner of one backpack, the anchor for a hastily thrown-up tarp, poked through the snow. Pete Hart, a buck ranger on his first NPS rescue, stuck his head into the small hole at the end of the trench. Hart would never forget the look in the young boy's eyes. Sharon, crowded against David, sat up. "We've been waiting for you to come for two days," she said. Their father lay slumped against a frozen wall.

Hart gently lifted Sharon from the hole. The rescue team quickly set up a tent. Stripped of their wet clothes, the kids were placed into dry sleeping bags. Hot soup was fixed and numb bodies massaged. Radios crackled; messages filled with both joy and sorrow flowed. Lou Whittaker would soon have to tell Mrs. Reddick that her husband—serving as a door against the blizzard died to save her children.

That Sharon and David lived is a testimony to their will to survive, a father's courage, and the mountain rescue teams that did what they do best.

Of the 2,244 climbers signed out for the summit of Mt. Rainier in 1968, this was the only fatality.

October 15, 1968
Yosemite National Park

"HE HEARD MADSEN SAY, 'WHAT THE F___'"

AN elite "brotherhood," the valley climbers kept vigil as Chuck Pratt and Chris Fredricks inched up El Cap's Dihedral Wall. First scaled only six years before, the 3,000-foot rock face had taken 38 days. Expecting now to do this giant in just five days, the two veteran "Big Wall" climbers didn't plan on the unseasonably early storm, or on a good friend dying while trying to help them.

Saturday the weather soured; after nearly 3 inches of rain fell, the snows came. At the park's 5,000-foot level, it had dropped to 24 degrees; Pratt and Fredricks were over 1,500 feet higher. The two young men, forced to stand in their painfully narrow web slings all night, pressed vainly against the frozen rock seeking refuge from the torrent. Their progress, measured between the puffs of mist blowing across the immense granite wall, was halting and slow. The brotherhood grew anxious.

At 20, Jim Madsen "was certainly one of if not the best and fastest climbers this country has produced." Having made the same, exacting climb before and understanding the demands his friends now faced, he wanted to help in any way he could. Armed with great skill and an intimate knowledge of the route, Madsen pressed the rangers into action at the top of El Capitan.

Burdened with ropes, climbing tackle, sleeping bags, food, and stoves, the crack team of rescuers reached the top just before midnight. Between drizzle, snow, and sweat, they were drenched when they finished the 9-mile hike in.

At first light, Madsen prepared to rappel down and make voice contact with the wet men far below. If they asked for help or sounded too weak to ascend, he would continue down 600 more feet to their tiny ledge. Then, if deemed critical, a small mechanical winch would be flown up to Yosemite from Sequoia, 150 miles away. After tying to a 3-foot-thick pine only 6 feet from the edge of the 3,000-foot cliff, Madsen threw a 150-foot rope over. With 45 pounds of survival gear strapped on his back, he started down.

> Price came scrambling up from the ledge with a look of horror in his face and said, "Madsen fell." He did not know how it had happened, if the sling had broken or what, only that Madsen had lost his rappel and fallen. He said he heard Madsen say, "What the fuck," and then yell. The rope then snapped upwards and Price heard the two noises of Madsen hitting on the way down.

Incredibly, a highly experienced Jim Madsen had somehow slipped off the very end of his rope, although he had tied a small safety knot in it. He was the fourth climber to die in Yosemite Valley. Chuck Pratt and Chris Fredricks completed their climb, without needing any of the assistance that had been offered.

```
                    November 3, 1968
                 Yosemite National Park
----------------------------------------------
```

"WE CANNOT LAST ANOTHER NIGHT. GET US HELP TODAY."

WARREN Harding's simple plea into the sodden CB radio was probably the last thing the two park rangers wanted to hear. Bob Pederson and Pete Thompson knew that the 44-year-old master climber and his 28-year-old partner, Galen Rowell, were gambling with the late-season weather when they ventured onto the unclimbed south face of Half Dome. The curving, 2,000-foot cliff, the lesser-known side of the world-famous Sierra monolith, is a 75-degree wall lacking in ledges and shelter. Now, just over two weeks after would-be rescuer Jim Madsen fell almost 3,000 feet, and nearing the end of a record-breaking 51 missions for the year, YOSAR—Yosemite Search and Rescue—

faced one of its greatest challenges: to save someone trapped in the middle of a Big Wall.

For six days, Harding and Rowell inched up the seemingly endless south face. After spending each long night awkwardly hanging in homemade hammocks, painfully flattened against the rock, the two were now forced onto an intimidating 1,000-foot blank wall. One particularly demanding section would later be described by Rowell as "the most spectacular sixth-class lead I have ever seen," while Harding, one of this country's most celebrated climbing elders, would call it "his most strenuous lead."

Despite the hardships and their average of only two solid rope lengths per day, the veterans expected to summit in a few more days. As Rowell marveled at the setting sun's shades of orange and red, he warily inspected the cirrus mare's tails overhead—a harbinger of imminent weather change. He recalls:

> Waking at midnight, I heard a new sound outside. It was the running of water and dripping of raindrops upon our hammocks. I went back to sleep, not worried because the weather forecast carried no prediction of a storm and therefore this must be a local disturbance. But several hours later, I realized my down footsack and jacket were soaking up water. . . . The tightly woven fabric let water soak in, but would not let it out. Pools formed at the bottom of the hammocks. We had to puncture holes to let water out. By dawn we were both soaked to the skin. Snow covered all the mountains in the high country. The rain became sleet and then turned into snow.

In a little over 24 hours, nearly 2 inches of rain fell in the valley; the snow line dropped to 7,000 feet—1,000 feet below where the two men were just beginning to realize how desperate their situation was. Weather worsened and the wet snow fell thicker and thicker. Incredibly, it soon stuck to the smooth, almost vertical granite around them. Both men shook all day with cold "and looked for a blue spot somewhere in the sky. It never came. We passed a second night in the storm. A sleepless, cold, wet ordeal. Fourteen hours of November darkness."

Day eight dawned, the second since the storm began, and with it came the quiet, knowing fear that they might not survive. Rowell, with all his clothing thoroughly drenched, didn't want to "hang in one place and freeze to death, as I thought we might after another night in the storm. Dying without an effort to escape seemed a most unforgivable thing." With toes and fingers completely numb, he chose somehow to force his way down the 1,400 feet of snow-covered cliff. After rappelling only 80 feet and with his frozen boots sliding crazily on the ice-covered rock, he knew his only chance lay in going back up to Harding.

Not only was his body freezing, but so was his rope; the ends of the nylon were rapidly hardening to the cliff. Worse, ice jammed the small teeth in the critical gripping part of his metal ascenders—they kept slipping off his now-frozen link to Harding, 80 feet above. Finally switching to thin cords knotted around the stiff rope, he managed to work his way back up, taking nearly two hours for what should have been a quick, easy climb.

When he heard a faint shout from far below, Harding turned on their CB radio. Rowell soon overheard his climbing partner say, "We cannot last another night. Get us help today. A helicopter if possible. We are very, very cold."

Rangers Pederson and Thompson, alert to the unfolding nightmare far above, made two phone calls that later proved critical in saving Warren Harding and Galen Rowell. The first was a request for a fire helicopter from Sequoia National Park, 150 miles to the south. The second was to Royal Robbins, a friend of the park and probably the most experienced Big Wall climber in the world. From nearby Modesto, Robbins, along with Al Steck, another mountaineering great, arrived shortly before the small chopper.

First on top of Half Dome late that afternoon was Ranger Pederson and Camp Four volunteer Joe McKeown; they located a spot to drop the sling-loaded supplies and then quickly put in needed anchor bolts. Ranger Thompson and Royal Robbins soon arrived. Robbins believed that the best way to save the men was to be lowered the 600 feet with a load of hot soup, parkas, and gloves. He didn't consider a second rope—a safety line—necessary, but he was quickly overruled.

On top of the frigid peak, as if in the middle of a cosmic balance beam— sun sinking in the west, full moon rising in the east—Robbins, an old friend of the two men below, started over the 2,000-foot cliff. Rowell vividly remembers:

> About an hour after dark I heard a strange noise, so I unzipped the hammock and saw a man being lowered on a rope not a hundred feet above us. . . . I yelled up, "Are you one of the guys from that chopper?" He was wearing a full down parka with a hood, carrying a walkie-talkie, a large pack and had a headlamp strapped to his forehead. From now on if I ever envision a guardian angel it will be in this form.

February 25, 1969
Sequoia National Park

"ANOTHER TWENTY FEET AND WE WOULDN'T HAVE MADE IT!"

LYING in a hospital bed, Navy Lieutenant John McDaniel was glad to be alive. He and his copilot had been searching for a downed A-4 jet when their own single-prop-engine Skyraider quit.

"We had very little forward speed" and no place to land. "I had about five seconds to make a decision and luckily spotted a small ledge. I figured it was the only place in the whole world and headed for it. We barely made it to the ledge. I pulled back, we nosed up and dropped in."

Escaping almost certain death, the two pilots found themselves sideways on the 60-degree shoulder of Mt. Kaweah, a 13,802-foot peak 12 miles west of Mt. Whitney. Facing deadly avalanches from above, four long hours passed.

Master Sergeant Guy Roberts, leaping 8 feet from the hovering chopper, plunged to his armpits in the deep snow. With more than 800 jumps in 26 years, the 47-year-old Pararescue paramedic was on his first mission since leaving Alaska. "I think the cold weather in the Sierras is much more noticeable."

Roberts stabilized the men's injuries. Now, faced with darkness before they could be lifted out, the survival instructor had medical supplies, rescue gear, and a radio quickly thrown to him.

Seeking insulation from the cold, the three men used parachute cushions and bits of padding to fashion crude beds inside the twisted "Spad." Crawling into down sleeping bags, they tried to stay warm as it sank to 10 degrees below zero. Leaking aviation fuel kept them from lighting a cigarette or starting a stove.

"Even inside the plane the temperature was below freezing and our injuries made it impossible to get a comfortable or restful position in our cramped quarters." Gale-force winds swept across the frozen open ridge. Through the night, a large four-engine "Hercules" circled far overhead, flying radio cover for the three men huddled below.

Dawn came and so did gentler winds. With Air Force Major Roy Dreibelbis at the stick of the twin-engine "Husky," the rescue crew quickly hoisted the three nearly frozen men to safety.

March 12, 1969
Point Reyes National Seashore

"FLAPPED HIS ARMS LIKE A BIRD AND JUMPED OFF THE CLIFF"

THE sixties was an era of drugs and a time most rangers of that period will not soon forget. Park Ranger Jim Liles remembers:

> I was the veritable lone ranger one weekend when an acquaintance came galloping in on his racing mule, all lathered up from a hard six-mile ride from the coast. He brought the news, relayed by hikers, that a fellow had fallen off of a sea-cliff and was in bad shape, with the tide coming in.
>
> I radioed for the local rescue unit to roll, grabbed my SCUBA gear and wet suit and jeeped down the Bear Valley Trail, scattering a few returning hikers along the way. At trail's end the only souls in sight were a couple of elderly hikers, urgently waving me to their vantage point, fifty-sixty feet above the sea.
>
> The beach was fully awash with no sign of anyone in the water, but the couple insisted that they watched the victim wash out to sea and "that was him—right out there." They were pointing urgently at the head-sized float-bulb on some sea kelp a few hundred yards off shore and were so insistent that I *do* something that I donned my gear and entered the sea via the sea tunnel [blowhole] at the mouth of Bear Valley.

I made it out to the kelp patch and dove repeatedly till out of air—and also daylight. The "blowhole" was by now fully charged by the tide and impossible to escape through—the way in was not going to be the way out. A direct cliff assault was also out of the question, as my rescue unit back-up never arrived. As I was assessing the seriousness of my situation, an approaching helicopter appeared off Double Point. Chief Ranger Phil Ward had radioed the Coast Guard. The chopper was a most welcome sight and I was slung aboard in moments.

I was of course questioned about undertaking a solo rescue attempt (was not the first time, nor the last). Sometimes—as any good ranger knows—"you gotta do what you've gotta do."

Incidentally, the victim's body washed ashore a week later. Investigation showed the guy had taken an LSD flight. Witnessed by the old couple from a distance, this lone hiker had appeared, removed all of his clothing, "flapped his arms like a bird and jumped off the cliff."

```
June 14, 1969
Great Smoky Mountains National Park
----------------------------------------
```

THE LARGEST SEARCH IN PARK SERVICE HISTORY

CLAIRVOYANTS called; so did the White House. Green Berets volunteered; so did YMCA Indian Guides. The FBI stood ready to assist; so did corporate jets. The sky was scanned for buzzards circling, the ground for telltale bear droppings. At the peak of the operation, more than 1,400 searchers—flying in excess of 1,100 sorties and driving over 70,000 miles—looked. But not one track, not a scrap of cloth, nor a clue of any kind has ever been found of the seven-year-old boy.

Dennis Martin, along with his dad and grandfather, had been enjoying Father's Day weekend camping near the famed Appalachian Trail. He and his nine-year-old brother were playing with other children when they decided to sneak back through the woods and surprise their elders. Dressed in a bright red T-shirt and khaki shorts, the boy was missed in less than five minutes; at 4:30 P.M., Dennis completely vanished.

Ranger Larry Nielson set the search into motion, but the 2.5 inches of rain that night didn't help; tracks and scents disappeared, roads and paths turned to mud. Flood-swollen streams—Little River, Spence Field, Anthony Creek, and Little Bald—were combed. Fifty-one students on a field trip from Florida were pressed into service. Boy Scouts hiked west on the Appalachian Trail, others went east. Horsemen and a helicopter showed up.

By day four the search force had ballooned to 615, not including medical and food volunteers, such as the Red Cross and Minnie Pearl's Fried Chicken. Fortunately there were few accidents and donated food was always in abundance.

Special Forces brought in their communications van and a special phone line was installed. Two "Hueys" and two "Jolly Green Giants" whisked a small army of volunteers over the rain-soaked ridges and bramble-filled gullies.

A psychic from Michigan claimed that the boy would be found "five miles southeast from area last seen on a stream by a waterfall and that white pine trees are in the area." She said her dreams "had come true before." A Tennessee Highway Patrol helicopter flew over the hillsides; Dennis's distraught father called from it with a small bullhorn, but he couldn't be heard over the roar of the engine. Bear and boar droppings were examined; buzzards were watched.

On day seven the Green Berets rappelled a man with a chainsaw onto a ridgetop to cut a new heli-spot. Two more communications trucks and 5,000 gallons of much-needed aviation fuel arrived. Two hundred Tennessee Guardsmen at summer camp were called in and bivouacked nearby. The Coast Guard Auxiliary surveyed the shores of nearby Lake Fontana in their private boats.

Thinking ahead, Chief Ranger Lee Sneddon set up Plan A—IF FOUND ALIVE, the radio code was to be 10-100-A; Plan B—IF FOUND DEAD, it was 10-200. Almost 800 searchers were instructed to consider rigor mortis the only sure sign of death. For anything less certain, a Special Forces medic would be lowered into the site to secure the boy in a litter and fly out with him.

One week after Dennis disappeared, probably the largest search force ever to blanket a national park was in full motion. It would seem to almost double overnight. At least 57 different rescue squads from Tennessee, Georgia, Kentucky, and North Carolina were present. Two more thunderous, twin-bladed Chinooks arrived, joining at least six other large military helicopters in ferrying around many of the estimated 1,400 people.

Six television and 10 radio stations interviewed search officials for the evening news, while 10 newspapers kept the search in the morning headlines. Advice poured in from everywhere, including a telegram from Mascot, Tennessee.

> Take several friendly dogs including the boy's own, put package containing food and plastic raincoat around neck. Release dogs 1–2 miles apart. Be sure dogs are lost same as Dennis. By chance one may find his trail and follow him for friendship. Dogs . . . released by helicopter.

From the nation's capital, famed medium Jeanne Dixon provided predictions to search headquarters, and other psychics aided from Los Angeles and New Orleans. One caller insisted that the searchers "start looking in trees—stop looking on the ground."

Finally, the chief ranger asked local radio and TV stations to report that no more help was needed. Only bona fide searchers were allowed closer than 5 miles from the 57-square-mile search zone. On the morning of June 23, Operations Chief Jim Wiggins and Plans Chief Marion Myers redeployed the searchers: Start from where the boy was last seen and re-cover the area. Seven new heli-spots were built for the increased manpower needs.

Unfortunately, the first scent dog to be used didn't arrive until day nine. Despite the confusing odors of more than 1,400 searchers and the destruction wrought by many inches of rain, a police dog from South Carolina was finally used, but "with negative results." Two more offers from dog owners were accepted the next day.

A three-year-old boy wearing a red T-shirt was seen nearby. Rangers investigated and asked his surprised parents to change his shirt. An odor of decay reported near the park boundary turned out to be a dog carcass. Mission leaders knew it was over.

At sunset on June 29, the largest search effort in NPS history shut down. Although this probe will never officially end, the fate of little Dennis Martin will never be known.

June 15, 1969
Mt. Rainier National Park

"ROCK!"

MT. RAINIER'S north side, especially Curtis Ridge, has long been a rescuer's nightmare because of its difficult approaches, sheer frozen slopes, and treacherous rock fall. Access from below is hindered by technical, very steep cliffs. Dropping down to a victim from above is equally demanding and hazardous.

Getting a late start, the five friends proceeded up the ridge's challenging gullies; the sun was already loosening the frozen earth. Tired and perhaps careless after several hard days of climbing, the two rope teams strayed from the safer route onto much steeper, boulder-studded terrain. At 12,000 feet the angle increased, and so did the missile-like stones shooting past.

George yelled "Rock!"—just before he plunged down the 300-foot ice chute. Killed outright when he struck a pointed outcrop, the 37-year-old now dangled from one end of the rope; two others, battered and dazed, were still tied to the other end.

Three frightened men soon sat huddled on a small ledge below a crumbly, 150-foot cliff. The warm air loosed a constant and deadly rain of rotten rock on them. Their failure to return set off the now all-too-familiar rescue "alarm."

By late afternoon, a park rescue team had managed to struggle to Liberty Cap. Upon clearing weather, they were quickly joined by three others airlifted up from below. Working their way down a dangerously narrow finger of snow, the rangers made voice contact with the victims. Because of the precarious spot, the rescuers asked for a chopper and a "horse-collar" hoist out. Their answer: The winds were still far too "squirrely"!

More rescuers, courtesy of a Coast Guard helicopter, arrived from above; after great difficulty they reached one survivor. Pete, minus ice axe and crampons and using a safety rope to guard the tricky ascent, painfully climbed from his dangerous perch despite a dislocated right arm and limited vision.

One by one, the remaining three men were pulled to safety and airlifted out the next day.

With the calming of the mountain's rough air—along with the impressive dedication of a great many rescuers—George's body was eventually lifted off the deadly, knife-edge ledge.

In 1969, there were 2,441 attempts to climb 14,410-foot Mt. Rainier— 1,647 were successful.

August 2, 1969
Rocky Mountain National Park

LONGS PEAK NAVY

MORE than halfway up the 1,600-foot sheer east face of Longs Peak, the 16-year-old was pounding his third anchor into the granite when his second one popped out.

Over the next 27 hours, one of the most difficult rescue missions ever performed in the Rocky Mountains would unfold. With a fractured skull, femur, and tibia, the young man's life would soon be literally in the hands of the rescue team.

After tumbling 8 feet, Kordell Kor crashed into his partner. Struck on the shoulder and stunned by the sudden blow, 15-year-old Mike let go of the safety

The east face of Longs Peak, Rocky Mountain National Park, has been the scene of numerous dramatic Big Wall rescues over the years. LEW DAKAN PHOTO

rope and Kor continued to ricochet down the cliff. Severely burning his hand as the rope pulled from his grasp, Mike somehow slowed his friend by biting the rope and then finally pinned it against the rock with his cheek. Luckily, after plunging over 100 feet, Kor stopped just a few feet short of a larger, more deadly ledge.

Strapped into a stretcher, Kor was lowered 550 feet on the end of a ⁵⁄₁₆-inch steel cable, hand-carried down a steep and treacherous scree and snow slope, rowed across Chasm Lake in a six-man raft by the "Longs Peak Navy," and airlifted from beneath the 14,256-foot peak by an Army "Huey" helicopter.

For this rescue, nearby climbers fixed ropes up a deadly, rock-filled gully. A doctor climbed to where Kor lay delirious. Pack horses and a human train of 12 hauled the heavy rescue equipment. A second doctor tended Kor from the base of the cliff; he ceased breathing at least once. A Denver Police helicopter guided the Huey to the hospital.

Young Kordell Kor would climb again—only because of the heroic efforts and expertise of a fine-tuned "rescue machine."

```
December 30, 1969
Glacier National Park
```

UNIT CITATION

MT. CLEVELAND SEARCH AND RECOVERY TEAM
GLACIER NATIONAL PARK

FOR efforts far beyond the line of duty in the search and recovery of five missing climbers during the period January–July 1970.

On January 2, 1970, a search operation was initiated to locate five young mountain climbers, ages 18 to 22, who were overdue from a planned six-day winter climb of Mt. Cleveland—the highest peak in Glacier National Park. The extremely rugged terrain of the mountain, which has an elevation of 10,448 feet, involved highly skilled alpinists to carry out the search and rescue mission. Constant threats of avalanches were encountered. The remoteness of the area presented monumental logistics problems. The exemplary leadership and magnificient [sic] teamwork by the participants in the emergency effort under the most adverse and dangerous conditions prevented loss of life and injury to the search and recovery party. The team worked tirelessly to locate the lost climbers. Following the suspension of search efforts on January 9, 1970, due to adverse weather conditions and avalanche danger, a recovery effort was accomplished in the early summer by the team of employees from Glacier National Park and several Canadian National parks. The recovery effort was completed without an injury to the rescue team on July 3, 1970. In recognition of commendable teamwork, involving dedicated and courageous effort during an emergency situation and in the face of serious hazards, the Mt. Cleveland Search and Rescue Team is granted the **Department of the Interior Unit Award for Excellence of Service.**

Rogers C. B. Morton
Secretary of the Interior

Rangers, spotting the first victim in the roof of a fissure at the foot of the avalanche and suspecting the five climbers were still connected by their ropes, developed an original method of reaching them. Using the intense pressure of cascading water, the rescuers funneled the melting snow into fire hoses and hydraulically "drilled" the young men from their frozen graves.

The Department of the Interior's Unit Award, signed on April 5, 1971, recognized the truly international spirit of SAR cooperation: two American parks and two Canadian ones. U.S. Park Service personnel actively involved in this mission were Willie Colony, Jerry DeSanto, Doug Erskine, Larry Feser, Bob Frauson, Fred Goodsell, George Lowe, Mike Lowe, Riley McClelland, and Rick Reese.

Rangers, using fire hoses and cascading snow melt, hydraulically dug 25 feet straight down into the avalanche to locate the five buried climbers.
GLACIER NATIONAL PARK RESEARCH LIBRARY

SAR training blossomed and commercial groups began teaching the subject around the country in the 1970s. Here, the Ropes that Rescue, Ltd. group instruct Arizona Department of Transportation engineers over Grand Canyon National Park's Marble Canyon in 1995.

CHAPTER 8

1970–1979

The Amalgamated Brotherhood of Alpine
Body Snatchers—our way of coping when
dealing with the horrors of the
park's all-too many traumatic and
grisly deaths.

—retired Yosemite Ranger Coyt Hackett

DURING the 1970s, search and rescue in both the United States and the National Park Service came of age.

NATIONAL-LEVEL SAR

Helicopters from five western military bases (Carson, Lewis, Luke, Mountain Home, and Sam Houston) began flying highway-related medevacs, premature-infant shuttles, and related remote-area SARs in the fall of 1970. To this day, Military Assistance to Safety and Traffic (MAST), created in November 1973 when Public Law 93-155 was signed by the president, proves a godsend to much of rural America.

Nine men from five states, meeting in Salt Lake City on November 30, 1970, recognized the need for SAR coordination and intra-agency liaison at a national level. The National Association of Search and Rescue (NASAR) was born. Originally labeling themselves the National Association of Search and Rescue Coordinators (NASARC), the group of state emergency officials elected Hal Foss, Washington's SAR coordinator, as its first president. In 1997 at NASAR's 28th annual conference, dozens of SAR groups and agencies were represented.

In the fall of 1973, the federal government created ICSAR, or Interagency Committee on Search and Rescue. Because of both historical and current SAR duties, the commandant of the Coast Guard was designated as the sponsor of the intra-agency group. Following the National Search and Rescue Plan, first published in March 1956 and implemented that July, ICSAR's mandate still is to coordinate SAR at the Washington level without usurping day-to-day missions and operations. Original ICSAR signatories were the Departments of Interior, Transportation, Commerce, and Defense; the Federal Emergency Management Agency; the Federal Communications Commission; and the National Aeronautics and Space Administration.

On June 1, 1974, the Air Force Rescue and Coordination Center (AFRCC) combined the three somewhat independent, regional (Western, Central, and Eastern) Air Rescue and Coordination Centers into one operation for the Lower 48.

Alaska, the Pacific, and offshore continental waters remained separate. In addition to facilitating SARs around the United States, the AFRCC enhanced communications, standardized procedures, and improved economy of operations. The NPS uses the AFRCC's services and resources extensively.

BIG WALL RESCUES

For years, injured and dead victims were lowered down cliffs by rope. It wasn't until rock climbing mushroomed in the late 1950s, however, that the need for both long raisings and lowerings began. In his book, *Camp 4*, climbing historian Steve Roper defines "Big Wall" as a "multi-day effort involving direct aid on a large and steep rock wall" and then cites the first Big Wall climb as the five-day ascent of Yosemite's 1,200-foot Lost Arrow Chimney in September 1947.

Ranger Jim Reilly administers medical aid to Peter Ourom 2,000 feet up the face of Yosemite's El Capitan on June 2, 1981.
JOHN DILL PHOTO

Ten years later, the state of mountaineering was pushed forward when the first Grade VI (most complicated) climb was completed on the northwest face of Yosemite's Half Dome on June 28, 1957. Fortunately for both climbers and rangers, no one needed help. Technique, expertise, and equipment were marginal at best for reaching someone stuck midway on a vertical, half-mile-high cliff. Preparation for such a scenario began in isolated cases around the country, for instance when Yosemite Ranger Buck Evans built a rescue winch by modifying an existing one from a boat trailer in the fall of 1958.

There were several dramatic Big Wall rescues in the mid- to late 1960s, including the several-day, 1,900-foot lowering of an injured man off the nightmarishly dangerous north face of Grand Teton in August 1967. On this mission, recognized by both *Reader's Digest* and Vice President Hubert Humphrey as "impossible," the rangers of Grand Teton pulled off one of the most spectacular SARs in history. This was soon followed by the November 1968 lowering of Royal Robbins down to Warren Harding and Galen Rowell, both suffering hypothermia on Yosemite's Half Dome. And the next summer, a technically exacting, 550-foot lowering of a 16-year-old "cliff rat" off the east face of Rocky Mountain National Park's Longs Peak took place.

When an injured climber was saved from the sheer, 1,500-foot face of Yosemite's Lost Arrow on April 6, 1970, the era of "Big Wall rescues" arrived in the busiest climbing area in the country. In reaction to such brutal missions, Yosemite created a rescue site in the park's Camp Four in December 1970. Climbers got free, unlimited camping and rangers gained access to many of the world's best rock jocks, who were soon needed to save each other.

On September 22, 1972, one of the most involved Big Wall rescues took place when a climber was lowered off the vertical face of El Capitan. Requiring two days to engineer on the top of the 2,800-foot face, it took Jim Bridwell 90 minutes to accompany the stretcher down the often overhanging 1,800 feet. Using a 4,400-foot rope, this was the longest single-rope, single-station litter lowering in U.S. history.

On October 5, 1976, two men were lowered 1,400 feet at night with the aid of an 8-million-candlepower "Carolina Moon" courtesy of the U.S. Coast Guard and its four-engine HC-130 circling close over Mt. Watson for several hours. Although routinely used on rescues at sea, the dazzling lamp had never been employed on a mountain SAR. A similar use of the light was made at least once again that year, on Washington's Mt. St. Helens on November 8.

Dangling rescuers and victims below a moving helicopter is a common tactic in Europe and Canada and was dramatically employed by the military in Vietnam. In the parks, there were a handful of attempts to use this lifesaving technique in the 1960s and 1970s. Usually this was done by "lassoing" someone from the open door of a small chopper. Until May 28, 1978 . . .

Fighting fading daylight, a crewman from California's Lemoore Naval Air Station lowered himself out of the "Angel" onto Yosemite's imposing Clouds Rest. Clipping onto the dying man, the medic cut the climber loose from his granite perch and stepped into space several thousand feet up. Upon a safe landing, these brave aviators heralded in the Park Service's now often used "short-haul," or "Big Wall Fly Away." They earned the first and only non-DOI **Valor Award.**

Because of its own internal restrictions, the NPS could not use its own smaller, single-engine helicopters for such striking assistance due for fear of one engine failing. Finally, based on the consensus of an FBI-hosted, week-long October 1979 gathering of a dozen civilian pilots, the cream of this country's urban fire and law enforcement helicopter expertise, as well as a Yosemite SAR ranger (the author), the DOI's Office of Aircraft Services finally sanctioned NPS choppers for rescue short-hauls and insertions.

ADVANCED EMERGENCY MEDICAL SERVICES

In 1910, the American Red Cross began teaching first aid as a national program, and by 1917 it had found its way into the national forests. Over that decade, both forest and park staffs were acquiring these principles. Bolstered also by skills gained during World War II, these rangers continued to practice basic first aid for the next 50 years.

In January 1968, rangers at Mt. Rainier began more sophisticated medical training through the University of Washington. Coordinated by Mount Everest climber and former Rocky Mountain National Park seasonal ranger Dr. Tom Hornbein, it was a 110-hour course in "Winter Survival and Medical Emergencies—Advanced Shock Treatment." Other than the standard Red Cross–type first aid and an occasional short session specific to an area, this was the first elevated medical instruction in the NPS and among the earliest in the nation. In the early 1970s, Emergency Medical Technician (EMT) training began springing up countrywide.

In response to the need for more first-aid skills, principally in the more remote sections of the system, the NPS graduated 23 rangers from its first EMT class on November 18, 1972. Taught by Vietnam-experienced Navy corpsmen at North Carolina's Camp Lejune, the 100-hour program included childbirth, dislocation reduction of joints, intravenous (IV) use, and practical field drug therapies.

On January 24, 1976, rangers and rescuers entered Sequoia's Lost Soldiers Cave for a spelunker with a broken back. In such a difficult place,

Ranger-paramedic Mead Hargis preparing to go over a 1,500-foot cliff in Yosemite National Park to rescue a climber suffering from extreme heat in the summer of 1980.
NPS PHOTO/AUTHOR'S COLLECTION

the gravity of the injury hit with Ranger John Chew, who then provided the energy for the creation of the NPS's now well-established "Park Medic" course. Developed by Sequoia and Yosemite—both areas having some legal autonomy due to their status as exclusive jurisdiction—the complicated program grew and is now available throughout the NPS. First taught by California's Fresno Medical Center, 20 rangers graduated on June 6, 1978.

MANAGEMENT OF SAR

For years the Pacific Northwest's Bill Syrotuck (1930–1976), a mathematician by education and an SAR dog-handler by avocation, compiled statistics on "lost person" behavior. Syrotuck and his wife, Jean, and Hank and Janet Wilcox developed ways of searching while still assigning mathematical chances for locating a victim. After three years of training in this new technique, they announced their availability to law enforcement agencies. In July 1965, they were assigned their first search when officials believed someone was missing from a Seattle-area train wreck. Although no one was found, the German Shepherd Search Dog Committee also had its first search.

In response to theories and principles largely developed by Bill Syrotuck to aid SAR officials in finding people more quickly and efficiently, the "Managing the Search Function" course was created. On January 27–29, 1974, rangers from the West met in Sequoia National Park for the prototype class taught by Bill Syrotuck, Bill Wade, and others. On May 6, 1974, the second class began at the Grand Canyon's NPS Training Center. The first "Managing the Search Function Instructor Workshop" graduated 33 people on September 15, 1978. It was refined over the next few years. In the following two years, more than 500 received this training. Now taught worldwide, the program brings discipline and science to what once was solely "seat of the pants" search management.

CAVE RESCUE

Steve Smith, a California fireman and a rescue coordinator for the National Speleological Society, launched the nation's first "Cave Rescue Symposium." Underground SAR and its specialized principles were advanced by this training. Aiding Smith were instructors with considerable experience in SAR and medicine: Bill Clem, Steve Hudson, Tom Vines, and Great Britain's Dr. John Franklin, as well as NPS employees Ron Kerbo and the author. This groundbreaking effort took place for a week in San Antonio, Texas, in June 1976.

MILESTONES OF THE 1970s

1970	NPS's 281 units receive 172,004,600 visitors.
July 15, 1970	Ft. Sam Houston is named pilot test site for Military Aid to Safety and Transportation (MAST) project.
November 25, 1970	Three die when NPS plane sinks in 400 feet of Lake Mead; diving bell is brought from Florida for search.
Spring 1971	Professional Ranger Organization (PRO) is formed; it fails.
May 1971	Aerospatiale Llama pulls climber off Mt. Everest at 23,000 feet—highest helicopter rescue mission on record.
June 8, 1971	Southwest Regional Office hosts first NPS SCUBA Conference; primary focus is to revise diving guidelines.
October 23, 1971	John Jones, 70, a California hunter, is reported missing near Utah's Capitol Reef National Park. Nearly 17 years later, May 14, 1997, his remains are found in a remote area of the park.
April 6, 1972	First official count of Death Valley's highly endangered Devils Hole Pupfish is made (38 are seen) by Lake Mead Rangers Acree and Dimont.
June 25, 1972	Man is killed and eaten in Yellowstone by grizzly bear. It may be a precedent-setting tort case.
August 1, 1972	Largest SAR cache in NPS burns down when arsonist sets fire to NPS barn and stables in Yosemite Valley.
Winter 1972	American Rescue Dog Association is formed.
1973	Based in Washington, D.C., U.S. Park Police obtain two B-206 helicopters—used on numerous SARs in area.
August 31, 1973	Lake Mead Park Ranger T. K. Brown dies of a heart attack while on scuba training dive in Ringbolt Rapids.
July 1974	Yosemite begins charging for rescues; this will not last long, as administrative difficulties creep in.
September 12, 1974	*Sierra*, an 11-part television series, debuts; it sensationalizes SAR efforts of Yosemite rangers.
February 8, 1975	SAR use of satellites for communications begins during search for downed aircraft in Yosemite.

MILESTONES OF THE 1970s

March 20, 1975	Sixteen die in Air Force C-141 crash in Olympic.
September 12, 1975	Eight people, including six from NPS, die in plane crash in proposed Lake Clark National Park—final impetus for NPS to join DOI's Office of Aircraft Services.
November 29, 1975	Massive, earthquake-caused tsunami kills two on beach of Hawaii Volcanoes National Park.
June 3, 1976	Buddy Woods lands helicopter at 20,300 feet on Mt. McKinley—breaks record for North American altitude landing.
July 1, 1976	Largest search in North America begins when 10-year-old boy is lost in Nova Scotia—5,000 people involved.
July 4, 1976	Celebrating U.S. Bicentennial, four hang gliders sail from top of Mt. McKinley; slightly injured, one person falls 800 feet on takeoff—30 days up, 30 minutes down.
July 31, 1976	Five-hundred-year flood in Big Thompson Canyon near Rocky Mountain National Park kills 145. Park takes lead, reacting in force.
October 10, 1976	NPS fields first SAR Overhead Team when retarded youth is lost in Lassen. Rescue uses rangers who have extensive large-fire experience; Dick McLaren is "SAR Boss."
December 9, 1976	Six-month-long salvage of plane with estimated $300,000 worth of marijuana and two dead pilots in wilds of Yosemite sparks Sylvester Stallone's movie *Cliffhanger.*
June 15, 1977	Two climbers fall 3,000 feet on a remote snowfield in Alaska's Glacier Bay National Monument; they are still there.
October 1, 1977	Association of National Park Rangers is born in Jackson Hole; brings heightened awareness of park ranger profession. Author is first president.
1978	The Western International Search and Rescue Advisory Committee (WISARAC) is founded by the states of Idaho, Montana, Oregon, and Washington. The group facilitates information between agencies responsible for air search and rescue and now includes several Canadian provinces as well.

MILESTONES OF THE 1970s

January 3, 1978	Responding to a downed plane, four rescuers are killed in a helicopter crash in Great Smoky Mountains.
1979	Based at Washington's Ft. Lewis, eight Army Chinook helicopter missions are flown for Mt. Rainier in support of park's demanding high-altitude SAR operations.
March 4, 1979	Willi Unsoeld, popular environmentalist and world-renowned climber, dies in avalanche on Mt. Rainier.

Rescuer Jim Bridwell nears the bottom of El Capitan after being lowered 1,800 feet from the ledge where Neal Olsen was injured. NPS PHOTO

April 6, 1970
Yosemite National Park

"WE DROPPED HIM!"

"**A TERRIBLE** scream rang up out of the void, and Bridwell's shocked voice thundered from the radio." Everyone froze. Jim Bridwell, a legend among the world's great rock climbers, was in the middle of one of the "hairiest," most technically demanding cliff rescues ever performed anywhere.

To the ancients of Yosemite, the 1,400-foot long "Lost Arrow" was frozen in stone. Aimed skyward, its 300-foot tip splits 75 feet away from the main wall and then tapers to a V notch hundreds of feet down. The vertical face then continues plunging to a jumbled, brush-covered base more than 1,000 feet below.

Twenty-year-old Roy Naasz and Andy Embick, 19, were a rope-length from the top of the "Arrow Direct," their goal for the past three tough days. Devoid of cracks, the face of glaringly white granite was one of the most challenging climbs in the country; it had been conquered for the first time only two years before.

Naasz studied his next move intently. Hammering his third pin in, a 2-inch-wide piton called a "bong," he cautiously shifted his weight onto the thin nylon loop that dangled off it.

As if on a triggered trapdoor, he dropped into 1,200 feet of nothing. Rock climbers call this "getting air time," but the former high school gymnast got more than a quick thrill. His rope soon snapped taut as he skidded down the rough, crystal-studded cliff face. Smashing into the tiny ledge 25 feet below, aptly called "Second Terror," Naasz hung limply at the end of the thin life line, his femur and ankle shattered. Embick climbed out for help.

Wayne Merry, former park ranger and director of the Yosemite Mountaineering School, and Lloyd Price, his chief climbing guide, flew by park helicopter to the rim above the Lost Arrow.

> Lloyd and I roped into the notch real fast and climbed to Salathe ledge with sleeping bags and medication, getting there pretty close to dark. It was cold as hell—seems like it was about 17 degrees or so. Roy was straight down, 90 feet below Salathe. It was so steep you couldn't see him from the ledge.
>
> We tossed a rope down into the gloom and I went down to Roy, who looked very tiny and very exposed on that wall, with a real white face and big eyes . . . sitting tied-in on a little ledge just about the size of his hips and legs.
>
> The ledge was so small that there was no way I could stand on it, so I just stood in the slings with my shoulders level with him. I got out the Demerol. There was a little wind, and so darn cold I was afraid the drug might freeze in the needle, but it didn't. I gave it in the shoulder. It hit him fast, and almost immediately he leaned over and barfed on my boots.

Yosemite Falls roared; frigid winds blew . . .

By midnight, Price was so cold he needed to go to the rim to warm up; he actually tied his hands to the ascenders to do so. His replacement out on the Arrow, Herb Swedlund, became "desperately entangled" in the nine ropes running from the rim. Swedlund would later describe the confusion of lines as resembling a "direct hit on a spaghetti factory." Eventually, over 3,500 feet of nylon rope were "tied" to this rescue operation.

At sunrise the gray-shadowed rock wall started humming with action and color; Merry and Swedlund welcomed the six other climbers. Place anchors. Rig pulleys. Play ropes out. Take the stretcher down to the victim. They knew what to do, and they did it well.

Getting Naasz into the Stokes basket "was quite a feat, as the bad leg was on the side against the cliff . . . and they just had to dangle on the ropes while loading him in."

On the rim, Yosemite Rescue Ranger Pete Thompson directed the placement of more anchors and ropes. Price designed an elaborate hoisting system. Eventually, through a sophisticated combination of ropes and pulleys, Naasz would be pulled from the outside of the base of Lost Arrow and then lifted 400 feet vertically while simultaneously being hauled 200 feet sideways. This seldom-done, elaborate maneuver would require the ropes and stretcher to turn a 90-degree corner while suspended over 1,000 feet above the rocky slabs below. Few rescue techniques require greater skill, coordination, effort, and luck.

Now, at midmorning and with more than 25 people involved on the cliff, the delicate operation began. Again, Bridwell's voice came over the two-way radio, this time hastily clarifying his earlier announcement. They hadn't really *dropped* him, but only toppled him a foot onto a ledge. Everyone relaxed a little.

By sunset, 30 hours after he probably should have died, Roy Naasz was in the Yosemite Hospital. He would climb again.

Even years later, Wayne Merry would remember: "While we were working we heard radio talk that Governor Ronald Reagan and his entourage were in the Valley and were watching us through binoculars. Instantly and simultaneously, five arms shot up with an internationally recognized hand signal." Someone later swore, "Damn . . . we shoulda mooned him!"

```
           July 11, 1970
     Imperial County, California
  --------------------------------------
```

GAS, HEAT STOPS RESCUE ATTEMPT
FOR TWO MARINES

WINTERHAVEN (UPI)—High temperatures and poisonous gas Sunday stalled efforts to rescue two marines missing and presumed dead in a maze of tunnels in an abandoned gold mine near this community.

Officials said the missing men and two other marines, all stationed at the nearby Yuma Marine Corps Air Station in Arizona, climbed down into the mine Saturday.

Imperial and Los Angeles County Sheriff's deputies said temperatures at the bottom of the 600-foot shaft the men entered reached more than 150 degrees Sunday. The surface temperature stood at 115. Deputies said the mine was full of carbon monoxide gas from a fire in the shaft last week.

"They were taking me to a level where they had been before" (survivor) Fontana said. "We started getting dizzy and all messed up. Lopez passed out on us."

—*Las Vegas Review-Journal*, 7-13-70
(reprinted by permission
of United Press International, Inc.)

Leaving his three companions to explore deeper into the Senator Mine, the 19-year-old marine was quickly overcome by fumes in a lateral tunnel. His friends, climbing out to summon help, returned with two deputies. Because their air packs lasted only 35 minutes, however, the officers were unable to reach the victim.

One of the marines then "fought his way by the deputies" and worked his way back to his downed comrade. Deputies tried to drop an air pack through a crevice to the second ill-fated marine but were forced to retreat before they were successful.

When Lake Mead Rangers Don Chase, Rick Gale, and Jerry Phillips—summoned because they had favorably impressed the nearby Mohave County (Arizona) sheriff on a recent "simple mine shaft recovery"—arrived at the scene, they joined 14 other rescue organizations trying to reach the two downed men.

Phillips worked on the Incident Command Team, bringing order to a chaotic operation while Chase and Gale were lowered into the "hell hole." The two rangers, unable to use standard rescue breathing tanks because of insufficient air, wore larger scuba tanks designed for diving but not for the many noxious gases they encountered.

At one point, Gale vividly remembered, he had "to take my tank off over my head, wiggle it through a narrow crack and then crawl through sideways behind it." Chase recalled "a lot of rope and cable work to reach the victims and a very long and arduous haulout."

On July 15, 1970, Imperial County Sheriff-Coroner Raymond B. Rowe awarded the three rangers a **Certificate of Appreciation** "in recognition of outstanding service and accomplishment."

October 23, 1970
Yosemite National Park

"THEY WERE TEN DAYS OVERDUE
AND HAD 1,600 FEET TO GO!"

TRULY an epic, the first ascent of the 2,200-foot Wall of the Early Morning Light—one of the most demanding and intimidating rock faces in the world—was a testimony to endurance and talent.

At 47, Warren Harding was the undisputed "hard man" of Yosemite Big Walls. Along with his partner, 27-year-old Dean Caldwell, the superclimber wrote on their registration card that they were going to haul 300 pounds of gear, including food for 12 days "and some emergency supplies"; they expected to be off El Capitan by October 31. On November 9, with Harding and Caldwell only halfway up, the park's rescue ranger, Pete Thompson, began to get nervous.

Planning on 12 days to ascend the unclimbed 2,200-foot "Wall of the Early Morning Light,"
Dean Caldwell (left) and Warren Harding actually required 27 days. Meeting them on top
were 19 rescuers and 1,900 pounds of gear. PETE THOMPSON COLLECTION

They had been up for many days longer than anyone had ever been on a wall before, their rations should have been critically short, they reported that their feet were numb, their gear got wet when it rained and that they were suffering from open sores brought on through lying in wet bags during the first big storm. They were ten days overdue and had 1,600 feet to go!

Two days later, faced with six massive, unseasonable wet-weather fronts rolling in from the Pacific, the climbers were asked if they could rappel off if needed.

Impossible! Caldwell's last comment that night, heard through the park's sophisticated electronic listening device, was, "We know that our asses are in a sling." Appreciating the double entendre from a thousand feet above, Thompson knew Caldwell could have been "merely referring to his belay seat, or that they were in trouble." That night, nearly an inch of rain soaked the valley—but up above, snow soaked the two climbers.

Caldwell and Harding were still 1,800 feet from the top, having made only 400 feet in the last six days. In fact, they averaged a mere 85 feet each day of the climb. Ranger Thompson, charged with protecting "life and limb," knew that a rescue had to be mounted now or it might be too late. "Feeling that it would be better to have the equipment poised on the top prior to the advent of a major storm which might preclude the possibility of flying equipment to the top, I carried forward arrangements." It was a very difficult decision for Thompson, one that would later be loudly—and unfairly—criticized by the "victims."

With the U.S. Army graciously volunteering six hours of helicopter time, 19 men and 1,900 pounds of rescue equipment were lifted to the top. "Of course, by that time the weather had stabilized nicely and our two friends on the wall . . . were beginning to move nicely." On November 18, 27 days after starting up and without ultimately needing a rescue, Harding and Caldwell "peered over the top to find some seventy newsmen peering back."

November 25, 1970
Lake Mead National Recreation Area

DIVING BELL IN THE DESERT

WHEN Chuck Rowland came to, he was already totally underwater. Fumbling with his seatbelt, the pilot somehow forced a door open and swam upward, where he was quickly rescued by the tour boat "Echo." The crew vainly looked for his passengers. And for the next 13 days, one of the most unusual searches in NPS history took place.

NPS Patrol Plane N-736 was only a few hundred feet up when it left the west end of Boulder Canyon. Those aboard were observing terrain likely to be affected by underground nuclear explosions at the nearby Nevada Test Site. The small Cessna 206, catching a sudden and violent desert downdraft, crashed and quickly sank 390 feet; Rowland escaped—the three others didn't.

The Atomic Energy Commission was sure that Theos Thompson, one of its three commissioners, and two of his key staff were at the bottom of the lake. Fearful of losing another scientist to China, and of the ever-mounting international antagonism toward nuclear testing, the AEC needed to be certain.

Near one of Lake Mead's deepest spots twists the steep-sided and submerged bed of the Colorado River. Somewhere among these drowned hills and dead cliffs lay a small plane. Were there still three men strapped inside, or had they somehow escaped only to quickly sink and drown?

Park Dive Officer Weir and Clark County Sheriff's Sergeant Leemon met with Harry Wham. Wham, a member of the World War II famed Underwater

Demolition Team and an advisor for Lloyd Bridges's *Sea Hunt* TV series, knew this was far beyond their combined capabilities. The Department of Defense volunteered.

Crude but intricate preparations were hastily made for Ocean Systems, a Navy contractor, and acknowledged deep-diving experts. Buoys, moorings, and thousands of feet of cable were placed as anchors against the unpredictable desert winds. A flat barge, large enough to cradle a portable decompression

With a diving bell (upper right) flown in from Florida, the Lake Mead patrol plane (left) is recovered from 400 feet of water. Three died but the pilot escaped. DON WEIR PHOTO

chamber, with a crane sturdy enough to lift a ton of diving bell—or an airplane—was built from scratch. The Florida-based, mixed-gas, deep-sea divers would have to manage with the makeshift rig.

Through the use of state-of-the-art electronics such as side-scanning sonar, radar, and underwater TV cameras, as well as old-fashioned common-sense, intuition, and hard work, a tiny bottom "blip" was swiftly found. That was the easy part.

Six days, almost exactly to the minute, after the crash, a military C-141 set down at nearby Nellis Air Force Base. Onboard, along with the rest of the crack team of underwater professionals, was a collection of unique underwater search "hardware" never before seen in the desert.

N-736, even though located electronically, now needed to be pinpointed to the foot by the small, two-person diving bell. Working from it at a depth of 400 feet, divers had only 20 minutes before they would need to be brought back to the surface and decompressed. They worked in the cold darkness, surrounded by thousands of pounds of water pressure, attaching heavy, steel hoisting lines. If the plane dropped . . .

After the bell's six round-trips and the divers' numerous decompressions, a cable was finally secured to a strut and the plane's small lifting eye. Gently encouraged off the lake bottom, it then took nearly three hours before the red and white tail of N-736 broke the surface. Uttering something about national security to the numerous rangers who were providing logistical support, the AEC "clamped the [publicity] lid on," including confiscation of all their film.

Commissioner Thompson and his special assistant, Lieutenant Colonel Jack Rosen (U.S. Army Retired), were still inside. Bill A. Smith, a private contractor assigned to the AEC, was not.

Park Ranger Gene F. Gatzke was the National Park Service team leader on this unique mission.

June 19, 1971
Grand Teton National Park

"PROBABLY
THE WORST SINGLE ACCIDENT"

"PROBABLY the worst single accident in the history of the park" is how Chief Park Ranger Frank Betts described the bizarre deaths of the three skilled mountaineers.

Several parties had signed out to climb 10,500-foot Symmetry Spire. After reaching the top, they all were in various stages of descending the steep, snow-filled gully by glissading—a quick way of "skiing" downward on the feet while dragging an ice axe along behind to serve as a brake.

Robert Deal was the first to lose control. After sliding down and around a prominent rock outcropping, the 28-year-old disappeared from the view of teammate Richard DaBell. A 19-year-old college student, DaBell quickly determined that Deal had tumbled into a partially hidden, water-carved snow cavern.

Roping up, DaBell lowered himself through a near-freezing waterfall only to see his partner tightly wedged between rocks. Unable to reach Deal, the would-be rescuer swiftly grew numb from the icy water showering down. Team leader William Radtke joined DaBell and was able to reach the still form of his friend Deal. Knowing it was too late, the two violently shivering men scrambled from the crevasse and learned that help had been sent for.

The second party, including 30-year-old Minneapolis policeman Ron Ottoson, halted above the rock ledge and yelled to the third party to stop. Despite the frantic warning, however, 36-year-old Wayne Creek could not slow down and he, too, slid into darkness. Then, his father looked on in sheer terror as nine-year-old Luis Y. Barrando plunged into the hole.

Ottoson, believing he had heard a faint reply to his shouts, threw a coil of rope into the crevasse. Feeling no tugs on this lifeline, he then rappelled the 20 gloomy feet only to find the two climbers tightly buried up to their necks in white. The falls had created a small avalanche and the wet snow was compacted around the three; their arms were pinned tightly to their sides.

"The unfortunate thing about this avalanche," Chief Ranger Betts later explained, "was that it also dammed up the stream so that the water level rose over their heads and both drowned."

Horrified at watching the two die in front of him, Ottoson desperately grabbed for nine-year-old Luis's helmet, but the strap broke. Frantically the policeman then tried lifting the boy up by his nylon jacket, but it slowly peeled off the small body.

Led by Ranger Bob Irvine, the park's seasoned rescue team reached the now-quiet scene at 6:30 that night. Having been dispatched for one victim, they were shocked to learn of the other two. Irvine, a veteran of hundreds of rescues, rappelled in but could no longer see anyone—snow and water covered all three.

A recovery team of 12 arrived the next morning. Donning a wet suit, District Ranger Tom Milligan dropped into the narrow, slushy moat. The dammed-up water had drained overnight, such that two of the dead climbers were clearly visible. Despite harrowing conditions, including the icy torrent falling from above, the seasoned Milligan was able to attach a nylon sling to one victim. Other rescuers, working together like the veterans they were, engineered a rope system to pull the body from its watery grave. This took most of the day, and the rangers elected not to try for the remaining two until the following day.

Eight of the team started down the second night with one victim, while the remaining four rangers made the watery trap safer by removing a large, snowy overhang from its edge. On the third day, Ranger Milligan again went into the hole. By noon the second body was removed. Milligan thought he could see the last body but could not quite reach it.

Rather than drop into the watery grave to use the same dangerous technique a third time, they tried to reach the remaining climber by "drilling." Using an 85-foot fire hose and the force of falling water from the same stream that had originally drowned the three, they dug to the creek below. They ended successfully only a few feet from Robert Deal.

In a July 12 letter to Secretary of the Interior Rogers C. B. Morton, Ron Ottoson and his teammate, James Hovoda, wrote:

> It is a credit to yourself and to our National Parks system
> that such high caliber personnel staff these areas. We wish
> to express our sincere appreciation for being able to witness
> their very inspiring team while operating on a mountain res-
> cue mission.

DaBell, Radtke, and Ottoson received **Carnegie Hero Commission Bronze Medals** for trying to save the three mountaineers.

The 12 members of the Grand Teton Mountain Rescue Team received DOI **Special Achievement Awards** of $150, except for Rangers Irvine and Milligan, who received $250.

```
              July 15, 1971
          Carbon County, Montana
-----------------------------------------
```

"CREWS PLUCK INJURED
CLIMBER FROM MOUNTAIN"

PARK Ranger Griffiths described the accident scene like this.

> ledge is located on the Northwest Face of Silver Run Peak
> (12,500 ft.) which . . . has not been ascended. This face is
> characterized by large towers, a maze of steep ridges, inun-
> dated by steep talus couloirs . . . interrupted periodically by
> cliffs of 150 to 300 feet high. The rock appeared to be . . .
> weathered granite which was friable in nature. . . . The face
> dropped approximately 3000 feet from the summit . . . 0.8 of
> a mile . . . and the slope averaged about 60 degrees.

The *Salt Lake Tribune* described the rescue like this.

> Red Lodge, Mont.—Gayle Zachary, a 22-year-old Girl Scout
> counselor who spent 79 harrowing hours on a 12,610-foot
> Montana mountain, was reported in good condition Monday
> after a dramatic rescue.
>
> The Boise counselor was stranded Thursday evening
> when she tumbled and slid down a rocky embankment to a
> nearly inaccessible spot on a cliff.
>
> Miss Zachary and a fellow counselor, Leslie Appling, 18,
> Hillsborough, Calif., had set out on a four-hour hike from a
> scout base camp at 11 A.M. Thursday.

> ### Above 10,000 Feet
> They were last seen by their hiking party at 1 P.M., waving
> from the top of a steep rocky slope on Silver Run Peak. The
> girls had climbed to above the 10,000-foot level by 6 P.M.
> when Miss Zachary fell.
>
> The first report that the hikers were missing came in the
> middle of the night Thursday and search efforts by horseback
> and air began early Friday.
>
> Efforts were fruitless, however, simply because the
> searchers were looking well below the 10,000-foot level.

> ### Walks into Camp
> "We didn't believe they would be as high as they were," said
> district ranger Gary Wetzsteon. "There was no rhyme or rea-
> son why they should be there."
>
> Wetzsteon said the searchers were finally made aware
> of Miss Zachary's location when Miss Appling walked into
> base camp at 1 P.M. Friday.

She boarded a helicopter with Carbon County Sheriff James Echler and Wetzsteon directed them to the spot where the injured Miss Zachary had been since late the day before, without food or water.

Wetzsteon described the section of the mountain as quite treacherous and said no one could figure out how the women got there.

"The climbers all said it was impossible," he said.

The first to reach the injured hiker were two climbers from the National Park Service, stationed at nearby Yellowstone National Park.

Weak, Dehydrated

They were helicoptered to near the summit of the mountain and then climbed down.

The two—Tom Griffiths and Dick Goss—said they found the young woman weak, dehydrated, and badly bruised but said she perked up when they "poured some lemonade down her."

The men put the woman in a large sleeping bag to ward off the near-freezing nighttime temperatures and the next morning began the harrowing descent down the sometimes vertical mountainside.

Several other climbers had joined the party by then, including Billings, Mont., physician, Dr. Warren Bowman.

Lands on Nubbin

The rescue workers said in the course of bringing her down they made three drops of 300 feet and four of about 150 feet, sometimes carrying the girl piggy-back.

One of the most dramatic events of the rescue operation came at the bottom of the precipice when Vietnam veteran pilot Jim Sanchez of Steamboat Springs, Colo., brought his helicopter dangerously near the rocks and lifted the woman to safety.

Rescue worker Joe Regan of Billings said Sanchez landed "on a nubbin, with the roters [sic] nearly touching rock." He added, "I could hardly believe it."

Regan said if the pilot had not landed, Miss Zachary would have had to have been carried across a long series of treacherous boulder fields.

When the helicopter finally landed here at 8:15 P.M., all the battered hiker could say was, "I've never felt so dirty. I've never been so happy to be alive."

—*Salt Lake Tribune*, 7-20-71
(reprinted by permission)

August 14, 1971
Rocky Mountain National Park

14-YEAR-OLD LOWERED 850 FEET
ON RANGER'S BACK

RESCUING the daring young climber—injured at 13,000 feet—required a spectacular 850-foot lowering off an overhanging cliff; a bold, extremely perilous nighttime climb of 1,500 feet; use of the Secretary of the Interior's helicopter; and the "Longs Peak Navy."

Chris Chidsey badly fractured his right leg while scaling the difficult east face of Longs Peak. The injured youth, assisted to the relative security of a large ledge by his doctor-father, now needed the herculean efforts of a crack rescue team to be moved any further.

By 7 that night, veteran rangers were ready to roll. Luckily for them and for Chidsey, Interior Secretary Morton was in the park when word of the young man's plight reached headquarters. It would be dark before a chopper from Denver or Ft. Collins could get there so Secretary Morton quickly volunteered his B-1 helicopter and pilot and then closely monitored the night's unfolding drama through a borrowed park radio.

Airlifted to a tiny rock shelf by fading light, Rangers Larry Van Slyke and Walt Fricke were forced to finish climbing the icy 900-foot Lamb's Slide after dark. "I wanted to rope up on the traverse but Walt just laughed and started off. Where it is about a foot wide with 800-foot exposure, I remember telling Walt that if I fell that I would come back and haunt his ass until he died." Reaching the boy after some difficulty, the two rangers spent a cold night preparing for the most dangerous part of their mission.

By first light, the rest of the team climbed into position and skillfully rigged a lowering system 1,000 feet long. Then, using a "tragsitz"—a leather and buckle device designed for one person to ride piggyback on another—Fricke, with Chidsey tightly strapped to his back, slowly scrambled onto the lip of the overhanging cliff and gently eased into space.

In a nearly picture-perfect operation led by Steve Hickman, the well-drilled rescue team on top lowered the two to the snowfield below. So sheer was the rock wall that Fricke touched only twice during their 850-foot descent. Once safely down, Chidsey was piggybacked to Chasm Lake where a rubber raft—the Longs Peak Navy—ferried him across. Chidsey's painfully long odyssey to the waiting ambulance finally ended after a torturous 5-mile horseback ride.

Walt Fricke received the **Department of the Interior Valor Award,** and he, Paul Anderson, Mike Donahue, Steve Hickman, Bob Pederson, Charles Post, Clarence Serfoss, and Larry Van Slyke were named in a **DOI Unit Award for Excellence of Service.**

```
        January 21, 1972
    Rocky Mountain National Park
```

ICICLES HUNG FROM FROZEN BEARDS

DOOMED before they left the road, the two Colorado State University students were dead before they were missed . . .

They were prepared more for a gala than for a gale; stuffed in Joan's small daypack were a dress, nightgown, cosmetics, and extra lingerie, but no sleeping bag, extra warm clothing, or survival necessities. Fred carried steaks, eggs, and two sleeping bags, but no stove, fuel, or water. They failed to register with anyone.

Their goal was Chasm Lake Cabin, a stoveless, barren rock shelter built above treeline in the frigid shadow of Longs Peak. There at 11,590 feet, hurricane winds are winter's rule—a cruel trial for raw beginners on recently rented skis.

Searchers performed "far beyond the call." Numbering more than 125 at one time, they included rangers, deputies, and mountain rescue groups from around the state. Green Berets from the Army National Guard and search-dog teams from Washington volunteered. Armed with skis and snowshoes, helicopters and snowmobiles, rescuers spent days battling the mountain. Windblown snow covered ski tracks within minutes and swept them clean the next day. Statewide front-page news pictured bone-weary volunteers with icicles hanging from their frozen beards.

Exactly what had happened to the two young people, who were just out to play, will never be known. The thin air and the brush-studded uphill slog probably proved overwhelming. Four miles from where they started, they abandoned their frustrating skinny cross-country skis, a practice common among novice skiers. With storm clouds and darkness closing in, they fought their way upward toward the bleak rock refuge on foot. Crossing the steep snowfield below the cabin, Fred probably hurt himself when he slid into the large boulders below. Then, it was up to Joan.

After helping her friend into his sleeping bag—one not designed for snow and wind—the nearly exhausted young woman probably went for help. Without skis and blinded and confused by wind and storm, she plunged downhill through the waist-deep snow. Shortly afterward, Fred left his crude shelter and followed. Desperate to escape the storm's fury, Joan nestled in the lee of a boulder.

On the fifth day of the search and less than a half mile from the road, her frozen body was found still huddled against the huge rock. Eight months later, Fred's remains were discovered a mile upstream from his girlfriend's.

June 25, 1972
Yellowstone National Park

GRIZZLY MEAL

THE bear that ate Harry Walker weighed just 232 pounds. The 25-year-old, job-less construction worker from Alabama ignominiously became the first person known to have been killed by a Yellowstone grizzly since 1942—the fourth in the park's 100-year history.

From the moment Walker and his high school buddy hitchhiked into the park, the two did everything wrong. They unlawfully pitched their tent in a restricted area after disregarding advice from a concession employee; they ignored fresh bear scat near camp; they littered the site with smelly scraps and dirty cooking utensils; and they left open food when they went hiking.

Shortly past midnight, the two campers were talking as they returned to their isolated hideaway, 600 yards beyond the huge summer crowds of the world-famous Old Faithful geyser.

> We stopped and I heard something in front of us. Just as he shined the light [we] could see . . . a bear, coming at us. Approximately 5 feet away. And I immediately dove to my left and sorta rolled down the embankment. I got back on my feet and was running and then I stopped and paused for a second and I could hear a lot of commotion and I heard Harry hollering "help me, Crow help me." And I hollered back, "Is there a bear there?" And that's all—he didn't respond anymore.

"Crow" collapsed when he stumbled into the Old Faithful Inn; within min-utes the search for hapless Walker was in high gear. Ranger Gerry Tays will never forget that very long night.

> We gathered along the boardwalk in the geyser basin and split up into 3-person parties. One ranger in the middle with a light was accompanied by rangers on either side with rifles/shotguns. . . . Our first obstacle was to leave the safe-ty of the boardwalk and in the blackness of the night make our way through the geyser basin.
>
> Needless to say, it was probably the scariest assignment I have ever been on, because unlike most other rescue activ-ities that require specific skills that you can count on, this exercise required no particular technical skills and success was largely left up to fate. It was difficult to hear any move-ment in the woods over the sound of your own heart beating and the deep breathing of your two partners.
>
> At one point during the wee hours Tom and I found ourselves walking side by side along the boardwalk having just returned from an unsuccessful search of the hillside.

> Tom, walking on my left, had a shotgun in his right hand, the barrel pointing down. Without warning the gun went off, blowing a large hole in the boards right next to my left foot. Tom, reacting to an array of mind-scrambling feelings, was through for the night. We put him in a stokes litter, covered him with a blanket, and told nurse Kathy Loux to keep an eye on him. He was literally a basket case.

At first light Harry Walker was found 50 yards below camp—everything between his pelvis and heart was gone. Hoping to catch the killer bear, rangers anchored three wire snares to lodgepole pines. Within 24 hours, a 20-year-old female grizzly—left ear tag no. 1792—was caught and quickly dispatched. An autopsy confirmed that she had eaten on Walker.

Although Walker had done almost everything illegally, his family sued the federal government.

Over the years there have been legal challenges involving bear attacks in national parks: *Rubenstein v. U.S.*, *Claypool v. U.S.*, *Johnson v. U.S.*, and *Martin v. U.S.* Under the Federal Tort Claims Act, private citizens have the right to sue the United States; liability generally depends upon the law where the alleged negligence occurred. In Montana, where natives seem to relish an occasional brush with a grizzly, the case might easily have gone in favor of the National Park Service. Walker's family, recognizing this frontier mentality, however, asked for and received a change of venue—to a more "civilized" San Francisco.

The man who heard this case, Judge A. Andrew Hauk of the District Court for the Central District of California, ruled that technology such as radio collars readily existed for keeping minute-by-minute track of wild animals, as seemingly evidenced on numerous *Wild Kingdom*–type television shows. Judge Hauk found in favor of Walker and awarded $87,417.67, saying the "Park Service willfully failed to warn decedent of a dangerous condition." The government appealed.

On December 3, 1976, Judges Barnes, Ely, and Van Pelt of the U.S. Court of Appeals for the Ninth Circuit declared that a "mistake has been committed" and that the original verdict "should be reversed and dimissed." Case closed.

In the spring of 1977, Alabama's influential Senator Allen introduced a private relief bill into Congress to award the Walker estate $87,000 for the loss of Harry. These special measures are seldom challenged; congresspeople defer to the good intentions of their peers and pass them without seeking public input. There is neither testimony nor the normal review process that accompanies a routine money authorization. If enacted, this bill would still have inferred that the United States was liable for Walker's death!

Once Wyoming's conservative Senator Wallop was apprised of Walker's flagrant misdeeds, the private relief bill never came to the Senate floor for a vote.

September 22, 1972
Yosemite National Park

LONGEST SINGLE-STAGE ROPE-LOWERING IN MOUNTAINEERING HISTORY

AT sunrise, while leading the difficult, 27th pitch on The Nose of El Capitan, Neal Olsen pulled a boulder of granite down onto himself. Just glancing off his head and back, it struck his right leg, smashing it badly. By 7:30 that morning, Yosemite SAR Officer Pete Thompson was organizing one of the most demanding rescues in North American mountaineering. Before it was over, two nights and 40 hours later, the 20-person rescue team would perform the longest rope-lowering in history: 2,600 feet.

UNIT CITATION
EL CAPITAN RESCUE TEAM
YOSEMITE NATIONAL PARK

in recognition of the high degree of professionalism and valor exhibited by all who took part in the rescue operations which saved the life of Mr. Neal Olsen.

The rescue of Mr. Neal Olsen from The Nose of El Capitan in September marked a new level in mountain rescue. A rescue of this nature had never before been attempted over such a steep terrain. The publicity resulting from the incident was worldwide. Six persons were lowered over the cliff to perform first-aid and litter evacuation while a fourteen-man crew remained on top to perform all aspects of support of equipment lowering, safety belaying, and rope management. These functions were accomplished without a single error or fault. Additional support was also required to haul equipment, pack it to the area, maintain communications, organize and order food, and provide other logistical support. Without this assistance the operation would have been delayed. Since part of the rescue operation was performed at night a special lighting system was devised which contributed significantly to the success of the rescue. In recognition of their outstanding teamwork and dedication to duty, the El Capitan Rescue Team of Yosemite National Park is granted the **Unit Award for Excellence of Service** of the Department of the Interior.

Rogers C. B. Morton
Secretary of the Interior

A recent fire had destroyed the Yosemite SAR cache, including all of its long ropes. Thanks to the efforts of Tubbs Cordage and the California Highway Patrol, El Toro Marine Air Station was able to fly new ones from San Diego to the summit of El Capitan that night.

The operation was engineered on top by John Dill and Lloyd Price. They knotted well over a mile of yachting rope together to make two 3,000-foot lengths. One rope made a directional change at the victim's tiny ledge nearly 800 feet below; the other ran straight from the edge of El Capitan to Olsen's wire litter and rescuer Jim Bridwell. Once under way, it took only 90 minutes for the two to be lowered the remaining 1,800 feet of sheer cliff.

```
December 1, 1972
Yosemite National Park
```

DOUBLE SUICIDE OR SUICIDE-HOMICIDE?

YOSEMITE park rangers truly believe that California is the "land of weirdos and wackos"; Bruce Norris simply validated their belief. Rescuers never did learn, however, if his pretty girlfriend willingly joined in when the young student physicist hurled himself over the third highest waterfall in the world.

At the base of 1,623-foot Yosemite Falls, an inverted "snow cone" grows almost every year. The steep, often 100-foot-high mini-glacier springs from the wind-driven spray of the world-class waterfall plunging from far above. This same freezing mist also coats the surrounding ledges and brush with treacherous, clear ice.

After struggling up the 4 miles of trail to the top of the waterfall, several visitors found two sets of clothing neatly folded just beyond the guardrail of the falls overlook. After carefully retrieving the strange find, which included high-top lace boots, the anxious hikers started down to report their discovery.

Simultaneously, but 2,000 feet lower, another couple could make out a nude body on the far side of the impassable, water-choked gorge between the falls. Scanning upstream, they then spotted a second flesh-colored splotch, stark against the "snowcone." After bushwhacking their way back up to the path, they accidentally met the first party on their way to the ranger station.

Officials, realizing no lives were to be saved even if they hurried, knew caution was paramount for retrieving Norris and his dead companion from one of the most dangerous spots in the Sierra.

Before first light, a team of 12 rangers wound their way up the trail to clean up after the grim ritual. Some, dispatched to the crime scene above, dangled off the lip of the 1,600-foot cliff to inspect the wall below with binoculars. Investigators spotted Norris's body now partially obscured by frozen mist, but could find no further clues to what had happened.

Other rangers, many donning scuba wet suits to work under the cascade tumbling from far above, dealt with headaches of their own. Three of the recovery team, roped together to climb on the huge "snow cone," dodged large sheets of falling ice. So dangerous were these frozen, sail-like chunks that it became one ranger's sole duty to scan the cliffs above, hoping to give ample warning before they struck somebody below.

The body recovery team, in black neoprene wet suits and orange plastic helmets, swinging metal ice axes and trailing brightly colored climbing ropes, somehow looked obscene against the white and gray. For two days this ranger force endured freezing spray and near-gale-force winds, ducked large hunks of ice peeling from far above and dodged death over ice-covered cliffs—all for Norris.

February 7, 1973
Northern Nevada

TWO RANGERS KILLED IN PLANE WRECK

RANGERS Ron Trussell and Jake Metherell, en route in Jake's single-engine Mooney to a conference in Boise, were an hour west of southern Utah's Cedar City when they vanished from radar. Trussell, 34, was a supervisor at Bryce Canyon, and Metherell, 45, was a resource specialist at nearby Curecanti National Recreation Area.

Faced with darkness and worsening weather, Metherell told the Salt Lake Flight Service Station that he was dropping from 14,500 to 12,500 feet just before 6 P.M. When the little plane disappeared 10 minutes later, it was somewhere southwest of Elko, Nevada.

The Civil Air Patrol promptly began routine airport checks while querying for other helpful information. Based on data and the best guesses available, the search focused on the rugged, highly remote Ruby Mountains of northern Nevada. Because of poor weather, CAP and local pilots conducted a limited air probe over the next two days. Snowstorms kept everyone grounded the following 48 hours, but on the 12th and 13th, six pilots were up and at it again.

With conditions improved by late on the 14th, Grand Teton Chief Ranger Frank Betts launched in his private plane, as did Glen Canyon's Warren Adams in the National Park Service patrol plane.

In addition to the intensive air effort, a skilled mountain climbing team was flown in that evening: Grand Teton Rangers Tom Milligan (leader), Pete Hart, and Ralph Tingey, as well as Rocky Mountain National Park's Walt Fricke, Bob Haines, and Steve Hickman. Driven to 9,000 feet by Snow Cat, the group spent three days skiing the most probable search area. A wreck was actually found, although it soon proved to be a plane located six years before.

On February 17 and 18, more than 15 search craft crisscrossed above the high desert. They stretched to the north of Elko in case Metherell had managed to skim below the radar and between the peaks of the isolated area. After 12 days and no further clues, the mission was scaled down on the 19th.

On April 3, the two rangers were found; they had been hidden by deep snows in a remote canyon in the Rubies for nearly two months.

While on duty 100 days after this accident, a pilot and three more NPS employees would die in another plane wreck in the West on May 19. Studying bighorn sheep in Canyonlands National Park, pilot and Moab-based owner-operator Dick Smith (25), Utah State graduate student John C. Ebersole (26), Capitol Reef National Park biologist William D. Cooper (30), and Las Vegas–based NPS

Research Biologist Chuck Hanson (52) were killed when their Cessna 185 smashed into a remote canyon 23 miles southwest of the airport. Why Smith, a veteran of the redrock of southern Utah with 6,668 hours of flight time, crashed will never be known.

```
June 3, 1973
Zion National Park
```

UNIT CITATION

FOR
SEARCH AND RESCUE TEAM
VIRGIN RIVER NARROWS, ZION NATIONAL PARK

IN recognition of the hazardous search and rescue mission performed by a three-man scuba team from the Division of Resources Management and Visitor Protection in order to save two Zion National Park visitors, threatened with possible loss of life or serious injury, while hiking the Virgin River Narrows.

The team entered the North Fork of the Virgin River June 6, fully equipped and prepared for an extended search. From an air reconnaissance of the river June 5, it was apparent the team would have to swim several miles through unpredictable river currents and be required to be self-supporting in bringing out the stranded party. Due to the remoteness of this area, the only communication was by radio through aircraft patrol. After 32 hours the rescue team located the hikers, Bob and Harry Pattison. They had been stranded by high water for five days and were suffering from exposure and lack of supplies. The team, using scuba equipment, a four-man rubber raft and ropes, evacuated the hikers through the Canyon Narrows. They arrived safely at roads-end late on June 7. In recognition of outstanding teamwork and dedication to duty, the Virgin River Narrows Search and Rescue Team is granted the **Unit Award for Excellence of Service of the Department of the Interior.**

Rogers C. B. Morton
Secretary of the Interior

Park Rangers Peter Allen and Ken Morgan were from Lake Mead and maintenance man Seth Phalen was from Zion.

Although scuba tanks were initially considered, they were never taken into The Narrows. The floating rescue team faced numerous hazards, including the chilling 38-degree floodwaters and isolation from the outside world, except for when the contact plane flew over the 1,000-foot-deep, 50-foot-wide gorge. The greatest dangers the three faced, however, were the large logjams that suddenly appeared around the sharp bends in the river—the threat of being sucked into and fatally entangled under one of these "strainers" of debris was ever present.

January 16, 1974
Grand Teton National Park

THREE DIE IN AVALANCHE

TRIGGERED by the two lead skiers, the snow slab that swept three unseasoned young men to their deaths was some 250 yards wide and 3 feet deep. According to veteran Winter Ranger Pete Hart, "the party ascended the wrong slope at the wrong time."

Searchers practice probing a snow slope in Rocky Mountain National Park in 1968.
ROCKY MOUNTAIN NATIONAL PARK RESEARCH LIBRARY

Skiing up from Amphitheater Lake, the 11 trainees had already crossed the most demanding obstacle of their route: the delicate traverse below the north face of Disappointment Peak. They and their leader were members of the National Outdoor Leadership School (NOLS) Teton Winter Mountaineering Expedition. NOLS, a developmental program focusing on motivation through fun in the wilderness, has a long history of caution and good judgment on such trips.

They started onto the moraine below Teton Glacier. When the avalanche cut loose, Wes was leading, followed closely by Mike Moseley. Both were pulled 500 feet downhill by the wave of white. Wes survived, miraculously "swimming" on top; firmly entombed, however, 24-year-old Moseley had perished by the time he was dug out some 20 minutes later. Tom, the expedition's leader, was carried 50 feet; buried to his waist upright on a large boulder, he watched the others disappear below.

Bart Brodsky was alone in the middle of the moderately steep slope when struck by the huge slab. Although he was pulled only 50 feet, the 18-year-old was dead when he was freed 25 minutes later. Peter, Donald, and David were within two steps of the slide's edge when they were engulfed. The first two were just under the surface and were dug out immediately—alive; 20-year-old David Silha was uncovered within eight minutes—dead.

Even with CPR, as well as other heroic measures used for more than an hour that frozen afternoon, the three young men could not be revived. Tom and Wes skied out for help, and the following morning, the shocked, numb climbers bore their lifeless comrades to Delta Lake, where they were soon lifted out by helicopter.

Predictably, avalanches are always unpredictable. Contributing to the mishap was the subzero cold spell of the preceding week, along with high winds and recent heavy snowfall. A highly unstable wind-slab condition developed on this steep, southeast slope at the 10,000-foot level. After examining the situation carefully, Grand Teton National Park's Board of Inquiry could make "no determination as to fault of leadership in this accident."

July 8, 1974
Yosemite National Park

"RESCUE IN THE GORGE"*

THE four-man crew stood wordlessly before Lieutenant Commander John Morse . . . at the Naval Air Station. . . . It was 4 A.M. The idling engine of "Angel 4," a twin-engine UH-1N helicopter of the search-and-rescue unit, seemed to stress the silence that covered the base.

"We'll be going into this deep, narrow gorge after a kid who's sitting on a rock in the river," he said. "At least we hope he'll still be there when we arrive. The situation is very tight; no space to maneuver. Wind and water go down the gorge like coal down a chute. Everything has got to work perfectly, ship and crew."

During the 100-mile, one-hour flight . . . Morse mulled over the perils of the mission. On the previous evening, he had [talked] . . . with Pete Thompson, the search-and-rescue specialist . . . had reported . . . Tyler Seal would be spending his second night stranded on a rock in the raging Tuolumne River in Muir Gorge. The gorge was at least 800 feet deep, with almost sheer granite walls that narrowed to a width of about 28 feet at the river. Rescue by winch-equipped helicopter was the only way to save Seal. "It's a hairy situation," Thompson had said.

[Tyler] looked at his watch. . . . He had been on the rock for 24 hours. He decided to remain there until morning. If no help came by dawn, he would slip off the rock and try to make it to the gorge wall. He had no way of knowing that a waterfall, which would surely batter him to death, was just around the bend.

High above Tyler—and now miles away—an exhausted Rick [hiking companion] had arrived at the ranger station where Pete Thompson and Richard Smith were on duty. It was 5 P.M. The rangers immediately called for a civilian helicopter. By 6:15, Rick and Ranger Smith made the first pass over the gorge.

After the chopper had landed . . . Smith radioed Tyler's position and predicament . . . and described the difficulties confronting a rescue operation. They agreed that Rick and Smith should climb down into the gorge and spend the night near Tyler. . . . Thompson would ask the Navy if it could send a rescue helicopter.

"Angel 4" dipped into Yosemite Valley early the next morning to pick up Pete Thompson. The ranger quickly briefed the crew on the problem, emphasizing that every minute was precious because of steadily increasing wind velocity. Crew chief Hart, 24, looked at 20-year-old Chavers. "Well, Sid," he said, "you've been waiting to make your first cable rescue. This one's a beauty."

Pilot Morse made one pass over the gorge, then another pass through the gorge at about 400 feet. He quickly weighed all the factors—air temperature, hovering altitude, gross weight of the helicopter, wind velocity, canyon dimensions—that would affect the operation. Because every extra pound subtracted from flying stability, Ranger Thompson was off-loaded on a little plateau about 1800 feet from Tyler Seal. "Okay," Morse announced finally. "We're going in."

As the helicopter sank into the gorge, each man assumed specific responsibilities. Pilot Morse played the craft's controls against the winds, and kept an eye on the south wall. Co-pilot Griesbach visually measured the distance between the rotor blades and the north wall, and at the same time scanned instruments and gauges. If one of the two engines failed, the ship might crash in the bare seconds it would take for the other engine to pick up the engine load. Chavers put on his harness and stuffed a second harness into his pocket. Jones reported the movements of the ship's tail.

Crew chief Hart, flat on his belly, his helmeted head sticking out the starboard door, directed Morse to a position 75 feet above the stranded hiker. "Forward, Mr. Morse," he said into his helmet mike. "Ten yards at 12 o'clock . . . easy forward . . . a little more to the left, Mr. Morse."

"Easy . . . easy . . . HOLD! You're right on the money. I'm opening the hoist boom, and Chavers is going out."

Hart used his electrically controlled winch to lower Chavers. "He's half-way down . . . you're drifting, Mr. Morse . . . easy forward and left . . . HOLD! He's three quarters down . . . he's turning . . . he's there!"

"The kid is buckled . . . I have a thumbs-up from Chavers . . . the cable is about to pick up the weight—NOW!"

Morse had to be instantly aware of the need to compensate for the additional weight of some 185 pounds imposed on one side of the ship. Hart moved the winch lever to its top speed. "He's halfway . . . three quarters . . . he's in!"

Morse was proud of his crew. . . . In 3500 flight hours, including search-and-rescue in Vietnam, he had never flown a more dangerous mission.

*Excerpted with permission from "Rescue in the Gorge" by Joseph P. Blank, *Reader's Digest,* March 1974. Copyright © 1974 by The Reader's Digest Association, Inc.

September 12, 1974
Sierra National Park

SIERRA: **THE TELEVISION SHOW**

SET in fictitious Sierra National Park, NBC's 11-episode *Sierra* series dramatized the work of National Park Service rangers. Filmed largely in Yosemite and inspired by the real-life adventures of the park's staff, Executive Producer Robert Cinader had tried to match the success of his previous television hits, *Adam 12* and *Emergency.*

First episode—9/12/74	Last episode—12/12/74
Theme song "Sierra" written by	John Denver
Theme song "Sierra" sung by	Denny Brooks
Technical Advisor	Ranger Jack Morehead

From 8 to 9 each Thursday evening (opposite *The Waltons, Paper Moon,* and *The Odd Couple* and followed by *Ironside),* Chief Ranger Jack Moore and his fun-loving but hardworking staff wrestled with

the conflict between trying to preserve the natural beauty of the wilderness and accommodating the flood of tourists wanting to utilize the resources of the park. The campers, skiers, hikers and climbers came in all shapes and sizes. Some were friendly, some stubborn, and some nasty and cruel.

The principal cast, in order of Universal's billing, was:

Ranger Tim Cassidy	(Starring)	James Richardson
Ranger Matt Harper	(Starring)	Ernest Thompson
Chief Ranger Jack Moore	(Also Starring)	Jack Hogan
Ranger Julie Beck	(Also Starring)	Susan Foster
Ranger P. J. Lewis	(Also Starring)	Mike Warren

The Rangers, the series pilot directed by Christian Nyby II, was first released by Universal Studios on Christmas Eve 1974. Three of the original cast changed during production, so the made-for-TV movie had to be redone. In this as well as the weekly episodes, there was a mostly unbelievable SAR mission woven in between Cruncher—the park's troublesome bear who would cleverly break into cars—and the clownish antics of Rangers Cassidy and Harper.

Yosemite's chief ranger was Jack Morehead; *Sierra's* was Jack Moore. From a distance, real ranger J. T. Reynolds often passed for P. J. Lewis. True-life Ranger Warren White was credited in the pilot for playing a ski patrolman. A few other rangers and a number of local climbers made respectable money as extras and rescue stuntmen.

In 1981, Thompson won an Academy Award for Adapted Screenplay for *On Golden Pond.* Warren became Officer Bobby Hill in the 1980s *Hill Street Blues,* and Hogan served for two years as Judge Smithwood in *Jake and the Fatman.* Richardson died several years later in his own rescue drama near Mammoth Mountain south of Yosemite.

Despite *Sierra's* questionable plots, laughable acting, and needy story lines, the short-lived television series was an interesting—albeit minor—addition to the history of NPS search and rescue.

Ranger Roger Rudolph swings out to Lost Arrow during the pilot for the short-lived Sierra, *a television series dramatizing the rangers of Yosemite National Park, summer of 1974.*
AUTHOR'S PHOTO

```
                September 14, 1974
        Lake Mead National Recreation Area
```

UNIT CITATION

SEARCH AND RESCUE TEAM, ELDORADO FLOOD
LAKE MEAD NATIONAL RECREATION AREA

FOR efforts performed beyond the line of duty in the search
and recovery of flash flood victims and property during
September–October 1974.

On September 14, 1974, a flash flood swept through the
Eldorado Canyon Resort, Nelsons Landing, on Lake Mohave
killing nine persons and causing $500,000 in property dam-
age. Search and rescue operations were directed toward removal of debris, using heavy equipment and cranes. Excavated
material had to be carefully examined for victims and property as it was removed. Scuba divers searched the harbor
area under extremely hazardous conditions. Air and water
craft searched the lake surface while other team members
were involved with gathering witnesses' statements, assisting relatives and friends of the victims, keeping records of
lost and recovered property, working with the news media
and providing information. Team members worked from dawn-
to-dark for a period of four weeks in this hazardous operation
without further serious accidents or injuries. In recognition
of their outstanding teamwork and dedication in response to
one of the worst natural disasters in a National Park Service
area, the Eldorado Canyon Search and Recovery Team is
granted the **Department of the Interior Unit Award for
Excellence of Service.**

Thomas S. Kleppe
Secretary of the Interior

At the height of the operation, 21 agencies were involved. Seventy-nine
National Park Service Search and Recovery Team members are named in the
Unit Award.

```
                March 20, 1975
            Olympic National Park
```

C-141 "STARLIFTER" CRASH

WITH its 10-man crew and six Navy passengers, the huge, 110-ton "Starlifter"
neared the end of a routine cargo flight from the Philippines. At 37,000 feet for
most of its 16-hour journey, MAC 40641 descended to 10,000 feet and was then

given a heading of 150 degrees to skirt the populous Seattle area, inbound for McChord Air Force Base, headquarters of the 8th Military Airlift Squadron. Reaching his new altitude, the aircraft commander, 28-year-old First Lieutenant Earl Evans, was quickly cleared down to 5,000 feet.

With only 10 minutes until touchdown, the instructions were clearly acknowledged: "40641 is out of ten at 0556Z." This was the plane's last recorded transmission before crashing into the snow-covered, 7,300-foot-high ridge of Inner Constance two minutes later. When the 145-foot aircraft hit the wall at nearly 250 knots, it triggered a massive avalanche. There were no survivors—men and metal cascaded to the frozen valley below.

Just before midnight, less than 47 minutes after the giant plane vanished from radar, a Coast Guard chopper from Port Angeles was in the air; it was promptly beaten back by thick clouds and heavy snows down to the 500-foot level. Far overhead, above the storm, an HC-130 "Hercules" soon began listening for signals from its ill-fated big brother. As day broke, the search intensified.

Army, Navy, and more Coast Guard helicopters arrived, as did McChord's disaster response team of 25 doctors, radio operators, truck drivers, and other support personnel. Forty skilled mountain rescue volunteers and park rangers mobilized at the Coast Guard station. Everyone waited for better weather and word from the search crew circling high above the storm. Finally, just before dark, the wreck was sighted through the broken clouds.

Debris and bodies were scattered down the length of the steep 1,900-foot-high slope, from the flight deck to the large vertical T of the tail section. The plane's navigator, still strapped in his seat, was recovered first, but because of colossal avalanche hazards as well as the specialized climbing skills needed on the rugged peaks, it was another two months before the second body would be found. The plane's flight recorder—and its last victim—weren't located until late the following June.

On September 1, more than five months after the crash and after approximately 200 people representing numerous federal, state, and local groups had spent nearly 30,000 hours on this mission, the Upper Dungeness River Drainage was reopened to the public.

Naming 27 people, the Secretary of the Interior granted a **Unit Award for Excellence of Service** for the Olympic National Park **Recovery and Salvage Operation.**

```
                    June 16, 1975
                Yosemite National Park
        ----------------------------------------
```

DEATH OF AN ANGEL

SCRAMBLING off a short climb on El Capitan, Peter Barton slipped and fell 150 feet. His stunned companion wanted to believe that there were still faint signs of life in the broken body of his friend.

Launching quickly to the alarm, Gordon Sibel, hovering just above Barton and the jumbled base of the 3,000-foot, sheer wall, was unable to land the park helicopter. From inside the ship, Ranger Dan Sholly, looking at hundreds of feet of treacherous cliffs over which a stretcher would need to be lowered, called for an "Angel."

Godsends to rescue agencies in California, the fleet of twin-engine UH-1 "Huey" helicopters—"Angels"—from the San Joaquin Valley's Lemoore Naval Air Station had flown hundreds of park rescues since 1961. Angel 6, with its 270-foot cable hoist and 1,100-hp engine, was only 45 minutes away.

Moments after this dead climber was hoisted into the Navy helicopter at the base of El Capitan, one of its two engines quit and the million-dollar craft crashed and burned.
MARK FORBES PHOTO

Sholly, clambering up through an 800-yard maze of truck-sized boulders and a jungle of gnarly oaks, found Barton dead. Twelve other rescuers soon reached the scene. They zipped the well-liked, young redhead into the black body bag, moved to a nearby level spot for the Angel's easy cable pickup, and waited.

Lieutenant Tom Stout commanded Angel 6; built like his name, the red-bearded, young lieutenant had performed numerous rescues for the park. Joined at the controls by John Sullivan, Stout had the mission and ship well in hand. In the back, Ranger Paul Henry and the three crewmen prepared to lift the body aboard.

On his second slow pass over the scene, Stout pulled a "hover check"; after rising 300 feet to guarantee sufficient power for the operation, he slowly lowered Angel 6 to within 20 feet of the dead climber. After swiftly hooking the thin wire cable to the stretcher, Sholly gave a thumbs-up to the crew chief above.

Just as the litter was being secured to the ship, R/R (Reporting Ranger Sholly) heard a sudden change in engine sound as if the ship was shutting down after landing. At this same time R/R observed the ship tilt back and forth and drop a few feet in altitude, causing the rotor blades to come close to the ledge. At this point the helicopter tilted strongly to its port side, and "rolled" into a spiral descent down the cliff making what appeared to be at least two full 360-degree turns before it went into the trees, approximately 500–600 vertical feet below R/R's position and then out of site. The victim was still secured outside the helicopter when last seen.

Peter Barton and the $1.2 million Angel were burned to ash, but miraculously nobody onboard was seriously hurt. Barton's was the second of three climbing deaths in Yosemite in three days.

August 1, 1975
Grand Canyon National Park

WANDERED FOR 20 DAYS IN CANYON

LINDA only wanted to hike down to Supai Village. Now, with 7 miles behind her and less than one relatively easy mile to go, she came to a fork in the broad, sandy trail. Unfortunately, the 25-year-old nurse took the wrong path. "I never got to the village. . . . It just started getting very dark. I laid down . . . but I was too scared to sleep."

Rugged and remote, the area is a stunning collection of orange-toned sandstone cliffs and gorges. In 1880 the Army Corps of Engineers found the new, 60-square-mile reservation too rough to survey accurately. Home today to 350 Supais, the tiny community at the bottom of the Grand Canyon is isolated from the outside world except for one telephone and an 8-mile trail.

In a postcard mailed to her parents the day before her hike, Linda had written of her proposed trip to the secluded village. Lost that first day and not due back to Pittsburgh for two more weeks, more than 17 long days—and longer nights—would pass before anyone would even miss her.

Three days after veering the wrong way, she finally found a tiny trickle of water in a crack in the rocks; "it took her 45 minutes to fill her eyeglasses case." Without those precious drops, she would have been dead in a few short days. "I just kept wandering and wandering. . . . Being without water is truly frightening."

"For the first four days I tried screaming, but that didn't help. Your voice doesn't carry that far."

Daydreams blurred to nightmares. The 100-degree, ovenlike heat drove her to seek lifesaving shade. She felt the bone-chilling nights the most frightening, however. "There was always a continuous buzz or hum at night."

Linda was finally reported missing by her anxious parents. Her dust-covered car was promptly identified at the trailhead. A day into the search, Hardy Jones, a local Supai, reported to mission leader Dick McLaren that footprints were spotted "where nobody should be." All that day and into the evening, the faint tracks of the woman's crepe-soled shoes were skillfully followed. At sunrise "they heard her hollering."

Now 21 pounds lighter, Linda had been lost for 20 days.

September 12, 1975
(pre) Lake Clark National Park

SIX NPS EMPLOYEES AND
TWO OTHERS KILLED

LABELED the "Alaskan Alps," the countless granite spires and plunging waterfalls of the Chigmit Mountains are awesome. Only an hour southwest of Anchorage, these 4 million acres of grandeur were under study as a possible national park. The 27-year-old captain of the 20-year-old, single-engine DeHavilland knew they couldn't see all the proposed area on this trip but he wanted his seven passengers to see as much as possible.

Hired by the Alaska Task Force of the National Park Service for a routine familiarization flight, James Smelcer, an experienced pilot with 2,096 hours and an N-64392—a recently converted seaplane with 7,117 hours—lifted off at 1:30 P.M. The normal orientation called for them to go through Merrill Pass, south to Lake Clark, and then return to Anchorage via Lake Clark Pass.

Captain Smelcer, after burning nearly half of their six hours of fuel and blessed with clear weather and a lack of turbulence, slowly worked his way back home, 150 miles away. The plane, observed from the ground by a wildlife photographer, was last seen snaking along below the jagged peaks only 400 feet above the glacial green waters of Twin Lakes.

When the DeHavilland Beaver failed to arrive as scheduled, company officials assumed that it was safe at Twin Lakes and did not report it missing until just past noon the next day. Military and Civil Air Patrol aircraft then searched more than 1,000 square miles before sighting wreckage 14 miles from Port Alsworth at 5:30 P.M. With daylight quickly fading, two Air Force Pararescue PJs readied to parachute onto the steep, heavily wooded mountainside.

The damage was impressive. They found the plane's clock stopped at 4:51 P.M. and its tachometer jammed at 1,850 rpm. The prop, moving at nearly full speed when it struck, cut one 14-inch tree in half while an engine gouged a twenty-foot-long furrow in the rocky slope before it too died. The fuselage was crushed upward and buckled, the top severed behind the trailing edge of the wing.

"This was not a survivable accident; all aircraft occupants were killed on impact," according to the National Safety Transportation Board. The official accident report went on to state that "control was lost when the pilot became preoccupied while conducting sightseeing activities and inadvertently stalled the aircraft."

Along with Captain Smelcer, six National Park Service employees were killed: Rhonda Barber, Carol Byler, Janice Cooper, Dawn Finney, Keith Trexler, and Clara Veara. Also onboard that day was Jane Matlock of the Bureau of Land Management. Parajumpers almost parachuted onto this wreck, but changed their minds at the last moment.

```
November 29, 1975
Hawaii Volcanoes National Park
```

TWO KILLED BY TIDAL WAVE

WITHIN seconds of the earthquake, the sea quietly, subtly rose. Without warning, a monstrous wave sired by this seismic belch raced inland. The tsunami that swallowed the 32 terror-stricken campers just before dawn was 30 feet high.

Some 100,000 quakes rattle Hawaii each year; most are never felt. At 3:36 A.M. a sharp roller shot beneath the Big Island; the tremor registered a magnitude of 5.7. Seventy minutes later, residents were once again rudely jarred from a fitful sleep. This jolt began with violent ground pitching, but instead of subsiding after a few seconds, the intensity swelled to 7.2. The earthquake that struck from deep within the molten core of Kilauea Crater that Saturday morning was the Islands' most powerful shock of this century.

Out of the darkness rose the deafening roar of rocks crashing off the nearby volcanic cliffs, and then the campground simply vanished beneath the foaming, dark waters. The sea approached faster than the startled campers could escape. A huge, rolling wave sucked up people, horses, boulders, and trees and blended them into a churning, doomed mass. The energy carried the highest swells a quarter of a mile inland. At least two more large waves battered the Halape coast before the disaster was over, scant minutes after it had begun.

Of the campers caught on the beach that morning, 30 survived; one was killed outright and one was never found.

```
January 24, 1976
Sequoia National Park
```

UNIT CITATION

FOR
RESCUE TEAM
SEQUOIA AND KINGS CANYON NATIONAL PARKS

IN recognition for efforts performed in connection with a cave rescue in Sequoia and Kings Canyon National Parks.

On January 24, 1976, members of the rescue team at Sequoia and Kings [sic: Canyon] National Parks were confronted with the challenge of safely evacuating a person immobilized by injuries from deep within Lost Soldiers Cave. The injured man had to be transported through more than 400 hundred [sic] feet of narrow passageways with a vertical ascent of 170 feet. Many passages were narrow and twisting, the smallest barely 12 feet [sic: inches] wide and the route to the surface involved vertical lifts of 30 and 60 feet. The cave temperature of 42 degrees, dampness, and lack of any natural light posed additional problems. Over a period of 22 hours rescue personnel provided painkilling medication, constructed a spine board, and several rope and pulley systems were prepared to effect transport up vertical walls as well as through the narrow passageways. Upon returning to the cave entrance the victim was moved ¾ of a mile down the trail to an awaiting ambulance. In recognition of the high degree of professionalism and considerable skill demonstrated during this difficult rescue, the Sequoia and Kings Canyon Rescue Team is granted the **Department of the Interior Unit Award for Excellence of Service.**

Thomas S. Kleppe
Secretary of the Interior

Excluding members of the original caving party, this rescue involved at least 18 people. Those who actually entered the cavern included a registered nurse and a medical technician from Tulare District Hospital; a number of local volunteer climbers; and Park Rangers John Chew, Paul Fodor, Alden Nash, and Dick Powell.

When first told of the difficult mission, Dr. Harold Jakes, a local Tulare Hospital physician who had been an advisor to many Sequoia park rangers, said there were only three choices: Leave the victim in the cave for six months until he healed, tunnel through 200 feet of solid rock, or risk breaking the 45-year-old man's back again by dragging him through the passages.

Because of this rescue, John Chew, articulated the need for more advanced medical training for park rangers and joined with Yosemite staff in developing the Servicewide Park Medic Program.

June 2, 1976
Denali National Park

NORTH AMERICAN ALTITUDE
LANDING RECORD

SLOWLY and cautiously, Buddy eased the skid onto the icy, windswept slope. Intent on reaching the two injured women, the new altitude record he was setting was quickly forgotten.

Mt. McKinley was inundated in the Bicentennial year; more than 500 climbers tried for the top. More than 300, including the four who spent a month dragging their 60-pound hang gliders to the summit of the 20,320-foot peak, made it; 4 died and 33 needed rescuing, including Jenifer Williams and Paula Kregel.

Just 500 feet short of the top, the Denali-76 Women's Expedition turned around and started down. Suffering from near-complete exhaustion and oxygen starvation, one of them stumbled; roped together, the four climbers plunged 400 feet down the steep, frozen slope. Two stood up and two didn't. Kregel remembers:

> It must have been days ago that we fell from 20,000 feet, days since the other two girls had gone for help, no word, Jenifer still can't move, thought her back or neck broken, fuel's gone, little food, can't get Jenifer down without killing her. She keeps talking about dying anyway. Sleep, got to stay warm.

Ray "Pirate" Genet and Warren "Buddy" Woods formed an odd but perfectly matched rescue team. Genet, owner of a local climbing service, had been to the top of McKinley 19 times. Woods, owner of a local flying service, was one of the best bush pilots in the Far North. When the call for help came, they responded. Phoning the Anchorage airport, Genet located Woods on a Denver-bound jet; he had the plane stopped as it taxied for takeoff.

Woods's chief mechanic ferried extra fuel and Genet onto the 7,000-foot-high Kahiltna Glacier. Woods stripped his turbine-converted Hiller helicopter of cargo sling, seats, a winch, a counterbalance—everything not essential to the rescue mission. When the altimeter exceeded 12,000 feet, the insurance on both him and his helicopter was no longer in effect. Woods didn't start out to prove anything; two people were in need and he thought he could help.

Woods flew to the 16,000-foot level and deposited four more jerry-cans of fuel. Now, needing to know what Ray Genet had volunteered him for, he lifted off and labored upward.

"My mouth began to go dry as I came out of 17,000 feet. . . . My climb rate was beginning to deteriorate noticeably. . . . By the time I got 19,000, the roll rate of the machine was getting very sluggish." After two confidence-building practice touchdowns at 19,600 feet, Woods knew the rescue was possible. Descending to the 7,000-foot mark for fuel and Genet, it was now the legendary mountaineer's turn.

Flying back up, they spotted the injured party. Woods tried to hover, but churning snow blinded him. Two heart-stopping attempts later, Genet gingerly stepped out of the tiny helicopter at 20,300 feet—20 feet from the top. Cautiously lifting off again, Woods then dropped down for a second rescuer and additional equipment.

Jenifer Williams, reportedly with neck and back injuries, "turned and saw Ray Genet striding down on us like an angry Olympic god." Only 800 feet from the roof of North America, the monster of a man gently carried the injured woman to the waiting ship. With the second record-setting round-trip success-fully completed, the two women were soon safely en route to the Anchorage hospital in the mechanic's small airplane. The rescue cost $8,640.87.

For his efforts in rescuing Williams and Kregler, Warren "Buddy" Woods received the **Robert E. Trimble Award** from the Helicopter Association Inter-nationale. Established in 1961, this prestigious award recognizes exceptional ability and good judgment in high-altitude flying in the course of providing an outstanding service to others.

Woods died several years later in a plane crash while ferrying equipment into a remote village in the Alaskan backwoods. Genet also died several years later in a small ice cave after having reached the top of the highest mountain in the world.

In a daring, May 1971 rescue on the southeast face of 29,028-foot Mt. Everest, an Aerospatiale SA-315 Lama helicopter landed at 23,000 feet to set the world's altitude record for landing on a rescue mission.

July 31, 1976
Rocky Mountain National Park

IT CAME WITHOUT WARNING,
AND 145 DIED

THE flood that ravaged Big Thompson Canyon was the greatest natural cala-mity to hit Colorado. By 9:30 that night, a freak thunderstorm dropped more than 11 inches of rain on the steep Rocky Mountains 75 miles northwest of Denver. A normally civilized river at the bottom of the narrow abyss suddenly became a tidal wave of deadly terror. An estimated 5 million tons of water roared at freight-train speed through the gorge. Without warning, nearly 2,000 people were locked in the winding, 30-mile-long canyon.

Neither campers nor residents, only a few scant feet above the normally shallow Big Thompson River, knew what hit them. One couple was eating when their Winnebago began to shake; opening the door, they plunged into water up to their chests. Another couple, feeling their small trailer being lifted and swept away, broke the windows out to escape. An 89-year-old woman stood on a table and then clung to a ceiling light throughout the horror-filled night "while the boiling waters swirled about her legs." One lucky survivor described cars and trailers as "toys in a bathtub."

Rocky Mountain National Park's first hint of the disaster unfolding 2 miles outside its eastern gate was at 9:48 P.M., when the local sheriff's department urgently asked for bulldozers. Two minutes later, the park's dispatcher was requested to reach anyone possible by radio—"they had a real serious emergency on U.S. 34 and needed rescue people." Thirty-two minutes later, the sheriff's lieutenant on scene pleaded for "anything that can move earth."

That night, 29 park employees worked their way down into Big Thompson Canyon; during the next 36 hours, a total of 54 saw emergency service along the swollen river. "The Park threw every available piece of machinery and every seasoned man they could spare into the desperate effort to save lives and property." Their mountain rescue experience paid off when rangers swung numerous victims across the raging torrent on lifesaving ropes.

As one of the few public agencies at the now unreachable upper end of the canyon, the staff of Rocky Mountain National Park worked wherever they could see a need. Some led survivors out of the gorge; herded by rangers at both ends of the line, large groups of disoriented and terrified people were forced up the steep, rain-slickened walls. Rocks and water were cascading down everywhere and had turned each tiny gully into a swollen, life-threatening challenge.

Hundreds were brought to safety in this way. Veteran Climbing Ranger Larry Van Slyke marked out helipads and gave signals to pilots to assist in their nearly impossible landings. He would later describe the constant explosions of thunder and the lightning striking all around as "truly terrifying."

With the canyon full of summer visitors from all over the country, it was impossible to know exactly who was where. A body was found partially buried under a jam of twisted logs and debris, while another was removed from nearly 2 feet of silt that had filled an overturned vehicle. A third was found tangled in the limbs of a fallen tree. Some, such as the local sheriff's patrolman who was responding "Code 3" up the canyon when he was hit by the black, 19-foot wall of water, were never found.

Horrified and helpless, Chief Ranger Dave Essex watched as an older couple struggled to ford a swift-flowing side gully. The black torrent flipped their vehicle over; he got out, she didn't. As a rope was thrown to the man, he suddenly disappeared into the darkness, swept to certain death. "We dug her out."

One deputy coroner grimly reported taking footprints of several dead children, hoping to eventually identify them through hospital records. Others were somehow miraculously alive; a five-month-old boy—alone and uninjured—was found lying atop an exposed boulder in the middle of the swollen river.

More than a dozen helicopters from nearby Ft. Carson and the National Guard flew in, despite narrow canyons and unpredictable winds. These ships were joined by others from Denver hospitals, the Red Cross, and private companies. To learn the status of the many clusters of isolated, terrified survivors, leaflets were dropped: A large "A" meant medical aid, "F" food, "W" water, and "OK" for no immediate care necessary. More than 1,000 people were eventually airlifted from their nightmare.

Nearby, CB radio operators proved invaluable; for most of the time they were the only link to the outside world, feeding vital information to relatives, law enforcement, and rescue workers. Hundreds of visitors traveling with CB units in their vehicles offered assistance. One local CBer—"Grandma Base"—stayed on the air for 25 consecutive hours.

With 145 people killed (6 still missing), 400 homes completely washed away, and another 138 seriously damaged by flooding, President Gerald Ford declared the region a disaster area.

At the DOI's 1976 Awards Convocation, Secretary Thomas S. Kleppe said, "It will never be known how many lives were saved by the quick, efficient, and diligent-response by NPS personnel." In recognition of this epic effort, "all persons, including employees and family members of Rocky Mountain National Park who participated in this operation," were granted the **Valor Award.**

Governor Richard Lamm issued Rocky Mountain National Park the **State of Colorado Governor's Citation** on September 3, 1976.

```
October 5, 1976
Yosemite National Park
```

"BUTCH, YOU MOTHER F_____, HE'S DEAD, GET ME OUT OF HERE"

DISASTER struck 1,200 feet below the top of the overhanging face of Mt. Watkins, an awesome white granite dome at the eastern end of Yosemite Valley. When Bob Locke's few skimpy anchors pulled free of the thin crack, swinging him into the cliff's knife-edge corners, he chopped his rope in two. Plummeting another 200 feet, only luck—and a thin accessory line—kept the seasoned climber from smashing to certain death on the rocks 1,500 feet below.

Lowering himself, Chris Falkenstein somehow managed to maneuver his gravely injured partner onto a tiny ledge and then into a sleeping bag. A veteran Big Wall climber, Falkenstein then retreated off the sheer face by a series of harrowing rappels using pieces of frayed rope tied together. When he reached a phone at 5 P.M., he sounded the alarm. Yosemite's rescue "machine"—blessed with mild weather, a full moon, and Jim Daugherty, the park's Vietnam-veteran chopper pilot—quickly shifted into high gear.

Orchestrated by SAR Officer Tim Setnicka and aided by Ranger Rick Smith, 11 men and nearly a ton of gear were shuttled to the nearby peak, a 25-minute round-trip. After five hours of precision flying, most of it after dark, Daugherty off-loaded the last man just before midnight. Meanwhile, a Coast Guard four-engine HC-130 "Hercules" and its eight-man crew arrived from San Francisco and circled the team 1,000 feet below. Onboard was a "Carolina Moon."

Manufactured and nicknamed in North Carolina, the powerful 8-million-candlepower spotlight was designed for mercy missions on the open seas, not in the mountains. Mt. Watkins's sheer cliff face, like a colossal drive-in movie screen, would soon be flooded in brilliant light for half of each of the giant plane's two-minute orbits.

Once a spot on the lip of the cliff directly above the victim had been pinpointed, Setnicka's rescue plan called for lowering Dale, a professional climber, and Butch, a ranger and EMT. After two false starts, Locke's ledge was finally located and the critical descent began at 1 A.M. As the Hercules orbited "low and slow" overhead, more than 8 million candles of light bathed the huge white wall.

Just before Dale went over, Butch primed him on what to do as he neared the victim: Yell to him, and if no answer, put a hand inside the sleeping bag to test for body heat. A supremely confident Dale responded, "Piece of cake," and then spent a long 75 minutes being slowly lowered nearly 1,300 feet—most of it free hanging. At exactly 2:48 A.M. and probably triggered by the lights and shadows of both "full moons" dancing surreally around him, Dale began shrieking over the parkwide radio: "Butch, you motherfucker, he's dead, get me out of here." A second climber was soon lowered to the tiny ledge to join the unnerved Dale. Twelve hours later, raised by a carnival of ropes and rescuers, Bob Locke finally reached the summit of Mt. Watkins.

October 10, 1976
Lassen Volcanic National Park

MATT GOT LOST . . .

MATTHEW, his younger twin brothers, and his father were returning from Butte Lake after camping for two days. When they arrived at the Cinder Cone Trail junction at 3:00 P.M., the doctor and his twin sons decided to scramble to the top. Tired, 16-year-old Matthew wanted to return to their car less than 2 miles away. His father agreed to meet him there. But the teenager got lost.

Matt suffered from dyslexia and couldn't read well. Not versed in survival skills, the boy had a poor sense of direction and became disoriented easily. Saying that his son was shy, Matt's dad didn't believe the boy would ask for help either; he would not respond if his name were called out.

Within 24 hours of the alarm, there were 14 searchers on the dust-covered trails and jeep roads, five German Shepherd search-dog teams from the South Lake Tahoe–based WOOF, and a Forest Service helicopter that scanned the rugged, moonlike lava fields. Good weather held: maximum 68 degrees, minimum 32 degrees.

Based on alerts from the air-scenting dogs the night before, WOOF focused on the inhospitable lava beds, a forbidding maze of razor-sharp rocks and deep crevices. If Matt had fallen into one of these cracks, and especially if he had injured himself, he would not be visible from the air. After a particularly difficult but thorough search effort, officials reasoned that the boy could not have gone too far into the lava fields.

With people spaced 100 feet apart, rescuers concentrated on a grid search through the trees. Two men began examining Butte Lake by boat, checking the shoreline to see if the boy had fallen in. Two prison crews from the Conservation Service, a mobile field kitchen, and a drinking-water truck from the Forest Service were brought in. By the end of the fourth day, 100 ground searchers were working out of the improvised base camp.

After five nights out, Matt was found alive; his body's core temperature had dropped to a life-threatening 82 degrees and he suffered from frostbite and dehydration. En route to the hospital, CPR had to be administered three times. Young and strong, Matt soon recovered without any lasting ill effects.

For probably the first time in NPS history, a National Class I Fire Overhead Management Team had been brought in specifically to run a major search. Grand Canyon's Dick McLaren was the search boss; Lee Shackleton, plans chief; Norm Clark, service chief; and Jack Fields, line boss. At the peak of the search, at least 225 people representing 15 agencies; choppers from the Forest Service, Coast Guard, and National Guard; and eight dog teams from as far away as Seattle were involved.

December 9, 1976
Yosemite National Park

DOPE LAKE:
THE ORIGINAL *CLIFFHANGER*

IF the vintage airplane's starboard engine hadn't literally fallen off high above the eastern edge of the Sierras, *Cliffhanger,* Sylvester Stallone's 1993 $73 million movie, may never have been filmed. The blockbuster's story model, a 1940s-era Lockheed Lodestar gutted for smuggling drugs, was stuffed with dozens of bales of high-grade marijuana when it smashed through the pines and sank into the freezing waters of a shallow, high mountain lake.

When Seattle's John Glisky crashed with his illegal cargo a few miles south of Yosemite Valley, he had just flown the twin-engine craft in from Mexico and was headed for an obscure landing strip in isolated northern Nevada. The fate of the red, white, and blue N-80BD, fictitiously registered in Florida, and its two male occupants remained unknown until late the following month. On January 29, 1977, hikers stumbled across a wing and a piece of tail section near the remote, 11,000-foot-high Lower Merced Pass Lake.

Joe Evans was one of the first two rangers on the scene, courtesy of a helicopter out of nearby Lemoore Naval Air Station. Sixteen years later, Evans ironically would be credited for his aid in making *Cliffhanger* while serving as chief ranger of Rocky Mountain National Park. Along with Ranger Bruce McKeeman, he knew that with most of the plane underwater, there were no survivors. They did, however, find several burlap sacks of waterlogged marijuana.

Sealed under a foot of ice and now snowbound, the wreck was more than a dozen demanding miles by foot from the nearest road and seemingly secure from assault. Headquarters elected to wait for spring to unlock the mysteries of the ill-fated plane.

In late February, reports of unusual vehicle activity at a generally deserted trailhead, along with quiet gossip among the local mountaineers, began filtering in to park officials. When a Fresno dive shop finally reported granite-loving Big Wall climbers trying to rent scuba gear, rangers at last knew they had trouble.

Paul Henry twinkles as he recounts how he and five armed fellow rangers surprised the enterprising entrepreneurs as they feverishly mined for plunder on the snow-covered, 2-acre lake. When the Navy chopper popped over a low rocky ridge like a Vietnam gunship, the climbers below scattered like a "covey of quail." Everything from chainsaws to sleeping bags was dropped and abandoned.

Despite wild rumors, no one will ever know how much "Yosemite Gold" was harvested before park rangers "took back" Lower Merced Pass Lake; guesses range up to $150,000. A few once-penniless climbers, however, soon bought new cars and took costly vacations. On June 16, the pilots' bodies were recovered. In addition to *Cliffhanger,* at least one book, Jeff Long's 1987 *Angels of Light* (McGraw-Hill), is loosely based on Yosemite's "Dope Lake."

May 23, 1977
Yosemite National Park

DEATH OF SOME RESCUERS

HIGH on a cliff, two ill-prepared young rock climbers, saddled with inexperience and trapped by recklessness, cried out in the dark.

It was 3 in the morning when the six rescuers started up the Yosemite Falls Trail. All accomplished Big Wall climbers, their mood was relaxed and confident. Just how hard could a rescue on the "YPB," a beginner's climb, be? Zigzagging up the broad path, they moved easily, their headlamps bobbing eerily in the mist that swirled around them. Light rain added to the air of excitement as they moved higher, wind and trickling water mingling with the fading sounds of an occasional car from below.

Jack Dorn, like everyone else in Camp Four—the climber's campground— lived for the challenge of the Yosemite walls. A veteran of the valley's demanding granite, Dorn was also on the park's semivolunteer rescue team. In exchange for a free camp spot and his expertise on the rocks, the 30-year-old was to be available for plucking wimpy kids from cliffs.

Perhaps he got lost listening to tunes on his portable tape cassette, had partied too long, climbed too hard or just maybe, he didn't notice the winding trail turn to the left.

Why Jack Dorn, responding to pleas for help in the middle of the night, walked off the well-worn path and plunged 600 feet to an instant death, no one will ever know . . .

Dorn, one of the 110 rescues the park handled that year, was rumored to be one of the many Yosemite Valley entrepreneurs who "struck it rich" from the marijuana aboard the ill-fated twin-engine plane lost in Lower Merced Pass Lake on December 9, 1976. There are some who think his death was more than accidental.

Beginning with Herb Sortland, who died on January 25, 1925, Jack Dorn was the 14th person to be killed while involved in an NPS SAR. Nine more would sacrifice their lives for their fellow-man before pilot Clayton Reed and observer James Matthews ran out of fuel over an extremely isolated section of the Everglades on October 2, 1991.

The two Civil Air Patrolmen were searching for a small fishing boat reported to be in distress. The two 70-year-old volunteers were concentrating on a nightmarish maze of shallow bays and mangrove-covered keys near Everglades City. Reed and Matthews crashed only 3 miles and two minutes away from the stranded fishing guide and his two customers. Killed on impact, the two men in their tiny Cessna 172 were not found for 15 days. Despite the involvement of at least four ships, 15 aircraft, and numerous agencies, the downed CAP plane had nearly succeeded in disappearing into the Everglades.

June 27, 1977
Yellowstone National Park

MAULED BY GRIZZLY,
MAN NEEDS 1,000 STITCHES
AND SEVEN OPERATIONS

AT 800 pounds and 7 feet tall, the grizzly bear is power incarnate. Even its former label, *Ursus horribilis* (now *arctos*), demands respect. Its name derives from its often silver-tipped or frosted hair. The grizzled giant is the Lower 48's largest meat-eater.

In early 1977, Yellowstone began examining grizzly behavior in the interest of preventing bear-man conflicts. Over the years, all too many travelers had dueled with the beast—and lost. Dr. Barrie Gilbert, a 40-year-old Salt Lake City biologist, along with undergraduate assistant Bruce Hastings, was conducting the study. "Bruce and I knew something about previous bear maulings, but we wanted to learn more about the animals' behavior patterns and exactly what circumstances can lead up to an attack."

After nearly three weeks of looking, the two scientists hiked into another section of the park's rugged backcountry. On the afternoon of June 26, the park's radio log notes, "Gilbert advises he sighted a grizzly just west of Big Horn Pass." Splitting up the next morning, the two men returned to watch the sow and her three cubs.

Within minutes, Gilbert "heard a low whoof come from a brushpile 40 feet away. It was half snarl and low growl . . . a grizzly was after him. He whirled and ran for a spindly fir tree. 'My God, I've gotten too close.'" Ironically, Dr. Gilbert was only moments away from becoming a near-fatal case study in his own research.

"If I live to be 1000 . . . I'll never forget the sound its teeth made as it tried to bite through the base of my skull. The pain was unbearable. . . . I'll always remember the foul breath of the bear as it ripped my face apart." Half of Gilbert's face was gone, his left eye was missing, what remained of his nose was right of center, and his scalp was almost totally torn off.

Hiking back to join his mentor, Hastings stumbled onto the attack. Unsure of what to do, the young man somehow scared the animal off. The park's radio log entry for 10:50 A.M. says, "Emergency, Emergency—we need a helicopter."

Within an hour, Yellowstone's chopper had the isolated mauling scene in sight, and within another 60 minutes, six Smokejumpers from the nearby Forest Service base had also parachuted onto the rocky ridgetop. After being mede-vaced out, Gilbert was stabilized at the local clinic and then flown on to Salt Lake City, where he underwent nearly 12 more hours of emergency work.

After two months, Dr. Gilbert had received more than 1,000 stitches and undergone seven operations. He still had more to go . . .

January 3, 1978
Great Smoky Mountains National Park

FOUR RESCUERS LIVE . . . AND FOUR DIE

ONE leg pointed the wrong way. Jagged ends of collar and shoulder bones grated harshly. Blinding pain exploded from his broken back. Still, 33-year-old Park Ranger Bill Acree knew he had been blessed. Unlike four others trapped with him in the mangled machine, he was alive, but just barely.

The MAST (Military Aid to Safety and Transportation) helicopter, an Army "Huey" out of Ft. Campbell, was one of three above the 4,732-foot-high Parson's Bald that morning. Captain Dunnavant, having just spotted the tar-get—a small, twin-engine commuter plane that had disappeared the night before—was trying to land an Army medic and two park rangers when there was a loud "pop."

> The pilot yelled "May Day" four times into the radio . . . Just before crashing, they recalled tightening their seat belts, getting braced, and feeling the nose of the helicopter rise. Then the crash! There were . . . parts, trees, and the ground all mixed together in a blur, with sounds of ripping and crushing metal. The helicopter came to a standstill upside down, nose down, with the jet engine still running. The main rotor blade was hanging in a large oak tree above and behind the fuselage.

Faced with a second, more unthinkable fate, Acree knew they had to exit the still-pulsating wreckage immediately. With the ship's 1,100-hp motor still going (it ran for two more hours), he was terrified of burning alive from a rup-tured, nearly full aviation fuel bladder.

> I remember dropping down towards the broken window, all the while trying to be very careful as my leg kept flip/flopping like a dead fish, and my back kept grating. . . . I discovered my arms had difficulty in working properly—that my collar bones were broken (I discovered this by seeing the broken bones moving under the skin).

Air Force Sergeant Phillip Thurlow was jammed in the left "hellhole" with jagged bits of the high-powered search light. He suffered five splintered ribs, a fractured clavicle, ruptured biceps, and numerous lesser injuries. His door had ripped off when they had crashed through the trees, he crawled out on the uphill side. Barely able to move, he was too badly injured and dazed to assist.

With Acree no longer blocking his escape, Ranger Dave Harbin released his safety harness and painfully worked his way free of the twisted metal. Even with a fractured rib, contused lung, rent ligaments, dislocated shoulder, broken elbow, and torn muscles, Harbin was still the most mobile of the four survivors.

Four rescuers died on this mercy mission in Great Smoky Mountains National Park.
BILL ACREE COLLECTION

Army paramedic Chris Wyman was behind the helicopter's jump seats and had survived the impact with only a grossly fractured femur and facial lacerations; he was helped out the same broken window that Acree had tunneled through. Since Wyman's leg wouldn't work, he told Harbin how to turn off the engine. Unable to do so because the entire cockpit was crushed into the frozen ground upside down, Harbin then looked to the paramedic's leg. After finishing a makeshift splint, Dave assisted the medic upslope.

About then Army Paramedic Collier arrived on the scene by a jungle penetrator [device on a cable to go through the forest cover of Vietnam] from another helicopter. He was injured on the descent by tree limbs and by being dropped several feet. Even though they were both injured, Collier and Harbin immediately went back to the wreckage/danger zone and worked Acree onto a broken stretcher that was aboard the helicopter. Since Harbin did not have the strength in his injured arms to lift his end of the stretcher, they dragged it up the slope as far as they could until more help arrived.

Collier made an assessment of the injuries and began treating Wyman for shock and splinting broken bones.

Ranger Lowell Higgins and two volunteers, following a trail of aircraft parts and clothing strewn from suitcases, quickly found the small airliner, the object of the initial search.

The wings and tail sections were broken off ... and shredded. One engine had been on fire but it was not immediately possible to determine if that was the cause or the result of the crash. The middle of the fuselage was fairly well intact but the top and nose section was crushed. The fuselage was resting upside down with five bodies generally around or under the front.

The **Blanchfield Medical Center Heliport** at Kentucky's Ft. Campbell was formally dedicated in honor of Army Captains John Dunnavant and Terrance Woolever and Sergeant Floyd Smith, all killed in the line of duty while performing this rescue. Ray Maynard, a 62-year-old lieutenant colonel in the Tennessee Wing of the Civil Air Patrol who was also aboard the ill-fated helicopter, was posthumously awarded the CAP's **Distinguished Service Medal.**

May 28, 1978
Yosemite National Park

CITATION FOR VALOR

LEMOORE SEARCH AND RESCUE HELICOPTER CREW
UNITED STATES NAVY

FOR heroic rescue of a critically injured climber which occurred in Yosemite National Park, California.

Early in the afternoon of May 28, 1978, two mountain climbers were working their way up the sheer face of Quarter Dome, a cliff at Yosemite National Park, and had reached a position about 2000 feet above the valley floor. While seeking a place to rest, Gary Gissendaner, who was about 70 feet above his partner, suddenly lost his footing and fell, hanging on his rope in mid air, to within 10 feet of his companion, who was able to let him gently drop to a 3 by 5 foot sloping ledge. It was 5 P.M. by the time the authorities could be summoned, and darkness was beginning to close in. The Park Rangers called for a Navy Search and Rescue Helicopter crew from Lemoore Naval [Air] Station. The team arrived at 6:25 P.M., made a quick reconnaissance, and planned the rescue. Their decision was to employ a special technique, developed at their Station. "Cliff evolution," the method they employed, requires that a member of the team rappell down a rope from the aircraft to the accident scene, stabilize the accident victim, and attach him to ropes from the helicopter. The rescuer and the rescued are then flown at the end of ropes to a landing area where they are gently let down. The situation at the accident scene was especially dangerous and tricky. To reach the injured man the aircraft commander, Lt. Sullivan had to edge his craft to within 5 feet of the cliff face and hover for 22 minutes—a harsh test for both man and machine. Co-Pilot Lt. Swain, eyes glued to a battery of gauges, was calling out critical readings, while Crewman Deciccio lay on his stomach on the floor, helmeted head stuck out the door, advising the pilot on how close he was to the rock face. Crew Chief Revels rappelled down a 300-foot rope to reach the victim while Corpsman Delgado held tightly to Revels' belay rope ready to take action in case of mishap. When Revels reached Gissendaner he attached ropes from the aircraft to him. Pilot Sullivan eased the helicopter from the rock face and had to compensate for the weight of the two men as he lifted them from the ledge. In four to five minutes, Lt. Sullivan gently laid his human cargo to earth in a nearby meadow. The rescue was completed, and the members of the five-man team had worked as one in an effort to save another. **Valor Awards of the Department of the Interior** are granted to John A. Sullivan, Donald A. Swain, John A. Deciccio [sic], Benny C. Revels, and Herman A. Delgado, Jr., United States Navy.

Cecil D. Andrus
Secretary of the Interior

The Navy crew is the only non-DOI unit ever to receive a **DOI Valor Award.**

July 15, 1978
Yosemite National Park

DAVID DIDN'T WANT TO BE A FATHER

SUSAN, only three weeks away from having their first child, watched her husband shoulder his heavy orange backpack and disappear down the Ililouette Trail. Despite being fully equipped for a four-day hike—even down to a fishing license—David never intended to see the heart of the Sierra. The 25-year-old father-to-be, within just minutes after his wife drove off on that Saturday morning, turned around and headed for Bangor, Maine.

Susan reported him missing when he was a day overdue. Distraught as she sat in the tent-cabin in Curry Village, she frequently broke into tears as rangers questioned her. No, David didn't have much hiking experience, although he had been a YMCA Indian Guide. Yes, he was thin and good-looking, his hair brown and receding. A tan corduroy patch on the left knee of his baggy cotton work pants would stand out. In spite of the six stars distinctively molded into the middle of his boot soles, the size-10½ Lowa Scouts would unfortunately make very common prints. One ranger even noted, on the fifth page of the Lost Persons Questionnaire, that David was "looking forward to fatherhood—taking Lemaze classes."

By coaxing Susan to describe everything from his equipment (adequate) to his religious beliefs (none), investigators formed a fair impression of the missing man. Susan, however, was less certain of his plans. When she was taken back to the trailhead—the point she had last seen him—she indicated that he was "going that way," waving her hand vaguely toward shadowed peaks rising to the east.

Rangers spent 10 intense days trying to second-guess David. Nearly 50 searchers from five California mountain rescue teams donated their time and risked their necks. Radio relay teams were placed on peaks. Trackers methodically followed several sets of 10½ size boots. Helicopters crisscrossed the densely wooded granite benches, and observers, including David's father, peered into the shady, deep gorges of the Merced drainage.

Rescue Ranger John Dill, pursuing a novel investigative search angle, made hundreds of phone calls to hikers who had obtained permits for that part of the park; he firmly established times, places, and observations. After cross-referencing his data, Dill was certain that David had not gotten very far on his trip.

On August 1, two weeks after his disappearance and only days before the baby's birth, David's unsigned postcard from Maine was received by a good friend of his. The missing man, eventually "surfacing" and confronted by frustrated investigators, announced cavalierly that fatherhood terrified him and he wanted out.

David was cited by the court for "creating a hazardous or offensive condition"—a Disorderly Conduct violation of the Code of Federal Regulations—and was fined $500 by the U.S. Magistrate.

December 27, 1978
Grand Canyon National Park

SEARCHING FOR THE HAVASUPAI INDIAN

REED Watahomigie's ancestors were already farming in the mile-deep canyon when the Spaniard Cardenas "discovered" it in 1540. A Havasupai ("people of the blue-green water") Watahomigie was quiet and proud. Having lived there his whole life, the colorful 60-year-old Supai was a local "fixture." Everyone knew him and they often turned their heads when he became falling-down drunk.

Christmas Day saw him in the Bright Angel Lounge drinking hard. Two days later he was observed nearby, passed out. He "was having trouble breathing and 'didn't look like he was gonna' make it.'" For some reason this went unreported. Four weeks later, Watahomigie's worried sister noted his absence.

Rangers skied and searched by horseback; deputies walked and searched from helicopters. Structures offering even minimal shelter from the nearly 0-degree cold were painstakingly combed, from haylofts in wooden mule barns to half-filled culverts along train tracks. Everything was checked and rechecked.

Tribal president Wayne Sinyella, along with 30 friends and relatives, volunteered to do a circular search around the cluster of wooden shacks of Supai Camp, Watahomigie's home. Completing only a third of their sweep, they quickly agreed that a person could walk right past a body and not see it. They would return when the 3 feet of snow was gone. Wind blew, snow drifted, and . . .

. . . three more months passed.

Requested by the Bureau of Indian Affairs, there was a new push to find Reed; 64 people joined in—BIA, Supai, NPS, four-wheel drivers and others scoured Grand Canyon Village again.

Officials instructed that the "spacing of the searchers on foot should be altered according to terrain so that every rock, tree, depression in the ground, etc., can be scanned." Look for bits of cloth, hats, boots, medicine bottles, or anything indicationg Reed had passed by. The "possibility of coyotes, dogs, birds and other animals scattering bones and clues should also be considered."

Even though the searchers were very thorough in their efforts—"bones believed to be nonhuman" . . . clothing scraps . . . false teeth—little of value was found.

Nearly five months after Reed Watahomigie disappeared and more than 5 miles from where he was last seen, the body of the once proud Havasupai was found by accident 250 feet below the rim of the Grand Canyon near Yaki Point.

```
                June 22, 1979
           Mt. Rainier National Park
     -----------------------------------------
```

"I'D PROBABLY DIE. I DIDN'T WANT TO DIE."

DESPITE the blinding pain, the 34-year-old physician knew his time was running out. Without help—and soon—John Donlou wouldn't see daylight. "When I saw the sun sinking down below the clouds, I gave up hope." Struck by a 300-pound block of falling ice, the anesthesiologist from Los Angeles suffered crushing fractures of the shoulder and arm; he was dying at the 12,500-foot level of Liberty Ridge, a knifelike crest of 60-degree, ice-covered walls plunging 3,500 feet to the Carbon River below.

At 9:30, as day dissolved to dark, Rangers Jean Paul "JP" de St. Croix and Garry Olson found themselves being lifted high onto the peak by a twin-bladed Army Chinook; the pilot, fighting 25-mph wind gusts and fading light, struggled to keep control. With a landing on the treacherous terrain virtually impossible, the veteran rescuers anxiously readied for a tricky lowering to the sloping ice on the end of a Vietnam-era jungle penetrator.

Olson and de St. Croix, told not to wear their pointed crampons inside for fear of puncturing vital electrical cables, couldn't even be roped together during the winch lowering. The rangers were to step onto the steep, frozen face—with the frightening exposure below them—without the security of either ice-biting crampons or a safety line. Even a small slip on the near-vertical wall could be fatal.

First down, Olson was dragged over the sharp ridge several times before freeing himself from the thin cable. Threatened now by the rotors' powerful downwash, he cautiously kicked several steps into the hard snow before finally mooring himself with his ice axe. De St. Croix was no luckier; he too was bounced around the slope while trying to get off the hoist's narrow, 50-pound metal seat.

Military helicopters, like this Army Chinook with a long line at 13,300 feet on an August 1997 body recovery on Mt. Rainier, are critical to SARs. Dr. Donlou owes his life to a similar helicopter and its dedicated, expert crew.
MIKE GAUTHIER PHOTO

Rapidly roping to each other as the ship hovered loudly nearby, the two men moved up to Dr. Donlou and drove an anchor into the ice for protection. With no time for medical niceties, they promptly lifted the injured man to his feet and primed him for the exacting, 75-foot lift. Considerably weakened, Donlou collapsed several times and had to be held up. Overhead, the crew, dueling with the failing light, struggled to bullseye the hoist's seat onto the table-sized ledge. Finally, de St. Croix climbed down a dozen feet, snagged the quarter-inch cable with his ice axe, and swung it over to Olson.

In spite of the darkness and the chopper's hurricane-like winds engulfing them, the two rangers—unknowingly having just earned DOI **Valor Awards**—engineered the semi-immobile doctor into the hovering Chinook. With the critically injured climber secure inside, the ship's crew skillfully lowered the jungle penetrator twice more for the nearly frozen rescuers.

Dr. John Donlou, who was flown directly to Tacoma, eventually had to have his lower right arm amputated.

Grand Teton Ranger Janet Wilts employes a short haul in 1993, like the one that saved Nicola Rotberg seven years before. RENNY JACKSON PHOTO

CHAPTER 9

1980–1989

The saving of human life will take
precedence over all other management
activities.
—NPS <u>Management Policies</u>, 1988

PARACHUTING AND NPS SEARCH AND RESCUE

Parachuting plays an entertaining but important role in NPS SAR. In October 1965, oblivious to legal and Native American cultural and religious ramifications, the author, a brand-new "buck" ranger, dragged his faded green parachute up southern Utah's remote, 290-foot-high Rainbow Bridge. I prepared to leap from the world's largest natural arch. Only the sudden vision of dying on the rocks in the gorge below kept the 24-year-old from making NPS history as the Park Service's first "broken" BASE jumper.

That ignominy is shared by two 26-year-old Southern California skydivers who threw themselves from Yosemite's sheer El Capitan on July 24, 1966. One suffered a cracked ankle and was found next to a road; the other, with a fractured leg and foot, had to be carried down by rangers between the huge boulders and twisted oaks from the base of the 3,200-foot cliff: "The air currents were really tricky. We didn't expect anything like it."

BASE stands for Building Aerial Span Earth. In vaulting from cliffs and bridges, this relatively small but eccentric slice of the skydiving community poses problems while providing arresting (pun intended) rescues for park rangers. At least 12 NPS areas have endured BASE jumpers: Amistad, Arches, Black Canyon of the Gunnison, Canyon de Chelly, Glacier, Glen Canyon, Grand Canyon (off Navajo Bridge), Jefferson Expansion, New River Gorge, Statue of Liberty (1912, before it became an NPS area in 1924), Yosemite, and Zion.

Until Yosemite's mid-1960s daredevils, all those who had jumped into park areas had done so from planes, either as stunts or from ailing crafts. The earliest is probably Army Lieutenant William A. Cocke's 1932 step from 16,000 feet into a blizzard high over Sequoia National Park. It took two months to find his comrade, who remained with their tiny plane. "I felt I would rather hit bad country in a chute than in a plane—so I told him to throttle down. Then I jumped."

Among the more infamous leaps was one onto the top of 865-foot Devils Tower by 30-year-old Charles Hopkins. This, his 2,348th parachute jump, was a publicity stunt for Rapid City, South Dakota, on October 1, 1940. When those in charge of the national monument yelled up, "How will you get down?" Hopkins's shout down was a cocky "Why worry about getting off? It's no problem, is it?"

Five days later, he was lowered off the geological wonder by a team of eight talented mountaineers from around the country.

Hundreds of military planes crashed in this country while on maneuvers during World War II. Many of these were in national parks. Sadly, only a few of those aviators used parachutes. In May 1943, one avoided crashing with his B-17 into the wilds of Yellowstone when the plane's intercom screamed, "This is it! Get out!" His ten confederates perished. A year later—in two separate midair collisions involving four B-24s and 28 men high above Joshua Tree and Death Valley National Monuments—only two lucky souls were able to get free and jump; the rest died. In June of that year, when the pilot of their B-24 bomber ordered them to leap to safety, three young men bailed out over the Grand Canyon, prompting both a giant air search and a unique ground rescue.

Rick Sylvester skis off the top of Yosemite's 2,800-foot-high El Capitan on February 1, 1972. Five years later he would double as James Bond in The Spy Who Loved Me *by skiing off a cliff in Canada.*
RICK SYLVESTER COLLECTION

In the intense, Cold War era of the 1950s and 1960s, others were forced to parachute into the remote areas of our parks. On October 4, 1956, three of the four men in the two Air Force F-89 "Scorpion" fighters that collided over Olympic National Park bailed out and they survived. The fourth, remaining aboard the crippled craft, was found still strapped into his seat.

Possibly the most enigmatic survival story during this time is that of Lieutenant David A. Steeves. The 23-year-old rookie jet pilot, experiencing a cockpit explosion in his T-33 trainer, ejected at 400 mph and 33,000 feet. That May morning in 1957, he came to rest in the craggy, snowbound heart of California's Kings Canyon. It would be 54 days before he would crawl his way to freedom. To this day—even though his shattered canopy was found many years later near the place he had finally drifted—his jet plane lies somewhere among the 13,000-foot peaks.

Parachutes were first used on an SAR in 1940, when Chet Derry leaped into history—and Montana's Bitterroot National Forest—for the world's first rescue jump. Smokejumpers first fought fires in a national park (Lincoln Peak Fire—Glacier) as early as August 25, 1945. The author, however, can find no evidence of an SAR jump in a national park until 1963. The earliest such para-jump (PJ) occurred when a "Cold War" B-47, suffering a midair collision over eastern Idaho, crashed into Yellowstone's frozen backcountry. Two Air Force PJs dropped onto the mangled giant to find three of the plane's four crewmen dead. The fourth, punching out just moments before the flying warship "pan-caked" into the lodgepole forest, walked out unscathed.

Perhaps the world's most remembered BASE jumper is Rick Sylvester. On February 1, 1972, he sailed off the edge of Yosemite's El Capitan. Kicking free of his skis, he headed his parachute to the meadow below and landed in a tree. On Sylvester's first try, he had trouble with his cameras, so he stole a second jump. Five years later he duplicated the feat by skiing off a cliff in Canada while doubling as 007—James Bond—in *The Spy Who Loved Me*.

During the late 1960s and over the following 10 years, park staff in Yosemite played "cat-and-mouse" with an occasional cliff-jumper. Starting in 1978, however, the daredevils began to seriously flaunt their illegal jumps. In September 1979, six were finally arrested after a near-disaster involving one ranger on the edge of a 3,000-foot cliff. For administrative control as well as to prevent injury, the park's chief ranger, Bill Wendt, permitted up to 12 "certified" parachutists to fling themselves from El Capitan without reprisal.

On August 1, 1980, parachuting off El Capitan was made "legal" in a three-month experiment. Citing concerns for a pair of nesting, endangered peregrine falcons, reasonable reins were placed on the jumpers. Soon, however, there was so much abuse by the rowdy skydivers—including riding bicycles and "pogo-sticking" off as well as mass jumps by many more than the stipulated maximum of a dozen per day—that "trial" terminated after only 68 days.

At 876 feet above West Virginia's New River, the steel bridge spanning the New River Gorge National River is a natural for BASE jumpers. Established in November 1978, the park takes the brunt of daredevils. Surely before it was even opened to traffic in 1977, someone had parachuted off the 1,700-foot-long bridge. The commercial prospects, however, quickly dawned on the locals, and the first "Bridge Day," with two jumpers, was on October 10, 1980.

Bridge Day, the third Saturday of October, is now an international spectacle and a big money-maker. In 1993, with some 125,000 people looking on, 458 registered chutists made 502 jumps. This was surpassed in 2003 when 346 people used their nylon and canvas rigs 836 times (the most to date). All of this "color" is complemented by hundreds of similar spirits: rappellers, rope-climbers, bungee-jumpers, and tyrolean traversers (a clothesline-like method of using a rope to go from one side to the other). The first and only death occurred on October 10, 1987. And each year, the taxed staff in that park provide a yeoman's job in SAR.

As an example, in 1993, 102 parachutists landed in the park and required rescue by NPS personnel. A bungee jump was made by seven people in a cus-tom-made metal basket that plunged 850 feet into the gorge to a point 25 feet above the river before springing back. Miraculously, only one person was injured in the stunt. On Bridge Day '94, "there were only sixty water landings, one tree landing, and 12 injuries (seven requiring local hospitals to set broken bones)."

Despite cold temperatures, erratic winds up to 25 mph, and minor rain showers, the 1996 event took on an added dimension when 1 U.S. senator, 10 gubernatorial candidates, and several other political aspirees attended the event to campaign and shake hands.

Exiting a low-flying plane on November 22, 1980, a 33-year-old man was killed trying to land on the 17-foot-wide top of the 630-foot-high Jefferson National Expansion Memorial Arch in St. Louis. His intention may have been to use a second parachute to leap from the curving steel structure. Instead, he slid grossly down the arch's concrete and metal column and became the first recorded death involving BASE and the NPS. The next fatality, on October 10, 1981, prompted an exceptionally perilous body recovery off the 2,200-foot volcanic walls of Colorado's Black Canyon of the Gunnison. Using a cabled winch, the Rocky Mountain Rescue Group lowered two men 1,100 feet down the crumbly cliff for the canopy-shrouded body of a 27-year-old Sooner Parachute Club member.

In the 1980s, BASE stuntmen were hard on the NPS. In Yosemite National Park alone, there were at least 11 rescues of jumpers, including three deaths, at a cost of some $35,000.

Rangers and the Coast Guard routinely join forces at San Francisco's Golden Gate National Recreation Area for search and rescue. STEVE GAZZANO PHOTO

MILESTONES OF THE 1980s

1980	NPS's 333 units receive 300,300,000 visitors. *Wilderness Search and Rescue*, written by Yosemite Search and Rescue Officer Tim Setnicka, becomes SAR bible for next decade.
January 13, 1980	Chiricahua National Monument Ranger Paul Fugate goes on a hike; despite a massive search, he is never seen again.
August 11, 1980	Longest rappel and single-rope ascent in NPS history, a world record at the time—2,649 feet down the overhanging granite face of Yosemite's El Capitan.
June 21, 1980	Greatest mountaineering disaster in North American history kills 11 climbers on Mt. Rainier when snow area collapses.
September 11, 1980	Aiding a climber, five rescuers are killed in a Coast Guard helicopter crash in North Cascades National Park.
June 14, 1981	First "save" by Forward Looking Infra Red (FLIR).
December 15, 1981	A rescue involving a downed aircraft begins on Mt. McKinley. Precedent-setting lawsuit results: *Clouser v. U.S.*
February 21, 1982	The NPS's first **Exemplary Act Award** for an SAR is earned by six NPS employees for treacherous scuba search for diving victim at Amistad Recreation Area in Texas.
May 1982	Denali Medical Research Project begins at 14,300 feet on Mt. McKinley's West Buttress. It saves many lives.
May 25, 1982	Forty-six senior SAR people are graduated from first Park Service–wide "Managing Emergency Operations Course."
July 1982	Longest rappel and single-rope ascent in the world to that date made up and down Mt. Thor on Canada's Baffin Island—3,250 feet.
September 9, 1982	First "save" by COSPAS-SARSAT—satellite SAR system. While looking for a plane missing since the previous July, another craft, with survivors, is found in British Columbia.
Fall 1983	"Computer SAR age" arrives when search modeling and determination of the Probability of Detection Program for finding a lost person is first used on an NPS search at Grand Canyon. CASIE-II is still being used by searchers around the country.

MILESTONES OF THE 1980s

June 2, 1984	First North American Technical Rescue Symposium takes place at South Lake Tahoe, California.
October 18, 1984	Laura Bradbury disappears from Joshua Tree. The three-year-old's picture is placed on grocery bags regionwide—reputed to be the first such use in the U.S.
1985	There are 187 SARs in Yosemite, costing $379,415— including $63,014 in uncompensated donated time— the highest to date. By contrast, in 1975, there were 107 SARs, costing just $49,002.
September 23, 1985	Sixteen handlers and 13 canines begin searching some 80 high-rises leveled in the magnitude 8.1 Mexico City earthquake. Shenandoah's Assistant Chief Ranger Bill Pierce and dog handler Marian Hardy help facilitate U.S. response. Two weeks later, rangers will lead 21 dog teams to Puerto Rico for victims of massive mudslides.
June 18, 1986	Twenty-five die in midair collision over Grand Canyon.
April 27, 1987	A 920-foot-long and 775-foot-high tyrolean off Devils Tower, an NPS record. On August 8, the world-record tyrolean will be engineered off Mt. Aerosmith on Vancouver Island, British Columbia—5,000 feet long with a 2,800-foot drop.
June 28, 1987	After Ben Johnson dies in Grand Teton, his estate argues he would "not have died but for the Park Service's negligent failure to . . . regulate . . . climbing activity . . . initiate a [timely] rescue . . . and conduct a reasonable rescue effort." On November 13, 1991, the 10th Circuit Court of Appeals will grant judgment for the United States, stating it "would jeopardize the Park rangers' autonomy to make difficult, individualized search and rescue decisions in the field. We seriously doubt Congress intended to expose these decisions to the second guessing of courts far removed from the exigencies of the moment."
September 1987	Devils Tower Superintendent Bill Pierce is elected president of the National Association of Search and Rescue (NASAR). He will serve until September 1990.

MILESTONES OF THE 1980s

May 31, 1987	NPS recognizes need for Washington-based Park Service emergency services coordinator; Butch Farabee is first to serve in this position. Because of cutbacks, the post will be discontinued in 1997.
March 4-5, 1988	First ASTM (American Society for Testing and Materials) organizational meeting for rescue takes place in St. Louis. Seven subcommittees are formed. The need for nationwide "standards and guidelines" was seen as early as 1983 when groups advertisied "certification" in high-angle rescue.
May 26, 1988	At 18,000 feet on Mt. McKinley, Army High Altitude Rescue Team (HART) pilot Myron Babcock executes world's highest helicopter hoist. He will duplicate feat two days later at same spot.
April 2, 1989	Ome Daiber—"Father of American Mountain Rescue"—dies at 81 in Seattle.
April 3, 1989	Wastl Mariner—"Father of Mountain Rescue"—dies at 80 in Austria.
Summer 1989	Mt. McKinley is attempted by 1,007 climbers, the most to date.

The third Saturday of October is Bridge Day over the New River Gorge. One day a year hundreds of BASE jumpers leap from the 876-foot high span. Note the people looking over the bridge railing. NPS PHOTO

```
                 January 13, 1980
             Chiricahua National Monument
     --------------------------------------
```

PARK RANGER . . . STILL MISSING

SAYING he was off "to do a trail," the 42-year-old ranger quietly walked out of the park's small visitor center.

The 11,000-acre Chiricahua National Monument, a part of the Forest Service until 1924, is a beautifully rugged blend of dark hidden canyons and weirdly shaped, rocky spires. Once the impregnable retreat of the Chiricahua Apache, this secret corner of Arizona has always been steeped in intrigue. When the intelligently eccentric Paul Braxton Fugate, still wearing his gray uniform with its gold ranger badge, vanished in the cold shadows of that winter afternoon, he only added to the mystery.

That first night, the park's meager staff made a hurried search of nearby buildings, campgrounds, and paths. By late the next day, 20 people and a search dog from a local U.S. Customs unit had been pressed into the hunt. Severely restricted by the terribly rugged lay of the land, no more than two dozen people could search at any one time during the next three weeks.

Boulder-filled washes and winding, secluded trails were scanned from the air and then inspected again from the ground. Obvious hiking hazards and the area's many natural traps were rechecked as many as four times. Special teams, equipped with safety masks and trained to enter abandoned mines spent days probing nearby shafts and collapsed tunnels full of questionable air.

As the weeks passed without even a scrap of a clue, it grew increasingly evident that Fugate was probably not in the park. Had something heinous taken place?

Cochise County Sheriff's detectives thought that the ranger may have taken his own life; or that he had stumbled into a gay lovers' quarrel or, even more likely, an illegal-drug transaction. Two monument employees were questioned under hypnosis; one believed he had seen Fugate sitting between two men in a pickup truck near the area that Sunday afternoon. A police artist drew sketches, and bilingual "wanted" posters were sent throughout the Southwest and into Mexico. The reward eventually rose to $20,000.

Late in 1982, a Wisconsin lowlife boasted of "killing a cop" and hiding the body somewhere in the Arizona desert. Polygraph tests were given and failed. Companions of the suspect soon grew nervous, evasive, and uncooperative. Private investigators and detectives intensified their efforts, but nothing further could ever be proven.

In December 1985, Paul Fugate was declared legally dead.

February 19, 1980
Sleeping Bear Dunes National Lakeshore

CITATION

UNIT AWARD FOR EXCELLENCE OF SERVICE
SLEEPING BEAR DUNES NATIONAL LAKESHORE STAFF

IN recognition of the exceptional teamwork demonstrated in an unusual search and rescue effort.

On February 19, 1980, a call for assistance was received at the office of the Sleeping Bear Dunes National Lakeshore. An avalanche had occurred about one mile north of the Dune Climb. A group of young people had been hiking in the park. Three of the youngsters had been swept down a 250-foot slope when an overhanging cornice on which they had been standing gave way. Two of the youngsters had ended up on top of the avalanche while Daniel Culp, age 11, became buried in six feet of the snow. The Lakeshore staff had spent many hours preparing a workable search and rescue plan for an emergency of this nature even though this type of incident was rare for them. Within minutes, the plan went into action. Rangers were dispatched to the scene to assess the situation. Telephones began to ring in various homes and offices according to previous planning. The community and all agencies contacted responded. A radio communications relay was set up because of the difficult terrain. Another ranger arrived to assist with the Command Post and traffic control. Lakeshore maintenance crews rushed to the scene and began the necessary probing and shoveling. Other searchers followed. The atmosphere was one of positive cooperation and prompt response by all contacted. After approximately two hours, young Daniel was found and rushed to the hospital. His core body temperature had dropped to 89 degrees, indicating that hypothermia had begun. Chances for survival under these conditions are usually slim; however, because Daniel was found so soon and proper emergency medical treatment was administered on the scene, he survived. Prior planning, the establishment and maintenance of relationships with cooperating agencies and individuals, and a professional approach to the problem were the key factors in the success of this rare mission. In recognition of the superior efforts of a well organized team, the staff of the Sleeping Bear Dunes National Lakeshore is granted the **Unit Award for Excellence of Service of the Department of the Interior.**

Cecil D. Andrus
Secretary of the Interior

```
                May 28, 1980
        Grand Canyon National Park
----------------------------------------
```

JUST ANOTHER LIFE-AND-DEATH MISSION

IN 1980, Grand Canyon National Park performed 137 helicopter medevacs. With the gracious permission of author Barbara Trecker, the following excerpts from her June 1981 *Reader's Digest* Drama in Real Life article, "Rescue in the Grand Canyon," describe just one.

Ahead—at mile 179.2—lay the most treacherous stretch of all, Lava Falls, one of the fastest navigable rapids in North America, where the river drops 37 feet in 150 yards.

Lava Falls took less than a minute to get through, with the boat dropping into a hole of churning water. Everyone was soaked through. But the sun was bright, the scenery breathtaking, and Ryan had never felt so alive.

Ryan and his son were on the beach. . . . Chuck thought he had found a good place to camp. "How's this look?" he asked.

No answer. He turned around and saw his father lying face up on the sand . . . in a split second he knew something was wrong . . . he wasn't breathing. Chuck . . . started screaming for help.

Ryan was already blue. He had no pulse and no respiration. [Dr. Edward Lefrak], 37, immediately began external heart massage while Trudy [Mrs. Lefrak, RN] gave him mouth-to-mouth resuscitation. Lefrak, a leading cardiovascular surgeon, had come on this trip . . . from the pressures of performing 500 open-heart operations a year. . . . Never did he dream he would be giving cardiopulmonary resuscitation at the bottom of the Grand Canyon!

"It doesn't look good," Lefrak said . . . fibrillated. . . .

Twelve minutes passed, 15 minutes . . . about given up hope.

And then Ryan suddenly came back to life. His face went from dark blue to pale pink. Lefrak detected a faint pulse. Ryan gasped, then took a few shallow breaths.

For the first time in almost 20 minutes, Lefrak and Trudy relaxed, but only for a moment. "We've got to get him to a hospital," Lefrak said. But then it dawned on him—they were stuck at the bottom of a 200-foot inner gorge. . . .

Guide Mike Harris suggested they try to signal with a mirror to any plane passing above. . . . They spread a red canvas on the ground in an X shape and held small mirrors ready. They waited. And waited. But it was after 5 P.M. and most planes that ferry tourists over the canyon had stopped for the day.

Then Mike remembered that the Park Service Patrol was somewhere in the area.

The patrol covers a 225 mile stretch of water. It would be a miracle if they were close by.

Mike Harris told his ... brother ... find the patrol. Mark climbed into the raft and set off. About half an hour out, straining his eyes in the fading light, he rounded a corner and caught a glimpse of boats bobbing in the river. ...

Grand Canyon helicopter during a medevac of an injured river runner in 1992. Similar missions are performed dozens of times each year. KEN PHILLIPS PHOTO

[Ranger Sam] West went to his ground-to-air, commercial-airline-frequency radio with trepidation. For three hours that afternoon it had been on the fritz. He switched it on—and right away he heard a pilot talking! Sam broke in. ...

[The pilot] called Los Angeles, and L.A. relayed the message to the Grand Canyon Park Service Dispatch. ...

... sunset was 7:27 P.M. ... barely an hour left of usable light. After that, the canyon would be pitch dark, and no pilot in his right mind would take a chopper down inside its walls.

Pilot Tom Caldwell was preparing to put the helicopter away ... when the message came through at 7:25. Paramedic [Ranger] Michael Smith ... quickly loaded on an ECG defibrillator, ECG monitor, oxygen, a stretcher and medical supplies. Then they jumped in and Caldwell started up the Bell Jet Ranger 206.

... 80 nautical miles away ... it would take 45 minutes to reach the spot ... after 8 P.M. ... hovering over the canyon. ...

... the last light was rapidly disappearing ... his chief's last words: "I think it's going to be too dark when you get there, but it'll be entirely up to you to decide."

... six minutes for the treacherous descent from the top of the inner gorge. Straining his eyes to pick out familiar landmarks, flying slowly in an oval, he circled and let down step by step. The shadows worried him. What appeared to be shadow could be the canyon wall.... Gently he set the chopper down. "... five minutes before we're in total darkness," Caldwell said.

Smith ducked under the whirring blades and ran to Ryan.

Total darkness enveloped the canyon just as the helicopter emerged from the river gorge. Smith ... monitoring Ryan ...

Suddenly Ryan started to roll and kick. "He's not getting enough oxygen," Smith shouted. "He's out of control!"

Ryan kicked a foot under the bulkhead and nudged the power stick. The chopper shot straight up. Caldwell grabbed the stick, reduced altitude and leveled off. Ryan quieted. At 9:30 P.M. Caldwell brought the copter down on the helipad.

... Jerry Ryan woke up in the hospital.

```
             July 4, 1980
      Organ Pipe National Monument
-----------------------------------------
```

26 ILLEGALS LEFT TO DIE IN DESERT HEAT

QUICKLY climbing the sagging wire fence late July 3, the 26 El Salvadorans were among the 7,000 hopefuls who sneak across the park's 30-mile Mexican border each year. Eagerly seeking their own Independence Day, the desperate, illegal aliens had paid the two "coyotes"—smugglers—$1,200 each for the dream.

"Coyote" Preciado walked behind, cautiously erasing the telltale tracks near the jeep roads. "Coyote" Negro set a fast pace: People struggled and fell behind, little groups split off, and everyone grew unsure which way to go. By noon the next day the 20 gallons of life-sustaining water was nearly gone, and the 110-degree air and the superheated ground started taking their deadly toll.

Carlos forced them to urinate in a bottle and rationed it back out by dabbing their lips and faces with it. Some drank perfume, others aftershave. Everyone was covered with cactus thorns. Some died. Yolanda begged to be killed and put out of her misery, as did Maria. A few, tormented by the sun, huddled under the spindly desert brush; they lay alongside those who had already died.

At 8 P.M., one smuggler was found staggering along State Route 85; near death, he told the Border Patrol nothing of the others.

At 2 the next afternoon, a second man was caught and the horrible tragedy unfolded. A rapidly formed rescue force of Customs, NPS, Border Patrol, and Pima County Sheriff's deputies swooped into this terribly harsh area, known locally as "Camino del Diablo"—the Highway of the Devil.

Eight people, only half a mile west of the area's main road, were quickly found by the low-flying Border Patrol plane. Two young men were dead; they had burned a power pole while praying for help. "Survivors cried 'Eres Dios! Eres Dios!' and begged for water when discovered." Informed of even others still to the southwest, the searchers—trackers, motorcyclists, horsemen, and helicopters—spread out.

Just after dawn, an 18-year-old boy was found dead alongside an empty gallon water jug a short distance from the main road. Flagging the boy, Ranger Thompson and the pilot hurried back into the air to search for the living.

At 9:08 A.M., nine women and one man were spotted on a rocky, sunbaked ridge. Seeking moisture, one had stuffed a small cactus into her mouth. Close by, in the stingy shade of a few scraggly trees, lay three more women—alive. Yolanda, who had begged to die earlier, was among them.

In fleeing from the impending civil strife of their homeland—trading their life savings for a dream—13 lived and 13 died.

September 11, 1980
North Cascades National Park

FIVE RESCUERS KILLED IN "FIREWOOD ONE"

AFTER the Canadian reported his partner seriously injured, the Whatcom County Sheriff requested help out of Whidbey Island Naval Air Station, 50 miles from Seattle. A chopper was the only way to snatch the climber from the rugged terrain that held him.

The Navy, respectful of the low clouds and quick-moving rain storms then assaulting northern Washington, was reluctant to launch. The sheriff eventually persuaded them to fly, however, and a large, twin-bladed CH-46—"Firewood One"—lifted off with a six-man crew. En route they picked up Deputy Hurlbut to help pathfind between the unfamiliar 8,000-foot peaks. He settled in just behind the pilots, one of the safest places in the huge Sea Knight.

Clouds cloaked the mountaintops as they neared Perfect Pass. While circling Baker River searching for a plan, the pass partially cleared, so they eased into the "sucker hole." As they felt their way through the thick mist, it silently closed in around them.

Judging from the badly twisted remains, Firewood One first hit ground at the rear loading ramp, just before a 50-foot rotor blade chopped the cockpit off. Metal—and men—had flown everywhere.

One sailor had been catapulted from the rapidly disintegrating aircraft onto a cliff face 200 yards away. Another's head and arm had been severed by whirling debris. The pilot, dead of a broken neck, was still strapped to his seat. Two men somehow survived.

The copilot was unable to use the voice-activated Electronic Locator Transmitter (ELT) with either of his broken arms and Deputy Hurlbut was also too injured to help. The other ELT had triggered at impact and, though it worked properly, it failed to pinpoint them in the cloud-shrouded Cascades.

The next morning, two climbers stumbled onto the carnage. After minding the living and finding the dead, they called for help. The Canadian Armed Forces Base in British Columbia, originally unaware of the missing helicopter, quickly took to the air in a CH-46 and reached the scene along with other teams from the area. The rescue helicopter demanded near-perfect piloting. The mission, handicapped by the worsening weather, was finally pulled off under conditions generously described as marginal at best.

According to Park Ranger Bill Lester, "The Canadians hoisted the last survivor into their helicopter while hovering in a cloud!"

Killed in Firewood One that day were Dan Mahoney, Pat Kidgell, Roy Lewis, Tom Sanders, and Rick Kubal. Two bronze plaques memorializing these final heroics rest in the park's Marblemount Visitor Center and on a boulder near the scene of the accident in Perfect Pass.

November 9, 1980
Grand Teton National Park

A NIGHT IN VALHALLA—
AN EVENING WITH SUSAN

VETERAN Park Ranger Ralph Tingey remembers it this way:

Despite snow covering the higher peaks and the climbing season being long gone, Gaylon and James had hiked up Valhalla Canyon to climb the Ice Gully on the Enclosure, a lesser peak of the Grand Teton. Cheerfully accompanying them was their inexperienced friend Susan, a 22-year-old nurse from Pocatello.

The next morning snow was falling and the wind was blowing, so rather than climb, the party began to hike out. The rock and scree were covered with an icy crust of snow about seven-inches deep, and the party was using ice axes and crampons to descend.

At about 9 A.M. at the 9,000-foot level, just as the canyon steepens to about thirty-degrees, the young woman was bypassing a large boulder. She stepped down lightly onto the frozen surface and planted her axe, but her crampons slipped, and the ice axe did not hold. As she began to slide down the icy slope, she tried to arrest herself, but lost it. As though in an enormous slippery slide she cascaded 300 feet down the gully into rocks which stopped her . . . instantly and painfully. Her partners thought she had broken her hip, so one went for help while the other covered her with sleeping bags and attended to her.

Gaylon arrived at Park Headquarters just before noon and reported the accident. Walt Dabney and I decided to call the local contract helicopter and fly up to see if we could lift Susan out that day. We also called Hill Air Force Base in Ogden, Utah to order a MAST helicopter with a hoist to evacuate her because the smaller ship could not land on the steep mountain side.

Walt and I dressed for the winter mountains and packed small day/first aid packs so that we would be light enough for the chopper. Roger Kjerstad, the local pilot arrived wearing a plaid wool hat, and a sheepskin jacket, the dress of the local ranchers, and flew us up in the little Bell. We were quite used to this as it seemed like rescues always happen in storms. The wind was blowing snow, and any flying, let alone landing was very risky. They let me out at the base of the Canyon where it dumps into Cascade Canyon, so that only one person at a time would have to get out on the dangerous terrain.

Walt flew up and was let out; Roger then returned for me. The blizzard itself was fierce, but the turbulence of the ship's blades made any landing on the steep slope impossible. So, knowing there was a critically injured victim needing help below, I threw my pack out—and then watched as it slid down the gully. I jumped about ten feet out of the helicopter onto the slope; my crampons stuck, and I walked down and retrieved my pack. There was no hope for the little Bell to lift us out that day.

When I got to the tent it was a collapsed flapping mess like a sheet in a hurricane. Walt was inside assessing Susan while her partner huddled outside. Since the tent was not big enough for all of us we had him hike out down the canyon. It took us quite a while to chip a small tent platform out of the slope, and we never got it larger than just a few feet across. When we set up the tent, half of it hung off the edge much like a hammock. We got Susan comfortable in a sleeping bag, cooked some soup, and waited for the Air Force.

About dusk, the large helicopter tried to reach us but the blizzard conditions prevented it from getting close. Dejectedly we watched it, droning like a giant dragonfly, turn and fly away. We then prepared for the nocturnal vigil. It was difficult to keep Susan warm at times, so we had her drink a lot of liquids through the night. This also produced the very natural results, and sometime in the middle of the night Nature called . . . loudly.

There was a kink, however; she could not move, and because of the nature of her injuries and the inclement weather, we did not want to lift her outside. So a "Thunder

Mug" was prepared from the top of a Sigg Tourist Cooker. To prevent the pottie from overflowing, a gauge was installed in the form of my right thumb. As the warm pee worked its way up, I could tell when the pot was full, passed it to Walt for emptying out the tent door, and went to round two. . . . it was a great system.

The next morning the helicopter came in, hovered, lowered a cable and Susan was spirited off into the skies by "Our Nation's Finest." Walt and I opted to walk home rather than brave the helicopter's ride out. Whenever I get a chance not to ride in a helicopter, I take it!

Susan had three fractured vertebrae, a broken pelvis, and a pneumothorax of one lung.

June 11, 1981
George Washington Memorial Parkway

THE YOUNG WOMAN WAS THE SIXTH TO DIE

THE young woman was the sixth to die on the swollen river in just two weeks. Moments after finding her, almost under the spray of the treacherous falls, a teenage boy was seen floating through the rapids above. Would he be the seventh?

When Kirby's voice came over the radio, Rangers Kopczyk and Duffy and Park Policeman Madden had just found the 19-year-old woman, missing now for more than four days. The three, in their small Zodiac rescue boat when the River Rescue Team leader called, anchored her and started quickly upstream to look for the youth.

Ranger Jones, meanwhile, launched a canoe from the other side of the gorge to help in the emergency. "I watched Jones enter the river and start into the S-turn. He hit some violent whirlpools and capsized almost immediately, and had considerable trouble keeping his head above water."

Ranger Kirby instructed the three in the Zodiac—unable to see the quickly unfolding drama because of the rocks and rapids—to go to Jones's aid. But after being hit by a huge wave, their motor stalled. Completely at the river's mercy now, the boat crew watched—and then relaxed as a nearby kayaker raced in to pull the struggling ranger from the Potomac. Assessed by an EMT from the assisting Park Police helicopter, Jones seemed okay.

A boy fitting the description of the missing youth was soon sighted scrambling off a small rock island in the midst of the rapids. The searchers, unable to establish verbal contact with him, believed he was indicating that he was the subject being looked for and that he would be able to make his way back to the Maryland shore safely. Everyone returned to work.

At 5 P.M. two people reported that they had been waiting for their friend at the base of the S-turn since 1:30. Suspecting that the almost legendary undercurrents had taken another one, the searchers resumed. For two more days they climbed up and down the cliffs and crawled over the water-worn boulders lining the shore. The rescue boat and volunteer kayakers scoured the swirling eddies and pools while the Park Police helicopter looked where it was too dangerous or impossible to reach.

Late that same day, the river tragically gave up its seventh victim in just two weeks.

The River Rescue Team of Great Falls Park received a **Unit Award for Excellence of Service** "in recognition of the outstanding team work, dedication to duty, skill and personal bravery. "

June 21, 1981
Mt. Rainier National Park

AMERICA'S DEADLIEST
MOUNTAINEERING ACCIDENT

IT seemed bitterly cold at Camp Muir, as it always does at 4 A.M. The six guides and their 23 clients, practicing forced breathing and rest-stepping, started to move slowly and steadily upward. Lamps and lightbeams bobbed up and down; colorful nylon ropes—linking body to body—hissed quietly as they slithered along on top of the frozen snow. Cautious climbing kept the lifelines from being stepped on by the knife-sharp crampons.

No one had been successful in reaching the 14,410-foot summit from the peak's south side during the previous week. Cool, wet weather had made climbing conditions unseasonably difficult at the higher elevations. Today, however, hopes were high that they would be luckier than other recent parties.

Ninety minutes into the five-hour ascent, guide Chris Lynch and his three clients turned and headed down. The others continued, taking a customary break on the Ingraham Flats; all too soon, they had to push on toward Disappointment Cleaver.

Under the lower edge of the Cleaver, the group stopped to examine the changing snow conditions of the route before them. Professional guides John Day, Mike Targett, and Peter Whittaker, after cautiously probing ahead for avalanches, reluctantly decided to halt the climb. Slope exposure, lack of good trail, and their clients' inexperience made their decision prudent. The three guides started back.

"There was a loud crack and a snap. The thing I remember vividly was everybody going, 'Ooooh,' kind of like they were watching a Fourth of July display. For an instant, no one moved as the ice roared down the glacier . . . the guides yelled, 'Run'!"

The swath from the frozen debris—100 yards wide and 75 feet deep—was devastating. Survivors, shocked almost to nausea as they watched their new friends get buried, numbly assessed the huge pile of icy rubble; they knew they were the lucky ones.

For the next two days, highly trained rescue personnel from the National

Park Service, the Rainier Mountaineering climbing service, and the Mountain Rescue Council searched. Soon, they too stopped; there was little chance of recovering the bodies. Only a pack, an ice axe, and a headlamp were ever found.

In one eternity-lasting moment, 11 fragile lives were entombed under mountains of ice—America's deadliest climbing accident.

The world's deadliest mountaineering accident to date took place on Russia's Lenin Peak on July 13, 1990: An avalanche killed an international team of 40 climbers.

```
                    October 10, 1981
    Black Canyon of the Gunnison National Monument
    ----------------------------------------
```

DEATH WAS A RESULT OF
AN ILLEGAL PARACHUTE JUMP

DEATH was a result of an illegal parachute jump into the canyon; a violation of CFR 36 2.2(b). The Board also reviewed a tape of the actual incident showing the jump and the actual impact suffered by the victim. The tape clearly shows Larry Jackson taking the four steps and leaping of his own free will into space off the cliff. The chute did deploy and apparently glided into the wall and struck the wall.
—NPS Board of Inquiry, November 12, 1981

The veteran skydiver—with more than 600 jumps to his credit—probably died slowly of internal injuries when he smashed into the 2,200-foot-high Painted Wall that Saturday morning. Jackson, a 27-year-old Sooner Parachute Club member and avid BASE jumper, had been among four who illegally vaulted from a 1,600-foot TV tower in Oklahoma City two months earlier.

Seeking favorable winds, at least a dozen people searched among the junipers of the quiet little monument's north rim for a good launch pad. Later that night, the six adventurers, the park's first documented parachutists, rehearsed their story in case they were stopped and vowed to stick together despite what might happen the next morning.

Karl was the first to dive into the narrow gorge; landing safely on a sandbar beside the river, he waited for Jackson. Almost 30 minutes passed before the supermarket manager threw himself off the brush-covered edge. Some say he stumbled as he went over; others

> stated Jackson did not "track" [steer] properly and was remaining close to the wall. After his chute deployed, Jackson glided toward the wall, struck the face, slid down the wall between 50 and 100 feet, where the parachute hung on a rock outcropping, leaving Jackson dangling there, approximately 1,000 feet from both the rim and floor.

Via CB radio with the far side, the group quickly learned that Jackson was in desperate trouble. Mindful of their pact, the remaining jumpers elected to continue and "determine his condition as they floated past." None of the four saw Jackson during their fleeting pass and, after waiting more than an hour and then deciding their friend was beyond help, they finally advised rangers of the mishap.

> A woman came in and said she wanted to see a ranger. . . . she stated that she was taking pictures at an overlook on the South Rim with a telephoto lens when she saw what she thought was a parachute hanging on the wall. Ranger [Duncan] Burchard questioned her as to whether she was sure that she saw a parachute; she said not but it looked that way.

The "Good Samaritan" was actually the mother of the fourth jumper, and the sketchy information she gave was just the beginning of a series of intentional deceptions over the course of the investigation. As the drama unfolded, officials repeatedly wondered at the group's nonchalance toward Jackson's death. Without knowing the fate of their friend, they clambered from the bottom of the half-mile-deep canyon, loaded their gear, and headed for a motel. "When we get there, we take showers, marvel at our good fortune at having made a nighttime climb out of the Black without injury, and fall asleep."

From a vantage point across the half-mile-wide canyon, Ranger Burchard zeroed in with his telescope. It soon became distressingly clear that there was a body dangling 1,000 feet above the river. This was confirmed presently as Superintendent Joe Kastellic and helicopter pilot Burt Metcalf hovered dangerously near the still form draped below the white nylon shroud. To reach the dead man would be a Big Wall mission of the first magnitude; outside expertise would need to be brought in.

For the nine members of Colorado's Rocky Mountain Rescue Group who arrived later that night, reaching the victim would be a particularly interesting challenge. For the team, founded in 1953 and composed of veterans of hundreds of other mountain missions, this would be the first major vertical long wall use of their cable winch technique, a system involving more than 10,000 man-hours in development.

Once over the 2,200-foot cliff, and ably assisted by six members of the nearby Western State College SAR Team, the group from Boulder lowered Walt Fricke and Steve Poulsen to the parachutist in just an hour. The two master mountaineers worked quickly under extremely dangerous conditions: loose rock, high winds, and awkward communications, not to mention dangling nearly a quarter mile above the river. Fricke and Poulsen, after dropping down the height of the Empire State Building while optimistically armed with first-aid gear, weren't surprised to find Larry Jackson dead. "That was the easy part," according to team leader Louis Dahm. "It took us more than three more hours to get the body up."

Later that day, but before Jackson had been brought to the top, local police would stop several club members as they were preparing to quietly leave the area in two private airplanes. The five surviving jumpers were eventually fined $50.

At least four other BASE parachutists had been rescued, all in Yosemite, prior to Jackson. Probably the very first two were on July 24, 1966, when they each suffered broken legs and ankles. One had to be carried down from the base of 2,800-foot El Capitan and the other landed alongside the road. On June 20, 1980, another one was carried out from the rocks at the bottom of the half-mile cliff after breaking her back. On August 2, 1980, the government spent $174.93 to fly a jumper from the top of El Capitan after he developed life-threatening anaphylactic shock from a bee sting.

December 15, 1981
Denali National Park

CLOUSER/SCANLON v. UNITED STATES OF AMERICA

AT 1 P.M., a sightseeing aircraft charter out of the little bush-hamlet of Talkeetna crashed at the 10,000-foot level of Mt. McKinley's frozen Kahiltna Pass. The Cessna pilot and his three clients from Indiana were soon reported overdue from their short trip. An Air Force C-130, diverted by the Alaskan Rescue Coordination Center, heard the downed aircraft's distress signal at 6 P.M. The flight crew of the circling Hercules, spotting small lights flashed from below, knew that someone had survived the tragedy.

Of the four men on the small plane that Tuesday afternoon, one died shortly after impact, a second perished several days later, and the pilot and Michael Clouser survived. Eventually, Clouser would lose a large part of both feet as well as many of his 10 fingers and would, along with the family of the deceased Patrick Scanlon, bring suit against the U.S. government—the National Park Service, the Army, and the Air Force.

The Rescue Coordination Center alerted the Army at Fairbanks's Ft. Wainwright to ready its High Altitude Rescue Team (HART) and then, just before midnight, finally notified Denali National Park. HART's two Chinooks, hoist-equipped veterans of other similar rescues, did not launch until the next morning because of the weather and unidentified equipment problems. Later, in the district court trial of Case No. A83-637, the Honorable Andrew J. Kleinfeld of the District of Alaska didn't find this explanation to be credible: "This was an extremely serious delay."

On Wednesday, three private pilots tried to land at the crash site or drop supplies, but none was successful because of locally severe turbulence. On what Judge Kleinfeld would later call the "critical day," the Army's large helicopters didn't arrive above the wreck until just before noon. He would write in his summary decision of April 23, 1987, that they "failed to exercise reasonable care" by wasting precious daylight as well as following "an imprudent plan which no reasonable person would have adopted."

After picking up two park rangers and several Air Force Parajumpers, HART also soon found the air over the downed aircraft to be too turbulent to land. One of these pilots would later testify that while trying to hover, the ship's instruments were shaking so wildly they could not be read, and that the needle in the rate-of-descent indicator was pegged at 3,000 vertical feet per minute.

In his decision however, the judge contended that the single most inexcusable part of the rescue effort was the failure to drop any survival gear to the victims. He noted:

> Most striking to me, [they] did not drop any survival gear. I just cannot imagine how human beings in the safety and warmth of the helicopter, a large heavy Army chinook, flying over those people, realizing that the weather was picking up and they could not land how they could fly over that and not so much as drop a knap sack to these people.

Weather kept the giant helicopters from getting within several miles of the site on Thursday and again on Friday morning, the 18th. On the 17th, a group of mountain climbers from Talkeetna, calling themselves the "Mountain Maniacs," were dropped off lower on the glacier and began a slow, difficult climb to the crash site.

> They hiked up the mountain through the blizzards and the dark, endangering their own lives in order to accomplish this rescue. It is striking that despite the tremendous advantage in equipment, money, facilities, and training that the military had, the people who actually reached the site first and rescued the survivors were the Mountain Maniacs. That shows the seriousness with which they took their task.

By late Friday, the weather cleared enough; the climbers and one chopper reached the wreck and removed all four victims.

In Judge Kleinfeld's summary decision, he noted the existence of Alaska's "Good Samaritan" law but held that the basis of liability was "not the rendering of emergency care, but the failure to render emergency care." He then went on to say that under the same law, liability for civil damages as a result of gross negligence or reckless or intentional misconduct was possible. "And I have found gross negligence in the failure to make a drop of supplies." Judge Kleinfeld then found that

> an appropriate award for Mr. Scanlon's pain and exacerbation of pain and suffering because of the failure to make a supply drop was $36,000. I determined that by the rough justice often used in Alaska State Court at jury trials of looking at it as approximately 18 hours [estimated time between the crash and death] and approximately $2,000 per hour.

With regard to Clouser, the judge wrote, "his injuries other than the broken tooth and cuts and bruises were proximately caused by the failure to make a supply drop . . . [and] by the breach of duty of reasonable care and gross negligence of the United States."

Much to the shock and dismay of many knowledgeable rescuers, as well as the people most intimately involved in this perilous mission, Michael Clouser was awarded $135,420 for past medical expenses, $600,000 for lost wages, and $600,000 for pain and suffering. Judge Kleinfeld's decision was never appealed.

```
                 December 31, 1981
           Joshua Tree National Monument
      --------------------------------------
```

CITATION

UNIT AWARD FOR EXCELLENCE OF SERVICE
RATTLESNAKE CANYON RESCUE TEAM
JOSHUA TREE NATIONAL MONUMENT

IN recognition of a high degree of professionalism and dedication in saving a woman's life.

On December 31, 1981, at approximately 5:00 P.M., a female visitor and companion were on a day hike in the Rattlesnake Canyon area of Joshua Tree National Monument. While attempting to climb down a rock wall, the female visitor lost her footing and fell approximately 25 feet sustaining life threatening injuries. The companion was able to make it out of the area and contact Rangers for help. A rescue team of Rangers was immediately dispatched to the accident scene over extremely rugged and dangerous terrain, carrying technical equipment and essential medical supplies. The rescue team reached and stabilized the victim but the seriousness of her medical injuries precluded evacuation over the rugged terrain. An air lift was requested but not possible due to poor weather conditions. The rescue team remained with the victim monitoring life signs continuously until her evacuation could be accomplished by air lift on the afternoon of January 1, 1982. The medical skills and decisiveness of the rescue team undoubtedly saved the victim's life. For an extremely high level of dedication to service, teamwork, and professionalism, the Rattlesnake Canyon Rescue Team is granted the **Unit Award for Excellence of Service of the Department of the Interior.**

James G. Watt
Secretary of the Interior

This rescue operation involved more than 200 man-hours by 25 people. The national monument, recognizing a need for a more structured and sophisticated rescue capability, formally created JOSAR—Joshua Tree Search and Rescue.

January 3, 1982
Yosemite National Park

11-YEAR-OLD SURVIVES SUBZERO ORDEAL

DONNY was fast asleep in the backseat of his stepdad's small plane when it hit the frozen, windswept peak.

> When I woke up it was light, but the top of the plane was cov-
> ered with snow . . . windows were broken and snow had come
> in the plane, mostly in the front seat. I was very cold and
> very, very hungry. I tried to put my boots on, but my pants
> were frozen to my legs. I called to my Mom and Ron and
> shook them, but they did not respond. I knew they had died.

Smashing head-on into White Mountain, the brown and white Grumman lay unrecognizably shattered at 11,200 feet. Six feet of snow fell on the steep, avalanche-prone slope; windchill dove to minus thirty degrees. Slowly freezing to death, 11-year-old Donny huddled alongside his lifeless parents in the frigid fuselage.

> I tried to get a sleeping bag out, but all the luggage had
> frozen together. I curled up in some sleeping bag pads and
> tried to get warm. Once I looked for my Mother's purse to see
> if she had some crackers but there was too much snow. I ate
> some snow but did not know where any food was.

A well-oiled "search machine"—critically hampered by continued brutal weather, a shattered energency Electronic Locating Beacon, and confusion about the pilot's amended flight plan—looked for the missing aircraft for four days. Only the tip of the ship's vertical fin poked above the storm's white after-math, a nearly invisible clue for straining observers to spot from the air.

Despite the heroics of many, including Navy helicopter crews who ducked in and out of the Sierra's quick-moving snow-squalls and rangers like Chas and Anne Macquarrie who plunged up to their waists to break trails and ulti-mately lifted the little boy from his trap, SAR Ranger John Dill and ITAP fi-nally found Donny.

Interum Track Analysis Program (ITAP) is a computerized record of a plane's radar image, a system so advanced it wasn't available at every FAA facility. To retrieve this electronic log, one exact location and time must be known; those points were the 37-year-old pilot's 3:30 P.M. takeoff from the Mammoth Airport.

After tedious hours of plotting, Dill discovered a small but highly crucial error in ITAP's first analysis. Racing ahead of a second forecasted blizzard, he graphed the corrected data on a topographic map to within ± 100 feet. Armed with Dill's more accurate information, Lemoore's "Angel 3" flew a reduced search area. Battling 30-mph winds, searchers found Donny alive, but seri-ously frostbitten, on the fifth pass over the barren ridge.

```
January 13, 1982
Washington, D.C.
```

AIR FLORIDA . . . FLIGHT 90

THIRTY seconds after lifting into the blizzard, 79 people on the Boeing 737 were trapped at the bottom of the ice-choked Potomac River. One of the most dramatic rescues ever began to unfold.

Despite the blowing snow and half-mile visibility, the Tampa-bound jet was cleared for takeoff at 3:59 that afternoon. After reaching 150 mph at 340 feet, the giant plane suddenly "fell from the sky." Skimming the top of the commuter-jammed 14th Street Bridge, it surgically sliced the roofs off eight cars—and the heads of several people—before plunging into 30 feet of blackness. Only the tip of the craft's tail marked the tragedy below—that is, until six people broke the icy surface and began screaming.

Professionals and volunteers, paralyzed by Wednesday's peak-hour traffic and now framed by the bridge's twisted carnage, soon jammed the edge of the frozen river. Frustrated would-be rescuers focused on those desperate few clinging to the plane's tail and to each other. Improvised lifelines were repeatedly thrown into the water, but only a near-miracle could save those six now.

Don Usher, a Vietnam veteran with 1,150 combat flying hours, was quietly monitoring the hangar's police radio when he heard the news. The 31-year-old

With the chopper under the control of U.S. Park Police pilot Don Usher, officer Mel Windsor pulls in one of the five survivors of the plane that crashed through the frozen surface of the Potomac River. U.S. PARK POLICE/CHARLES PEREIRA PHOTO

U.S. Park Police helicopter pilot, with Rescue Technician Mel Windsor madly scrambling onboard, swiftly lifted "Eagle One" into a blizzard and a nightmare. The **DOI Valor Citation** reads, in part:

> Amid freezing temperatures and blowing snow, Officer Windsor exited the helicopter while in flight, throwing a flotation ring and two life vests to the survivors. While standing on the skids, holding onto the helicopter, he dropped a rescue rope. . . . Despite severe weather conditions, Officer Usher lifted the helicopter and raised the victim out of the water, transporting her. . . . "Eagle One" returned to the wreckage and rescued three more survivors in similar fashion. A fifth victim in a life vest was unable to continue her hold onto the wreckage as "Eagle One" returned. . . . After several failed attempts with the lifeline, Officer Usher lowered the helicopter to a point where the skids were immersed in the icy waters enabling Officer Windsor to pull the woman onto the skid with him.

A fifth victim was pulled to safety by M. L. Skutnik, a commuter who jumped in after seeing the woman lose her grip on Windsor's rope. The sixth person to reach surface that day, a 34-year-old Virginia man, kept passing the lifeline off to others instead of using it himself. Hopelessly snagged on the plane, he slipped beneath the watery slush before Usher and Eagle One could return for him.

On January 22, 1982, Secretary of the Interior James Watt presented Officers Don Usher and Melvin Windsor with the DOI's **Citation for Valor.**

On April 9, 1982, both policemen received the first ever **International Federation of Air Line Pilots Associations Polaris Award** for heroism. Named for the North Star, Polaris "implies permanence and unchanging values." The silver medal carries the federation's crest and depicts the polestar constellation with Polaris itself indicated by a diamond.

Both men received **Carnegie Medals** and $2,000 as well as the **Crew of the Year Award** for 1982 from the Helicopter Association International.

Don Usher received the **National Association for Search and Rescue Zimmerman-Rand Award for Valor.**

Sheet-metal worker Roger W. Olian was awarded the **Carnegie Medal**; he had "tied a makeshift line around his waist and entered the ice-clogged water" to try to save airline attendant Kelly L. Duncan. M. L. Skutnik III, a 28-year-old office services assistant, was awarded the **Carnegie Medal** for trying to rescue Priscilla K. Tirado, one of the five survivors of the Air Florida crash.

FOUR WENT DOWN . . .
THREE CAME UP

WHEN their friend didn't surface, the three men alerted the park. Rangers Gibbons and Igo and Administrative Officer Peregoy dove into the cold lake twice that first day. After searching outside the submerged three-story powerhouse, they went inside. The three park divers, prudently realizing that there was a need for unique skills beyond their own abilities, cautiously backed out, and Regional Marine Archeologists Lenihan, Murphy, and Nordby were called. As members of the Park Service's internationally recognized Submerged Cultural Resources Unit (SCRU), these professional underwater scientists brought technical scuba expertise to the mission. They possessed the necessary confidence gained through years of difficult and tricky underwater dives, including significant experience in very hazardous cave-diving in remote parts of the world.

The divers strained for a slight glint of metal from the dead man's tank. Slowly swimming through the darkened rooms, they warily felt their way between the confusion of cables and pipes. Eighty feet down and unable to even see their fingertips, they carefully avoided kicking up the fine, blinding silt. To ensure their direction and balance and to discern up from down, they unreeled a line behind them as they swam. They felt their way from room to shadowy room, zigzagged from wall to wall, searched along metal cages, groped under staircases, and squeezed into long, narrow generator tunnels.

On the second dive of the third exhausting day, the victim was discovered wedged between a wire switch cage and an interior wall. Afraid that even one careless movement would turn the already marginal visibility into total darkness, Lenihan slowly and carefully spent several minutes to free the body from its tight spot.

The Exemplary Act Award of the Department of the Interior was given "in recognition of the heroic acts carried out in a professional manner and in severe jeopardy of their lives . . . in hazardous underwater conditions, to Messrs. Mark W. Igo, Daniel J. Lenihan, Larry E. Murphy, Larry V. Nordby and Daniel Peregoy, and Ms. Deborah A. Gibbons." This was the first time this newly created award was given.

June 29, 1982
Rocky Mountain National Park

MISSING CHILDREN ARE COMMON—
BUT NEVER ROUTINE

THE trembling voice instantly tipped off the radio dispatcher that this phone call was serious. Based on Mrs. Baldeshwiler's description of her son's scant clothing, rangers soon concluded that the 12-year-old was ill-prepared to be out very long, particularly with the intense afternoon thunderstorms that had been occurring recently.

Understandably distraught, his mother claimed that the evening before, Robert had watched a slide program on the park and became "obsessed with climbing mountains and sliding snowfields." He asked his parents to rent technical equipment for him. As a compromise, however, the family hiked up Flattop Mountain instead.

Rangers immediately went out that first night, and for the next six days one of the largest searches in National Park Service history was undertaken. Covering 50 square miles, it involved difficult and extensive high-angle rock and snow, thick timber, impenetrable brush, marsh, streams, and alpine tundra. It ranged in elevation from 8,000 feet to 12,400 feet. Before it ended, nearly 1,000 people would be involved, including volunteers, dog teams, military air support, catering services, and search-strategy experts from around the country.

By the end of day two, more than 100 searchers were in the field, supported by a large Chinook helicopter from Ft. Carson, 90 portable two-way radios from Idaho, and a Colorado-complex base unit to handle the complicated radio transmissions. They concentrated on the incredibly rough terrain from treeline to the Continental Divide. They walked gullies, couloirs, and snowfields. Pilots, flying far too close to the canyon walls, slowly scanned each dark gully and light snowfield.

Denver's Channel 7 News helicopter searched Forest and Spruce Canyons. Ranger Larry Van Slyke was called in from Grand Canyon as the search's plans chief. Six dog teams were deployed, and one of them was kept near the heliport to respond immediately to any clue. On day four, with almost 250 people out, a climber elsewhere in the park broke an ankle and personnel and a helicopter were diverted to that rescue.

Strain creased the faces of frustrated searchers. Lack of sleep and the taxing labor of scrambling up and down boulder fields and through solid forest soon took their toll. Nothing concrete was found, and without any real clues to go on, the search officials started demobilizing. At sunset on the sixth day after Robert's disappearance, the search was suspended.

Five days later, hikers found the bloody visor of a white hat at the top of a steep, 1,300-foot snowslide and a tiny, crumpled body among the wet gray boulders at the bottom.

July 22, 1982
Bandelier National Monument

A BEAUTIFUL PLACE TO POISON HERSELF

DETACHED from the rest of the monument, the Tsankawi is a rugged series of high mesas and deep canyons. In an area with no roads and only a few ill-defined game trails, finding the intended suicide would take time, and search leader Bob Belden didn't have time.

Having recently attended a course in "mantracking," Rick Mossman and Ed Greene had learned the ancient art from its guru: retired Border Patrolman Ab Taylor. Locating a starting track, the two skillfully followed an "invisible" trail, an upturned pebble here and a faint scuff mark there. When they lost the next clue, they would methodically and patiently return to the last one. Often they had to get on their hands and knees to gain just the right sunangle to make out the woman's almost imperceptible track.

After three hours of painstaking effort, they found a comatose 24-year-old in a small, nearly hidden cave. Without the specialized tracking techniques they had learned from Taylor, the search would have taken days, and the woman would not have survived. Four days later she regained consciousness.

Rangers Belden, Greene, and Mossman received **Exemplary Act Awards** for their lifesaving efforts.

November 27, 1982
Kings Canyon National Park

VICTIM "MOONS" RESCUE HELICOPTER

MIKE, 24, and Paul, 21, wanted to "bag" Mt. Mendel over the long Thanksgiving weekend. Departing Southern California's Edwards Air Force Base the day before the holiday, the two climbers headed for the 13,691-foot Sierra peak, 100 miles to the north. Although experienced and well equipped, they weren't quite prepared for the monstrous blizzard that hammered them late that Saturday afternoon.

After summiting, 80-mph winds and a whiteout struck the pair just below the top. They attempted to bivouac, but the storm grew even more severe and the climbers again started down. Faced with potential avalanches and fearing falls into icy crevasses, Mike and Paul felt their way down the glacier in the dark. Blinded by the chaos and confused by the peak's many ridges, they missed their camp with all of their gear. On the edge of Evolution Lake, they found themselves stranded on the wrong side of the mountain.

Managing somehow to dig a tiny snow cave with their ice axes, they huddled together for the next six nights. Their only rations were seven candy bars and some nuts; their only equipment, heavy down jackets and foul weather gear. Off and on for days, they could hear the storm roaring outside. An avalanche swept over their frozen hole, temporarily collapsing it and burying what little of the much-needed gear they had left.

On Tuesday, after Paul's mother reported him two days overdue, the Inyo County Sheriff and rangers from Sequoia National Park launched a search. Deep snows and deadly slide conditions hindered ground parties, and marginal flying weather throughout the high mountain range limited air activity.

On December 2, nine days after leaving home and five days after being forced to bivouac, the two crawled from their small shelter when they heard what they thought was a helicopter. Not seeing it, Mike returned to the cave and fell asleep until after dark. When he awoke, he found his partner still gone. Paul, too exhausted to make his way back to the hole, lay in a snowy ditch some 400 yards away.

At midmorning the next day, "Angel-1," a Lemoore Naval Air Station SAR "Huey," lifted off from park headquarters with Ranger John Kraushaar onboard. Relying on Kraushaar's knowledge of the peak-studded backcountry and using instruments to feel their way along, they searched for Mt. Mendel between the blowing clouds. Lieutenant Helms, while slowly crossing the frozen lake, saw fresh tracks. Soon he spotted a partially disrobed climber in the waist-deep drifts.

Paul, who was standing barefoot in the snow and hallucinating, would later apologize to Kraushaar for "mooning" them as they first approached. He said "he did this because an earlier helicopter had landed and the pilot had told him to take his boots and clothes off and to stand on the ridge for 5–6 hours."

July 14, 1983
Grand Teton National Park

WET-SUITED RANGERS PROBE
WATER-FILLED SNOW CAVE

PLEASURABLY tired after reaching the top, Mark and Robert slowly worked their way down the rocky slope below the Lower Saddle. The longtime climbing friends from Washington, despite leaving ice axes at home and now forced to skirt the recent storm's icy buildup, were thrilled with having "bagged" the 13,770-foot Grand.

Somewhat off-route as they dropped toward the lower headwall, the two chose to correct the error by plunge-stepping and glissading across a moderately steep snowfield. Robert accomplished the tricky traverse. A not-so-lucky Mark, losing his balance in a gust of wind and then falling into a sitting position, began to slide.

Not yet grasping the crisis as he slid past other mountaineers, Mark smiled and said hello. When he saw the rocks rushing into view, he flipped over and frantically dug in with his elbows and toes, but he vanished through a manhole-sized opening in the lower snowfield. He had fallen into a stream that tumbled 20 feet and then cascaded over a small waterfall. A witness to the tragedy quickly reached the valley and notified park officials.

Five two-man teams, including several park divers, formed at the rescue cache. Rich Perch and Randy Harrington were the first crew, Leo Larson and diver Scott Berkenfield the second. Racing against darkness, only the first group flew in. After a two-hour slog, they reached the scene. Without warm wet suits and with the torrent at its day-ending crest, the two rangers halted for the night.

Under the snow the next morning, rescuers discovered two tunnels; the shafts, less than 36 inches high when they split, rejoined 20 feet farther on. The cave wound its way down along the rocks to where the stream surfaced 50 yards lower—it was suicide to enter the tiny hole through which Mark had disappeared.

Rangers Craig Patterson (left) and Scott Berkenfield entered the water- and slush-filled snow cave numerous times before finding the dead mountaineer.

LEO LARSON COLLECTION

Stripped to the waist, searchers dug an entrance from the side through 18 feet of solid snow. Five hours later, Berkenfield and Craig Patterson were cautiously lowered through the tiny gap.

> Craig and I went downstream—nothing. Upstream, the cave varied so we could walk, down to so tight we had to lie in the water and pull ourselves uphill. The current was so strong that while in the water, when we pulled on rocks two feet in diameter, they rolled from under us.
>
> We decided we would go upstream on our bellies until we put our faces in the water; at that point we would turn around. We knew as the day wore on the current got worse. We kept patting each other on the leg to reassure ourselves that we were OK as we slithered along. Just as we reached the set limits—as well as our own psychological ones—we found Mark.

August 12, 1983
Yosemite National Park

PINNED TIGHTLY UNDERWATER FOR 25 MINUTES

EVEN in late summer's low water, the Merced River can be deadly for rafters. Boulders and submerged obstacles mold deceptive currents and form dangerous "hydraulics"; fallen trees become fatal "strainers." Pete was lucky he saw her. Donna was luckier—underwater now for 10 minutes, only her arms and head were visible.

Donna's husband, struggling to shore after their tiny rubber boat flipped over, flagged down a radio-equipped bus and reported that his 40-year-old wife had been swept in the chilly water. Four minutes later, Ranger Pete Dalton arrived.

> While I searched the area around the "Big Hydraulic," I observed a life jacket float by. . . . I proceeded . . . checking any strainer that might have trapped . . . 100 yards upstream on river right I observed what appeared to be Donna . . . wrapped around a submerged log . . . under 1½ feet of swift moving water, in one of the river's main channels . . . arms and head were the only portion of her body visible.

The river, narrowing by 5 feet farther downstream, raced through floating debris and tumbled, creating jams of "strainers." Lodged 40 feet away, a deep channel separated victim from rescuer.

> I attempted to swim across the channel to an eddy . . . directly above where the victim was trapped . . . half way across . . . I realized that even with the appropriate gear; wet suit, fins and life jacket, the exposure to the "strainers" . . . down stream . . . would be high risk.

The rescuers knew of dramatic saves of people submerged in cold water for up to 45 minutes and battled to release the woman from the river's death-like grip. Their **Valor Award** reads in part:

> In the extremely swift current . . . [Colliver and Dellinges] managed to get hold of the victim . . . found it extremely difficult to maintain their positon and . . . pull the victim free. . . . If they lost their position . . . they would be carried downstream and become entrapped in a maze of log strainers located just below the surface . . . understanding, they gave one final effort.

After 25 minutes underwater, Donna Skinner survived.

On August 12, 1983, Secretary of the Interior Don Hodel presented **Valor Awards** to Rangers Gary Colliver, Pete Dalton, and Dan Dellinges. On November 22, 1983, NPS Director Russell Dickenson granted a **Unit Award for Excellence of Service** to 22 people of the Yosemite SAR team.

```
         October 9, 1983
      Shenandoah National Park
----------------------------------------
```

RANGER ZIEMANN SAID,
"IT WAS AS NASTY AS IT COULD GET."

SOMEWHERE up on Old Rag Mountain, 18-year-old Shawn Crawford was dying, and those looking for him knew it. The conditions that plagued the 130 searchers in the 2-square-mile area couldn't be worse: 5 inches of rain in 24 hours, 45-degree temperatures, visibility down to 15 yards, wicked winds, thick brush, steep cliffs, and ankle-breaking, loose rocks.

The young man, lightly dressed in jogging shorts and a sweater and without any emergency gear, started off the 3,000-foot summit shortly after noon that Sunday. Sighting north on his compass, he intended to bushwhack his way back to Weakley Hollow. When his three companions walked into the parking lot several hours later, their ill-prepared friend from West Virginia was not there.

An Incident Command Team was established and Ranger Mike Hill took charge early the next morning. Investigators began to develop a background profile, additional searchers hastily combed Shawn's most likely routes, and three dog teams tried to work the areas of greatest probability. "The terrain on the upper one-third of the mountain was very difficult with large rocks, ledges, laurel thickets and sheer dropoffs making searching with dogs almost impossible." The dense fog—a ceiling to 1,000 feet and 40-foot visibility—prevented vital aircraft support.

The weather grew even worse over the next two days, but searchers worked tirelessly through the long nights. Hill knew that if they could just surround Shawn and keep him from wandering out of the area or even attract him with bright lights, they might save him. After seven "alerts" by the dogs, a vertical line search—five teams roping off the cliff at line-of-sight intervals—began.

Late Tuesday night, a battered Shawn was found crumpled on a tiny ledge 250 feet below the top of the mountain; hypothermic and unconscious, he lay convulsing from a life-threatening head injury. Ranger Ziemann and Madison County paramedic Lewis Jenkins medically stabilized and then expertly "packaged" him for the tricky litter evacuation to follow.

Rescuers, already exhausted and now fighting darkness, an unrelenting downpour, near-zero visibility, dense brush, muddy slopes, and steep cliffs, struggled through the next 11 hours hand-carrying the critically injured boy a relatively short 2,500 yards to a waiting ambulance. Shawn Crawford is alive today because of the luck of youth and a very tenacious and dedicated search team.

More than 1,200 hours of highly skilled effort were contributed by neighboring rescue groups. Shenandoah National Park was granted a **Unit Award for Excellence of Service** by Secretary of the Interior William S. Clark.

December 8, 1983
Grand Canyon National Park

HELICOPTER CRASHES UPSIDE DOWN
INTO THE COLORADO RIVER

THE 400-foot cable stretched tightly from cliff to cliff. Anchored 35 feet above the muddy brown waters, it was invisible in the flickering afternoon shadows of the mile-deep gorge.

"Doc" banked sharply out of the narrow side canyon and headed down-river. To his left sat Bill Lamb, a BLM (Bureau of Land Management) district manager from Utah; behind them both was Charlie Houser, a top administrator from Washington. The two officials were comparing this remote part of the park with a nearby area recently designated for wilderness status. Skimming along 30 feet above the water, their brightly colored Bell-206 could be heard before it was seen.

In the rapidly fading light, Heidi Herendeen and John Pittman readied the cable car for the evening's scheduled sediment sampling. Hanging above the silt-filled river was part of the young couple's job with the U.S. Geological Survey. As Herendeen neared the coffin-sized trolley, Pittman refueled its small gas engine.

Hearing the echoes ricocheting off the towering rock walls, the two anxiously looked upstream for the swiftly approaching ship. When it rounded the corner and came into view, Pittman and Herendeen knew they were fewer than 20 seconds from disaster.

After striking the engine cowling, the 1-inch-thick cable slammed into the helicopter's rotor mast. The 2,500-pound machine stopped cold, rolled to its right, and then dropped into the quickly moving river. Landing upside down in 15 feet of water, it started to float slowly downstream. Instinctively, Pittman dove out of the way when he heard the explosive report of the snapping line; the heavy cart, catapulted into the air, landed within a foot of where Herendeen had ducked.

Pittman jumped into the frigid water and assisted the struggling pilot. Then Herendeen jumped in and grasped the aircraft skid with one hand and some shoreline brush with the other; desperately she fought to keep the helicopter from disappearing downstream.

Bill Lamb somehow slid free of his shoulder harness from inside the water-filled cockpit and looked around for Houser. He found the unconscious man still buckled in the rear—upside down and underwater. Lamb, grabbing the trapped man's helmet to keep his head up, couldn't unbuckle the seatbelt. While he held Houser above water, Pittman made several dives to find the release. Lamb finally pulled Houser out, pushed him onto the belly of the ship, and successfully gave him mouth-to-mouth resuscitation.

Heidi Herendeen, William Lamb, and John Pittman received **DOI Valor Awards** from Secretary of the Interior Donald P. Hodel. Charles "Charlie" Houser died several days later.

```
                  December 29, 1983
                  Olympic National Park
-----------------------------------------
```

CITATION FOR VALOR
RICHARD W. THOMAS

IN recognition of the heroic act performed in Olympic National Park in the rescue of two small children from the waters of Lake Crescent.

During the early morning hours of December 29, 1983, a family of five in a small sedan traveling east around Lake Crescent skidded on the slick roadway. The vehicle made a 180-degree turn and plunged into 30 feet of icy cold water. The mother, father, and a 4-year old daughter were able to escape through the windows as the car submerged. However, the 5-year-old daughter and 20-month-old son were still trapped inside. Shortly thereafter, off-duty Park Ranger Richard Thomas received a telephone call at home informing him of the accident, but with no real details provided. He immediately put on his wet suit and responded to the call, arriving at the accident approximately 10 minutes later. At the scene, he was advised that two small children were still trapped inside. Immediately taking command, he directed onlookers to care for surviving family members. Ranger Thomas, realizing the survival chance for the children was approaching the maximum period, even for a cold water drowning, knew his immediate response was essential. He made the decision to make a solo dive rather than wait 30–45 minutes until another diver arrived. He dove in and located the vehicle resting on its top in 30 feet of 43-degree water. He found one child inside the vehicle and took him to the surface. He re-entered the water for a second solo dive to search for the other child. He located her approximately 30 feet from the submerged vehicle, 10 feet deeper in the lake. He brought the child to the surface. While near exhaustion from the deep, cold water dives, Ranger Thomas proceeded to direct and administer CPR at the accident scene and in the ambulance en route to the hospital. CPR was continued for approximately one hour until both children were delivered to the Emergency Room Staff at Olympic Memorial Hospital in Port Angeles, Washington. Both children were revived but unfortunately died later that same day from injuries sustained in the accident. For his courage and complete disregard of his own safety, Richard W. Thomas is granted the **Valor Award of the Department of the Interior.**

Donald Paul Hodel
Secretary of the Interior

Richard Thomas was killed on June 22, 1984, while participating in a Civil Air Patrol search and rescue training mission.

February 13, 1984
Denali National Park

DEATH OF A "SAMURAI WARRIOR"

NAOMI Uemura is among the great adventurers of all time—period. Yet, outside of Japan where he was a national hero and before he became international news on Mt. McKinley, few knew the name of this mountaineer. Among his many feats, he:

- was the first person to reach the highest point on five continents, including 29,028-foot Mt. Everest, four of these ascents were solo.

- made the longest solo dogsled trip on record, more than 7,444 miles in 313 days, from Greenland to Alaska.

- was the first person to solo to the North Pole, covering 500 miles in 55 days by dogsled.

- rafted 3,782 miles down the Amazon River by himself.

- walked the length of Japan, 1,700 miles.

- made the first successful solo climb of Mt. McKinley.

A prosperous writer of children's adventure books, the 5-foot-4 Uemura was truly a giant of a person. In 1970, just 10 feet below the summit of Mt. Everest, he stopped and slowly motioned to a countryman to pass ahead. With this modest courtesy, Uemura granted to his friend the honor of being the very first Japanese to stand on the highest point on earth.

Nearly 14 years later, this time loaded down with raw caribou meat, seal oil, and whale blubber, and defending himself from countless fatal crevasses with two 17-foot bamboo poles lashed to his waist, Naomi Uemura worked his way up 20,320-foot Mt. McKinley. Climbed only three times in the winter and never by someone alone, the highest point in North America has some of the world's most unpredictable and deadly weather.

On his 43rd birthday—February 12, 1984—Uemura, after being continually hammered by hurricane winds and blinding blizzards and forced on several occasions to desperately claw out tiny snow caves in order to save his life, became the first to reach the top of "Big Mac" in the winter—by himself.

Despite the faulty radio transmissions on the morning after his victory, Uemura haltingly conversed with two countrymen being flown over the cloud-shrouded mountain by Lowell Thomas, Jr. Although hidden from their view and severely hindered by the poor reception, they understood his triumph, that he had descended to 18,000 feet, and that he was planning on meeting the pickup plane in two days. But Naomi Uemura didn't show up.

On February 16, bush pilot Thomas and professional mountaineer Harry Johnson, along with fellow aviator Doug Geeting, again braved the mountain. The turbulent weather that engulfed them was chancy at best.

> Geeting spotted what he believed to be Uemura waving from
> a snow cave at the 16,400-foot level on the West Buttress.
> . . . flew around the site several times . . . most of his passes
> he saw Uemura slide his head and upper body out of the snow
> cave and wave. . . . Geeting and Uemura had agreed . . . Uemura
> would make no movement if he needed help, Geeting
> assumed . . . Uemura was . . . in good condition but was pinned
> down . . . by very strong winds.

Although everyone expressed some degree of concern for Uemura, they also knew he was wise to stay put. Considering his 20 years of almost unparalleled mountaineering and survival experience and enough food and fuel for several more days, few seriously doubted a favorable outcome. They also knew that a rescue in those conditions would have been impossible. Uemura, the recipient of Japan's **Kikuchi Kan Award,** England's **International Award for Valor in Sport,** and the **American Academy's Achievement Award,** had no choice—he *"had* to descend on his own."

For the next three days the weather remained poor. Flirting with certain disaster themselves, Thomas and Geeting both spent several hours each day nursing their small planes as close to Uemura's obscured descent route as they dared. Because his much-needed snowshoes were spotted at the 14,300-foot level, and because it was believed he had been seen at 16,400 feet, it was assumed that he was cautiously holed up somewhere in between. However, the rescuers also knew that most of this short distance was a 1,500-foot, frozen, treacherous, 60-degree ice wall. There was little to do but wait and trust Uemura's rare and tested ability.

A break in the storm finally arrived on the 20th, and both Geeting and Thomas were dodging the clouds buffeting the mountain as soon as there was daylight. Uemura's route was searched several times, but they saw nothing—not even tracks in the fresh snow. Finally blessed with good weather, he should have been moving if he were capable, so fear for Uemura mushroomed. "[I]f he were travelling down the mountain, Geeting and/or Thomas *would have* seen him."

That same morning, chopper pilot Ron Smith brought a powerful high-altitude Bell 212 in from Anchorage. With veteran Rescue Ranger Bob Gerhard onboard, he proceeded to Uemura's base camp, where they picked up two climbers: Eiho Otani, a photographer and good friend of the missing man, and Jim Wickwire, an attorney from Seattle and for decades one of the world's elite mountaineers. The four flew to where Geeting had last seen Uemura. The helicopter, too heavy to safely land on the narrow, windswept ridge, descended 2,000 feet to where Uemura's snowshoes still poked mutely from the snow. Otani and Wickwire off-loaded their expeditionary winter gear, oxygen bottles, and a radio.

With the helicopter lighter and much more maneuverable, Smith gingerly touched down at 16,400 feet, as well as at a second snow cave a thousand feet higher. With the ship slowly hovering nearby, Gerhard literally dug through both camps for clues. On this day the three aircraft flew 14 hours; if Uemura had been active, he would have been spotted. Below, Wickwire and Otani found evidence that their friend had not returned to this cave after leaving for the top; he was still somewhere above.

Good weather lasted only a day; night brought a return of the same poor weather that had already frustrated the rescuers. Despite the marginal flying conditions over the next five days, both Geeting and Thomas boldly felt their way toward the often obscured 20,320-foot peak. Along with a third fixed-wing pilot, Dan Ashbrook, they had varying but significant degrees of success, and less likely escape routes were examined and eliminated.

> Wickwire and Otani . . . able to climb . . . getting low on food and fuel . . . weather was marginal . . . but the strong winds had subsided. At noon on 2/25, they left . . . camp at 14,300 feet and climbed for five hours to the West Buttress at 16,200 feet. About 100 feet north of the top of the ridge . . . found a snow cave . . . used by Uemura. They found . . . caribou bone . . . fuel can . . . food bags. The fuel can had definitely *not* belonged to Uemura [they] guessed [he] had salvaged the fuel from . . . above. . . .

A climbing team from Uemura's own Meiji University Alpine Club arrived 12 days after he had vanished to look for their revered alumnus. Four of them flew to the Kahiltna Base Camp a few days later. After nearly two weeks on the mountain, they reached the 17,200-foot level, where they found a snow cave with a number of items that belonged to their missing hero. It was assumed that Uemura had not descended below 17,200 feet but was instead somewhere above. Thousands of climbers have ascended this route since, but no further clue has ever been found.

In a letter to the author, Park Ranger Bob Gerhard indicated that he believes Uemura

> stopped to burrow into a crevasse or dig a small cave somewhere between the summit and Denali Pass. He made it through the night. . . . With several days of conditions where he could not travel I suspect he just ran out of steam and got covered over.

Flight time logged was 67.9 hours. Eiho Otani and Jim Wickwire received the American Alpine Club's prestigious 1985 **David A. Sowles Memorial Award** for their efforts in trying to find the "Samurai Warrior."

May 5, 1984
Montgomery County, Maryland

FIVE OF SEVEN BOATERS DROWN

INNOCENTLY, the young men, most of them members of the Army's nearby elite ceremonial 3rd Infantry Regiment, launched their small inflatable boat into the flood-swollen Potomac. Almost casually, they approached the deceptive Brookmont Dam, later described as "unquestionably one of the most dangerous obstacles to recreational boating on any river anywhere." Two hundred rescuers, including Park Police helicopter pilot Ed Cronin and Officer Wilbur Land, tried to save the seven novice rafters.

Low-head dams demand respect, and this one, within sight of the nation's capital, is "one of the most horrible places imaginable on a river." Because of the recent late-spring rains, the small concrete-and-rock dam created a unique washing machine–like hydraulic so overwhelming that it wouldn't release its doomed captives once they were cycled into it.

Cronin and Land, in the first of three mercy choppers to reach the scene, spotted the terrified seven churning around in the foaming backwash below the dam. Commencing the exacting mission, "Eagle One," with its rescue net dangling 40 feet below, began skimming the water.

The aircrew, blaring from the ship's loudspeaker, directed those underneath to "get in the net." The Billy Pugh, a cargolike rope device acquired after the 1982 ill-fated Air Florida crash, at first partially "collapsed in the water when two panicked rafters lunged for it at the same time." Eagle One finally lifted up carefully—one exhausted boater lay inside the rescue net while a second weakly clutched the outside.

Unfortunately, the second man lost his feeble grip and plunged backward. Cronin, depositing the first half-drowned man, returned for the one now bobbing along below. Quickly scooped up, he was deposited on a small rocky island in the middle of the river. Now using the deserted inflatable boat to sight in on, they flew back, hoping to find the others.

Cronin and Land cautiously brought the lifesaving net within inches of a panic-stricken third man. Without warning, an oil drum suddenly exploded from the foaming turbulence and hammered the hapless rafter. Sucked under several times by the nightmare hydraulic, only his orange life jacket popped to the surface. "We made numerous orbits in the hopes of seeing one of the persons reappear. We saw none."

October 18, 1984
Joshua Tree National Monument

THREE-YEAR-OLD GIRL DISAPPEARS

RUGGED and remote, the Morango Basin, millions of acres of Southern California's high desert, is a seductive blend of beauty and mystery. Good people go there to relax; misfits go to hide. It's a place where little children vanish.

The little blond girl, wearing a matching purple blouse and pants, a kelly-green sweatshirt, and rainbow-colored flip-flops, was last seen in the Indian Cove Campground at 4:30 P.M. Eight-year-old Travis remembered hearing his sister jabbering while he was inside the chemical toilet; he later recalled the door slamming on the women's bathroom next to him.

Within five hours of Laura Bradbury's disappearance, one of the nation's most heartrending missing-child dramas was in high gear. A team of skilled volunteers from the Mountain Rescue Association, San Bernardino County, Rescue Dog Association, as well as military helicopters from nearby Twentynine Palms, swooped into the area. Experienced in such searches, seasoned park rangers coordinated the mission.

For the next three days this talented force—numbering in excess of 270 people at one time—concentrated on more than 11 square miles of jumbled boulders and joshua trees. Sophisticated state-of-the-art search technology was used: computers, aircraft, human trackers, specially trained dogs, and electronic devices able to distinguish body heat from nearby, sun-warmed rocks.

The area was covered thoroughly several times by pros on foot, on horseback, and from the air. Trackers strained to see tiny footprints, climbers pored over the cliffs, lookouts on rocky high points watched and listened. Laura's mother rode through the area pleading into a loudspeaker. Each day the campground was combed once again. But they all somehow knew she wasn't there.

More than 400 concerned callers told the sheriff to examine the small toilets, although they had been drained that first day. More than 50 detectives chased innumerable leads, including a check of some 4,400 locally known sex-offenders. After the authorities released a composite drawing of a strange man in a blue van, nearly 800 calls were received in two days. One official believes that they had heard from more than 200 psychics. Private detectives were hired by the family. The brown-eyed Laura appeared on millions of grocery bags and milk cartons nationwide—the first such use of this method. A "no strings attached" reward of $25,000 was offered. It was never collected.

On March 22, 1986, a child's bone skullcap was found 2 miles away and was tested for blood and DNA clues. In December 1990, it was concluded that it was very likely Laura's. It is now a death investigation, not a missing person one.

October 21, 1984
Haleakala National Park

SHARON FRACTURED HER PELVIS

SHARON fractured her pelvis and broke her ankle when she fell. Either the shock from the 30-foot drop or the cooling spray of the 50-foot waterfall would quickly kill her. Considering the jagged rocks and steep cliffs and her position only inches from another 30-foot fall, the surest—probably the only—way to save her life was by helicopter.

With veteran Hawaiian pilot Tom Hauptman at the controls, Rangers Bednorz and Cabatbat, dangling from the end of a 150-foot rope, were soon swung onto the slippery, algae-covered ledges. The 30-year-old was strapped skillfully to a stretcher and, with a practiced hand, Hauptman lifted her from the deep gorge.

Ranger Perry Bednorz was granted an **Exemplary Act Award** by Western Regional Director Howard Chapman. Ranger Kimo Cabatbat, owing to his modesty, didn't submit himself for any form of recognition. Tom Hauptman, not an employee and thus ineligible for this award, received only the "high" of saving Sharon's life.

June 21, 1985
Isle Royale National Park

THE WRECK OF THE *MISCONDUCT*

LAUNCHING at 6 that night, the 28-foot, wood-hulled *Misconduct* headed east from Houghton for the open waters of Lake Superior. Bound for the island, only 15 miles south of the Canadian border, were two adults and six children ranging in age from 4 to 12. The operator, having made this 72-mile trip before and seduced by the mild waters and gentle breezes, elected not to monitor the regional weather forecasts on the boat's marine radio.

Just short of midnight they hit the dense fog bank and the heavy seas broadcasted—but missed—earlier. The operator, believing they were elsewhere, steered into Isle Royale's Conglomerate Bay, southwest of Middle Island Passage. Referring to the new radar onboard, the captain said that "he was not totally familiar with the equipment." He soon corrected the error and then made both radar and visual contact with the proper navigational buoy. With seas rolling a dozen feet high, however, he quickly lost this critical reference. The boat didn't have a chance.

After the *Misconduct* violently struck the rocks, the gale-driven seas jammed it into a cleft on the tiny island. With its bottom ripped out, the little craft quickly filled with water. Terrified and now battling whitecapping 12-foot rollers, the adults somehow engineered the six children onto the fog-shrouded crag. Knowing how lucky they were just to be alive, they managed to salvage much-needed survival gear, including a portable marine-band radio.

Within two hours of the wreck, Isle Royale's well-tested rescue machine was in high gear. Boats, crews, and support personnel mobilized, and the *Lorelei,* the park's 31-foot Bertram, with veteran rangers Jay Wells and Stu Croll, launched into the stormy night.

At about 0230, the *Lorelei* and crew arrived near Middle Island Passage. It was raining and the seas were extremely rough, I [Chief Ranger Croll] estimated the waves to be 12–14 feet. A spot light would not penetrate the thick fog. Our hailer was heard by the victims but we could not hear them or tell where they were even though they had several flashlights and were yelling, due to the thick fog, wind and heavy seas.

I was operating the boat and Jay was trying to keep us off the same rock and other reefs by using the radar. Making turns in heavy seas when it is pitch black and with your running lights reflecting off the thick fog is nearly impossible. You judge the next swell and wave, basically by feel—it gets harrowing to say the least.

Luckily, we could pick up the bell buoy on radar and occasionally hear its clanging but by now our four deck hands were completely sick and not of much use. At 0330, I broke off rescue operations since we did not know where the *Misconduct* or the victims were exactly located and the safety of the *Lorelei* and its occupants was getting more tenuous each time we came about.

By 0500 the fog began to lift so the search was resumed, however, sea conditions had not improved. At 0530 visual contact was made. This was the first time that we knew what side of the small island the *Misconduct* had sunk. They were lucky, had it been the other side, the boat would have been torn apart and the passengers thrown into the lake and washed away from the island. Surface water temperature that night was about 34 degrees.

We decided, because of the sea conditions, the now-posted gale warnings, windchill factors and concern for the victims having to wait 24 more hours before rescue, to ferry emergency gear via a swimmer tied to a nylon line. Jay, wearing a dry suit, entered the water and fought his way onto the rocks. After many trips between 0630 and 0730, sleeping bags, a park radio, tarps and food were transferred to the victims who were wet but in good spirits. Jay returned and all further rescue attempts were suspended until the ugly sea conditions abated.

Patience was not a trait on everyone's part. The victims reported they were very annoyed at the park service for not rescuing them earlier. It simply was too rough to put a small boat in the water and ferry people back to the larger rescue boats without seriously risking injury to someone. Attempts were made at 1230 and 1430 on Saturday afternoon, but again they had to be abandoned due to heavy seas. At 1210 the winds shifted abruptly from the southeast to the west and began to build; gale warnings were in effect for western Lake Superior.

At 1615 the *Lorelei,* operated by Paul Gerrish and myself, and a 16-foot outboard with Maintenancemen Doug Boose and Lee Jameson onboard, returned. Winds were blowing steadily from the west at 40 knots, gusting to 55 knots. At 1642, protected by Middle Island, the 16 footer safely landed. For the next 30 minutes eight people transferred to the Bertram . . . and by 1735, the rescue was over.

Twenty-one Park Service people aided the *Misconduct,* and the cost came to $2,500. Beginning in 1877 with the 204-foot wooden side-wheeler *Cumberland,* 10 ships over 200 feet in length, including two 525-foot Great Lakes ore freighters, have sunk on the rocks of Isle Royale National Park.

June 30, 1985
Golden Gate National Recreation Area

EXEMPLARY ACT AWARD
DENNIS R. GLASS

IN recognition of the heroic act performed at Ocean Beach, Golden Gate National Recreation Area on June 30, 1985, which resulted in the saving of a life.

Park Lifeguard Dennis R. Glass responded to a report of a drowning victim, twelve year-old Kenna Golden, along Ocean Beach. Lifeguard Glass arrived on the scene and immediately swam through the surf approximately 125 yards to Ms. Golden, who was in a semi-conscious state, being supported in the water by two San Francisco firemen. By this time the firemen were exhausted and cold. Taking command of the situation, Lifeguard Glass placed a rescue buoy around Ms. Golden to provide buoyancy and maintain her position in the surf. He advised the firemen that he believed Ms. Golden would not survive the swim to shore, and that the Golden Gate rescue boat would arrive shortly to transport her to shore. After caring for Ms. Golden until the rescue boat arrived, Lifeguard Glass, with the assistance from Lifeguard Steven Prokop, placed Ms. Golden in the rescue boat. By this time there were five firemen in the surf, three needing assistance to shore. Lifeguard Glass assisted one of the three firemen to shore.

Kenna Golden was unconscious when the rescue boat reached shore. She was immediately transported to a medical facility where she was in a coma for a period of time, and then fully recovered.

For his prompt, expert actions, which resulted in the saving of a girl's life, Dennis R. Glass is granted the **Exemplary Act Award of the Department of the Interior.**

Howard H. Chapman
Regional Director, Western Region

July 27, 1985
Yosemite National Park

TWO SIMULTANEOUS MAJOR RESCUES

FROM Saturday night through Sunday morning, the park's rescue group reacted to two SARs, not a rare occurrence in one of the busiest parks in the system. Complicated at the outset by both bad weather and darkness, either mission would have been notable. Occurring nearly concurrently, however, the rescuers did a heroic job of reaching and evacuating two dead, two critically injured, two ill, one moderately injured, and two very weary visitors

HALF DOME RESCUE
At 9:30 P.M., word was received that five people had been struck by lightning on top of 8,842-foot Half Dome. Two were killed outright (one falling 1,800 feet to the base), two were severely hurt, and one suffered only moderate injuries. After notifying the park dispatcher, Colin Campbell and Scott Jackson headed for the scene, 5 long, uphill miles away. They climbed the wet, twisting trail on the peak's backside as fast as the storm-darkened night would allow.

Three ranger-medics, carrying only essential emergency medical gear, also started up the 11-mile trail from the valley floor; seven more rangers with additional equipment soon followed.

Through distinguished effort, Rangers Campbell and Jackson reached the scene shortly after midnight. Rapidly surveying the injured, they laid out a helicopter landing zone. Because of deadly, often invisible hazards, choppers are used in mountains at night only on the gravest of missions—this was one.

With the weather clearing temporarily, a Medi-Flight helicopter made a tricky moonlit landing on the world-famous rock with ranger-medic Gary Colliver onboard. Working in the cold and wet they stabilized the three victims, two of whom had critical injuries from the lightning. Lifted from the summit, the three were then flown to the valley and further treated. Soon, the two victims deemed too seriously injured for the limited resources of the little local clinic were helivaced from the park.

Later that morning, while the park's second major rescue was going on elsewhere, an expert climbing team retrieved the two people killed by lightning. One body recovery required a very difficult effort at the base of Half Dome, an area typified by loose rock and precipitous terrain. This mission lasted more than 15 hours.

TENAYA CANYON RESCUE

Thirty minutes into the Half Dome rescue, word was received that a party of four, hiking from Tioga Road to the valley, were both lost and in serious trouble—two of them were epileptic and had no medications. Having anticipated an easy trip, they also carried no food, spare clothing, or other essentials.

An extremely rugged eastern extension of Yosemite Valley, Tenaya Canyon has seen dozens of the unlucky over the years. With their stunning appearance, the steep, several-thousand-foot, polished granite walls running the canyon's 10-mile length form a subtle, natural trap for the unwary.

The CB radio's weak batteries and the solid rock cliffs prevented this critical link from being comprehensible. Rangers only learned that there had already been one epileptic seizure and that there was at least one additional injury in the group.

Acting on this meager information, seasoned rescue hand Ron Mackie headed down from Olmstead Point. Along with medic Scott Emmerich, the two rangers were in search of four wet, lost, and injured people. Shouldering medical gear, food, and vital equipment, they were responding to an incident that generally demands several times their number. The lightning strike on Half Dome had created an overwhelming manpower demand elsewhere.

The missing party left their flashlights on, and a spotter on a distant point overlooking Tenaya guided the rangers toward them. At 7 A.M., after scrambling most of the night through tricky, extremely treacherous terrain, the two groups joined.

A twin-engine rescue helicopter—an "Angel"—from Lemoore Naval Air Station evacuated the party later that morning.

While performing under the able command of Ranger Jim Reilly, 59 people on the Yosemite rescue team were named in an **Exemplary Act Award** for these two missions.

During these two simultaneous operations, three stricken hikers were lifted from Half Dome while four more were rescued from Tenaya Canyon. Although the use of helicopters made the two missions look easy, they were anything but. When the two rescues were launched, severe thunderstorms had just moved through the area.

A massive callout of manpower was made in order to organize and provide logistical support to both a ground search and an evacuation of two sets of victims. Removing three seriously injured people from Half Dome by hand-carried litters is a difficult and complex technical problem requiring upwards of 40 rescuers. Removing two or more litter-patients from wild Tenaya Canyon would have required equally large numbers of strong backs.

In 1985, Yosemite rangers responded to 187 SAR missions in all.

July 29, 1985
Capitol Reef National Park

TWO RANGERS SAVE 14 LIVES

WITH little warning, the afternoon thunderstorm swiftly turned the normally peaceful Fremont River into a deadly torrent. Park Rangers Ken Kehrer and Larry Vensel warned visitors at Fruita Campground of likely flash floods. While patrolling, they soon observed an alarmingly unexpected rise in the muddy waters. Presently, logs and heavy debris began richocheting from bank to nearly overflowing bank.

After recalling 12 kids and their leaders tenting close to the once quiet river, Kehrer and Vensel rushed back to the group camping area. En route, the park radio blared that the water level had jumped 2 more feet and a major cascade now gushed from the nearby, upstream gorge. They arrived just as the deluge jumped the north bank and began racing through the tents. Ripping open several of the shelters, the rangers led the terrified youngsters out of the knee-deep water only moments before a 5-foot crest roared through.

With the children safe, the pair returned to the main camping area to look for others in trouble. They crossed the road bridge just before it collapsed and was swept downstream. Ranger Vensel waded through the still-rising flood to a travel trailer, where he found an elderly woman trapped. He helped her to safety just before her small mobile home bobbed up and floated off.

Nearby, Ranger Kehrer helped an older man escape from his stalled truck. Slowly struggling through waist-deep water, they were forced to retreat to the downstream side of a nearby tree after encountering treacherous footing. Vensel, himself driven to seeking the top of a large vehicle, noticed that the two men were having considerable difficulty. Leaving his safety, he fought his way over to Kehrer, where he helped ward off the chunks of debris racing past the frightened man. Campers came to the aid of the three by throwing them a rope and a garden hose.

Rangers Kenneth Kehrer and Larry Vensel were awarded the **DOI Medal of Valor** by Secretary of the Interior Donald Paul Hodel.

September 11, 1985
Grand Teton National Park

RESCUERS BATTLE 90-MPH WINDS
TO SAVE TWO CLIMBERS

CAUGHT in a savage, early fall blizzard, two parties desperately tried to retreat from high on the Grand Teton. Woefully ill-equipped for the storm, the five climbers—three from Jackson Hole and two from Seattle—endured a forced night bivouac at 13,000 feet in the Upper Saddle. Continuing down at first light, they soon chose the wrong route. Now stranded at the top of a 300-foot cliff, they spent the rest of the day vainly hunting for a way through the broken rock. All began to sufferer the deadly effects of frostbite and hypothermia.

Park Rangers "Renny" Jackson and "Woody" Woodmencey left Jenny Lake at noon that day to look for one of these parties, now overdue according to their permit. Earlier, Jackson had tried to fly into the area, but the helicopter had to turn around because of 60-mph winds—under full power, the ship was unable to go forward.

The two rangers carried fully equipped winter survival and rescue packs to the Lower Saddle. While breaking trail through snowdrifts 3 feet deep, they made the 7-mile march and its 5,000-foot elevational gain in the almost super-human time of five hours. Contacting a team of descending climbers, the rangers were told the two parties had not returned to the Lower Saddle the pre-vious day and that conditions above were too severe to even attempt to aid them. Jackson and Woodmencey, followed from below by Rangers Leo Larson and Randy Harrington, pressed forward into these same terrible circumstances.

They reached the Lower Saddle just before 6 P.M. It was brutal: blowing snow, poor visibility, and single-digit temperatures made even more torturous by the 90-mph winds. Despite the nearly impossible odds, the two climbed higher, hoping to find the missing mountaineers in the Owen Couloir. They forced their way up and over the demanding terrain, made extremely difficult and technically hazardous by the snow and ice covering the rock. Finally, after reaching the 12,400-foot level, darkness forced a retreat by headlamp to the raw refuge afforded by the Lower Saddle.

At 9 P.M., Woodmencey left his relative safety to help guide Harrington and Larson up the unstable, steep cliffs below. Glancing upward at just the right moment, he spotted a faint glow from far above; it blinked three times in the outdoorsman's standard plea for help. Nearly blinded by the swirling blizzard, he acknowledged the signal from overhead with three long flashes of his own light.

Woodmencey, mistakenly believing that the blinking distress signal had come from the Black Dike Traverse, relayed his sighting to Jackson. The pair immediately put together packs and started for the source of the dim light. They intended to have Harrington and Larson stay at the Lower Saddle and help guide them from below and, once the lost mountaineers were located, bring additional equipment.

Jackson and Woodmencey waited at the Black Dike Traverse while the two rangers below struggled with enormous loads of rescue gear. When they reached them, the small mountain of weight was divided among the four. Battling high winds, darkness, and blowing snow, the exhausted rangers made the risky ascent to the Owen Couloir at 12,500 feet. They then crossed over into the Wall Street Couloir, where ropes were anchored on the most airy, perilous sections.

The four rangers established faint voice contact with the missing climbers at just after 1 A.M. on the 13th. Thirty minutes later, after rappelling and sliding down treacherous, ice-covered rocks, they reached a nearly inco-herent Paul Johnson.

For the next 45 minutes, Johnson was given initial care. The rangers learned that there was another climber alive 150 feet below. Rappelling down once again,

Woodmencey found a seriously frostbitten Greg Findley tied to a single shaky anchor with his frozen rope tangled around him. Secured from above, Woodmencey assisted Findley back up the tricky rock face to the others.

Sometime just before dark, Findley and Johnson had left Nils Green and Ken Webb higher up in the gully; hypothermic and unable to move, both had been semiconscious—or worse. John Atthowe, the third climber in the party from Wyoming, unable to cling to his hold any longer, was seen skidding over the cliff below.

Ranger Jackson knew that Findley and Johnson had to be rewarmed immediately if they were going to survive. Green and Webb, left above 10 hours before in an advanced state of exposure, were probably beyond help. Renny Jackson knew that searching higher under such extreme, life-threatening conditions would greatly multiply the chance of killer rockfall. He also guessed that there was little or no hope for the climber who had fallen.

For the next three hours, rescuers focused on rewarming the two frozen men; Johnson and Findley lay in sleeping bags with rangers on either side of them. Jackson, tending the little gas stove all night, made hot drinks. Everyone tried to stay warm in the cutting, penetrating cold. Windchill was -30 degrees.

With the coming light of dawn, the nearly frozen team leapfrogged down the couloir using ice-covered ropes. Jackson fixed anchor lines while Woodmencey, Larson, and Harrington helped the two survivors each step of the way. Miraculously they all safely reached the Lower Saddle, where the storm had subsided enough to permit helicopter flights and the assistance of other rescue team members.

Rangers Randy R. Harrington, Reynold G. "Renny" Jackson, Leo L. Larson, and James T. "Woody" Woodmencey were awarded **Department of the Interior Valor Awards** for saving Greg Findley and Paul Johnson.

September 19, 1985
Mexico City, Mexico

MEXICO CITY EARTHQUAKE

WHEN the dust settled, the largest city in the world lay stunned; the first shock was 8.1 on the Richter scale, the second, 7.5. An estimated 9,000 people died, 30,000 were injured, and countless lives were altered forever.

More than a dozen countries sent help—the world literally came to the rescue. Venezuela and Spain arrived with 60 men each and tons of heavy rescue equipment. Very sophisticated electronic listening and video gear came from Germany, while the United States responded with the "Flying Doctors" and additional miniature eavesdropping equipment. Switzerland, France, Canada, Italy, Russia, and Algeria collectively sent upwards of 50 search-dog teams.

This disaster struck while many U.S. rescue experts, including some of the best dog-handlers, were in Nashville at the National Association of Search and Rescue Conference. Just before midnight on the 20th, the initial callup for dogs from the federal Office of Foreign Disaster Assistance reached them in Tennessee.

After a night of frantically turning Nashville upside down for veterinary supplies, freeze-dried food, water-purification devices, surgical gloves, and a multitude of other things, the advance team of four dogs was on an Air Force transport.

Providing coordination for Aly, Bourbon, Pepper, Sardy, and their handlers was Marian Hardy, a seasoned canine volunteer. Shenandoah National Park Assistant Chief Ranger Bill Pierce was along to provide liaison with the government. Already onboard the C-141 StarLifter with their specialized seismic and video equipment were federal mine officials from Pittsburgh. After the first day, additional dogs were requested by the U.S. embassy and nine more arrived on the 23rd.

Working in units of three or four dogs, the U.S. team was dispatched to widely scattered neighborhoods to determine if and where there were survivors. They were to search damaged or collapsed buildings where people might be trapped—alive. Dogs crawled through tunnels, climbed onto ledges, and picked their way over broken concrete, glass, and twisted metal. They were lowered into pits and hoisted up by cranes. Once they had provided a strong "alert," the animals were moved on to the next site, leaving the dangerous rubble removal to thousands of human hands.

Working for five long days, 16 handlers and their 13 canines searched 80 buildings. They found dozens of corpses, numerous possible live finds, and six known survivors.

An estimated 100 rescuers—ordinary people—were killed while trying to help their fellow citizens.

Coordinated by Bill Pierce and Marian Hardy, 13 dog teams searched the rubble of the Mexico City earthquake, which claimed 9,000 dead and 30,000 injured people.
BILL PIERCE COLLECTION

October 7, 1985
Ponce, Puerto Rico

"THE WORST TRAGEDY
TO EVER HIT OUR ISLAND"

FOR 30 hours tropical storm Isabel terrorized the tiny, nearly helpless island of Puerto Rico. When it was over, upwards of 700 people were gone, buried under countless tons of rock, mud, and building debris. Calling it "the worst tragedy to ever hit our island," Governor Rafael Colon turned to the United States for aid.

A call for help from the State Department was waiting for Bill Pierce when he arrived home near Shenandoah. The assistant chief ranger had just attended a high-level review of lessons learned during the Mexico City earthquake. Having just spearheaded this country's search-dog response to that disaster only three weeks earlier, Pierce knew who and where the experts were.

Almost before the collapsing limestone and clay ridge had settled, rescuers could hear scattered, muffled cries from beneath their feet. A few lucky survivors were pulled from the rubble during those first horrible hours. Friends and strangers frantically clawed with hands and picks. Chainsaws and bulldozers cautiously inched toward those thought to be still alive, hopelessly entombed in their flimsy, cardboard-like houses. But after nearly 36 hours, the pleas from below diminished to silence.

The first six U.S. dog teams, scheduled in Puerto Rico more than 24 hours earlier but delayed by federal confusion and disaster inexperience, finally arrived at 6 P.M. on October 9. Veteran searchers themselves, dog-handler Marian Hardy and Park Ranger Skip Wissinger surveyed the quickly hardening mudflows—some 40 feet deep—and set tomorrow's action plan. They phoned Pierce and requested more help, and then at dawn, aided by sophisticated electronic "listeners" from the Corps of Engineers, the six teams from Maryland and Virginia went to work.

On October 11, a second U.S. contingent—15 dog teams and 10 rangers—arrived in Ponce. Under the incident commander, Park Ranger Ken Hulick, handlers from the District of Columbia, Maryland, New York, North Carolina, Pennsylvania, Tennessee, and Virginia spent the next five days hoping for life-saving "alerts" from their dogs.

These 21 dog teams, now combined into four primary work units, faced extreme heat and humidity. They searched in shifts during the day, while electronic devices, needing silence, "listened" at night. By the time this U.S. team left San Juan on the 16th, 40 bodies had been located by "alerts" and another 137 possibles were flagged for the continued digging. There were no live finds.

For their humanitarian efforts, 10 rangers and 21 handlers and their dogs were formally recognized by Puerto Rico's **Amantes de Animales.** The red, white, and blue–ribboned medals awarded to the group read "Heroes en Puerto Rico—October, 1985."

<pre>
                  June 13, 1986
       Lake Mead National Recreation Area

</pre>

RANGER KEPT HIM FROM FALLING OFF

MICHAEL, balancing on a 1-foot-wide, 4-foot-long, sloping ledge, stood trapped—600 feet high. Time grew critical; without water and with the desert heat nearing 100 degrees, the 16-year-old became more desperate.

Michael's friend, risking a fatal plunge to the rocks far below, somehow managed to scramble to safety and describe his companion's dire state to Ranger Pete Dalton.

Led by Bill Briggs, the NPS rescue team faced an intense undertaking on the sheer rock wall and treacherously loose sandstone. Arriving at 6, after racing against the rapidly fading light, they quickly started up the near-vertical face.

Their movement soon grew slow and tedious; safe anchor points were almost impossible to find in the crumbly cliff. Fist-sized rocks, knocked loose by the terrified boy above, whistled down past them—some didn't miss. Rather than risk their whole team, Dalton and Briggs decided to climb on alone. Darkness settled in.

As the two rangers moved up the steep face, the route grew even less stable. Chunks pulled out when grabbed, flakes wobbled when stepped on. The men inched upward smoothly, cautiously.

Just after midnight, six agonizing hours after starting, Briggs and Dalton reached the boy who was now seriously dehydrated and semiconscious. Finding the frighteningly narrow ledge to be very unstable, the two rescuers feared it might give way from their movements and added weight at any second. After treating Michael for heat exhaustion and shock, Ranger Dalton wedged his body next to the boy to keep him from falling off.

Twelve hours after starting this dangerous mission, Briggs and Dalton watched as the teenager was safely winched into a hovering Marine Corps helicopter from Yuma.

On September 30, 1987, Secretary Donald Hodel presented Park Rangers William Briggs and Peter Dalton each with the **Valor Award** of the Department of the Interior "for their courageous actions and the great personal risks they took."

<pre>
                  June 18, 1986
           Grand Canyon National Park

</pre>

25 KILLED IN MIDAIR COLLISION

AT 9:30 A.M., two local sightseeing aircraft—a 20-place airplane and a 5-place helicopter—collided in midflight. Momentarily "swallowed" by the immense walls of the mile-deep Grand Canyon, the pilots probably never even saw each other.

Just as the emergency blared over their radio, chopper pilot Morris and Rangers Kuncl and Peterson spotted the column of black smoke to the west. High above the gorge for another medevac, it took them less than five minutes to reach the flaming wreckage. Though highly experienced, the three men weren't prepared to see people still strapped to their seats, burning in the plane below.

When it became apparent that no one had survived, Peterson was dropped off at the grisly scene and paramedic Kuncl completed the evacuation of a sick Chinese diplomat. Twenty more minutes passed before anyone discovered that a second aircraft—a helicopter—was also involved. Debris was scattered across a mile of desert floor.

Over the next several hours, the local sheriff's office, Federal Aviation Administration, National Safety Transportation Board, Department of Public Safety, and Arizona National Guard arrived. So did at least 60 people from the nation's press.

For three days, veteran investigators painstakingly sifted through the still-smoldering scene collecting evidence. Officials methodically removed the charred bodies and recorded the seats they were found in, hoping to learn why these 25 had died.

At the command post, complicated logistical needs were met, including coordinating four helicopters, feeding the many rescuers and investigators, obtaining a temporary morgue, and providing crucial communications with the accident site 26 miles away. A team of Critical Stress Debriefing experts was brought in to help workers deal with the emotions caused by the disaster.

Because most of the victims were foreign, the State Department and several embassies became involved. Hundreds of phone calls to relatives and friends around the world taxed the few telephone trunk lines into the park. Press conferences were given and numerous media photo pools sent out grim footage for the nation's nightly news. And finally, after the initial shock of the incident had waned, the park coordinated a community-wide memorial service with more than 300 people in attendance.

Naming 24 people, Secretary of the Interior Donald P. Hodel granted a **Unit Award for Excellence of Service** to the Grand Canyon Air Disaster Incident Command Group.

July 14, 1986
Grand Teton National Park

PARK'S FIRST HELI-RAPPEL AND SHORT-HAUL SAVES A LIFE

AFTER "bagging" the 12,605-foot summit of Mt. Moran, Nicola Rotberg and her climbing companion began to descend the peak's steep upper snowfield late in the afternoon. Within minutes the two women slipped. Cascading down the sun-sculpted glacier for nearly 2,000 vertical feet, they plunged into the frozen moat at the bottom. One died outright; one almost died.

Fifty minutes before sunset, park communications received word of the misadventure. Within minutes, a local Bell 206 helicopter was in the air. Rescuers soon grasped the gravity of the cry for help: rugged terrain, dwindling light, and life-threatening injuries. They must risk rappelling from the hovering chopper onto the dark mountainside if the young woman were to live. They also knew that this technique had only recently become operational; it had never been used on an actual mission in the Tetons.

Rangers Dan Burgette, Renny Jackson, and Steve Rickert lifted off for the accident site at 9 P.M. Ten minutes later, with the ship straining at this altitude and with Burgette supervising, Jackson and Rickert executed a flawless, 150-foot rappel. Dropping to within 40 feet of the motionless Rotberg, they found her unconscious.

The only way to get the dying woman to advanced life-support that night was to hurriedly try a second, but previously unused, technique—a short-haul: lower a rope from the helicopter, attach it to a stretcher, and then slowly fly away from the glacier face with the victim dangling 100 feet below the tiny but powerful machine.

After going for extra equipment, the ship returned to the mountain scene, where Burgette lowered the stretcher to the rescuers below. With speed and skill gained from years of lifesaving work in the mountains, Jackson and Rickert splinted the critically injured Rotberg and "packaged" her for the tricky short-haul pickup.

At 9:40 P.M., the chopper maneuvered noisily into place one final time. Darkness obscured the rescuers below. Burgette, unable to see his teammates and forced to rely blindly on precise radio reports, signalled for Rotberg to be hooked to the thin nylon lifeline. Forcing the hovering little craft up and away, the wary pilot slowly flew the litter four miles to a waiting ambulance.

Doctors at the Jackson Hole hospital, determined that Rotberg had numerous acute injuries along with a life-threatening, low core body temperature of 83 degrees. There was no question: If the woman had not been rescued from the remote peak that night, she certainly would have died.

Rangers Burgette, Jackson, and Rickert received a **Department of the Interior Exemplary Act Award** for saving the life of Nicola Rotberg.

July 20, 1986
North Cascades National Park

LETTER TO PARK SUPERINTENDENT
JOHN REYNOLDS

DEAR MR. REYNOLDS:

. . . as a member of the Skagit County Rescue Unit, I was in a Crevasse Rescue exercise jointly between our personnel and the Back Country Rangers of your Park. On my way back down the trail from Boston Basin I stepped on a large rock that suddenly gave way, toppling me and it into Midas Creek and trapping my right leg above the ankle. I was waist-deep with the rock on me just above a 20-foot waterfall. I was holding on to some scrub branches to keep from pulling myself and the rock over the falls.

Your employee, Christy Fairchild, was the only other climber present and upon her seeing me get into this predicament she immediately waded back across the fast-flowing creek and secured a rope around my chest so that I would not drown or go over the waterfalls. This involved considerable danger to her as she needed to cross and recross this fast-flowing creek.

After doing this she got her ice-axe and attempted to pry the rock off my leg; she was unsuccessful in doing this, but somehow or other, with some super-human effort, was able to move the rock (it took three rescuers later on to lift it) partially off of my leg so that some of the weight of the rock was borne by the stream bed. I think this saved my foot from being crushed or permanently injured as I laid in that position for approximately one and one-half hours until more help could arrive. During that time period Christy used our radio to summon help and guide the rescue helicopter to the area. If she had not been present to console me and assure me help was coming, I don't know what might have happened as I was in great pain and suffering from shock.

Under the supervision of William Lester, a helicopter was dispatched carrying climbing rangers, Jeff Clark and Saul Weisberg, who, upon their arrival, were able to, with the help of Trail Crew Maintenance Man, Artie Olson and a man named Daryl Baker, lift the rock off of me and get me into the helicopter. This was done with great expedition and humaneness and I wish to express my thanks to them also. The helicopter pilot is also to be thanked as he landed on a narrow ledge to pick us up.

However, the purpose of my writing this letter is to inform you and the National Park Service that you have an extraordinarily courageous and efficient employee in Christy Fairchild, without whose aid and comfort I might not be alive today.

John R. Sullivan

Christy Fairchild was granted a **Department of the Interior Exemplary Act Award.**

October 15, 1986
Yosemite National Park

INCREDIBLE SURVIVAL STORY—
BUT BOTH LEGS HAD TO BE AMPUTATED

OFTEN called pretty, the whiter-than-normal granite cap of Mt. Clark is visible from many parts of the park; the view from the top is a striking panorama of the surrounding wilderness. First climbed in 1866, the knife-edge arêtes leading up the 11,522-foot peak demand respect but are commonly done without a rope.

Lemoore Naval Air Station "Angels" have been used for SAR in California, including the one for Kalantarian, since the mid-1960s. This photo is from the summer of 1980. AUTHOR'S PHOTO

Headed for the summit, Michael Kalantarian, alone and running way behind schedule on the second of his two days off, knew that he was pushing his luck when he encountered the steep icy slab partway up. Unroped and forced to move onto even steeper rock, the 30-year-old soon slipped and tumbled 70 feet to the rocks below.

Draped over a brushy pine tree when he woke, he had been out for an hour. Bleeding from his head and suffering from a broken wrist and shattered ankle, he was unable to walk or even stand to get his bearings. Kalantarian was alone, seriously injured, and far from any trail. His food, tent, and sleeping bag, as well as additional gear for survival, were 3 miles away; help was even farther.

"'All I could do was crawl,' he said. 'The pain was intense at first . . . but it was so cold that after a while I couldn't feel it.'" Temperatures plunged to 15 degrees; after losing his hat, he wrapped a cotton sweatshirt around his head to keep the lifesaving heat in. He spent days dragging himself through torturous terrain; he sought sunny open areas for their warmth and, at night, hunted for thirst-quenching water.

Two days after he hadn't shown up for work, Kalantarian was finally reported missing. At first, searchers didn't know where to look. Upon critical detective work and interviewing numerous hikers as well as a friend of the missing man, Incident Commander John Dill focused his attention on the western drainages of Mt. Clark.

Climbing teams checked the remote peak's summit as well as others nearby to see if the unregistered hiker had been successful or had changed his destination. One witness was hypnotized to see if she could recall helpful details. Helicopters worked constantly to shuttle ground searchers into areas of high probability.

Trackers found fresh footprints matching the pattern of the missing man— they headed up the mountain. A discarded boot discovered on the peak's heavily forested lower slopes and a cap located higher up finally gave Dill proof that Kalantarian was somewhere nearby. Hair samples and the hat were sent to a Fresno forensics lab for a more positive identification.

By the time Kalantarian's drag marks through the woods were located and the lucky man was found alive—six days after he had fallen—100 searchers, four helicopters, six dog teams, and at least 18 agencies had been involved in the search.

```
                 May 24, 1987
         Lava Beds National Monument
   --------------------------------------
```

CITATION

FOR VALOR
STEPHEN W. UNDERWOOD

IN recognition of his courageous action resulting in the rescue of two rockslide victims.

A rockslide within a lava tube collapse pit at Lava Beds National Monument trapped two male park visitors under heavy lava rock within a space approximately two feet high, three feet wide, and four feet long. Over a two-hour period, Resource Management Specialist Stephen Underwood and volunteers moved enough lava rock to create an access to the cavity in which the victims were trapped. The first victim was extricated and evacuated with shock symptoms and abrasions. The other victim remained trapped with the upper part of his body in the cavity and his legs pinned, although not crushed, by the rock slide. Crawling into the hole and over the upper body of the victim, Mr. Underwood calculated the precise amount of movement needed to lift the rocks, one by one, without creating sliding which would have crushed both of them. Working in a confined area that could only be lighted by a flashlight, for approximately one and one-half hours in a cramped position under tons of unstable rocks, Mr. Underwood jacked and shored the lava. Mr. Underwood remained calm, exhibiting unusual courage as he directed the cutting of shoring materials, jacked the rocks, and installed the shoring unaided. A slight miscalculation on his part in jacking the heavy rocks could have resulted in a severe injury or death. Mr. Underwood was finally able to stabilize enough rock to enable extrication of the victim on a backboard. The victim was evacuated by helicopter to a Medical Center in Klamath Falls. For his courageous action and the great personal risk he took, Stephen W. Underwood is granted the **Valor Award of the Department of the Interior.**

Donald Paul Hodel
Secretary of the Interior

Underwood also received the **Carnegie Hero Award.**

Off duty, 25-year-old Police Officer Mathew H. Rokes was also granted the **Carnegie Hero Award** for his efforts in rescuing 15-year-old John R. Adams, Jr.

```
June 28, 1987
Grand Teton National Park
```

JOHNSON v. USA—
A PRECEDENT-SETTING COURT CASE ON SAR

ON November 13, 1991, Monroe McKay, chief judge of the 10th Circuit Court of Appeals, granted summary judgment in favor of the United States in a lawsuit that had potential for profoundly affecting—and seriously impeding—mountain search and rescue on a nationwide scale.

Ben Johnson, the plaintiff, contended,

would not have died but for the Park Service's negligent failure to: (1) adequately regulate recreational climbing activity in Grand Teton National Park; (2) initiate a rescue effort after . . . initial report; and (3) conduct a reasonable rescue effort after . . . second report.

The least experienced of the four climbers, Johnson finally reached the top of 11,938-foot Buck Mountain at midmorning. Savoring their hard-earned success, the young men then started down via the relatively easy east face. Leaving first, the two most seasoned hikers safely reached the bottom of the nontechnical route at noon.

Following within minutes of the others, Johnson and his partner, Daniel, soon strayed onto more difficult ground. Blocked by dangerous terrain, they searched for an easier route. Prudently, Daniel eventually halted on a small ledge in sight of those below. Johnson, occasionally in voice contact but lost from view of the other three, continued down alone.

Several hours after Ben Johnson should have joined them, one of the hikers reported his companions as "off course and stuck, but . . . he believed there was a ranger in the area." Two-way radio messages confirmed that Ranger Randy Harrington had indeed encountered four climbers at the peak's base on their way out. Believing erroneously that the overdues were by now relatively safe, rangers advised the worried friend to return and wait.

Just before dark, the two hikers finally comprehended the significance of the mistake and reported the error. Ranger Pete Armington, the park's experienced SAR coordinator, soon had a team working its way up the peak's crumbly, deadly slopes.

After hours of climbing in the dark, rescuers safely retrieved Daniel from his trap but were unable to locate the man's missing partner. Then, just past dawn, a body lying in a shallow pool of melted snow was spotted from the air. Johnson had slipped on a steep rock bank and had died of hypothermia the previous night.

Judges McKay, Barrett, and Brorby said that if the plaintiff's argument had been accepted, it "would jeopardize the Park rangers' autonomy to make difficult, individualized search and rescue decisions in the field. We seriously doubt Congress intended to expose these decisions to the second guessing of courts far removed from the exigencies of the moment."

August 13, 1987
Cape Cod National Seashore

"I'M NOT LETTING GO OF MY MOMMY"

AIMEE and her mother almost drowned in the Atlantic Ocean that afternoon. Their thank-you letters to the park say it all.

> Without their teamwork and know how I wouldn't be writing this letter today and my daughter's life would have been cut short at a mere 11 years. The day was just like any other first day of vacation—filled with excitement and anticipation.
>
> The sign was posted—NO SWIMMING, DANGEROUS WAVES—so we decided to just relax on the beach and collect shells for a couple of hours. . . . I never saw waves so big. . . . So Aimee and I started to walk along the shore line in water and foam no higher than our ankles. Some how, Aimee tripped and fell sitting with her back to the ocean—I yelled for her to get up, we were no further apart than three or four feet. She was on the edge of the beach—beyond this point the sand dropped down the bank where the waves were crashing. She fell backwards . . . sucked . . . into the white water.
>
> I saw her surface behind the wave. I jumped in . . . the waves pounded us from both directions. We went under several times. A man . . . saw us and jumped in to offer us his help.

I just knew I had to keep Aimee up and to tell her when the waves were coming so she was ready and never to let her go. . . . This man tried to keep us up. I just prayed to God to help me hold onto my baby.

Then all of a sudden Mark was there and said something to the effect, "Hang on, we'll get you back." I just knew we were being helped . . . then I was aware of a few people out with us, there were a few maneuvers with the life belt—and ropes and instructions to hang onto a torpedo type float.

My daughter, crying, "I'm not letting go of my mommy," repeatedly, and the kind voice reassuring her we wouldn't be separated—the other man who now also had to be rescued telling the lifeguards to get us in first—then we were told to hang onto the floats and we were being towed to shore.

We were in—we were safe—and all things considered, in fair shape. Mark stayed with us the whole time, talked to my daughter who was petrified . . . he was able to calm her and reassure her. He saw to it I got the oxygen to straighten my jangled nerves. . . . He couldn't have been more caring or concerned.

Thank you are just two short words. I look into my daughter's face knowing she was almost lost to me. So again, I say thank you for being there. Thank you for putting your lives on the line for us. Thank you from the bottom of my heart.

Sincerely,
Bonnie Jones

Dear Mark,

Hi, how are you. I'm just fine now. I just wanted to say thank you for saving my moms life and mine. And thanks for being with me the hole time and for cheering me up. Were thinking of coming back to Cape Cod. We might even come back to the same beach because I'm not afraid of the water any more because I'm learning how to swim. Isn't that great. Tell all the other lifeguards that I said thanks for saving our life.

Sincerely
Aimee Jones

PS. Thanks again. I appreciated it very much.

Mark D. Griffin was the primary responding lifeguard and Don Socorelis was the man who jumped in to help.

February 10, 1988
Yellowstone National Park

WHEN THE YOUNG MAN FELL
INTO THE 180-DEGREE WATER

WHEN the young man fell into the 180-degree water of the hot pool, he suffered second- and third-degree burns over 90 percent of his body. In spite of the heroic efforts of his friends and the rangers who had to battle their way through the blizzard that night, he died.

Pitching camp near Shoshone Lake, the five cross-country skiers were only 200 yards from an active geothermal basin. Long after daylight had ended, one of the three men in the group went exploring alone. The others never did learn exactly what happened—they just heard him scream and watched him stagger into camp. Quickly comprehending that this was a life-and-death emergency, they knew that if their scalded friend had any chance for survival, they would have to ski for help, which was 10 miles away.

Faced with high winds and a mounting ground blizzard, the two men started out. Soon exhausted, one turned back; the other struggled into Old Faithful at 4 A.M. and reported the accident. Two rangers quickly readied their emergency equipment and consulted a doctor by phone about handling the extensive burns. When they took off on their snowmobile, they were guessing as to exactly where the injured man lay.

Along with two volunteers, the two rangers motored nearly 7 miles before the drifts stalled them. Skiing the rest of the way through the predawn storm, they broke trail in the knee-deep snows. Twenty more skiers, carrying additional equipment including a toboggan, soon followed. A third ranger, actually a little closer but initially unavailable, started out at daybreak.

Faced with what they soon guessed to be the inevitable, the dying man's companions still valiantly fought for his life. Because they had run out of water and were unable to get their stove to melt snow, they thawed it in their mouths to give him life-sustaining liquids. Conscious and talking, he was in extreme pain and seriously dehydrated.

Fourteen long hours after he fell into the near-boiling water, he convulsed; his life signs soon ceased. Desperately his friends began CPR. Arriving soon afterward from Shoshone Lake, Bonnie Gafney did what she could to assist in the last-ditch efforts. Rangers from Old Faithful joined in when they reached the scene.

Once they had ensured that all vital signs were absent for a medically significant time and had consulted with a doctor by radio, the exhausted rescuers stopped their lifesaving attempts. Because of the weather and the approaching night, it took 24 more hours before the dead man could be flown out by helicopter.

May 26, 1988
Denali National Park

AT 18,200 FEET—THE WORLD'S HIGHEST HOIST

ONLY "Mayday, Mayday" was in English. Rangers scrambled to find someone who spoke Korean to translate the rest of the fear-laden message sent from many miles away high on the mountain.

Days late in starting, Sung Hyun Baek tried to catch up with his climbing team. Scaling the Cassin Ridge alone and facing exhaustion, he luckily met several members of another party of Koreans. Attempting anything on the highest mountain in North America is difficult and daring at best, but the steep Cassin is spectacularly challenging. Bivouacked at the 18,200-foot level, the Koreans found they had no rope and only one day of food left.

The Mayday, according to the translator, had come from a countryman suffering from "high altitude sickness, frostbite on one leg and frostbite on the hands." Furthermore, according to the report, Baek was unable to use his fingers and could not walk.

Although part of the upper mountain was clear, lowering clouds on the Cassin Ridge prevented veteran bush pilot Jay Hudson from getting his small Cessna 206 close to Baek that night. At the controls and with Ranger Ralph Moore and a Korean onboard, Hudson tried again the next morning. Finally successful in locating their tiny target, the trio circling above somehow coached Baek out to the end of the ridge, just below his small camp.

By a quirk of good fate, two powerful Army Chinook helicopters from the 242nd Aviation Company of Fairbanks's Ft. Wainwright were already in Talkeetna, the area's remote climbing headquarters, to fly out the park's high-altitude medical research camp. Pilots Kirk Brown and Myron Babcock, with the Rescue Coordination Center at Elmendorf Air Force Base approving the tricky mercy mission, launched.

One of the huge twin-rotored ships hovered at 18,200 feet; a thin steel cable extended 80 feet to raise the waiting climber. Extra food and CB batteries were then lowered for the others. These two helicopter crews had just performed the highest hoist rescue in North America, probably the highest in the world.

Minutes later, a neurosurgeon, who had coincidentally been working at the nearby high-altitude medical lab, examined the reportedly serious "victim." No frostbite on the feet, no symptoms of swelling of the brain, and only the tips of two fingers were gray.

One day after helping his fellow countryman get winched off Cassin Ridge, 27-year-old Hyun Young Chung suffered a stroke. Six days later, Chief Warrant Officer Myron Babcock flew his Chinook back to the *same* spot to perform a second record rescue hoist. Babcock was named **Army Aviator of the Year** by the Army Aviation Association of America. During the previous 14 years, the High Altitude Rescue Team had made more than 46 rescues off Mt. McKinley.

August 30, 1988
Southern California

LOST MARINE

IT was almost two full days before anyone missed Jason Rother, who had been left alone at the end of night maneuvers at Southern California's Twentynine Palms Marine Corps Training Center. More than three months passed before the young lance corporal from Company K was found.

JOSAR (Joshua Tree Search and Rescue), shown here on an earlier rescue, led and coordinated the 1,750 soldiers who looked for Lance Corporal Jason Rother. NPS PHOTO

Racing against desert daytime ground temperatures in excess of 150 degrees, the Marine Corps launched a search for the 19-year-old. Using missile-equipped antitank vehicles with sophisticated heat-imaging equipment along with infrared night-vision goggles, they soon found Rother's pack, helmet, and flak jacket. Nearby, an arrow of stones pointed toward the east. By dawn, nine helicopters and a spotter plane were in the air; by 9:30 that night, search dogs from the California Rescue Dog Association and four park rangers from nearby Joshua Tree National Monument had joined the search.

On September 4, the effort was at its peak. In addition to the four rangers, nearly 1,750 soldiers, seven dog teams, 140 hours of aircraft flight time, and officials from both state and local law enforcement were part of the massive, but ultimately futile search. By the end of the day, desert survival experts gave Rother no chance, and the active phase of the large-scale effort was halted. Many of the local military command believed that Rother was AWOL; this may have contributed to their lack of success.

Rother's family appealed to prominent congressional leaders, including Senator John Glenn, a former marine, to reopen the case. On October 24, after intense media scrutiny and Washington pressure on the Marine Corps headquarters, the search was reactivated. Joshua Tree's chief ranger, Paul Henry, a veteran of numerous desert searches, was named incident commander.

No longer pressured by life or death, Ranger Henry engineered Operation Desert Search, "one of the most thought-out search efforts in the history of this country." Some 146 square miles of difficult and blistering desert terrain were carefully inspected. At least 16 agencies, including 14 dog teams, 28 trackers, 105 State of California personnel, 109 marines, 20 federal personnel, five helicopters, a C-130 "Hercules," and 40 ground vehicles, were committed to the two-and-a-half-day mission. More than 5,000 man-hours were expended; the helicopter effort alone consisted of 141 sorties of four to six hours each. For all of this hard work, one boot print, a rock arrow, a practice hand grenade, and a foul odor were all that was found.

On December 3, the San Bernardino Sheriff's Office search and rescue team, while on a routine training mission focusing on the original search, finally found Lance Corporal Jason Rother's body.

February 23, 1989
Denali National Park

WINDS MAY HAVE REACHED 200 MPH

WINTER ascents of the highest mountain in North America have been accomplished only a handful of times. Lying just below the Arctic Circle, 20,320-foot Mt. McKinley demands the world's most accomplished and daring mountaineers.

Lining his little plane up on the long white "runway," Doug Geeting landed the four-man Japanese Winter Expedition on the Kahiltna Glacier. Only two days before, he had placed an Austrian team at the same 7,200-foot-high base camp. When he lifted off once again, the veteran bush pilot must have marveled at just how determined groups like this were.

Both climbing parties moved quickly and smoothly over the frozen glaciers and windswept ridges. Unroped, however, they would risk plunging into the ever-present hidden crevasses. Stomach problems forced one of the Japanese to retreat, but within 72 hours, the rest had gained more than 7,000 feet on Big Mac.

At the 14,200-foot level, the Japanese dug small snow caves and watched as the Austrians struggled up the 50-degree, 1,000-foot cliff of ice before them. Along with the camouflaged crevasses, ground blizzards, zero visibility, cyclone winds, lack of oxygen, and 40-below-zero temperatures, the intimidating frozen wall was just one more obstacle to surmount.

The Austrian mountaineers "tightroped" along the narrow ridge, which was only a dozen feet wide in places between 16,000 and 17,000 feet—on their right, a 2,000-foot drop; on their left, 5,000 feet of air. A false step, one gale-force gust, a slip of any kind . . .

On February 22, despite heavy winds and poor visibility, the Austrians reached the top and then hastily retreated to the base camp. Awaiting their chance, the Japanese were eager to climb through Denali Pass and push for the mountain's final 2,000 feet. Their team was strong, but the mountain was stronger.

The weather service in Anchorage that week measured the winds at 17,000 feet at 100 mph. Later they would declare that this speed could easily double when funneled through the peak's highest pass. With little protection the climbers faced a hurricane. By their due-out date of March 3, the Japanese Winter Expedition had not been seen or heard from in more than 10 days.

Responding to the National Park Service's call for help, one of the world's most accomplished mountain rescue operations quickly went into high gear in Talkeetna. HART, the Army's special High Altitude Rescue Team, arrived from Ft. Wainwright. Aptly nicknamed, HART consists of powerful CH-47 choppers, well-trained crews, and seasoned pilots. Chief Warrant Officer Myron Babcock, a Chinook pilot for 16 years, would later recall downdrafts of more than 2,000 feet per minute. "Sometimes we had no aircraft control!" The year before, Babcock had been named Army Aviator of the Year for two other daring rescues from almost the same spot.

A four-engine C-130 provided coordination and communications cover far above the maddening clouds. Observers in a small twin-engine plane tried to approach, but turbulence and extremely poor visibility forced pilot Lee Savoda back, miles away from the scene. Nearby, the talented but stubborn Doug Geeting kept trying to edge his small aircraft in closer.

Television crews and reporters crowded into Talkeetna; additional phone lines had to be arranged for. Dr. Peter Hackett, a Mt. Everest climber and world authority on high-altitude medicine, designed emergency medical protocols should the three men be found. The Alaska Mountain Rescue Group was put on standby. A crack 17-man rescue team from Japan arrived, as did Air Force Parajumpers. Park rangers, local climbing guides, and the recently successful Austrians united, ready to go when the weather broke. Even for these professionals, however, there was little to do but wait.

Finally, on March 10, three reddish forms were spotted at the bottom of steep Denali Pass. The consensus was that, even if the objects were not the missing climbers, there was no chance they could be alive elsewhere. Rescue leader Ranger Bob Seibert, unwilling to continue jeopardizing searchers, at least until the severe weather eased, reluctantly suspended the heroic efforts.

Three days later, the red dots were positively identified as the missing men—still roped together. With considerable danger to themselves, the special mountaineering team from Japan eventually reached and removed their dead countrymen.

In 1989, of the 1,009 mountaineers who attempted Mt. McKinley, 360 of them were foreign, as were 7 of the 13 people who had to be rescued. Including the 3 from Japan, 6 died that season.

In 1990, Japanese climbers installed an anemometer at the 19,400-foot level of Mt. McKinley to measure wind speeds every six minutes for one year. Upon their return the following year, they found that the cables securing the gauge had snapped and that the metal pole supporting it was badly bent.

```
            May 20, 1989
    Cape Hatteras National Seashore
-----------------------------------------
```

THEY SAVED FIVE PEOPLE

WAVES broke 10 to 12 feet high at the sandbar; low tide rushed seaward at 3 to 4 knots. In 15 years of lifeguarding, the director of Rescue Operations for the Nags Head Fire Department had rarely seen such severe conditions as existed that day. N. H. Sanderson would later declare, "This . . . rendered any swimming rescue virtually impossible, especially a multi-victim rescue. I am sure Anderson realized this but still, without hesitation, went to the troubled swimmers assistance."

When Ranger "Hank" Anderson arrived, the five swimmers were already 100 yards off the beach. Desperately clinging to a short surfboard, they battled the rough seas trying to stay abovewater. Anderson saw that the men were caught in a dangerous riptide and were becoming numb from the 65-degree water; one man was waving his arm for help. Moments after arriving, Anderson grabbed a surf-rescue buoy and entered the water.

> I swam out to the subjects and was told 1 person was missing, Chris Jackson. Subjects were panicked, had swallowed a lot of seawater, and some could not swim due to leg cramps. I put 2 subjects on the Boogie Board and 3 on the swim buoy. I kept the group together and calmed them down. Nags Head Rescue had dispatched a jet ski from the beach operated by Mirek Dabrowski. Dabrowski was able to reach us and towed the surf buoy back to shore. He then returned to the surf and towed in the last 2 subjects.

Lifeguard Sanderson would conclude:

> I learned that one of the victims began to panic because of the pounding of the waves, as well as exhaustion. Anderson was able to calm and reassure this subject to a point where he could continue to be towed to shore. Although appearing extremely exhausted, Anderson assisted with the other victims until all were transported to medical facilities.
>
> I feel confident that all of these individuals would have perished had it not been for the courageous actions of Mike Anderson and Mirek Dabrowski.

On March 8, 1990, Henry "Hank" M. Anderson III received the DOI's **Valor Award** from Secretary Manuel Lujan.

June 10, 1989
Hawaii Volcanoes National Park

UNIT CITATION

PARK RANGER RESCUE TEAM
HAWAII VOLCANOES NATIONAL PARK

ON June 10, 1989 a Hawaii Scenic Air Tour plane with eleven persons on board disappeared over the island of Hawaii. On June 12, 1989 the emergency locator for the plane was picked up and the plane was found on the face of the vertical head wall of Waipio Valley. The valley at the crash site is over two thousand feet deep, with highly vegetated vertical walls, and just over 75 yards wide. The plane was located 900 feet above the floor of the valley. The delay between the estimated crash time and the receiving of the signal from the emergency locator gave hope that a survivor of the crash may have activated the devise.

Hawaii County Civil Defense requested that the Drug Enforcement Helicopter transport a back-up team of park rangers from Hawaii Volcanoes National Park to the scene the morning of June 13.

By noon of June 13, Hawaii County Fire Department, a military special operations team, state and county law enforcement agencies had been unable to access the site. At this time the three park rangers, utilizing a combination of helirappeling, long line insertion and one-skid helicopter landing, led a rescue team into the crash site. The team successfully gained access to the crash site and rigged fixed lines to carry out recovery operations from. It was immediately apparent that there were no survivors, however, by the end of the day the remains of six of the passengers were recovered and removed from the site. Using the techniques established this first day of operations and receiving on site support by members of this ranger team, the Hawaii County recovery effort had removed all the human remains that could be located as well as much of the actual wreckage.

The combined competence and skill of each of the individual Rangers, resulted in the successful completion of a mission that was outside of the abilities of any other agency in the State of Hawaii. In recognition of outstanding teamwork and dedication to public service, the Park Ranger team who led this effort are granted the **Unit Award for Excellence of Service of the Department of the Interior.**

Manuel J. Lujan
Secretary of the Interior

Dangling beneath the chopper were Park Rangers Jeffrey B. Judd, Scott W. Lopez, and John A. Machado; Hawaii County firefighter Mike Tomich; and

Richard White of the State Department of Land and Natural Resources. At the ship's controls was Tom Hauptman, a Vietnam War pilot and president of Pacific Helicopter Tours.

```
                    August 9, 1989
                 Big Bend National Park
        ----------------------------------------
```

ONE MORE RED CROSS

"LIMA 82," coming in hot, hovered at full power; the wheels of the sleek Blackhawk hung over the 700-foot drop. Rangers, leaping catlike from the door, dropped onto the table-sized rock.

Unable to scramble free of the 6-foot-wide ridgetop until the chopper left, the rescuers lay face down and fought the hurricane blast from the big machine's main rotor. Lifting off, the three-man crew started for Panther Junction and the next team.

Lima 82, a powerful weapon in the War on Drugs, was already a veteran. After only five months along the Mexican border, the 1,700-hp helicopter had its victories "growing" on its door: six marijuana leaves, three cocaine plants, and two red crosses. Courtesy of the U.S. Customs Service, 14 rescuers had just been spared a very tough, very hot, eight-hour hike. Lima 82 had just earned one more red cross.

Kelly Hogan, a 27-year-old graduate student from Sul Ross, was studying the effects of pesticides on peregrine falcon eggs. His plan, depending on how far down he found the nest, was to either continue to the bottom or ascend his rope back to the top. The rope was 500 feet long, the cliff 700.

When he reached the nest at 3:30 P.M., Hogan collected his samples. As he later explained, either "an equipment failure or sudden shock on his climbing rope caused him to release himself." He fell about 40 feet, stopping when he smashed into the wall.

Balancing on a foot-wide ledge, he radioed his support crew for help. His back and shoulder hurt, but he said he was okay. "Okay" meant three fractured thoracic vertebrae.

Rescue leader Charlie Peterson checked, rechecked, and then rechecked again: people—knots—anchors—the 1,200-foot lowering rope. The team was ready. Then, testing his radio one last time, Ranger Clyde Stonaker started over the edge.

Within three hours of his brush with death, Hogan, hooked to the lowering rope with Stonaker, stood safely at the bottom of the 700-foot cliff. "I would not have been able to last the night if you had not gotten me down."

October 22, 1989
Wind Cave National Park

MOCK SEARCH TURNS INTO THE REAL THING

NEARING the end of an intensive eight-day class on caving, NOLS, the National Outdoor Leadership School, went underground early that Sunday morning to conduct a simulated rescue. One instructor went off into the maze of narrow dark passages and "got lost." Then, after receiving final instructions and being duly challenged, several teams of NOLS students systematically fanned out.

Close to noon, Rachel and Scott, finished with inspecting the Cataract Room, separated to probe smaller side leads for the still-missing "victim." Expecting to return shortly, the pair of novice cavers left their packs, water, and extra carbide fuel in the main corridor. The 18-year-old woman, having already earlier traded away a troublesome light, soon ran out of water for her one liquid-generated gas lamp; her extra light was back in her pack.

After too quickly giving up on Scott and then feeling her way around in the dark for what must have seemed hours, Rachel was able to finally relight her lamp after she had carefully urinated into the light's small container. In unfamiliar territory and without the caver's routine two sources of backup light, she continued to move on rather than wait for assistance.

When NOLS realized that Rachel was missing, they abandoned their mock rescue for the real thing. Ninety minutes later they told the Park Service about their new victim. Implementing the Incident Command System, rangers set up teams of NOLS students, employees, and local cavers. By 9 that night, 50 people and one search dog had been committed to the mission.

By the time the search was escalated, Rachel had already crawled out of what would soon be considered the primary search area. And, with her extra fuel left behind, her light went out one final time. Continuing to feel along in the dark, she soon lost her hard hat and the useless light down a limestone fissure. Rachel ended up squirming down through a narrow crack into an unmapped passage in the lower section of the cave.

> The call went out for more cavers/searchers and teams were fed, rested and rotated as they searched the area where she disappeared, a 3-D maze, into Monday morning." Just before midnight that evening, voice contact was finally made with the missing woman.
>
> "[Rachel] would never have been found except she was hitting a rock against a rock wall and the search party heard the sound. If [she] had been sleeping or unconscious when the search party had gone by, she probably never would have been found." The passage she was in was not on the map.

Official reports indicate that "a total of 110 searchers for 1,800 man-hours and about $30,000 were spent in the search."

Rangers from Pennsylvania's Delaware Water Gap National Recreation Area rescue a trapped trucker, circa 1977. POCONO PRESS/STEVE BLAKLEY PHOTO

CHAPTER 10

1990–1999

The successful ranger must be honest,
courteous, and patient and at the same
time firm, equal to emergencies, and of
good judgement. He must be impartial to
all, cognizant of his responsibilities,
and loyal to the Service he represents.

—Director Stephen T. Mather, Report of
Director of National Park Service: 1918

SPACE-AGE TECHNOLOGY

In 1970, Congress enacted Public Law 91.596 of the Federal Aviation Act. Although given a grace period, U.S. registered aircraft were mandated to install Emergency Locator Transmitters (ELTs). When two congressmen, including Louisiana's Hale Boggs, disappeared in 1972 in remote Alaska—prompting a 39-day, yet unsuccessful, search—Congress finally cracked down. A relatively unrefined ELT, designed to activate after a crash and transmit signals, soon began to appear in small privately owned planes. Initially, ELT signals were tri-angulated by handheld antennas; they are still detected by special receivers installed in aircraft.

ELTs save lives; they are also frustrating. Most ELT "alerts" are false, created by pilots who fail to disarm the device when parking or who activate their sensitive electronics upon making a hard landing. Rapid SAR response to plane wrecks is crucial. Studies show that only 20 percent of injured crash victims survive the first 24 hours and only 50 percent of those not hurt live beyond 72 hours, mostly due to psychological trauma.

A satellite system for locating downed aircraft was proposed to NASA as early as 1957, and a patent for the concept was issued in 1962. Finally, in November 1979, a Memorandum of Understanding was signed by the United States, Soviet Union, Canada, and France for the joint formation of the COSPAS-SARSAT Program.

The Soviet Union launched its first SAR satellite (COSPAS I, the English phonetic spelling of a Soviet acronym meaning "the Space Project for Searching for Vessels and Aircraft in Distress") in June 1982, followed in 1983 and 1984 with one satellite each year. The United States then launched SARSAT I (SAR Satellite-Aided Tracking) in March 1983 and a second one in December 1984. These satellites bounce the 121.5- or 406-MHz ELT signals back down to earth-based terminals. These are credited with nearly 4,000 saves since September 9, 1982, the date of the first successful rescue using satellites.

In addition to ELTs, there are EPIRBs (Emergency Position Indicating Radio Beacons). Designed for small watercraft, they are the maritime equivalent of ELTs. The most recent advent of technology, however, and the one with the most potential widespread application to land SAR, is the PLB (Personal Locating Beacon). Intended to be transmitted up to commercially available satellite systems as well as COSPAS-SARSAT, the PLB is a several-pound radio, small and portable enough for backpacks, snowmobiles, fishing creels, or dune buggies. In 1997, there were 400 PLBs in use, mostly on Alaska's remote North Slope.

In 1979, the United States, Union of Soviet Socialist Republics, Canada, and France joined together to form COSPAS-SARSAT. This SAR satellite system has saved nearly 4,000 lives.

Now no longer mandatory, two-way radios were first required of all parties making a summit bid of Alaska's 20,320-foot Mt. McKinley as early as the late 1960s. Although somewhat abused on occasion during the seventies and eighties, for example when some "important" mountaineer would "cry wolf" or when a hiker in the Grand Canyon declared an "emergency" and then demanded assistance, usually in the form of a helicopter, the private radiophone saved numerous lives over the years. Technically illegal but tacitly allowed, boaters on the Colorado River in the mile-deep Grand Canyon routinely carried compact ground-to-air aviation radios for talking to a passing jumbo jet 35,000 feet overhead.

In 1997, Grand Teton National Park's veteran SAR and climbing ranger Mark Magnuson claimed that visitor reliance on the cellular phone is "the most significant technological impact" they've seen. And this sentiment is shared by all the other wild areas of the system. One of the earliest SARs involving the cellular phone experienced by the NPS took place in the Great Smoky Mountains on May 25, 1990. The upset caller had been walking "in circles" for hours after leaving the Appalachian Trail. At first the park's radio dispatcher thought it was just a crank call. Once he was convinced it was not, however, Ranger Bobby Holland was able to direct the lost person out of the wilds of the most heavily visited area in the National Park System.

INCIDENT COMMAND SYSTEM

The National Park Service is responsible for visitor and resource protection and enjoys a well-earned reputation for this competence. This obligation includes not only search and rescue but also law enforcement, fire, natural and manmade calamities, and special events as well. Over the years the NPS has overseen oil spills, presidential visits, plane wrecks, rock concerts, manhunts, earthquakes, and agency restructuring. These challenges are now managed by the Incident Command System (ICS).

Incident Command is a management system now universally used by emergency response agencies throughout the nation. Conceived in 1970 during the conflagrations in Southern California during which firefighters from more than 500 agencies had great difficulty working together, it incorporates common terminology and standardized resources (equipment, manpower), organizational structure, command, basic procedures, and decision-making.

Following the infernos of 1970, the director of the California Department of Conservation appointed a task force to resolve the problem. Out of that counsel came FIRESCOPE (Firefighting Resources of Southern California Organized for Potential Emergencies). Initiated in 1972, FIRESCOPE was a research project of the U.S. Forest Service; it had six funding partners: California's Department of Forestry and Office of Emergency Services; the Los Angeles City Fire Department; and the Los Angeles, Santa Barbara, and Ventura County Fire Departments.

The magnitude of the event dictates the degree and breadth of the Incident Command organization. The most complicated are Type I incidents—a complex situation in which resources must be drawn from all sources. Such international headline newsmakers as the 1988 Yellowstone fires and Hurricane Andrew necessitate such a reaction. Type II incidents are so demanding that they generally and quickly overwhelm the local, first responding agency; they include the same affairs as a Type I Team will respond to, but are of lesser size and reach. Type III and IV occurrences are usually handled by in-house, "initial-attack" resources.

OTHER ICS MILESTONES

September 16, 1972	Yellowstone, using "lessons learned" from the recent California fires, manages the Second World Congress on Parks with its several hundred dignitaries by proto-type ICS.
May 6, 1974	First NPS "Managing the Search Function" Course begins; employing fire protocols, it stresses incident manage-ment for SAR.
October 10, 1976	When a boy gets lost in Lassen, NPS fields first SAR Overhead Team, using men from several parks who have extensive large-fire experience. Dick McLaren is "SAR Boss."
November 16,1980	Yosemite employs a Unified Command for a major rock-slide that killed three people and injured six others.
1981	ICS is formally adopted by Southern California fire agencies. Santa Monica Mountains National Recreation Area also ratifies ICS.
March 5-7, 1983	Queen Elizabeth visits Yosemite; NPS uses ICS.
1985	NPS formally adopts Incident Command System as a management procedure for emergency operations and in February the NPS begins identifying instructors for ICS.
June 23, 1988	Shoshone fire is ignited by lightning and becomes first of many "Yellowstone Fires of 1988." At its peak, there are 9,500 firefighters, including 4,146 from the military, on scene as well as in 117 aircraft. Ultimately 25,000 people will fight the conflagration that will burn 793,880 acres in the park. Managed under a Unified Area Command with park ranger Rick Gale as Incident Commander, 14 of the country's 18 Type I Teams are deployed during the almost four-month battle. Cost of fighting the fires is estimated at $120 million.
March 24, 1989	*Exxon Valdez* oil spill; nearly 600 NPS employees even-tually respond when 11 million barrels of crude oil oblit-erated 1,244 miles of pristine Alaska shoreline. On-scene staffing and cleanup efforts will occur through the summer of 1991.
December 1990	NPS trains two Type II All-Risk Management Teams; Rangers Bill Blake and Hal Grovert are named Incident Commanders.

OTHER ICS MILESTONES

August 1991	Based on recommendations from the *Exxon Valdez* oil spill critique, NPS organizes federal government's first national Type I All-Risk Incident Management Team with veteran Park Ranger Rick Gale named as first Incident Commander.
November and December 1991	First deployment of NPS Type I Team; 50th anniversary of bombing of Pearl Harbor.
August 24, 1992	Hurricane Andrew strikes southern Florida; about 350 NPS employees will eventually be used in the NPS Type I Team response.
March 1993	Second national All-Risk Incident Management Team is formed; Park Ranger Bill Pierce is named as Incident Commander.
July/August 1994	"Operation Future," a downsizing effort by the NPS, is initiated; Rick Gale and the NPS Type I Team are used.

Having just exited a helicopter, a rescuer moves toward a "victim" on the cliff in this June 19, 1986, training exercise in Yosemite. For 15 seconds the rescuer is "caught" between the rock and the chopper. One mistake could be fatal.

NPS PHOTO

OTHER ICS MILESTONES

Summer 1995	President Clinton visits Grand Teton and Jim Northup leads NPS Type I Team to help manage the presidential vacation.
Spring 1996	Type I Team is dispatched to Mescalero Apache Indian Reservation to aid during calamitous floods; Jim Northup is incident commander.
Summer 1996	President Clinton vacations in Grand Teton and once again Jim Northup and NPS Type I Team manage it. Their detail is extended when the plane carrying Secret Service support crashes.
January 1, 1997	Catastrophic floods hit Yosemite; from January 11 to February 2, Zion's chief ranger, Steve Holder, leads the NPS Type I Team to assist in rebuilding destroyed infrastructure.

MILESTONES OF THE 1990s

June 26, 1990	Three NPS fire "Alpine Hotshot" crewmen earn both DOI and Agriculture **Valor Awards** for a rescue during a fire.
July 13, 1990	Forty people are killed on USSR's Lenin Peak—world's worst tragedy in civilian mountaineering history.
1991	Record year for NPS search and rescue incidents: 6,414.
August 15, 1991	A depth of 436 feet is reached in Death Valley's Devils Hole by Alan Riggs of the U.S. Geological Survey and National Speleological Society divers Sheck Exley and Paul DeLoach. This is a cave-diving record for the United States.
September 24, 1991	NPS Scuba Advisor Jim Stewart is made an honorary park ranger by NPS Director Ridenour and receives the **DOI's Conservation Award** for his leadership and assistance.
Summer 1992	Worst SAR season in Mt. McKinley's climbing history: 13 die, with 22 rescue efforts involving 28 people.
1993	Record year for NPS search and rescue costs: $4,700,142.
May 28, 1993	Stallone's *Cliffhanger*, set in Rocky Mountain, opens at theaters.

MILESTONES OF THE 1990s

June 3, 1993	On a training mission, Denali Mountaineering Ranger Daryl R. Miller is short-hauled (dangled 100 feet below Aerospatiale Lama 315B helicopter) from 14,200-foot level of Mt. McKinley to its summit at 20,320 feet—highest short-haul on record.
June 6, 1993	Illegal "landing" of 298 Chinese in Gateway National Recreation Area; 10 die and 288 are rescued, treated, and/or arrested.
September 1993	Paul Anderson, NPS Alaska deputy regional director, is elected for first of four terms as president of National Association of Search and Rescue.
November 2, 1993	British Royal Marines set a world-record rappel of 3,627 feet in a U.K. potash mine.
1994	Most climbers ever to attempt Mt. McKinley: 1,277.
July 3, 1994	Yellowstone seasonal ranger Ryan F. Weltman, 22, dies while on boat patrol on Shoshone Lake. He is the park's second ranger to die in the line of duty in 1994.
Memorial Day 1995	Lifeguards at Stinson Beach in San Francisco's Golden Gate National Recreation Area pull 38 people from a series of rip currents that developed when 6 to 8-foot waves rolled in the afternoon—largest single-day rescue total for the beach since the park assumed jurisdiction over the area in 1976.
November 21, 1995	Man filming a soft drink commercial bungee-jumps from helicopter hovering 900 feet above Bryce Canyon.
1996	From 1932 through 1996, 87 climbers have been killed on the slopes of 20,320-foot Mt. McKinley; 34 are still there.
	Record year for NPS search and rescue deaths: 297.
	Staff of Lake Mead responds to 332 SARs (176 boat), 442 emergency medical cases beyond basic life support, and 36 deaths.
	Thirteen NPS areas are formally certified as ex officio members of national Mountain Rescue Association.
May 11, 1996	ValuJet Flight #592 crashes 15 miles from Miami, killing all 110 people onboard. Five people from Everglades National Park and Big Cypress National Preserve are directly involved with the recovery efforts.

MILESTONES OF THE 1990s

August 6, 1997	Korean Airlines 747 crashes on fog-shrouded approach to Guam International Airport, striking the ground 750 yards from the NPS War in the Pacific National Historical Park. Approximately 220 people are killed on impact. Units of the NPS respond and aid in rescue efforts.
August 12, 1997	Eleven hikers drown after being surprised by a flashflood in a narrow canyon that empties into Arizona and Utah's Glen Canyon National Recreation Area. There are 29 NPS employees on the subsequent 10-day search.
September 12, 1997	While searching for a missing 73-year-old hiker in Olympic National Park, three rescuers die and five others are seriously injured when the helicopter they are in, crashes on takeoff.
1998	Only 420 climbers reach the summit of Mt. McKinley during the regular climbing season, a success rate of only 36 percent. The average stay by each is 21 days. Korean Kim Hong Bin succeeds despite not having either hand.
	Lost: A Ranger's Journal of Search and Rescue, written by former park ranger Dwight McCarter, is published about SAR in Great Smoky Mountains NP.
May 17, 1998	Craig Dahl is tenth person killed by a grizzly bear in Glacier NP since 1910. DNA confirms which bears ate concession employee.
May 26, 1998	Mike Vanderbeek, volunteer climber for Denali NP dies and is never found.
August 1998	Ranger/paramedic Scott Wanek is struck by lightning while on a high-altitude rescue in Rocky Mountain NP. He escapes with only minor injuries.
May 2, 1999	Glacier Bay seasonal Scott Croll and his pilot are lost out of Juneau, Alaska. Neither men nor their plane has been found.
May 19, 1999	Three British climbers are rescued from the 19,500-foot level of Mt. McKinley. Ranger Billy Schott earns **DOI Valor Award**. They perform a 10,000-foot vertical short-haul off of mountain, taking 30 minutes.
July 30, 1999	Hiker lifted off Mt. Whitney, high point in Lower 48 by Navy helicopter.
September 25, 1995	Ten people killed in a sightseeing plane over Hawaii Volcanoes NP. The Piper Navajo Chieftain is located at 10,500 feet of the 13,600-foot mountain.

April 29, 1990
Ft. Jefferson National Monument

CITATION

FOR VALOR
IAIN "AL" C. BROWN AND CAROLYN P. BROWN

IN recognition of the heroic acts performed at Fort Jefferson National Monument in Dry Tortugas, Florida, which resulted in the rescue of three fishermen from a sinking vessel in stormy seas.

On the morning of April 29, 1990, Park Rangers Al Brown and Carolyn Brown responded to a radio distress call from a vessel with three persons on board. The vessel was taking on water quickly through a large hole in its hull and was in danger of sinking. To reach the sinking vessel, the Rangers set out directly into the full force of 20–25 knot winds. Ranger Al Brown was at the helm and realized that any false move could bring down upon them the full and certain wrath of the 10-foot seas towering above their 18-foot patrol boat. Being washed overboard or capsized by the violent breaking waves provided a clear threat to their own survival. The likelihood of being found and rescued in these kinds of sea conditions was not reassuring. The Rangers reached the vessel just as it was about to go down. In violent, breaking seas, Ranger Carolyn Brown pulled the three men from the water into the patrol boat. Ranger Al Brown then skillfully maneuvered to allow a U.S. Coast Guard helicopter to lower a rescue basket to evacuate one of the men who was suffering a heart attack. For their courageous actions accomplished at considerable risk to their own personal safety, Iain "Al" Brown and Carolyn P. Brown are granted the **Valor Award of the Department of the Interior.**

Manuel Lujan, Jr.
Secretary of the Interior

July 14, 1990
Sequoia National Park

SECOND LIGHTNING DEATH ON MT. WHITNEY

THEY felt a buzzing through their boots and felt their hair stood on end. And then, along with the frightening electricity came the rain. Therefore, taking cover in the small abandoned building nearby that afternoon seemed prudent to the 13 hikers.

The two-room structure, solidly built of quartz-manzonite granite and roofed by sturdy sheet metal, has attracted thousands of "peak-baggers" since its erection in 1909. On top of 14,495-foot-high Mt. Whitney, this relic of a Smithsonian Institution science experiment is literally the highest point in the Lower 48.

Within 15 minutes the sheltered party heard several loud booms; the dim interior of the stone hut crackled and hummed. With a flash, a glowing basketball of electricity started to bounce from wall to wall. The favored ones, stunned for a few eternity-like seconds, received only minor burns, one suffered third-degree burns on both shoulders, and one went into full cardiac arrest.

Among the lucky hikers, one young woman carried a ground-to-air, two-way radio, insisted upon by her pilot-father. A Forest Service helicopter, notified by Air Traffic Control after they were alerted by a passing plane, was diverted from a fire 20 miles away for the dangerous landing on top. Bringing in rescuers and taking out the most seriously injured, pilot Frank Shafer made two more difficult touchdowns before it grew dark.

Rotating as they grew tired, the group gave CPR to the dying 26-year-old for almost six hours. Despite the heroics of friends as well as the daring of rescuers, however, Matthew Nordbrock was pronounced dead in a hospital far below.

Sunday morning brought two Air National Guard Chinooks, one of the few helicopters capable of landing so high. With a quality effort hallmarked by professionalism gained through years of teamwork, the Chinook crews successfully completed the rescue mission started more than 12 hours before.

Thirty minutes before Nordbrock was electrocuted and only half a mile away, another party was also struck by lightning. Hunkered down between the large white boulders, Terry Nabours was using a thin, metallic sheet of plastic to escape the rain. When he was hit, the 32-year-old stopped breathing—twice. Revived twice, he then somehow walked down 6 miles and 2,000 vertical feet before being evacuated by a fourth helicopter. Painfully suffering from ever-increasing back spasms at every step, Nabours was later diagnosed as having a fractured spine.

Sierra District Ranger Paul Fodor would later say that this "rescue ranks as the largest of its kind in the park's history. It was also one of the most hazardous."

July 16, 1990
Death Valley National Monument

LIGHTNING FLASHES GUIDE THE WAY

TEN minutes before midnight, Chief Ranger Dale Antonich and Rangers Mark Maciha and Terry Harris took a report of two visitors stuck somewhere on a cliff over Badwater, the lowest point in the United States. Complicating Antonich's decision to act that night was a murderous thunderstorm rapidly rumbling in from the north.

They interviewed a companion of the hikers; all three men were German and spoke little English. For some foolish reason the stranded duo had begun scrambling down the treacherous, 5,300-foot drop from Dante's View to Badwater only a few hours before dark. When last heard yelling, they were stuck 500 feet above the floor of Death Valley. The two wore only shorts and T-shirts, hadn't eaten for 17 hours, and had probably already run out of what little water they carried.

Because of the perilous perch, length of exposure, and the major electrical storm now overhead, the rangers knew that immediate action was necessary if they were to save the two men. Antonich, Harris, and Maciha started up the crumbly cliff; headlamps and lightning flashes guided their way over the rocky face.

A marginal route on the nasty cliff was made even more tricky by 70-mph winds, a deluge, and a dangerous increase in localized lightning strikes. Alternating leads as they ascended the slippery, almost living slope, the rangers found the way to be nearly impossible—conditions were life-threatening to everyone on the mountain that night. The rescuers stopped to think.

Antonich made one more attempt; protected by a thin lifeline, he somehow reached the victims and hastily readied them for their climb out. When a 200-pound rock tumbled from above, he shielded the two men with his body. Despite suffering a large bruise and narrowly escaping death, he persisted in guarding the Germans from falling hazards during the rescue. His efforts were frustrated by loose rock, heavy rain, high winds, and a language barrier.

After three frightening hours on the treacherous cliff, the three rangers finally guided the Germans to safety. The probability of the two surviving, had the rescuers not persevered that night, would have been low; floods would have flushed them from their ledge, or exposure and a rain of rocks would have taken their toll.

According to the citation presented by Secretary of the Interior Manuel J. Lujan, Jr.

> All three rangers placed their lives on the line that night, under dangerous environmental conditions and, in very rugged terrain, to make a successful rescue. For their courageous actions in rescuing two visitors stranded on a rock face, Mark J. Maciha, Dale J. Antonich, and Terry L. Harris, are granted the **Valor Award of the Department of the Interior.**

March 31, 1991
Carlsbad Caverns National Park

GREATEST U.S. CAVE RESCUE
SINCE FLOYD COLLINS

LECHUGUILLA is arguably the most beautiful cave in the world. Exploding with rare, fantastic formations—some previously unknown to science—the labyrinth, formed by hydrogen sulfide rising from oil deposits deep below, is awesome in every respect. *National Geographic* compared the 1986 findings in the cavern to having "just discovered the Grand Canyon in this day and age." Surveyed to a depth of 1,568 feet below the New Mexico desert, Lechuguilla is the deepest cave in the United States and, with more than 100 miles of currently measured passageway, the third longest.

To protect this world-class wonder while allowing for scientific and technical exploration, the Lechuguilla Cave Project (LCP), composed of dedicated cave researchers from around the country, was formed under the auspices of the National Park Service.

Emily Davis Mobley, a member of the LCP, was one of five cavers intent on "pushing" and mapping passage nearly 2 miles from the entrance and 1,000 feet below the surface. When the 40-year-old from New York squeezed down through the 36-inch-wide metal highway culvert that guards Lechuguilla's only known opening, the most heralded American cave rescue since Floyd Collins was set in motion.

After 16 hours underground and having fallen short of its preset goal, the weary team started out at 6:30 that Easter morning. Mobley, climbing up a 10-foot slope through a rocky breakdown, grabbed a block she had used as a handhold on her way in; the 70-pound boulder pulled loose and tumbled onto her lower leg. Physician and team member Steve Mosberg quickly diagnosed the injury as a simple break; there was no vascular or neurological compromise.

The subject of the deepest rescue in NPS history, Emily Mobley was lucky. The 173 people who struggled to help her during this intensely demanding, 91-hour rescue were luckier, for several reasons.

1. Her injuries were not life-threatening.
2. She was with experienced cavers/rescuers.
3. She was herself an experienced caver/rescuer.
4. A medical doctor was present when she was hurt.
5. Pain medications were almost immediately available.

The 173 rescuers used more than 9,000 feet of rope to retrieve Emily Mobley, shown here being pulled across a pit in Lechuguilla Cave, New Mexico. STEVE SONNTAG PHOTO

6. The passageway out was generally open and reasonably large.
7. The cave is largely dry, and at 68 degrees, relatively warm.

Using more than 9,000 feet of rope, the route out required more than 50 hauling sections. The magnitude and complexity of this mission warranted a Multi-Agency Incident Overhead Team with Big Bend's chief ranger, Phil Koepp, as incident commander. In addition to the National Park Service, the National Cave Rescue Commission, the Eddy County/New Mexico Rescue Service, the Bureau of Land Management, and the Bureau of Indian Affairs participated. The rescue of Emily Davis Mobley cost approximately $230,000.

May 5, 1991
Olympic National Park

CITATION

FOR VALOR
CLAYTON P. BUTLER

IN recognition of his courageous actions in rescuing a swamped kayaker in distress in turbulent waters of the north Pacific Ocean off the coast of Olympic National Park.

On the afternoon of May 5, 1991, Park Ranger Butler was notified of a swamped kayaker in the Pacific Ocean approximately 100 yards off shore in the Kalaloch Area of Olympic National Park. Ranger Butler was also advised that a strong current was taking the victim out to sea. Realizing that he had to act quickly because hypothermia comes rapidly in the cold north Pacific waters, he donned a wet suit and responded to the area. When he arrived at the beach, Ranger Butler realized the situation had been further complicated when the victim abandoned his kayak and attempted to swim toward shore. At great risk to his own life, Ranger Butler tied a rescue line to himself and swam through extremely turbulent seas to the victim. When he made contact with the victim, the victim was in the first stages of hypothermia and efforts at saving himself had become futile. Ranger Butler was able to secure the rescue line to the victim and both were pulled to shore. For his heroic actions with disregard for his personal safety, Ranger Clayton P. Butler is granted the **Valor Award of the Department of the Interior**.

Manuel Lujan, Jr.
Secretary of the Interior

On May 31, 1991, Ranger Clayton Butler received the **West Olympic Penninsula (Washington) Law Enforcement Officer of the Year Award**.

July 3, 1991
Denali National Park

\-

HIGHEST TECHNICAL ROPE RESCUE
IN NORTH AMERICA

KRZYSTOF Wiecha left his camp at 17,000 feet and headed slowly for the top, 3,300 feet above. Hoping to complete the round-trip in eight hours, the lone climber carried just a few extra clothes, one chocolate bar, and a liter of juice. Within sight of his goal and with little warning, the weather abruptly changed and blowing snow plunged the visibility to almost zero. Wiecha, quickly forced to bivouac without shelter or needed equipment, was stranded 400 feet below the summit of the highest mountain in North America.

Dangling below Denali National Park's powerful Llama helicopter, Valor Award recipient Daryl Miller is about to set down on top of 20,320-foot Mt. McKinley in a 1993 training mission.
STEVE GORHAM PHOTO

Ten minutes after 6 the next morning, Park Rangers Daryl Miller and Jim Phillips learned of the drama unfolding far above. For 48 more hours, sharp winds, 2 feet of new snow, and near-zero cloud conditions foiled all rescue efforts. Hope began to fade.

Late on the afternoon of the sixth, the weather finally stabilized enough for Jay Hudson to launch his Cessna 206; Wiecha was spotted at the 19,800-foot level—alive. Jim Hood, piloting the park's contract turbo high-altitude rescue helicopter, lifted out of Talkeetna and headed for the top of the continent.

Fearing that the marginal weather would keep them from landing, the rescue team first dropped survival gear to the solitary figure. Despite the vital supplies landing within 10 feet of him, Wiecha was unable to move to grab them, and the lifesaving bundle slowly tumbled down the icy ridge. As conditions improved momentarily, Phillips was cautiously landed at 19,500 feet; Miller soon followed. It was -15 degrees and the frigid, unstable air continued to gust. Flying conditions were questionable at best. Quickly climbing the frozen slope, the two rangers found Wiecha exhausted, dehydrated, hypothermic, and complaining of a numb foot.

Phillips and Miller swiftly engineered two directional pendulums to avoid a large crevasse system; three hours and six lowerings were required to get their victim to the 19,500-foot level and the waiting helicopter.

As the storm worsened again, the two rescuers were forced to make a dangerous descent to 17,000 feet. Miller and Phillips, faced with developing the potentially fatal complications of ascending too rapidly, remained trapped there for three days by hurricane-force winds and 4 feet of new snow.

The 28-year-old Wiecha lost both feet to frostbite. While most rescues require the heroics of many people, Wiecha is alive today only because Daryl Miller, Jim Phillips, and Jim Hood, without regard for their own safety, professionally effected the highest technical rescue in North America.

Park Rangers Daryl Miller and Jim Phillips received **Department of the Interior Valor Awards** for this rescue.


```
             August 12, 1991
     Glen Canyon National Recreation Area
------------------------------------------------------------
```

EIGHT SURVIVE FLASH FLOOD
IN 200-FOOT-DEEP SLOT CANYON

EIGHT members of the Berry family were reported overdue from a long hike in White Canyon, a twisting, uniquely narrow groove in the southern Utah sandstone. The party consisted of two older adults and six children ranging in ages from 9 to 17. All were in thin swim clothes, since the day-long trip requires a lot of floating through pools chilled in the sunless deep slot canyon.

At midnight on the evening after receiving the alarm, Ranger Kerry Haut and his wife, Deanne, located the hikers in The Black Hole—a water-filled cut often less than 4 feet wide and nearly 200 feet deep. The Hauts could communicate only by yelling down into the gorge. Declining assistance, the Berrys chose to stay put.

Early the next morning, the ravine "flashed" before the stranded party could move on. Ranger Haut sped back to the flooded canyon and found the family desperately clinging to the now slippery rocks. Up to his chest in foaming brown water, the elder Berry was balanced on a boulder with a death grip on his nine-year-old grandson. The 63-year-old later said that the two of them had almost been swept away several times, and that he had held on to the boy's trunks to keep the rushing waters from pulling the terrified lad downstream. Out of sight, the others were finally found clutching tiny holds on the smooth canyon walls; each thought the other had been flushed away and lost.

Ranger Kerry Haut, racing the forecasted treacherous thunderstorms and flash flooding, led a multiagency rescue. By 7:30 that night, technical climbers finished bringing everyone out, just as rain began falling again.

Summer 1992
Denali National Park

MORE TRIED . . . AND MORE DIED

DENALI'S 1992 climbing season broke two records: More tried and more died. Coming from 23 different countries, 1,070 people wanted to reach the summit of Mt. McKinley, 61 more than the previous high in 1989. Only 515 reached the top of the North American continent.

In fewer than 60 days, in what proved to be the most trying and intensive rescue season ever, the park's ranger staff conducted 22 SAR missions involving 28 people and 13 deaths. These operations cost the NPS $206,000, the military $225,345, and ultimately the taxpayers $431,345. They attracted unprecedented attention by the international media. South District Ranger J. D. Swed was featured in radio and television interviews, as well as in numerous newspaper and magazine articles, describing the heroic efforts of the rescuers and the tragedy of the injured and dead.

In a 10-day blizzard in early May—accurately forecast by the National Weather Bureau—7 people perished and 11 others needed saving in the "worst storm to hit the mountain in ten years." In a 24-hour period at the 7,200-foot base camp, 60 inches of snow fell while 110-mph winds battered those hunkered at 14,000 feet. The weather prediction and park staff's warning of climbers about the impending storm almost certainly saved scores of others.

This was the second year that the turbine-powered Aerospatile Lama helicopter was used on Mt. McKinley. In his second season, pilot Bill Ramsey was successful in a bold rescue—among others—of three Koreans at 17,700 feet on Cassin Ridge. For the first time in the park's history, "short-hauls," or live-slinging below the chopper, were used for extracting two Americans from the 11,000-foot mark on the East Buttress. This ship saved six people as well as probably six others who were near death.

On September 25, the town of Talkeetna, the jumping-off spot for most Denali expeditions, dedicated a memorial to those mountaineers who have lost their lives in the Alaska Range. Located in the town's small cemetery, the statue depicts two climbers making their way up a white pole signifying snow-covered, 20,320-foot Mt. McKinley. Between 1932 and 1992, 75 lives ended on its slopes; 32 of these are still up there.

Ranger Ronald Johnson was awarded the **Department of the Interior Valor Award** for his rescue efforts during his 24-day patrol on the mountain. He was involved in saving 13 people as well as trying to recover 7 others who were killed.

A **Unit Special Achievement Award** was granted to the Talkeetna ranger staff of Scott Beatty, Ron Johnson, Daryl Miller, Jim Phillips, Roger Robinson, Kathy Sullivan, and J. D. Swed for their contributions during these demanding months.

June 27, 1992
Lake Meredith National Recreation Area

SPECIAL ACHIEVEMENT AWARD

PATRICK McCRARY, SUPERINTENDENT

SUPERINTENDENT Pat McCrary is hereby recognized for his . . . dedication and services to the community of Fritch, Texas following a natural disaster which struck the town in June, 1992.

Superintendent McCrary especially distinguished himself following the events of June 27, 1992 when at least three tornados devastated the community of Fritch. He has subsequently been recognized by community leaders for his assistance in establishing an effective incident command system within the still standing park service administrative building and his subsequent coordination and mobilization of National Park Service and other rescue personnel immediately following the tornados. In the hours and days following the catastrophe, Superintendent McCrary exhibited a sense of leadership and competence which distinguished himself, the staff of Lake Meredith . . . and the National Park Service.

Equally important, Superintendent McCrary demonstrated a personal dedication to the emergency situation which has resulted in his being recognized by community leaders for his tireless personal labors throughout the long days following the emergency. His personal concern for the victims of the storm and his efforts to assist the people of Fritch in their struggle for recovery has also been recognized by individuals and the community as being above and beyond that . . . expected under these circumstances.

The National Park Service is therefore honored to recognize the achievements of Superintendent McCrary and is

pleased to present him with a commendation, and a monetary award, in acknowledgement of these accomplishments.

John E. Cook
Regional Director, SWR

Three documented tornadoes struck Fritch that evening, although some
people claim to have seen more. Most of the $50 million in damages was caused
by one cell, rated by the National Weather Service as F4 on a scale of F1 to F5;
it was 1 to 1½ miles wide. More than 300 homes in Fritch were destroyed, but
miraculously—thanks partly to the early-warning alerting of the town's tornado
sirens—nobody died and only seven people were hurt.

Among other well-deserved kudos, Pat McCrary received letters of appreciation from Texas Governor Ann W. Richards and U.S. States Congressman Bill
Sarpalius of the 13th District.

```
         August 24, 1992
          South Florida
-----------------------------------------
```

HURRICANE ANDREW AND THE NATIONAL
ALL-RISK MANAGEMENT TEAM

LEAVING a swath of destruction and death, Hurricane Andrew bulldozed its
way into National Park Service history.

Andrew was the third most powerful hurricane to reach North America in
the 20th century. Exceeded only by the 1935 Labor Day storm and by Hurricane
Camille in 1969, the Category IV hurricane was a "tornado 25 miles wide."
Small and intense, the fast-moving cyclone passed directly over Biscayne
National Park, plowed its way across the center of the Everglades, and then
brushed Big Cypress's southern tip. Winds of 150 mph and gusts up to 175 mph
were recorded before the Miami-based National Hurricane Center's anemometer blew away.

Damage in southern Florida was $25 billion; 123,000 homes and 82,000
businesses were destroyed. Of the 258 employees in the three NPS areas
affected, 101 lost their homes and 75 more suffered major property waste. In
addition to incalculable natural and cultural resource impacts, an estimated
$52 million in damages were sustained by the parks' infrastructures. "Tito"
Rohena, a Ft. Jefferson National Monument employee released from duty to
take care of his family, was one of the 41 people to die because of Andrew.
Anger, fear, and disbelief prevailed.

Once the magnitude of the catastrophe had become evident and the three
areas began digging out, the Park Service's first national All-Risk Management
(ARM) Team, an outgrowth of years of refining the Incident Command System
but only formalized the year before, was activated. Deployed only once before—
for the 50th anniversary of the bombing of Pearl Harbor—Andrew became the
team's first disaster mission. It would not be its last.

By all accounts, Ranger Rick Gale and his "Gray" Team—named for its aging cadre as much as to differentiate it from the soon-to-be-established second ARM Team—met its two top priorities: to mitigate existing personal and emotional trauma and then to aid the three areas in returning to normalcy. Although rotating in and out as the weeks passed, the Gray Team's initial command structure was:

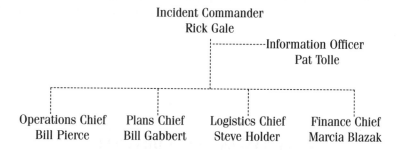

Incident Commander
Rick Gale

Information Officer
Pat Tolle

Operations Chief
Bill Pierce

Plans Chief
Bill Gabbert

Logistics Chief
Steve Holder

Finance Chief
Marcia Blazak

For more than three months, with the last of the ARM Team leaving on December 4, some 350 people—from scientists to heavy-equipment operators—had labored long and hard caring for the NPS family.

September 23, 1992
Yosemite National Park

WORLD-RECORD RAPPELS

A 42-year-old Colorado man died while rappelling off El Capitan, sliding mostly out of control for 2,600 feet down a nylon rope. The victim, who was attempting to make one continuous rappel, was not familiar with his U-shaped descending gear and had failed to properly adjust its metal spacing bars for a controlled, safe rate of drop.

This same single-line unbroken rappel was first successfully made in 1980. A group of 18 people, mostly eastern cavers, rigged a 4,400-foot Pigeon Mountain Industry (PMI) static rope to make the measured 2,649.3-foot drop. Taking just 17 minutes, the first descent was made by Steve Holmes on August 11.

Over the next three days, eight others, including the author, also backed off the top of El Capitan; seven of them climbed back up the same rope during that week. Although short-lived, the world records for both the longest rappel and the return trip were also set. BASE jumpers, legally parachuting off The Nose of El Capitan during that time, would fall past the cavers as they went up the thin rope.

In July 1982, with Steve Holmes once again leading, 13 men and 2 women set another world-record rappel of 3,250 feet. They lowered off the unclimbed west face of Mt. Thor in Canada's Auyittuq National Park on Baffin

Island; for more than 2,000 feet they never touched the cliff wall. All but two people used the 3-pound, 26-inch, U-shaped descending racks specially designed for this adventure.

Ultrarapid rappels were unsafe and unlikely on Mt. Thor because of a spot on the cliff where the rope rubbed the rock. The fastest descent for the remaining 2,800 feet below this point, using the 280-pound, custom-made, 5,280-foot PMI rope, took six minutes. Thirteen people on this team subsequently made still-existing world-record ascents—the fastest in one hour, 58 minutes, and 57 seconds.

October 10, 1992
Zion National Park

CHIEF RANGER'S MOST DIFFICULT RESCUE IN 29 YEARS

ANCHORING their 150-foot rope to a stubby, 2-inch-thick piñon pine, David and his two companions prepared to lower themselves to the sandy floor of Russell Gulch. His friends safely rappelled into the sandstone slot. However, the inexperienced 220-pound Salt Lake City attorney stumbled and slipped. Severely jolted, the shallow-rooted tree jerked out. Tumbling over backwards, the 33-year-old hiker fell onto a sloping, flat rock.

Having landed on his back and suffering severe head trauma after falling through the air for nearly 30 feet, David stopped breathing at 15 minutes past 3 that Saturday afternoon.

Among the dozen or so in the gorge that day was a physician. Detecting a weak pulse and with his victim's airway rapidly swelling shut, the doctor engineered a breathing tube from the handle of a plastic milk jug. Lifesaving ventilations were begun with this makeshift tool while someone scrambled out for help. At the remote trailhead, a locked government truck was found; breaking a side window, they used the two-way radio to summon aid.

When they received the urgent call at 4:45 P.M., rangers immediately requested the short-haul team from Grand Canyon National Park and a hoist-equipped helicopter from Nellis Air Force Base in Las Vegas, more than 100 miles away. Two hours later the huge Blackhawk, after picking up Chief Ranger Larry Van Slyke, orbited overhead.

According to Van Slyke, one of the Park Service's most seasoned rescuers—the steep, funnel-shaped ravine posed one of the most difficult rescue problems he had seen in 29 years: a four-sided, shadow-filled slit 20 feet wide and 150 feet deep.

As if he were slowly being threaded through the "eye of a rocky needle," Sergeant Tony Keller was lowered to the desperate scene below. Joining the doctor, the paramedic prepared the dying man for evacuation. As a backup in case David couldn't be lifted from the hole that night, four park rangers, including paramedic Sherry Collins, had also started in from the Wildcat Canyon Trailhead with additional equipment. Day turned to night.

Whirling just above the now-obscured buttes of Zion, the chopper crew effected their tricky task using Desert Storm–era night-vision goggles. With only a dozen feet of main-rotor-blade clearance, the hovering helicopter, once again rethreading the eye of the rocky needle, pulled a 250-foot hoist, the full length of the ship's cable. Although he still had a weak pulse upon arriving at nearby St. George 40 minutes later, David was soon pronounced dead.

The crew of the Blackhawk received **DOI Exemplary Act Awards.**

November 21, 1992
Hawaii Volcanoes National Park

THREE CRASH INSIDE ERUPTING VOLCANO

THE dramatic rescue of two Paramount Pictures cameramen and their pilot who crashed in the erupting Kilauea led to this letter to the editor in the January 10, 1993, issue of the *Hawaii Tribune-Herald*. It was written by J. B. Stokes, president of the Citizens Against Noise.

Fumes and acid rain generated by the volcano ruined two private helicopters and $30,000 worth of park equipment, including gas masks, breathing apparatus, respirators, and rescue equipment. The camera crew did not have a film permit since it was not expected to land its helicopter within park boundaries. However, it did pay for one of the helicopters associated with the three-day rescue operation. It is not often that the National Park Service receives such lauded, unsolicited appreciation. The small park staff has been coping with constant fires, lava flows, increased visitation to a dangerous area, special events held by native Hawaiians exercising traditional and spiritual practices, as well as routine park operations.

As long as we're on the subject of heroes . . . I'd like to mention just a few of my own. The Hawaii Volcanoes National Park staff, Hawaii County Civil Defense Director Harry Kim and his CD staff . . .

Special kudos go to NPS rangers Neil Akana, Robin Cooper, Greg Herbst, and Jeffrey Judd—four people who risked their lives for 30 non-stop hours in acid-laden fumes and zero visibility.

Several more heroes worth mentioning are pilot Don Shearer and NPS ranger Paul Ducasse (who landed inside Pu'u O'o under extremely hazardous conditions to rescue the paramount pilot on Saturday, November 21); pilot Tom Hauptman (who, with NPS ranger Jeff Judd, drop-rescued a lifeline to the last survivor inside Pu'u O'o during virtual "whiteout" conditions on Monday, November 23); geologist Margaret Mangan of the U.S. Geological Survey (for telling the rescuers what to expect once inside the vent); the Red Cross (for helping to support the command post at Kalapana) . . .

Finally, the biggest hero throughout remains NPS Chief Ranger Jim Martin, who skillfully pulled off this most impossible, worst-case scenario rescue effort without the loss of one single life. He accomplished this challenge with much grace and heart, and in doing so, garnered even more respect from his co-workers, friends, and the public.

As Big Islanders we must all learn to cherish and conserve Hawaii's most spectacular natural resource—Hawaii Volcanoes National Park, and especially those individuals and dedicated NPS employees who work in some way every day to protect Volcanoes and the other fine heroes mentioned above. . . . You've made every one of Big Islanders most proud indeed.


```
February 20, 1993
Craters of the Moon
National Monument
```

WINTERFEST

WHEN the severe winter storm arrived, the park's staff was preparing for "Winterfest," a day of snow-sculpting, crafts, cross-country ski lessons, sledding, sleigh rides, food, and search and rescue demonstrations. The storm brought 40-mph winds, heavy snow, and whiteout conditions for five hours.

Automobiles and trailer trucks were stranded along Highway 20/26, which passes through the park. The timing was excellent; because of the preparations for the festival, the entire staff was working and fully prepared for blizzard conditions. Hot food and drinks had been prepared, and the Butte County SAR team and sheriff's department were on-site with radios and cold-weather rescue gear anticipating the day's demonstrations.

Park staff and county units rescued a number of motorists and led them back to the visitor center. A total of 45 people were stranded there, since highways in all directions were closed. Until the storm broke in midafternoon, the park offered horse-drawn sleigh rides to the marooned visitors.

March 13, 1993
Great Smoky Mountains National Park

CITATION

UNIT AWARD FOR EXCELLENCE OF SERVICE
GREAT SMOKY MOUNTAINS NATIONAL PARK

IN recognition of outstanding organizational cooperation and team efforts demonstrated by the National Park Service employees involved in emergency search and rescue operations March 13 through March 18, 1993, as a result of a record snowfall known as the "Blizzard of 1993" which paralyzed the Great Smoky Mountains National Park.

A snowfall of the century, with sub freezing temperatures, began on March 12, 1993. It continued unabated 3 days, through Sunday, March 14, and deposited from 2 to 5 feet of snow in the lower elevations and up to 9 feet with 12-foot drifts in the higher elevations of the Park and throughout the mountain areas of North Carolina and Tennessee. Downed trees destroyed electrical lines, interrupted communications, and seriously hampered snowplowing operations to clear roads and initiated search and rescue operations for 183 visitors trapped in the campgrounds and along the 939-mile backcountry trails system. It would be impossible to list the individual acts of cooperation, physical hardships, and determined efforts that Park personnel and volunteers accomplished to provide support and assistance in the evacuation of visitors. Several employees cleared downed trees and literally shoveled their way out to report for duty. Deteriorating weather conditions of low clouds, fog, and plummeting temperatures exacerbated the life-threatening urgency of the rescue operations, dictating that rescue personnel work long, stressful days. It also increased the personal discomfort and danger to rescue teams in waist-deep snow on the backcountry trails. The blizzard claimed over 230 lives from Florida to Maine; but through the cooperative efforts of involved Park employees, assistance provided by the North Carolina National Guard, Tennessee National Guard, and the 101st Airborne Army unit, all of those stranded in the Park were rescued and evacuated without loss of life. The outstanding cooperative efforts of Park employees for the successful rescue operations were far beyond that normally expected and created long-lasting pride in Great Smoky Mountains National Park and the National Park Service. For outstanding teamwork and dedication, the staff at Great Smoky Mountains National Park is granted the **Unit Award for Excellence of Service of the Department of the Interior.**

Bruce Babbitt
Secretary of the Interior

```
                    May 11, 1993
               Canyonlands National Park
       ----------------------------------------
```

37 RESCUED FROM 23 RAFT WRECKS

OUT of the 54 private river-running permits issued for Cataract Canyon between May 11 and Memorial Day, 23 rafts and kayaks wrecked. Park rangers rescued and/or aided 37 people during this time. Another five large commercial rafts flipped, dumping an additional 19 people into the flooded river. Most of these accidents occurred on the Colorado's notorious Big Drop 2.

With the river flowing at 65,600 cubic feet per second (cfs), the highest since the 1984 record of 110,000 cfs, temporary restrictions were implemented on May 18 to prohibit rowing trips without a motorized support vessel at least as big as a 22-foot Baby J-rig. No single-boat trips were authorized, regardless of the size of the craft. In addition to these regulations, river rangers established a small camp below the canyon's Big Drop Rapids to assist both private and commercial boaters after they attempted to run this celebrated stretch of Class V whitewater.

On the afternoon of June 3, rangers recovered the body of a 52-year-old resident of nearby Moab. An experienced commercial river-runner, the victim had hiked into the canyon intending to swim the park's 13 miles of rapids. When found, he was still wearing a full wet suit, life jacket, and one swim fin. This was the fourth death in Cataract Canyon that year; two people are still missing.

```
                    May 28, 1993
             Rocky Mountain National Park
       ----------------------------------------
```

CLIFFHANGER: RAMBO ON A ROCK

OPENING on Memorial Day weekend 1993, Sylvester Stallone's film *Cliffhanger*—a good-guy v. bad-guy, dope-dealing, search and rescue adventure—was labeled "Rambo on a Rock" by movie buffs. Director Renny Harlin's $73 million TriStar blockbuster was set in Rocky Mountain National Park, although this "action machine" was filmed in the Italian Dolomites. Spectacular scenery, simple plot.

Good guys Gabe (Sylvester Stallone), Hal (Michael Rooker), and Jessie (Janine Turner) play members of the Rocky Mountain Rescue Group, a real SAR team in Colorado. After Hal's girlfriend slips through his outstretched hand and plunges 4,000 feet to an obvious end, Gabe becomes an emotional cripple and drops out. Guilt-ridden but soon chided back into action by Jessie, his lady and rescue chopper pilot, Gabe goes on to do battle in the frozen Rockies with "a megaviolent gang of thieves who are out to recover the $100 million swag they lost in a plane crash."

Cliffhanger's original premise, credited on the big screen to John Long—legendary rock climber–gone–Hollywood—had its genesis in a real-life

Yosemite SAR drama. On December 9, 1976, a 1940 Lockheed Lodestar, after having its 2,500-hp starboard engine fall off over the eastern Sierra, crashed into a shallow lake in the park's snow-covered backcountry. Packed with an estimated several thousand pounds of high-grade marijuana, the plane's treasure shortly became a prize for local entrepreneurs.

More than 30 "rock jocks," including climbing big-leaguers Ron Kauk and Jim Bridwell, labored on the movie's many action-packed scenes. Kauk, who stunt-doubled for both Hal and Jessie, and Bridwell, who helped orchestrate the film's many heart-stopping moments, were genuine key players in numerous Yosemite Big Wall rescue dramas during the 1970s and 1980s.

Joe Evans, Rocky Mountain National Park's true-life chief ranger and a veteran of the five-month Lower Merced Pass Lake dope-recovery mission, was given special acknowledgment in the movie's ending credits. Look at the film's Rocky Mountain Rescue Group brown arrowhead closely; it easily passes for the National Park Service's federally protected symbol.

And so, except for those who provided technical assistance for *Cliffhanger* or who were in the park at the time of the original criminal fiasco, there is little further link between fact and fiction. Because of the plot's origins, SAR theme, quasi-NPS connection, and several of the men involved in its creation, *Cliffhanger* portrays an interesting moment in NPS search and rescue history.

Commercial diver Bob Tostenson prepares to look for dope and bodies. The crash of the twin-engine plane in Yosemite's back-country was probably the seed for Sylvester Stallone's Cliffhanger *movie.*

NPS PHOTO

```
                     June 6, 1993
              Gateway National Recreation Area
          ----------------------------------------
```

298 ILLEGAL CHINESE ALIENS RESCUED

JUST before 2 A.M., U.S. Park Police officers heard a number of people calling for help from the ocean near New York's Ft. Tilden. Investigating, they confronted a madhouse of confusion. Dozens of illegal Chinese immigrants floundered in the surf; there were sick and dead people everywhere. Two hundred yards away, the *Golden Venture,* a 130-foot, Honduran-registered coastal trawler, lay grounded on a tidal mudflat.

Within an hour at least 250 police officers, 52 ambulances, four helicopters, and scores of firefighters were pulling swimmers from the 53-degree waters. When the epic drama was finally over, 10 aliens had drowned, 29 were hospitalized for hypothermia (5 would later escape and disappear), and 259 were in the custody of the Immigration and Naturalization Service.

Captain Tobin, the Indonesian skipper of the ship's 10-man crew, was taken into custody. Questioning revealed that the 298 immigrants had been jammed onboard the small ship for up to 112 days. Originating in Bangkok, they went on to Singapore, Kenya, South Africa, and finally to rendezvous with another ship in the mid-Atlantic. This connection never materalized, and Captain Tobin was ordered by gang bosses to proceed on to the United States. He stopped protesting when a gun was put to his head.

Immigration officials believe that dozens of such ships have delivered illegal aliens from China to the United States. in the past year as part of a multimillion-dollar smuggling operation based in Manhattan's Chinatown. It's known that these immigrants had to pay upwards of $30,000 for passage on the *Golden Venture.*

On November 10, 1993, chief of the U.S. Park Police, Robert Langston, honored members of the New York Field Office for their roles in rescuing the immigrants. Cited were Officer Daniel M. McFadden, **Medal of Honor;** and Sergeant Patrick Broderick and Officers Clay Rice, Grant Arthur, Barry Smith, Steven Divivier, and David Soma, **Awards of Merit. Lifesaving Awards** were presented to Sergeant John Lauro and Michael Lanfranchi, and the **Chief's Certificate** was given to Officer John Marigliano.

Additionally, a **Unit Citation** naming 46 officers, many of them recognized above, was presented to the New York Field Office, under command of Captain Tom Pellinger, for their assistance with the *Golden Venture.*

On November 22, 1994, Officers Broderick, Divivier, Lanfranchi, Lauro, McFadden, Smith, and Soma received the **Department of the Interior Valor Award** from Secretary Bruce Babbitt.

July 15, 1993
Zion National Park

TWO DIE—PARK SUED FOR $25 MILLION

NEARLY paralyzed, he watched his father swirl face down in the frigid pool only feet away. The horrified 14-year-old struggled against the powerful current of the narrow creek. Scant yards into the Mormon Church–sponsored quest, 37-year-old Kim had vaulted into the icy waters to free David; the trip's leader had a dangerously snagged backpack strap. But something went horribly wrong as two of the group's three adults whipped around in the foaming, bed-sized whirlpool. Kim died, not David. Tragically, in less than two hours, 27-year-old David would also suffer a savage death in the shadows of the rocky abyss.

One of southern Utah's most treacherous canyoneering descents, the middle of Kolob Canyon is a quarter-mile-long, water-carved gouge in the sandstone plateau. Some sections never see the sun; torturously tight, the cleft is often less than 6 feet wide at stream level. With walls worn smooth by eons of summer floods and winter melts, the 300-foot-deep gorge is steep. There are at least a dozen waterfalls, two of which plunge 130 feet before they vanish into shady holes below. The echoes bouncing off the walls and the din of cascading torrents make normal speech impossible.

Along with three leaders, the five teenagers from Salt Lake City were on a four-day scramble through Kolob and its more famous lower extension, The Narrows. In preparation for their adventure, they had been introduced to the basics of rappelling—off a stadium bleacher. Now, dressed in wet suits and with their water-absorbing down sleeping bags and designer jeans wrapped loosely in flimsy plastic garbage bags, they felt ready to challenge the chasm.

Although he had traversed the watery slot several years before, David was relying solely on being able to tie ropes to rock nubbins and rusty, already-in-place metal rings for the canyon's numerous drop-offs. The group carried no bolts or other artificial anchors for use in going down the water-polished cliffs. Even if they knew how, they had no gear for climbing back out. Once over the first falls and after pulling their nylon ropes down behind them, they were totally committed to the gorge. A fatal error . . .

With one dead and the team unable to retreat because of the short but unclimbable falls above them, they could stay put or push on. David, claiming to know an escape downstream, ushered them off the dryness and safety of a small logjam. After propping Kim up, the two men rigged a line to lower the teens over the next pour-off. The first boy over the edge was the dead man's son.

Half-swimming, half-standing, they were seldom able to even crawl onto the slick, polished rock to get out of the numbing waters. Wedged loosely together, each could shuffle only a few steps at a time. Bewildered and shivering in the humid cold, the seven struggled slowly on. After only two hours—and just 50 yards—they reached the fourth drop, a 15-footer; they had pulled their ropes irretrievably from the cliffs behind them. By this point, all but two of their backpacks were lost to the stream.

> From the lip of the falls, [David] tested the force of the
> whirlpool at its base, tying a rope to his pack and throwing

the pack into the pool. The pack got sucked under and could not be pulled free. [David] decided he had to try anyway. He wanted to swim the pack to shore where it could serve as a safety anchor for the others. He leaped in, and just when it seemed he had it handled, the pack slipped and the current sucked him under again.

David floated free, face down. In the decision of his life, Mark knew he had to remain with the five boys rather than aid a good friend. "It was very difficult," he would confess later. Since the party had signed out for four days, and with the two leaders dead within hours of starting the ill-fated trek, the six survivors would not be missed for some time.

Trapped between waterfalls, they were locked in an overhanging alcove not much bigger than a prison cell. With only damp wet suits to combat the constant chill of both the stream and the sunless hole, they were forced to sit with their tennis shoes in the cold, moving water. For a few brief minutes each day the sun would hit the far wall; the six would take turns standing in the creek at that spot to gather what little warmth and comfort they could. Terribly cramped, they huddled on small boulders yanked from the stream. The smallest boy lay across the laps of the other five when they tried to settle in for the excruciatingly long nights.

They quietly shared a few raisins, oatmeal packets, and what other meager rations hadn't been lost in the chaos. They prayed and sang hymns and used two of their three matches trying to light driftwood for a signal fire. The waters in the narrow stream in which they were trapped rose and fell. Four days passed . . .

Twice, a helicopter flew low and slow overhead. The boys used their last match on an inner tube, but they were too far down and the black smoke wasn't seen. When rescuers in the chopper spotted masses of colorful gear bobbing in the shadows below and then a lifeless form in a black wet suit, they at first feared that all were dead. And they may have been if the park's rescue team hadn't gone into high gear. Zion's chief ranger, Larry Van Slyke, was later told that if another night were to pass, one or more of the weaker kids would not have lived through it.

In January 1994, attorneys for the group filed for $24,556,813 in damages. This wrongful-death suit focuses on the park's role and responsibility in issuing the trip's backcountry permit. On June 19, 1994, the United States agreed to an out-of-court cash settlement of $1.49 million for the 13 claimants.

March 11, 1994
Shenandoah National Park

TWO EMPLOYEES INJURED
ON TWO SEPARATE SARs

SEARCH and rescue is dangerous; there is an inherent risk for injury and death every time one person goes to the aid of another. The following two SAR missions, coincidentally in the same park and on the same blustery weekend, illustrate this potential. Fortunately, the injuries to the two rangers were not far worse.

At suppertime, the park received a report that two students from a Smithsonian Institute Conservation and Research Center study group had failed to return from a data-collecting hike on the Knob Mountain Trail. The two women, ages 25 and 22, both from Philadelphia, had started from a roadside trailhead that morning and were to have completed the 2-mile circuit and returned by 1:30 P.M.

Indications were that both women were dressed appropriately for the weather. Afternoon temperatures reached the low fifties but plunged into the teens at night. Three search teams were deployed into the area. Snow cover ranging up to 18 inches hampered rescue efforts, as did numerous swollen streams along the Jeremy's Run Trail. Rangers located two sets of footprints in the snow around 7 P.M. and followed them throughout the backcountry area. After stalking the wandering women by headlamp for nearly eight hours, searchers found the two off the trail. Both were wet and cold, but in good condition. They had to be ferried across eight thigh-deep streams on their carryout.

During the search, Ranger Janice Pauley lost her footing on glaze ice and slid 50 feet down the frozen trail before striking a tree and suffering complete fractures of the radius and ulna of her left arm. She was evacuated and taken to a hospital.

At about 4 P.M., on March 12, a 55-year-old man from near Washington, D.C., was on the Appalachian Trail at Marys Rock Mountain, a mile south of Thornton Gap, when he slipped on ice-glazed snow, slid about 150 feet, struck several rocks and logs, and suffered a fractured collarbone and numerous minor injuries. The trail at that point was completely drifted in, with 2 feet of solid ice and snow on a 45-degree slope. A crew was called in to chop a trail across the frozen path; axe-edged firefighting tools called "pulaskis" were used to carve the way. The park's technical rescue team then reached, stabilized, and raised the man to the highway and a waiting ambulance, which took him to a nearby hospital.

While setting up for the specialized evacuation and before hooking himself in that night, Ranger Bob Martin slipped and slid 60 feet, striking a tree. He suffered ankle and spine injuries and was removed to the same hospital. Because of the two employee injuries in two back-to-back SARs during the weekend, the park soon reviewed its rescue procedures to improve safety measures.

May 21, 1994
Denali National Park

FIRST NPS EMPLOYEE TO DIE
ON PEAK IN 40 YEARS

ALMOST exactly 40 years before, after reaching the 20,320-foot summit of Mt. McKinley, Ranger Elton Thayer fell to his death at the 14,000-foot level. He is still up there.

Late Saturday morning, Kee-Won Kim, 27, an accomplished climber and volunteer on the park's eight-person mountaineering patrol on Mt. McKinley, left the team's camp at the 14,200-foot level. Along with his friend, Sang Myeung Lee, 25, he intended to climb a 75-degree, sloping ice wall on the West Buttress, the peak's most popular route. From Pusan, South Korea, Kim had been selected as a member of the patrol based on his considerable experience in the Alaska Range. He had reached the top of the highest point in North America in 1992 and 1993 and was on the very difficult Mt. Foraker for two climbs. After several Korean climbers died on the peak in 1992, District Ranger J. D. Swed traveled to South Korea to address safety with several climbing groups. Arrangements were made at that time for a member of their federation to join an NPS patrol to gain experience and pass knowledge along to countrymen.

Despite winds of 50 mph, near-whiteout conditions, and temperatures plunging to 50 degrees below zero, the two somehow battled their way to the top of the route around 16,000 feet at 10 P.M. After they failed to return, however, the remaining patrol members below began a search for the Koreans at 2 in the morning.

At 6 A.M., they found Lee's body attached to the fixed lines that assist climbers in moving up and down a steep, 700-foot section of the West Buttress route. He had fallen and probably died of hypothermia. There was no sign of NPS volunteer Kim, but searchers did find an ice axe and a section of NPS rope near the top of the fixed lines. Deteriorating weather forced suspension of the ground efforts later that morning. An air search was to be initiated as soon as winds and visibility permitted.

Poor weather on Monday stymied the air search for Kim. Although conditions were marginally acceptable early in the day, winds increased to near-hurricane force and visibility dropped considerably soon after the park helicopter and a fixed-wing aircraft reached the search area. On Tuesday evening, climbers discovered the body of Kee-Won Kim below the 16,000-foot level in a rock band between the ice-climbing route he had completed and the fixed ropes on the head wall of the West Buttress.

Kim was anchored into the snow and apparently had not fallen. The cause of death and the events leading up to the accident will never be known. His death was the first among park staff and volunteers working on Mt. McKinley since 1954, when Ranger Elton Thayer died on Muldrow Glacier.

July 29, 1994
Grand Canyon National Park

IT'S A DARN BUSY PLACE

AMONG the old-timers in the park, legend has it, the record number of times for launching the park's helicopter in one day into the nearly mile-deep, often brutally hot abyss to bring out an injured or ill person was 12 during a July inferno in the mid-1980s. Although the following is probably not a record for emergency responses at the Grand Canyon, this short summary was taken almost verbatim from the National Park Service's Morning Report. Provided by E. Brennan and written by Bill Halainen, it's pretty impressive.

Rangers managed seven separate emergency medical and SAR incidents in the inner canyon on July 29. Two people requiring advanced life-support measures were flown out of the Phantom Ranch area early that morning. Shortly thereafter, rangers received a report of a possible cardiac arrest on the South Kaibab Trail. While the victim was being evacuated, another report came in, this time of a 46-year-old man experiencing shortness of breath and chest pain on the Bright Angel Trail. Rangers who went to his aid determined that he was suffering from exhaustion and mild dehydration and helped him walk out of the canyon.

The next incident involved a group of stranded hikers who had run out of food and water while attempting to hike a difficult and seldom-traveled route along the Little Colorado River. During this mission, which culminated in the group's evacuation, a report was received of a hiker with a possible lower leg fracture about 2½ miles down the North Kaibab Trail. A litter evacuation and medevac were required to bring the victim to the Grand Canyon Clinic.

At 8 P.M., a ranger on patrol on the Bright Angel Trail was advised that a hiker had collapsed at about the 3-mile point. Advanced Life Support (ALS) measures were required for the victim, including oral and IV rehydration. While this incident was going on, dispatch received a 911 call reporting a hiker who had collapsed and was unconscious and unresponsive a mile and a half down the South Kaibab Trail. Rescue crews found the victim to be severely dehydrated but conscious and alert. ALS measures were begun and a litter team evacuated the patient to the rim.

August 12, 1995
Mt. Rainier National Park

TWO RESCUE RANGERS FALL TO THEIR DEATHS

JOHN Craver navigated cautiously down the dangerously steep, frozen face of Emmons Glacier. Four miles long and well over a mile wide, the Emmons is among the largest ice streams in the Lower 48 and the route of the first ascent of the peak in 1855.

"I had both feet down, took a step, and I was airborne." Craver's two partners, instinctively hurling themselves against the slope, watched as the colorful nylon rope stretched between them quickly snapped taut. The 40-year-old restaurateur, now 50 feet lower and only 900 feet from the top, lay with a crushed ankle. Erroneously reported to a ranger at Camp Muir as "shocky," Craver was in serious but not really critical condition that afternoon.

Sean H. Ryan, a 23-year-old recent graduate of the University of California, was a first-year climbing ranger with 11 ascents of the peak and was well qualified under the park's criteria for climbing rangers. Philip J. Otis, a 22-year-old Student Conservation Association aide from Minneapolis, had climbed Mt. Rainier once and had little actual experience on steep ice and snow. Ryan was very eager to go on the rescue and Otis was excited about being along.

Accompanied by a local weekend SAR volunteer, the two strong young men started toward the injured Craver at 7 P.M. Within 30 minutes, an ill volunteer turned around and started down to their base at Camp Schurman. The two park employees continued on into the night. They were tasked to climb to the injured man, stabilize him, and stay the night until a second rescue team arrived from Camp Muir sometime before dawn. Weather permitting, an Army helicopter would be "on station" early in the morning.

When Craver's two companions arrived at Camp Muir, they said that they had left him alone with all the extra clothes and food they had available. This led to additional concern that the injured Craver was now alone; Ryan and Otis kept climbing. At 11:25 P.M., Ryan radioed that they were near 12,900 feet, that it was cold and windy, but they were going to continue on. He also indicated that they were having a crampon problem. He said they could see where Craver was

The Emmons Glacier is among the largest glaciers in the Lower 48 and the route of the first ascent of Mt. Rainier in 1855. This climbing party is very near where Ryan and Otis fell to their deaths, circa 1994. MIKE GAUTHIER PHOTO

reported to be and they expected to reach the hurt man around 1 A.M. because the climbing was going slow. All attempts to contact the two men after that last transmission were unsuccessful.

Leaving Camp Muir just after midnight, the second rescue team reached Craver five hours later; Ryan and Otis had never arrived. Within hours the Chinook helicopter, with more climbing rangers to assist, evacuated Craver. In the meantime, the park's radio center reported that a climbing party had found an NPS ice axe and part of a crampon near the 13,000-foot level of nearby Winthrop Glacier. A thousand feet below lay the two bodies of the young rescuers.

In 1995, Mt. Rainier National Park saw four deaths and 30 SARs.

1995
National Park Service

LESSER-KNOWN SAR AREAS
AND THEIR EMERGENCY WORKLOAD

THE National Park Service experienced 24,663 emergency medical incidents in 1995, among which were 1,228 people needing Advanced Cardiac Life Support, 762 other Advanced Life Support cases, and 330 fatalities. Most important, however, the 2,509 formally trained personnel in the NPS Emergency Medical System can proudly and legitimately claim 619 saves: those people who would have died without the field care of dedicated NPS men and women.

Also in 1995, there were 3,725 SAR efforts in the National Park System. Areas such as Yosemite, Grand Canyon, Mt. Rainier, Lake Mead, Shenandoah, Great Smoky Mountains, Grand Teton, Rocky Mountain, Golden Gate, Cape Cod, and Denali routinely and justifiably received recognition for their hard work and heroic efforts. But there are others as well. The following are a few selected incidents from National Park Service sites not generally credited with much of a search and rescue workload.

Acadia National Park (Maine): On January 8, a 50-year-old climber fell 70 feet and severed his spinal cord on impact. After a difficult and hazardous approach, rescuers moved both themselves and equipment up a frozen fixed line and stabilized him. An Army medevac helicopter was able to winch the injured man aboard.

Voyageurs National Park (Minnesota): On January 28, at the request of the Ontario Provincial Police, park rangers directed the rescue of a seriously injured woman in a snowmobile accident on the Canadian side of the park's international border. After rangers stabilized the woman, who could not feel her legs, park pilot Scott Evans flew the park airplane to meet the life-flight helicopter from Duluth and successfully guided it onto the scene.

Kalaupapa National Historical Park (Hawaii): On January 28, three men in a small inflatable raft attempted to paddle out to a small island off Oahu but were blown out to sea. A Coast Guard search was begun, but no signs of them were found over the next four days. On February 1, a psychic advised searchers that two of the three men were clinging to rocks on the northeast side of the Kalaupapa Peninsula. Rangers searched the entire area but found nothing.

Obed Wild and Scenic River (Tennessee): Rangers and local rescue squad members were involved in two searches during the first week of March. The first involved a kayaker who had tried to paddle a river during flood conditions and was temporarily lost. The second involved a couple in a tandem canoe who were also lost but were successfully located upstream of their intended takeout.

Whiskeytown-Shasta-Trinity National Recreational Area (California): On March 21, the park was asked to look for two men who were overdue from a four-wheeling expedition into the area. Efforts were hampered by 60-mph winds and a subsequent blizzard and hailstorm. The next morning, the park received word that the two men had become stuck between two trees behind one of their homes and could not extricate themselves. They ended up breaking one of the windows and crawling out. In doing so, however, they managed to roll their vehicle down an embankment and into the creek bottom.

Redwoods National Park (California): On March 23, the park assisted the local county and Coast Guard in rescuing four overdue and very inexperienced rafters on Redwood Creek. Concern was heightened by unusually high water and deep snows in the area. The wet and weary crew was soon located and escorted out by the park's search party.

Dinosaur National Monument (Colorado): On March 28, the park was asked to assist in the search for three overdue and inexperienced river rafters on BLM's Yampa River, 9 miles outside the park. Stranded between serious rapids, the three were quickly located by helicopter the next morning, midway through the 3-mile-long gorge. One of the park's river rangers was airlifted in to assist them. The park ranger piloted the rafters' 1944-vintage, military surplus rubber raft through the worst of the remaining rapids. The rescue was paid for by the Colorado Search and Rescue fund, made possible by a 25-cent fee on all Colorado recreation licenses.

Upper Delaware Scenic River (New York/Pennsylvania): On March 28, an Alzheimer's patient was reported missing. After a hasty search by locals, the park was asked to assist, and a command center was set up in the North District ranger station. By the time he was safely found late the next afternoon, the operation had involved 120 people and included dog teams, helicopters, and fixed-wing aircraft to search the 50 square miles of highly wooded terrain.

Gates of the Arctic National Park and Preserve (Alaska): On April 11, Craig Johnson, the park's ranger/pilot in a wheeled aircraft, along with state troopers, began a search for four snowmobilers overdue from a trip into the park. One had tried returning home, a distance of 175 miles but found their cached gasoline stolen. Eventually, Johnson found both sets of snowmobiles and dropped them food and a radio before they could be picked up by a ski-equipped airplane.

Lava Beds National Monument (California): On April 17, a 27-year-old man became separated from his party in one of the largest caves in the park. After a six-hour search by friends and rangers, the man was found at the end of the cave, about 6,900 feet from the entrance. He had broken his flashlight and had become disoriented.

Guadalupe Mountains National Park (Texas): On April 21, the park began searching for a 14-year-old boy lost on a trip into the rugged high country; he had neither water, light, nor jacket. The expected high winds and resulting windchill would push temperatures from the thirties down to a very dangerous level. Guadalupe often experiences winds in excess of 100 mph. The boy, suffering from hypothermia, was later found after he had hiked 16 miles.

Mount Rushmore National Memorial (South Dakota): On May 12, a 12-year-old boy became separated from his school group on Harney Peak and was missing in the rugged wilderness immediately adjacent to the park. Rangers covered many miles of difficult terrain, and on May 14, located the boy's tracks in the snow. Seasonal Ranger Brian McMahon found the boy alive and doing well two days later, although he had frostbitten feet and hypothermia. With 8 inches of new snow, as well as cold and wet weather, searchers had had little hope of finding him alive.

Hawaii Volcanoes National Park (Hawaii): On May 21, two stranded hikers who had intentionally left the trail in an attempt to take a shortcut back to the rim of Kilauea became lost and began yelling for help after wandering around for three hours. Because of their inaccessibility and precarious location, a hazardous, long-line rescue by helicopter was required to evacuate them.

Rangers from West Virginia's Harper's Ferry join with local fire departments and practice advanced high line techniques. Historic Harper's Ferry is in the background.

REED THORNE/ROPES THAT RESCUE LTD.,
COLLECTION

Delaware Water Gap National Recreational Area (Pennsylvania/New Jersey): After spending the first six days of June looking for a 76-year-old fisherman last seen along a creek just outside of the park, the park suspended its search. Representing 38 agencies, more than 322 volunteers, dog teams, divers, and Civil Air Patrol and state police aircraft were involved in the effort. In November the man's remains were found in the park, but outside the original area.

Glacier Bay National Park (Alaska): On June 15, after tangling their fishing net in their boat prop on the Alsek River about a mile upstream of the ocean, two men swamped their small craft and had to swim ashore in the frigid waters. With neither wearing life jackets, one made it and one didn't. After an intensive search by rangers, the Alaska State Troopers, and the Coast Guard, the missing man was not found and was presumed drowned.

Big South Fork National River and Recreation Area (Tennessee/Kentucky): On June 16, rangers spent a long night searching for a 13-year-old boy who had not returned to his campsite. When found the next morning, he had covered a distance of almost 20 miles.

Gulf Islands National Seashore (Mississippi/Florida): On June 26, two lifeguards, despite a very rough and dangerous sea off the beach they were assigned to guard, successfully rescued three swimmers who were in desperate trouble. A fourth swimmer, later found drowned, had disappeared and could not be located.

Indiana Dunes National Lakeshore (Indiana): On July 1, an 11-year-old girl was lost in the surf of Lake Michigan. An extensive search was conducted by park lifeguards. She was found two hours later, drowned. In the meantime, the park was also looking for a seven-year-old missing from a nearby breakwater. Also at the same time, lifeguards saved another swimmer in the area. Because of the Fourth of July weekend and the excellent weather in the Chicago area, the park experienced some of its heaviest visitation ever. At one time, park traffic was backed up 20 miles.

Perry's Victory and International Peace Memorial (Ohio): On July 2, high winds and waves on Lake Erie caused eight power- and sailboats to drag their anchors and drift in against a park seawall. Five of the boats, which were repeatedly smashing against the concrete wall, had people trapped onboard. Park staff and personnel from several local agencies rescued 14 people.

Jefferson National Expansion Memorial (Missouri): On July 7, a two-year-old child visiting the arch with her family ran ahead of the group and fell into the North Reflecting Pool. A worker on the grounds heard the mother yelling for help, dove into the pond, retrieved the child, and cleared her airway with back blows, restoring her breathing. The family refused ambulance transport.

Great Sand Dunes National Monument (Colorado): On July 8, rangers learned that a backpacker was severely hypoglycemic and suffering from food poisoning. Rangers responded on horseback and foot; one ranger ran 4 miles to assist.

Evacuated by horse, the woman was transported to a hospital. At 3 A.M. the next morning, a report was received from her party of 10 that they now suffered from a lack of food and water. After a four-hour search, six were found. Two more were located later, having walked 12 miles during the night. All were dehydrated.

Mesa Verde National Park (Colorado): On July 10, while playing a joke on their students, one instructor pretended to be pushed over a cliff by another instructor. The teacher jumped onto a ledge, but then actually fell 35 feet into the canyon. He suffered a fractured hip and arm, two broken shoulders, and closed head injuries.

Blue Ridge Parkway (North Carolina/Virginia): On July 12, a 23-year-old man suffered a broken leg and head trauma in a fall near White Rock Falls. He was carried out by rangers and members of a local rescue squad and flown to a university hospital for surgery. He had been drinking extensively since the previous evening.

Chickasaw National Recreation Area (Oklahoma): On July 23, rangers saved a man suffering from hypothermia after clinging to a life preserver when his 14-foot boat sank in a sudden thunderstorm.

Cape Lookout National Seashore (North Carolina): On August 5, a 32-year-old woman set out to swim across Berden Inlet, a distance of 1 mile. Companions lost sight of her and a park and Coast Guard search, using a large vessel and three helicopters, ensued. Hours later she was located; she had been blown into open water.

Carlsbad Caverns National Park (New Mexico): On August 7, a 40-year-old caver was extricated from Lechuguilla Cave after sustaining broken ribs in a fall. It took 28 rescuers to bring the injured man out—1½ miles and 1,000 vertical feet.

Everglades National Park (Florida): On August 8, two park rangers in two airboats responded to a call for help from a team of four Navy SEALs embarked on a cross-country trip through the park. Flooded sawgrass, temperatures, and humidity were too much for the two sets of kayakers. Few visitors attempt to cross this remote wilderness.

Biscayne National Park (Florida): On September 3, a 36-year-old scuba diver disappeared in 60 feet of water from a party of four friends. A search, using park, Coast Guard, and county vessels; Coast Guard and private helicopters and aircraft; and Coast Guard divers, was begun. His body was found the next day.

Haleakala National Park (Hawaii): On September 5, a nude and inebriated swimmer was swept over three waterfalls, including one nearly 100 feet high. An intensive search was begun but was soon called off on account of poor visibility. At 4 A.M. the next morning, a resident 3 miles from the gorge called to report that there was a man wearing only one sandal sitting in his front yard. The bruised and scratched victim had survived the waterfalls as well as five hours in the shark-infested waters off the coast.

<u>Katmai National Park and Preserve</u> (Alaska): On September 17, an off-duty park volunteer was swept downstream while crossing a flooded creek just above a dangerous, unboatable sandstone gorge. Severely hampered by rain and wind and after an intensive effort by helicopters, airplanes, and dog teams, rescuers found no trace of the 39-year-old native of India. Her backpack was discovered 5 miles downstream of where she had fallen in.

<u>Buffalo National River</u> (Arkansas): On November 4, a 20-year-old man fell 20 feet at the mouth of a cave, sustaining internal injuries, broken ribs, and a punctured lung. He was eventually stabilized and carried down a drainage to a waiting helicopter.

<u>Washington Monument</u> (District of Columbia): On November 20, the elevator in the famous 555-foot monument malfunctioned, trapping 28 people in the shaft for nearly 30 minutes. Repair crews maneuvered the disabled car to the 280-foot level, where all passengers disembarked and descended the steps to the base.

<u>Arches National Park</u> (Utah): On November 25, a 13-year-old boy was running along the top of a sandstone fin when he lost his footing and fell 75 feet to the ground, landing on sand between two rock outcroppings, missing both by inches. He suffered open fractures of the femur and humerus and was evacuated by park staff.

<u>White Sands National Monument</u> (New Mexico): On December 5, two photographers became disoriented and began hiking toward the remote sections of the park and into the White Sands Proving Grounds and a highly dangerous area of unexploded military ordnance. They were eventually found after they had walked through 13 miles of soft sand.

These incidents were culled from the Washington Office of Ranger Activities' *Morning Reports* for 1995. They paraphrase accounts much better written by Delaware Water Gap's Bill Halainen.

```
                    July 20, 1996
             Kings Canyon National Park
     ----------------------------------------
```

VETERAN BACKCOUNTRY RANGER VANISHES

THE scribbled note tacked on the door of the Bench Lake Ranger Station, tucked on the remote granite high above the south fork of the Kings River, said he was going "on a 3–4 day patrol." Fit and gregarious, although somewhat moody, 54-year-old Randy Morgenson had long ago chosen to safeguard the solitary chunks of the Sierra Nevada. One of the Park Service's best backcountry rangers with 35 seasons—28 in Sequoia and Kings Canyon—was now missing.

On his last radio contact, Morgenson indicated that he was at 12,100-foot Mather Pass, an outlying but well-traveled spot above treeline along the Pacific Crest Trail. In the early afternoon of July 23, Kings Canyon District Ranger

Coffman was notified that his senior employee had not been heard from for three days. The Rae Lakes ranger was assigned to make the long hike to Morgenson's cabin on a "welfare check" of his comrade.

In midafternoon on July 24, Coffman, a paramedic and skilled search leader, flew into Bench Lake, and by dusk he, along with four other seasoned backcountry rangers, made plans to begin scouring likely areas at first light. Morgenson's patrol district covered more than 80 square miles; knowing that the ranger was far too experienced for something not to be seriously wrong, the search for him quickly escalated in this rugged expanse.

By the fifth day, 16 agencies; 94 people; five helicopters including 1 aircraft equipped with Forward Looking Infra Red (FLIR), capable of night operations; and eight dog teams were involved. Friends from around the country volunteered. With no clues and all reasonable spots in the huge, hazardous tract of granite and forest exhausted, the effort was scaled back and finally demobilized on August 3. The search was as massive as the area.

Incident investigators were assigned to follow up with friends, relatives, and numerous other potential leads. Morgenson was entered into the computerized national missing person's network. Bulletins were sent to law enforcement agencies, and notices with his photo were posted at trailheads throughout the area and beyond to inform visitors. His canvas patrol cabin was checked for leads, his handwriting was analyzed, and documents were studied by crime labs. Personal effects, including his pickup truck, were inventoried.

Hospitals, airports, train and bus stations, banks, motels, and other nearby businesses where Morgenson may have traded were contacted. Backcountry permit-issuing stations for the Pacific Crest Trail, from the Mexican border to Yosemite, were queried to determine who might have been traveling in the park during this period. Finally, almost five years to the date of his disappearance, Randy Morgenson was found in a remote part of the park on July 15, 2001, where he had apparently fallen.

October 5, 1996
New River Gorge National River

KAYAKER PLUMMETS OVER WATERFALL AND IS TRAPPED

At 4:20 in the afternoon, three people in two canoes and a whitewater kayak accidentally went over 30-foot Sandstone Falls on New River. Lucky to survive the plunge, two of the boaters were able to save themselves with minimal injuries. The third, however, became stranded in the middle of a boulder garden on a small rock jutting just above water at the base of the falls.

Over the next nine hours, a team of park rangers worked with local emergency service agencies in bidding for the life of this third victim before he lapsed into hypothermia and slid unconscious into the foaming torrent. Even though helicopters were en route, the closing darkness soon prevented their use.

Because the temperature dropped to nearly 40 degrees and the victim was constantly sprayed by water from the falls, the SAR team feared that he would be unable to last through the night on his sloping rock and would end up in the cold water. They also feared hypothermia, the darkness, and a dangerous boulder field through which the waterfall was channeled. With boats positioned downstream but not in line of sight of the victim, the lifesaving strategy boiled down to attempting anything short of causing extreme danger for the rescuers.

The roar of the waterfalls prevented voice contact, but lights were positioned on the victim, and some hand communication was possible. At the request of the park, the Army Corps of Engineers closed down its gates in the upstream Bluestone Dam, which succeeded in lowering river flow at Sandstone Falls just after midnight.

Two rangers were able to precariously move to a position at the top of the plummeting river and propel a rope to the barely mobile victim. Another ranger was then able to slowly force his way through the channel of water to reach the man and stabilize him to the nylon line. The hapless kayaker was then removed from his perch.

The entire rescue took place at night in an extremely hazardous site in the middle of the largest falls on the New River. With boats operating in darkness and personnel at the top of the falls, there were no further injuries or accidents. Fear that the victim would be unable to maintain a hold on the spray-shrouded rock until daylight had forced rangers to make several daring attempts at rescue, and the final try was successful. Because of the heroic efforts of the SAR team, a life was saved.

Dave Bartlett (incident commander), Cindy Bradley, Peggy Brown, Mark Carrico, Bill Handy, Jim Light, Mike Peck, Harry Perkowski, Kinsey Shilling, Donald Sledge, and Andy Steel were all SAR team members named in the **Exemplary Act Award.** Ranger Kinsey Shilling also received the **DOI Valor Award.**

December 14, 1996
Lake Meredith National Recreation Area

SHE REPORTED HER ENTIRE FAMILY MISSING

LAKE Meredith, north of Amarillo, is the largest body of water in the Texas Panhandle. Constructed in 1962 and contrasting spectacularly with its surroundings, the manmade reservoir lies in the windswept region for which the high plains is so well known.

As noon approached that Saturday, a severe cold front—a Blue Northern—roared out of Oklahoma. Those who started out on this unusually calm, winterlike day on Lake Meredith quickly saw the water whipped into 5-foot frothy waves by winds of 60 mph. Forty-one-year-old Robert Britten, an Amarillo dentist, called his wife by cellular phone and told her it was getting choppy and that he and their three young sons (11, 9, and 8) were finished duck hunting and were now heading back across the lake. He said they were okay and that once they had loaded their 14-foot aluminum runabout, they'd be home shortly. At 4:45 P.M., Mrs. Britten reported to rangers that her entire family was missing.

Park Rangers Pam Griswold and Carl Dyer were there in less than 45 minutes, in spite of the howling gale and treacherous "high seas." Before the day was over, more than 125 searchers were in the field. The body of 11-year-old Philip was reclaimed by rangers after dark that first evening, and that of Dr. Britten, the next morning. Still missing in the vast, windswept search zone were nine-year-old Patrick and eight-year-old Ben.

Most of the park staff's grueling search was conducted during blustery cold and stormy conditions typical of the area. On a few days, wind and waves were so bad that it was unsafe to send out boats and the area was scanned from land. Helicopters were used and fixed-wing aircraft flew daily for a month. Diving conditions were so dangerous that only those capable of working in the frigid, dark, and brush-clogged waters took part. Sonar search patterns were run and rerun. Scent dogs were brought in from as far away as Illinois. The shoreline was constantly swept and the brush-filled coves were scoured after each windstorm.

The body of Patrick was recovered on March 1; 145 days after he died, Ben, the youngest of the three brothers, was found on May 7. The search was the longest and most extensive ever carried out at Lake Meredith. The enormity of the tragedy struck a deep blow to the citizens of the Texas Panhandle and maybe the most touching for the staff of the park. More than 6,000 people attended the memorial service, and the city of Amarillo observed a moment of silence in their memory. National Park Service employees from across the nation responded by writing cards and letters to Mrs. Britten. The story made national news and dominated the local media until the last little boy was found.

August 12, 1997
Glen Canyon National Recreation Area

ELEVEN DIE IN SLOT CANYON

BASED on "scenic beauty, lots of deep and dark narrows, challenges of passage, and interesting geology," Antelope Canyon is described as one of the best hikes in the Four Corners area by Michael R. Kelsey, author of *Canyon Hiking Guide to the Colorado Plateau* and perhaps this country's most knowledgable canyoneer. Beginning as a small gully on the Navajo Reservation just east of Page, Arizona, and emptying into Glen Canyon's Lake Powell, it is a snaky, normally dry, 5-mile stretch of water-carved sandstone. Tortuously tight with some spots never seeing the sun, it is often less than 5 feet wide and more than 100 feet deep, with numerous short drop-offs requiring a rope. The 11 trekkers who died in the desert's gash that day were swallowed by a 10-foot wall of water, funneled undetected from a cloudburst a few miles upstream. They never knew what hit them.

Since the ill-fated hikers were swept away from the Navajo Reservation in Arizona's Coconino County, some of them even ending up several miles away in Glen Canyon National Recreation Area, a joint and coordinated interagency SAR operation was initiated. It ultimately involved 29 NPS employees, as well as dozens of others from the state and county, the tribal police, the county SAR team, and the Page fire and rescue department. Also employed were dog teams, divers, boats, and several helicopters. Once the first sweep of the constricted canyon was made, the mission became "weird, surreal, nightmarish, scary, unbelievable . . ."

This injured hiker, shown being lifted out of Arizona's snake-like Antelope Canyon in 1993, was far luckier than the 11 who were swept to their deaths in this same spot in 1997. REED THORNE/ROPES THAT RESCUE LTD. COLLECTION

The flood deposited up to 5 feet of silt and left a debris field on the lake, which formed an almost solid mat of compressed and entwined vegetation likened to wet baled hay. This refuse cover, up to 6 feet thick, floated on several feet of water, which in turn capped a second layer of flotsam. The surface of this thin arm of the lake was so thick and solid that full sheets of plywood were placed for searchers, divers, and scent dogs to work from.

Struggling through the rank debris involved searchers in full wet suits sweating in tepid water and chest-deep compressed matter, using handtools to cut through the filth and gloved hands to break large chunks apart to move it out of the way so that it would not fill in behind the divers and encase them. The heat in the canyon was extreme and the water temperature in the upper eighties.

Rescuers endured large numbers of dead frogs, fish, lizards, rats, and an unexpected amount of both animal and human waste. All searchers were required to take precautionary immunizations for Hepatitis A. When small spaces in the debris were opened and probed, the submerged corpses burst up through the solid scum, directly in the faces of those looking for them in the dark water. Thanks to the August sun, the warm water, and the added heat from the rapidly decaying debris, the bodies were already in an advanced state of decomposition. Even veteran rescuers, accustomed to bizarre and ghastly conditions, called the search in this narrow slot canyon "pure hell."

September 6, 1997
Olympic National Park

THREE RESCUERS DIE IN HELICOPTER CRASH

OLYMPIC National Park is nature at its grandest. Designated as both a Biosphere Reserve and a World Heritage Site by the United Nations, it is over 1,400 square miles of incomparable wet wilderness, a roadless domain of near-record numbers of spruce, hemlocks, alders, and cedars. In some places the canopy of the rainforest is so dense that falling snow does not reach the ground. In temperate valleys, carpets of moss, accented by head-high ferns, silence the footfalls of the few hikers who explore it. On rocky ridges and dozens of tree-less peaks, patchy snowfields dominate; glaciers cling to the highest. Some-where in this grandeur, John Devine lies unfound.

Considered a strong, avid hiker, 73-year-old Devine was last seen on the far northeastern boundary of the park, intent on wandering the densely wooded slopes of 6,797-foot Baldy. The week-long search for the local man involved more than 150 people from a dozen rescue groups, including several from Canada; five dog teams; a Civil Air Patrol plane; and five helicopters led by a Coast Guard chopper equipped with heat-sensing infrared. The search was costly in more ways than one.

At 4 in the afternoon of the fifth day of the effort, 35-year-old Kevin Johnston, a contract pilot from Oregon, poised his seven-passenger Bell 205 for takeoff. The helicopter, ferrying eager rescuers, squatted momentarily in the rugged, bowl-shaped cirque; mist intermittently shrouded the ragged ridges above. Ironically, just days before, the press quoted one search leader as say-ing cloudy skies and cooler weather made helicopter operations safer.

Eight people were onboard the chopper when it crashed. The ship had lifted up slightly and was hovering low as the pilot made his last-minute checks when it inexplicably rolled to its side. Massive, whirling rotor blades splintered, and deadly pieces of metal shrapnel shot out at the next searchers waiting to board. Three people died and five others were seriously injured in those fleeting moments. If it hadn't been for the quick reactions of those on the ground wait-ing their turn who dove for cover and then rapidly and expertly rendered life-saving first aid, the death toll could have been much greater.

In addition to the pilot, 31-year-old Taryn Hoover, a seasonal employee of Olympic National Park from Waldron, Washington, and Rita McMahon, 52, a member of West Coast Search Dogs, a volunteer search and rescue group from Aberdeen, Washington, died in the crash.

Was the crash due to pilot inattention or error? Was there too much weight for the ship to safely lift at that elevation? Could some piece of the multimillion-dollar machine have malfunctioned? Was tainted gasoline a factor? As of this writing, this terrible tragedy is still under investigation.

```
              September 24, 1997
            Glacier National Park
    -----------------------------------------
```

SECONDS AFTER JUMPING,
HIS PARACHUTE SNAGGED ON THE CLIFF

JAMES Kauffman, with some 50 parachute cliff jumps to his credit, almost experienced his last death-defying stunt that autumn day.

At 10,014 feet, Mt. Siyeh is among the highest peaks in the Northern Rockies of the United States. From its knife-edge summit, hikers, surely drained from a rugged 5,000-foot climb in elevation, savor almost every billion-year-old mountain in the park, as well as those in southern British Columbia and Alberta. Below, three of the park's 50 named glaciers can be seen. At the base of the peak's 4,000-foot north face is vivid-blue Cracker Lake. Beside these glacier-fed waters, one of Kauffman's ground crew anxiously waited for his friend to come flying off the gray limestone wall above.

With conditions perfect and a burst of adrenaline, the 40-year-old skydiver hurled himself over the lip of the park's fifth highest mountain. He counted to five and pitched his pilot chute from his hand. When he released the kite-sized device designed to drag the main canopy from its container, he mistakenly positioned himself unsafely. When his parachute jerked open, he was 40 feet away from the jagged wall, headed in the wrong direction. Before he could correct, Kauffman slammed into the rocky face.

Unable to control the drop, he struck the gnarly cliff, bounced clear, and fell free for a moment, parachute partially inflated. Kauffman couldn't turn around before again striking the rock face, this time smashing his right lower leg. He glanced off the harsh surface one final time, then swung back into the wall a third time when his parachute snagged above. He had stopped but didn't know for how long. With only three shroud lines and just inches of nylon keeping him from sliding to his death down the crumbly, 3,000-foot cliff, Kauffman was in life-and-death trouble. He later declared, "The seconds and minutes passed very slowly" while waiting for the rescue team.

After Kauffman's friend at Cracker Lake talked to someone using the same CB radio channel who then relayed the emergency call through 911 to the park, officials finally learned of the bizarre events taking place in their backyard.

Charlie Logan is a veteran ranger with hundreds of risky rescues to his credit; he will surely remember this one for years. After being flown to the summit, the experienced mountaineer, with Kim Peach assisting, quickly rappelled down 275 of the cliff's nearly 3,000 feet of vertical rotten rock. Worried about loose boulders striking Kauffman, the rescuer stopped 10 feet short and sized up the scene. Because he feared that the parachute would rip free at any moment, Logan quickly tied the now-safe jumper securely to himself.

Kauffman was cited into court; he forfeited his skydiving equipment and was ordered to reimburse the park for its $6,457 rescue.

May 24, 1998
Denali National Park

VOLUNTEER RESCUER
HAS NEVER BEEN FOUND

THERE were 9 major mountaineering incidents in Denali National Park in 1998 involving 17 climbers. The park spent over $181,000 for SAR activities while the military contributed another $321,500. Park staff, volunteers and several highly skilled helicopter pilots saved 8 lives. Some climbers did not make it, however.

Daniel Raworth was descending the icy, snow-covered ridge at the 16,200-foot level of the West Buttress, generally considered the easiest climbing route to the top of the 20,320-foot high Mt. McKinley. Every one of the more than half-dozen ways to the top of the continent is extremely difficult and poses its own unique hazards, even for the most seasoned mountaineer. There are many places on this ridge where the frozen pathway narrows dangerously down to only a few feet in width. Expert climbers proceed cautiously here and make each step very precisely and deliberately. Death is nearby.

During this month of May, weather conditions on the mountain were incredibly bad with winds often reaching hurricane force and temperatures dipping to 60 degrees below zero. This was the first time since records were kept that no one had reached the summit during the month of May and at the time of these two accidents, over 465 climbers were stacked up at various elevations on the mountain, all waiting to make the ascent.

To help manage the ever-increasing numbers of climbers attempting Mt. McKinley during the spring and summer, the National Park Service establishes a six-week long semi-permanent camp at the 17,200-foot level of the mountain, at the top of the West Buttress. This camp was within a one-half mile of where the two accidents had taken place and is temporarily staffed during the relatively short climbing season by veteran Mt. McKinley climbers including, often, a medical doctor.

At approximately 2 P.M., volunteers Mike Vanderbeek and Dr. Tim Hurtado had just finished a 7-day patrol at the 17,200-foot camp and were descending the steep ridge. Vanderbeek radioed Lead Mountaineering Ranger Daryl Miller at the 14,200-foot ranger camp from below "Washburn's Thumb," saying they had just witnessed a climbing fall.

Why Daniel Raworth, a 25-year-old Canadian from British Columbia, slipped and fell no one will ever know for sure. He tumbled and slid down the

80-degree slope, coming to rest on the shadowed north side of the West Buttress. If the young man did not die in the fall, his life ended soon after coming to rest on the ice at the 15,000-foot level. Even without an injury, survival under these conditions is tricky at best without shelter or heat.

Vanderbeek, a 33-year-old resident of Talkeetna and Outward Bound Coordinator for Alaska, requested permission to "take a look" from what he described as easy terrain. Miller, a close friend of Mike agreed but requested Vanderbeek return to the top and report his findings. As a favor to Ranger Miller, Vanderbeek had given up a paying guiding trip to help out as a volunteer on the mountain during this heavy climbing season.

Mike and Tim started to make an unroped descent off the ridge when Vanderbeek fell on the icy slope, 750 feet below the point at which Rowarth had fallen. Hurtado, who had quickly put an ice screw into the ice and attached himself to it after witnessing his partner fall, started screaming for help as their single park radio was still attached to Vanderbeek. Two climbers who had volunteered their assistance, Adrian Nature and Rowan Laver subsequently heard the shouts and rescued Hurtado. The three climbers then descended down to look for Vanderbeek, using ropes and ice screws. The day's first victim, Raworth could not be located until late that night due to the 80-mph winds and whiteout conditions. Hurtado, a physician pronounced him dead at the scene.

At 16,000 feet, the team was forced to burrow into the snow and spend the night in storm conditions. The next morning they ascended several hundred feet to the ridge and then down climbed 2,000 feet to the 14,200-foot ranger camp. The missing rescuer's pack had been found about twenty feet away from where Raworth had come to rest, but there was no sign of Mike. Some 45 people spent an exhaustive three days under horrendous conditions searching by ground and by air. Rescuers camped in snow caves during the worst of the storms and up to a foot of new snow fell on them. Although they found Mike Vanderbeek's equipment, to date, his body has not been recovered.

June 11, 1998
Mt. Rainier National Park

TEN CLIMBERS CAUGHT IN AVALANCHE

WHEN "Gator" overheard the emergency call on his radio he strapped on his snowboard; from the summit of Mt. Rainier it took the seasoned climber just 26 minutes to ride down 3,000 feet to the accident scene. During the mountaineering season, Search and Rescue Ranger Mike Gauthier never seems to be really off duty—even on his days off!

At 1:45 P.M., an avalanche swept two rope teams off "the nose" of Disappointment Cleaver. The first report indicated many climbers might be dead. Gator, quickly on scene and able to make an immediate size-up for those already gearing up below, reported that two separate groups with up to 10 climbers, were missing. The scene was extremely hazardous with 40-degree icy slopes, 20-foot vertical rock bands, exposure to more avalanches, and then a 300-foot drop to the glacier below.

Like a well-oiled machine, emergency operations for the park went into high gear. The park assembled rangers from Camps Schurman and Muir, Mountain Rescue Association volunteers, local guides and two helicopters to assist. Gator along with RMI Guides Randolf and Eichsner, hurried to assess the situation and bring chaos to order.

One group of victims was dangling off a refrigerator-sized rotten rock; the other clung to a cliff or dangled on a rope which was dangerously frayed down to its inner strands and pulled tight over a sharp rock held by just one anchor. Patrick Nestler, a 29-year-old client, had fallen substantially farther than the others and was below the rest of his group.

This avalanche was described as a "wet, loose snow slide" and only a small trigger was necessary to start the white mass moving. Senior guides said the area had no avalanche activity for over 20 years. The two rope teams were clipped into the same fixed line when they were hit from above. A wave of snow caught the first group popping two of the anchors. The slide continued, pulling the second rope team down the 40-degree slope. One guide and one client were caught on a rope above the cliff. Three clients and one guide clung to the top of the cliff, tangled in the rocks and ropes. Three clients dangled below them on a cliff of ice and snow, while Nestler hung beneath a second rock band. From above, a near-freezing waterfall of snowmelt covered the climber.

SAR teams were inserted on to the mountain's steep, ice-covered slopes with both Army and private helicopters. Some of the rescuers climbed to the accident site to assist with the raising evacuation while other teams headed to the base of the cleaver to assist with the lowering of Nestler. Rescuers negotiated the cliff securing the injured and triaging the patients. Most victims had combinations of serious hand and leg injuries, as well as three who were already hypothermic. Rescuers were racing the nightfall.

To get to Nestler the others on his rope had to be raised first. Then, the best way for him to go was down. As quickly as possible Nestler was lowered off the cliff, taken across the bergschrund and evacuated to the waiting Army Chinook where he was pronounced dead.

July 10, 1998
Capitol Reef National Park

MAJOR FLASH FLOOD INVOLVING 100 PEOPLE

CAPITOL Reef, proclaimed a national monument in 1937, gets its name from the dome-shaped or capitol-like white-cap rock of Navajo Sandstone, coupled with the "reef" of rocky cliffs which are a barrier to travel. The 242,000 acre park preserves the 100-mile-long Waterpocket Fold, a warp in the Earth's crust. Although the area only averages 7 inches of precipitation annually with one inch

This $60,000 Humvee was hit by a 10-foot-high wall of water in Canyonlands National Park in 2002. The occupants were unharmed after floating in the flashflood for nearly two miles.
PHOTO BY RANGER STEVE YOUNG

of rain falling in July, water is the major force sculpting the area. Summer thunderstorms and powerful downpours at any time are always a challenge to the park staff.

That Friday noon, a localized squall dropped a quarter inch of rain in 20 minutes. Within moments, sheets of water ran off of every rock and slope and serious floods began racing down through the normally bone-dry canyons along the park's Scenic Drive. Grand Wash, a popular hike for many of the area's half-million visitors, quickly became a river and flowed at a probably record level. Water was 12 feet deep and spread 230 feet wide where the canyon opens out near Utah Highway 24 and empties into the Fremont River. Culverts overflowed, covering the area's only major road to a depth of three feet and resulting in a three-hour road closure that backed up traffic about a mile in each direction. The Narrows of Grand Wash was twenty feet deep.

Park personnel from four divisions responded, evacuating visitors and their vehicles from the canyons and closing the drive and its three spur roads. A visitor waiting for his family to complete a hike was stranded in his pickup truck at the Grand Wash parking lot when flowing water surrounded him. The five members of his family hiking in the wash climbed to high ground and waited for the water to recede, hours later. At the other end of the wash, ranger Paulina Russell escorted three visitor vehicles out of the canyon, narrowly beating the flood headwall by less than a minute. She then held the cars in a high spot between two flowing washes until the next morning.

In Capitol Gorge, another group of visitors was quickly stranded. A midsize RV occupied by a German family was exiting the canyon on the dirt road as it follows the wash bottom and met this flood's five-foot deep headwall, head on. Brown, silt-laden water immediately washed over the hood of the RV, obscuring the view out the windshield. It rotated the heavy machine 180 degrees, and then floated the terrified visitors onto some rocks. Another 23 people in several vehicles had to wait at high points within this canyon until they were reached by a rescue team led by Lamont Chappell in a road grader. Flood waters reached 7 feet deep in Capitol Gorge. In all, approximately 100 people and 40 vehicles were evacuated over a seven-hour period.

The following day, a second thunderstorm struck. This time Sulphur Creek, normally only a trickle of water, flowed 8 feet deep. Twenty visitors swimming near a waterfall on the Fremont River initially disregarded rangers' warnings about the wall of water racing toward them, as it was sunny and 90 degrees at the time. Moments later, they learned the rangers were right and scrambled out of the way at the last second.

December 27, 1998
Zion National Park

LOWERED 600 FEET IN THE DARK

TWENTY-FIVE-YEAR old Vince Gonor and his 20-year-old climbing partner, Leif Enbertson, both from Corvallis, Oregon, were climbing near Moonlight Buttress in the park's main canyon, late in the afternoon. Gonor was a somewhat seasoned Yosemite Big Wall climber and aspired for a slot with YOSAR, the park's prestigious search and rescue team. On this trip, Vince had intentionally left his helmet behind but had insisted his partner wear a hard hat since this was the young man's first major ascent.

More experienced, Gonor led the way up the first 200 feet of the red sandstone cliff to a brush- and-rock-covered ledge. Reaching the first shelf, they shifted their vertical path a few feet and then headed up again. Although the pair soon suspected as much, they were on the wrong ascent route and not even close to where they should have been. By being so far off route, their climbing holds soon became more difficult to find.

In the next 30 feet, Gonor placed two devices for security. Ten feet above this last point of protection he slowly put his weight on a fishhook-like piece of hardware while trying to place a similar one above his head, and out of sight over a slight bulge. Gonor was not comfortable with what he was about to trust his life to. He had to either go up or down and finally committed to the piece with his full body weight. It popped out. With the sudden shift in weight, the hook he had been standing on also pulled loose and the veteran climber fell 20 feet, striking his unprotected skull against the sloping wall.

Knocked unconscious for at least 15 minutes, Gonor was now dangling upside down in his harness; he was convulsing and seizing from the head injury. Rescuers would be amazed at how much blood was lost. Enbertson was somehow able to get his partner upright and placed against the wall and then rappelled 200 feet down for help. Getting to the road and alerting a passing climber who had just finished a nearby ascent, Enbertson then climbed back up and proceeded to lower Gonor to their previous ledge.

At 6:15 P.M., the Zion technical rescue team was in motion. As Assistant Chief Ranger Dave Buccello would later say, "If it weren't for our team climbers Bo Beck, Karl Hammer, and Dean Woods, we might not have been able to save Vince." Gonor lay with a potentially fatal head injury, 600 feet from the canyon floor.

Buccello, a ranger and paramedic, ascended the lines which Hammer and Woods had fixed, and packaged the victim. Then, aided from afar by lights from the park's fire truck and the beams from their own tiny headlamps, the team lowered the litter 600 feet to dozens of waiting hands at the bottom. After roping the victim across the 45-foot wide Virgin River, the operation was completed at 3 A.M.

In intensive care for at least two weeks and on a ventilator for much of this time, Vince Gonor made a full recovery. In addition to the complicating factors of such a hazardous rescue at night, rescuers had to deal with freezing temperatures, wind, and rock fall.

February 6, 1999
Yosemite National Park

HER RESCUE ROPE WAS CUT IN THREE PLACES

SO intense was the rain and sleet, soil liquefied and flowed out from under their boots as they climbed. The headlamps on their helmets, half-filled by water blown inside their so-called sealed reflectors by the gale, had to be emptied. The team's two-way radios were almost useless; the voices squawking from them were distorted and hard to understand. Despite the near-freezing temperatures, sweat literally ran off the rescuers. Even so, each adjusted their 50-pound pack; each slowly inched further into the blustery gloom.

At three that afternoon, someone had finally heard Mitch Griffin literally screaming for his life. In two more hours it would be pitch black, even without the major storm now engulfing them. The 17-year old off-trail hiker was trapped and lay injured at the top of 300-foot-high Lower Yosemite Falls. In all of Yosemite, this is one of the park's most dangerous and inaccessible spots. The young man, caged beneath 2,000-foot high cliffs and suffering a broken wrist and a dislocated ankle, was terribly lucky he had not fallen quickly to his death on the rain-slicked, highly polished granite. Why didn't he slide into the flood-filled chasm at his feet? Go over Lower Yosemite Falls? Or succumb to exposure and hypothermia in the wet, near-frozen night?

Loosened by the torrential winter downpour, boulders rumbled and crashed down around them. In the dark and with the wind-mixing echoes, it was impossible to tell where the next rock would land. Or who might get hit. It was terrifying to this 6-person rescue team and hanging below them, Ranger Mary Hinson feared a piece of granite shrapnel might crush her thin nylon lifeline and plunge her into the watery gorge below.

Getting to Mitch was problematic but team leader Keith Lober would get it done. With the overhanging cliffs, it was impossible to climb directly to the teenager. The SAR team hiked two miles up the trail only to then have to descend 1,200 feet directly into the bowels of the Inner Gorge. To reach the river's edge required serious "down climbing" and about 400 feet of rappelling. Werner Braun, a world-class climber and SAR Technician, led the way as he was the only one who had actually been to this spot. Unroped, he clambered up and down the steep rain-soaked, brush and boulder-covered slope. Rock fall was constant. While Hinson was rappelling down, a missile shooting out of the dark sliced her rescue rope in three places, almost cutting it in two.

In addition to broken bones, Mitch suffered from hypothermia, his core body temperature dangerously reduced by the wind and water. After attending to the rapidly deteriorating youth, the team cautiously moved him across the slippery, algae-covered granite and readied him for the 350-foot drop to the dozen team members waiting at the bottom. Rescuer Mark Garbarini was attached to the stokes litter and he and Mitch were methodically lowered to the spray-covered jumble of rocks at the base of the waterfall.

Mitch Griffin is alive today *only* because of the dedicated, heroic, and self-less actions of the Yosemite SAR Team. On October 30, 2000, Rangers Mary Hinson and Keith Lober received **DOI Valor Awards** and SAR team members Werner Braun, Mark Garbarini, Jay Salvedge, and Jo Whitford each received a **DOI Citizens Award for Bravery**.

```
          May 2, 1999
        Near Glacier Bay
    National Park and Preserve
```

SECOND GENERATION NPS EMPLOYEE LOST

THIRTY-FOUR-YEAR old Scott L. Croll, just beginning his third season as a Biological Science Technician at Glacier Bay National Park, along with his friend and pilot David McKenzie, 51, were lost on a short flight between Haines and Juneau. Despite having been warned several times about the weather, McKenzie said "I can make it."

Scott was an accomplished writer and a published photographer as well as an avid climber, mountaineer, kayaker, and sailor—once helping sail a small boat 4,200 miles to Tahiti. Raised in a National Park Ranger's home, he began his all-too-short career in parks while in high school with the Student Conservation Association in North Cascades.

The small, four-place Piper Comanche was last reported over Berners Bay in the Lynn Canal, flying in a snow squall. It is likely the plane went down—either on nearby land or in the water—shortly after McKenzie's last radio transmission, since a call from another aircraft a few minutes later went unanswered. Numerous agencies and volunteers—including Scott's brother Perry—logged over 75 flight hours, focusing on the areas of highest probability between the two towns. Coast Guard and NOAA mapping ships participated, including using side-scanning sonar. Mountains and difficult terrain, heavy forest cover, and deep snows seriously hampered finding the two missing men.

Air and water temperatures, averaging in the thirties, greatly reduced survivability probabilities so on May 6, the Coast Guard and Alaska State Troopers suspended the search following several days of intensive air, water, and ground efforts. To date, Scott L. Croll and David McKenzie or their aircraft, have not been located.

Not long after the accident, the Haines newspaper wrote:

> On June 11, 1999, a sturdy little hawthorn tree was planted in Little City Park in honor and memory of David McKenzie, *Eagle Eye* reporter [the newspaper] and private pilot and Scott Croll who was a mapper with . . . Glacier Bay National Park. To choose a hawthorn tree was most suitable to remember the vitality each man had for life. They both contributed significantly to the lives of those around them. These two never met a stranger, friend, family, child, or new acquaintance that didn't know immediately they had met a kindred spirit.

Scott is the son of Ellen and Stu Croll, a 29-year employee of the NPS.

June 28, 1999
Grand Canyon National Park

NO TIME TO TAKE A BREATHER

IN 1999, the men and women of the National Park Service responded to 4,387 separate search and rescue incidents, involving over 4,500 people, including 195 deaths. That year, Grand Canyon National Park, which is generally considered the busiest SAR area in the system, handled 325 missions, including 85 heat-related incidents, and 8 deaths.

Despite taking extraordinary measures to educate people and to warn visitors to the park about the dangers of summertime heat, rangers at Grand Canyon know they will face a tough day when the temperature at the river and Phantom Ranch reach 110 degrees, which it often does. On one day in that summer of 1999, they handled the following:

It began at 8 A.M. that morning when a distress call was received from Crystal Rapids on the Colorado River. Surprisingly to the staff, the incident did not involve someone being injured as a result of a boat running the most demanding rapids in the park. Rather, the rangers began their day needing to evacuate a 47-year-old woman who was already suffering from dehydration associated with heat exhaustion.

A hiker called from the Hermit Trail Trailhead at the west end of the Village to report having discovered the body of a female hiker on the Tonto Trail, three-quarters of a mile west of Hermit Creek. The reporting party was camping at Hermit Campground and was out on an early morning walk when he came across the body of a 46-year-old hiker, soon learned to have been from Las Vegas, Nevada. She had run out of water and died of heat-related complications during an extended five-day trip in the Inner Canyon.

A 49-year old woman who was a passenger on a commercial river tour needed to be evacuated from Phantom Ranch. She was suffering from hyponatremia or low sodium, a relatively common heat-related problem associated with travelers inside the reflector-like walls of the Inner Gorge.

Two river parties advised Phantom Ranch rangers that they had seen a red tarp with a large "H" made of rocks on it near the mouth of Red Canyon, or Hance Rapids. A 51-year-old woman was evacuated with a knee injury. The "H" is a standardized symbol for needing assistance as well as often identifies the spot for a helicopter to safely land.

A teenage boy suffering from dehydration was evacuated from the Bright Angel Trail, the most popular route in the Canyon. He had stupidly attempted a rim-to-rim hike with only three tangerines to provide fluids! He reported vomiting 10 times along the 22-mile hike. His parents had dropped him off on the North Rim, then had to drive several hundred miles to the South Rim to pick him up. They are lucky to see him alive again.

A diabetic patient was evacuated from Phantom Ranch due to his inability to control blood glucose levels in the heat.

The two helicopters the park was using that day, each of which cost $2500 per hour to operate, were very busy . . .

June 30, 1999
Sequoia National Park

RESCUED FROM HIGHEST POINT
IN LOWER 48 STATES

FORTY-SIX-YEAR-OLD Henry Rendler of San Jose, California (near sea level), along with four other family members started the 22-mile roundtrip hike to the top of Mt. Whitney (14,494 feet) on a Sunday. They planned on spending three nights working their way to the top of the highest point in the Lower 48 States. When anyone hikes to above 10,000 to 12,000 feet, there is a need for the body to adjust to the radical differences in altitude and the Rendler party was well aware of this life-or-death precaution. Although they allowed more time than most to make the ascent, it would soon prove not long enough.

Luckily for Mr. Rendler, he was discovered on the peak's summit by an off-duty member of the Inyo County Search and Rescue Team at just after 1 P.M. He was disoriented and in immediate need of medical assistance. The off-duty official cell-phoned the sheriff's office in Bishop, who in turn called Sequoia National Park. Rendler's condition declined rapidly—an hour after the initial call he was incoherent, and in less than three hours, he was suffering from convulsions. Rendler had High Altitude Cerebral Edema or HACE.

HACE is a life-threatening medical condition that is a complication of going too high too fast. Symptoms include severe headache and mental dysfunction with hallucinations, bizarre behavior, coma, and ultimately and, often quickly, death. Administering oxygen is a stop-gap measure, but the only real treatment is to get to lower elevations swiftly.

Flying the man off was the only way to save his life. To find a machine capable of this extreme challenge required a helicopter powerful enough to reach this elevation in temperatures in excess of 100 degrees in the valley directly below them. Altitude and heated upslope drafts made it impossible for all but the most specialized aircraft to produce the tremendous mechanical lift necessary for both landing and taking off.

Launching from nearly 100 hundred miles away, the Vietnam-era "Huey" from Lemoore Naval Air Station arrived on scene first and dropped off much-needed oxygen and a litter, but could not set down due to the high temperatures. A California Army National Guard Chinook from Stockton was also en route to the scene as officials learned the victim was rapidly deteriorating. The crew of "Angel 6," recognizing the dire urgency and knowing if Rendler was to live they had to somehow land on the peak, stripped their chopper down to the bare minimum by leaving both vital gear and personnel lower on the mountain.

In what would prove a very daring rescue, the Navy was somehow able to land and more importantly, take off. Rendler was airlifted from the summit at 4:30 P.M. as he neared death. His breathing stopped several times and had to be assisted during the short flight to nearby Lone Pine, 10,000 feet lower. Stabilized there by hospital staff, the very sick man was then flown by a pressurized airplane to more advanced treatment. Despite being but minutes from dying, Henry Rendler is alive today due to the cooperation and heroic efforts of all individuals involved including the Inyo County Sheriff's Office, Lemoore Naval Air Station, California Army National Guard, and Sequoia National Park.

December 30, 1999
Near Canyonlands National Park

PARACHUTIST SNAGS ON OVERHANGING CLIFF

MARILYN (Mari) Schroering, a recent graduate of the Air Force Academy and now a 24-year-old C-130 military pilot, was making her fourth BASE jump of the day. BASE stands for Building, Antenna, Span, and Earth and down through the years has been tried in at least 12 units of the National Park System. Illegal within Canyonlands National Park near Moab, Utah, it is permissible on lands adjacent to the park and the scene of this accident. This was the tenth BASE jump of her career and all seemed to be going well as she confidently launched herself off the 500-foot high overhanging sandstone cliff.

Upon opening the specially engineered parachute, Schroering mistakenly turned the wrong way and quickly slammed into the cliff. Her nylon canopy collapsed over a sharp, sofa-sized rock and she now dangled 270 feet from the top of the red wall. She was tangled in the cords from her equipment, with one leg bent painfully upwards to her shoulder. Her two-inch wide chest harness was pressed against her throat and she could barely breathe. Until she was rescued eight hours later, she'd muscle herself up on the chute's thin lines every few moments for a count of four or five and take as many quick, deep breaths as she could and then slowly lower herself back into the same very awkward position. Any sudden jerking on her part could plunge her to the bottom, 250 feet below.

The rescue was run as a joint operation between the park and Grand County Search and Rescue. Due to the close working relationship between the local sheriff's department and rangers—where each agency must rely on the other in this relatively isolated section of Southern Utah—this kind of cooperation is routine and born of necessity.

Schroering was now trapped beneath an overhanging roof and halfway down the 500-foot cliff; it was impossible to reach her from below. Anyone getting to her would need to dangle in mid air and would somehow have to work their way onto the more-than-vertical cliff face, 25 feet away. Initially, a rescuer rappelled down to her but she and the cliff proved impossible to reach. Rather than rappel, Ranger George Paiva was lowered to a spot 25 feet out from Mari; he dangled in mid air 250 above the rocks below.

Paiva assessed this precarious situation, now compounded by darkness and cold. A ranger with strong technical rescue skills, he somehow got a rope to the terrified woman. Once to her, he clipped himself to her harness and then with a knife cautiously cut her loose of her parachute. Most importantly, this freed her from the webbing which was suffocating her. She now hung suspended from his climbing rig. Repeatedly she sobbed, "I don't want to die." Slowly and efficiently, the team at the top raised the pair to safety.

After the mission was over, Frank Mendonaca, Commander of Grand County Search and Rescue, an organization which routinely completes challenging rescue operations, stated this was the most difficult technical rescue he had ever been involved with. On September 4, 2002, Canyonlands National Park Ranger George Paiva was awarded the **Department Of Interior's Valor Award**.

BASE jumper Mari Schroering (in kneepads in center) moments after being lifted to the top of the 500-foot cliff she was snagged on.

PHOTO BY RANGER LARRY VAN SLYKE

Grand Canyon National Park SAR helicopter crashed on the park's North Rim on October 16, 2003. Everyone walked away form the accident. GRAND CANYON NATIONAL PARK PHOTO ARCHIVES

```
Flags should be flown at half-staff
immediately until further notice.
```

—Director Fran Mainella,
September 11, 2001

NATIONAL PARK SERVICE RESPONDS TO TERRORISM

The National Park Service and its employees answered the September 11, 2001, "Attack on America" in an unprecedented fashion. Four minutes after the jetliner struck the Pentagon, both "Eagle 1" and "Eagle 2" were over the burning building. The two are part of the United States Park Police fleet of five helicopters based in Washington, DC.

Moments later, the Pentagon's Air Traffic Control directed Eagle 1 to assume control of the air space around the Pentagon after heavy smoke from the crash site forced the abandonment of their nearby tower. Eagle 2 quickly landed to assist the now-arriving fire and military medical personnel with loading the most seriously injured. They flew the first two victims away from the Pentagon and to a local hospital. While circling overhead and directing rescue efforts from the air, Eagle 1 began to provide immediate, live downlink video images to federal, state, and local emergency command posts now mobilizing.

From her office within sight of the Pentagon, National Park Service Director Fran Mainella quickly pledged full support of the agency's resources and within hours, both the service's National Type I Incident Management Team and United States Park Police Chief's Command Post were activated, overseeing an immediate and unified response: "Operation Secure Parks." In addition to the immediate emergency assistance provided by NPS personnel, the safety of our country's greatest symbols of freedom, such as the Statue of Liberty, Liberty Bell, White House, Mt. Rushmore, USS *Arizona*, Lincoln Memorial, the Arch in St. Louis, and Washington Monument, became paramount.

Many of the United States Park Police officers at the New York Field Office witnessed the attack and within minutes of the first plane striking the Tower One, they responded. Marine Patrol vessels were sent immediately from Gateway National Recreation Area to the Statue of Liberty and were on scene within 20 minutes, enforcing a security zone around the island. Officers on Liberty Island began an immediate evacuation of visitors.

The second jet passed directly over Liberty and Ellis Islands, striking the Tower Two. All off-duty NPS personnel were recalled and Liberty Island was cleared of all staff and residents. A detail of Park Police officers responded to

Federal Hall (three blocks from Ground Zero) to secure the site; it ended up being a refuge by approximately 150 people fleeing the nightmare of the falling towers. Others went to guard the critical Verazzano Bridge as well as Fort Wadsworth which houses the U.S. Coast Guard Command Center for New York Harbor. When Tower Two collapsed, a medical triage center was established on Ellis Island. Service staff provided assistance and emergency aid to over 100 wounded, now trickling in from the Trade Center area.

That first day, national parks in New York City, Boston, Philadelphia, and Washington, D.C. closed down as soon as the threat was recognized. The Park Police provided escorts to both the President and the Secretary of State as well as evacuated the Secretary of the Interior and the Director of the NPS. For 14 days, the Park Police helicopters provided around-the-clock aerial security to the nation's capital.

Rangers and other Service staff mobilized on the National Mall, the home of American icons like the Washington Monument and Lincoln Memorial, and began to guard them. Boat crews from Fire Island National Seashore transported firefighters from New Jersey to aid at the Twin Tower crash site. Rangers from Gateway National Recreation Area were dispatched to control crowds forming along the Sandy Hook shoreline to view the altered New York City skyline. Teams of rangers also provided support and eventual evacuation of at least 50 children from the Pentagon's Day Care Center.

All across America, the National Park Service provided critical assistance. Rangers in Florida secured beaches to safeguard the Space Shuttle and performed perimeter control for a nuclear power plant. In Hawaii, they controlled a road to a vital radar site for the Federal Aviation Administration. Fort Point National Historic Site was temporarily closed down due to its proximity to the Golden Gate Bridge. Twenty-four hours a day, rangers guarded (and still do) 8 of this country's largest dams including Hoover, Glen Canyon, Shasta, and Coulee. They worked with the FEMA in New Jersey, New York, and Washington, D.C., and soon were asked to be Sky Marshals.

During the first year following the attack, one-third of the agency's 1,500 law enforcement rangers saw duty outside their park. At any given time, even at the end of 2004, approximately 80 rangers were still away from home, assigned to nearly 20 high-risk sites around the country including strategic dams; the president's retreat at Camp David; and the Main Interior Building in Washington, D.C.

A further reflection of this country's concern for preparedness was the service's role in the XIX Winter Olympics in Salt Lake City in 2002. Approximately 150 employees spent 17 days providing security and visitor information. At the request of the Secret Service, 100 law enforcement rangers with winter and snow expertise assisted with perimeter control in the rugged settings of four outdoor athletic venues. They often worked the midnight shift, traveling by ski, snowshoe, and snowmobile.

Rangers were well recognized for their expertise by both the Secret Service and officials of the Olympics. The national news routinely spotlighted this winter and snow prowess as well as routinely gave credit to those men and women who provided a quality interpretive contact at the Games' visitor centers and information booths.

MILESTONES OF THE 2000s

2000	There are 4,869 SAR incidents in NPS, up 482 from 1999.
January 31, 2000	Alaska Airline flight #261 crashes off Anacapa Island, killing all 88 people on board. Channel Islands NP responds.
March 29–30, 2000	Lifeguards at San Francisco's Golden Gate NRA made 23 surf rescues.
April 5, 2000	Kieran Burke was last seen in Curry Village. He was never found. There have been at least 27 people lost and never seen again in Yosemite National Park.
June–July 2000	Rangers in Rocky Mountain NP conduct six major technical rescues in 19 days, including one death from falling 600 feet.
November 11, 2000	Park Police Eagle Two short-hauled worker from a 200-foot high phone tower in Virginia.
April 30, 2001	Park responds to a Personal Locator Beacon activated because a skier was merely feeling "anxious" and wanted out of the backcountry of Wrangell-St. Elias NP.
July 8, 2001	Park Police search for and locate an Alzheimer's patient at the Vietnam Veterans Memorial in Washington, DC.
September 11, 2001	NPS responds to "Attack on America" in unprecedented fashion.
November 12, 2001	Grand Canyon NP firefighters detailed to a fire in Kentucky save the life of a helicopter pilot who had crashed and was trapped. Both earn **DOI Valor Awards**.
December 3, 2001	185 Haitian illegal immigrants run aground in Florida's Biscayne NP, 39 had to be rescued from the surf. This was the second such incident in less than a week.
2002	*Submerged: Adventures of America's Most Elite Underwater Archeology Team*, written by retired ranger Daniel Lenihan, chief of the NPS Submerged Cultural Resources Unit is published. During his career, Dan was involved in many underwater SARs.
April 6, 2002	Four people killed in a plane wreck in Sequoia National Park. The search lasts five days. One passenger onboard as a birthday present from his parents.

MILESTONES OF THE 2000s

April 15, 2002	Winds gust over 91 mph on Lake Mead, creating havoc for boaters with several boats sinking and at least 7 people needing rescuing by helicopter.
July 25, 2002	Thunderstorm dumps 1 inch of rain in Capitol Reef NP in just a few minutes. The park only received 1.63 inches in their "water year." The average is 7 inches.
January 29, 2003	A victim of 1992's Hurricane Andrew is found in Biscayne NP.
February 2003	NPS from park areas spend weeks searching for pieces of shuttle Columbia.
May 1, 2003	Aron Ralston amputates his arm near Canyonlands NP; it's recovered on May 4.
October 2003	Hurricane Isabel strikes East Coast. At one time over 250 NPS staffers are in cleanup of at 27 NPS areas "hit." Cape Hatteras NS suffers $28 million in damages.
October 16, 2003	Used on hundreds of rescues, Grand Canyon NP's McDonnell Douglas 900 Explorer (no tail rotor) helicopter, crashed on a fire recon.
2004	*High Country,* written by former ranger Nevada Barr, is published. Her heroine, Ranger Anna Pigeon, is involved in a crime with backdrop of a plane crash in backcountry of Yosemite NP. Story is based on real events in park in 1976–77.
May 2, 2004	SAR legend, retired ranger Doug McLaren dies; he gave 40 years to NPS.
June 8, 2004	Sequoia/Kings Canyon NPs performs first actual shorthaul rescue for employee injured in Tehipite Valley, a remote section of Kings Canyon.
July 15, 2004	A major SAR begins for a 17-year-old in Joshua Tree NP; Jeff Ohlfs is IC. At least 30 news agencies follow story. The boy is found dead on July 23.
July 17, 2004	California's Lemoore Naval Air Station deactivates its detachment of rescue helicopters, after serving the San Joaquin Valley and "High Sierra" for over 30 years.
August 13, 2004	Hurricane Charley strikes Florida and Dry Tortugas NP.

MILESTONES OF THE 2000s

August 16, 2004	Major flooding kills two in Death Valley NP; park shuts down for week.
mid-September	Hurricane Ivan strikes Gulf of Mexico damaging several park areas.

----

88 PEOPLE DIED

A "thank you," calmly said at 4:20 p.m., was the last radio transmission from Alaska Airlines Flight 261, only moments before it hit the water in a steep dive. The MD-83 aircraft, en route from Puerto Vallarta, Mexico, to Seattle, with an intermediate stop in San Francisco, carried 2 pilots, 3 cabin crew, and 83 passengers. Observed by other nearby aircraft as well as monitored on radar, the disaster was also witnessed by Drew Gottshall, a 45-year-old maintenance man for Channel Islands National Park.

> I was putting in a trail sign on the Lighthouse Trail, on the eastern portion of East Anacapa Island . . . I heard the aircraft, looked up, and followed its path visually till it hit the water, approximately 2.7 miles north of Anacapa.

"Tree," as Gottshall is known to friends and coworkers, immediately notified the park's radio dispatcher.

> The plane made a quick entry into the water upon impact, and disappeared (he was 240 feet above the ocean). I did not see much wreckage at all . . . it was four or five seconds after seeing the plane hit the water before I heard the sound.

Hours passed before Tree would finally learn it was an airliner, initially thinking it was probably a military jet.

Although the weather was clear, the seas were rough and the wind-swept swells were very high. Within five minutes, the *Calogera A*, a local fishing boat,

Channel Islands "Ocean Ranger" spent two days patrolling the area where Alaska Flight 261 went into the ocean. CHANNEL ISLANDS NATIONAL PARK PHOTO ARCHIVES

was on scene; there was an oil slick and some debris, but little else—certainly no survivors. Responding along with other rescue agencies, Channel Islands National Park had launched its largest vessel, the 100-foot-long *Ocean Ranger*. From port in Ventura, the *Ocean Ranger* would normally take ninety minutes to get to Anacapa. Once on station, they spent a long night slowly motoring the search area, gathering wreckage, clues, and human remains.

Everyone would soon be very grateful the park had not launched any of its smaller boats. A monstrous "rogue" wave, coming from out of nowhere smashed into them. One of the 7-person crew yelled "oh shit . . . hang on" as the 25-foot-high wall of black water threatened to almost swallow the ship. Pitching and rolling and with little time to take a breath, the crew immediately found itself seeming to freefall straight down the backside of the freak wave. As quickly as it hit, it was gone. One young ranger broke her leg when the *Ocean Ranger* hit the bottom of the trough. They all agree, however, they were lucky they hadn't capsized, adding to the horrendous tragedy unfolding around them.

On January 31, 2001, the Air Line Pilots Association International awarded its **Gold Medal for Heroism** to the two pilots for their response to the emergency. This was the first time the association had made this award posthumously; it has been given out only 12 times since 1952. The National Transportation Safety Board would declare they "had never heard a more professional crew, from start to finish."

Investigators would eventually determine the catastrophe might have been averted if the jackscrew system and associated nut threads in the horizontal trim stabilizer of the Alaska Airline's MD-83 had been but lubricated more frequently.

February 19, 2000
Ozark National Scenic Riverway

FIVE-YEAR-OLD BOY IS BUT ONE
OF 4,869 MISSIONS THAT YEAR

WHEN his father entered Coalbank Cave to illegally harvest bat guano for fertilizer, 5-year-old Philip wandered off into the rugged, wooded area of the park. Even though only underground for 10 minutes, when Mr. Leuckel emerged from the cave that late Saturday afternoon, he found his son gone. After searching until dark he quickly notified the sheriff's office which in turn contacted the park, local volunteers, and several other federal, state, and county agencies. The park assumed management of the incident.

Temperatures that night dropped into the low 20s and with the darkness, came the fog and wet. The boy was wearing only a light jacket. Serious injury—or worse—was very possible due to hypothermia and exposure. With the nearby Current River also in flood stage, accidental drowning was another major concern, as well. To compound matters, search authorities would learn the youngster might not respond to their calls and shouts.

Four dog teams, a helicopter with sophisticated thermal imaging capability, and several hundred volunteers persistently searched through the night. They knew they were racing time. The joint Intermountain Region-Midwest Region All-Risk Incident Management Team responded the next morning. The regional Air Force Rescue and Recovery Center was contacted, and they dispatched Civil Air Patrol units from St. Louis and Cape Girardeau, an army helicopter from Fort Riley, and two military search teams to the area.

Just after noon the next day, searchers checking an abandoned hunting cabin about two-and-one-half miles from the cave found the young Leuckel sheltered in the building. Demonstrating a will to survive, he had discarded his soaked clothing and had crawled between two old foam mattresses with a blanket to stay warm. The lad said he had heard searchers calling and the helicopter as it passed overhead, but had not responded.

In the year 2000, the men and women of the National Park Service handled 4,869 search and rescue missions, including 244 deaths and another 5,210 people. The little lost 5-year-old boy from Van Buren, Missouri, was but one of them.

June–July 2000
Black Canyon of the Gunnison National Park

TWO MAJOR TECHNICAL RESCUES

LOCATED in west-central Colorado, the Black Canyon of the Gunnison was set aside on March 2, 1933. It has been said that "no other canyon in North America combines the depth, narrowness, sheerness, and somber countenance" that it does. It is 53 miles long, with 12 miles within park boundaries. The Gunnison River drops an average of 95 feet per mile, one of the greatest rates of fall for any river in North America. The Canyon is 2,200 feet deep in places and from rim-to-rim it narrows to 1,300 feet wide. The hard crystalline volcanic rock of the two-million-year old gorge is not for beginner climbers. The following SAR missions constitute two of the most significant technical evacuations in the park, hinting at the very real dangers faced by the dedicated rescuers in the area.

June 17: Twenty-year-old Zach Alberts was leading the very difficult Cruise Route, an advanced climb rated at 5.10 (the most difficult at that time would have been 5.13). The young man was 10 feet above his last piece of safety protection when he lost his footing, slipped and fell 20 feet, fracturing both ankles. After climbing back up to the rim at 9:30 P.M., Alberts's partner contacted Seasonal Ranger Ed Delmolindo, an experienced rock climber himself. The later in the day it begins, the more difficult the rescue—a "Murphy's Law."

Delmolindo treated Alberts's injuries and along with others, carried him piggyback down to the bottom of the gorge and spent a long night waiting for daylight. An EMT from the local community college then assisted the injured young man back up the 1,500-foot North Chasm Wall. Even with the two broken ankles it was deemed easiest and safest to secure the victim to the rescuer's chest harness, straddle him, and then "walk" the injured climber back up. Once the raising began, it took 25 rescuers over five hours to complete.

July 9: It was raining intermittently when 41-year-old Martha Moses fell while leading a climb up Cruise Gully. Initially she and her partner had started another, more difficult route, the Leisure, but elected to back off of it. Moses was climbing 50 feet above her first safety point when she lost her footing on the wet rock; falling and tumbling about 80 feet, she sustained an open skull fracture. Her partner contacted Ranger Ed Delmolindo, who responded along with an EMT from the local volunteer ambulance squad. Much like the demanding Alberts rescue of three weeks before, it was now dark.

The night-time litter evacuation involved lowering her down the remainder of the gully in a now steady rain, accompanied by dangerous lightning and continuous, even more potentially fatal falling rock shooting out of the night from above. Moses, once at the bottom and safely off the climb, was "repackaged" and along with an attendant, was then raised over 900 feet up the North Chasm Wall to a rim out-of-sight and far above. At 8 that morning, a helicopter then evacuated her to Grand Junction, 60 miles away where she successfully underwent surgery. This demanding search and rescue operation took 12 hours and involved 50 rescuers, including a number of local volunteer SAR teams.

August 2, 2000
Yosemite National Park

WHEN RANGERS TURNED ON THEIR LIGHTS, SHOTS RANG OUT

RESCUERS always risk accident or injury when trying to save someone and to some degree, it "goes with the territory." Every SAR mission poses a real chance for mishap because of rain, snow, lightning, wind, heat, rock fall, swift water, equipment failure, darkness, helicopter crash, animals, and a dozen other concerns, mostly uncontrollable. But when the victim injured at the top of the cliff above them has a semi-automatic handgun and is shooting it, "life and death" for the SAR team takes on a whole new meaning.

Rangers on the night shift heard gun fire and quickly pinpointed the yells for help coming from the cliff bands above the Yosemite Chapel. Although not totally rare, people becoming trapped or injured on the steep, tree- and cliff-covered slopes below the South Rim of the Valley are not all that common either. It was 8 P.M. that Wednesday and the park was just beginning to settle in for the evening.

When investigators began shining powerful lights on the cliffs hundreds of feet above them, additional shots rang out. Even with the constant background din of vehicles and campers preparing for the night throughout the valley, to those at the scene there was no mistaking the distinct *cr-a-a-ck* that guns make.

Many rangers wear multiple hats and in this incident they would be now responding as both rescuer and as a law enforcement officer, a combination not often faced by these men and women.

Reacting to their police training, they instinctively took available cover and employed a loudspeaker to make contact with the man on the cliff, subsequently identified as 22-year-old Johnathan Haft, of Beverly Hills. Rangers would ask Haft questions about his circumstances as well as to give instructions; he responded to them by using the flash from his camera. He indicated he was slightly injured and that he had reached his present location by scrambling down through the broken cliffs from the Four Mile Trail. He also gave conflicting answers to other key questions, prompting extra caution by the responders. Further investigation and rescue efforts were delayed by darkness.

At first light a powerful telescope was used to locate Haft, who was wearing camouflage clothing and carrying a daypack and semiautomatic handgun. Rangers used the public address system to instruct him to disassemble the handgun, separate the parts of the weapon, place the daypack out of reach, and put his hands on his head. Haft complied with these commands. Employing the park's helicopter, Rangers Keith Lober, Steve Yu, and Michael Nash then helirappelled to the site, secured Haft's weapon, and escorted him on foot safely to the Valley floor. He told them he'd gotten stuck while attempting to climb directly back up to Glacier Point to get his car. Johnathan Haft was charged for weapons violations and for disorderly conduct by creating a hazardous condition.

In the year 2000, the search and rescue staff of Yosemite National Park responded to 147 missions, which involved 9 deaths, 82 people who were hurt or injured, and 65 people who were not hurt but needed technical assistance.

January 17, 2001
Haleakala National Park

THEIR VEHICLE WAS ABOUT TO GO UNDER

Rangers practice entering submerged vehicle at SCUBA refresher at Lake Mead in 1982.

PHOTO BY RANGER DAVE MCLEAN, LAKE MEAD
NATIONAL RECEPTION AREA

RANGER Jonathan Liakos was patrolling in the Lelekea area of the Hawaiian park when he spotted an open-topped Jeep on an embankment half in and half out of the ocean. Waves were cresting at five feet, the shoreline consisted of slippery, almost unmanageable round rocks on a steep slope, and there were two people still in the brightly colored rental car.

Both occupants seemed confused and unsure of what to do. As each successive wave battered the Jeep, it was pulled further down into the water. The ranger noted that neither occupant was wearing a seatbelt and that the Jeep was teetering and rocking and in serious danger of rolling over. His greatest fear was if the four-wheel drive vehicle should overturn, the two occupants could be crushed by the roll bar or be pinned underwater and drown before they could be pulled free of the submerged car.

Liakos leaped into the surf to pull the passenger—Susan Richardson—from the Jeep, timing his actions between wave surges. At the same time, he directed driver John Chance, also of Texas, to fasten his seatbelt in the event the Jeep rolled over before Liakos could get him out. The open vehicle filled with water and waves were crashing into it broadside. Due to the car's angle, Chance soon could not safely escape. The ranger grabbed a length of rope from his patrol vehicle and ran it from his large suburban to the smaller Jeep. Then, aided by two area residents, he pulled the Jeep and its driver back up to the roadway. The two Texas visitors said they'd done lots of off-road driving back home and felt very comfortable in leaving the road to drive along the rocky beach. Amazingly, John Chance was able to restart the Jeep and drive from the scene.

January 31, 2001
Mammoth Cave National Park

PULLED THROUGH 1450-FOOT, WATER-COVERED CRAWLWAY

RESCUERS face few challenges more daunting than trying to save a seriously injured person from deep within the earth. When the cavern has pits, waterfalls, streams, and long partially water-filled passages, it gets enormously more complicated.

On that Wednesday afternoon, park hydrologist Joe Meiman advised rangers that Dr. Chris Groves, a 42-year-old geology professor from Western Kentucky University, had been seriously injured in Sides Cave, located on the park's eastern boundary. Meiman, Groves, and park employee Brice Leech had been retrieving scientific data from the cave when the accident occurred. Professor Groves was attempting to go around Safety Dome on a rock ledge when it broke free from below him and he plunged 30 feet. The 30 inches of water at the bottom barely cushioned his fall.

Getting to the injured Groves was a blur for Meiman, who to this day is not sure how he down climbed the Dome's slippery wall. He fully expected "to be met by a crimson wash" when he arrived. All but the seat of the victim's coveralls were underwater. "When I pulled Chris from the water his eyes were wide open, water drained from his mouth and nose, and he was not breathing. A small trickle of blood from a cut under his left eye was running down his face. He immediately started breathing and coughing."

Although the extent of his injuries was not known completely at the time, Dr. Groves had suffered four broken ribs, a fractured collar bone, a punctured lung, cuts and bruises as well as being disoriented and somewhat in shock. This was all compounded by the 100% humidity and the near-50-degree air and water temperatures.

As a waterfall sprayed down on them and after a two-hour struggle, Groves was pulled out of the pit. Leech stayed while Meiman went for help. It had taken the researchers an hour to reach Safety Dome, including crawling through the cave's 10-inch high, partially water-filled opening. And, the accident site was at the wrong end of a 1,450-foot "wet crawl," a low, tight passage with up to 10 inches of stream covering the bottom.

More than 100 rescuers from Mammoth Cave National Park, the Technical Rope and Cave Emergency Response Team based in Kentucky, and the National Cave Rescue Commission out of Indiana, responded and immediately went into action.

This would prove a particularly demanding rescue because first they had to cross the pit and then traverse the water-covered 1,450-foot long passage and finally, exit the cave through the tiny opening. As the litter traveled the length of the low tunnel, rescuers either crawled on their hands and knees or slid on their stomachs while the stretcher rode on their backs to keep the injured man as dry as possible. The threat of hypothermia was ever-present and even though the cavers wore protective wetsuits, teams of four were forced to relieve each other frequently throughout the night. After what surely seemed like 14 very tortuous hours, the rescuers were met with success the next morning at 4 A.M..

June 25, 2001
Yellowstone National Park

THE UNKNOWN GOOD SAMARITAN

THE Grand Canyon of the Yellowstone plunges 1,000 feet; it was down cut rapidly more than once, perhaps by great glacial outburst floods. Hot water acting on the area's world-famous volcanic rock created the gorge's rainbow of muted pastel colors, and the river's yellow banks at its distant Missouri River confluence occasioned the Minnetaree Indian name that early French trappers translated as *roche jaune*—yellow stone.

Twelve-year-old Andrew Fortier was visiting the park with his brother and parents and had stopped at Artist Point on the south rim of the Grand Canyon of the Yellowstone to view the Lower Falls. After enjoying the spectacular vista, the family began walking back to their vehicle trying to beat the darkness, since it was already 8 P.M.. The two boys were off-trail and on the downhill side, throwing sticks. Trying to encourage their sons to move along a little faster on the path back to the parking lot, the parents were several dozen feet ahead of the youngsters when they heard the unmistakable cries for help.

Andrew had accidentally slipped on some loose gravel and slippery pine needles into a steeply sloping, V-shaped water-worn gully; he tumbled about 15 feet before he was able to grab onto a rock, which slowed him but did not stop him. Because of the crumbly rocky sides of the chute, he then slid another ten feet before he was again able to grab onto a flimsy quarter-inch root sticking out from the thin mineral soil. It held. So did he.

If Andrew's grip on his fragile handhold failed or if the tiny wooden stick were to pull free or break, he would continue to slide down the gully and over an abrupt edge just 30 feet away. It was then a free fall for another 200 feet onto the boulders along the river, with nothing in between to interrupt his fall and save him.

Andrew's screams quickly attracted other park visitors who improvising, tried tying T-shirts together to reach him. Although well intentioned this effort soon proved of little value. The unusual commotion also grabbed the attention of a 30-year-old tour guide, Michael Doran, of Eaton, Ohio, who accurately assessed the situation. Thinking smartly, he asked a nearby RV owner for a line. He had no rope, but he was able to quickly put his hands on a long extension cord. Grabbing the make shift rope Doran ran to the rescue. At this point an unknown visitor joined forces with Doran and volunteered to go down the extension cord to the terrified boy. Cautiously moving down the crumbly slope, he reached a point where he could reach Andrew and tie the cord around him. Doran and others then raised the two of them; the unknown man helping Andrew along.

When rangers arrived, the rescue was over; the Good Samaritan was no where to be found and his identity remains a mystery to this day. Other than shaken, Andrew was unharmed; he would live another day to throw more sticks along with his brother. . . .

January 21, 2002
Crater Lake National Park

SEARCHERS CAUGHT IN AVALANCHE

CRATER Lake National Park, established in 1902 as this country's sixth national park, consecrates one of the great sceneries of the world, including the deepest lake in the United States. Highlighted by its cobalt-blue water, Crater Lake is arguably at its most spectacular in the winter, draped in white. When 33-mile Rim Drive, which circles the lake, is closed and snow covered, it is truly a grand trip for cross-country skiers.

Portlanders Kate Gessford, 21, and Dave Schuler, 24, began their adventure on Thursday and planned for two nights out, finishing on Saturday. The following Monday they didn't show up as planned, and the park began a search for the now overdue skiers. Seasoned rescuers fully appreciate that the success and speed of a trip such as theirs depends on skill levels and conditioning, as well as the many variances of the weather and terrain. Factors like these help determine when and how to begin looking for lost people.

During the initial search that afternoon, Ranger Randy Benham and volunteer ski patroller Bill Bloom were traversing the East Rim Drive ski trail about three miles east of park headquarters. Along the way they had joined up with Richard Ward, 32, and Kris Fisher, 28, park visitors from Klamath Falls. As they skied the narrow tracks of the man in front, they were suddenly and with but a moment's notice, violently swept off their feet by an avalanche that had released on a steep slope from about 100 feet above them.

Benham and Ward were lucky and somehow ended up on the surface but Bloom and Fisher had disappeared. Most people die quickly when buried by the cement-like weight of an avalanche. Knowing full well that time is critical, the two survivors immediately began looking for their partners. Seeing just the tip of a ski pole sticking up, they dug out Fisher, who was head down in 6 feet of snow and under for about 10 minutes.

Shaken but alright, the lucky skier now eagerly joined the search for volunteer Bill Bloom. After what must have seemed like an eternity to Bloom but what really was only 40 minutes, he was located by using avalanche beacons and snow probes. He was solidly entombed beneath 6 feet of frozen debris and on the verge of blacking out. Bloom was already suffering from mild hypothermia. After rewarming, the four were able to ski out with the aid of other rescue personnel who were now on the scene.

The original victims, Schuler and Gessford, were still missing and the search for them was now severely complicated by low clouds and fog, approximately 40 inches of fresh snow, and by many new areas of high avalanche risk. Just before dark on Wednesday, searchers located the two, both uninjured, several miles east of park headquarters. Their progress had been slowed by the great snowfall, and that they both had also been caught in an avalanche; luckily buried only waist deep. The young couple was found just one day before a major blizzard was forecast to hit the area, with up to four feet of new snow and strong winds predicted. Employees from Mt. Rainier and Lassen Volcanic assisted as did personnel from the Umpqua National Forest and local snow-cat operators.

January 28, 2002
North Cascades National Park

RESCUED AND THEN ARRESTED
FOR DRUG SMUGGLING

NORTH Cascades contains some of America's most breathtakingly beautiful scenery—high jagged peaks, ridges, slopes, and countless cascading waterfalls. The park encompasses at least 318 glaciers, more than half of all glaciers in the Lower 48. Known generally as North Cascades National Park, there really are two other lesser-known areas here also: Ross Lake and Lake Chelan National Recreation Areas. In these 684,000 acres, with 90 percent designated as wilderness, there is only one year-round road. The area is so rugged, particularly in the winter, you would have to be either desperate or a fool to try and smuggle dope in from Canada through here. William Karras was one . . . or the other.

The 34-year-old would-be entrepreneur was intent on bringing in 16 ounces of "BC Bud"—marijuana grown in British Columbia and valued at $4,000. When he left Canada he had a backpack full of winter camping equipment, as well as a hardware-quality one-man plastic raft. To save time and to make his life easier, Karras had put his gear into the small boat and towed it along the frozen edge of boulder and stump-studded Ross Lake. That is until the cheap raft with all of his food and survival equipment sank.

Dressed appropriately for the weather at the very beginning of his three-day adventure, Karras apparently forgot to check the long-range forecast. After he stole into the United States from British Columbia, a major arctic system blew into northern Washington, with 40-mph winds, 10-degree temperatures and over a dozen inches of new snow, with about that same amount already on the ground. With most of his gear now underwater, he had little or no equipment with which to face the blizzard and if it had not been for rescuers, he would have died from either greed or ignorance during his survival epic.

Alerted that Karras was overdue, Park Rangers Hugh Dougher, John Madden and Galen Clark finally found him after a 10-hour search by helicopter, ski, and boat. He had hiked down 40 miles of seasonally closed road from Canada through increasingly deeper snow and deteriorating weather. At one point he sought refuge from the freezing wind and cold in a steel bear-proof box of a boat in a campsite along the shore. He told Ranger Madden that he could only endure 45 minutes in the icebox-like shelter before the piercing cold drove him to keep going. When his trail was finally "cut," the rangers could easily see that his footsteps were increasingly wandering and that he was suffering from the effects of fatigue and the cold. He later declared he knew if he stopped moving he would die. When found, he was suffering from an ankle injury, frostbite, and hypothermia but ultimately refused definitive medical care.

Not only did questioning by the rangers soon reveal that Karras had somehow struggled 72 miles through the rugged North Cascades in a major winter storm over a three-day period, but that he had several kilos of dope on him. The marijuana was seized and the criminal—either lucky or unlucky, depending on one's point of view—confessed to previous successful efforts. He was arrested and charged with smuggling and distribution. At least on this near-death saga, all of his hard work was for naught. . . .

April 17, 2002
Cuyahoga Valley National Park

WENT OVER 65-FOOT-HIGH WATERFALL

CUYAHOGA Valley National Park, authorized in 1974 and only a few miles from both Cleveland and Akron, protects 33,000 acres along the banks of the Cuyahoga River in northern Ohio. In 2002, almost 3,200,000 visitors explored the area's rural landscapes, including 20 miles of the Ohio & Erie Canal, a key to the settlement of the valley in the 19th and early 20th centuries.

Five boys, ages 12 and 13, climbed to the top of the park's 65-foot high Brandywine Falls late in the afternoon and slipped through the fencing which closes the area off immediately above the drop. As the kids were playing with a raft that had been brought along, one of the 13-year olds walked to the edge of the falls and began throwing things off. Either ignoring or unaware of the uneven and slippery surfaces, he soon lost his footing while trying to dislodge a log stuck at the edge of the falls and went over.

Two visitors, Matthew Whited and Michael Cagey, were at the falls with their children and saw the young boy slip over the edge and tumble into the pool at the bottom. Cagey called 911 on his cell phone. Whited entered the cold water and quickly made his way to the boy, who was now floating face down. The rescuer, fearing the boy may have suffered a broken spine, cautiously turned the lad over and then swam to the edge of the stream, supporting the boy's neck and back as he went. He rested the boy's head on a rock and let his body float in the water, gently holding him up from below. The 13-year old wasn't breathing, so Whited gave him two rescue breaths and compressions. The boy vomited and resumed breathing on his own; Cagey entered the water to help Whited. The stream was rising, so one of them grabbed a life preserver floating nearby, placed it under the boy's neck, and moved him up on the slightly submerged rock shelf.

Rangers Cheryl Hess and Cindy Swaggard were notified by park dispatch and responded; when they arrived, Swaggard managed the scene. Hess activated the county SAR team, of which she was an active member, and then assisted in the rescue as well as coordinated a landing site for the medevac helicopter. The two rangers acted as relays for teams on both sides of the falls due to the large number of agencies involved and their lack of common radio frequencies. Once the seriously injured boy was stabilized and placed in a litter, he was lifted from the vertical gorge by a high-angle technical raising system. The boy was aboard the helicopter less than 90 minutes after he had fallen.

Rescuers Whited and Cagey were then extricated. Cagey had sustained an injury to his left ankle during the rescue. At least 60 firefighters, SAR and EMS personnel and police officers from 12 neighboring agencies responded to Brandywine Falls.

2003

A TYPICAL YEAR IN NATIONAL PARK SERVICE
SEARCH AND RESCUE

OUR national park areas are busy and sometimes dangerous. The following information was taken from the official *National Park Service Search and Rescue Report for Calendar Year 2003*. This data is not intended to be all-inclusive but rather meant to provide the reader some insight into just how active the people of the service are.

*****

Number of recreational visits to national park areas in 2003:   266,099,641
Number of search and rescue (SAR) incidents: 3,108

Number of people who died?:   124
Number of people who were ill or injured?:   1,199
Number of people who were not ill or injured?:   2,162
Number of lives actually saved because of
  National Park Service intervention?:   427

A total of 3,251 people are individually identified in this report and they were doing the following activities when they became lost and/or needed to be rescued: There were 926 people day hiking, 711 motorboating, 446 were swimming, 338 hiking overnight, 186 using nonmotorized boats, 102 were rock climbing while roped, 55 were using horses and mules, 40 were traveling in a vehicle, 34 were climbing on steep snow or ice, 28 committed suicide, 23 flew in an airplane, 19 were fishing, and 1 was snowboarding.

Another 342 people were hang gliding, parachuting, bicycling, canyoneering, caving, scrambling off the trail, hunting, gathering plants, skiing, SCUBA diving, murdered, snowshoeing, snowmobiling, committing a crime, surfing, or we just do not know.

For those park visitors who were lost, 1,831 were found within 24 hours, 55 within 48 hours, 5 were located after seven days, and 16 are still out there. There were 276 people who were under 13 years of age and there were 189 who were over 60. Most (1,521) were found within one mile of where they were last seen but at least 15 people had traveled more than 20 miles before being found! **(When you realize you are lost, stop where you are!)**

What contributed to the problem and why did these people get into trouble? At least 673 individuals were in poor physical condition; 658 exercised bad judgment or had insufficient information; 347 were the victims of an equipment malfunction or problem; 335 had insufficient equipment, clothing, or experience; 262 fell; 241 suffered from heat, cold, poor visibility, or wind; 162 were overtaken by darkness; 35 were on drugs; 10 were struck by lightning; and 6 were involved in a snow avalanche. Factors for the remaining 641 people include bees, snakes, and bears; fire; flood; and falling rock with 411 classified as "unknown" (i.e., the reporting park either didn't indicate or didn't know).

The total cost for search and rescue within the NPS for 2003 was $3,468,255!

January 29, 2003
Biscayne National Park

REMAINS FROM VICTIM
OF HURRICANE ANDREW FOUND

FORTY-ONE people were known to have died in Hurricane Andrew, which struck southern Florida on August 24, 1992. It was the third most powerful hurricane to reach North American in the 20th century. More than 10 years later, the remains of one of the missing victims of the storm were found on Elliot Key in Biscayne National Park.

Archeologist Brenda Lazendorf and biological technician Toby Obenauer were looking for remnants of an old railroad in the area when they discovered a human skull and long bones. Dental records soon revealed these were the remains of Gus Lorences. Lorences was killed when he and two companions tied up their boat on the Key, intending to ride out the storm. They made the fatal mistake when they assumed the vicious winds would turn a different direction than what they did. During the hurricane, Lorences went out on deck to secure lines and was swept away. Another person on the boat was killed by flying debris. The sole survivor remained inside the boat throughout the hurricane.

```
        April 26, 2003
  Near Canyonlands National Park
```

TO SURVIVE HE HAD TO AMPUTATE HIS OWN ARM

```
It's 3:05 on Sunday. This marks my 24-hour
mark of being stuck in Blue John Canyon.
My name is Aron Ralston. My parents are
Donna and Larry Ralston of Englewood,
Colorado. Whoever finds this, please make
     an attempt to get this to them.
```

```
—Aron Ralston videotaping his own death
```

ON Saturday, the 27-year-old avid and highly accomplished outdoorsman from Colorado was solo canyoneering in a remote area just outside the western edge of Canyonlands National Park. After mountain-biking 15 miles to the upper end of the snake-like gorge, the experienced "slot rat" intended to spend a long day of a dozen rugged miles climbing and squirming his way down between narrow, towering walls. Slot-canyon hiking is a highly specialized sport. At its extreme, it demands sophisticated climbing, caving, and often even swimming-through-mud skills; it is for only the most advanced adventurer.

In 1998 Ralston, a mechanical engineer by education and a salesman at an Aspen outdoor equipment company, had embarked on three climbing projects: scale all 59 of the 14,000-foot peaks in Colorado, both in the summer and the winter as well as summit the highest point in every state. He was in exceptional physical condition and was preparing to climb Mt. McKinley. Aron Ralston, a rural search and rescue volunteer and generally very responsible in his outdoor pursuits, violated the most cardinal of wilderness rules on this five-day outing from work: **He failed to tell anyone where he was going.**

Only 15 minutes into the scramble down Blue John Canyon, in a 3-foot wide and 100-foot deep section of the slot, a red sandstone boulder weighing some 800 pounds and about "the size of a large bus tire" he was crawling over, teetered and slid down several feet. Before he could react, Ralston's right arm was pinned tightly to the wall, just above the wrist. He was unable to pull free and was trapped standing up. Within 20 minutes, his right thumb was a sickly gray; there was no feeling in his hand at all.

Fear, frustration, and rage coursed through Aron immediately. Almost as quickly, however, he countered these emotions; the mechanical engineer and seasoned outdoorsman, forced himself to analyze the problem. As he recounts in his memoir, *Between a Rock and a Hard Place:*

> Without enough water to wait for a rescue, without a pick to crack the boulder, without a rigging system to lift it, I have one course of action. I speak slowly out loud: "you're gonna have to cut your arm off."

It would be another 48 hours, however, before Aron would seriously consider amputation as his only salvation.

Aron Ralston would be trapped for 5 long nights. He would go over 125 hours without sleep, nearly 50 hours without fresh water while judiciously storing his urine in his now depleted water containers, and be pinned for some 115 hours before he would finally cut himself free. He alternated between trying to raise the boulder with rope and makeshift pulleys and chipping at the rock with his pocket knife. He was already now saving the smaller, two-inch and less dull of his two blades for the inevitable operation.

On Tuesday morning, he ran out of water. "I wonder what kidney failure will feel like. Not good, probably . . . It's gonna be a rough way to die." On Thursday, Canyonlands National Park and the Emery County Sheriff's Office were notified that the climber was missing and overdue; they swung into action. That same morning, Ralston realized his ultimate survival required drastic action and even at that, it just might prove too late.

His lower arm was now totally gangrenous—it was dead. He would be too, if something wasn't done soon.

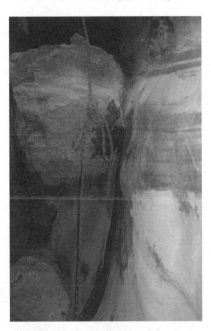

The 800-pound rock that pinned Aron Ralston down for six days.

CANYONLANDS NATIONAL PARK PHOTO ARCHIVES

> Out of curiosity, I poke my thumb with a knife blade twice . . . like it is dipping into a stick of room-temperature butter, and releases a telltale hissing. Escaping decomposition gases are not good: the rot has advanced more quickly than I guessed.

Aron Ralston, forced by sheer desperation into probably one of his last moments of mental and emotional clarity, accidentally grasped that he could now break the bones in his forearm. *"Like bending a two-by-four held in a table vise."* Doomed otherwise, he didn't hesitate. "I put my left hand under the boulder and push hard, harder, HARDER!" One bone snapped, then the other. After an hour of cutting and hacking, it was finished. Aron had completely amputated his arm below the elbow using only his pocketknife!

Ralston, applying a tourniquet and administering first aid and unable to go back up the short distance he had traversed 6 days before, somehow then worked his way down through the slot, including a 65-foot rappel at the end. Six hours later he exited the gorge and within several more hours was spotted by a searching Utah Public Safety helicopter.

On May 4, with great logistical and mechanical difficulty, while understanding the unfortunate need to foil the gruesome but inevitable "souvenir hunters," rescuers from both the park and county recovered the remains of Aron Ralston's arm.

All quotations in this story attributed to Aron Ralston are from *Between a Rock and a Hard Place,* Atria Books (September 2004).

July 26, 2003
Grand Teton National Park

ONE OF THE MOST EPIC RESCUES
IN AMERICAN MOUNTAINEERING

RANGER Tom Kimbrough, a 30-year veteran of mountain rescue would say, "This might be the most spectacular rescue in the history of American mountaineering . . . [for] . . . people being extricated and the way the helicopters worked and how fast the boys did it."

Lightning kills dozens of people in the United States every year. Rescuers recover the body of a woman climber near Moab, Utah in August of 1995. She died instantly from lightning.
PHOTO BY RANGER LARRY VAN SLYKE

At 3:35 P.M. that Saturday, 25-year-old Erica Summers from Idaho Falls was killed outright when the lighting bolt struck above them. Near her at the 13,000-foot level of the Grand Teton were 12 other climbers in several teams. When the 911 cellphone call came in 11 minutes later, CPR was in progress on Summers, 27-year-old Rodrigo Liberal dangled unconscious and upside down in the middle of a rock face, three other climbers were seriously injured and three more, even though they had been anchored to the rock, had been "blasted" off their ledge and over a cliff and were missing.

It was now raining, the rocks were slippery and many of those at this spot on the 13,770-foot high peak were relatively novice to mountaineering. The day before, the climbers—mostly friends and coworkers from Idaho—had been cautioned about late-afternoon thunderstorms and advised to get an early start or not go at all. Given their location, sheer numbers, and skill level and with even 30 minutes notice about the storm they would not have been able to move to a safer location. Several of them later commented, "[The storm cell] didn't look that bad," or "We've been in way worse weather."

Rangers would quickly mobilize for one of the most complex rescues in the history of the park. When the report first came in Brandon Torres, who would become the Incident Commander for this nightmare, was actually on the phone with a worried mother who had a missing 12-year-old child. Before long, this mission would include two powerful helicopters, each borrowed from neighboring agencies and coming with their own several-person helitack crew, one regional air ambulance, three ground ambulances and at least a dozen highly skilled rangers and climbers from around the area.

Wind, more thunderstorm cells, approaching darkness, and peak-shrouding fog greatly worried Ranger Renny Jackson, among the world's elite of mountain rescue and a veteran of many-hundreds of Teton emergencies. On the mission's first aerial recon, he "came upon a horrific scene." And when Renny saw Liberal dangling from his harness and suspended upside down in mid-air, he recalled the almost-mythical mountaineering sagas of the Alps, embodied by the 1975 Clint Eastwood epic, *The Eiger Sanction.*

Slowly, despite being initially forced back in one particularly bad "cloud event," pilot Laurence Perry was able to cautiously insert 11 rangers on top of the accident scene via short-haul. Perry would lift two rangers at a time, suspended below the helicopter on a 100-foot long line, and place them directly on the small ledges of the cliff face.

Ranger Leo Larson, among the first to unhook from the chopper and another Grand Teton rescue legend, found it difficult to make sense of the scene. "It was hard, initially, to triage the people." For over three hours, Liberal swung free while being bent nearly double on the vertical wall before being reached by rescuers. The three climbers, who had been blasted off their ledge and "lost," were found seriously hurt 60 feet below. When their rope became tangled in the rocks and crevices, they escaped from plunging over the edge of a much higher cliff.

But everyone knew their task and fell to it. Anchors were set, stranded climbers retrieved, medical assessments were performed and the injured that were all perched on cliff faces, were readied for a tricky aerial evacuation in the fading light.

One by one, the injured climbers were short-hauled to the Lower Saddle, where they were relayed to another helicopter and flown to the valley floor. Liberal was packaged into a litter mid-face on Friction Pitch and quickly but efficiently raised by hand to a ledge 60 feet above. With daylight almost gone and with literally only minutes to spare, Liberal, the last patient to be removed from the mountain, was slung from the accident site to a spot where he was then transferred to a waiting medevac helicopter. He was raced to a regional trauma center. Everyone other than the Erica Summers, the young woman who died instantly from the lightning bolt, survived. That was the eleventh major SAR in Grand Teton National Park that year and the third fatality.

July 31, 2003
Yosemite National Park

NEVER FOUND, THEY ARE STILL "OUT THERE"

ON August 10, the massive search to locate 46-year-old Fred Claassen from Livermore, California, was scaled back. For five days, an intense combined effort by Yosemite and neighboring Mono County, had involved upwards of 140 people. Claassen had begun his four-day solo hike from Twin Lakes, a popular trailhead north of the park boundary. His itinerary included travel on glaciers and hiking into the heart of some of the most rugged terrain in the park. Extensive air searching by helicopters from five different agencies resulted in no clues nor did the dog teams or the over 100 interviews conducted by investigators of the two agencies. It is believed that Fred Claassen is still "out there."

Fred Claassen is but the latest of at least 27 people who are known to have vanished while in Yosemite National Park. Although most disappeared while hiking somewhere in the area, at least four were last seen going over a waterfall or through a rapids in the park.

1. F. P. Shepherd—last seen June 17, 1905, hiking away from Glacier Point.
2. Frank Koenman—last seen about June 10, 1925, in a tent in Curry Village.
3. Godfrey Wondrosek—reported missing on April 26, 1933, from Camp 7.
4. Norris Parent—last seen July 9, 1941, hiking in Shepherd's Crest area.
5. Emerson Holt—last seen July 18, 1943 one mile west of Merced Lake.
6. William H. Dickenson—May 27, 1945, his car was found in the Merced River.
7. Malcolm McClintock—last seen August 7, 1948, hiking to Glacier Point.
8. Louis Miller—last seen September 9, 1950, fishing near Dana Meadows.
9. Walter A. Gordon—last seen July 20, 1954, hiking on the Ledge Trail.
10. Orvar F. van Lass—last seen October 9, 1954, hiking near Sugar Pine Bridge.
11. Tom Opperman—last seen September 17, 1967, hiking to Merced Lake.
12. Nelson H. Paisley—last seen June 2, 1969, being swept down Merced River.
13. Christine Fuentes—last seen June 18, 1970, going over Vernal Fall.

14. Jerome R. Oldiges—last seen June 20, 1970, in Merced River near Cascades.
15. Steven H. Brown—last seen July 1, 1970, going over Waterwheel Falls.
16. Dikran Knadjian—last seen July 24, 1972, moving around Curry Village.
17. Fred W. Comstock—last seen November 30, 1975, hiking near Vogelsang.
18. Jeff Estes—last seen May 24, 1976, hitchhiking on the Tioga Road.
19. Susan Schantin—last seen May 14, 1981, maybe murdered on Wildcat Creek.
20. Stacy Arras—last seen July 17, 1981, leaving the Sunrise High Sierra Camp.
21. Timothy J. Barnes—last seen July 5, 1988, hiking out of the Tuolumne area.
22. Donald W. Buchanan—last seen November 11, 1988, hiking near Half Dome.
23. David P. Morrison—last seen May 25, 1998, hiking toward Half Dome.
24. Kieran Burke—last seen April 5, 2000, moving around Curry Village.
25. Ruthann Rupert—last seen August 14, 2000, traveling in Yosemite Valley.
26. Walter H. Reinhard—last seen September 19, 2002, hiking near White Wolf.
27. Fred Claassen—last seen July 31, 2003, hiking into the park on the East Side.

May 4, 2004
Wrangell-St. Elias National Park
and Preserve

JASON HAS NEVER BEEN FOUND

AT over 13 million acres, Wrangell-St. Elias National Park and Preserve is larger than the two states of Maryland and Vermont, combined. One glacier, the Malaspina, is bigger than Rhode Island. This is North America's mountain kingdom, containing the largest assemblage of glaciers and its greatest collection of peaks over 16,000 feet in elevation.

On Tuesday, May 4, Jason Harper hired an air taxi to drop him off at Windy Ridge for a climb of 16,237-foot Mt. Sanford, located in the northern portion of the park. When pilot Harley McMahan returned to pick him up at the appointed time five days later, Harper didn't show. McMahan scoured the immediate area on foot, and looked from the air for several more days, notifying officials of the missing man on May 12. An immediate investigation was launched in the air and on the ground. In the ensuing days, Alaska State Troopers, the NPS, the Air National Guard Rescue Coordination Center, volunteer mountain rescue teams and other climbers from throughout Alaska joined the effort.

While park pilots flew the climbing route and possible exit paths, Harper's car was located and inventoried for possible clues. A Pavehawk helicopter with a large C-130 flying cover and refueling assistance, responded. The Harper family had planned a reunion in Utah on May 12 and when Jason didn't show, his father and brother flew to Anchorage to assist. The next day, Thursday, both the NPS and McMahan flew numerous sorties along the climber's path on Mt.

Sanford. They then looked at other ways off the mountain. Meanwhile the Pavehawk, equipped with heat-detecting FLIR—Forward-Looking InfraRed— flew the route to the summit; they found some evidence of previous climbing parties, none linked them to Harper. Helicopters from Denali National Park and the Alaska State Troopers came. Fortunately, the weather remained favorable.

Friday, planes and helicopters blanketed the area and the young man's father was flown over the probable route. Two sets of dog teams from Anchorage were brought in. They made a visual search of the area while the dogs sniffed for human scent. Tracks found leading downhill from Windy Ridge faded. Denali's high-elevation Llama rescue helicopter shuttled 6 expert climbers to near the icefall on the Sheep Glacier. After splitting into two teams, they scoured the upper and lower sections of the icefall; they cautiously wound their way down through the blocks of broken ice. Safety concerns prevented them from inspecting the crevasses very thoroughly. They were extracted.

That afternoon the lower team found a base camp Jason had made during his summit attempt. He made his camp in a snow shelter built by a climbing party several weeks before. He then left most of his camping gear secured in the snow shelter, and headed up the mountain in a presumed fast, light, one-day summit attempt. Harper did not return and in the subsequent days the shelter collapsed, making it undetectable from the air.

Twelve days after Jason Harper was last seen, and without further clues to direct the effort, the search for the young mountaineer was scaled back.

May 27, 2004
Lava Beds National Monument

CAVE WAS SEARCHED
THREE TIMES FOR THE TWO KIDS

AT first glance the land looks barren, covered by scrawny grasses and clumps of sagebrush growing here and there among the black rock. Closer examination reveals much more. Lava Beds National Monument in northern California was set aside on November 21, 1925, to recognize the incredibly rugged and diverse results of volcanism, as well as to provide insight to the rich history of the Native Americans of the area.

When lava streams from a volcano it is about 1800 degrees Fahrenheit. The outer edges of the flow cool rapidly and begin to slow down and harden while the rest of the red-hot magma inside remains fluid and fast moving. As this river of lava cools and drains away, a tunnel is often left. There are more than 300 such lava tubes or caves with names in the park's 46,500 acres, Catacombs Cave is but one of them.

While on a school outing in the park and exploring this popular attraction, 11-year-olds Kyra and Timothy squeezed and stumbled into a greater adventure than they bargained for when they separated from their group that Thursday afternoon. Catacombs Cave is much more than just a straight tun-

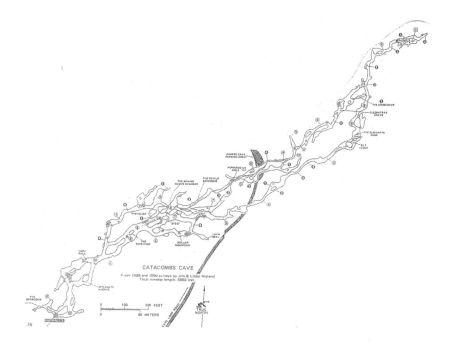

There were almost 7000 feet of underground passage for the two children to get lost in.
LAVA BEDS NATIONAL MONUMENT PHOTO ARCHIVES

nel and includes branches and passageways with a total length of nearly 7,000 feet. Its ceiling height ranges from 12 feet to less than a foot, and rough, knife-sharp lava makes footing and sections of the subway-like cave extremely difficult to access. The black of the rock is intense; it seems to almost absorb light.

Confused, the two kids soon became exhausted at the far end of the cave. They were in a remote section of the tube not shown on most cave maps and had somehow dared to squeeze through a tight passage much smaller than the average-sized adult. The sound dampening nature of the volcanic rock would restrict their yells and that of the searchers and greatly contributed to the delayed discovery time.

Rescuers at first disregarded the small opening off the larger passage as being just too tiny and unattractive for both kids to have shinnied through; the entire cave was searched three times before they were finally found. Fortunately for all, the children had remained calm and stationary the entire time. Kyra and Timothy, when located 26 hours after being reported missing, were cold, tired, and hungry, but otherwise in good condition.

Over 75 people were dedicated to the search effort on the surface and in Catacombs and in several of the surrounding caves. There were rescuers from federal, state, and local agencies including CARDA dog teams; California Highway Patrol aircraft; Modoc, Siskiyou and Klamath County Sheriff's Office SAR teams; park personnel; as well as numerous cavers from the surrounding areas.

A DIFFERENT KIND OF RESCUE

GLEN Canyon National Recreation Area is over 1,250,000 acres in size and encompasses the nation's most rugged canyon country. Lake Powell, located on the Colorado Plateau and straddling the Arizona and Utah borders, stretches 186 miles behind Glen Canyon Dam with almost 2,000 miles of shoreline when at its maximum height. Sections of this beautiful area are as remote as any place within the Lower 48 States.

Dangling Rope Marina, up lake thirty miles by boat as well as almost two hours from the nearest road, lost complete power on Monday morning of the major Fourth of July weekend, the park's busiest time. The entire marina and developed area were affected by the outage. Accessible only by water, it is a highly popular refueling and supply stop for boaters on Lake Powell, and is a necessary gas station for many of the numerous day-use visitors traveling over 50-lake miles to Rainbow Bridge.

At first, park officials hoped the problem was temporary but as the 100-degree day wore on, the seriousness of the situation became apparent. Power failure resulted in all water, sewer, communication, fire suppression and fuel delivery systems being totally shut down. Since gasoline could not be dispensed, well over 400 people in approximately 100 boats were left stranded without gas on the last day of the three-day weekend. In addition to the many boaters who were unable to return to their camp sites, day travelers not prepared for an overnight stay now faced unanticipated but very basic needs such as food, water, shelter, and medication.

At times, nearly 50 boats per hour were arriving in search of fuel and/or supplies. With very limited shade on the docks and no relief elsewhere, children and the elderly were particularly vulnerable to the triple-digit heat. Some people abandoned their vessels to be evacuated in tour boats or with passersby. Due to limited docking space, others had to leave the immediate area and were forced to "bivouac" along the shoreline to await the return of services. An almost martial law-like atmosphere had to soon be employed.

An Incident Command System was implemented by the park to manage the many needs of visitors as well as personnel resolving the crisis while also trying to evacuate those who requested it. A large generator system, potable water tanks and portable vault toilets were brought in from 150 miles away—entailing a major movement of equipment and technical specialists by truck, barge and helicopter to the isolated site. Several large houseboats in the area were chartered and tied at the marina to provide temporary accommodations, shelter and toilet facilities. The area's concessionaire, unable to keep refrigerated perishables, supplied free meals and gave away food to those stranded.

Rangers, park volunteers, concession employees and maintenance personnel spent two days and nights aiding park visitors during this incident. It was 36 hours before the NPS and a private electrical contractor, especially brought in for this emergency, located and repaired a break in the three-quarter-mile long underground power line.

ACKNOWLEDGMENTS

The 469 contributors listed below certainly have to be the most impressive "Who's Who" in SAR and/or the NPS that one writer could ever hope to assemble between two book covers. Some are still working; many, including the four directors of the NPS, were at least semi-retired when I first contacted them. Sadly, all too many have died since I began this project in 1982. Ranger John Bingaman, with pen actually to paper, suffered an eventually fatal stroke while writing me of a rescue he made in Yosemite in 1929.

Several widows of "old-time rangers" were very grateful that the mostly unsung efforts of their husbands, as well long-gone friends of yesteryear, would be remembered. To these women, as well as all our other silent partners, I wonder how many countless times we have overlooked your efforts—when you "manned" the park radio, comforted parents of the lost child, brought order to chaos, and made the SAR easier and better in a thousand ways.

Fearing that I have overlooked even one person, I am indebted to all who helped me with my labor of love. I count myself blessed in having crossed paths with you and pray that I have done you justice.

Joe Abrell	Bob Bendt	Phyllis Broyles	John Cook
Dutch Ackart	John Benjamin	Rod Broyles	John Cook, Sr.
Bill Acree	Gordon Best	Fred Brueck	Alan Cox
Lew Albert	Frank Betts	Dave Buccello	Elbert Cox
Bea Anderson	Kathy Betts	George	Robert Craig
Bill Anderson	Irene Bingaman	Buckingham	Paul Crawford
Mrs. Jack	John Bingaman	Dave Butts	Paul Crews
(Dusty)	Fred Binnewies	Dick Burns	Bob Crisman
Anderson	Scott Birkenfield	Harvey Butchart	Stu Croll
Paul Anderson	Bruce Black	Bill Butler	Joanne Cross
Rick Anderson	Norm Blair	Mike Butler	John Crowley
Tony Anderson	Bill Blake	Gilbert Calhoun	Kim Crumbo
Dale Antonich	Hugh Blanchard	Chris Cameron	Carrie Dabney
Les Arnberger	Gil Blinn	Jim Carrico	Walt Dabney
Rob Arnberger	Les Bodine	Nash Castro	Lewis Dahm
Chris Andress	Tony Bonnano	Joe Cayou	Mary Dahm
Russ Appel	George Bowen	Kimo Cebhart	Rob Danno
Ken Ashley	Gordon Boyd	John Chapman	Dan Davis, Jr.
Alan Atchison	Dick Boyer	Scotty Chapman	Dan Davis, Sr.
Lloyd Athearn	Jim Brady	Don Chase	Jack Davis
George Baggley	Bob Branges	John Chew	Mrs. John Davis
Howard Baker	Bill Briggle	Kathy Clark	Bob DeArmond
Gene Balaz	Leroy Brock	Dorothy	Frank Deckert
Doug Barnard	Chester Brooks	Cochrane	Stella Degenhardt
Steve Battista	Bill Brown	Randy Coffman	Ed Delmolindo
Ann Baugh	Gary Brown	Bruce Collins	Lenny Dems
Glen Bean	Joe Brown	Wayne Cone	Jerry DeSanto
Betty Beard	Lawrie Brown	Scott Connelly	Jim Detterline
Miles Becker	Mrs. Charlie	John Conoboy	Russ Dickenson
Bill Beer	Browne	Dr. Hull Cook	Leo Diedrich

Jan Dick
John Dill
Greg Dillman
Norm Dodge
Craig Dorman
Hugh Dougher
Linda Douglas
Roy Dreibelbis
Maury Ducasse
Bill Dunmire
Bob Dunnagan
Jim Dunning
Tom Durant
Linda Eade
Bill Ehorn
Jay Eichenhorst
Tom Ela
Lauren Elder
Beth Elliott
Doug Erskine
Dave Essex
Joe Evans
Gary Everhardt
Bill Everhart
Boyd Evison
Herb Evison
Sheck Exley
Mrs. Fred (Nell)
  Fagergren, Sr.
Christie Fairchild
Archie Ferguson
Gary Ferguson
Larry Feser
Boyd Finch
Mike Finley
Pat Fletcher
Paul Fodor
Mark Forbes
Ray Foust
Bob Frauson
Mike Freeman
George Fry
Steve Frye
Arnold Gaffrey
Mary Liz Gale
Rick Gale
Glenn Gallison
Walt Gammill
Ken Garvin
Luis Gastellum
Mike Gauthier
Bob Gerhard
Bego Gerhart
Karl Gilbert
Patrick Gilbo

Jim Godbolt
John Good
Russ Grater
Pat Grediagin
Tom Griffiths
Hal Grovert
Fran Gruchy
Dick Guilmette
Les Gunzel
Coyt Hackett
Paul Haertel
Aubrey Haines
Lou Hallock
Dwight Hamilton
Warren Hamilton
Jerry Hammond
Bob Haraden
Marian Hardy
Rich Harned
Bryan Harry
Dick Hart
Pete Hart
Ruben Hart
Tom Hartman
George Hartzog
Jeff Heater
Carl Heinrichs
Jean Heller
Wayne Hembre
John Henneberger
Paul Henry
Steve Hickman
Bob Hill
Ken Hill
Martha Lynn Hill
Mike Hill
Mary Hinson
Scott Hinson
Anne Hirst
Lloyd Hoener
Bob Hoff
Ray Hoffman
Steve Holder
Hunter Holloway
Carl Holmberg
Tom Hornbein
Bob Howard
Homer Hoyt
Doug Hubbard
Steve Hudson
Jack Hughes
Ken Hulick
Mark Igo
Bud Inman
Phil Iversen

Don Jackson
Harold Jakes
Greg Johnston
Hank Johnston
Paul Judge
Dave Karraker
Andy Kauffman
Paul Kaufman
Glen Kaye
Abbe Keith
Dennis Kelley
Ron Kerbo
Paul Kirkland
Tim Kovacs
Steve Knutson
Bob Koch
Marcia Koenig
Tim Kovacs
Jim Koza
Sue Kozacek
Marilyn Kwock
John Krambrink
Bill Kratch
Ernie Kuncl
Ed Kurtz
Fred Lalone
Mike Lalone
Bill Larson
Leo Larson
Rick LaValla
Bob Lee
Jimmy Lee
Bill Lester
Jay Liggett
Grannie Liles
Jim Liles
Keith Lober
Clyde Lockwood
Rod Losson
Kathy Loux
Rudy Lueck
Ron Mackie
Barry Mackintosh
Mrs. Preston Macy
John Madden
Charles Maddox
John Mahoney
Mary Maruca
Steve Mark
Dick Marks
Bob Marriott
Debbie Martin
Dick Martin
Jim Martin
Steve Martin

Paul Mathis
Carol McCoy
Dave McCoy
Lois McCoy
Pat McCrary
Lyle McDowell
Chuck McHugh
Bob McIntyre
Mamie McIntyre
Bruce McKeeman
Laurie McKnight
Alvin McLane
Dick McLaren
Doug McLaren
Paul McLaughlin
Steve Medley
Ann Meroney
Wayne Merry
Joe Mieman
Dave Mihalic
Jerri Mihalic
Daryl Miller
Ken Miller
Tom Milligan
Cornelius
  Molenaar
Dee Molenaar
Dave Moore
Terris Moore
Jack Moorhead
Dave Morris
Rick Mossman
Vincent Murone
Bob Murphy
Mrs. Ray (Liz)
  Murphy
Ray Murry
Ken Morgan
Alden Nash
Dave Nathanson
Coleman Newman
Dick Newgren
Pete Nigh
Rick Obernesser
Jeff Ohlfs
Bill Orr
Clarence Osborne
Leigh Ortenburger
Dave Panebaker
Dale Pate
Craig Patterson
Gordon Patterson
Tom Patterson
Howard Paul
George Pavia

Tom Pellinger	Matt Ryan	Sutherland	Bill Wade
Charles Pereira	George Sainsbury	Denice Swanke	George Wagner
Adolph Peterson	Pete Sanchez	Steve Swanke	Carl Walker
Bob Peterson	Rick Sanger	J.D. Swed	Ron Wallace
Charlie Peterson	Shirley Sargent	Brian Swift	Kennan Ward
Pat Phelan	Al Schneider	Larry Tagg	Phil Ward
Jim Phillips	Bob Scott	Gerry Tays	Doug Warnock
Ken Phillips	Dorothy Scott	Ralph Tingey	Bradford
Bill Pierce	Ted Scott	Tom Thomas	Washburn
Nancy Pimental	Bob Seibert	David Thompson	Frank Weingart
Cleve Pinnix	Cliff Senne	Jim Thompson	Bob Weldon
Ruby Presnall	Tim Setnicka	Lynn Thompson	Jay Wells
John Preston	Elaine Sevy	Pete Thompson	Don Weir
Steve Pyne	Alice Siebecker	Ted Thompson	Bill Wendt
Jim Randall	Chuck Sigler	Ron Thoreson	Bill Whalen
Rick Reese	Lee Shackleton	Reed Thorne	Bob White
J. T. Reynolds	Steve Shackleton	Scott Thybony	Lowell White
John Reynolds	Bruce Shaw	Bill Torode	Lou Whittaker
Doug Ridley	Deirdre Shaw	Lisa Towery	Lee Whittlesey
Andy Ringgold	Larry Shepherd	John Townsend	Bob Wightman
Don Ripley	Kay Shevlin	Bernie Trudell	Paul Williams
John Rittenour	Charlie Shimanski	T. J. Tucker	Butch Wilson
Tom Ritter	Dan Sholly	Tom Tucker	Redman Wilson
Bob Rockwell	Karrie Skinner	Rob Turan	Kittredge Wing
Steph Rogers	Susan Skrove	Bill Tweed	Bonnie Winslow
Gene Rose	Bob Smith	Don Utterback	Steve Winslow
Judy Rosen	Rick Smith	Blake Vande	Conrad Wirth
Sally Ross	Irene Stachura	Water	Elaine Wolf
Homer Rouse	Dick Stenmark	Gail Van Slyke	Terry Wood
Ginny Rousseau	Norm Stephan	Larry Van Slyke	Les Womack
Mel Ruder	Jim Stewart	Bill Vargas	Doyal Yaney
Melanie Ruesch	Deryl Stone	Phil Veluzat	Larry Young
Joe Rumburg	Gary Stork	Tom Vines	Bill Zauche
Ray Rundell	Howard Stricklin	Mary Volceka	
Walter Rutowski	Mrs. Walt	Leonard Volz	
John Rutter	(Roberta)	Carolyn Vujec	

I want to thank the following for their editorial assistance:

Jan Eagle	Bill Halainen	Vicki Scott
Mike Ebersole	Patsey Morris	Laura Soulliere
Karan English	Joann Speelman	Connie Vallie

APPENDIX I

This is a record of formal awards and recognitions earned by (1) NPS employees for SAR work anywhere and (2) anyone performing an SAR within the National Park System. It does not include valorous law enforcement incidents.

Unless otherwise noted, the date given is the date the event occurred, not when the award was granted. Two asterisks (**) indicate that the incident has been described elsewhere in this book.

1879–1886. Walnut Canyon National Monument—Custodian Neil Erickson—**Special Congressional Medal**—"for valorous service in the United States army" from 1879 to 1886, "during which he took part as scout in the campaign against Geronimo, the Apache chieftain." Accompanied by a pension, the honor was given to Erickson as well as 31 Navajo Scouts, in an intertribal ceremony in Gallup in August 1926 by New Mexico Governor A. T. Hannett. Erickson "was the only white man presented with the award."

1888, August 9. Yellowstone NP—Army Private John Coyle—**US Lifesaving Service Silver Medal**—saved a young woman from serious injury after she almost fell into a near-boiling geyser.** Congress passed the Life-Saving Act on June 20, 1874; First and Second Class Medals were established. First Class was for a rescue of extreme daring and Second Class was for those slightly less heroic. Congress then changed these classifications in 1882, renaming the former award the Gold Lifesaving Medal and the latter award the Silver. The first to be honored with medals were the Clemons brothers—A.J., Hubbard, and Lucian—who, on April 30, 1875, rescued two people from the 450-ton *Consuelo*, a schooner laden with block stone that wrecked on the shores of storm-tossed Lake Erie.

1907, August 12. Yosemite NP—Students J. Parks Jones and Harry L. Masser—**Carnegie Hero Awards (Bronze)**—rescued 17-year-old Bertha Pillsbury from drowning in the Merced River.** Established by Andrew Carnegie on April 15, 1904, the "Carnegie Hero Fund Commission was created to recognize outstanding acts of selfless heroism performed in the United States and Canada." Rescuers receive a medal and, for acts in which disabling injuries are sustained, a supplemental continuing grant. If the rescuer dies, financial assistance may be provided to surviving dependents. For acts in which no disability is sustained, gifts for education or other worthy purposes may be awarded. The first to be honored by the commission was 17-year-old Louis A. Baumann, Jr., for saving a fellow-worker from drowning.

1919, August 6. Glacier NP—Lawyer Herbert A. Friedlich—**Carnegie Hero Award (Silver)**—rescued 21-year-old man from an impending fall after he had climbed 350 feet up Pinnacle Wall.**

1923, June 24. Yosemite NP—Housewife Mary Blanche Nelson—**Carnegie Hero Award (Bronze/$1,000)**—saved a 14-year-old boy from drowning in the Merced River after he fell in while fishing.**

1929, July 2. Mt. Rainier NP—Temporary Ranger Charles E. Browne—**Presidential Appointment as Permanent Ranger** (President Herbert Hoover granted it on September 27, 1929); "The first citation for heroism ever issued by the Department of the Interior . . ." (issued on July 24, 1929); a "promotion and pay increase . . ." (from $1,740 to $1,800 per annum); and the Seattle Mountaineer's **1929 Acheson Cup**—week-long rescue/recovery of two men on a guided mountain climbing trip.** The Mountaineers' 1922 *Annual Report* states, "The exquisite sterling silver trophy [Acheson Cup] presented by Thomas J. Acheson is to be awarded each year to the Washington member accomplishing the most notable achievement in mountaineering for that year."

1929, July 2. Mt. Rainier NP—Guide Ray Strobel—**Demolay Medal**, by Tacoma's Fredric W. Keaton Chapter of the Order of the Demolay, the first time to a living person and only the 12th ever to be awarded. (Awarded 5-10-30.) See above.

1929, August 18. Yosemite NP—Time-keeper Jay Booth Meredith—**Carnegie Hero Award (Posthumously/Bronze Medal)** and "until further notice $80 a month for the support of herself and three children, not to extend however, beyond twelve years or the date of her remarriage"—died while saving 16-year-old student from drowning in Merced River.

1930, July 5. Sequoia NP—Trail Crew—**Letters of Commendation from NPS Director**—("It is time to start a roll of honor for special citations." Acting Director Cammerer)—extensive search for youth on side of Mt. Whitney. Special praise was given to noted Sierras mountaineer, trail crewman Norman Clyde.**

1931, July 4. Mt. Rainier NP—Mountain Guides Clem Blakney, William Butler, and "Swede" Willard; Rangers Charles Browne and Larry Devlin—**Letter of Commendation from Secretary of the Interior** (Ray Lyman Wilbur)—recovered body from deep crevasse after extensive effort.** In a letter to the park's five heroes, Wilbur said:

> Through the Director of the National Park Service I have learned of the heroic conduct of the party which recovered the body of Robert Zinn after the tragedy on Mount Rainier, and particularly of the courage displayed.
>
> On behalf of the United States Government I want to thank you for your exceptionally meritorious service, and personally to congratulate you on your conduct during the trying situation.

1932, June 2. Hawaii NP—Civilian Rikan Konishi—**Silver Trophy** from Hilo Japanese Contractor's Association—recovered two victims of "unrequited love affair" from bottom of Kilauea Crater.**

1933, Summer. Yosemite NP—13-year-old Robert M. Irwin—**"Medal"**—saved 11-year-old girl from drowning in Merced River.

1934, August 2. Acadia NP—Civilian Christine Stewart—**Carnegie Hero Award (Silver and "$500 for a worthy purpose as needed")** and civilian Ellen Geaney—**Carnegie Hero Award (Bronze and "$500 for a worthy purpose as needed")**—unsuccessfully attempted to save 31-year-old Emily McDougall from drowning in treacherous Atlantic Ocean surf near Thunder Hole.**

1935, July 12. Yellowstone NP—Seasonal Radio Technician Richard Lillig—given a permanent position with the NPS for saving the life of Harvey Crowder, a Mt. Sheridan Fire Lookout.**

1936, January 19. Mt. Rainier NP—Temporary Ranger William Butler—**Presidential Appointment as Permanent Ranger** (President Franklin Roosevelt) for rescue/recovery efforts of Delmar Fadden.**

1936, January 19. Mt. Rainier NP—Delmar Fadden Rescue Team—**Resolution by Seattle Chamber of Commerce:**

> That the Seattle Chamber of Commerce expresses its admiration for the high quality of character displayed by all of the rescuing party and that the Chamber bring their feat to the attention of the proper governmental agency, or other national organization, for fitting and deserved recognition and citation. March 3, 1936.

1937, January 29. NPS CCC Camp Sp-10, Gooseberry Falls, MN—CCC employee Anthony Jakes—**U.S. Treasury Life Saving Medal**—saved two boys who fell through the ice while skating on Lake Superior.

1938, July 3. Rocky Mountain NP—Superintendent David H. Canfield—**Denver Post's Gallery of Fame**—coordinated one of park's most intensive and complicated searches.** The "Gallery of Fame" was started in 1933 by the *Denver Post* as "An Appreciation for Some Public or Private Act or Benefaction Performed in the Current Week." The citation under David H. Canfield's photo reads:

> Superintendent, Rocky Mountain National Park, who had charge of the long search for Alfred Beilhartz, 4½, lost along the Roaring River in the mountains above Estes Park. Although the lad was not found, the search was inspiring in realizing the general human sympathy of the participants and the ability of the park service to organize such a united expedition.

1939, June 26. Yellowstone NP—Laborer William L. Nelson—**Carnegie Hero Award**

(Posthumously/Bronze), CCC enrollee Brutus C. Johnson—**Carnegie Hero Award (Bronze/ $250)**, and Vaughn H. Roley—Nelson died while trying to rescue Roley who had been overcome by hydrogen sulfide at the bottom of a 27-foot-deep hole. Johnson attempted to rescue Nelson but was overcome also and pulled out. Roley in the meantime revived and retrieved Nelson.

1939, August 7. Rocky Mountain NP—Civilians Robert Boyd and Robert C. Lewis, Jr. and Ranger Ernest Field—**Denver Post's Gallery of Fame**—lowered mountain climber 1,500 feet in "a rare feat in the history of mountain climbing." (Entered on 8-12-39.)**

1940, February. Mt. McKinley NP—Park sled dog Tige—**Dog World International Diploma of Honor**—saved life of Park Ranger John C. Rumohr. Rumohr and his dog team and sled had broken through the ice on Toklat River into 6 feet of water. Tige excited the rest of the dog team and they were able to pull the sled to firm ice.

1940, September 13. Rocky Mountain NP—CCC employee M. W. Whitaker—**$50 Certificate**—located body of man missing for more than a week.

1941, October 1. Devils Tower, NM—John R. Durrance, M.D.—American Alpine Club's **1986 David A. Sowles Memorial Award**—helped rescue parachutist from the top of the tower. (Awarded 1986.)** In 1981, the American Alpine Club established this award, conferring it "from time to time on mountaineers who have distinguished themselves, with unselfish devotion at personal risk or at sacrifice of a major objective in going to the assistance of fellow climbers imperiled in the mountains." Sowles, a 29-year-old "mountaineer's mountaineer," was killed in the Alps in 1963.

1942. Mt. Rainier NP—**Mountain Troops Memorial**—located on the trail to Alta Vista, this plaque honors the 10th Mountain Division who trained in the park in preparation for their role in World War II.

1943, April. Olympic NP—Ranger Dewey Webster—**Award of Outstanding Achievement, $25 War Bond,** and "**Received Personal Letter of Appreciation from Secretary Ickes**"—located Navy plane missing for several months. (Awarded 5-22-44.) Dewey Webster was one of just three DOI employees and the first from the NPS to receive the department's

Award of Outstanding Achievement in the first year of the federal government's newly created Suggestions System inaugurated in November 1943. The $25 War Bond included in the award, as stated in the "Report of the Interior Department Suggestions Committee—November 1943 to June 1944," was "contributed jointly by three employee unions in the Department: the American Federation of Government Employees, the National Federation of Federal Employees, and the United Federal Workers of America."

1943, November 19. The first "routine" honors of any kind bestowed by DOI were in three simultaneous ceremonies in Washington, DC; Denver, CO; and Portland, OR.

1944, June 20. Grand Canyon NP—Ranger Ed Lawes—"**Promoted for Exceptionally Meritorious Service**" (promoted 1-3-47)—rescued three trapped Army aviators who had parachuted onto North Rim.**

1944, September 18. Mt. McKinley NP—Ranger Grant Pearson—**Army Medal of Freedom**—for 44 days, led 43 men to crash site of C-47 where 19 soldiers lay buried under avalanche. Medal was presented by Major General Howard A. Craig.**

1946, July 9. Yosemite NP—Civilian Orville Dale Loos—**Carnegie Hero Award (Post-humously/Bronze)**—swept over 325-foot Vernal Falls while trying to save 12-year-old Keen Freeman.**

1946, December 10. Mt. Rainier NP—Ranger William J. Butler—**DOI Distinguished Service Award, US Navy Distinguished Public Service Certificate** (Navy's highest civilian award), **NPS Superior Accomplishment Pay Increase**, and a check for $5,000 from appreciative relatives (was returned uncashed)—persisted in locating Marine Corps aircraft with 32 men onboard.** Allowed under the provisions of Section 14 of the 1946 Public Law 600—Honor Awards—the Department of the Interior presented the first Distinguished Service Award (DSA) at the First Honors Convocation on April 28, 1948. Assistant Chief Ranger Bill Butler's gold-embossed DSA and accompanying gold medal were presented personally by Secretary of the Interior Krug on October 24, 1948, at a Superintendent's Conference at the Grand Canyon.

1946, December 10. Mt. Rainier NP—a **Marine Memorial** commemorating the loss of 32 soldiers on the slopes of South Tahoma Glacier was placed at Round Point; relatives of the victims meet each year and place flowers on the plaque. (See above.)

1949, February 7. Western Parks "Operation Snowbound" Unit—**DOI Unit Citation for Meritorious Service** (George H. Beaton, Frank Benda, Clarence Bengston, and Adolph Opalka)—Glacier NP, along with other DOI units in the West, provides "assistance to snowbound human and animal victims of unprecedented snowstorms and their aftermath in our western states."

1949, June 28. Yosemite NP—Rangers Marshall B. "Buck" Evans and Duane D. Jacobs—**DOI Meritorious Service Awards**—found two missing sisters after extensive search. (Awarded 10-16-50.)** Permitted under the same public law as the DSA, Evans and Jacobs are the first NPS employees personally honored with DOI's second highest tribute, the Meritorious Service Award; they received a silver-embossed certificate and a silver medal.

1949, July 21. Civilian Leroy J. Maloy—**Boy Scouts of America Certificate for Heroism**— "In Recognition of his effective and heroic action in saving the life of an Unknown Child." At the time he rescued this child from Kings River just outside of Kings Canyon National Park, Maloy was a stock packer for his family's Sierras pack station. Later joining the NPS, he eventually retired from Sequoia National Park.

1949, August 30. Acadia NP—Civilian John Large Harrison—**Carnegie Hero Award ("Bronze Medal and $500 for a worthy purpose as needed")**—attempted to save woman drowning in turbulent Atlantic Ocean near Otter Cliffs.**

1950, November 21. Grand Teton NP—Ranger Blake Vande Water—**DOI Distinguished Service Award**—during blizzard, climbed Mt. Moran for 19 victims of airplane wreck. (Awarded 9-27-51.)**

1950, November 21. Grand Teton NP—Chief Ranger Paul Judge, Ranger Blake Vande Water and civilian Paul Petzoldt—**Denver Post's Gallery of Fame**. (Entered 12-2-50.) (See above.)

1950, November 21. Grand Teton NP—Civilian Paul Petzoldt—**DOI Conservation Service Award**. (Awarded 5-20-52.) (See above.) Not a federal employee, Petzoldt was eligible only for the DOI's highest civilian recognition, the Conservation Service Award.

1951. Lake Mead NRA—Hoover Dam employee Robert W. Brumback—**DOI Distinguished Service Award**—saved three boys from drowning in lake. (Awarded 5-20-52.)

1951, May 20. Sequoia and Kings Canyon National Parks Rescue Team (12 men were named)—**DOI Unit Award for Meritorious Service**—rescued fisherman from Kaweah River. (Awarded 12-8-53.)** Permitted under Section 14 of 1946 Public Law 600, this is the first NPS *unit* award for valor—in any form. The actual commendation presented to Sequoia Super-intendent E. T. Scoyen by Secretary of the Interior Douglas McKay uses the two terms "Unit Citation" and "Unit Award" interchangeably. A "silver medal" was also presented to the park at this time. More than four years later (May 24, 1955), Rangers Thomas Adams, Richard Black, Richard Boyer, and Sequoia's contract physician, Dr. Raymond Manchester, were presented individual **Unit Award Certificates** for the "extraordinary risk which you all took to reach the injured men, in complete darkness. As a result, the final hours of Mr. Crawford were eased and no doubt the life of Mr. Brazil was saved."

1952, August 16. Grand Teton National Park Mountain Rescue Team (six men named)—**DOI Unit Award for Meritorious Service** and **NPS Certificate of Honor Award**—attempted rescue of mountain climber James Ayer. (Awarded 12-14-54.)**

1953, April 9. Petrified Forest NM—Ranger Clinton G. Harkins—**DOI Distinguished Service Award**—unsuccessful attempt to rescue the manager of Painted Desert Inn from a fire. (Awarded 12-8-53.)

1953, July 14. Grand Teton National Park Mountain Rescue Team (nine men named)— **DOI Unit Award for Meritorious Service**— 20-hour rescue of Norma Hart from the top of the Grand; she had a broken back. (Awarded 6-28-54.)**

1954, July 30. Grand Canyon National Park Rescue Team—**DOI Unit Award for Meritorious Service**—extensive search and recovery of missing Seasonal Ranger Ronald T. Berg. (Awarded 5-16-55.)**

1955, May 6. Mammoth Cave National Park Rescue Team (five men named)—**DOI Unit**

Award for Meritorious Service—rescued man trapped in a cave many miles from the park. (Awarded 3-12-56.)**

1955, June 28. Grand Teton National Park Mountain Rescue Team (eight men named)—**DOI Unit Award for Meritorious Service**—battling a treacherous blizzard, they recovered Fred Ford, a dead mountain climbing guide. (Awarded 4-23-57.)**

1955, August 19. Lake Mead NRA—Lifeguards Ruth M. Heard and Sylvia S. Reeves and Seasonal Ranger John R. Herse—**DOI Citation for Distinguished Service**—rescued four people. (Awarded 3-12-56.)**

1956, May 30. Rocky Mountain NP—Seasonal Rangers Frank Betts, Robert Frauson, Jerry Hammond, and Norman Nesbit—**DOI Valor Awards**—rescued youth from cliff in extensive lowering mission. (Awarded 4-23-57.)** These four rangers, along with Cahoon (below), received the first Valor Awards presented to *NPS* employees. The first two Valor Awards given to any DOI employee were on May 16, 1955, at the DOI's 15th Honors Convocation in Washington, D.C.

1956, June 10. Cape Hatteras NS—Seasonal Ranger Jack W. Cahoon—**DOI Valor Award**—saved man drowning in stormy surf. (Awarded 4-23-57.)

1956, June 30. Grand Canyon NP—Rangers Robert Bendt and Daniel Davis—**DOI Meritorious Service Awards**—for recovery efforts of the 128 people killed in a midair collision over the park.**

1956, June 30. Grand Canyon NP—From the 14th Aviation Company at Ft. Huachuca, AZ; Army Captain Walter E. Spriggs, Jr.; First Lieutenant Paul F. Walker; and Chief Warrant Officers Howard L. Proctor, James T. Spearman, Jack L. Carey, and Billy L. Pearman—**Distinguished Flying Crosses**.** (See above.)

1956, June 30. Grand Canyon NP—On August 2, 30 military officers and enlisted men, including Air Force helicopter pilots from Luke Air Force Base and other personnel from Arizona's Ft. Huachuca, were decorated.** (See above.)

1956, October 4. Olympic NP—Coast Guard Lieutenant Commander David Gershowitz (USCG helicopter pilot's license #7)—**US Air Medal**—cited for several Coast Guard rescues,

including the midair crash of two Air Force "Scorpion" Jet Fighters over the park.**

1956, October 31. Yosemite NP—Ranger John Bingaman—**DOI Meritorious Service Award**—presented upon retirement, specifically mentions the park's April 7, 1928, Wilbur and Ring rescue.**

1958, June 9. Castillo de San Marcos, NM—William H. Manucy, Jr.—**DOI Valor Award**—saved small child and her mother from drowning.

1958, June 21. Everglades NP—Ranger Clifford W. Senne—**DOI Valor Award**—saved four-year-old girl from an alligator-infested pool. (Awarded 9-5-58.)**

1958, August 11. El Morro NM—George D. Carter, Jr. and Lyle E. Jamison—**DOI Valor Awards**—saved man who fell 40 feet into crack. (Awarded 4-27-59.)

1958, August 19. Yosemite National Park Mountain Rescue Team (nine rangers named)—**DOI Unit Award for Excellence of Service**—rescued 17-year-old off 1,000-foot cliff. (Awarded 11-12-59.)**

1959, June 18. Glacier NP—Ranger Donald Dayton—**DOI Valor Award**—shot grizzly bear attacking a man. (Awarded 4-11-60.)**

1960, March 9. Grand Teton NP—Rangers Stan Spurgeon and Gail Wilcox (Posthumously)—**DOI Valor Awards** and **Carnegie Hero Awards (Bronze/$500)** and, to Mrs. Wilcox, $60 per month for two years)—Wilcox died trying to rescue fellow ranger John Fonda while Spurgeon nearly died trying to rescue Wilcox. (Awarded 4-19-61.)**

1960, March 9. Grand Teton NP—Rangers John Fonda and Gail Wilcox (Posthumously)—places on Jackson Lake, Fonda and Wilcox Points, named in their honor. (See above.)

1960, May 17. Mt. McKinley NP—Helicopter pilot Link Luckett—**Carnegie Hero Award (Silver / $500 and "$700 to reimburse him for pecuniary loss")**—participated in spectacular rescue of John Day, Pete Schoening, and brothers Lou and Jim Whittaker after landing at the 17,200-foot level.**

1960, May 26. Arlington, VA—Park Policeman Frank E. Papuga—**DOI Valor Award**—halted runaway 10-ton truck by leaping into cab. (Awarded 1-16-61.)

1960, June 22. Natchez Trace Parkway—Caretaker Harvey Brown—**DOI Valor Award** and **Carnegie Hero Award (Bronze $500)** and civilian S. Lamor Hinton—**Carnegie Hero Award (Bronze/$500)**—rescued two young women from drowning. (Awarded 1-16-61.)

1960, July 10. Takoma Park, MD—-Park Policeman James D. Finch—**DOI Valor Award**—saved five people from burning home. (Awarded 1-18-62.)

1960, November 13. Mt. Rainier NP—Ranger William Butler—recognized for his years of search and rescue effort by being the subject of Ralph Edwards's nationally televised *This Is Your Life*. He received a Ford Falcon Stationwagon, binoculars, a movie projector, and a charm bracelet to commemorate that night. Butler allegedly locked himself in a bathroom after taping the show and would not come out until his wife, Martha, promised they would return home at once so he could get back to his elk-hunting camp.

1961, August 15. Olympic NP—Coast Guard Lieutenant Lee Levy—**US Coast Guard Commendation Medal**—helicopter pilot of dangerous medevac during raging forest fire at dusk while in blinding smoke.

1961, October 30. City of Refuge NHP—Maintenanceman Henry C. Hua—**DOI Valor Award** and **Carnegie Hero Award (Bronze/ $500)**—rescued five men from boat being forced onto rocks. (Awarded 8-6-62.)

1962, July 27. Grand Teton National Park Mountain Rescue Team (eight men named)—**DOI Unit Award for Meritorious Service**—difficult and hazardous body recovery of one Appalachian Mountain Club member and the rescue of nine others from Teepee Glacier on the Grand Teton.

1963, June 27. Glacier NP—Volunteer scuba diver Tom Dumay—Columbia Falls High School established **Tom Dumay Memorial Scholarship**—Dumay died in Lake McDonald while searching for missing boy.**

1964, August 16. Isle Royale NP—Fire Control Aid Gordon Haber—**DOI Valor Award**—saved park ranger who grabbed 2,400-volt electrical line. (Awarded 7-15-65.)

1964, August 27. Big Bend NP—Caretaker Merechildo L. Ybarra—**DOI Valor Award** and **Carnegie Hero Award (Bronze/ $750)**—rescued 17-year-old boy from burning overturned truck. (Awarded 7-15-65.)

1965, August 1. Grand Teton NP—Civilian pilot Bob Schellinger—Helicopter Association Inter-national (HAI) **Helicopter Pilot of the Year Award**—rescued two climbers at the 9,700-foot level at dusk. Established in 1960, the Pilot of the Year is the oldest of HAI's 12 awards. It recognizes an outstanding single feat performed by an active civilian helicopter pilot during the year or extraordinary professionalism over a period of time.

1966. Yosemite NP—Rangers Frederick T. Anderson, Gary N. Brown, and David W. Huson—**DOI Valor Awards**—given for the combination of three separate cliff rescues that saved five climbers in Yosemite Valley. (Awarded 6-8-67.)

1966, March 19. Death Valley NM—Seasonal Ranger Robert K. DeVine—**DOI Valor Award** and **Carnegie Hero Award (Bronze/$750)**—narrowly rescued driver of burning fiberglass sports car. (Awarded 11-10-66.)

1966, May 21. Fire Island NS—Maintenanceman Ashley N. Smith and Seasonal Ranger William E. Shaner—**DOI Valor Awards (Posthumously)** and **Carnegie Hero Awards (Posthumously, Bronze/$750 and $80 per month to the widows)**—all three died trying to save a young swimmer caught in turbulent surf. (Awarded 11-10-66.)**

1966, May 21. Fire Island NS—Civilians James C. Del Giudice and James C. Lawler—**Carnegie Hero Awards (Bronze /$750)**. (See above.)

1966, July 16. Ft. Matanzas NM—Ranger D. L. Huggins—**DOI Valor Award**—using a small boat, he rescued five people in high seas after professional rescue unit could not do so. (Awarded 12-12-67.)

1966, Summer. Mt. McKinley NP—Ranger Wayne Merry—**Special Achievement Award** ($500)—developed two slide and tape programs for teaching climbing safety and mountain rescue.

1966, Summer. Mt. Rainier National Park Ranger Division—**DOI Unit Award for Excellence of Service**—recognized for busy SAR season.

1967, February 6. Washington, D.C.—Park Policeman Carl R. Holmberg—**Valor Award**—rescued woman who attempted suicide by jumping into tidal basin. (Awarded 12-12-67.)

1967, March 27. Washington, D.C.—Park Policeman Robert K. Cornwell—**Valor Award**—rescued woman attempting suicide in Potomac River. (Awarded 12-12-67.)

1967, August 21. Grand Teton NP—Rangers Hans M. Ermarth, Robert W. Irvine, Richard L. Reese, Leon R. Sinclair, Ralph H. Tingey, and Ted L. Wilson—**DOI Valor Awards**—rescued two people from Grand Teton; lowered one of them over 1,800 feet. (Awarded 6-4-68.)** The letter from Vice President Hubert H. Humphrey said, in part, "I still don't see how you did it, but I am told that Mr. Campbell will live, so I guess you did!"

1967, August 21. Grand Teton NP—Mountain Rescue Support Team (eight men named)—**DOI Unit Award for Excellence of Service.** (See above.)

1967, August 21. Grand Teton NP—Civilian helicopter pilot Robert K. Schellinger and climbing guide Leigh N. Ortenburger—**Letters of Commendation from Secretary of the Interior.** (See above.)

1967, December 12. NPS Midwest Regional Office—Ranger Ernest Field—**DOI Distinguished Service Award (Posthumously)**—recognized for extensive contributions to SAR over the years, including coauthoring early mountain rescue book, *Mountain Search and Rescue Operations*, in 1958. (He died 6-4-62.)

1968, April 15. Mt. Rainier NP—**T-33 Accident Memorial: Dedicated to Colonel Wilfred B. Crutchfield and Major Ivan E. O'Dell**—placed in the Paradise Inn is a plaque dedicated to the two Air Force pilots killed in an aircraft accident on the mountain.

1968, May 23. Lake Mead NRA—Ranger Joe Cayou—**DOI Valor Award**—in a strong gale, dove under capsized sailboat for trapped man. (Awarded 12-11-68.)**

1969, August. Hawaii Volcanoes NP—Rangers Johnny Hauanio and Dave Morris; Maintenanceman Bill Halm—**NPS Special Achievement Award** ($200)—crossed day-old lava flow to rescue three trapped people. Morris stated, "Why Jim [Superintendent Tobin] chose to write

us up for S.A.A., rather than valor or courageous act awards was never explained, nor has it ever seemed important to me . . . we were too broke to question the source."

1969, August 6. Isle Royale NP—Dennis A. Long—**DOI Valor Award (Posthumously)** and **Carnegie Hero Award (Posthumously/ Bronze)**—saved drowning woman and then drowned. (Awarded 6-30-70.)

1970, January 2. Glacier NP—Mt. Cleveland Search and Recovery Team—**DOI Unit Award for Excellence of Service**—for six-month-long recovery effort for five victims of winter avalanche.**

1970, February 5. Grand Teton NP—Ranger Doug McLaren—**DOI Meritorious Service Award**—cited for contribution to mountain rescue and receiving previous five Unit Awards for Excellence of Service.

1970, March 22. Pinnacles NM—Ranger James M. Langford—**DOI Valor Award**—rescued man from 600-foot cliff in dark. (Awarded 6-7-71.)

1970, May. Yosemite NP—Civilian engineer Harlan E. Shoemaker—**NPS Appreciation Award**—aided in the rescue of a climber who had fallen 270 feet. According to NPS Associate Director Dan Tobin, Jr., Shoemaker "exhibited bravery, tenacity, and clear thinking in the face of crisis."

1970, May. Yosemite NP—Civilian engineer George R. Wolf—**NPS Appreciation Award**—rescued small boy who was being carried down a stream toward a 25-foot waterfall. In the same ceremony as Harlan Shoemaker, Dan Tobin said Wolf was recognized "for courageous disregard of his own safety and for saving a life."

1970, July 7. Yosemite NP—School teacher Edward Jack Miller and student William G. Worthington—**Carnegie Hero Awards (Bronze)**—attempted a very technical rock rescue for fellow climber Hallard B. Kinnison who had fallen onto a ledge on a 750-foot cliff.

1970, July 11. Lake Mead NRA—Rangers Donald Chase, Richard Gale, and Jerry Phillips —**Certificate of Appreciation from Imperial County, CA**—for successful body recovery of two dead marines trapped deep in an abandoned mine in Southern California.**

1971. Mt. Rainier NP—Ranger William Butler—former Ranger Dee Molenaar's book, *The Challenge of Rainier*, was dedicated—"To Bill Butler—Who for over 30 years was wherever help was needed on the mountain . . . a legend in his time."

1971, June 19. Grand Teton NP—College student Richard W. DaBell, Policeman Ronald F. Ottoson, and Engineer William H. Radtke—**Carnegie Hero Awards (Bronze)**—attempted to rescue three people who fell into ice- and water-filled crevasse.**

1971, June 19. Grand Teton Rescue Team (12 men named)—**NPS Special Achievement Awards** for $150 each; $250 for Milligan and Irvine. (See above.)

1971, July 2. Grand Teton NP—Seasonal Ranger Edward A. Wilson—**NPS Special Achievement Award** for $150—rescued seven people trapped on Snake River at night.

1971, August 14. Rocky Mountain NP—Seasonal Ranger Walt Fricke—**DOI Valor Award**—accompanied a youth in a litter down a 1,000-foot cliff. (Awarded 8-30-71.)**

1971, August 14. Rocky Mountain Rescue Team (nine men named)—**DOI Unit Award for Excellence of Service**. (Awarded 8-30-71.) (See above.)

1971, August 31. Sequoia NP—Ranger Larry D. Weede—**DOI Valor Award**—rescued seven-year-old from treacherous river. (Awarded 6-15-72.)**

1972, June 21. Rock Creek Park—Park Policeman Stephen G. Livesay—**DOI Valor Award**—rescued woman trapped in submerged car. (Awarded 6-19-73.)

1972, September 23. Yosemite NP—El Capitan Rescue Team—**Unit Award for Excellence of Service**—lowered climber almost 2,200 vertical feet in a three-day effort.**

1972, September 24. Grand Teton NP—Seasonal Ranger Edward A. Wilson—**DOI Valor Award**—rescued two men from Snake River. (Awarded 6-19-73.)

1973, May 28. Lake Mead NRA—Ranger Ted W. Miller—**DOI Valor Award**—rescued drowning man at Katherine. (Awarded 6-27-74.)

1973, June 3. Zion NP—Virgin River Narrows

Search and Rescue Team—**DOI Unit Award for Excellence of Service**—Lake Mead Rangers Peter Allen and Ken Morgan and Zion Mainten-an-ceman Seth Phelen floated for two days through The Narrows during flash flood looking for survivors.**

1973, June 26. Thornton State Beach, CA—State Park Ranger Steve R. Gazzano (later to become NPS Ranger)—**State of California Medal of Valor**—rescued drowning 17-year-old boy from heavy surf.

1974, April/May. Haleakala NP—Ranger Edward K. Pu, Sr.—**DOI Valor Award**—on three separate occasions rescued people drowning in rough surf at the park's isolated Seven Pools. (Awarded 12-4-75.)

1974, July 17. City of Refuge NHP—Ranger Walter P. Kaniwa—**DOI Valor Award**—saved two people after boat exploded. (Awarded 12-4-75.)

1974, September 14. Lake Mead NRA—Eldorado Canyon Search and Recovery Team (79 people named)—**DOI Unit Award for Excellence of Service**—21 agencies united in search and recovery efforts after a locally intense flash flood killed nine people in narrow canyon.**

1974, September 24. Near Blanding, UT—Natural Bridges NM Ranger Michael J. Gilbert—**DOI Valor Award**—part of regional rescue team who saved BLM Ranger Steven A. Rivas, who was trapped under 3-ton boulder in remote canyon of southern Utah. Two other BLM employees received Carnegie Hero Awards.

1975, March 20. Olympic NP—Recovery and Salvage Operation (27 people named)—**DOI Unit Award for Excellence of Service**—searched five months for 16 victims of an Air Force C-141 Starlifter crash.**

1975, March 20. Olympic NP—C-141 Peak, the 7,339-foot point of the collision is dedicated, at least unofficially, by The Mountaineers, to the 17 servicemen killed in the Starlifter crash.

1975, March 26. Medora, ND—Theodore Roosevelt NM Maintenancemen Donald R. Chambers and Jerry E. Goldsberry and Ranger Martin C. Ott—**DOI Valor Awards** and **Carnegie Hero Awards (Bronze/$1,000)**—rescued 34-year-old man trapped underground in a collapsed building in a small community near park headquarters.

1975, June. Olympic Staff—Washington State's **Snowshoe Thompson Award**—given for "outstanding, unique, and/or unusual rescue." Complicated and humorous set of missions during the year.**

1976, January 24. Sequoia National Park Mountain Rescue Team—**DOI Unit Award for Excellence of Service**—rescued injured man from deep in technically difficult Soldier's Cave.**

1976, April 29. Golden Gate NRA—Ranger James E. McOwien—**DOI Valor Award**—rescued 20-year-old woman who survived jumping from Golden Gate Bridge into San Francisco Bay (220 feet).

1976, June 2. Denali NP—Civilian pilot Warren "Buddy" Woods—Helicopter Association International's (HAI) **Robert E. Trimble Memorial Award**—landed at 20,300 feet (North American altitude landing record) to rescue two injured climbers.** The HAI "Robert E. Trimble Award honors . . . pilot who is especially distinguished in mountain flying . . . established in 1961 to focus attention on a pilot who has . . . exceptional ability and good judgement in high altitude flying."

1976, July 31. Rocky Mountain NP (29 people named and "presented to NPS employees and family members")—outside of park—**DOI Valor Award**—rescue and recovery efforts in devastating Big Thompson Canyon flood, which killed 139. (Awarded 12-7-76.)**

1976, July 31. Rocky Mountain NP Search and Rescue Team—outside of park—**State of Colorado Governor's Citation**—signed by Governor Richard Lamm on September 3, 1976. (See above.)

1976, December 30. Washington, D.C.—Park Police helicopter pilot Earl Cronin and Officer High C. Irwin—**DOI Valor Awards**—saved distraught woman who had attempted suicide in Potomac River. (Awarded 5-17-78.)

1977, August 10. Chesapeake and Ohio Canal NHP—Maintenanceman Cecil L. Tucker—**DOI Valor Award**—saved two small children from drowning in Potomac River. (Awarded 5-17-78.)

1978. Great Smoky Mountains NP—Ranger Bill Wade **NASAR Fellow Award**—for training committee assistance.

1978, January 2. Washington, D.C.—Park

Policeman Albert F. Jez—**DOI Valor Award**—rescued numerous persons from two burning buildings. (Awarded 10-10-79.)

1978, January 3. Great Smoky Mountains NP—Army aviators John L. Dunnavant, Floyd Smith, and Terrance K. Woolever **(Posthumously)**—dedicated **Blanchfield Medical Center Heliport** at Ft. Campbell, KY, in their honor—killed while trying to rescue five people who had crashed in a small commuter plane.**

1978, January 3. Great Smoky Mountains NP—Civil Air Patrol Lieutenant Colonel Ray Maynard—awarded the CAP **Distinguished Service Medal (Posthumously)**—for contributions from November 1964 to January 1978, as well as for the rescue attempt above.**

1978, April 14. Gulf Islands NS—Maintenanceman Timmy A. Gray—**DOI Valor Award**—rescued semiconscious six-year-old from riptide. (Awarded 10-10-79.)

1978, May 2. Yosemite NP—Student Bradley Mentzer—**Carnegie Hero Award (Posthumously/Bronze)**—drowned trying to save 16-year-old fellow student who had fallen into river below Merced Falls.

1978, May 28. Yosemite NP—Lemoore Search and Rescue Helicopter Crew, United States Navy (John A. Deciccio, Herman A. Dolgado, Jr., Benny C. Revels, John A. Sullivan, and Donald A. Swain)—**DOI Valor Awards**—rescued climber from Cloud's Rest by hovering while the crew chief rappelled 300 feet to victim. (Awarded 10-10-80.)** This U.S. Navy helicopter crew was the first and only non-DOI unit to ever receive DOI Valor Awards.

1978, July 20. Yellowstone NP—School teachers Sammy K. Christiansen and Darrel L. Gibbons—**Carnegie Hero Awards (Bronze)**—launched two canoes into severe windstorm on Lake Shoshone to rescue three people after their craft had capsized.

1978, September 4. Golden Gate NRA—Park Policeman Steven S. Prickett—**DOI Valor Award**—rescued child and then saved a second potential rescuer from heavy surf at Ocean Beach. (Awarded 10-10-79.)

1979. Albright TC—Instructor James Brady—**NASAR Fellow Award**—for NASAR Conference support.

1979, June 10. Cape Hatteras NS—Ranger

John J. Troy—**DOI Valor Award**—rescued three people on two separate efforts from surf.

1979, June 22. Mt. Rainier Rescue Team—Rangers Jean Paul de St. Croix and Gary D. Olson—**DOI Valor Awards**—lowered onto knife-edge ice ridge at 12,500 feet at night for injured climber.**

1979, September 12. Washington, D.C.—Park Policeman Chester M. Hendrickson—**DOI Valor Award**—dropped from USPP helicopter into Anacostia River for person attempting suicide by jumping in.

1980. Yosemite NP—Ranger Charles R. "Butch" Farabee—**NASAR State Award, California**.

1980. Great Smoky Mountains NP—Ranger Bill Wade—**NASAR State Award, Tennessee**. NASAR's State Award is "to the individual or organization making the most significant contribution to search and rescue within a NASAR member state. Nominations for the state awards will be sent to the governors of the respective states for approval."

1980. Albright TC—Instructor James Brady—**NASAR Fellow Award**—for SAR training.

1980. U.S. Navy Crew Chief John Bazan—Yosemite NP Search and Rescue Officer Tim Setnicka's book, *Wilderness Search and Rescue*, has dedication "For John Bazan." Bazan, a good friend of NPS SAR, died in a helicopter accident off the coast of Florida in 1979.

1980, February 6. Washington, D.C.—Park Policeman Phillip W. Cholak—**DOI Valor Award**—saved fellow officer from burning vehicle after collision during high-speed chase. (Awarded 10-21-80.)

1980, February 19. Sleeping Bear Dunes Staff—**DOI Unit Award for Excellence of Service**—11 staff and 29 others saved 11-year-old boy from six-foot-deep snow avalanche.**

1980, May 25. Canyonlands NP—Ranger James K. Braggs—**DOI Valor Award**—cut woman free from under capsized boat while they floated through rapids on Colorado River. (Awarded 10-21-80.)

1980, August 5. Sleeping Bear Dunes NL—Ranger Stephen E. Yancho—**DOI Valor Award**—saved teenage boy from drowning in heavy waves. (Awarded 10-21-80.)

1980, August 26. Grand Teton NP—Jenny Lake Mountain Rescue Team (Convocation program names six rangers: Barbara Eastman, Tim M. Hogan, Robert W. Irvine, Reynold G. Jackson, Leo L. Larson, and Peter N. Wallis)—**DOI Valor Award**—rescued two climbers during blizzard. (Awarded 12-2-81.)** Also nominated for International Valor Award.

1980, Summer. Grand Teton NP—Jenny Lake Rescue Team (named 20 people)—**DOI Unit Award for Excellence of Service**—recognized team for "exceptional performance which involved more than 30 different, highly technical and complex rescue missions."

1980, September 11. North Cascades NP—Helicopter Detachment "Whidbey Angels" (Dan Mahoney, Pat Kidgell, Roy Lewis, Rick Kubal)—**Bronze Plaques** in Marblemount Visitor Center and on boulder near Perfect Pass.** One plaque reads:

> While on a rescue mission, "Firewood One," an HC-46 [sic] Helicopter from Whidbey Island Naval Air Station crashed at Perfect Pass. Five crewmen died. Their mission had been to evacuate an injured climber from Mt. Redoubt. "So Others May Live" is the motto and spirit of the Whidbey fliers. The sacrifice that "Firewood One" made to those values is carried on, Whidbey is still flying "So Others May Live."

1981, January 1. Lassen NP—Ranger George R. Giddings—**DOI Valor Award**—rescued two people who fell through ice of Manzanita Lake. (Awarded 12-2-81.)

1981, February 20. West Potomac Park—Maintenanceman Melvin A. Lewis—**DOI Valor Award**—saved fellow electrician from electrocution. (Awarded 12-2-81.)

1981, May 2. Lassen NP—Secretary Sarah L. Miller—**DOI Valor Award**—rescued man trapped in rain-swollen culvert; both were swept through it but she was still able to save him. (Awarded 9-20-83.)

1981, May 23. George Memorial Parkway—River Rescue Team, Great Falls Park (13 people named)—**DOI Unit Award for Excellence of Service**—received for accumulated superior conduct for SAR operations during the spring.**

1981, June 21. Mt. Rainier—**1981 Climbing Disaster Memorial**—placed on the wall of the Paradise Visitor Center is a plaque commemorating 11 climbers who were killed in the worst mountaineering tragedy in North American climbing history.

1981, July 12. Zion NP—Ranger Roy Given—**DOI Valor Award**—saved two small children from a flash flood as he was running in front of it warning people to get out of the way. (Awarded 9-20-83.)

1981, August 19. Acadia NP—Ranger Victor Rydlizky—**DOI Valor Award**—in heavy seas and amidst treacherous rocks, helped rescue man clinging to overturned kayak. (Awarded 9-20-83.)

1981, September 16. Rock Creek Park—Maintenancemen Frank Hart, John W. Klepp, Calvin D. Yates, and Park Policeman John P. Farrell—**DOI Valor Awards**—saved four from auto submerged in water-filled creek. (Awarded 9-20-83.)

1981, December 31. Joshua Tree Rescue Team (15 people named)—**DOI Unit Award for Excellence of Service**—after stabilizing woman who had fallen, they lowered her 500 feet down cliff.**

1982, January 13. Washington, D.C.—Park Policemen Donald Usher and Mel Windsor—**DOI Valor Awards**, **Carnegie Hero Awards ($2,000)**, Helicopter Association International's **1982 Crew of the Year Award**, and International Association of Air Line Pilot's **Polaris Awards**—dramatic rescue in the frozen Potomac River of five people from an Air Florida plane crash. (DOI Valor citations Awarded 1-13-82.)**

1982, January 13. Washington, D.C.—Pilot Donald Usher—**NASAR 1982 Zimmerman-Rand Award for Valor**. (See above.) "This award is presented to a person who, by being involved in a lifesaving SAR effort, exemplifies the selfless, perhaps risky commitment embodied in the motto of NASAR: 'That Others May Live.' It is not presented posthumously."

1982, February 21. Amistad RA—Archeologists Daniel J. Lenihan, Larry E. Murphy, and Larry V. Nordby; Rangers Deborah A. Gibbons and Mark W. Igo; and Administrative Officer Daniel M. Peregoy—**DOI Exemplary Act Awards**—located body of missing scuba diver in abandoned, submerged powerhouse.**

1982, April 25. Cuyahoga Valley NRA—Ranger Matthew G. Bland—**DOI Exemplary Act Awards**—assisted woman who had fallen onto rocks.

1982, June 16. Ft. Jefferson Staff—**DOI Unit Award for Excellence of Service**—in 60-mph winds, six staff and two Denver Service Center employees responded to save numerous boats and reduce victims' confusion and resulting chaos.

1982, July 22. Bandelier NM—Rangers Robert E. Belden, Edward J. Greene, and Rick L. Mossman—**DOI Exemplary Act Award**—searched for and then found a potential suicide victim.**

1983. Delaware Water Gap NRA—Superintendent Bill Wade—**NASAR Hal Foss Award**—When Hal Foss died in 1974, he was the State of Washington's director of emergency operations; he tirelessly furthered SAR. "The Hal Foss Award is the most prestigious award presented by NASAR. It is a national award given to the individual or organization that has made the most significant contribution to search and rescue on a national basis."

1983. Shenandoah NP—Ranger Bill Blake—**NASAR State Award, Virginia**.

1983. Delaware Water Gap NRA—Ranger Bill Wade—**NASAR Fellow Award**.

1983, January 26. Whiskeytown Rescue Team (10 people named)—outside of park—**DOI Unit Award for Excellence of Service**—cited after they "struggled through waist high water and mud" to save eight people trapped by floodwaters and landslides.

1983, February 2. Lake Mead NRA—Hoover Dam Police Officer Carl W. Davis—**DOI Valor Award**—rescued man trapped in burning sports car two miles east of the dam. (Awarded 4-24-85.)

1983, April 30. Buffalo River NR—Ranger Richard E. Brown—**DOI Valor Award**—saved a couple trapped in river rapids who were being crushed against rock by canoe. (Awarded 4-24-85.)

1983, June 17. Yosemite NP—Ranger Charles M. Peterson—**DOI Valor Award**—while using scuba to clear water-filled highway culvert, saved fellow-ranger John Daley, who had been sucked into pipe. This dramatic effort was recreated in fall 1992 on a 15-minute segment of *Heart of Courage*, a Discovery Channel television documentary. (Awarded 4-24-85.)

1983, July 3. Assateague Island NS—Ranger Kenneth Zimmerman—**DOI Exemplary Act Award**—rescued two men from surf; "for his immediate and skillful response to this emergency, reflecting the highest and best traditions of the National Park Service."

1983, July 8. Canaveral NS—Scott's Bluff NM Rangers Richard H. Helman and Kathleen F. Spellman and Canaveral NS Ranger Curtis C. Weikert—**DOI Exemplary Act Award**—helped rescue four people who were drowning in Mosquito Lagoon.

1983, July 13. Whiskeytown NRA—Ranger Henry J. Chojnacki—**DOI Valor Award**—rescued drowning woman who had been sucked 10 feet into powerhouse discharge tube. (Awarded 4-24-85.)

1983, July 17. Yosemite Staff (18 NPS people named along with staff of Yosemite Medical Group, Lemoore NAS Helicopter Unit, and Modesto Mediflight Unit)—**DOI Unit Award for Excellence of Service**—saved victim of a fall from Washington's Column in Yosemite Valley.

1983, August 12. Yosemite NP—Rangers Gary Colliver, Peter Dalton, and Dan Dellinges—**DOI Valor Awards**—successfully rescued lady who had been trapped underwater for 25 minutes. (Awarded 4-24-85.)**

1983, August 12. Yosemite Staff—**DOI Unit Award for Excellence of Service**—resuscitated woman. (See above.)

1983, August 18. Yosemite NP—Maintenanceman Edwin L. Appling—**DOI Exemplary Act Award**—rescued man trapped on dam in Merced River.

1983, September 18. Western Regional Director Howard Chapman presented NASAR with **Special Commendation**—for assistance on preparing much used "Managing the Search Function" Course.

1983, October 10. Shenandoah Search and Rescue Unit—**DOI Unit Award for Excellence of Service**—intensively searched for, and then saved lost 18-year-old boy.**

1983, October 23. Point Reyes NS—Rangers Lee Shenk and Bryan Sutton—**DOI Exemplary Act Award**—rescued man from drowning in rough surf.

1983, December 8. Grand Canyon NP—Geological Survey employees Heidi H. Herendeen and John Pittman and Bureau of Land Management District Manager G. William Lamb—**DOI Valor Awards**—rescued man strapped in helicopter upside down in river; Lamb, also one of helicopter's occupants, joined in effort. (Awarded 4-24-85.)**

1983, December 29. Olympic NP—Ranger Richard W. Thomas—**DOI Valor Award**—using scuba, located two infants trapped in vehicle 30 feet down; kids died later in day. (Awarded 4-24-85.)** Thomas died June 22, 1984, while on a Civil Air Patrol SAR training mission.

1984, January 11. Cuyahoga Valley NRA—Ranger Thomas A. Cherry, III—**DOI Exemplary Act Award**—while off-duty in Harpers Ferry, WV, saved man who was choking.

1984, February 13. Denali NP—Civilians Eiho Otani and Jim Wickwire—American Alpine Club's **1985 David A. Sowles Memorial Award**—tried to find Naomi Uemura, missing Japanese climbing hero.**

1984, May 5. Yosemite NP—**DOI Exemplary Act Award** (25 people named)—evacuation of fall victim from the Ledge Trail.

1984, May 11. Washington, D.C.—Park Policeman Richard J. Murphy—**DOI Valor Award**—saved man from fire-engulfed truck ignited by fireworks explosion in parking lot of RFK football stadium.

1984, July 25. Mt. Rushmore NM—Ranger Frank Bounds—**DOI Exemplary Act Award**—using CPR and first aid, saved one-year-old boy who suffered both cardiac and respiratory arrests several times.

1984, August 22. Salinas NM—Maintenanceman Earl F. Ferguson, III—**DOI Valor Award**—rescued man from truck caught in flash flood. (Awarded 4-24-85.)

1984, October 9. Picture Rocks NL—Maintenance Mechanic Vernon M. Kirkens—**DOI Exemplary Act Award**—administered lifesaving first aid to man with diabetic complications.

1984, October 21. Haleakala NP—Ranger Perry Bednorz—**DOI Exemplary Act Award**—rescued falling victim from base of waterfall.**

1985. Great Smoky Mountains NP—Ranger Duane Alaire—**NASAR Fellow Award**—for Conference Committee assistance.

1985, January 21. Indiana Sand Dunes NL—Ranger Colette H. Daigle-Berg—**DOI Exemplary Act Award**—while a passenger herself, provided more than two hours of first aid at scene of two-train collision in Gary, IN.

1985, January 25. Yellowstone NP—Rangers Tom Black, John Donaldson, Sandi Fowler, and James Sweaney—**DOI Exemplary Act Award**—rescued woman from car overturned in freezing Yellowstone River.

1985, May 6. Lake Mead NRA—Ranger Robert W. McKeever—**DOI Exemplary Act Award**—rescued man drowning in turbulent lake.

1985, May 26. Buffalo River NR—Civilian D. Robert Young, Jr.—**Carnegie Hero Award (Bronze/$2,500)**—saved drowning woman.

1985, June 12. Hawaii Volcanoes NP—Italian scientist Dr. Dario Tedesco—**DOI Secretarial Commendation** and nominated for **Fred Packard International Valor Award**—saved companion who was sinking into volcanic lava. The Fred Packard International Merit Award is a valor award created in 1980 by the IUCN's World Commission on Protected Areas "to honour parks personnel for acts of unusual courage involving a high degree of personal risk in the face of danger."

1985, June 30. Golden Gate NRA—Lifeguards Dennis R. Glass, Steven Prokop, and Scott E. Urban—**DOI Exemplary Act Award**—rescued drowning 12-year-old and the two firemen who tried to assist.**

1985, July 27. Yosemite Rescue Team (59 people named)—**DOI Exemplary Act Award**—resolved two very difficult technical rescues in different parts of the park at the same time.**

1985, July 29. Capital Reef NM—Rangers Ken Kehrer and Larry R. Vensel—**DOI Valor Awards**—rescued 14 people from flash flood that raced through campground. (Awarded 9-26-86.)**

1985, August 10. Indiana Dunes NL—Ranger Gordon R. Zwick—**DOI Exemplary Act Award**—helped rescue drowning 12-year-old boy.

1985, September 11. Grand Teton NP—Rangers Randy R. Harrington, Reynold G. Jackson, Leo L. Larson, and James T. Woodmencey (Jenny Lake Rescue Team)—**DOI Valor Awards**—in a vicious blizzard, rescued two climbers from high on Grand Teton peak. (Awarded 9-26-86.)**

1985, October 8. Ranger Ken Hulick as incident commander and Dick Barr, Jan Hill, Mike Hill, Rusty Loran, Skip Wissinger, and Denny Zieman—Puerto Rico—**"Heroes en Puerto Rico" Medal**—NPS employees coordinated 13 American dog teams searching for victims of massive mudslide.**

1985, December 19. Indiana Dunes NL—Rangers Robert D. Carnes and Darlene Mandel—**DOI Exemplary Act Awards**—while off-duty, gave lifesaving assistance to victims of a train-vehicle accident.

1986. Shenandoah NP—Ranger Bill Pierce—**NASAR Fellow Award**—for contributions as a conference track leader.

1986. Glacier NP—Ranger Charles Logan—**NASAR Fellow Award**—for contributions in membership recruitment.

1986. Yosemite NP—SAR Technician John Dill—**NASAR Fellow Award**—for extensive contributions to the Technical Rescue Symposium.

1986, June 13. Lake Mead NRA—Rangers William Briggs and Peter Dalton—**DOI Valor Awards**—rescued youth from 600 feet up on crumbling cliffs. (Awarded 9-30-87.)**

1986, June 13. Lake Mead NRA—Ranger Peter Dalton—**NASAR 1987 Zimmerman-Rand Award**. (See above.)

1986, June 18. Grand Canyon Air Crash Incident Command Group (24 people named)—**DOI Unit Award for Excellence of Service**—coordinated recovery efforts of 25 people killed in an aircraft collision over Grand Canyon.**

1986, July 14. Grand Teton NP—Rangers Daniel L. Burgette, Reynold G. "Rennie" Jackson, and Steve W. Rickert—**DOI Exemplary Act Award**—rescued victim of 2,000-foot fall down Skillet Glacier by using sophisticated helicopter short-haul techniques.**

1986, July 20. North Cascades NP—Seasonal Ranger Christy Fairchild—**DOI Exemplary Act Award**—rescued man trapped in river with rock on top of him.**

1986, July 25. Fire Island NS—Volunteer-in-Park Jared Cumming—**DOI Exemplary Act Award**—rescued man drowning near Watch Hill Marina.

1986, July 26. Yosemite NP—Ranger Mead Hargis—**DOI Exemplary Act Award**—rescued four people from burning airplane.

1986, August 8. Rock Creek Park—U.S. Park Policeman Richard A. Deriso—**DOI Valor Award**—rescued occupants of vehicle being swept down flood-swollen stream. (Awarded 9-30-87.)

1986, September 11. Glacier NP—Ranger Brian Kuhn—**DOI Exemplary Act Award**—efficiently handled hiker who had been seriously mauled by grizzly bear in backcountry.

1987. Shenandoah NP—Ranger Bill Pierce and Mather TC Director Bill Wade—**NASAR Honor Society (Angels of the High Lonesome)**—for serving on Board of Directors.

1987. Mather TC—Superintendent Bill Wade—**NASAR Service Award**.

1987. Shenandoah NP—Ranger Bill Pierce—**NASAR State Award, Virginia**.

1987, May 24. Lava Beds NM—Ranger Stephen W. Underwood—**DOI Valor Award** and **Carnegie Hero Award ($2,500)**—rescued 15-year-old boy from a ceiling collapse in a lava tube cave. (DOI Valor citation awarded 9-30-87.)**

1987, May 24. Lava Beds NM—Off-duty Police Officer Mathew H. Rokes—**Carnegie Hero Award ($2,500)**. (See above.)

1987, July 14. Grand Teton NP—Rangers Neil Akana, George Angelo, Ken Dwyer, Missy Epping, Rocky McCreight, and Scott McHowell—**DOI Exemplary Act Award**—successfully resuscitated a 67-year-old man who was in full cardiac arrest.

1987, December 22. George Washington MPW—Civilian Bruce Dobbs—Kiwanis International's **Robert P. Connelly Heroism Award** and **Carnegie Hero Award ($2,500)**—this 46-year-old jogger rescued man trapped in car overturned in Potomac River. Kiwanian Connelly, 32, lost his life trying to rescue a crippled woman who had fallen in the path of an onrushing passenger train in 1966. "For service beyond the call of duty."

1987, December 28. Blue Ridge Parkway—Ranger Bloomfield B. Cantrell—**DOI Exemplary Act Award**—persisted in searching for 15-year-old boy who was subsequently found alive in snowstorm.

1988, February 3. Washington, D.C.—Park Policemen John W. Damadio and John P. Farrell (his second)—**DOI Valor Awards**—saved intoxicated man after he had vandalized and set fire to a service station gas pump. (Awarded 9-30-88.)

1988, February 10. Philadelphia, PA—Maintenancemen Walter L. Anderson and William M. Hundzynski—**DOI Valor Awards**—rescued six people from burning vehicle. (Awarded 3-8-90.)

1988, May 26. Denali NP—Army Pilot CW-4 Myron Babcock—**Army Aviator of the Year Award**—on separate days, pulled two climbers from 18,000-foot ridge with military helicopter hoist (world altitude record for hoist operations).**

1988, June 11. Death Valley NM—Ranger Kent Mecham—**DOI Exemplary Act Award**—rescued and administered lifesaving first aid to man who would have died from sunstroke.

1988, June 18. Chattahoochee River NRA—Rangers David Atkins, Mark Ballard, and Bethany Taylor—**DOI Exemplary Act Group Award**—saved three people from drowning near Devil's Stair Step Beach.

1988, August 3. Great Smoky Mountains NP—Rangers Dennis R. Brewer and Bobby W. Holland—**DOI Valor Awards**—refueling during a SAR, saved crew and other injured rescuers from burning Army Blackhawk helicopter that had crashed into gas pump. (Awarded 3-8-90.)

1988, September 7. Idaho—Joe Bueter (Ozark NSR) and Greg Cravatas (Cuyahoga Valley NRA)—**Special Achievement Awards**; Jerry Brown, Larry Burnham, Rich Drummond, Bill Rodgers, Ron Siller, Jeff Sullivan, Russell Wright (Ozark NSR), and Tom Henry (George Washington Carver NM)—**DOI Exemplary Act Group Award**—helped save the life of a 22-year-old firefighter critically injured in the Eagel Bar fire in western Idaho.

1988, September 15. Glacier NP—Christopher J Purke—**DOI Exemplary Act Award**—while working on the Red Bench fire, saved fellow fireman from being crushed by falling burning snag.

1988, December 3. Grand Teton NP—Jenny Lake Rescue Team—American Alpine Club's **1988 David A. Sowles Memorial Award**—for "many years of service to the mountaineering community."

1989, April 21–26. Denali NP—Civilian David Nyman—**Carnegie Hero Award ($2,500)**—eventually saved his injured climbing partner after he had been buried by eight separate avalanches.**

1989, May 5. Glen Echo Park—Park Policemen David E. Duffey and William H. Lovegrove—**DOI Valor Awards**—rescued two people from roof of submerged vehicle in rain-filled parking lot. (Awarded 3-8-90.)

1989, May 20. Cape Hatteras NS—Ranger Henry M. Anderson, III—**DOI Valor Award**—rescued five people from treacherous seas. (Awarded 3-8-90.)**

1989, June 10. Hawaii Volcanoes National Park Ranger Rescue Team—**DOI Unit Award for Excellence of Service**—Rangers Jeffrey B. Judd, Scott W. Lopez, and John A. Macheeo were named for extracting 10 bodies from airplane crash in Waipo Valley when no other local agencies could do so.**

1989, June 23. Rock Creek Park—Park Policeman Charles W. Herrera—**DOI Valor Award**—entered rain-swollen creek to look for occupants of submerged vehicle. (Awarded 3-8-90.)

1989, July 26. Bryce Canyon NP—Rangers Kenneth Kehrer, Keathleen Lee, Scott Lowery, William Miles, Charles Passek, Susan Ream, Richard Reich, Sarah Rotch, and Laurie Taylor—**DOI Exemplary Act Award**—provided lifesaving CPR to victim of lightning strike.

1989, August 10. Yellowstone NP—Ranger Rob Danno—**DOI Exemplary Act Award**—saved a family of three from drowning after their vehicle had been washed off the road and into the Gibbon River by a mud slide. (Awarded 11-22-89.)

1989, October 13. Yosemite NP—Ranger Daniel K. Horner—**DOI Valor Award**—rescued climber on 2,800-foot cliff after rappelling out of helicopter with stretcher and medical equipment onto tiny ledge. (Awarded 3-8-90.)

1989, October 17. San Francisco, CA—Park Policeman Michael J. Falzone—**DOI Valor Award**—rescued four people after searching five buildings collapsed in earthquake. Awarded 5-8-91.)

1989, October 17. San Francisco, CA—Park Policemen Norman S. Hinson and Raymond M. Rapp—**DOI Valor Awards**—rescued 12 people after searching 10 buildings collapsed in earthquake. (Awarded 5-8-91.)

1989, October 17. San Francisco, CA—Park Policewomen Lisa A. Dunlap and Rachel R. Luce—**DOI Valor Awards**—located two dead victims from building collapsed in earthquake. (Awarded 5-8-91.)

1989, October 17. San Francisco, CA—US Park Police, San Francisco Field Office—**DOI Unit Award for Excellence of Service**—for response to devestating earthquake at afternoon shift change.

1990, February 6. Lake Clark NP—Ranger Leon Alsworth and administrative employees Norm Jacko, Mark Mullins, and Kathie Painter—**DOI Exemplary Act Award**—fought house fire in -32-degree temperatures in remote park community of Port Alsworth.

1990, March 18. Jacksonville, FL—Michael H. Bureman—**DOI Valor Award**—rescued two occupants of vehicle just before it exploded.

1990, April 10. Golden Gate NRA—Ranger Terry G. Swift—**DOI Valor Award**—rescued swimmer drowning in surf at Stinson Beach.

1990, April 22. Panama City, FL—Archeology Technician David M. Brewer—**DOI Exemplary Act Award**—while assisting Florida State Marine Laboratory, participated in rescue of three people who had been swamped by huge ocean wave. (Awarded 9-24-90.)

1990, April 29. Ft. Jefferson NM—Rangers Carolyn P. Brown and Iain "Al" Brown—**DOI Valor Awards**—rescued three fishermen from a boat sinking in 10-foot seas.**

1990, June 24. Yosemite NP—Ranger Colin Campbell—**DOI Exemplary Act Award**—persevered in looking for missing man and ultimately saved his life after he had fallen 75 feet and lain for six days with gangrenous broken leg.

1990, June 26. Tonto National Forest—Alpine Interagency Hotshot Crewmen James Mattingly, William Moe, and David Niemi—**DOI** and **Department of Agriculture Valor Awards**—provided decisive leadership and assistance to a prison inmate fire crew after it had experienced six fatalities and other serious injuries when they had become trapped in an unexpected flashover on the Dude fire.

1990, June 26. James Mattingly received Boise Interagency Fire Center's **Employee of the Quarter Award** for "calm leadership and professional skill at a time of 'great danger and stress.'"

1990, June 26. Tonto National Forest—Michael S. Beasley, James R. Higgins, J. Mark Kaib, and NPS Alpine Interagency Hotshot Crew—**DOI Exemplary Act Award**. (See above.)

1990, July 4. Jefferson NEM—Rangers Shawn M. Frensley and John C. Tesar—**DOI Exemplary Act Awards**—provided immediate lifesaving attention to victim of heatstroke at Veiled Prophet Fair.

1990, July 16. Death Valley NM—Rangers Dale J. Antonich, Terry L. Harris, and Mark J. Maciha—**DOI Valor Awards**—rescued two men off high cliff during hurricane-like thunderstorm. (Awarded 5-8-91.)**

1990, November 18. Mammoth Cave NP—Small craft operator Steve V. Brooks—**DOI Valor Award**—saved woman whose friend had driven his truck into a rain-swollen river. (Awarded 5-5-92.)

1991. Grand Canyon NP—Ranger Michael Ebersole—**NASAR State Award, Arizona**—for contributions in developing computer software for Probability of Detections and related land-search technology.

1991, April 22. Costa Rica—Ranger Anthony Bonanno—**Certificado de Reconocimiento**—provided major assistance during the 7.4-magnitude earthquake that struck Costa Rica while he was assisting with training there: "por su colaboracion, dedicacion y alto espiritu de servicio durante la emergencia de abril de 1991."

1991, May 5. Olympic NP—Ranger Clayton P. Butler—**DOI Valor Award** and **West Olympic**

Peninsula Law Enforcement Officer of the Year Award—donning a wet suit, he swam through turbulent seas to rescue an endangered swimmer who had abandoned his kayak. (DOI Valor citation awarded 5-5-92.)**

1991, June 14. Yosemite NP—Rangers Kim R. Aufhauser and Joseph Sumner—**DOI Valor Awards**—saved life of man who had lost his footing and was trapped on a ledge near a dangerous waterfall. (Awarded 5-5-92.)

1991, June 15. Chesapeake and Ohio Canal NHP—Ranger Christopher Lea—**DOI Valor Award**—rescued kayaker trapped against boulder in rapids on Potomac River. (Awarded 5-5-92.)

1991, June 15. Chesapeake and Ohio Canal NHP—Rangers Michael L. Larsen and Robert Leaver—**DOI Exemplary Act Award**. (See above.)

1991, July 4. Denali NP—Rangers Daryl R. Miller and James R. Phillips—**DOI Valor Award**—rescued an injured climber from 19,500-foot mark of Mt. McKinley. (Awarded 11-22-94.)

1991, July 4. Denali NP—Ranger Daryl Miller—**The International (Targa D'Argento) Silver Plaque Award for Alpine Solidarity in Search and Rescue**—for a person who has "carried out perilous rescue operations, risking one's life in favor of another's life," and presented by the president of Italy. (Awarded in Italy 9-23-96.) This was the first time in the award's 25-year history that an American was selected.

1991, July 19. George Washington Memorial Parkway—Maintenanceman Kevin Price—**DOI Valor Award**—saved the life of a U.S. Park Police officer who was trapped inside his cruiser after being involved in a five-car collision. (Awarded 5-5-92.)

1992. Southwest RO—Ranger Duane Alaire—**NASAR Service Award**.

1992, January 11. Big Thicket NP—Rangers Jeffrey W. Goad and Randolph B. Neal—**DOI Exemplary Act Award**—saved elderly man living in nearby private mobile-home park from an arson fire.

1992, January 15. Great Smoky Mountains NP—Rangers Steven P. Kloster and Jack Piepenbring—**DOI Exemplary Act Award**—assisted in evacuation of a downed military fighter pilot.

1992, March 17. Ft. McHenry NM—Ranger Hugh E. Manar—**DOI Exemplary Act Award**—by performing CPR, saved life of the park's 39-year-old concession employee.

1992, April 12. Big Bend NP—**DOI Exemplary Act Award**—(27 people, including 16 NPS employees, named)—for saving the life of one student and medically assisting 10 others in a remote, 16-person schoolbus rollover.

1992, May 11. Denali NP—Ranger Ronald F. Johnson—**DOI Valor Award**—while racing with the "worst storm in 10 years" on Mt. McKinley, rescued two climbers at 17,000 feet. (Awarded 11-22-94.)**

1992, May 24. Canaveral National Seashore—Ranger Benjamin H. Hansel, III—**DOI Exemplary Act Award**—rescued two swimmers from rough surf off Klondike Beach. (Awarded 7-23-92.)

1992, June 26. Grand Teton NP—Rangers James T. Dorward and Steven W. Rickert—**DOI Valor Awards**—saved life of injured climber. (Awarded 11-22-94.)

1992, June 26. Grand Teton NP—Pilot Willard Eldredge—**DOI Exemplary Act Award**—flew helicopter on above short-haul rescue.

1992, July 4. Yosemite NP—Ranger Daniel K. Horner—**DOI Valor Award**—rescued injured climber from Leaning Tower. (Awarded 11-22-94.)

1992, July 11. Upper Delaware SRR—Ranger Robert Weber, III—**NPS Fast Track Award**, **Distinguished Service Award** (Upper Delaware Council), and **Certificate of Special Congressional Recognition** (Congressman Maurice Hinchey)—saved 25-year-old man from drowning after his foot became wedged between rocks in the river.

1992, July 24. Manassas NBP—Civilian Carloyn F. Grubbs—**DOI Exemplary Act Award**—resident from Fairfax, VA, performed CPR on another park visitor.

1992, July 30. Yosemite NP—Rangers Michael D. Lalone and Kerry N. Maxwell—**DOI Valor Award**—rescued an injured hiker off sloping terraces below Half Dome. (Awarded 11-22-94.)

1992, August 6. Yosemite NP—Rangers John T. Dill and John A. Roth—**DOI Valor Award**—rescued an injured climber from face of El Capitan. (Awarded 11-22-94.)

1992, September 6. Big Bend NP—Ranger Marcos M. Paredes—**DOI Exemplary Act Award**—saved the life of a man drowning in Rio Grande River.

1992, September 15. Grand Canyon NP—Ranger Bryan K. Wisher—**DOI Valor Award**—saved 28 people during flash flood in campground at the bottom of the canyon. (Awarded 11-22-94.)

1992, September 17. Yosemite NP—Ranger Michael D. Lalone—**DOI Valor Award**—rescued climber at base of Half Dome. (Awarded 11-22-94.)

1992, October 10. Zion NP—Ranger Larry Van Slyke and Nellis Air Force Base Airmen Lieutenant Colonel Bob Ziehm (pilot), Captain Ron Newby (pilot), Staff Sergeant Tony Keller (Parajumper), Staff Sergeant Mike Starnes (hoist operator), Airman First Class Scott Carmack (medic)—**DOI Exemplary Act Award**—hazardous rescue of injured hiker from deep and dangerous slot canyon.**

1992, October 10. Zion NP—on March 10, 1993, Utah's U.S. Senator Harry Reid read a two-page citation into the *Congressional Record* specifically commending the above-named rescuers for their efforts.

1992, November 11. Hawaii Volcanoes NP—Ranger Paul Ducasse—**DOI Valor Award**—rescued one victim of a news helicopter crash from inside of Kilauea Crater. (Awarded 11-22-94.)

1992, November 21. Hawaii Volcanoes NP—Ranger Jeffrey B. Judd—**DOI Valor Award**—rescued last victim of a three-person helicopter crash from inside Kilauea Crater. (Awarded 11-22-94.)

1992, November 21. Hawaii—**Unit Award for Excellence of Service: Pu'u O'o Incident Response Team** (16 people named)—rescue of three aircraft victims from inside Kilauea Crater. (Awarded 9-10-93.)

1992, December 25. Golden Gate NRA—Ranger Stephen B. Prokop—**DOI Valor Award**—rescued man trying to drown himself. (Awarded 11-22-94.)

1992–1993. Cape Hatteras Group (Cape Hatteras NS, Fort Raleigh NHS, and Wright

Brothers NM)—**DOI Unit Award for Excellence of Service** (162 people named)—"outstanding teamwork and dedication to duty in response to emergency situations" during Hurricane Andrew, the "Storm of the Century," and Hurricane Emily.

1993. Isle Royale—Ranger Pete Armington—**SOI Award for Outstanding Contributions in Aviation Safety**—a guiding force in developing the lifesaving DOI/NPS Short Haul SAR technique. (Awarded 3-24-94.)

1993, March 13. Cape Hatteras NS—Maintenancemen Ed Bailey and Doug Blackmon and Ranger Ed Whitaker—**North Carolina's Governor's Award for Bravery and Heroism**—"Braving winds in excess of 65 mph, air temperatures in the low thirties, and soundside flooding between 3 and 5 feet deep, they located and safely evacuated 16 victims from nine vehicles trapped by wind-driven waters of the 'Storm of the Century' in Dare County, North Carolina."

1993, March 13–18. Great Smoky Mountains NP—**DOI Unit Award for Excellence of Service** (167 employees named)—"organizational cooperation and team efforts" for location and evacuation of 183 stranded visitors during the "Blizzard of 1993."**

1993, June 6. Gateway NRA—Park Policemen Patrick M. Broderick, Steven E. Divivier, Michael A. Lanfranchi, John A. Lauro, Daniel M. McFadden, Barry M. Smith, and David P. Somma—**DOI Valor Award**—assisted in rescue of 298 illegal Chinese aliens who grounded in the vessel *Golden Venture*. (Awarded 11-22-94.)**

1993, June 6. Gateway NRA—Park Policeman McFadden received USPP **Medal of Honor**; Officers Grant Arthur, Broderick, Divivier, Clay Rice, Smith, and Soma received USPP **Awards of Merit**; Officers Lauro and Lanfranchi received USPP **Lifesaving Awards**; and Officer John Marigliano received USPP **Chief's Certificate.** (See above.)

1993, June 18. Big South Fork NR—Ranger Carl F. Hicks—**DOI Exemplary Act Award**—saved two girls from drowning. (Awarded 7-26-93.)

1993, June 21. Buffalo NR—Ranger R. Joe Doster—**DOI Exemplary Act Award**—saved two children from drowning after kayak overturned.

1993, July 15. Zion NP—Kim Ellis—**Carnegie Hero Award**—the 37-year-old repair technician died while trying to save another leader in a young adult wilderness expedition down a water-filled, narrow slot canyon.**

1993, July 15. Zion NP—Mark S. Brewer—**Carnegie Hero Award**—the 35-year-old attempted to save Ellis (see above) by jumping into the turbulent canyon creek. Before the day was over two of the three adults on this trip would die.**

1994. Isle Royale—Ranger Pete Armington—**NASAR Hal Foss Award.**

1994, May 26. Chickasaw NRA—Ranger Richard P. Martin—**DOI Valor Award**—by diving in 15-foot waters, saved driver who had run off road and plunged into rain-swollen river. (Awarded 12-9-96.)

1994, September 23. Big Cypress NP—Forestry Technician Jack Finley—**DOI Valor Award**—by remaining inside after the crash, saved two from a burning, fully fueled CH-47 helicopter involved in fighting Blackwell fire near McCall, ID. (Awarded 12-9-96.)

1994, November 24. Olympic NP—Ranger Jack Hughes—**On the Spot Award**—received the park's in-house recognition for saving two teenage boys on separate rescues, both of whom were lost from Hurricane Ridge Snowplay Area.

1995, June 23. Olympic NP—Ranger Randall K. Flanery—**DOI Valor Award**—saved 12-year-old boy swept into Queets River. (Awarded 12-9-96.)

1995, August 2. Gateway NRA—Park Police Lieutenant Michael Fellner—**DOI Valor Award**—saved two people from drowning in surf off Jacob Riis Park. (Awarded 12-9-96.)

1995, August 12. Rocky Mountain NP—Ranger James L. Detterline—**DOI Valor Award**—saved two people, who had fallen into water, from going over 75-foot Horseshoe Falls in Roaring River. (Awarded 12-9-96.)

1995, November 20. New York City—Park Police Officer Steven J. Battista—**DOI Valor Award**—patrolling Staten Island, came across a house fire (later determined to be a three-apartment illegal rental) and rescued a person who was combative and had to be restrained from re-entering the burning building for valuables. (Awarded 3-4-99.)

1996, January 20. Voyagers NP—Ranger/Pilot Richard Scott Evans—**DOI Valor Award**—using a small plane and landing numerous times, rescued three snowmobilers trapped on Lake Namakan. (Awarded 12-9-96.)

1996, January 26. Washington, DC—Park Police Officer Jeffrey D. Muller—**US Park Police Medal of Honor** (only third time awarded, 1-30-97), **DOI Valor Award** (Awarded 9-23-96), and **National Law Enforcement Memorial Officer Of the Month**—saved a 79-year-old woman from drowning after the car she was in rolled backward into the nearly frozen Anacostia River at one in the morning. Swimming to the totally submerged vehicle, he used his pistol to break open a window. Hypothermic himself, he was able to extricate the woman who was now completely underwater.

1996, May 18. Buffalo NR—Rangers Charles J. Bitting, Anthony B. Collins, Teresa L. Friday, Gary F. Kiramidjian, Dale S. MacMillan, James S. West, Jeffery West, and Tracy L. Whitaker—**DOI Exemplary Act Award**—this NPS team, along with others from neighboring rescue groups, saved a missing spelunker who was found severely hypothermic in Cave Mountain Cave. (Awarded 9-23-96.)

1996, May 18. Buffalo NR—Civilian rescuers Era Krumwiede, Scamp Krumwiede, Skip Krumwiede, Garland Matloc, Thomas Moore, Lance Sholter, and Danny Smith—**DOI Citizens Award for Bravery**—(See above.) (Awarded 9-23-96.)

> The **Citizens Award for Bravery** is granted to private citizens for heroic acts or unusual bravery in the face of danger. Recipients have risked their lives to save the life of a Department employee or the life of any other person while on property owned or entrusted to the Department of the Interior. They receive a special certificate and citation signed by the Secretary of the Interior.

1996, July 10. near Chiricahua NM—Chief Ranger Rob Danno—**DOI Valor Award**—at night and without moonlight, helped save three Arizona Game and Fish employees who were trapped 800 feet up a 1200-foot cliff in a neighboring National Forest. With the aid of other NPS personnel and after rappeling down the crumbly rocky cliff, he orchestrated all of them

to be lowered to the floor of the rugged canyon. (Awarded 3-4-99.)

1996, July 23. Ozark NSR—Ranger Martin Q. Towery—**DOI Valor Award**—off duty, Towery rescued a non-swimming park visitor who had slipped from an inner tube and had become entangled in a large tree root in the park's Current River. (Awarded 3-4-99.)

1996, July 30. Gulf Islands NS—Ranger Tom Howell—Escambia County (Florida) Proclamation—"commends and congratulates him for risking his own life to rescue" two swimmers in the Gulf of Mexico. (Adopted 10-22-96.)

1996, October 6. New River Gorge NR—Dave Bartlett (Incident Commander), Cindy Bradley, Peggy Brown, Mark Carrico, Bill Handy, Jim Light, Mike Peck, Harry Perkowski, Kinsey Shilling, Donald Sledge, and Andy Steel—**NPS Team Exemplary Act Award**—saved kayaker in the middle of the night from an extremely hazardous situation at the largest falls on the New River.**

1996, October 6. New River Gorge NR—Ranger Kinsey Shilling—**DOI Valor Award**. (See above.) (Awarded 3-4-99.)**

1996, December 29. Yosemite NP—Rangers Charles "Rick" Foulks, Greg Magruder, and Deron Mills—**DOI Exemplary Act Award**—rescued two people trapped inside of vehicle submerged in the Merced River which was in flood stage and at 40 degrees. (Awarded 8-19-99.)

1997. Grand Canyon NP—(62 people named)—**Superintendent's Award for Team Excellence**—in 1996, the park responded to more than 200 heat-related emergencies, including four deaths. To prevent repeating the previous summer's catastrophe, the park staff implemented an intensive Hiking Safety Campaign the next year. Through many educational avenues and innovative preventative methods, the heat-related emergencies for 1997 were reduced by 25%; there were no associated deaths. (Awarded 2-25-97.)

1997, May 17. Lake Mead NRA—Brian T. Sanders—**Carnegie Hero Award**—19-year-old Sanders drowned after repeatedly diving for a friend who had jumped from a cliff. The two young men were found together in the 30-foot deep water.

1997, July 27. Perry's Victory and International Peace Memorial—Ranger Greg A. Johnston—**DOI Exemplary Act Award**—saved a man from drowning who had grown tired while trying to swim to an anchored boat in Lake Erie. (Awarded 9-4-97.)

1997, September 24. New York City area—Park Police Officer Daniel M. McFadden—**Federal Executive Board Award of Honor**—when he saw a vehicle on fire with two people trapped inside while he was going to work, McFadden "valiantly took swift and precise action by using a fire extinguisher from his vehicle to suppress the flames." The award was presented by CBS News Anchor Dan Rather aboard the U.S.S. Intrepid at the second annual ceremony of the Federal Executive Board of New York City.

1997, October 18. Yosemite NP—Arjuna D. N. Babapulle—**Carnegie Hero Award**—a non-swimmer, the 29-year-old electrical engineer drowned trying to rescue his wife from the cold water of Emerald Pool of the Merced River. She survived.

Park Policewoman Renee M. Abt—**DOI Valor Award**—information unavailable. (Awarded 3-4-99.)

Aquatic Park. Gardner Brad R. Benson—**DOI Valor Award**—information unavailable. (Awarded 3-4-99.)

Park Policeman Warren C. Boyer—**DOI Valor Award**—information unavailable. (Awarded 3-4-99.)

Yosemite NP. Steven J. Drager—**DOI Valor Award**—saved a drowning victim below Happy Isle Bridge. (Awarded 3-4-99.) (other information unavailable)

Park Policeman Patrick J. Fouty—**DOI Valor Award**—information unavailable. (Awarded 3-4-99.)

Gulf Islands NS. Thomas L. Howell—**DOI Valor Award**—information unavailable. (Awarded 3-4-99.)

1998, July 11. Kings Canyon NP—Ranger Richard A. Sanger—**DOI Valor Award**—rescued a hiker who was trapped in a rushing stream. As the victim states, "your poise and action was very impressive. You are a credit to your profession." (Awarded 3-4-99.)

1998, July 19. Yellowstone NP—Charles "Dino" Nicholau—**DOI Exemplary Act Award**—saved the lives of three members of a family from dying of carbon monoxide poisoning in their RV. (Awarded 6-2-02.)

1998, December 20.Lake Mead NRA—Rangers Paul G. Crawford, Jeffrey W. Goad, and Robert Moelder—**DOI Valor Award**—saved a sailboarder who was struggling in 50 mph winds in Boulder Basin, after his sailboard had blown away. (Awarded 10-30-00.)

1999, February 6. Yosemite NP—Rangers Mary Hinson and Keith Lober—**DOI Valor Award**—at night and in torrential, near-blinding rain, the rescue team including Hinson and Lober, climbed down 1200 feet to rescue a teen-age boy who had wandered from the trail and would have died during the night. (Awarded 10-30-00.)**

1999, February 6. Yosemite NP—SAR Team Members Werner Braun, Mark Garbarini, Jay Salvedge, and Jo Whitford—**DOI Citizens Award for Bravery**—(See above) (Awarded 10-30-00.)**

1999, May 20 & 21. Denali NP—Ranger William "Billy" E. Shott—**DOI Valor Award**—short-hauled beneath the park's high-altitude helicopter to rescue one individual at the 17, 000-foot level of Mt. McKinley (the highest such rescue in North America) and the next day was again short-hauled beneath the park's high-altitude helicopter to rescue another climber from a difficult ice coulior on Mt. Hunter. (Awarded 10-30-00.)

1999, May 30. Yosemite NP—Rangers Mary Hinson and Keith Lober—**DOI Valor Award**—rappelled from a helicopter onto a dangerous, sloping ledge near El Capitan , stabilized the victim of a hiking fall, and after spending the night, orchestrated the victim being "short-hauled" off by helicopter.(Hinson received a *second* **DOI Valor Award** at these ceremonies—See above.) (Lober received a *third* **DOI Valor Award** at these ceremonies for an incident involving a suicidal juvenile on Christmas Day, 1998.) (All the above awards presented on 10-30-00.)

1999, November 25. near St. Croix NSR—Ranger Rodney Turner—**Polk County** (Wisconsin) **Medal of Merit**—responding to a two-car accident outside of the park, Turner and another police officer saved two people, the first from a burning vehicle and the second from the other car in which the victim was trapped.

1999, December. Gulf Islands NS—Ranger Greg Johnston—**US Coast Guard Auxiliary Award**—recognized for his rapid response and assistance to an officer on board a USCG Auxiliary vessel which was patrolling near the park. The victim of the heart attack died. (Awarded 12-00.)

1999, December 30. Near Canyonlands NP—Ranger George Pavia—**DOI Valor Award**—lowered over a dangerous sandstone cliff to rescue a BASE jumper whose parachute was caught halfway down the 500-foot-high wall. (Awarded 9-4-02.)**

2000, April 18. Cape Krusenstern NM—Maintenancemen Archie R. Ferguson and Joseph Murphy—**DOI Valor Award**—with snowmobiles, worked their way across broken slabs of thin, floating sea ice, saving a man trapped two miles off shore. (Awarded 9-4-02).

2000, July 15. Yosemite NP—Civilian John McCoy—**DOI Citizen's Award for Bravery**—saved a woman whose vehicle had plunged into Tenaya Lake by pulling her free of the wreck and then providing emergency care when onshore. (Awarded 9-4-02.)

2001, April 22. New River Gorge NR—Ranger Mark Carrico—**DOI Valor Award**—rescued three men stranded on a large rock in the New River. (Awarded 9-4-02.)

2001, April 11—Pompano, FL—Park Police Major Thomas G. Pellinger—**DOI Valor Award**—while vacationing at the beach, he saved five young boys from drowning in two separate but contiguous back-to-back rescues. (Awarded 9-4-02.)

2001, June 7. Gulf Islands NS—Ranger Lawrence P. Bova—**DOI Valor Award**—he helped to rescue a swimmer who had been caught in a dangerous riptide created by a tropical storm which had already claimed three lives in the park. (Awarded 9-4-02.)

2001, June 7. Gulf Islands NS—Lifeguards Joseph R. Storti and Tony M. Thomas—**DOI Valor Award**—rescued a swimmer 75 yards from shore who'd been caught in a riptide created by a tropical storm which had already killed three in the park. (Awarded 9-4-02.)

2001, June 17. Big Thicket NP—Ranger Jared B. St. Clair—**DOI Valor Award**—saved two adults and an 11-month old infant swept from a sandbar into the fast moving current of Village Creek, which was ten times its normal flow. (Awarded 9-4-02.)

2001, July 8. New River Gorge NR—Ranger Charles W. (C.W.) Mitchem—**DOI Valor Award**—using a garden hose for a safety line and a door he ripped from its hinges as a float, he rescued two residents of a nearby town who were trapped in their home by floodwaters from a storm dumping 11 inches of rain in three hours. The house collapsed immediately afterwards. (Awarded 9-4-02.) (This is Mitchem's second **DOI Valor Award,** the first was awarded on 3-4-99 for saving a local police officer in 1998.)

2001, September 12. George Washington Memorial Parkway—Maintenance man Michael B. Whalen—**DOI Valor Award**—entered the waters of Dyke Marsh to save a lady attempting suicide. She struggled free and then ran into traffic, both narrowly being missed by oncoming vehicles. (Awarded 9-4-02.)

2001, November 12. Daniel Boone National Forest—Grand Canyon NP Emergency Medical Technicians and Firefighters Sean C. Cox and Michael P. Flynn—**DOI Valor Award**—rescued a trapped forest fire helicopter pilot from his crashed, burning aircraft. (Awarded 9-4-02.)

2002, January 27. Buffalo NR—Buffalo National River Search and Rescue Team (14 people named)—**DOI Team Exemplary Act Award**—saved a caver at the bottom of a dangerous vertical pit and who had been struck in the head by a rock. (Awarded 9-4-02.)

2002. Yosemite NP—Civilian Michelle Hobbs—**Yosemite National Park Search and Rescue Award for 2002**—aided a hiker at the base of Half Dome by performing CPR for 30 minutes until assistance arrived. (Awarded 2-3-03.)

2002. Yosemite NP—Civilian Timmy Sullivan—**Yosemite National Park Search and Rescue Award for 2002**—took charge and provided aid to an injured climber who had fallen on Cathedral Peak. (Awarded 2-3-03.)

2002. Yosemite NP—Civilians Johann Arberger, Ty Cook, and Scott Sandberg—**Yosemite National Park Search and Rescue Award for 2002**—aided a climber who had taken a fall on Higher Cathedral Rock. (Awarded 2-3-03.)

2002. Yosemite NP—Civilians Alexander Cooper and Bryan Palmintier—**Yosemite National Park Search and Rescue Award for 2002**—at night and during a snowstorm, scrambled up to Arrowhead Arete to aid two overdue climbers. (Awarded 2-3-03.)

2003, May 5. Canyonlands NP—Ranger Steve Swanke, Emery County (Utah) Sheriff's Deputies Kyle Ekker, Greg Funk, and Mitch Vetere, and Utah Highway Patrol Helicopter Pilot Terry Mercer—**State of Utah Award of Merit**—assisted in search for Aaron Ralston, who rescued himself after amputating his arm. (Awarded 11-6-03.)**

2003, July 6. Jefferson National Expansion Memorial—Rangers Robert Born, Daniel Stork, and Cuyahoga Valley NP Ranger Mark Plona—**DOI Exemplary Act Award**—saved the life of a 52-year-old man who had gone into cardiac arrest. (Awarded 3-14-04.)

2003, July 23. Glacier NP—Maintenance men Chris Burke and Mike Sanger—**DOI Valor Award**—credited with saving 39 people while at Granite Park Chalet after the Trapper Creek Fire, pushed by 70-mph winds, blew up and raced over them. (Awarded 2-2-05.)

2003, July 26. Grand Teton NP—Rangers Dan Burgette, Chris Harder, Craig Holm, Leo Larson, Jack McConnell, George Montopoli, Jim Springer, and Marty Vidak—**DOI Valor Award**—incredible rescue near summit of Grand Teton. (Awarded 2-2-05.)**

APPENDIX II

Search and Rescuers Killed in the Line of Duty

This is a record of rescuers of an organized response killed while involved in an NPS-related SAR. Two asterisks (**) indicate that the incident is described elsewhere in this book.

1925, January 25. Rocky Mountain NP—Volunteer Herb Sortland died trying to rescue Agnes Vaille during a winter ascent of Longs Peak.**

1947, June 22. Yellowtone NP—Maintenancemen John P. Baker, Vernon E. Kaiser, and Richard N. Ruckels suffocated in truck while trying to save people caught in blizzard on highway into park.**

1959, September 2. Mt. Rainier NP—Civil Air Patrolmen Charles Carman and Harold Horn were killed in light aircraft trying to assist party trapped on summit; their bodies are still there.**

1963, June 28. Glacier NP—Volunteer diver Tom Dumay drowned in Lake McDonald trying to recover body of little boy.**

1964, March 23. Great Smoky Mountains NP—Maintenanceman Frank Shults suffered fatal heart attack responding to plane crash in the middle of the night.

1966, May 21. Fire Island NS—Maintenanceman James Lawler and Ranger William Shaner drowned trying to save swimmers from a turbulent surf.**

1967, December 21. Death Valley NM—Richard Slates, volunteer Mountain Res-cue Association member from China Lake, slid to his death while on body recovery on Telescope Peak.**

1968, October 14. Yosemite NP—Climber Jim Madsen rapelled off the end of his rope while trying to rescue/assist friends on El Capitan; he fell 2,500 feet.**

1969, August 6. Isle Royale NP—Dennis Long drowned while rescuing a person in Lake Michigan.

1977, May 23. Yosemite NP—Camp Four volunteer climber John "Jack" Dorn fell to his death hiking up Upper Yosemite Falls Trail on a rescue of people trapped above Yosemite Valley.**

1978, January 3. Great Smoky Mountains NP—Army aviators John Dunnavant, Floyd Smith, and Terrence Woolever and Civil Air Patrolman Ray Maynard, rescue crew members of MAST helicopter, were killed responding to a downed commuter aircraft.**

1980, September 11. North Cascades NP—Coast Guard Pat Kidgell, Rick Kubal, Roy Lewis, Dan Mahoney, and Tom Sanders died in the crash of "Firewood One," a helicopter trying to rescue an injured climber.**

1991, October 2. Everglades NP—Civil Air Patrolmen James Mathews and Clayton Reed ran out of fuel and died in an airplane accident while searching for an overdue boat.**

1995, August 12. Mt. Rainier NP—Seasonal Climbing Park Ranger Sean H. Ryan and Student Conservation Associa-tion Aide Philip J. Otis fell and died while responding in a night blizzard to the victim of a broken ankle on Winthrop Glacier.**

1997, September 12. Olympic NP—Seasonal Park Ranger Taryn Hoover, helicopter pilot Kevin Johnston, and volunteer search dog handler Rita McMahon, were killed while participating on a search for a 73-year-old missing man. Additionally, five other seasonal and/or volunteer park employees were injured when the B-205 helicopter they were in crashed in the Olympic National Forest, just outside of Olympic National Park.

1998, May 24. Denali NP—Seasonal Climbing Ranger Mike Vanderbeek disappeared at the 16,000-foot level of Mt. McKinley while responding to a rescue of a climber who was ultimately found dead. Vanderbeek has been never found.**

APPENDIX III

ACAD — Acadia National Park
AEC — Atomic Energy Commission
AFRCC — Air Force Rescue and Coordination Center
ALS — Advanced Life Support
AMIS — Amistad National Recreation Area
ARCH — Arches National Park
ARM — All-Risk Management Team
AWOL — Absent Without Leave
BADL — Badlands National Monument
BAND — Bandelier National Monument
BASE — Building Aerial Span Earth
BIA — Bureau of Indian Affairs
BIBE — Big Bend National Park
BISC — Biscayne National Park
BLCA — Black Canyon of the Gunnison National Park
BLM — Bureau of Land Management
BRCA — Bryce Canyon National Park
BUFF — Buffalo National River
CACH — Canyon de Chelly National Monument
CACO — Cape Cod National Seashore
CAHA — Cape Hatteras National Seashore
CANY — Canyonlands National Park
CAP — Civil Air Patrol
CARE — Capitol Reef National Park
CAVE — Carlsbad National Park
CCC — Civilian Conservation Corps
CHIR — Chiricahua National Monument
CHIS — Channel Islands National Park
CMC — Colorado Mountain Club
COSPAS-SARSAT — Satellite Search and Rescue System
CQD — "stop sending and listen," radio distress signal
CRLA — Crater Lake National Park
CRMO — Craters of the Moon National Monument
CWA — Conservative Work Administration
CUVA — Cuyahoga Valley National Park
DENA — Denali National Park
DETO — Devils Tower National Monument
DEVA — Death Valley National Monument

DOI — Department of the Interior
DSA — Distinguished Service Award
ELT — Electronic Locator Transmitter
EMT — Emergency Medical Technician
EPIRB — Emergency Position Indicating Radio Beacon
ESAR — Explorer Search and Rescue
EVER — Everglades National Park
FAA — Federal Aviation Administration
FIIS — Fire Island National Seashore
FIRESCOPE — Firefighting Resources of Southern California Organized for Potential Emergencies
FLIR — Forward Looking Infra Red
FOJE — Fort Jefferson National Monument
GATE — Gateway National Recreation Area
GLAB — Glacier Bay National Park
GLAC — Glacier National Park
GLCA — Glen Canyon National Recreation Area
GOCA — Golden Gate National Recreational Area
GRCA — Grand Canyon National Park
GRSM — Great Smoky Mountains National Park
GRTE — Grand Teton National Park
GSSD — German Shepherd Search Dogs
GWMP — George Washington Memorial Parkway
GLCA — Glen Canyon National Recreation Area
HAI — Helicopter Association International
HALE — Haleakala National Park
HART — High Altitude Rescue Team
HAVO — Hawaii Volcanoes National Park
ICS — Incident Command System
ICSAR — Interagency Committee on Search and Rescue
IFP — Instrument Flight Plan
IKAR — Internationale Kommisia für Alpines Rettingwesen
ISRO — Isle Royale National Park
ITAP — Interim Track Analysis Program
IUCN — World Conservation Union
IV — intravenous

JOSAR	Joshua Tree Search and Rescue	OZAR	Ozark National Scenic Riverway
JOTR	Joshua Tree National Monument	PLB	Personal Locating Beacon
		PMI	Pigeon Mountain Industry
KATM	Katmai National Monument	PORE	Point Reyes National Seashore
KEFJ	Kenai Fjords National Park	PRO	Professional Ranger Organization
KICA	Kings Canyon National Park	RMRG	Rocky Mountain Rescue Group
LACL	Lake Clark National Park	ROMO	Rocky Mountain National Park
LAME	Lake Mead National Recreation Area	SAGU	Saguaro National Park
		SAR	Search and Rescue
LASS	Lassen National Park	SARDA	Search and Rescue Dogs Association
LABE	Lava Beds National Monument		
LAMR	Lake Meredith National Recreation Area	SCRU	Submerged Cultural Resources Unit
LCP	Lechuguilla Cave Project	SEAL	Sea, Air, Land Team
MACA	Mammoth Cave National Park	SEKI	Sequoia/Kings Canyon National Parks
MAST	Military Assistance to Safety and Traffic		
		SEQU	Sequoia National Park
MEVE	Mesa Verde National Park	SHEN	Shenandoah National Park
MOMC	Mount McKinley National Park	SLBE	Sleeping Bear Dunes National Lakeshore
MORA	Mount Rainier National Park		
MORESCO		SURF	Sheriff's Underwater Rescue Force
	Mountain Rescue and Safety Council		
		SWR	Southwest Region
MRA	Mountain Rescue Association	USCG	United States Coast Guard
NASAR	National Association of Search and Rescue	USGS	U. S. Geological Survey
		USLSS	United States Life Saving Service
NASARC	National Association of Search and Rescue Coordinators	USPP	United States Park Police
		WASO	NPS Washington Office
NAUI	National Association of Underwater Instructors	WHSA	White Sands National Monument
NOCA	North Cascades National Park	WICA	Wind Cave National Park
NOLS	National Outdoor Leadership School	WOOF	Wilderness Finders
		WRST	Wrangell-St. Elias National Park
NPS	National Park Service	YELL	Yellowstone National Park
NSS	National Speleological Society	YOSAR	Yosemite Search and Rescue
OLYM	Olympic National Park	YOSE	Yosemite National Park
ORPI	Organ Pipe National Monument	ZION	Zion National Park

REFERENCES

A key to abbreviations and acronyms used in these references is located in Appendix III.

SEPTEMBER 9, 1870   **(PRE) YELLOWSTONE NATIONAL PARK**
Haines, Aubrey L. "Lost in the Yellowstone: An Epic Survival in the Wilderness." Montana,
    Vol. 22. July 1972, pp. 31–41.

AUGUST–SEPTEMBER 1882   **YELLOWSTONE NATIONAL PARK**
"A Remarkable Story." *Avant Courier* (Bozeman, MT), September 7, 1882.
"CY-1993 Search and Rescue Report—by Incident Type." WASO Division of Ranger
    Activities. April 15, 1994.

FEBRUARY 21, 1884   **YELLOWSTONE NATIONAL PARK**
"CY-1991 Search and Rescue Report—by Incident Type." WASO Division of Ranger
    Activities. March 27, 1992.
"Park Notes." *Livingston (MT) Enterprise.* February 26, 1884.
"Up River Mishap, A Fatal Snowslide." *Livingston (MT) Enterprise,* February 23, 1884.
Whittlesey, Lee H. (YELL Archivist). Communications with author, November 5, 1993.
———. *Death in Yellowstone.* Boulder: Roberts Rinehart Publishers, 1995, pp. 73–74,
105, 157.

SUMMER 1884   **YELLOWSTONE NATIONAL PARK**
"Park Notes." *Livingston (MT) Enterprise,* August 4, 1884.

SEPTEMBER 23, 1884   **(PRE) ROCKY MOUNTAIN NATIONAL PARK**
"Longs Peak Deaths." ROMO Chief Ranger's files, p. 1.

AUGUST 9, 1888   **YELLOWSTONE NATIONAL PARK**
Haines, Aubrey L. *The Yellowstone Story: A History of Our First National Park.* Vol. I.
    Yellowstone: Yellowstone Library and Museum Association, 1977, p. 22.
Means, Dennis R. "A Heavy Sea Running: The Formation of the U.S.
    Life-Saving Service, 1846–1878." *Prologue: Journal of the National Archives,*
    Vol. 19, No. 4., Winter 1987, pp. 223–237.
"Park Notes." *Livingston (MT) Enterprise,* January 26, 1889.
"Report of the U.S. Life Saving Service, from FY 1889." Vol. I (1876–1903). National
    Archives, p. 59.

JULY 10, 1889   **(PRE) GRAND CANYON NATIONAL PARK**
Crumbo, Kim. *A River Runner's Guide to the History of the Grand Canyon.* Boulder:
    Johnson Books, 1981, p. 7.

JANUARY 1, 1890   **(PRE) GRAND CANYON NATIONAL PARK**
Smith, Dwight L., and C. Gregory Crampton, eds. *The Colorado River Survey.* Salt Lake
    City: Howe Brothers, 1987, p. 122.

JULY 27, 1891   **YELLOWSTONE NATIONAL PARK**
Whittlesey, Lee H. *Death in Yellowstone.* Boulder: Roberts Rinehart Publishers, 1995,
    pp. 173–176.

MARCH 14, 1894   **YELLOWSTONE NATIONAL PARK**
"Report of the Acting Superintendent of the Yellowstone National Park to the Secretary of
    the Interior—1895." YELL files.
Whittlesey, Lee H. *Death in Yellowstone.* Boulder: Roberts Rinehart Publishers, 1995,
    pp. 75–76. .

JULY 25, 1895   **(PRE) GRAND CANYON NATIONAL PARK**
"Killed by Lightning." *The Coconino (AZ) Weekly Sun,* August 8, 1895.

JULY 27, 1897   **(PRE) MT. RAINIER NATIONAL PARK**
"His Last Ascent." *Seattle Post-Intelligencer.* July 20, 1897.
Molenaar, Dee. *The Challenge of Rainier.* Seattle: The Mountaineers, 1979, p. 235.

DECEMBER 14, 1897   **YELLOWSTONE NATIONAL PARK**
"Acting Superintendent's Report for 1898." YELL Archives, p. 26.
Hofer, Edward. "Yellowstone Park Notes." *Forest and Stream*, December 19, 1897.

JULY 1, 1899   **YOSEMITE NATIONAL PARK**
"Ladies Showed No Fear." *San Francisco Examiner.* July 3, 1899.

JULY 30, 1900   **YELLOWSTONE NATIONAL PARK**
Haines, Aubrey L. *The Yellowstone Story: A History of Our First National Park.* Vol. I.
    Yellowstone: Yellowstone Library and Museum Association, 1977, pp. 118–119.
"Report of the Acting Superintendent of the Yellowstone National Park—1900." *Annual*
    Report to the Secretary of Interior. YELL Archives, n.d., n.p.
Whittlesey, Lee H. *Death in Yellowstone.* Boulder: Roberts Rinehart Publishers, 1995, p. 180.

JULY 6, 1901   **YELLOWSTONE NATIONAL PARK**
"Fell Waist Deep into Hot Mud." *San Francisco Chronicle*, July 10, 1901.

JULY 7, 1901   **YOSEMITE NATIONAL PARK**
"Drowned in the Rapids." *San Francisco Chronicle*, July 8, 1901.

FEBRUARY 17, 1904   **YELLOWSTONE NATIONAL PARK**
Haines, Aubrey L. *The Yellowstone Story: A History of Our First National Park.* Vol. I.
    Yellowstone: Yellowstone Library and Museum Association, 1977, p. 197.
Whittlesey, Lee H. *Death in Yellowstone.* Boulder: Roberts Rinehart Publishers, 1995, pp. 77–78.

JULY 26, 1904   **SEQUOIA NATIONAL PARK**
"From Lone Pine." *Inyo (CA) Independent,* July 22, 1904.
"Killed by Lightning." *Inyo (CA) Independent,* July 29, 1904.
"Mt. Whitney." *Inyo (CA) Independent,* June 26, 1903.
"Mt. Whitney Trail." *Inyo (CA) Independent,* August 26, 1904.

JUNE 5, 1905   **YOSEMITE NATIONAL PARK**
"Fell from El Capitan." *Gazette (CA) Mariposan,* June 10, 1905.

1905 OR 1906   **(PRE) GLACIER NATIONAL PARK**
Liebig, Frank F. *Early Days in the Forest Service.* Missoula: U.S. Forest Service, Northern
    Region, 1946, pp. 133–134.

AUGUST 12, 1907   **YOSEMITE NATIONAL PARK**
"Acts of Heroism: Carnegie Hero Fund Commission Summary: Harry L. Masser #429 and
    J. Park Jones #430." Pittsburgh: Carnegie Hero Fund Commission, n.d.

JUNE 17, 1909   **YOSEMITE NATIONAL PARK**
"Report of Acting Superintendent of Yosemite National Park to the Secretary of the
    Interior—1909." National Archives RG-79.
"Risk Lives in the Yosemite Search." *San Francisco Chronicle*, June 22, 1909.
"Search in Vain for Shepherd." *San Francisco Chronicle*, June 21, 1909.
"Tourist Is Lost in Wilds above Yosemite." *San Francisco Chronicle*, June 18, 1909.

AUGUST 14, 1909   **MT. RAINIER NATIONAL PARK**
Molenaar, Dee. *The Challenge of Rainier.* Seattle: The Mountaineers, 1979, pp. 235, 286.
"Seattle Girl Falls to Death on Mt. Rainier." *Seattle Post-Intelligencer.* August 13, 1912.

1909 OR 1910   **SEQUOIA NATIONAL PARK**
Halliday, William R. *Adventure Is Underground.* New York: Harper & Brothers Publishers,
    1959, pp. 15–26.

FEBRUARY 1, 1911   **CRATER LAKE NATIONAL PARK**
Hamilton, Eva. "The Disappearance of B. B. Bakowski." *Table Rock (OR) Sentinel.*
    Jacksonville: Southern Oregon Historical Society, September–October 1985, p. 3.

MAY 20, 1913   **YOSEMITE NATIONAL PARK**
"A. R. Pohli Falls to His Death in Yosemite." *San Francisco Chronicle,* May 21, 1913.

AUGUST 19, 1913   **GLACIER NATIONAL PARK**
"Dr. Fletcher Is Instantly Killed." *Helena (MT) Daily Independent,* August 21, 1913.

JUNE 14, 1914   **LASSEN PEAK NATIONAL MONUMENT**
Hill, Mary R. "Volcano: History and Geology." *Off Belay.* Renton, WA, April 1973, p. 6.
"Lassen Volcano Takes Human Life." *Mariposa (CA) Gazette,* June 20, 1914.

AUGUST 5, 1915   **YOSEMITE NATIONAL PARK**
Bolton, E., Mrs. "Yosemite Valley." *Mariposa (CA) Gazette,* August 7, 1915.

SEPTEMBER 3, 1915   **ROCKY MOUNTAIN NATIONAL PARK**
"Pastor's Fate Called Divine." Unnamed newspaper, n.d.
Rogers, Edmund (Superintendent). Letter to the Director. National Archives RG-79,
    July 21, 1932.
"Skeleton of Educator Is Found in Estes Park." *Denver Post,* July 10, 1932.

SEPTEMBER 8, 1915   **GRAND CANYON NATIONAL PARK**
"Crazed in Grand Canyon." *New York Times,* September 13, 1915.

MAY 26, 1916   **YOSEMITE NATIONAL PARK**
"Yosemite Valley." *Mariposa (CA) Gazette,* June 17, 1916.

AUGUST 12, 1917   **MT. RAINIER NATIONAL PARK**
"Girl Lost in Crevasse," *Seattle Post-Intelligencer,* August 13, 1917.
"Rescued from Crevasse by Guide on Mt. Rainier." *Seattle Post-Intelligencer,* September
17, 1916.

AUGUST 2, 1918   **ROCKY MOUNTAIN NATIONAL PARK**
"Superintendent's Annual Report to Secretary of the Interior—1918." National Archives
    RG-79, n.d.

AUGUST 6, 1919   **GLACIER NATIONAL PARK**
"Acts of Heroism: Carnegie Hero Fund Commission Summary: Herbert Aaron Friedlich
    #1726." Pittsburgh: Carnegie Hero Fund Commission, n.d.

JANUARY 1920   **YELLOWSTONE NATIONAL PARK**
Chief Ranger's Monthly Report—April 1920. YELL Archives, p. 19.

JULY 7, 1920   **YOSEMITE NATIONAL PARK**
"Rescuer Killed, Girl Dead." *San Francisco Chronicle,* July 8, 1920.

AUGUST 28, 1920   **SEQUOIA NATIONAL PARK**
"Fat Men Barred from Crystal Caves; Must Reduce." Unnamed newspaper, September 13,
    1920.

JULY 21, 1921   **CRATER LAKE NATIONAL PARK**
"Forests Aviator Forced to Land in Deep Crater." *San Francisco Examiner,* July 24, 1921.

JULY 25, 1921   **YOSEMITE NATIONAL PARK**
"S. F. Clubman Plunges off Yosemite Peak." *San Francisco Examiner,* July 27, 1921.

AUGUST 11, 1921   **YELLOWSTONE NATIONAL PARK**
"Two Escape When Plane Plunges into Yellowstone Lake." *Denver Post,* August 12, 1921.

AUGUST 13, 1921   **YELLOWSTONE NATIONAL PARK**
"Man Lost in Yellowstone Sends N Y Cry." *Baltimore Sun,* n.d.

SEPTEMBER 16, 1921   **ROCKY MOUNTAIN NATIONAL PARK**
"Elements Disinter Unknown's Body on Flat Top Mountain." *Rocky Mountain News*
    (Denver), September 19, 1921.

JULY 21, 1922   **YOSEMITE NATIONAL PARK**
"Young Lady Injured on Glacier Pt. Trail." *Mariposa (CA) Gazette,* July 29, 1922.

AUGUST 1, 1922 ROCKY MOUNTAIN NATIONAL PARK

"J. E. Kitts, Banker of Greeley, Instantly Killed by Lightning on Crest of Longs Peak Tuesday Afternoon." *Trail Gazette* (Estes Park), August 4, 1922.

"Woman Lives Following Lightning Stroke." *Trail Gazette* (Estes Park, CO), September 7, 1923.

SEPTEMBER 1923 GRAND CANYON NATIONAL PARK

"Asks Plane to Seek Canyon Explorers." *New York Times,* September 23, 1923, p. 1.

"Canyon Explorers Not Yet Heard From." *New York Times,* September 24, 1923, p. 2.

Emery, Steuart M. "Daring Scientists Conquer Grand Canyon's Wild Rapids." *New York Times,* November 11, 1923, Sect. 9, p. 3.

"Patrol Starts Hunt for Canyon Explorers." *New York Times,* September 25, 1923, p. 9.

JULY 13, 1924 YELLOWSTONE NATIONAL PARK

"Back over Brink of Grand Canyon." *Butte (MT) Miner,* July 15, 1924.

Whittlesey, Lee H. *Death in Yellowstone.* Boulder: Roberts Rinehart Publishers, 1995, pp. 91–92, 244.

JULY 25, 1924 MT. RAINIER NATIONAL PARK

"Denies Hurling Wife off Cliff on Mt. Tacoma." *Tacoma Ledger,* August 12, 1924.

"Rainier Visitor Falls to Death." *Seattle Post-Intelligencer,* July 26, 1924.

Tomlinson, O. A. (Superintendent). Letter to F. B. Kutz, Superintendent of Records, Long Beach Police Department. MORA SAR files, November 24,1925.

AUGUST 22, 1924 YOSEMITE NATIONAL PARK

"Girl Goes over Falls to Death." *Stockton Record,* August 22, 1924.

Mariposa (CA) Gazette. December 17, 1892.

"Yosemite Park Visitor Plunges over Falls." *Mariposa (CA) Gazette,* August 29, 1924.

AUGUST 24, 1924 GLACIER NATIONAL PARK

Secretary of Interior. Letter to Mrs. Dora B. Whitehead. National Archives RG-79, Box 253, September 16, 1924

JANUARY 12, 1925 ROCKY MOUNTAIN NATIONAL PARK

"Agnes Wolcott Vaille." *Trail and Timberline,* Denver: Colorado Mountain Club, No. 77. February 1925, pp. 2–9.

Blaurock, Carl A. "Tragedy on Longs Peak." *Denver Westerners' Roundup,* Denver: Denver Posse, September–October 1981.

"*Denver Post*'s Story of Hero Wins College Course for Him." *Denver Post,* September 20, 1925.

Moomaw, Jack C. (Ranger). *Recollections of a Rocky Mountain Ranger.* Longmont, CO: Times-Call Publishing Co, 1963, pp. 34–39.

"Official Report on Tragedy Pays Tribute to Courage of Miss Vaille." *Rocky Mountain News* (Denver), January 18, 1925.

JANUARY 30, 1925 (PRE) MAMMOTH CAVE NATIONAL PARK

Murray, Robert K., and Roger W. Brucker. *Trapped!* New York: G. P. Putnam's Sons, 1979.

JUNE 7, 1925 YOSEMITE NATIONAL PARK

"Weird Suicide Unearthed by Park Rangers." *San Francisco Chronicle,* August 19, 1925.

AUGUST 14, 1925 GLACIER NATIONAL PARK

"Annual Report—1925." GLAC National Archives RG-79.

"Searching Glacier for Missing Pair Gone Since Aug. 12." *Helena (MT) Daily Independent,* August 26, 1925.

JUNE 27, 1927 ZION NATIONAL PARK

Scoyen, E. T. (Superintendent). Letter to the Director. National Archives RG-79, July 13, 1927.

JUNE 29, 1927 YELLOWSTONE NATIONAL PARK

Hardy, Karl J. (Ranger). Canyon Ranger Station Logbook. National (YELL) Archives RG-79, June 29, 1927.

APRIL 7, 1928   **YOSEMITE NATIONAL PARK**
Bingaman, John W. Letter to Stephen T. Mather, National Archives RG-79, April 30, 1928.
———. "Accidents—Lost People—and Rescue." *Guardians of the Yosemite: A Story of the
     First Rangers.* Palm Desert: Desert Printers, 1961, pp. 31–32.
Leavitt, E. P. (Acting Superintendent). Letter to the Director. National Archives RG-79,
     April 10, 1928.
"Report of Trail Rescue on Ledge Trail, April 7, 1928." Memorandum to park files.
     National Archives RG-79, April 7, 1928.

DECEMBER 1, 1928   **GRAND CANYON NATIONAL PARK**
Albright, Horace M. (Director). Memorandum to Assistant Secretary. National Archives
     RG-79, March 30, 1929.
Lavender, David. "For the Sake of Fame." *River Runners of the Grand Canyon.* Grand
     Canyon: Natural History Assoc., pp. 78–84.
"Supplemental Memorandum Re Search for Glen R. Hyde River Party." Memorandum to
     park files from Superintendent (?). National Archives RG-79, December 29, 1929.
Thybony, Scott. "A River Mystery." *First Descents,* unpublished, 1987.
———. "What Happened to Bessie Hyde." *Outside,* October 1985, p. 108.

FEBRUARY 20, 1929   **GRAND CANYON NATIONAL PARK**
"Grand Canyon Nature Notes." Vol. 3, no. 8. GRCA files, February 28, 1929.
"Grand Canyon Rapids Drown Pair in Boat." *Phoenix Republic,* February 22, 1929.
"Testimony of Witnesses in Coroner's Inquest . . . in the Case of Glen E. Sturdevant."
     National Archives RG-79, February 23, 1929.

MARCH 6, 1929   **CARLSBAD CAVERNS NATIONAL PARK**
"Superintendent's Monthly Narrative Report for March." CAVE files, April 12, 1929.

JULY 2, 1929   **MT. RAINIER NATIONAL PARK**
Department of Interior Press Release. National Archives RG-79, July 24, 1929.
Molenaar, Dee. *The Challenge of Rainier.* Seattle: The Mountaineers, 1979, pp. 237–242.
Webster, Esther. "Penninsula Profile: Ex-Ranger Browne: Colorful Man." *Daily News*
     (Port Angeles, WA), December 9, 1973.

JULY 8, 1930   **ZION NATIONAL PARK**
Scoyen, E.T. (Superintendent). Letter to the Director. National Archives RG-79, Box 556,
     July 12, 1930.

AUGUST 4, 1930   **SEQUOIA NATIONAL PARK**
Ebersol, C. B. Letter to John H. Edwards, Assistant Secretary of the Interior from Carnegie
     Hero Fund Commission. National Archives RG-79, November 19, 1930.
"Hero Dares Explosion: Paralyzed Man Is Rescued." *Fresno Bee,* August 7, 1930.

AUGUST 26, 1930   **SEQUOIA NATIONAL PARK**
Clark, Samuel L. (Ranger). Letter to Lawrence F. Cook, Chief Ranger. National Archives
     RG-79, September 8, 1930.
"Fight Against Infection Lost Monday Night." *Fresno Republican,* September 3, 1930.
"Visalia Youth Makes 22 Mile Heroic Run." *Visalia (CA) Delta,* September 10, 1930.

NOVEMBER 17, 1930   **CRATER LAKE NATIONAL PARK**
"Bill Godfrey." *Medford (OR) Mail Tribune,* November 18, 1930.
"Godfrey of Lake Staff Succumbs." *Oregonian,* November 18, 1930.
Lueck, Rudy (retired Ranger). Letter to author, March 24, 1985.
Selinsky, E. C. (Superintendent). Letter to the Director. National Archives RG-79,
     November 19, 1930.

JUNE 28, 1931   **MESA VERDE NATIONAL PARK**
"Dr. Wilbur Operates to Save Man in Camp." Unnamed newspaper. National Archives
     RG-79, June 29, 1931.
"Secretary Wilbur Saves Man's Life by Operation," Unnamed newspaper (Associated
     Press). National Archives RG-79, June 29, 1931.

JULY 5, 1931   **MT. RAINIER NATIONAL PARK**

Butler, William. Letter to Ray Lyman Wilber [sic] (Secretary of the Interior). National
    Archives RG-79, September 6, 1931.
Molenaar, Dee. *The Challenge of Rainier.* Seattle: The Mountaineers, 1979, pp. 243–246.
Tomlinson, O. A. (Superintendent). Letter to the Director. National Archives RG-79, July 8,
    1931.

JULY 25, 1931   **ZION NATIONAL PARK**

Allen, Thos. J. (Superintendent). Letter to Mr. Allen. National Archives RG-79, n.d.

FEBRUARY 1, 1932   **SEQUOIA NATIONAL PARK**

"150 Planes to Join Search for Lost Fliers." *Fresno Bee,* February 4, 1932.
"Army Plane Lost Two Months Found near Oriole Lodge." *Fresno Bee,* April 2, 1932.
"Army Plans to Keep Searching for Lost Flier." *Tulare (CA) Daily Advance-Register,*
    February 24, 1932.
"Missing Army Flyer's Plane Found Wrecked." *Los Angeles Times,* April 2, 1932.
"Mountain Posse Fails in Search for Army Flier." Unnamed newspaper, February 13, 1932.
"One of Missing U.S. Army Fliers Found in Sequoia." Unnamed newspaper, February 2,
    1932.
"Technical Report of Aircraft Accident Classification Committee, April 1932." Files of U.S.
    Air Force HQHA Inspection and Safety Center, Norton Air Force Base, CA.
"Three Ground Parties Will Hunt Aviator." *Tulare (CA) Times,* February 25, 1932.
"Unsuccessful in Search for Son, F. A. Hoffman Returns to Tacoma." *Tulare (CA) Daily
    Advance-Register,* February 29, 1932.

MAY 10, 1932   **MT. MCKINLEY NATIONAL PARK**

Beckwith, Edward P. "Carpe, Koven Died in a Feat of Daring." *New York Times,* May 18,
    1932.
———. "Spadavecchia, Olton and Rescue Pilot Safe on Alaskan Glacier, Search Plane
    Reports." *New York Times,* May 21, 1932.
Lindley, Albert D. "Carpe, Koven Lost Hunting Companions." *New York Times,* May 19,
    1932.
"Plane Sees Searchers for Body of Koven." *New York Times,* August 11, 1932.
Sherwonit, Bill. "The 1932 Expeditions: Carpe and Lindley-Liek." *To the Top of Denali.*
    Anchorage: Alaska Northwest Books, 1992, pp. 61–79.

JUNE 2, 1932   **HAWAII NATIONAL PARK**

"Bodies Located on Floor of Volcano." *Hawaii Press (Hilo),* June 2, 1932.
"Bodies Retrieved from Pit in Harrowing Descent." *Hilo Tribune Herald,* June 13, 1932.
"Coroner's Jury Sworn in on Brink of Pit." *Hilo Tribune Herald,* June 5, 1932.
"Descent into Crater Today Is Postponed." *Hilo Tribune Herald,* June 9, 1932.
"Konishi Brings Bodies from Pit." *Hilo Tribune Herald,* June 12, 1932.
Leavitt, E. P. (Superintendent). Letter to the Director. National Archives RG-79, Box 313,
    June 14, 1932.
"Rikan Konishi Given Honors." *Hilo Tribune Herald,* June 21, 1932.

JULY 18, 1932   **ROCKY MOUNTAIN NATIONAL PARK**

Cook, Hull (physician). Letter to the author, April 10, 1995.
Detterline, Jim (ROMO ranger). Letter to the author, March 23, 1995.

JULY 19, 1932   **SEQUOIA NATIONAL PARK**

"Litter Crew Loses Grim Park Dash." *San Francisco Chronicle,* August 4 (?), 1932.

APRIL 19, 1934   **GRAND CANYON NATIONAL PARK**

"Two Parties Fight to Save Life of Injured Man in Grand Canyon." *Denver Post,* April 21,
    1934.

JUNE 22, 1934   **YOSEMITE NATIONAL PARK**

"Chief Ranger's Monthly Report—June." National Archives RG-79.
"Tenderfoot Rangers." *Los Angeles Times,* n.d.

JULY 6, 1934   **GRAND TETON NATIONAL PARK**
Fryxell, Fritiof (Ranger). "Various Notes: The Tragedies on the Grand Teton." *American Alpine Club Journal.* Vol. II, No. 3, n.d.

AUGUST 2, 1934   **ACADIA NATIONAL PARK**
"Acts of Heroism: Carnegie Hero Fund Commission Summary: Christine Stewart #2882 and Ellen Geaney #2883." Pittsburgh: Carnegie Hero Fund Commission, n.d.

JULY 25, 1935   **YOSEMITE NATIONAL PARK**
Bryant, M. D. Letter to Douglas H. Hubbard. National Archives RG-79, December 13, 1935.

JANUARY 19, 1936   **MT. RAINIER NATIONAL PARK**
Buchanan, Richard W. (Asst. General Manager, Seattle Chamber of Commerce). Letter to John Davis. MORA SAR files, March 3, 1936.
Cunningham, Ross. "Alpinists Fight Way toward Fadden's Body." *Seattle Post-Intelligencer,* January 30, 1936.
Davis, John M. (Chief Ranger). Letter to O. A. Tomlinson, Superintendent. MORA SAR files, February 10, 1936.
Molenaar, Dee. "Solo Winter Ascent of Rainier." *Summit Magazine.* Seattle. July–August 1971, pp. 19–23.
"Relief Crew Bringing out Fadden's Body." Unnamed newspaper, n.d.
"Rescue Hero Describes Icy Cold on Peak," *Seattle Post-Intelligencer,* February 2, 1936.
"Searching Party Reaches Body of Mt. Rainier 'Thrill Climber.'" *Washington Post,* February 1, 1936.
Tomlinson, O. A. "Superintendent's Monthly Report—January, 1936." National Archives RG-79, February 5, 1936.
Welch, Doug. "Fadden's Death Caused by Fall," *Seattle Post-Intelligencer,* February 2, 1936.

AUGUST 19, 1936   **GRAND CANYON NATIONAL PARK**
Purvis, Louis L. (CCC member). Letter to author, April 13, 1985
Tillotson, M. R. (Superintendent). Louis L. Purvis files. Letter to N. C. Duncan, September 17, 1936.

APRIL 21, 1937   **BOULDER DAM NATIONAL RECREATION AREA**
Cummings, Calvin R. (NPS Senior Archeologist). "The History of National Park Service SCUBA Diving." December 20, 1987.
"Monthly Report—April 1939." National Archives RG-79.
Phoenix Republic. April 22, 1937.
"Superintendent's Monthly Report—April, 1937." National Archives RG-79.

MARCH 1, 1938   **YOSEMITE NATIONAL PARK**
Bingaman, John. *Guardians of the Yosemite: A Story of the First Rangers.* Palm Desert: Desert Printers, 1961, p. 33.
"Fatal Aeroplane Fall at Wawona." *Mariposa (CA) Gazette,* July 30, 1926.
"Lights Clue to Air Liner." *San Francisco Chronicle,* March 3, 1938.
"Looting Adds to Storm Terror; 50 Planes to Hunt Lost Airliner." *San Francisco Chronicle,* March 4, 1938.
"Plane Crash Dead Moved." *Los Angeles Times,* June 15, 1938.
"S. F. Transport Plane, with Nine Aboard, Unreported on Los Angeles Flight." *San Francisco Chronicle,* March 2, 1938.
Tucker, Tommy (retired Ranger). Letter to author, August 31, 1988.
"Wreck Lies on Yosemite Peak," *Los Angeles Times.* 13 June 1938.

JULY 3, 1938   **ROCKY MOUNTAIN NATIONAL PARK**
"Bones Found in Park Spur Search for Boy." *Rocky Mountain News* (Denver), July 8, 1938.
"Denver Child Lost in Mountains." *Rocky Mountain News* (Denver), Sunrise Edition, July 4, 1938.

Fry, George W. (retired Ranger). Letter to author, June 23, 1986. "Park Search for Boy Ends." *Rocky Mountain News* (Denver), July 12, 1938.

Pike, Alberta. "Rangers to Divert River in Hunt for Lost Denver Child." *Rocky Mountain News* (Denver), July 5, 1938.

————. "Campers Face Probe in Lost Boy Case as Mystery Deepens." *Rocky Mountain News* (Denver), July 9, 1938.

JANUARY 25, 1939   **CARLSBAD CAVERNS NATIONAL PARK**

Boles, Thomas (Superintendent). "Monthly Report—January 1939." CAVE files, February 6, 1939, p. 13.

AUGUST 7, 1939   **ROCKY MOUNTAIN NATIONAL PARK**

"Denver Mountain Climber Dies after Rescue from Longs Peak," *Rocky Mountain News* (Denver), August 8, 1939.

Field, Ernest K. (Ranger). "Report on the Fatality in the Second Chimney on Longs Peak." *Trail and Timberline*. Denver: The Colorado Mountain Club, September 1939, p. 119.

"New Faces in the Denver Post Gallery of Fame." *Denver Post*, August 12, 1939.

AUGUST 28, 1939   **OLYMPIC NATIONAL PARK**

"Monthly Report: September—1939." National Archives RG-79.

"Woman Lost on Peninsula," *Seattle Post-Intelligencer*, n.d.

JUNE 15, 1940   **CRATER LAKE NATIONAL PARK**

Crouch, J. Carlisle (Chief Ranger). "Rescue of David C. Campbell and Kenneth E. Prince from the Crater: Memorandum to the Park Files." National Archives RG-79.

JULY 20, 1940   **MT. RAINIER NATIONAL PARK**

MacGowan, George (Secretary of the Mountaineers). Letter to Major O. A. Tomlinson, Superintendent. National Archives RG-79, August 16, 1940.

Patterson, Gordon K. (Ranger). Letter to Oscar A. Sedergren, Chief Ranger. National Archives RG-79, July 25, 1940.

AUGUST 11, 1940   **LAKE MEAD NATIONAL RECREATION AREA**

"Aviator Killed in Lake Mead." *Arizona Republic (Phoenix)*. August 12, 1940.

AUGUST 15, 1940   **CRATER LAKE NATIONAL PARK**

Crouch, J. Carlisle (Chief Ranger). "Rescue of George F. Gubser, Alfred B. Wiedman, and Norman C. Goesckel from the Crater: Memorandum to the Files." National Archives RG-79.

MAY 19, 1941   **GRAND TETON NATIONAL PARK**

Smith, Charles J. (Superintendent). "Letter to Lieutenant H. C. Leach, Company Commander, Company No. 5498, Jenny Lake, Wyoming." National Archives RG-79, May 22, 1941.

AUGUST 10, 1941   **MT. RAINIER NATIONAL PARK**

Seattle-Post Intelligencer. August 11, 1941.

————. August 12, 1941.

OCTOBER 1, 1941   **DEVILS TOWER NATIONAL MONUMENT**

Field, Ernie. "The Devils Tower Episode." *Trail and Timberline*. Colorado Mountain Club, December, 1941. pp. 167-169.

Joyner, Newell F. (Custodian). Memorandum for the Director. DETO files, October 10, 1941.

Riske, Milt. "Close Encounter at Devils Tower." *Denver Post: Empire Magazine*, October 1, 1978.

Zimmermann, Jeffrey. "Climbing on Devils Tower." *Summit Magazine*, December–January 1979, pp. 15–18.

OCTOBER 24, 1941   **KINGS CANYON NATIONAL PARK**

Boghosian, S. Samuel. "1941 Air Force Mission Leaves Saga of Death, Destruction in Sierras." *Fresno Bee*, October 22, 1972, p. A-24.

————. "The Day It Rained P-40s." *Air Combat: The Ghostly Warriors of World War II.* Canoga Park: Challenge Pubs, 1981, pp. 88-92.

JUNE 1, 1942   **(PRE) LAKE CLARK NATIONAL PARK**
Glines, Carroll V., and Wendell F. Moseley. "The Assault on Mount Redoubt." *Air Rescue.* New York: Ace Books, 1961, pp. 64–73.

JUNE 19, 1942   **GRAND TETON NATIONAL PARK**
"Superintendent's Annual Report: 1942." National Archives RG-79.

APRIL 1, 1943   **OLYMPIC NATIONAL PARK**
Gibbs, James A., Jr. "Lamut." *Shipwrecks of the Pacific Coast.* Portland: Binfords & Mort n.d, pp. 41–43.
Macy, Preston (Superintendent). "Memorandum for the Regional Director, Region Four." National Archives RG-79, April 9, 1943.
Noble, Dennis L. "Soviets on a Shoestring." *Proceedings.* Annapolis: U.S. Naval Institute, October 1989, pp. 140–141.

MAY 15, 1943   **SHENANDOAH NATIONAL PARK**
Broyles, Phyllis. Letter to the author, May 8, 1987.
Cline, A.B. "Little Doris Dean. [Poem]. Harrisonburg, VA: Charles Maddox Collection, n.d., n.p.
Freeland, Ed (Superintendent). "Memorandum for the Director." National Archives RG-79, June 10, 1943.

MAY 23, 1943   **YELLOWSTONE NATIONAL PARK**
Bartimus, Tad. "Park Fires Bring History to Light." *Post-Register.* Idaho Falls, ID. November 20, 1988, p. A-l.
Mitchell, Robin (B-17 historian). Letter to Timothy Manns, YELL historian. YELL Archives, January 6, 1989.
"U.S. Army Air Forces Report of Aircraft Accident." Files of U.S. Air Force HQHA Inspection and Safety Center, Norton Air Force Base, CA, June 3, 1943.

DECEMBER 5, 1943   **KINGS CANYON NATIONAL PARK**
"B-24 Crash Bodies May Never Be Found." *Fresno Bee,* August 1, 1960.
Brock, Leroy (Ranger). Communications with author, May 14, 1987.
Koch, R. W. "The Deadly Storm." *Air Combat: The Ghostly Warriors of World War II.* Canoga Park: Challenge Pubs, 1981, p. 61.
"Missing 17 Years." *San Francisco Chronicle,* July 29, 1960.
Osborne, Clarence. Letters to author, March 2 and April 7, 1986.
"U.S. Army Air Forces Report of Aircraft Accident." Files of U.S. Air Force HQHA Inspection and Safety Center, Norton Air Force Base, CA, December 12, 1943.
"'We Saw Bomber's 11,000-Foot Grave.'" *San Francisco Chronicle,* August 1, 1960.

JUNE 20, 1944   **GRAND CANYON NATIONAL PARK**
Butchart, Harvey. Letter to author, June 24, 1988.
"Canyon Climbers Save 3 Army Fliers." *New York Times,* July 1, 1944.
Hines, Paul, Jr. (S/Sgt.). "Greatest Rescue in History of Army Aviation Effected Friday." Cactus. Kingman (AZ) Army Air Field. National Archives RG-79, July 6, 1944.
MacRae, Allen A. Letter to Harvey Butchart. Butchart files, January 13, 1977.
"Ranger Monthly Report: June—1944." National Archives RG-79.
"Signals from Canyon Spur Fliers' Rescuers." *Phoenix Republic,* June 28, 1944.
"Three Stranded Fliers on Way out of Canyon." *Phoenix Republic,* June 30, 1944.

JULY 4, 1944   **JOSHUA TREE NATIONAL MONUMENT**
"U.S. Army Air Forces Report of Aircraft Accident." Files of U.S. Air Force HQHA Inspection and Safety Center, Norton Air Force Base, CA, July 5, 1944.

AUGUST 1, 1944   **DEATH VALLEY NATIONAL MONUMENT**
Cronkhite, Daniel. *Death Valley's Victims: A Descriptive Chronology 1849–1980.* Morongo Valley, CA: Sagebrush Press, 1981, p. 38.

Goodwin, T. R. (Superintendent). "Memorandum for the Director." National Archives
    RG-79, August 2, 1944.
"U.S. Army Air Forces Report of Aircraft Accident." Files of U.S. Air Force HQHA
    Inspection and Safety Center, Norton Air Force Base, CA, August 18, 1944.

SEPTEMBER 18, 1944   **MT. MCKINLEY NATIONAL PARK**
Fahlberg, Larry. "Denali's Eastern Shadow." *Off Belay.* Renton, WA. August 1980, pp. 17–18.
Pearson, Grant. "Bring Out the Bodies!" *My Life of High Adventure.* Engleung, NJ:
    Prentice-Hall, 1962, pp. 190–199.
"U.S. Army Air Forces Report of Aircraft Accident." Files of U.S. Air Force HQHA
    Inspection and Safety Center, Norton Air Force Base, CA, November 14, 1944.
Washburn, Brad. "The First Ascent of Mount Deception." *Sierra Club Bulletin,* 1941,
    pp. 94–104.
———. Communications with author, April 19, 1988.

JANUARY 20, 1945   **SAGUARO NATIONAL MONUMENT**
Severson, Ed. "Retired Air Force Chaplain Wins Memorial Peak for Downed Airmen."
    Arizona Daily Star, October 16, 1986.
Tagg, Larry. "Aircraft Accidents in Rincon Mountains." SAGU files. March 15, 1984.
Tagg, Larry. Letter to author, February 27, 1989.

FEBRUARY 7, 1945   **BIG BEND NATIONAL PARK**
Maxwell, Ross A. (Superintendent). "Memorandum for the Director." National Archives
    RG-79, July 15, 1948.
"Monthly Report: February—1945." National Archives RG-79.

DECEMBER 3, 1945   **CRATER LAKE NATIONAL PARK**
"Crater Lake National Park Incident Report." August 7, 1970.
"Department of the Navy Accident Report." Naval Historical Center, Washington, D.C., n.d.
"Navy Identifies Long Lost Skull." *Herald and News* (Klamath Falls, OR) , October 1, 1970.
Panebaker, Dave (Ranger). Letter to author, November 10, 1993.
"'Receipt for Property' for Skull, Human: 1 EA." Dave Panebaker files, August 20, 1970.

FEBRUARY 2, 1946   **YOSEMITE NATIONAL PARK**
"Skier, Lost in Sierras 11 Days, Found Alive." *San Francisco Chronicle,* February 14 (?), 1946.

JULY 9, 1946   **YOSEMITE NATIONAL PARK**
"Death at Yosemite Waterfall: Veteran Tries to Rescue Boy, Both Are Swept over Cascade."
    San Francisco Chronicle, July 10, 1946.
"Ranger Monthly Report: July—1946." National Archives RG-79.

AUGUST 13, 1946   **ZION NATIONAL PARK**
Smith, Charles J. (Superintendent). "Memorandum for the Regional Director." National
    Archives RG-79, August 19, 1946.
———. Proposed Prohibition on Climbing. National Archives RG-79, n.d.

AUGUST 24, 1946   **SEQUOIA NATIONAL PARK**
Wallace, Gordon (Acting District Ranger). "Memorandum to the Superintendent." National
    Archives RG-79, September 17, 1946.

DECEMBER 10, 1946   **MT. RAINIER NATIONAL PARK**
Garrett, Chick. "Bill Butler: The Living Legend of Mt. Rainier," *Seattle Post-Intelligencer,*
    March 1964.
Molenaar, "K." (former Ranger). Letter to author, April 6, 1986.
Preston, John C. (Superintendent). "Memorandum for the Director." MORA SAR files,
    September 17, 1947.
———. "Report: Lost-Search-Discovery: Marine Crops Transport Plane." MORA SAR files,
    July 29, 1947.

JUNE 20, 1947   **YELLOWSTONE NATIONAL PARK**
Merriam, Lawrence (Regional Director). Telegram to the Director. National Archives RG-79,
    June 25, 1947.

"Superintendent's Monthly Report: June 1947." YELL Archives.
"Three Are Killed in Heavy Snow at Yellowstone Park." *Wyoming State Tribune* (Cheyenne), June 23, 1947.
"Three Die in Blizzard on Cooke Route." Unnamed newspaper. National Archives RG-79, June 23, 1947.

OCTOBER 24, 1947   **BRYCE CANYON NATIONAL PARK**
"52 Die in Utah Air Liner Crash." *Salt Lake Tribune,* October 25, 1947.
Buckingham, George (Ranger). Letter to author, January 31, 1986.
Halliday, Bob. "Stricken Sky Giant Burned Half-Mile Path, Flew Apart." *Salt Lake Tribune,* October 25 (?), 1947.
"Memorandum for Superintendent, Zion and Bryce Canyon National Parks." National Archives RG-79, November 19, 1947.
Nash, Jay Robert. *Darkest Hours.* New York: Pocket Books, 1977, pp. 576–577.

MARCH 12, 1948   **(PRE) WRANGELL ST. ELIAS NATIONAL PARK**
Campbell, Larry. "Pilot Searches Mountain for 41-Year-Old Plane Wreck." *Anchorage Daily News,* August 9, 1989.
"Civil Aeronautics Board Accident Investigation Report No. 19752—Northwest Airlines, Inc." July 28, 1948.
"Plane, Carrying 30, Missing." *Ketchikan Alaska Chronicle,* March 13, 1948.
"Little Hope of Recovering Wrecked Plane." *Anchorage Daily Times,* March 15, 1948.
"Plane's Wreckage Spotted on Mt. Sanford." *Anchorage Daily Times,* March 13, 1948.
"Rites Planned from Airplane." *Anchorage Daily Times,* March 17, 1948.

JULY 21, 1948   **LAKE MEAD NATIONAL RECREATION AREA**
"Army Air Forces Report of Major Accident, No. 4-C-7-21-2." Files of U.S. Air Force HQHA Inspection and Safety Center, Norton Air Force Base, CA.
"B-29 Crashes in Lake Mead." *Arizona Republic* (Phoenix), July 22, 1948.
Dodrill, Ed. "Ex-B-29 Pilot Recalls Crash into Lake Mead." *Sun* (Las Vegas), June 30, 1986.

OCTOBER 5, 1948   **OLYMPIC NATIONAL PARK**
"2 Lake Crescent Anglers Missing." *Seattle Post-Intelligencer,* June 24, 1949.
"Army Flyers Found Unhurt." *Scattle Post-Intelligencer,* October 7, 1948.
Browning, Robert. "Mountain Rescue Party Finds Body of Young Climber." *Seattle Post-Intelligencer,* October 6, 1948.
Crapson, Major Herbert L. (Adjutant, United States Air Force). Air Rescue Services Regulation Number 55–21. "Operation." OLYM SAR files, January 17, 1949.

APRIL 27, 1949   **HAWAII NATIONAL PARK**
Oberhansley, Frank R. (Superintendent). "Memorandum for the Regional Director, Region Four." National Archives RG-79, April 30, 1949.

JUNE 28, 1949   **YOSEMITE NATIONAL PARK**
"Girl Found after Five-Day Ordeal in Yosemite's Wilds." *San Francisco Chronicle,* July 2, 1949.
"Yosemite Men Are Honored for Dramatic Rescue." *San Francisco Chronicle* (?), National Archives RG-79, October 17, 1950.

JULY 8, 1949   **GRAND CANYON NATIONAL PARK**
Crumbo, Kim. *A River Runner's Guide to the History of the Grand Canyon.* Boulder: Johnson Books, 1981, p. 12.
"He Died On His River . . ." *Desert Magazine.* Desert Palm: September 1949, p. 30.

JULY 31, 1949   **YOSEMITE NATIONAL PARK**
"'Copter Saves Injured Boy in Yosemite." *San Francisco Chronicle* (?), August 4, 1949.
"Fourth Helicopter Attempt Brings Injured Boy Out of High Sierra Mountains." *Mariposa Gazette,* August 4, 1949
"Helicopter Tries to Save SF Boy Hurt in Yosemite." *San Francisco Chronicle* (?), August 2, 1949.
"Second Helicopter Try Yosemite Rescue." *San Francisco Chronicle* (?), August 3, 1949.

OCTOBER 9, 1949   **ROCKY MOUNTAIN NATIONAL PARK**
Field, Ernest K. (Ranger). "The Devitt-Gerling Search." *Trail and Timberline*. The Colorado
    Mountain Club, May 1950, p. 22.
Marranzino, Pasquale. "Searchers Believe Two A & M Boys Have Perished in Icy
    Mountains." *Rocky Mountain News* (Denver), October 13, 1949.

JUNE 17, 1950   **GRAND CANYON NATIONAL PARK**
"Explorer Hollers 'Nuff; River Trips Abandoned." *Phoenix Republic,* June 20, 1950, pp. 1–2.
"Superintendent's Annual Report: 1950." GRCA files.

NOVEMBER 21, 1950   **GRAND TETON NATIONAL PARK**
Baker, Howard (Regional Director). Letter to Superintendent. GRTE SAR files, November
    27, 1950.
Bonney, Orin, and Lorraine Bonney. "Plane Crash On Mt. Moran." *Teton Magazine,*
    Jackson: Teton Bookshop, 1984, p. 16.
Denver Post. GRTE SAR files, November 23, 1950.
———. GRTE SAR files, December 2, 1950.
Judge, Paul (retired Ranger). Letter to author, n.d.
"New Faces in the Denver Post Gallery of Fame." *Denver Post,* December 2, 1950.
Wyoming State Tribune. May 20, 1951.

MARCH 2, 1951   **KINGS CANYON NATIONAL PARK**
Brock, Leroy (Ranger). Letter to Clay [Peters ?]. SEKI SAR files, July 20, 1961.
"Missing Plane." *San Francisco Chronicle,* March 4, 1951.
"Orosi Soldier Drowns on Hiking Trip in Sierra." *Fresno Bee* (?),June 7, 1951.
"River Victim Hunt Pressed." *Los Angeles Times,* June 9, 1951.
Smith, Robert J. (Ranger). Letter to Chief Ranger Irvin D. Kerr. SEKI SAR files, October 5,
    1954

APRIL 12, 1951   **MT. RAINIER NATIONAL PARK**
Butler, William (retired Ranger). Letter to author, May 19, 1987.
Molenaar, Dee. *The Challenge of Rainier.* Seattle: The Mountaineers, 1979, pp. 158–159.

MAY 20, 1951   **SEQUOIA NATIONAL PARK**
Black, Bruce W. (retired Ranger). Letter to author, May 25, 1988.
"Bob Crawford, Times-Delta News Editor, Dies After Fishing Accident." *Visalia Times-
    Delta,* May 22, 1951.
Boyer, Richard (Ranger). Memorandum to Chief Ranger Kerr, Boyer files, May 24, 1951.
———. Letter to author, May 14, 1988.
Department of the Interior, *Twelfth Honor Awards Convocation* [Program Booklet].
    Washington, D.C.: DOI. December 8, 1953.
McKay, Douglas (Secretary of Interior). "Unit Citation for Meritorious Service." Boyer files.
Wirth, Conrad L. (Director). Letter to Richard Boyer. Boyer files. September 28, 1953.

JULY 21, 1951   **YOSEMITE NATIONAL PARK**
"Couple Survive Plunge over Waterwheel Falls in Park." *Mariposa (CA) Gazette,* July 26,
    1951, p. 1.

JULY 19, 1952   **CRATER LAKE NATIONAL PARK**
"Report of: Murder of C. P. Culhane and A. M. Jones in Crater Lake National Park, on or
    about July 19, 1952." CRLA files.

AUGUST 16, 1952   **GRAND TETON NATIONAL PARK**
Accidents in North American Mountaineering: 1952. New York: American Alpine Club
    Safety Committee, 1952, p. 10.
"Denver Man Is Killed in Fall While Climbing." *Jackson Hole Guide,* August 21, 1952.
Department of the Interior, *Fourteenth Honor Awards Convocation* [program booklet].
    Washington, D.C.: DOI. December 14, 1954.

AUGUST 29, 1952   **HAWAII NATIONAL PARK**
Field, Ernest K. (Chief Ranger). "Memorandum to Acting Superintendent." National
    Archives RG-79, September 4, 1952.

Maier (Acting Regional Director). Telegram to the Superintendent. September 2, 1952.

Oberhansley, Frank R. (Superintendent). Telegram to Dr. W. Mark Smith. National Archives RG-79, September 1, 1952.

MAY 25, 1953   **KINGS CANYON NATIONAL PARK**

Bender, H.G. (Ranger). "Rescue of Downed Airmen-Paradise Valley Area." National Archives RG-79, May 26, 1953.

"Two Planes Crash—2 Die; 5 Bail Out." *San Francisco Chronicle*, May 26, 1953.

JULY 14, 1953   **GRAND TETON NATIONAL PARK**

McKay, Douglas (Secretary of Interior). "Unit Citation for Meritorious Service." GRTE SAR files.

McLaren, Doug (Ranger). Letter to author, May 2, 1991.

"Mountain Climber Injured in Fall from Teton Peak." *Wyoming State Tribune*, July 16, 1953.

FEBRUARY 15, 1954   **SOUTH PACIFIC**

Department of the Interior, *Twenty-Eighth Honor Awards Convocation* [program booklet]. Washington, D.C.: DOI. December 12, 1962.

Hirst, Anne. Letters to author, February 19 and 20, 1987.

"Superintendent's Monthly Report—March 1954." HAVO files, n.d.

Udall, Stewart (Secretary of the Interior). "Citation for Distinguished Service: Ernest K. Field." Hirst files, n.d.

MAY 16, 1954   **MT. McKINLEY NATIONAL PARK**

Accidents in North American Mountaineering: 1954. New York: American Alpine Club Safety Committee, 1954, p. 18.

"Alaska Plane Lost with 19." *Phoenix Republic*, November 8, 1952.

"Alaskan Storm Hampers McKinley Rescue Team." *Boston Daily Globe*, May 28, 1954.

"Injured Mt. McKinley Climber Tells of His Eight-Day Ordeal." *San Francisco Chronicle*, June 2, 1954.

"McKinley Climber Found Alive." *San Francisco Chronicle*, May 31, 1954.

"Rescue Party Slowed in Mt. McKinley Search." *San Francisco Chronicle*, May 28, 1954.

"Superintendent's Monthly Report—May 1954." DENA files.

JULY 30, 1954   **GRAND CANYON NATIONAL PARK**

Davis, Dan (retired Ranger). Letter to author, October 1, 1985.

"Park Aide Dies in Fall at Canyon." *Phoenix Republic*, August 2, 1954.

AUGUST 22, 1954   **ROCKY MOUNTAIN NATIONAL PARK**

Dalie, John T. "Lost Climber Watched Wind Scatter His Food." *Rocky Mountain News* (Denver), August 28, 1954.

Jones, Bill. "Climber's 'Return from Death.'" *Rocky Mountain News* (Denver), August 28, 1954.

"Long's [sic] Peak Climber without Food Six Days." *Denver Post*, August 28, 1954.

"Man's Body Found below 200-Foot Cliff." *Rocky Mountain News* (Denver), August 17, 1954.

APRIL 10, 1955   **GRAND CANYON NATIONAL PARK**

Beer, Bill. *We Swam the Grand Canyon.* Seattle: The Mountaineers, 1988.

"River Search Yields No Clue of Frogmen." *Arizona Daily Sun* (Flagstaff). April 18, 1955.

JUNE 28, 1955   **GRAND TETON NATIONAL PARK**

Department of the Interior, *Eighteenth Honor Awards Convocation* [program booklet]. Washington, D.C.: DOI. April 23, 1957.

"Mountain Climbing Guide Loses Life on Grand Teton." *Jackson's Hole (WY) Courier*, June 30, 1955.

AUGUST 19, 1955   **LAKE MEAD NATIONAL RECREATION AREA**

McKay, Douglas (Secretary of the Interior). "Citation for Distinguished Service." National Archives RG-79.

MAY 30, 1956   **ROCKY MOUNTAIN NATIONAL PARK**

"Rescuing Trapped Arvada Scaler Wins 4 Park Employees Citations." *Denver Post*, April 24, 1957.

Seaton, Fred A. (Secretary of the Interior). "Citation for Valor Award: Frank J. Betts."
    National Archives RG-79.
"Three Park Rangers to Get Awards." *Denver Post,* April 19, 1957.

JUNE 30, 1956   **GRAND CANYON NATIONAL PARK**
"67 TWA Crash Victims Laid to Rest Here as Hundreds Pack Cemetery." *Arizona
    Daily Sun (Flagstaff)* , July 9, 1956.
Davis, Dan (retired Ranger). Letter to author, October 1, 1985.
Gavin, Tom. "Climber Tells of Three Days on Narrow Ledge of Canyon." *Rocky Mountain
    News* (Denver), n.d.
————. "Swiss Climbers Worry about Grand." *Rocky Mountain News* (Denver), n.d.
Kazy, Ted. "Copter Reaches TWA Crash; Plans Made to Move Bodies." *Arizona Republic*
    (Phoenix), July 2, 1956.
McLaughlin, John S. "Memorandum to Regional Director, Region Three." July 18, 1956.
Nash, Jay Robert. *Darkest Hours.* New York: Pocket Books, 1977, pp. 563–565.
Sweitzer, Paul. "Grave Is Mute Reminder of Grand Canyon Air Crash," *Arizona Daily Sun*
    (Flagstaff), June 29, 1986, p. 1.

JULY 24, 1956   **SEQUOIA NATIONAL PARK**
Jakes, Harold. Letter to author, July 22, 1988.
"Leader Gives Full Account of Gary Rule." *Exeter (CA) Sun,* n.d.

AUGUST 19, 1956   **MT. RAINIER NATIONAL PARK**
Blinn, Gil (Ranger). Letter to author, April 15, 1956.
Cohen, Lucille. "Bloodhounds Enter Search for Boy Lost on Mt. Rainier." *Seattle Post-
    Intelligencer,* August 23, 1956.
Reed, Robert. "Boy 13, Found on Mountain, Brought Here," *Seattle Post-Intelligencer,*
    August 26, 1956.
"Richard Mizuhata." *Mountain Rescue Council Newsletter,* No. 13. Seattle. MORA SAR
    files, September 20, 1956.

OCTOBER 4, 1956   **OLYMPIC NATIONAL PARK**
"The Accident.*" Mountain Rescue Council Newsletter,* No. 15. Seattle. MORA SAR files,
    November 19, 1956.

MAY 9, 1957   **KINGS CANYON NATIONAL PARK**
Balaz, Gene (retired Ranger). Letter to author, March 10, 1986.
Koch, R.W. "The Strange Case of the Missing T-33." *Air Classics,* n.d., n.p.
Peters, William. "The Survival of Lt. Steeves." *Redbook,* December 1957.
San Francisco Chronicle. July 2, 1957, p. 1.
"Saturday Morning." *Denver Post,* October 14, 1978.

JUNE 25, 1957   **BIG BEND NATIONAL PARK**
Alpine (TX) Avalanche. July 4, 1957.
Broyles, Phyllis. Letter to author, July 23, 1989.
El Paso Times. July 2, 1957.

JULY 2, 1957   **GRAND TETON NATIONAL PARK**
Accidents in North American Mountaineering: 1957. Issue 10. New York: American Alpine
    Club Safety Committee, 1957, p. 14.
McLaren, F. Douglas (Ranger). "Annual Mountain Climbing Report—Grand Teton National
    Park." GRTE SAR files, n.d.

JULY 26, 1957   **YOSEMITE NATIONAL PARK**
Oakland Tribune. June 30, 1957.
San Francisco Chronicle. June 28, 1957.
————. June 30, 1957.
Tucker, Tommy (retired Ranger). Letter to author, June 18, 1988.

MARCH 31, 1958   **YOSEMITE NATIONAL PARK**
Accidents in North American Mountaineering: 1958. Issue 11. New York: American Alpine
    Club Safety Committee, 1958, p. 17.

Fresno Bee. April 1, 1958, p. 1-B.
San Francisco Examiner. April 1, 1958, p. 10.

JUNE 15, 1958   **CARLSBAD CAVERNS NATIONAL PARK**
Carlsbad (NM) Current-Argus. June 17, 1958.
Crisman, Bobby (Ranger). Letter to author, May 13, 1988.
Ela, Tom (retired Ranger). Letter to author, March 17, 1986.

AUGUST 19, 1958   **YOSEMITE NATIONAL PARK**
Anderson, Rick (Ranger). Letter to author, November 16, 1985.
Betts, Frank (retired Ranger). Letter to author, December 1, 1985.
Department of the Interior, *Twenty-Second Honor Awards Convocation* [program booklet].
    Washington, D.C.: DOI. November 12, 1959.
Preston, John (YOSE Superintendent). Commendation for Park Ranger Frank J. Betts.
    Frank Betts's files, August 27, 1958.
San Jose Mercury, August 22, 1958.

SEPTEMBER 1, 1958   **MT. RAINIER NATIONAL PARK**
Accidents in North American Mountaineering: 1958. Issue 11. New York: American Alpine
    Club Safety Committee, 1958, p. 9.
Blinn, Gil (Ranger). Letter to author, April 15, 1986.
Mountain Rescue Council Newsletter. Seattle. October 1, 1958.
Seattle Post-Intelligencer. September 3, 1958, p. 1.
————. September 4, 1958, p. 1.
Seattle Times. September 3, 1958, p. 1.

JUNE 18, 1959   **GLACIER NATIONAL PARK**
Department of the Interior, *Twenty-Third Honor Awards Convocation.* [program booklet].
    Washington, D.C.: DOI. April 11, 1960.

JULY 23, 1959   **GRAND CANYON NATIONAL PARK**
Davis, Dan (retired Ranger). Letter to author, October 1, 1985.
New York Times. July 31, 1959.
Savannah (GA) Morning News. 31 July 1959.
————. August 1, 1959.

JULY 23, 1959   **SEQUOIA NATIONAL PARK**
"Jet Helicopter Rescues Injured Lindsay Girl, 13." *Lindsay (CA) News,* July 28, 1959.

JULY 27, 1959   **BADLANDS NATIONAL MONUMENT**
Accidents in North American Mountaineering: 1959. Issue 12. New York: American Alpine
    Club Safety Committee, 1959, p. 20.

SEPTEMBER 1, 1959   **MT. RAINIER NATIONAL PARK**
Blinn, Gil (Ranger). Letter to author, April 15, 1986.
Molenaar, Dee. *The Challenge of Rainier.* Seattle: The Mountaineers, 1979, pp. 257–258.
"Mount Rainier Accident." *Mountain Rescue Council Newsletter.* Seattle. George Sainsbury
    files. No. 27. October 6, 1959.
Sellers, Bob (retired Ranger). Letter to author, April 30, 1986.

MARCH 9, 1960   **GRAND TETON NATIONAL PARK**
"Citation For Valor Award: Gale H. Wilcox," Secretary of the Interior Stewart Udall. April
    19, 1961.
Dickenson, Russell (Chief Ranger). "Memorandum to Superintendent: Park Accident
    Report." GRTE SAR files, April 4, 1960.
Jackson Hole (WY) Guide. March 17, 1960.
Spurgeon, Stanley (Assistant Chief Ranger). Statement. GRTE SAR files, n.d.

MARCH 19, 1960   **YOSEMITE NATIONAL PARK**
Accidents in North American Mountaineering: 1960. Issue 13. New York: American Alpine
    Club Safety Committee, 1960, p. 36.

"Man Dangles 2,800 Feet Above Yosemite Valley." Unnamed newspaper. National Archives RG-79, July 14, 1947

Merry, Wayne (former Ranger). Letter to author, April 2, 1989.

"Superintendent's Monthly Report: September—1948." National Archives RG-79.

MAY 17, 1960   **MT. MCKINLEY NATIONAL PARK**

Accidents in North American Mountaineering: 1960. Issue 13. New York: American Alpine Club Safety Committee, 1960, p. 44.

Champlin, Charles. "Intrepid Men vs. Mighty Mac." *Life*, June 6, 1960, pp. 24–31.

Crews, Paul B. "Accident on Mount McKinley." *Summit Magazine*, August 1960, p. 3.

———. "Ascent of Mount McKinley South Peak, May 17th, 1960." Unpublished draft. Paul Crews files, August 1960.

Molenaar, Dee. "The Mount McKinley Affair (As Viewed from the Ground) 1960." Unpublished account. Dee Molenaar files.

Wilson, Rodman, M.D. (accident witness and rescuer). "Mountain Medicine: Comments on the Rescue of Climbers on Mount McKinley in May 1960." *Alaska Medicine*, December 1960.

———. Letter to author, November 2, 1988.

AUGUST 4, 1960   **GRAND TETON NATIONAL PARK**

Accidents in North American Mountaineering: 1961. Issue 14. New York: American Alpine Club Safety Committee, 1961, p. 18.

McLaren, Doug (Ranger). Interview with author, October 5, 1986.

———(retired Ranger). Letter to author, October 8, 1993.

NOVEMBER 26, 1960   **DEATH VALLEY NATIONAL MONUMENT**

Accidents in North American Mountaineering: 1960. Issue 13. New York: American Alpine Club Safety Committee, 1960, p. 43.

Ryan, Matt. Transcribed Oral Interview by Herb Evison. Oral Interview Records, Harpers Ferry Center, November 13, 1962.

JUNE 18, 1961   **MT. RAINIER NATIONAL PARK**

Seattle Post-Intelligencer. June 20, 1961, p. 1.

Sellers, Bob (retired Ranger). Letter to author, April 30, 1986.

APRIL 19, 1962   **YOSEMITE NATIONAL PARK**

"Monthly Report of the Protection Division: April—1962." YOSE files.

San Francisco Chronicle. April 21, 1962.

FEBRUARY 1963   **DEATH VALLEY NATIONAL MONUMENT**

Liles, Jim (Ranger). Letters to author, February 6, 1986 and May 10, 1990.

FEBRUARY 12, 1963   **EVERGLADES NATIONAL PARK**

Miami Herald. February 13, 1963, p. 1.

New York Times. February 13, 1963, p. 1.

MAY 3, 1963   **YELLOWSTONE NATIONAL PARK**

"Log of Yellowstone National Park Headquarters Activities in Connection with B-47 Bomber Crash in Bechler River Sub-District May 3, 1963." YELL Archives.

Milligan, Tom (retired Ranger). Letter to author, February 7, 1994.

JUNE 27, 1963   **GLACIER NATIONAL PARK**

Anderson, William (Assistant Principal of Columbia Falls High School). Letter to author, May 24, 1988.

Dumay, Tony (brother of victim). Letter to author, March 16, 1987.

Hungry Horse News (Columbia Falls, MT). July 5, 1963.

Sellers, Bob (retired Ranger). Letter to author, April 30, 1986.

SEPTEMBER 2, 1963   **YOSEMITE NATIONAL PARK**

Merry, Wayne (former Ranger). Letter to author, April 2, 1989.

Szecsey, Paul (witness). Letter to Superintendent John Preston. National Archives RG-79, September 5, 1963.

MAY 31, 1964   **MT. RAINIER NATIONAL PARK**
Seattle Post-Intelligencer. June 2, 1964, p. 1.
———. June 3, 1964, p. 1.
Tacoma News Tribune. June 3, 1964, p. 1.

APRIL 23, 1965   **MT. RAINIER NATIONAL PARK**
"Tacoma Mountain Rescue Council Newsletter." May, 1965, p. 4.
Tacoma News Tribune and Sunday Ledger. April 25, 1965.

JUNE 20, 1965   **DEATH VALLEY NATIONAL MONUMENT**
"Devil's Hole Claims Two Lives." *NSS News,* Vol. 23, no. 8. Huntsville, AL, August 1965, p. 113.
Las Vegas (NV) Sun. June 22, 1965.
———. June 23, 1965.

SEPTEMBER 5, 1965   **ZION NATIONAL PARK**
"A Brief Outline of the Narrows 'Tragedy' of 1961." ZION files, October 1984.
Desert (UT) News and Telegram. September 19, 1961.
Salt Lake Tribune. September 7, 1965, p. 1.
———. September 8, 1965, p. 1.
———. September 19, 1961, p. 1.
"Zion Narrows," *National Park Service Courier,* October 1965, p. 4.

MAY 21, 1966   **FIRE ISLAND NATIONAL SEASHORE**
"3 Drown Trying to Save Youth." *Long Island Press,* May 22, 1966.
"3 L. I. Men Drown Trying to Rescue 2 Surfing Youths." *New York Times,* May 21, 1966.
Carroll, Robert. "3 Try to Save a Surfer and the Sea Wins." *New York Daily News,* May 22,
    1966, p. 2.
Department of the Interior, *Thirty-Third Honor Awards Convocation* [program booklet].
    Washington, D.C.: DOI. November 10, 1966.
"Drowned Rescuer's Body Recovered." *Long Island Press,* May 31, 1966.
"Letters to the Editor," *Long Island Press,* n.d.

JULY 15, 1967   **MT. RAINIER NATIONAL PARK**
"Mt. Rainier Yields Body of Young Girl." *Seattle Post-Intelligencer,* July 18, 1967.
Naot, Stan. "Third Feared Dead· Rainier Ice Cave Plunge Kills Two." *Seattle Post-
    Intelligencer,* July 17, 1967.

JULY 18, 1967   **MT. MCKINLEY NATIONAL PARK**
Merry, Wayne. "Disaster on Mount McKinley." *Summit Magazine,* December 1967, pp. 2–9.
Sherwonit, Bill. "The Wilcox Expedition Disaster, 1967." *To the Top of Denali,* Anchorage:
    Alaska Northwest Books, 1990.
Snyder, Howard H. *The Hall of the Mountain King.* New York: Charles Scribner's Sons, 1973.
Wilcox, Joe. "Storm of Storms." *Summit Magazine,* August–September 1980, pp. 13–19.
———. "A Study of Windstorms on Mt. McKinley." *Summit Magazine,* November–December
    1980, pp. 20–25.

AUGUST 21, 1967   **GRAND TETON NATIONAL PARK**
"Drama In Real Life: The Impossible Rescue " *Reader's Digest,* September 1969, pp. 50–55.
Fales, E. D., Jr. "Marooned at 12,000 Feet." *Popular Mechanics,* June 1969, pp. (?) 200.
"Gaylord K. Campbell Evacuation Trip Log," GRTE SAR files, n.d.
Humphrey, Hubert H. Letter to Rick Reese from the Vice President. Rick Reese files,
    September 19, 1967.
Reese, Rick. Letter to author, April 23, 1988.
Scott, Dixie. "Rescue in the Tetons." *Outdoor World,* Cleveland, TN: Preston Publications,
    July–August 1969, pp. 4–8.
Sinclair, Peter. "A Battle Between Man and a Mountain." *National Observer,* September 4,
    1967, p. 1.
Tingey, Ralph (Ranger). Letter to author, March 23, 1989.

JANUARY 27, 1968   **ROCKY MOUNTAIN NATIONAL PARK**
Griffiths, Tom (Ranger). "American Alpine Club—Mountain Rescue Association Accident
    Report." Griffiths's files, May 9, 1968,

Queal, Cal. "Night of Despair." *Denver Post: Empire Magazine,* February 22, 1970, pp. 9–12.

MAY 23, 1968   **LAKE MEAD NATIONAL RECREATION AREA**
Udall, Stewart (Secretary of the Interior). "Citation for Valor: Joe J. Cayou." 37th Honors
    Convocation, December 11, 1968.

JUNE 1, 1968   **MT. RAINIER NATIONAL PARK**
Accidents in North American Mountaineering: 1968. Issue 21. New York: American Alpine
    Club Safety Committee, 1968, p. 26.
Erskine, Doug (Ranger). Communications with author, May 1, 1989.
Hart, Pete (Ranger). Letter to author, February 24, 1989.
Molenaar, Dee. *The Challenge of Rainier.* Seattle: The Mountaineers, 1979, p. 276.
Whittaker, Lou (rescuer). Letter to author, n.d.
Yancey, Philip. Drama In Real Life: "Whiteout on Mt. Rainier." *Reader's Digest,* January
    1976, pp. 106–110.

OCTOBER 15, 1968   **YOSEMITE NATIONAL PARK**
Accidents in North American Mountaineering: 1968. Issue 21. New York: American Alpine
    Club Safety Committee, 1968, p. 18.
Pederson, Robert (Ranger). "American Alpine Club—Mountain Rescue Association
    Accident Report." YOSE files, November 30, 1968.

NOVEMBER 3, 1968   **YOSEMITE NATIONAL PARK**
Pederson, Robert (Ranger). "American Alpine Club—Mountain Rescue Association
    Accident Report." YOSE files, October 30, 1968.
Rowell, Galen A., ed. *The Vertical World of Yosemite.* "Rescue on the South Face of Half
    Dome." Berkeley: Wilderness Press, 1974, pp. 147–159.

FEBRUARY 25, 1969   **SEQUOIA NATIONAL PARK**
"Air Force Paramedic in Daring Rescue of VA-125 Pilots." *Golden Eagle.* Lemoore Naval
    Air Station, CA, March 6, 1969.
Visalia (CA) Times-Delta. February 27, 1969.

MARCH 12, 1969   **POINT REYES NATIONAL SEASHORE**
Liles, Jim (Ranger). Letter to author, December 14, 1989.

JUNE 14, 1969   **GREAT SMOKY MOUNTAINS NATIONAL PARK**
Beale, Merrill D. (Acting Superintendent). "Great Smoky Mountains National Park Incident
    Report—Lost Child." July 9, 1969.
GRSM Press Release. September 10, 1969.
Memorandum to Regional Director, Southeast Region from Superintendent, GRSM. October
    15, 1969.

JUNE 15, 1969   **MT. RAINIER NATIONAL PARK**
Accidents in North American Mountaineering: 1969. Issue 22. New York: American Alpine
    Club Safety Committee, 1969, p. 13.
Smutek, Ray. "SCREE: Rainier Climbing Record." *Summit Magazine,* May 1970, p. 34.

AUGUST 2, 1969   **ROCKY MOUNTAIN NATIONAL PARK**
"Climber, 16, Hospitalized after Fall." *Rocky Mountain News* (Denver), August 4, 1969,
    p. 5.
Fricke, Walt. "Case History No. 2." *Off Belay.* Renton, WA, October 1972, p. 10.
Van Slyke, Larry (Ranger). Communications with author, February 20, 1992.

DECEMBER 30, 1969   **GLACIER NATIONAL PARK**
"Report of the Mt. Cleveland Tragedy Involving Five Young Mountain Climbers, December
    26, 1969–July 3, 1970." GLAC files.

APRIL 6, 1970   **YOSEMITE NATIONAL PARK**
Merry, Wayne (former Ranger). Letter to author, April 2, 1989.
"Rescue." *Summit Magazine,* June 1970, pp. 36–37.
"Search and Rescue Incident Report No. 120137.37." YOSE SAR files, April 16, 1970.

JULY 11, 1970   **LAKE MEAD NATIONAL RECREATION AREA**
"Futile Attempt to Save Pal Costs Marine, 20, His Life." *Arizona Republic* (Phoenix). July
    13, 1970.
"Gas, Heat Stops Rescue Attempt for Two Marines." *Las Vegas Review-Journal,* July 13, 1970.
Rowe, Raymond B. (Sheriff-Coroner, Imperial County). "Certificate of Appreciation." Don
    Chase files, July 15, 1970.

OCTOBER 23, 1970   **YOSEMITE NATIONAL PARK**
"Search and Rescue Incident Report No. 100-461.55." YOSE SAR files, n.d.
Thompson, Petc (Ranger). Letter to author, November 23, 1993.

NOVEMBER 25, 1970   **LAKE MEAD NATIONAL RECREATION AREA**
Weir, Don (Ranger). Letter to author, October 17, 1990.
Weir, Donald H., and Gene F. Gatzke (Rangers). "National Park Service Aircraft Incident."
    Weir files, December 8, 1970.

JUNE 19, 1971   **GRAND TETON NATIONAL PARK**
"Carnegie Hero Fund Commission Case Summary: Drowning—File No. 52639." Pittsburgh:
    Carnegie Hero Fund Commission, 1971.
"Recognized for Rescue Work," *Jackson (WY) Hole News,* November 24, 1971.
"Tragedy in Tetons," *Jackson (WY) Hole News,* June 24, 1971.
"USDOI Recommendation for Monetary Award, Docket No. NPS/M-SA-72-32." October 18,
    1971. Edward Wilson files.

JULY 15, 1971   **CARBON COUNTY, MT**
Griffiths, Thomas W. (Ranger). Memorandum to Chief Ranger. Tom Griffiths files, July 23, 1971.

AUGUST 14, 1971   **ROCKY MOUNTAIN NATIONAL PARK**
Dunning, Jim (retired Ranger). Letter to author, May 9, 1989.
"Secretary Morton Honors National Park Service Team for Dramatic Rescue of Injured
    Youngster." Press Release, August 30, 1971.

JANUARY 21, 1972   **ROCKY MOUNTAIN NATIONAL PARK**
"Air, Ground Search Starts for 2 Students." *Denver Post,* January 25, 1972.
Barr, Lois, and Steve Johnson. "More Pack Gear Found." *Denver Post,* January 30, 1972.
"Body Found; Winter Hike Victim." *Denver Post,* August 5, 1972.
Fricke, Walt. "Ski Touring Tragedy in Rocky Mountain National Park." *Off Belay,* Renton,
    WA, April 1972, p. 50.

JUNE 25, 1972   **YELLOWSTONE NATIONAL PARK**
Brady, Jim (Ranger). Communications with author, March 5, 1994.
"The Death of Harry E. Walker Involving Bear Attack, June 25, 1972." Old Faithful
    Subdistrict Report No. 1419. YELL files.
Frakt, Arthur N., and Janna S. Rankin. *The Law of Parks, Recreation Resources, and
    Leisure Services.* Salt Lake City: Brighton Publishing Co., 1982, p. 296.
Tays, Gerry (Ranger). Letters to author, November 18, 1992 and December 7, 1993.

SEPTEMBER 22, 1972   **YOSEMITE NATIONAL PARK**
Farabee, Charles. Personal recollection of the author.
Morton, C. B. (Secretary of the Interior). "Award for Excellence of Service." Author's files.
Thompson, Pete (Ranger). "Rescue on El Capitan." *Summit Magazine,* October 1972,
    p. 1.
————. Letter to author, November 23, 1993.

DECEMBER 1, 1972   **YOSEMITE NATIONAL PARK**
Farabee, Charles (Ranger). "A Psychological Profile of the Death of Bruce Douglas Norris."
    An Original Paper for FBI National Academy 105th Session. Author's files, June 4, 1976.

FEBRUARY 7, 1973   **NORTHERN NEVADA**
"4 on Crashed Plane." *Salt Lake Tribune,* May 20, 1973.
Betts, Frank. Communications with author, February 25, 1993 and February 24, 1994.
"Bodies of Four Found at Plane Wreck." *Salt Lake Tribune,* May 21, 1973.

"Obituaries: John Ebersole." *Herald Journal* (Logan, UT), May 22, 1973.

Parker, William. "National Transportation Safety Board Accident Investigation: No. DEN 73-A-D050." June 22, 1973.

White, Betty. "Plane Carrying Rangers Lost Enroute to Idaho." *National Park Service Courier,* March 1973, p. 1.

JUNE 3, 1973   **ZION NATIONAL PARK**

"Las Vegan, Brother Rescued." *Las Vegas Sun,* June 8, 1973.

Morgan, Ken (Ranger). Letter to author, May 5, 1990.

Morton, Rogers C.B. (Secretary of the Interior). "Unit Citation for Search and Rescue Team." Ken Morgan files, n.d.

JANUARY 16, 1974   **GRAND TETON NATIONAL PARK**

"Superintendent's Board of Inquiry—Deaths of Bart Brodsky, Michael Moseley, and David Silha." GRTE SAR files, January 29, 1974.

JULY 8, 1974   **YOSEMITE NATIONAL PARK**

Williams, John J. "Drama In Real Life: Rescue in the Gorge." *Reader's Digest,* March 1974, pp. 66–71.

SEPTEMBER 12, 1974   **SIERRA NATIONAL PARK**

Brock, Tim, and Earle Marsh. *The Complete Directory To Prime Time Network TV Shows— 1946 to Present* (5th Ed.), New York: Ballantine Books, 1992, p. 803.

Farabee, Charles. Personal recollection of the author.

Miller, Paul (TV official). Letter to author, July 20, 1993.

SEPTEMBER 14, 1974   **LAKE MEAD NATIONAL RECREATION AREA**

Briggle, William J. (Superintendent). "Unit Award for Excellence of Service Nomination." LAME files, October 22, 1975.

Kleppe, Thomas S. (Secretary of the Interior). "Unit Citation: Search and Rescue Team, Eldorado Flood." January 30, 1976.

MARCH 20, 1975   **OLYMPIC NATIONAL PARK**

Andersen, Tony (Ranger). "Case Incident Report No. 4808." Olympic SAR files, March 31, 1975.

Bowen, George (Ranger). Letter to author, April 4, 1989.

"USAF Accident/Incident Report No. 75-3-20-1." Hq MAC, Scott AFB, Illinois, April 4, 1975.

JUNE 16, 1975   **YOSEMITE NATIONAL PARK**

Farabee, Charles. Personal recollection of the author.

————. "Search and Rescue Incident Report No. 8804-1033-100-110." June 16, 1975. YOSE SAR files.

Sholly, Dan (Ranger). "Case Incident Record No. 75-1107." YOSE SAR files, June 17, 1975.

AUGUST 1, 1975   **GRAND CANYON NATIONAL PARK**

Schroeder, John. "Searchers Find Woman Lost 20 Days in Canyon." *Arizona Republic* (Phoenix), August 21, 1975.

SEPTEMBER 12, 1975   **(PRE) LAKE CLARK NATIONAL PARK**

"Aircraft Accident Report: Ketchum Air Service, Inc. No. NTSB-AAR-76-6." National Transportation Safety Board, Washington, D.C. February 25, 1976.

Peterson, Bob (Director, DOI Office of Aircraft Services). Letter to author, September 15, 1992.

NOVEMBER 29, 1975   **HAWAII VOLCANOES NATIONAL PARK**

Kaye, Glenn (Ranger). "Earthquake! November 29, 1975." *Kilauea Times,* n.d. p. 4.

JANUARY 24, 1976   **SEQUOIA NATIONAL PARK**

Fodor, Paul (Ranger). "Case Incident Record No. 76-0053." SEKI SAR files, January 24, 1976.

Kleppe, Thomas S. (Secretary of the Interior). "Unit Citation for Rescue Team." SEKI SAR files, n.d.

Steinberg, Jim. "Rescue," *Advance Register* (Tulare, CA). January 26, 1976.

JUNE 2, 1976   **MT. MCKINLEY NATIONAL PARK**

Gerhard, Bob (Ranger). "Case Incident Record No. 1954." DENA files, June 3, 1976.

Greiner, James. "Touchdown at 20,300 Feet." *The AOPA Pilot,* Frederick, MD: AOPA Publishers, January 1977, pp. 41-44.

Van Aken, Ray. "Altitude Record Set during Mount McKinley Rescue." Off Belay, Renton, WA. April 1976, p. 43.

JULY 31, 1976   **ROCKY MOUNTAIN NATIONAL PARK**

Asbury, Tim. "Raging Torrent Rips through Canyon Area, Estes Park Provides Rescue." *Trail Gazette* (Estes Park, CO), Special Edition, n.d.

Department of the Interior, *Forty-Fourth Honor Awards Convocation.* Program Booklet. Washington, D.C.: DOI, December 7, 1976.

Murphy, Lou. "CBers 'Pitch In' to Assist as Disaster Hits Canyons." *Trail Gazette* (Estes Park, CO). Special Edition. n.d.

———. "Park Personnel Mobilize in Big Thompson Flood Disaster." *Trail Gazette* (Estes Park, CO). August 11, 1976.

Van Slyke, Larry (Ranger). Letter to author, May 15, 1988.

AUGUST 31, 1976   **GREAT FALLS PARK (GWMP)**

Untitled document. George Washington Memorial Parkway files, n.d.

OCTOBER 5, 1976   **YOSEMITE NATIONAL PARK**

Dillman, Greg (HC-130 crewman). Letter to author, July 1, 1988.

Farabee, Charles. Personal recollection of the author.

Setnicka, Tim. "Rescue on Mt. Watkins." *Search and Rescue Magazine,* Montrose, CA: Kelley Publishing, Fall 1978, p. 4.

OCTOBER 10, 1976   **LASSEN NATIONAL PARK**

"Narrative of Search for Matthew Smith, October 10–15, 1976." LASS files, n.d.

Orr, Bill (retired Ranger). Letter to author, February 2, 1986.

Schneider, Albert C. (Chief Ranger). Letter to Dick McLaren, Author's files, December 2, 1976.

DECEMBER 9, 1976   **YOSEMITE NATIONAL PARK**

"$ Fortunes Made From Drug Plane." *Mountain Magazine: #2,* London: Mountain Magazine, Ltd. July–August 1977, p. 12.

Connelly, M. Scott (Ranger). Letter to author, June 30, 1993.

Farabee, Charles. Personal recollection of author.

Henry, Paul (Ranger). Communications with author, November 15, 1993.

"Judgment and Probation/Commitment Order No. 78-0930M: Eastern District of California." October 25, 1978.

McKeeman, Bruce D. (Ranger). "Case Incident Record No. 77-0133." YOSE SAR files, January 29, 1977.

MAY 23, 1977   **YOSEMITE NATIONAL PARK**

Farabee, Charles R. (Ranger). "Yosemite Search and Rescue Incident Report." YOSE SAR files, May 23, 1977.

Koontz, D. (Ranger). "Case Incident Record No. 91-3334." EVER files, October 12, 1991.

JUNE 27, 1977   **YELLOWSTONE NATIONAL PARK**

"Communications Center Daily Logs: 1 June 1977—30 June 1977." YELL Archives.

Richey, David. "My God, I've Gotten Too Close." *Outdoor Life,* January 1978, p. 58.

JANUARY 3, 1978   **GREAT SMOKY MOUNTAINS NATIONAL PARK**

Acree, Bill (Ranger). Letter to author, March 16, 1992.

"Bodies of 9 Crash Victims Being Retrieved in Smokies." *Knoxville News-Sentinel,* January 5, 1978.

Higgins, Lowell K. (Ranger). "Case Incident Record No. 78-0025." GRSM files, January 7, 1978.

Moulden, Jan. "'It Happened So Fast,' Says Survivor of Helicopter Crash." *Knoxville News Sentinel,* January 5, 1978.

Williams, Renova W. (Civil Air Patrol). Letter to author, October 22, 1991.

MAY 28, 1978   **YOSEMITE NATIONAL PARK**

Andrus, Cecil D. (Secretary of the Interior). "Citation for Valor: LeMoore Search and Rescue Helicopter Crew: United States Navy." YOSE SAR files, October 10, 1979.

Farabee, Charles. Personal recollection of the author.
"Lemoore Crew Cited for Valor." Unnamed newspaper, November 24, 1979.
Setnicka, Tim (Ranger). "Case Incident Record No. 78-0851." YOSE SAR files, n.d.
"Spectacular Yosemite Rescue." Unnamed newspaper, May 29, 1978.

JULY 15, 1978   **YOSEMITE NATIONAL PARK**
"Lost Persons Questionnaire: David Cunningham." YOSE SAR files.
"Search and Rescue Incident Report #78-2325." YOSE SAR files.

DECEMBER 25, 1978   **GRAND CANYON NATIONAL PARK**
Kuncl, Ernest K. (Ranger). "Case Incident Record No. 0305." GRCA files, January 30, 1978.
Stiegelmeyer, David (Ranger). "Case Incident Record No. 2000." GRCA files, May 12, 1979.

JUNE 22, 1979   **MT. RAINIER NATIONAL PARK**
"Mount Rainier Park Rangers Receive Valor Award," *Off Belay,* Renton, WA, December
    1980. p. 33.
"Mt. Rainier NPS Rangers Receive Interior Department Valor Award." *Summit Magazine,*
    November–December 1980, p. 13.
Olson, Garry (Ranger). Letter to author, January 5, 1995.

JANUARY 13, 1980   **CHIRICAHUA NATIONAL MONUMENT**
"Dogs Aid Hunt for Lost Ranger." *Tucson Citizen,* January 23, 1980.
Hanley, Patrick F. (detective). "Case Incident No. 6004—Golden Gate National Recreation
    Area." CHIR files, July 15, 1980.
"Park Ranger Missing." *Tucson Citizen,* January 16, 1980.
"Ranger Still Missing." *Tucson Citizen,* January 17, 1980.
Scott, Charles E. (private investigator). Letter and chronology to USPP Captain Dave
    Lennox, CHIR files, October 29, 1985.
Scott, Ted R. (Superintendent). "Memorandum to General Superintendent, SOAR." CHIR
    files, February 14, 1980.
"Search Continues for Missing Ranger." *Daily Dispatch* (Cochise County, AZ). January 23, 1980.

FEBRUARY 19, 1980   **SLEEPING BEAR DUNES NATIONAL LAKESHORE**
Brown, Donald R. (Superintendent). "Unit Award for Excellence of Service Nomination."
    SLBE files, March 10, 1980.

MAY 28, 1980   **GRAND CANYON NATIONAL PARK**
Trecker, Barbara. "Drama in Real Life: Rescue in the Grand Canyon." *Reader's Digest,*
    June 1981, pp. 75–79.

JULY 4, 1980   **ORGAN PIPE NATIONAL MONUMENT**
"2 More Held in Alien Deaths." *Arizona Republic* (Phoenix), July 14, 1980.
"2 Salvadorans Perish in Desert; 7 Saved, 25 Lost." *Arizona Republic* (Phoenix), July 6, 1980.
"Aliens Left to Die in Desert—13 Perish." *San Francisco Chronicle,* July 7, 1980.
Lough, Detective (#443). "Pima County Sheriff's Department Case Number S/80-07-07-
    914." September 2, 1980.
Sahagun, Louis. "Smugglers Abandon 30 El Salvadorans." *Tucson Citizen,* n.d.
Thackery, Ted. "Aliens Robbed, Abandoned in Desert; 13 Die." *Los Angeles Times,* July 7, 1980.
Thompson, Paul R. (Ranger). "Case Incident Record No. 80-0093." ORPI files, July 14, 1980.

SEPTEMBER 11, 1980   **NORTH CASCADES NATIONAL PARK**
Lester, Bill (Ranger). Letters to author, July 1, 1990 and January 28, 1992.

NOVEMBER 9, 1980   **GRAND TETON NATIONAL PARK**
Tingey, Ralph (Ranger). "Case Incident Record No. 80-2494." GRTE SAR files, November
    11, 1980.
———. "A Night in Valhalla." Letter to author, June 2, 1989.

JUNE 11, 1981   **GREAT FALLS PARK (GWMP)**
Kirby, William (Ranger). "Case Incident Record No. 81-0108." GWMP files, June 14, 1981.

JUNE 21, 1981   **MT. RAINIER NATIONAL PARK**
Briggle, William (Superintendent). "Board of Inquiry." MORA SAR files, July 29, 1981.

"Tragedy for American Mountaineering." *Summit Magazine*, July–August 1981, p. 3.

OCTOBER 10, 1981   BLACK CANYON OF THE GUNNISON NATIONAL MONUMENT
"5 Chutists Cited for Illegal Jump." *Denver Post*, November 22, 1981.
Burchard, Duncan. "Case Incident Record No. 084." BLCA files, October 16, 1981.
Dahm, Lewis A. (Rocky Mountain Rescue Group Leader). Letter to Superintendent Joe
 Kastellic, October 25, 1981.
Flack, Ray. "Cliff Jump Defended by Chutist." *Denver Post*, November 21, 1981.
Kastellic, Joseph (Chairman). "Board of Inquiry into the Death of: Larry D. Jackson."
 BLCA files, November 12, 1981.

DECEMBER 15, 1981   DENALI NATIONAL PARK
*Michael W. Clouser, Thomas M. Scanlon, Personal Representative of the Estate of Patrick
 J. Scanlon, Deceased, v. United States of America;* Case No. A83-637; United States
 District Court, District of Alaska; April 26, 1987.

DECEMBER 31, 1981   JOSHUA TREE NATIONAL MONUMENT
Watt, James G. (Secretary of the Interior). "Unit Award for Excellence of Service." JOTR
 SAR files.

JANUARY 3, 1982   YOSEMITE NATIONAL PARK
Durr, Mike (Ranger). "Case Incident Record No. 82-0030." YOSE SAR files, January 27, 1982.
Steinberg, Jim. "Boy Survives Air-Crash Ordeal." *Fresno Bee*, January 9, 1982.
Vines, Tom. "SAR Case File: Downed Aircraft." *Response Magazine*, spring 1982, pp. 7–10.

JANUARY 13, 1982   WASHINGTON, D.C.
"Capital's Disaster Readiness Questioned." *Response Magazine*, winter 1982, pp. 18–19.
"Carnegie Hero Fund Commission Case Summary: Exposure-File No. 58225." Pittsburgh:
 Carnegie Hero Fund Commission, n.d.
Department of the Interior, *Special Honor Awards Convocation.* Press Release.
 Washington, D.C.: DOI, January 13, 1982.
Usher, Donald. Communications with author, July 5, 1986.
Watt, James G. (Secretary of the Interior). "Citation for Valor: Donald W. Usher." n.d.

FEBRUARY 21, 1982   AMISTAD RECREATION AREA
"Justification for Exemplary Act Award." NPS Southwest Regional Office Personnel files, n.d.

JUNE 29, 1982   ROCKY MOUNTAIN NATIONAL PARK
Essex, David J. (Chairman). "Board of Inquiry: Robert S. Baldeshwiler." ROMO SAR files,
 August 9, 1982.

JULY 22, 1982   BANDELIER NATIONAL MONUMENT
"Bandelier Employees Receive Department's Exemplary Award," *National Park Service
 Courier*, March 1983.
"Bandelier Rangers Cited for Life-Saving Actions." *Los Alamos* (NM) *Monitor*, January 19,
 1983.

NOVEMBER 27, 1982   KINGS CANYON NATIONAL PARK
"Case Incident Record #20-1790." SEKI SAR files, n.d.
Vines, Tom. "SAR Case File: Ordeal at Mendel Glacier." *Response Magazine*, spring 1983, p. 27.

JULY 14, 1983   GRAND TETON NATIONAL PARK
Berkenfield, Scott (Ranger). Letter to author, October 3, 1993.
Vines, Tom. "SAR Case File: Grand Teton Glissade." *Response Magazine*, spring 1984, p. 25.

AUGUST 12, 1983   YOSEMITE NATIONAL PARK
Chapman, Howard (Regional Director). Memorandum to Assistant Director. YOSE SAR
 files, October 25, 1983.
Dalton, Peter J. (Ranger). "Case Incident Record No. 83-8400." YOSE SAR files,
 September 2, 1983.
Hodel, Donald Paul (Secretary of the Interior). "Citation for Valor: Peter Dalton, Dan
 Dellinges, Gary Colliver." April 24, 1985.

OCTOBER 9, 1983   **SHENANDOAH NATIONAL PARK**
Pierce, Bill (Ranger). "Case Incident Record No. 1705." SHEN SAR files, October 21, 1983.

DECEMBER 8, 1983   **GRAND CANYON NATIONAL PARK**
Farabee, Charles R. Personal recollection of author.
Hodel, Donald Paul (Secretary of the Interior). "Citation for Valor: William Lamb." April
    24, 1985.

DECEMBER 29, 1983   **OLYMPIC NATIONAL PARK**
Hodel, Donald Paul (Secretary of the Interior). "Citation for Valor: Richard W. Thomas."
    April 24, 1985.

FEBRUARY 13, 1984   **MT. MCKINLEY NATIONAL PARK**
Bartley, Bruce. "Clouds Hamper Pilots' Efforts to See Climber." *Anchorage Daily News,*
    February 19, 1984.
Gerhard, Robert A. (Ranger). "Search and Rescue Report: Naomi Uemura Search: February
    20–26, 1984: CIR #840002." DENA files, May 10, 1984.
Gidlund, Carl. "Storm Stalls Search for Climber." *USA Today,* February 22, 1984.
Jenkins, Paul. "Mount McKinley Solo Climber Feared Dead." *Anchorage Daily News,*
    February 23, 1984.
Kraft, Scott. "Search Continues Despite Dimming Hope for Climber." *Anchorage Times,*
    February 23, 1984.
———. "Unlikely Heroes Gamble Lives." *Anchorage Times,* February 24, 1984.
Sherwonit, Bill. "Winter Solo Ascents: Waterman, Uemura, and Johnston." *To the Top of*
    Denali. Anchorage: Alaska Northwest Books, 1990, pp. 209–227.
Uemura, Naomi. "Solo to the Pole." *National Geographic,* September 1978, pp. 297–324.

MAY 5, 1984   **MONTGOMERY COUNTY, MARYLAND**
Land, William (pilot). "Supplementary Case/Incident Record No. 015737." U.S. Park Police
    files, May 5, 1984.
Vines, Tom. "Potomac River Tragedy." *Response Magazine,* fall 1984, pp. 15–18.

OCTOBER 18, 1984   **JOSHUA TREE NATIONAL MONUMENT**
Brinkmeyer, Ranger. "Case Incident Record No. 84-0392." JOTR SAR files, October 26, 1984.
Ciotti, Paul. "Mike Bradbury's Obsession." *Los Angeles Times Magazine,* July 20, 1986,
    pp. 10–29.
WASO Ranger Activities Division Morning Report No. 90-453. December 27, 1990.

OCTOBER 21, 1984   **HALEAKALA NATIONAL PARK**
Cabatbat, Kimo (Ranger). Letter to author, May 8, 1988.
Chapman, Howard H. (Regional Director). "Exemplary Act Award: Perry Bednorz:
    Haleakala National Park." HALE files, n.d.

JUNE 21, 1985   **ISLE ROYALE NATIONAL PARK**
Croll, Stu (Chief Ranger). Letters to author, October 19, 1990 and October 6, 1992.

JUNE 30, 1985   **GOLDEN GATE NATIONAL RECREATION AREA**
Gazzano, Steven (Ranger). "Exemplary Act Award Nomination." GOGA files, July 29, 1985.

JULY 27, 1985   **YOSEMITE NATIONAL PARK**
Riegelhuth, Richard (Chief Ranger). "Exemplary Act Award Nomination." YOSE SAR files,
    April 25, 1986.

JULY 29, 1985   **CAPITOL REEF NATIONAL PARK**
Hodel, Donald Paul (Secretary of the Interior). "Citation for Valor: Kenneth Kehrer, Jr., and
    Larry R. Vensel." September 26, 1986.

SEPTEMBER 11, 1985   **GRAND TETON NATIONAL PARK**
Armington, Pete D. (Ranger). "Case Incident Record No. 85-783." GRTE SAR files,
    September 24, 1985.
Department of the Interior, *Fifty-First Honor Awards Convocation* [program booklet].
    Washington, D.C.: DOI. September 26, 1986.

Piccoli, Joseph. "Rangers Say They Were Just Doing Their Job." *Jackson Hole (WY) Guide,*
   September 17, 1985.
———. "Two Saved, Three Die in Climbing Tragedy." *Jackson Hole (WY) Guide,* n.d.
Stark, Jack E. (Superintendent). "Award For Valor Nomination." GRTE SAR files, November 7, 1985.

SEPTEMBER 19, 1985   **MEXICO CITY**
Graham, Hatch, and Judy Graham. "SAR 'Quake' Dogs," *Response Magazine,* November–
   December 1985, pp. 7–11.
Pierce, Bill (Ranger). "Case Incident Record No. 501901." SHEN SAR files, October 7, 1985.

OCTOBER 7, 1985   **PUERTO RICO**
Graham, Hatch, and Judy Graham. "The U.S. Team in Puerto Rico." *Response Magazine,*
   July–August 1986, pp. 41–47.
Graham, Judy, ed. "US Dogs Search Puerto Rico Mudslide." *SAR Dog Alert,* Somerset, CA
   National Association of Search and Rescue, December 1985.
Hill, Michael (Ranger). "Case Incident Record No. 85-0001." WASO SAR files, December 10, 1985.

APRIL 16, 1986   **DENALI NATIONAL PARK**
Capps, Kris. "Icy River, Little Food Didn't Deter Survivor." *Daily News-Miner* (Fairbanks),
   May 31, 1986.
Griffiths, Tom (Ranger). "Case Incident Record No. 86-0063." DENA files, June 3, 1986.

JUNE 13, 1986   **LAKE MEAD NATIONAL RECREATION AREA**
Hodel, Donald Paul (Secretary of the Interior). "Citation for Valor: William Briggs and
   Peter Dalton." September 30, 1987.

JUNE 18, 1986   **GRAND CANYON NATIONAL PARK**
"Executive Summary—National Safety Transportation Board." March 17, 1987.
Farabee, Charles R. Personal recollection of author.

JULY 14, 1986   **GRAND TETON NATIONAL PARK**
Stark, Jack E. (Superintendent). "Exemplary Act Award Nomination for Steve W. Rickert."
   GRTE SAR files, September 12, 1986.

JULY 20, 1986   **NORTH CASCADES NATIONAL PARK**
Sullivan, John R. Letter to John Reynolds, Superintendent, August 26, 1986.

OCTOBER 15, 1986   **YOSEMITE NATIONAL PARK**
Rose, Gene. "Beating Odds, Elements: Hiker's Survival Called 'Incredible.'" *Fresno Bee,*
   October 23, 1986.
Vines, Tom. "The Mt. Clark Search." *Response Magazine,* March–April 1987, p. 12.

MAY 24, 1987   **LAVA BEDS NATIONAL MONUMENT**
"Carnegie Hero Fund Commission Case Summary; Cave-In—File 62524." Pittsburgh:
   Carnegie Hero Fund Commission. n.d.
Hodel, Donald Paul (Secretary of the Interior). "Citation for Valor: Stephen W. Under-
   wood." September 30, 1987.

JUNE 28, 1987   **GRAND TETON NATIONAL PARK**
*Hugh B. Johnson, Jr., as Personal Representative of the Estate of Ben Johnson, Deceased
   v. United States of America, Department of Interior;* Case No. 90-8060. United States
   Court of Appeals, Tenth Circuit; November 13, 1981.

AUGUST 13, 1987   **CAPE COD NATIONAL SEASHORE**
Griffin, Mark D. (Ranger). "Case Incident Record No. 87-0597." CACO files, August 13, 1987.
Jones, Bonnie. Letter to William Whigham, CACO files, August 18, 1987.
———. Letter to author, September 27, 1987.

FEBRUARY 10, 1988   **YELLOWSTONE NATIONAL PARK**
"Yellowstone Rangers Respond to Difficult Incident." *Response Magazine,* May–June 1988, p. 9.

MAY 26, 1988   **DENALI NATIONAL PARK**
Douglass, Linda. "The Best: HART Chief Is Aviator of Year." *Arctic Star* (Fort Wainwright,
   AK), February 10, 1989, p. 4.

Moore, Ralph (Ranger). "Case Incident Record No. 88-0033." Talkeetna Ranger Station (DENA) files, May 29, 1988.

AUGUST 30, 1988   **SOUTHERN CALIFORNIA**
Gercke, Herb. WRO Ranger Field Incident Report. December 5, 1988.
Hannigan, LCOL. Operation "Desert Search" Summary, JOTR SAR files.
Henry, Paul (Ranger). Communications with author, October 8, 1992.
Vines, Tom. "Sifting for Clues." *Rescue,* May–June 1989, p. 28.

FEBRUARY 23, 1989   **DENALI NATIONAL PARK**
Seibert, Robert (Ranger). "Case Incident Record No. 89-0007." Talkeetna Ranger Station (DENA) files, March 15, 1989.

MAY 20, 1989   **CAPE HATTERAS NATIONAL SEASHORE**
Anderson, Henry M. (Ranger). "Case Incident Record No. 42-2026." CAHA files, June 1, 1989.
Department of the Interior, *Fifty-Fourth Honor Awards Convocation* [program booklet]. Washington, D.C.: DOI. March 8, 1990.

JUNE 10, 1989   **HAWAII VOLCANOES NATIONAL PARK**
"Unit Citation—Hawaii Volcanoes National Park: Park Ranger Rescue Team." HAVO files. n.d.
WASO Ranger Activities Morning Report #89-134. June 16, 1989.
Wiles, Greg. "Four Plane-Crash Bodies Elude Retrieval Efforts." *Honolulu Advertiser,* June 15, 1989.

AUGUST 9, 1989   **BIG BEND NATIONAL PARK**
Peterson, Charlie (Ranger). "Case Incident Record No. 89-358." BIBE files, August 11, 1989.
———. Letter to author, January 28, 1989.

OCTOBER 22, 1989   **WIND CAVE NATIONAL PARK**
"BI—Lost Caver—Incompetent." *NSS News: American Caving Accidents 1989,* Part II. Huntsville, AL. December 1990, p. 346.

APRIL 29, 1990   **FT. JEFFERSON NATIONAL MONUMENT**
Lujan, Manuel, Jr. (Secretary of the Interior). "Citation for Valor: Iain 'Al' C. Brown and Carolyn P. Brown." DOI 55th Honors Convocation, May 8, 1991.

JULY 14, 1990   **SEQUOIA NATIONAL PARK**
Rose, Gene. "Rescue Wasn't Easy." *Fresno Bee,* n.d.
WASO Ranger Activities Morning Report #90-197. July 19, 1990.

JULY 16, 1990   **DEATH VALLEY NATIONAL MONUMENT**
Lujan, Manuel (Secretary of the Interior). "Valor Award." DEVA files.

MARCH 31, 1991   **CARLSBAD CAVERNS NATIONAL PARK**
Cahill, Tim. "Charting the Splendors of Lechuguilla Cave." *National Geographic,* March 1991, pp. 34–59.
Costello, D. M. "A History of the Davis Mobley Rescue Incident: Carlsbad [sic] National Park." CACA files, April 5, 1991.
Fee, Scott, and Jamie Fee, eds. *NSS News,* Huntsville, AL, May 1993, p. 1990.
Haederle, Michael. "Her Leg Crushed but Her Spirit Intact, Emily Mobley Is Rescued from America's Deepest Cave." *People Weekly,* April 22, 1991, pp. 46-48.
Mansur, Michael C. "Caver's Forum: Rescue in Lechuguilla—More of the Story." *NSS News,* Huntsville, AL. August 1992, p. 199.
Martinez, Anthony J. "Lechuguilla Cave Response." *Rescue,* July–August 1991, pp. 36–39.

MAY 5, 1991   **OLYMPIC NATIONAL PARK**
Lujan, Manuel, Jr. (Secretary of the Interior). "Citation For Valor: Clayton P. Butler." *Fifty-Sixth Honor Awards Convocation* [program booklet]. Washington, D.C.: DOI, May 5, 1992.

JULY 3, 1991   **DENALI NATIONAL PARK**
Medred, Craig. "Daring Rescue Works." *Anchorage Daily News,* July 8, 1991.
Swed, J. D. (Ranger). "Justification for Department of Interior Valor Award: Jim Phillips and Daryl Miller." Talkeetna Ranger Station (DENA) files, n.d.

AUGUST 12, 1991   **GLEN CANYON NATIONAL RECREATION AREA**
WASO Ranger Activities Morning Report #91-403. August 14, 1991.

SUMMER 1992   **DENALI NATIONAL PARK**
Schmitt, Jan. "SAR Log." *Response Magazine,* fall 1992, p. 30.
Swed, J. D. (Ranger). "Denali National Park and Preserve 1992 Mountaineering Summary." DENA files.
———. Letters to author, April 22, 1993 and October 7, 1993.

JUNE 27, 1992   **LAKE MEREDITH NATIONAL RECREATION AREA**
Cook, John (Regional Director). Special Achievement Award Statement to Superintendent Pat McCrary, November 12, 1992.
Richards, Ann (Governor). Letter to McCrary, December 11, 1992.
Sarpalius, Bill (Congressman). Letter to McCrary, August 10, 1992.

AUGUST 24, 1992   **SOUTH FLORIDA**
Davis, Gary E. "Executive Summary: Assessment of Hurricane Andrew Impacts on Natural and Archeological Resources of Big Cypress National Preserve, Biscayne National Park and Everglades National Park, 15–24 September 1992." EVER files.
Ring, Richard G. (Superintendent). "Superintendent's Annual Report 1992." EVER files.

SEPTEMBER 23, 1992   **YOSEMITE NATIONAL PARK**
Johnson, Brad. "Journal of the First Rappel and Climb of El Capitan, Yosemite National Park, Using a Single Static Rope, August 9–16, 1980: A Trip Report." Author's files, n.d.
Twilley, Dan. "Mount Thor: The One-Kilometer Rappel." *NSS News,* Huntsville, AL, November 1982, p. 287.
WASO Ranger Activities Morning Report #92-523. September 25, 1992.

OCTOBER 10, 1992   **ZION NATIONAL PARK**
Van Slyke, Larry (Chief Ranger). "Fatality Investigation of David Bryant Case Incident #92-2186." ZION files.
WASO Ranger Activities Morning Report #92-555. October 13, 1992.

NOVEMBER 21, 1992   **HAWAII VOLCANOES NATIONAL PARK**
National Park Service Courier February 1993, p. 18.

FEBRUARY 20, 1993   **CRATERS OF THE MOON NATIONAL MONUMENT**
WASO Ranger Activities Morning Report #93-82. February 24, 1993.

MARCH 13, 1993   **GREAT SMOKY MOUNTAIN NATIONAL PARK**
Babbitt, Bruce (Secretary of the Interior). "Unit Award for Excellence of Service." GRSM files, n.d.

MAY 11, 1993   **CANYONLANDS NATIONAL PARK**
WASO Ranger Activities Morning Report #93-316. June 4, 1993.

MAY 28, 1993   **ROCKY MOUNTAIN NATIONAL PARK**
Osius, Alison. "Real Cliffhangers: Climbers Are Key Players behind the Scenes at Cliffhanger." *Climbing,* June–July 1993, p. 38.
Sella, Marshall. "Yo, Renny, You Getting the Biceps?" *Outside,* June 1993, p. 53.

JUNE 6, 1993   **GATEWAY NATIONAL RECREATION AREA**
NPS Press Release. "USPP Chief Honors New York Field Office for Role in Chinese Immigrant Rescue." November 10, 1993.
WASO Ranger Activities Morning Report #93-323. June 7, 1993 and June 8, 1993.

JULY 15, 1993   **ZION NATIONAL PARK**
Buccello, Dave. (Investigating Ranger). "Supplementary Case Incident Record #93-1558." ZION files, August 20, 1993.
Smith, Christopher, and Ray Ring. "Whose Fault?" *High Country News,* August 22, 1993, pp. 1, 8–11.
Van Slyke, Larry (Chief Ranger). "Case Incident Record #93-1558." ZION files, July 13, 1993.
Willis, Clint. "Who's to Blame for Kolob Creek?" *Outside,* May 1994, pp. 27–28.

MARCH 11, 1994   **SHENANDOAH NATIONAL PARK**
WASO Ranger Activities Morning Report #94-118. March 17, 1994.
WASO Ranger Activities Morning Report #94-121. March 17, 1994.

MAY 21, 1994   **DENALI NATIONAL PARK**
WASO Ranger Activities Morning Report #94-232. May 22, 24, and 26, 1994.

JULY 29, 1994   **GRAND CANYON NATIONAL PARK**
WASO Ranger Activities Morning Report #94-440. August 2, 1994.

1995   **NATIONAL PARK SERVICE**
WASO Ranger Activities Morning Reports # 95-08, 37, 49, 107, 117, 119, 127, 129, 160,
    177, 183, 245, 275, 282, 314, 315, 355, 359, 361, 375, 404, 420, 435, 447, 513, 514,
    519, 590, 624, 633, 726, 747, 758, and 772.

AUGUST 12, 1995   **MT. RAINIER NATIONAL PARK**
Briggle, Superintendent, Mt. Rainier National Park. "Sean H. Ryan/Philip J. Otis Board of
    Inquiry." September 28, 1995.
Brown, Leslie. "Report Blames Ranger Deaths on Gear, Ice." *News Tribune*
    (Longmont, WA) October 17, 1995, pp. A1 and A3.
Clifford, Hal. "Tragedy on Mount Rainier." *Snow Country*, January 1996, pp. 82–89.

JULY 20, 1996   **KINGS CANYON NATIONAL PARK**
Randy Coffman (Ranger). "Case Incident Record No. 60-0474." July 23, 1996. SEKI SAR Files.

OCTOBER 5, 1996   **NEW RIVER GORGE NATIONAL RIVER**
Babbitt, Bruce (Secretary of the Interior). "Citation For Team Exemplary Act Award." n.d.,
    NERI files.

DECEMBER 14, 1996   **LAKE MEREDITH NATIONAL RECREATION AREA**
Foust-Peeples, Shanna. "Mrs. Britten Honors Searchers." *Amarillo Daily News*. June 13,
    1997, p. 1.
Wilson, Robert (Ranger). "Case Incident Record No. 96-0596." March 5, 1997. LAMR SAR
    Files.
———. "Supplement, Case Incident Record No. 96-0596." June 8, 1997. LAMR SAR Files.

AUGUST 12, 1997   **GLEN CANYON NATIONAL RECREATION AREA**
Good, Allison (GLCA Safety Officer). "Documentation of Flash Flood Incident: August
    12–22, 1997." Memorandum to GLCA Personnel Officer. October 3, 1997.
WASO Ranger Activities Report #97-454. August 12, 1997

SEPTEMBER 6, 1997   **OLYMPIC NATIONAL PARK**
Maynes, Barb (Public Affairs Officer). "Search Effort Expands for Missing Hiker in Olympic
    National Park; Obstruction Point Road to Be Closed." OLYM press release, September 8, 1997.
———. "Search Team Plans for Tomorrow; Obstruction Point Road Closes at Hurricane
    Ridge." OLYM press release, September 9, 1997.
———. "Ninety-Nine Ground Searchers, Four Helicopters and One Airplane Now Involved
    in Search." OLYM press release, September 9, 1997.
———. "Change in Weather Aids Searchers, Helicopters and Search Dogs." OLYM press
    release, September 10, 1997.
———. "Details on Yesterday's Helicopter Accident." OLYM press release, September 13, 1997.
———. "Search for John Devine Scaled Back; Investigators Examine Crash Scene." OLYM
    press release, September 14, 1997.

SEPTEMBER 24, 1997   **GLACIER NATIONAL PARK**
Charles Logan (Ranger). "Case Incident Record No. 97-1188." September 28, 1997. GLAC
    SAR Files.

MAY 24, 1998   **DENALI NATIONAL PARK**
Miller, Daryl (Ranger, DENA). Communications with author, September 1, 2004.
WASO Ranger Activities Morning Report #98-223. May 27, 1998.
WASO Ranger Activities Morning Report #98-223. May 28, 1998.

JUNE 11, 1998   **MT. RAINIER NATIONAL PARK**
Wilson, Kimberly A. C. and Scott Sunde. "How a successful climb suddenly turned deadly."
    Seattle Post-Intelligencer, June 13, 1998, pp. A1 and A5.
Gauthier, Mike (Ranger, MORA). Communications with author, January 13, 1999.

JULY 10, 1998   **CAPITOL REEF NATIONAL PARK**
WASO Ranger Activities Morning Report #98-391. July 16, 1998.

DECEMBER 27, 1998   **ZION NATIONAL PARK**
Buccello, David (Assistant Chief Ranger). "Case Incident Record #98-3017." ZION files,
    December 27, 1998.
Buccello, David (Chief Ranger, ACAD). Communications with author, September 10, 2004.
Mafly, Bryan. "The Rescuers." *Salt Lake Tribune*. May 25, 1999, pp. B-1 and B6.
WASO Ranger Activities Morning Report #98-773. November 13, 1998.

FEBRUARY 6, 1999   **YOSEMITE NATIONAL PARK**
Hinson, Mary (Ranger, LAME). Communications with author, August 20, 2004.
Lober, Keith (Ranger, YOSE). Communications with author, August 17, 2004.

MAY 2, 1999   **NEAR GLACIER BAY NATIONAL PARK AND PRESERVE**
Croll, Stu (retired Chief Ranger, ISRO). Communications with author, September 20, 2004.
WASO Ranger Activities Morning Report #99-156. May 7, 1999.

JUNE 28, 1999   **NATIONAL PARK**
Phillips, Ken (SAR Ranger, GRCA). Communications with author, August 15, 2004.
WASO Ranger Activities Morning Report #99-327. July 2, 1999.

JUNE 30, 1999   **SEQUOIA NATIONAL PARK**
Fister, Kris (Public Affairs, SEKI). Press Release: "Hiker Rescued from Summit of Mount
    Whitney," July 5, 1999.

DECEMBER 30, 1999   **NEAR CANYONLANDS NATIONAL PARK**
"Citation for Valor Award: George Pavia," Secretary of the Interior Gale Norton. September
    4, 2002.
Pavia, George. (Ranger, YOSE). Communications with author, August 20, 2004.
Swanke, Steve (Ranger, TELL). Communications with author, August 15, 2004

JANUARY 31, 2000   **CHANNEL ISLANDS NATIONAL PARK**
Fitzgerald, Jack (Chief Ranger, CHIS). "Case Incident Record #2000-0014." CHIS files,
    February 10, 2000.
Fitzgerald, Jack (Chief Ranger, CHIS). Communications with author, August 12, 2004.
Porterfield, Elaine and Hector Castro. "Pilots honored for heroism during crisis." *Seattle
    Post-Intelligencer*," February 1, 2001. n.p.
Setnicka, Tim (retired Superintendent, CHIS). Communications with author, August 10,
    2004.
Spears, Carol J. (Public Affairs, CHIS). Press Release: "National Park Service Employee's
    Statement as Witness to the Crash of Alaska Airlines Flight 261." February 1, 2000.
WASO Ranger Activities Morning Report #00-021. February 1, 2000.
WASO Ranger Activities Morning Report #00-021. February 2, 2000.

FEBRUARY 19, 2000   **OZARK NATIONAL SCENIC RIVERWAY**
WASO Ranger Activities Morning Report #00-072. March 2, 2000.

JUNE–JULY, 2000   **BLACK CANYON OF THE GUNNISON NATIONAL PARK**
Delmolindo, Ed (Ranger, NOCA). Communications with author, August 19, 2004.
WASO Ranger Activities Morning Report #00-395. July 14, 2000.
Winslow, Steve (Ranger, BLCA). Communications with author, September 10, 2004.

AUGUST 2, 2000   **YOSEMITE NATIONAL PARK**
WASO Ranger Activities Morning Report #00-472. August 11, 2000.

JANUARY 17, 2001   **HALEAKALA NATIONAL PARK**
WASO Ranger Activities Morning Report #01-021. January 24, 2001.

JANUARY 31, 2001   **MAMMOTH CAVE NATIONAL PARK**
Mieman, Joe (Hydrologist, MACA). Communications with author, August 22, 2004.
WASO Ranger Activities Morning Report #01-034. February 6, 2001.

JUNE 25, 2001   **YELLOWSTONE NATIONAL PARK**
WASO Ranger Activities Morning Report #01-311. June 27, 2001.

JANUARY 28, 2002   **NORTH CASCADES NATIONAL PARK**
Madden, John (Ranger, NOCA). Communications with author, September 10, 2004.
WASO Ranger Activities Morning Report #02-025. January 31, 2002.

JANUARY 21, 2002   **CRATER LAKE NATIONAL PARK**
WASO Ranger Activities Morning Report #02-018. January 25, 2002.

APRIL 17, 2002   **CUYAHOGA VALLEY NATIONAL RECREATION AREA**
WASO Ranger Activities Morning Report #02-119. April 25, 2002.
Welch, Mosie (Ranger, CUVA). Communications with author, August 26, 2004.

2003   **A TYPICAL YEAR IN NATIONAL PARK SERVICE SAR**
Clark, Kathy (NPS Emergency Reports Coordinator). "National Park Service Search and
    Rescue Report: 2003." March 31, 2004.

JANUARY 29, 2003   **BISCAYNE NATIONAL PARK**
WASO Ranger Activities Morning Report. February 26, 2003.

APRIL 26, 2003   **NEAR CANYONLANDS NATIONAL PARK**
Gerhart, Bego (Rescuer). Communications with author. August 17, 2004.
Ralston, Aron. Excerpt from *Between a Rock and a Hard Place.* New York: Atria Books,
    2004. *Outside Magazine.* September, 2004, pp. 54–62.
Swanke, Steve (Ranger, CANY). "Case Incident Record #0307000008." CANY files. May 1,
    2003.
Swanke, Steve (Ranger, CANY). "SAR Record #2003-008." CANY files. May 1, 2003.
Swanke, Steve (Ranger, YELL). Communications with author, September 1, 2004.
WASO Ranger Activities Morning Report. November 25, 2003.

JUNE 29, 2003   **GRAND TETON NATIONAL PARK**
Accidents in North American Mountaineering: 2004. New York: American Alpine Club
    Safety Committee, 2004, pp. 84-85.
Thuermer, Jr., Angus M. and Rebecca Huntington. "Climbers: Rangers Saved Us." *Jackson
    Hole News & Guide,* July 30, 2003. p.1.
Thuermer, Jr., Angus M. "Report: Rescued climbers ignored several warnings." *Jackson
    Hole News & Guide,* November 26, 2003. p.1.
WASO Ranger Activities Morning Report. August 11, 2003.

JULY 31, 2003   **YOSEMITE NATIONAL PARK**
Farabee, Charles R. Personal and original research by author. 2000-2004.
WASO Ranger Activities Morning Report. September 5, 2003.
YOSE Media Relations Office. Press Release: "Mono County/Yosemite National Park Seek
    Information About Overdue Backpacker." August 7, 2003.

MAY 4, 2004   **WRANGELL-ST. ELIAS NATIONAL PARK AND PRESERVE**
Alaska Region Press Room: "Search for Missing Climber Scaled Back: Update." May 16,
    2004.
WASO Ranger Activities Morning Report. May 19, 2004.

MAY 27, 2004   **LAVA BEDS NATIONAL MONUMENT**
Author(s) unknown. "Students found in cave after getting lost on field trip." Newspaper
    unknown. May 29, 2004. (forwarded to author by Art Allen on June 1, 2004.)
Dorman, Craig (Superintendent, LABE). Communications with author. September 3, 2004.
WASO Ranger Activities Morning Report. June 2, 2004.

GENERAL REFERENCES

Annual Report of the DOI. Administrative Report: Volume I-II, Washington, D.C.: GPO, 1912–1918.

Butcher, Devereux. *Exploring Our National Parks and Monuments.* Boston: Harvard Common Press, 1985.

Casewit, Curtis W. *The Saga of the Mountain Soldiers.* New York: Julian Messner, 1981.

Cronkhite, Daniel. *Death Valley's Victims.* Morongo Valley, CA: Sagebrush Press, 1981.

Everhart, William C. *The National Park Service.* Boulder, CO.: Westview Press, 1983.

First Annual Report of the National Park Service. Washington, D.C.: GPO, 1917.

Garrison, Lemuel A. *The Making of a Ranger.* Salt Lake City: Howe Brothers, 1983.

Henneberger, John W. *Chronology of the Ranger Story.* Corvallis, OR: 3256 NW Harrison Blvd., Author, 1996.

Jones, Chris. *Climbing In North America.* Berkeley: University of California Press, 1976.

Kane, Joseph Nathan. *Famous First Facts: Fourth Edition.* New York: T. H. Wilson Company, 1981.

Mackintosh, Barry. *The National Parks: Shaping the System.* Division of Publications and the Employee Development Division, National Park Service. Washington, D.C.: GPO, 1991.

Mazel, David. *Pioneering Ascents: the Origin of Climbing in America—1642–1873.* Harrisonburg, PA: Stackpole Books, 1991.

National Parks: Index 1991. Office of Public Affairs and the Division of Publications, National Park Service. Washington, D.C.: GPO, 1991.

Pyne, Stephen J. *Fire In America: A Cultural History of Wildland and Rural Fire.* Princeton, NJ: Princeton University Press, 1982.

Report of Director of National Park Service. Washington, D.C.: GPO, 1917–1950.

Roper, Steve. Camp 4: *Recollections of a Yosemite Rockclimber.* Seattle: The Mountaineers, 1994.

Voge, Hervey H. and Andrew J. Smatko, eds. *Mountaineers Guide to the High Sierra.* San Francisco: Sierra Club, 1972.

War Department Field Manual 70-10, *Mountain Operations.* Washington, D.C.: GPO, 1944.

INDEX